PHILIP'S

STREE

Buckinghamshire

and **Milton Keynes**

Amersham, Aylesbury, High Wycombe

C000259087

www.philips-maps.co.uk
First published in 1990 by Philip's
a division of Octopus Publishing Group Ltd
www.octopusbooks.co.uk
Endeavour House 189 Shaftesbury Avenue
London WC2H 8JY
An Hachette UK Company
www.hachette.co.uk

Fourth edition 2010
First impression 2010
BUCDA

ISBN 978-0-540-09299-4 (pocket)

© Philip's 2010

 Ordnance Survey®

This product includes mapping data licensed from
Ordnance Survey® with the permission of the
Controller of Her Majesty's Stationery Office.
© Crown copyright 2010. All rights reserved.
Licence number 100011710.

Contents

II Mobile safety cameras

III **Key to map symbols**

IV **Key to map pages**

VI **Route planning**

VIII Major administrative and Postcode boundaries

1 **Street maps** at 2⅔ inches to 1 mile

214 **Index** of towns, villages, streets, hospitals, industrial estates, railway stations, schools, shopping centres, universities and places of interest

Digital Data

The exceptionally high-quality mapping found in this atlas is available as digital data in TIFF format, which is easily convertible to other bitmapped (raster) image formats.

The index is also available in digital form as a standard database table. It contains all the details found in the printed index together with the National Grid reference for the map square in which each entry is named.

For further information and to discuss your requirements, please contact
philips@mapsinternational.co.uk

Mobile safety cameras

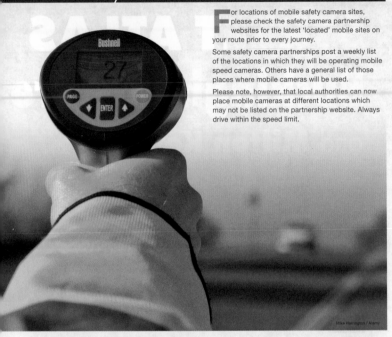

For locations of mobile safety camera sites, please check the safety camera partnership websites for the latest 'located' mobile sites on your route prior to every journey.

Some safety camera partnerships post a weekly list of the locations in which they will be operating mobile speed cameras. Others have a general list of those places where mobile cameras will be used.

Please note, however, that local authorities can now place mobile cameras at different locations which may not be listed on the partnership website. Always drive within the speed limit.

Mike Harrington / Alamy

Useful websites

Thames Valley Safer Roads Partnership
www.saferroads.org

Northamptonshire Casualty Reducton Partnership
reducingroadcasualties.com
www.northants.police.uk/default.aspx?id=275

Bedfordshire and Luton Casualty Reduction Partnership
www.drivesafely.org

Hertfordshire Safety Camera Partnership
www.hertsdirect.org/envroads/roadstrans/rsu/driving/safetycameras/hscpdetails/

London Safety Camera Partnership
www.lscp.org.uk

Surrey Safety Camera Partnership
www.surrey-safecam.org

Further information
www.dvla.gov.uk
www.thinkroadsafety.gov.uk
www.dft.gov.uk
www.road-safe.org

Key to map symbols

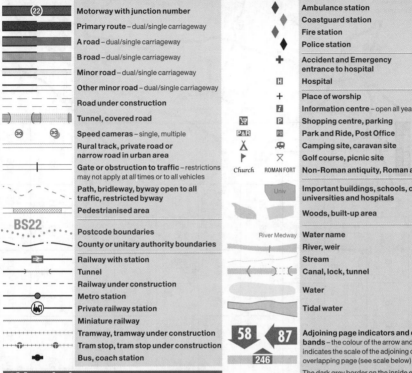

	Motorway with junction number (22)
	Primary route – dual/single carriageway
	A road – dual/single carriageway
	B road – dual/single carriageway
	Minor road – dual/single carriageway
	Other minor road – dual/single carriageway
	Road under construction
	Tunnel, covered road
	Speed cameras – single, multiple
	Rural track, private road or narrow road in urban area
	Gate or obstruction to traffic – restrictions may not apply at all times or to all vehicles
	Path, bridleway, byway open to all traffic, restricted byway
	Pedestrianised area
BS22	Postcode boundaries
	County or unitary authority boundaries
	Railway with station
	Tunnel
	Railway under construction
	Metro station
	Private railway station
	Miniature railway
	Tramway, tramway under construction
	Tram stop, tram stop under construction
	Bus, coach station

	Ambulance station
	Coastguard station
	Fire station
	Police station
	Accident and Emergency entrance to hospital
H	Hospital
+	Place of worship
i	Information centre – open all year
P	Shopping centre, parking
P&R / PO	Park and Ride, Post Office
	Camping site, caravan site
	Golf course, picnic site
Church / ROMAN FORT	Non-Roman antiquity, Roman antiquity
Univ	Important buildings, schools, colleges, universities and hospitals
	Woods, built-up area
River Medway	Water name
	River, weir
	Stream
	Canal, lock, tunnel
	Water
	Tidal water

58 ◄ 87 / 246 Adjoining page indicators and overlap bands – the colour of the arrow and band indicates the scale of the adjoining or overlapping page (see scale below)

The dark grey border on the inside edge of some pages indicates that the mapping does not continue onto the adjacent page

The small numbers around the edges of the maps identify the 1-kilometre National Grid lines

Abbreviations

Acad	Academy	Meml	Memorial
Allot Gdns	Allotments	Mon	Monument
Cemy	Cemetery	Mus	Museum
C Ctr	Civic centre	Obsy	Observatory
CH	Club house	Pal	Royal palace
Coll	College	PH	Public house
Crem	Crematorium	Recn Gd	Recreation ground
Ent	Enterprise		
Ex H	Exhibition hall	Resr	Reservoir
Ind Est	Industrial Estate	Ret Pk	Retail park
IRB Sta	Inshore rescue boat station	Sch	School
		Sh Ctr	Shopping centre
Inst	Institute	TH	Town hall / house
Ct	Law court	Trad Est	Trading estate
L Ctr	Leisure centre	Univ	University
LC	Level crossing	W Twr	Water tower
Liby	Library	Wks	Works
Mkt	Market	YH	Youth hostel

The map scale on the pages numbered in blue is 2⅔ inches to 1 mile
4.2 cm to 1 km • 1:23810

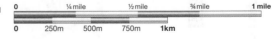

0	¼ mile	½ mile	¾ mile	1 mile
0	250m 500m 750m	1km		

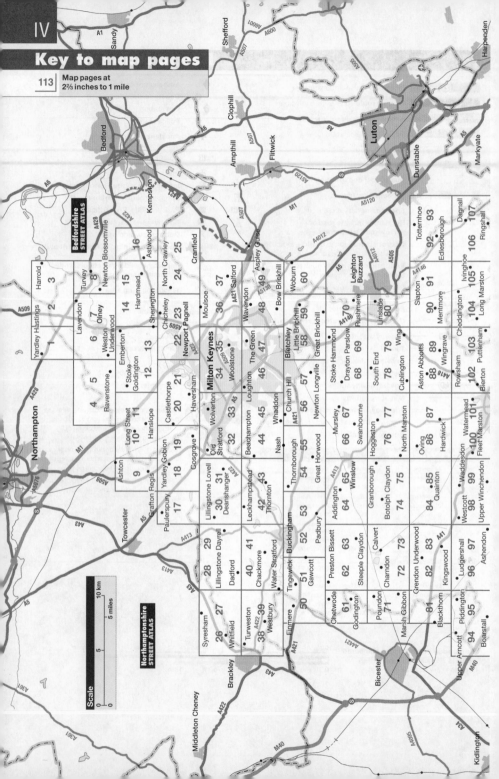

V

Hertfordshire STREET ATLAS

London STREET ATLAS

Surrey STREET ATLAS

Oxfordshire STREET ATLAS

Berkshire STREET ATLAS

St Albans
Hemel Hempstead
Watford
Rickmansworth
Redbourn
Kings Langley
Radlett
Bushey
Harrow
Ruislip
Hayes
Southall
Ealing
Brentford
Hounslow
Feltham
Ashford
Staines
Stanwell
West Drayton
Yiewsley
Cowley
Uxbridge
Harmondsworth

Felden 146
Bovingdon
Flaunden
Chenies 156

Northchurch 134 135
Berkhamsted
Ashley Green 144 145
Botley
Chesham 154 155
Latimer
Amersham
Maple Cross 178
Chorleywood 166 167

Aldbury 120 121
Little Gaddesden
Wilstone Green 118 119
Tring
Wigginton
Hastoe 132 133
Cholesbury
St Leonards

Aston Clinton 116 117
Weston Turville
Wendover 130 131
Ellesborough

Aylesbury 114 115
Stone
Bishopstone
Ford 128 129
Little Kimble

Upper Pollicott 110 111
Chilton
Chearsley
Cuddington
Westlington
Long Crendon 124 125
Haddenham 126 127
Kingsey
Thame

Brill
Oakley 108 109
Worminghall 122 123
Ickford
Wheatley
Shabbington
Tiddington
Milton Common 136

Horton-cum-Studley

Oxford

Lewknor 157
Christmas Common 168 169
Turville

Chinnor 147
Crowell
Henton 137

Bledlow Ridge 158 159
Stokenchurch

Naphill 160 161
West Wycombe
Lacey Green 148 149
Rout's Green

Prestwood 150 151
Speen

Great Missenden 152 153
Little Missenden

Lee Common 142 143
Chartridge

Longwick 138 139
Princes Risborough
Wendover Dean 140 141
Little Hampden

High Wycombe 172 173
Booker
Cryers Hill 162 163
Hazlemere

Loudwater 174 175
Beaconsfield
Amersham Old Town 164 165
Winchmore Hill

Chalfont St Giles 176 177
Seer Green
Chalfont St Peter
Gerrards Cross 188 189
Higher Denham

Iver Heath 200
Iver 206 207
M4 208

Slough 205
Wexham Street 198 199
Farnham Common
Hedgerley 186 187
M40
Wooburn Common

Lane End 170 171
Frieth
Maidensgrove 179
Fawley 180 181
Hambleden
Henley-on-Thames 191

Marlow Bottom 182 183
Lower Woodend
Mill End 192 193
Hurley

Marlow 194 195
Cookham Rise
Bisham
Little Marlow 184 185
Flackwell Heath

Taplow 196 197
Burnham
Cookham
Wooburn

Maidenhead 202 203
Bray

Eton Wick 204
Boveney 209
Windsor 210
Datchet 211
Old Windsor

Colnbrook 212 213
Upton
Dorney Reach

Lower Assendon
Mill End

Wallingford
Goring
Sonning Common
Reading
Twyford
Wokingham
Binfield
Bracknell
Wargrave

Abingdon
Didcot

Maidenhead

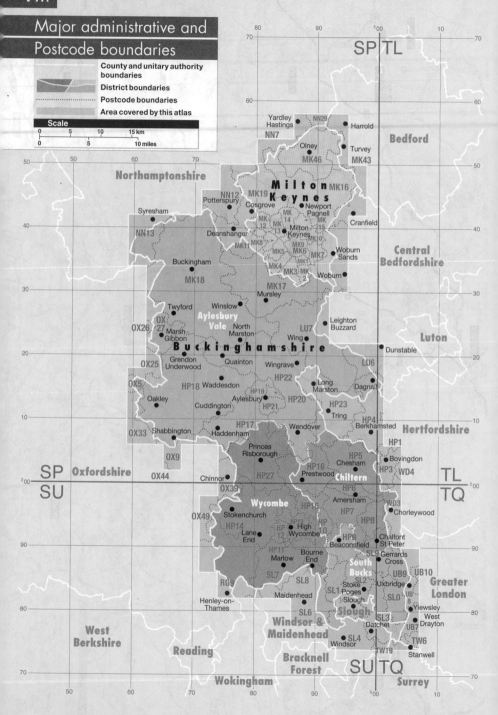

Major administrative and
Postcode boundaries

County and unitary authority boundaries
District boundaries
Postcode boundaries
Area covered by this atlas

Scale
0   5   10   15 km
0   5   10 miles

SP TL

SP SU

TL TQ

SU TQ

Milton Keynes
Aylesbury Vale
Buckinghamshire
Chiltern
Wycombe
South Bucks
Slough
Windsor & Maidenhead

Northamptonshire
Bedford
Central Bedfordshire
Luton
Hertfordshire
Greater London
Surrey
Wokingham
Bracknell Forest
Reading
West Berkshire
Oxfordshire

NN7
NN29
NN12
NN13
MK46
MK43
MK16
MK19
MK14
MK12
MK13
MK11
MK8
MK5
MK6
MK9
MK10
MK15
MK7
MK1
MK4
MK3
MK2
MK18
MK17

OX27
OX26
OX25
OX5
OX33
OX9
OX44
OX39
OX49

HP18
HP22
HP19
HP20
HP21
HP17
HP23
HP4
HP1
HP5
HP16
HP27
HP3
HP6
HP15
HP7
HP8
HP14
HP13
HP10
HP12
HP11
HP9
WD4
WD3

LU7
LU6

SL9
SL2
SL1
SL0
SL3
SL4
SL6
SL7
SL8

UB10
UB9
UB8
UB7

TW6
TW19
RG9

Yardley Hastings
Harrold
Olney
Turvey
Cosgrove
Newport Pagnell
Cranfield
Potterspury
Syresham
Deanshanger
Milton Keynes
Woburn Sands
Woburn
Buckingham
Twyford
Winslow
Mursley
Marsh Gibbon
North Marston
Wing
Leighton Buzzard
Grendon Underwood
Quainton
Wingrave
Dunstable
Waddesdon
Long Marston
Dagnall
Oakley
Aylesbury
Cuddington
Tring
Shabbington
Haddenham
Wendover
Berkhamsted
Princes Risborough
Chesham
Bovingdon
Chinnor
Prestwood
Stokenchurch
Amersham
Chorleywood
Lane End
High Wycombe
Chalfont St Peter
Marlow
Bourne End
Beaconsfield
Gerrards Cross
Henley-on-Thames
Maidenhead
Stoke Poges
Slough
Uxbridge
Datchet
Yiewsley
West Drayton
Windsor
Stanwell

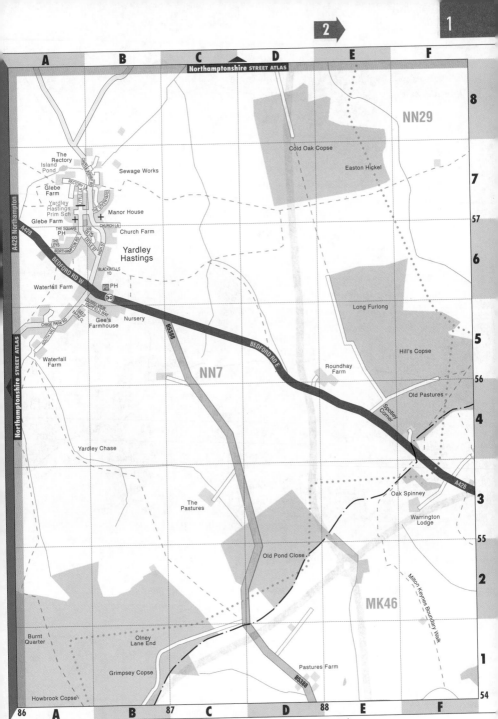

NN29

The Rectory
Island Pond

Sewage Works

Cold Oak Copse

Easton Hickel

Glebe Farm

Yardley Hastings Prim Sch

Manor House

Glebe Farm

Church Farm

Yardley Hastings

BLACKWELLS YD

Waterfall Farm

PO PH

Gee's Farmhouse

Nursery

Long Furlong

Hill's Copse

Chase Park Rd

BEDFORD RD E

Roundhay Farm

Old Pastures

Waterfall Farm

NN7

Spotley Corner

A428

Yardley Chase

Oak Spinney

The Pastures

Warrington Lodge

Old Pond Close

MK46

Milton Keynes Boundary Walk

Burnt Quarter

Olney Lane End

Grimpsey Copse

Pastures Farm

B5388

Howbrook Copse

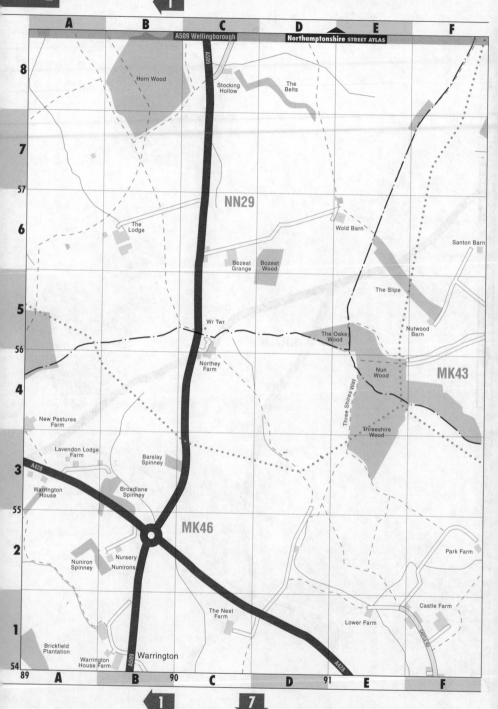

A509 Wellingborough

Northamptonshire STREET ATLAS

NN29

Horn Wood

Stocking
Hollow

The
Belts

Wold Barn

Santon Barn

The
Lodge

Bozeat
Grange

Bozeat
Wood

The Slipe

Nutwood
Barn

Wr Twr

The Oaks
Wood

Nun
Wood

MK43

Northey
Farm

Three Shires Way

New Pastures
Farm

Threeshire
Wood

Lavendon Lodge
Farm

Barslay
Spinney

A428

Warrington
House

Broadlane
Spinney

MK46

Park Farm

Nuniron
Spinney

Nursery
Nunirons

Castle Farm

The Nest
Farm

Lower Farm

Brickfield
Plantation

Warrington
House Farm

Warrington

A509

A428

CASTLE RD

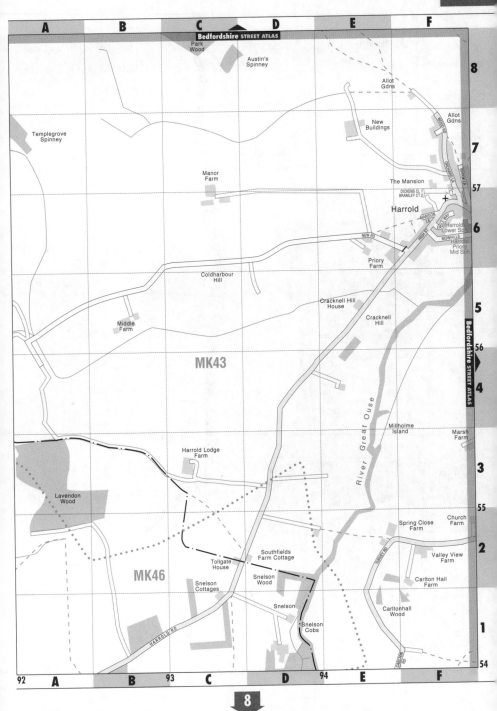

Bedfordshire STREET ATLAS

Bedfordshire STREET ATLAS

| | A | B | C | D | E | F |

Park Wood

Austin's Spinney

Allot Gdns

Templegrove Spinney

New Buildings

Allot Gdns

Manor Farm

The Mansion

DICKENS CL 1
BRAMLEY CT 2

Harrold

MANSION LA

Harrold Lower Sch

NEW RD

HIGH ST

MOWHILLS

Harrold Priory Mid Sch

Priory Farm

Coldharbour Hill

Cracknell Hill House

Cracknell Hill

Middle Farm

MK43

River Great Ouse

Millholme Island

Marsh Farm

Harrold Lodge Farm

Lavendon Wood

Spring Close Farm

Church Farm

Southfields Farm Cottage

Valley View Farm

Tollgate House

MK46

Snelson Wood

Carlton Hall Farm

Snelson Cottages

Snelson

Carltonhall Wood

HARROLD RD

Snelson Cobs

CARLTON RD

| 92 | A | B | 93 | C | D | 94 | E | F |

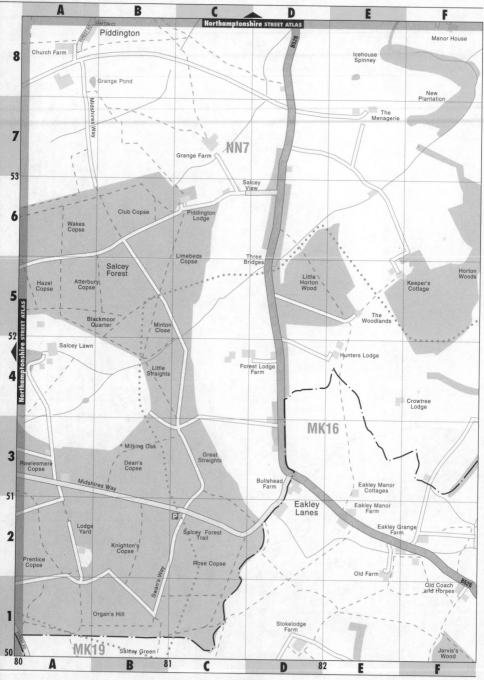

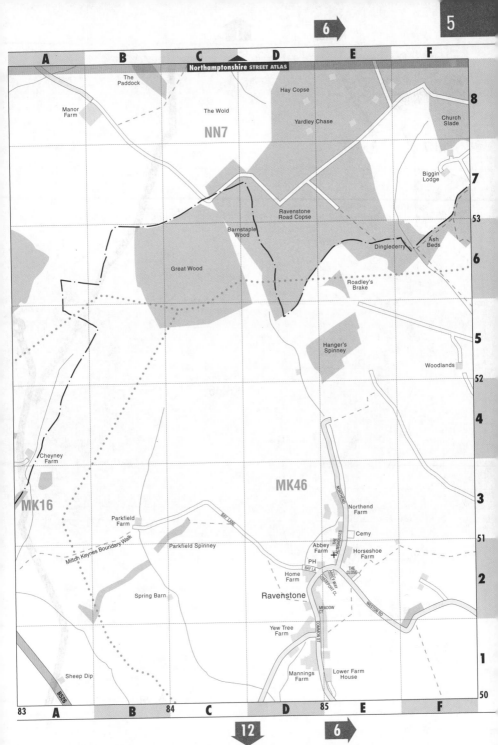

Northamptonshire STREET ATLAS

A | B | C | D | E | F

The Paddock

Manor Farm

Hay Copse

The Wold

Yardley Chase

Church Slade

NN7

Biggin Lodge

Ravenstone Road Copse

Barnstaple Wood

Ash Beds

Dinglederry

Great Wood

Roadley's Brake

Hanger's Spinney

Woodlands

Cheyney Farm

MK46

Northend Farm

MK16

Cemy

Parkfield Farm

Milton Keynes Boundary Walk

Parkfield Spinney

BAY LANE

Abbey Farm

Horseshoe Farm

THE CLOSE

PH

BAY LA

Home Farm

Spring Barn

Ravenstone

MEADOW

Yew Tree Farm

Mannings Farm

Lower Farm House

Sheep Dip

83 | 84 | 85

A | B | C | D | E | F

8
7
53
6
5
52
4
3
51
2
1
50

5

1

| A | B | C | D | E | F |

Howbrook Copse

Grimpsey Copse

Yardley Chase

8

Olney Park Farm

Olney Park Cottages

B5388

Olney Hyde

Church Slade

NN7

Smith's Farm

7

Court Farm

YARDLEY RD

53

Kilwick Wood

Sewage Works

6

Olney Ind Est

Warrington Road Farm

STILEBROOK RD

RABANS

ASPREYS

KIPPELL

DRIFT WAY

TILLY HILL

A509

5

SHORT MASSEY 1
CRAB TREE CL 2
SLATEPITS CFT 3
WOODPITS LA 4

Olney Mid Sch

HOPPERS

HAWKSWOOD

MAYBUSH WLK

KENSINGTON PL

MIDLAND RD

B5388

Dickens Spinney

52

MK46

OVERHILLS

FLAGGS MDW

STOCKEN

CHERRY ORCH

LONG LA

RISE

WEST

CLICKER TODD

POLES CL

Olney

Ousedale Sch Resr

Liby

4

Pheasants Nest

LONG LA

WHITMEES

DICKENS SPINNEY

Olney Inf Sch

JOHNSONS FIELD

SPRINGFIELD RD

COBBS GDN

THE OLD MEWS

ORCHARD RISE

ELMLEA

DELLS

The Alcove

ANDINGS CL

ASH LEA

HOLLOW

BEECH AVE

The Cowper & Newton Mus

3

Overbrook Spinney

STONE PIT CL

WESTON RD

SPRING LA

WELL CT

HIGH ST

Weston Park

51

Goosey Bridge

BRIDGE ST

The Wilderness

Sluice

2

PH

Manor House

Laundry Cottage

Otter Pool

Church Farm

Heron Water

HIGH ST

River Great Ouse

Emberton Country Park

Weston Underwood

1

THE CLOSE

Grebe Lake

Visitor Ctr

Snipe Pool

HARVEY RD

A509

The Willows

50

| 86 | A | B | 87 | C | D | 88 | E | F |

5

13

F3
1 FOUNTAIN CT
2 BERRELL'S CT
3 ROSE CT
4 MARKET PL
5 OSBORN'S CT
6 CHURCH ST
7 PEMBROKE HO
8 CHANTRY RI
9 CLAY PIT LA

10 PEBODY PL
11 STONEMASONS CL
12 WAGSTAFF WY

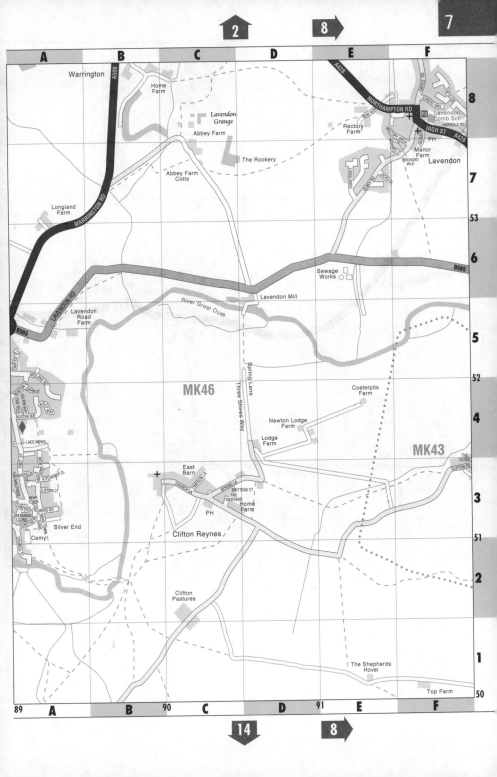

7

3

	A	B	C	D	E	F

8

New Barn

Snip Wood

Uphoe Manor Farm

Copymoor

Cemy

A428

7

New Park

THE DE LA

53

Cricket Ground

MK46

Cemy

6

Turvey House

Turvey Lower Sch

New Gains Farm

B565

Chantry Farm

HAWTHORN CL

Turvey

MORDAUNT

VINE ROW

MAY RD

CHURCH TERR

ELM WY

THE ROW

Turvey Bridge

CRANES CL

PO

ABBEY SQ

BEDFORD RD

THE GREEN

HIGH ST

A428

A428 Bedford

Cold Brayfield

Waterfield Farm

BRIDGE ST

BAMFORDS YD

Turvey Abbey

5

Brayfield Farm

MILL GN

LADYBRIDGE TERR

Ford

Bedfordshire STREET ATLAS

BRAYFIELD HO

BAKERS CL

52

Lodge

Long Belt

Abbey Farm

4

Newton Blossomville

Top Lodge

Mossy Bank Wood

PH

Newton Blossomville CE Sch

Turvey Cottage

River Great Ouse

CLIFTON RD

THE ROW

Woodside Cottage

Home Farm

BROOK LA

HARDMEAD RD

New Wood

3

Westfields Barn

MK43

Keepers Cottage

51

Turvey Hall

2

Newton Park

Gullet Wood

Clifton Spinney

Two Chimneys

Sheepwalks Spinney

1

Mast

Newton Wood

Turvey Lodge Farm

50

92	A		B	93	C		D	94	E		F

7

15

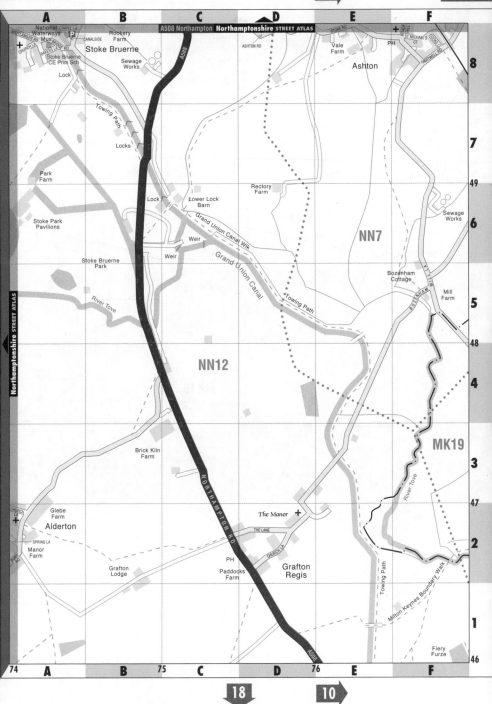

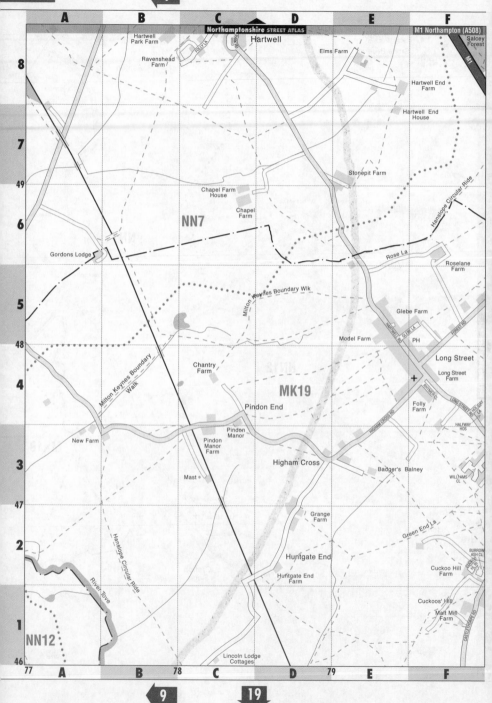

M1 Northampton (A508)

Salcey Forest

Hartwell Park Farm

Hartwell

Ravenshead Farm

Elms Farm

Hartwell End Farm

Hartwell End House

Stonepit Farm

Chapel Farm House

NN7

Chapel Farm

Hanslope Circular Ride

Gordons Lodge

Rose La

Roselane Farm

Milton Keynes Boundary Wlk

Glebe Farm

Model Farm

PH

Long Street

Long Street Farm

Chantry Farm

Milton Keynes Boundary Walk

MK19

Pindon End

Folly Farm

HALFWAY HOS

New Farm

Pindon Manor

Pindon Manor Farm

Higham Cross

Badger's Balney

WILLIAMS CL

Mast

Grange Farm

Green End La

BURROW ASH CL

Cuckoo Hill Farm

Hanslope Circular Ride

Huntgate End

Huntgate End Farm

Cuckoos' Hill

Malt Mill Farm

River Tove

NN12

Lincoln Lodge Cottages

9

19

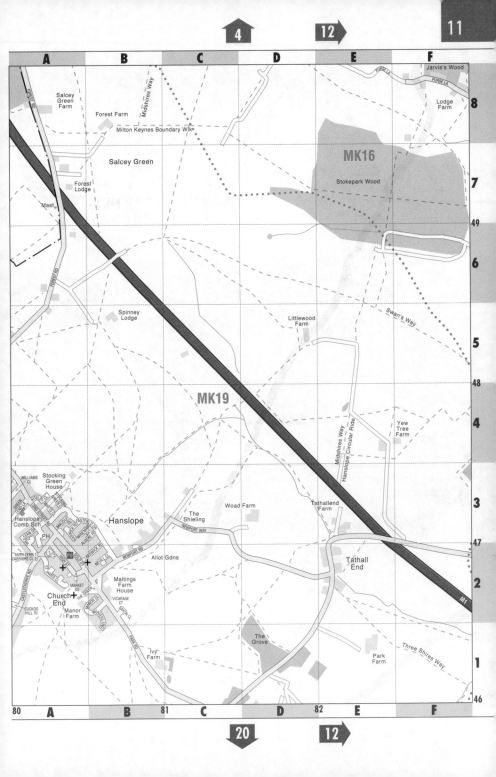

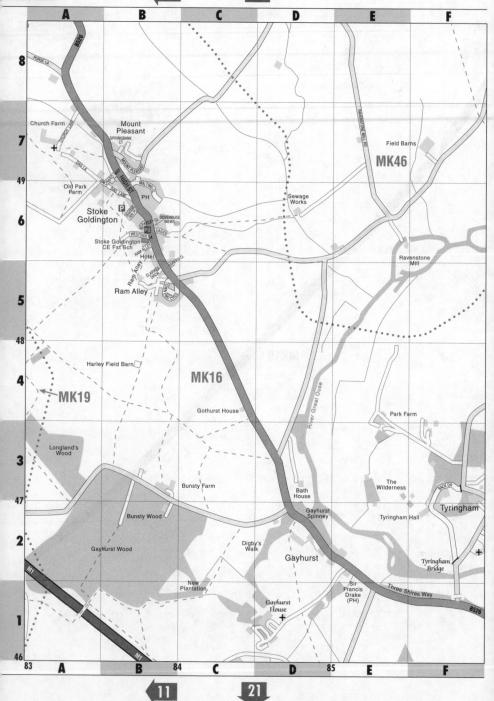

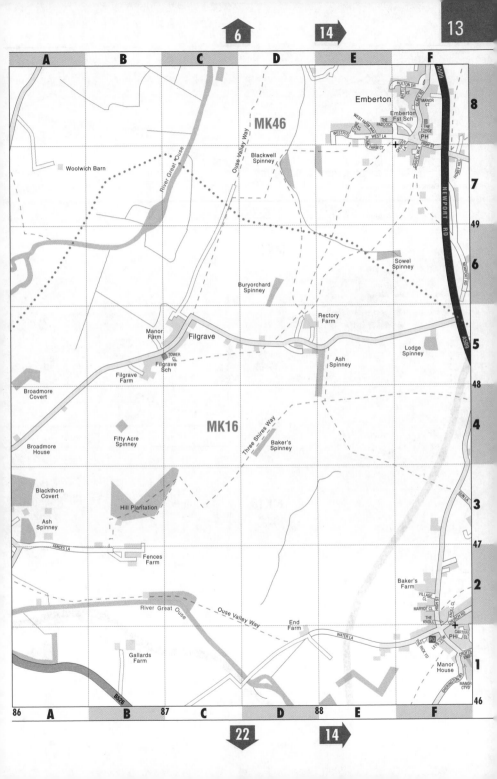

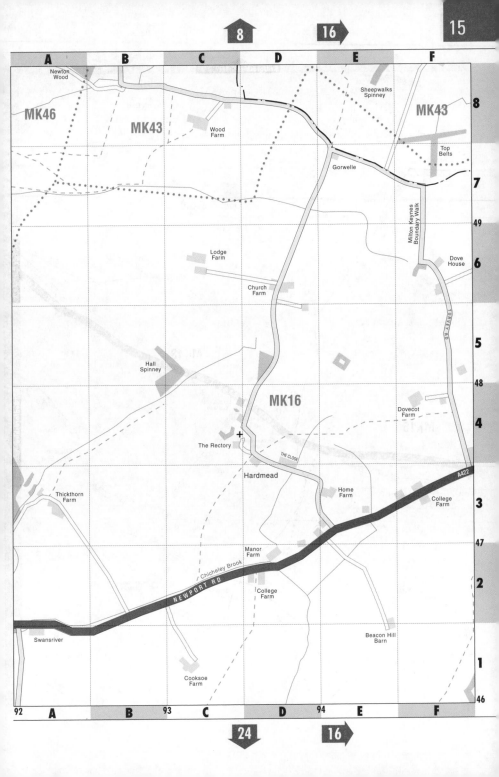

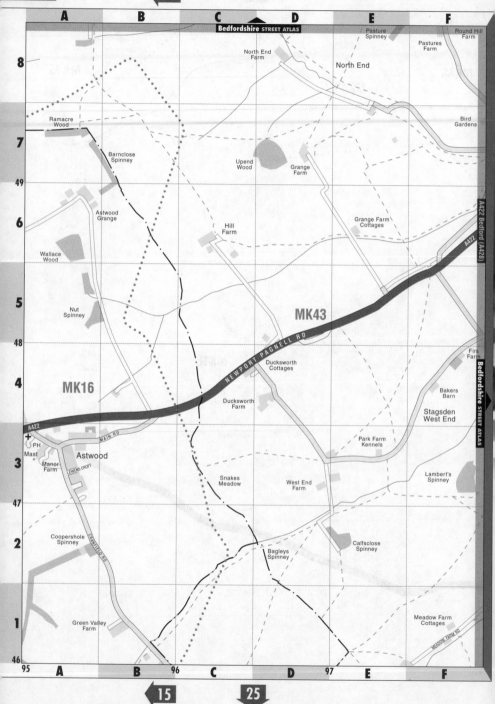

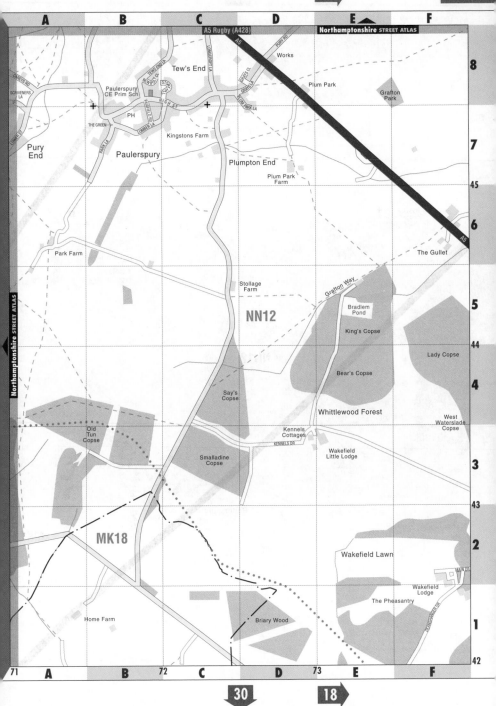

A B C D E F

A5 Rugby (A428)

Works

Tew's End

Plum Park

Grafton
Park

Paulerspury
CE Prim Sch

SCRIVENERS
LA

PH

THE GREEN

Pury
End

Paulerspury

Kingstons Farm

Plumpton End

Plum Park
Farm

NN12

Park Farm

Stollage
Farm

Grafton Way

Bradlem
Pond

King's Copse

Lady Copse

Bear's Copse

Say's
Copse

Whittlewood Forest

West
Waterslade
Copse

Old
Tun
Copse

Kennels
Cottages

KENNELS DR

Wakefield
Little Lodge

Smalladine
Copse

MK18

Wakefield Lawn

MAIN DR

Wakefield
Lodge

Home Farm

Briary Wood

The Pheasantry

The Gullet

A5

8 7 45 6 5 44 4 3 43 2 1 42

71 A B 72 C D 73 E F

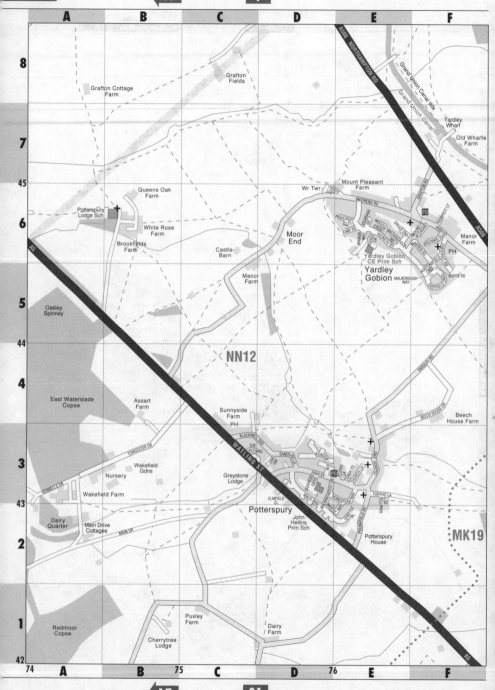

A B C D E F

8

Grafton Cottage
Farm

Grafton
Fields

A5(W) NORTHAMPTON RD

Grand Union Canal Wlk

Grand Union Canal

Yardley
Wharf

7

Old Wharfe
Farm

45

Queens Oak
Farm

Wr Twr

Mount Pleasant
Farm

MOOREND RD

Potterspury
Lodge Sch

6

White Rose
Farm

Moor
End

HIGHCROFT

PO

Brookfields
Farm

Castle
Barn

Yardley Gobion
CE Prim Sch

Manor
Farm

PH

Yardley
Gobion

MALBOROUGH
WAY

BUDGE RD

5

Oakley
Spinney

Manor
Farm

44

NN12

YARDLEY RD

4

East Waterslade
Copse

Assart
Farm

BEECH HOUSE DR

Beech
House Farm

3

TOWCESTER DR

Nursery

Wakefield
Gdns

Sunnyside
Farm
PH

BLACKWELL END

THE
ORCHARD

WATLING ST

SANDE PK

MEADOW

HIGH ST

PO

FURTHO LA

KENWELLS DR

Wakefield Farm

Greystone
Lodge

ELMFIELD
CL

Potterspury

John
Hellins
Prim Sch

GRAFTON RD

43

Dairy
Quarter

Main Drive
Cottages

MAIN DR

Potterspury
House

MK19

2

Redmoor
Copse

Puxley
Farm

Dairy
Farm

A5

1

42

74 A B 75 C D 76 E F

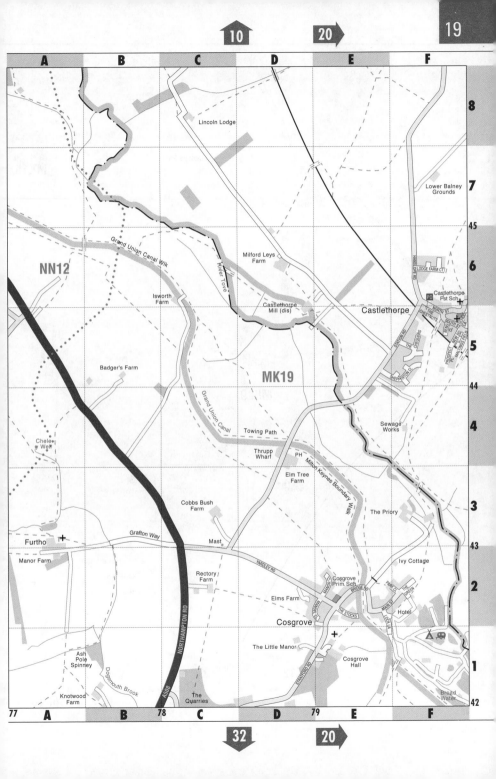

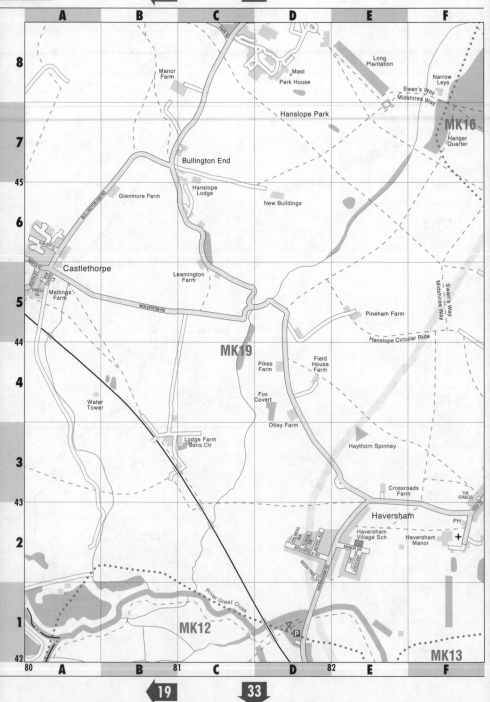

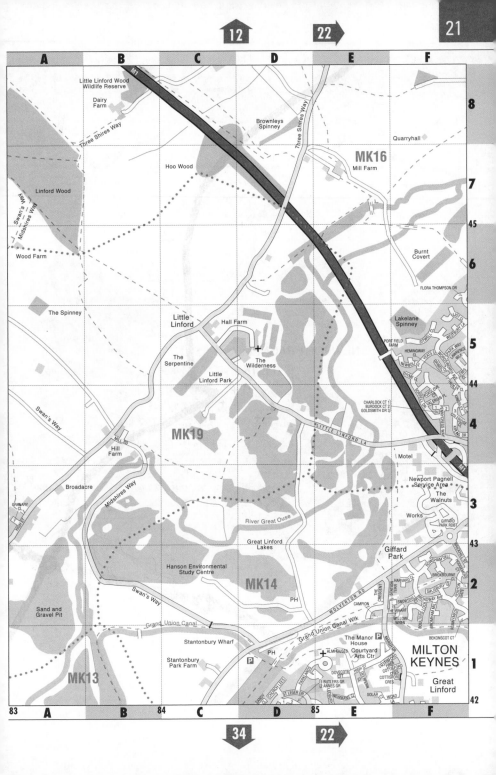

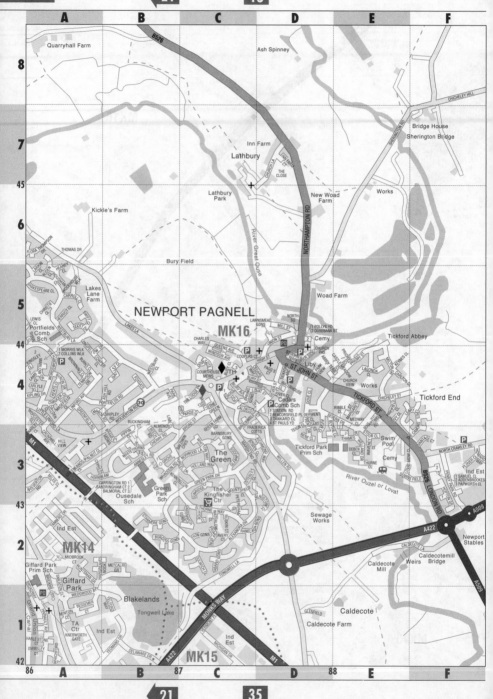

21

13

A **B** **C** **D** **E** **F**

8

Quarryhall Farm

Ash Spinney

CHICHELEY HILL

7

Inn Farm

Lathbury

Bridge House
Sherington Bridge

45

Lathbury
Park

New Woad
Farm

Works

Kickle's Farm

6

FLORA THOMPSON DR

THOMAS DR

Bury Field

River Great Ouse

NORTHAMPTON RD

Woad Farm

Lakes
Lane
Farm

5

NEWPORT PAGNELL

MK16

LAWNSMEAD
GDNS

NORTH
SQ

MILL ST

Cemy

Tickford Abbey

Portfields
Comb
Sch

44

CHARLES
WAY

QUEENS AVE

WINDSOR AVE

COOPERS LA

UNION ST

HIGH ST

1 POLLYS YD
2 OUSEBANK ST

CHURCH

Liby

ST JOHN ST

Works

Tickford End

4

COURTHOUSE
MEWS

LOVAT ST

BURY ST

CALDECOTE ST

CHURCH
VIEW

TICKFORD ST

30

BUCKINGHAM

ALMOND

CHERRY

GREEN LA

GREEN END

FREDERICK
COTTS

Cedars
Comb Sch

1 STATION RD
2 BEACONSFIELD PL DERWENT
3 TANKARD CL
4 ST PAULS YD

RIBBLE

MEDWAY

Swim
Pool

NORTH CRAWLEY RD

BARNSBURY
GDNS

The Green

Tickford Park
Prim Sch

Cemy

1 SAMUEL CL
2 ADDENBROOKES
3 PAPWORTH CL

3

CARRINGTON RD 1
SANDRINGHAM CT 2
BALMORAL CT 3

Ousedale
Sch

Green
Park
Sch

The
Kingfisher
Ctr

GREEN PARK DR

River Ouzel or Lovat

B526 LONDON RD

A509

43

Ind Est

ELTHORNE WAY

Sewage
Works

A422

2

MK14

MIDBROOK

Giffard Park
Prim Sch

Giffard
Park

BURGESS GDNS

Caldecote
Mill

Weirs

Caldecotemill
Bridge

Newport
Stables

Grand Union Canal

TA
Ctr

KNEBWORTH
GATE

1

Blakelands

Tongwell Lake

MONKS WAY

GLENFIELD

Caldecote

Caldecote Farm

HARLESTONE CT
OVERSLEY CL

Ind Est

Ind
Est

A422

MK15

M1

42

86 **A** **B** 87 **C** **D** 88 **E** **F**

21

35

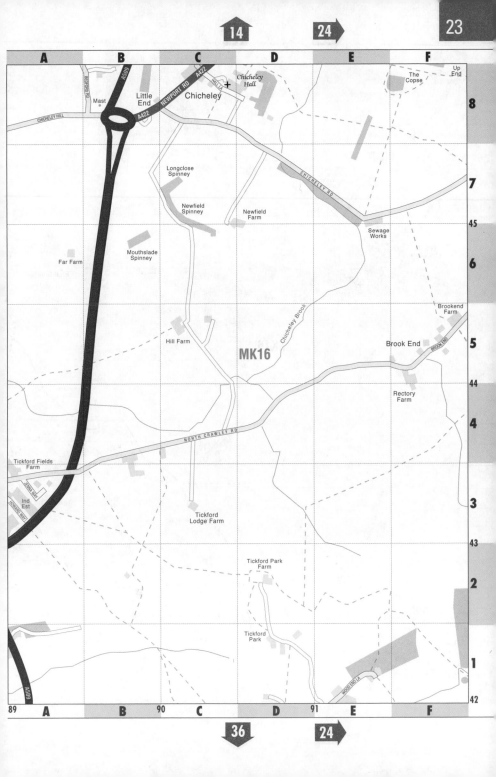

23
15

| A | B | C | D | E | F |

Up End

8

Little Crawley Farm

Horncastle Farm

7

Gumbrills Farm

Old Moat Farm

Chicheley Brook

Dollars Grove Farm

Dollars Grove

East End Farm

45

ORCHARD WAY

HACKETT PLACE

North Crawley

Crawley Grange

Quaker's Farm

6

HIGH ST

PH

BROOK END

North Crawley CE Sch

CHURCH WLK

Church Farm

CHEQUERS LA

Broadmead

Ford

Rookery Farm

Manor Farm

East End

FOLLY LA

MK16

Lodge Farm

Ringtail Farm

5

44

Ring Croft Farm

4

Hurstend Farm

Murtland's Farm

BRIDLE LANE

Rings Wharley Farm

Hurst End

3

Sewage Works

Wharley Farm

43

FEDDEN HO

WEST RD

INDICE RD

PRINCE PHILIP RD

THE DRIVE

Conference Ctr

MERCHANT LA

BENSON CL

REYNOLDS CL

HANDLEY CL

PINE CL

DUNCAN RD

MITCHELL RD

THE CRESCENT

EAST RD

LANCHESTER RD

COLLEGE RD

PO

2

The Cottage

Wharley End

Cranfield Univ

Liby

MK43

Moulsoe Old Wood

Chapelclose Spinney

Wharley End Farm

UNIVERSITY WAY

Cranfield Airport

1

Cabair Coll of Air Training

42

92

A

93

B

C

94

D

E

F

23
37

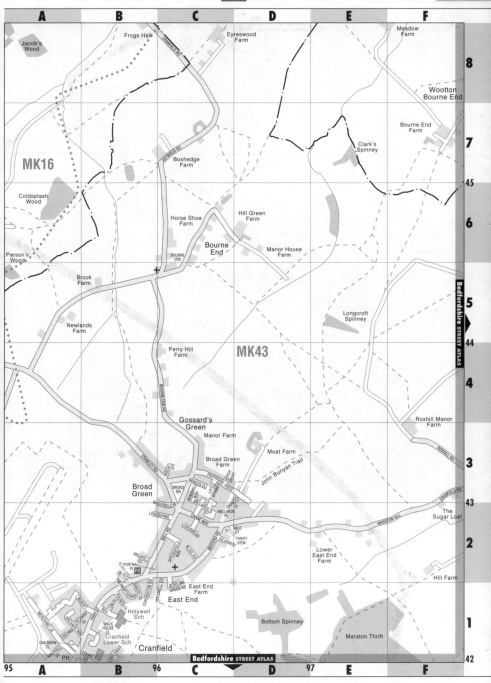

8
7
45
6
5
44
4
3
43
2
1
42

Bedfordshire STREET ATLAS

MK16

Jacob's Wood

Frogs Hall

Eyreswood Farm

Meadow Farm

Wootton Bourne End

Bourne End Farm

Clark's Spinney

Boxhedge Farm

Coldsplash Wood

Hill Green Farm

Horse Shoe Farm

Bourne End

Manor House Farm

Parson's Woods

Brook Farm

Longcroft Spinney

Newlands Farm

Perry Hill Farm

MK43

Roxhill Manor Farm

Gossard's Green

Manor Farm

Moat Farm

Broad Green Farm

John Bunyan Trail

The Sugar Loaf

Broad Green

Lower East End Farm

Hill Farm

East End Farm

East End

Holywell Sch

Walk House

Cranfield Lower Sch

Cranfield

Bottom Spinney

Marston Thrift

Oak Barn Cl

PH

Crowfield

B4525

Falcutt
Hall
Farm

Shortgrove
Wood

Staplegate
Farm

40

Crowfield

Whistley
Wood

B4525

Pimlico

Kiln
Farm

Radstone

Hoppersford
Farm

Wrighton's
Barn

A43

Coldharbour
Farm

NN13

Whitfield House
Farm

PH

CHESTNUT RD

THE AVENUE

FAIRFIELD DR

BEECROFT CT

Whitfield

Fox
Covert

Manor
Farm

Mill
Bridge

MILL RD

CHAPEL
LA

River Great Ouse

Sewage
Works

Ilett's
Farm

Sundale

Bushy
End Wood

Saw
Mill

Versions
Farm

Airstrip

NORTHAMPTON RD

TOP STATION
RD

A43

TURWESTON RD

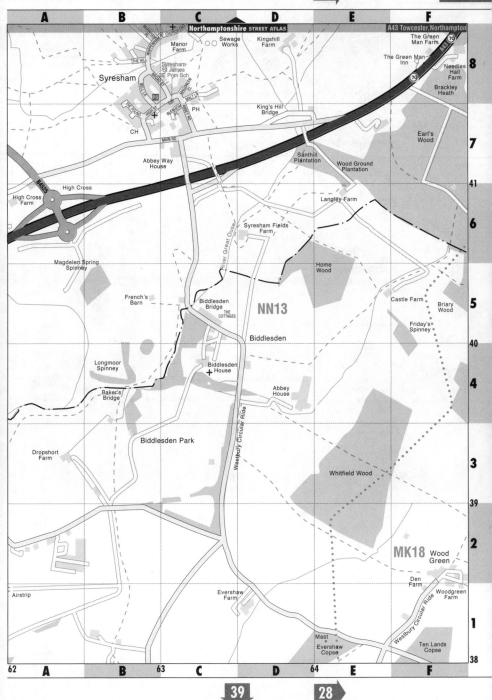

Syresham

Manor Farm

Sewage Works

Kingshill Farm

The Green Man Farm

The Green Man Inn

Needles Hall Farm

Brackley Heath

THE HILL

Syresham CE Prim Sch

BROAD ST

BELL LA

MAGDALEN CL

HIGH ST

BLENHEIM PL

CHAPEL RD

PH

PO

THE POUND

CH

MAIN RD

King's Hill Bridge

Earl's Wood

Abbey Way House

Santhill Plantation

Wood Ground Plantation

High Cross

B4525

High Cross Farm

Langley Farm

Magdelen Spring Spinney

Syresham Fields Farm

NN13

Home Wood

Castle Farm

Briary Wood

French's Barn

Biddlesden Bridge

THE COTTAGES

Friday's Spinney

Biddlesden

Longmoor Spinney

Biddlesden House

Abbey House

Baker's Bridge

Westbury Circular Ride

Dropshort Farm

Biddlesden Park

Whitfield Wood

MK18

Wood Green

Den Farm

Woodgreen Farm

Airstrip

Evershaw Farm

Westbury Circular Ride

Ten Lands Copse

Mast

Evershaw Copse

River Great Ouse

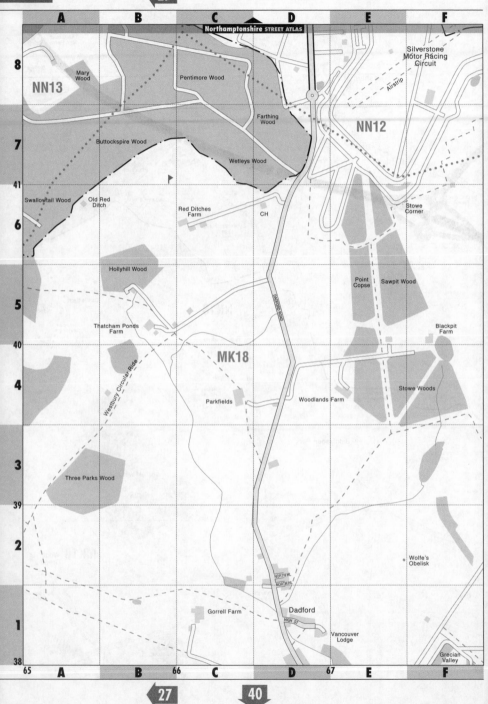

NN13

Mary Wood

Pentimore Wood

Silverstone Motor Racing Circuit

Airstrip

NN12

Farthing Wood

Buttockspire Wood

Wetleys Wood

Swallowtail Wood

Old Red Ditch

Red Ditches Farm

CH

Stowe Corner

Hollyhill Wood

Point Copse

Sawpit Wood

Thatcham Ponds Farm

Blackpit Farm

MK18

Westbury Circular Ride

Stowe Woods

Parkfields

Woodlands Farm

Three Parks Wood

Wolfe's Obelisk

NORTH HL

NORTH HL

Gorrell Farm

Dadford

HIGH ST

Vancouver Lodge

Grecian Valley

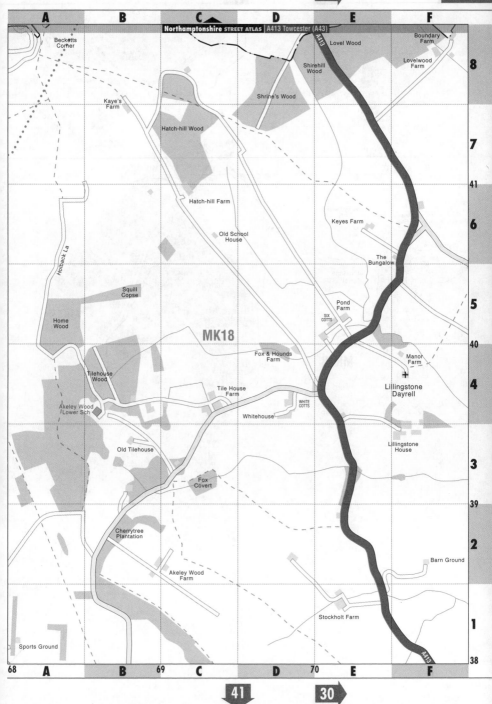

Northamptonshire STREET ATLAS A413 Towcester (A43)

A413

Becketts Corner

Lovel Wood

Boundary Farm

Lovelwood Farm

Shirehill Wood

Shrine's Wood

8

Kaye's Farm

Hatch-hill Wood

7

41

Hatch-hill Farm

Keyes Farm

Old School House

6

Holback La

Squill Copse

The Bungalow

5

Home Wood

Pond Farm

SIX COTTS

40

MK18

Fox & Hounds Farm

Manor Farm

Lillingstone Dayrell

4

Tilehouse Wood

Tile House Farm

WHITE COTTS

Akeley Wood Lower Sch

Whitehouse

Lillingstone House

Old Tilehouse

3

39

Fox Covert

Cherrytree Plantation

2

Barn Ground

Akeley Wood Farm

Stockholt Farm

1

A413

Sports Ground

38

68 **A** 69 **B** **C** 70 **D** **E** **F**

29
17

	A	B	C	D	E	F

8

Manor Cotts

Manor House

Briary Wood Farm

West Ashalls Copse

NN12

Hill Copse

Briary Lodge

East Ashalls Copse

DEANSHANGER DR

The Spinney

Long Copse

7

Manor Lodge

Forest Farm

41

6

Valley Farm

Bradley Fields Farm

Church Farm

CHURCH LA

BROOKSIDE

Wicken Wood

Lillingstone Lovell

Notamore Copse

Glebe Farm

Lilby Wood

MK19

5

Leckhampstead Wood

40

MK18

Hall Farm

4

Hill Farm

3

39

2

Wicken Road Farm

The Shaw

Park Copse

Brook House (Ruin)

WICKER RD

1

Lodge Farm

Limes End

Pottery Farm

CHAPEL LA

Leckhampstead House

LONG ROW

38

71	A	B	72	C	D	73	E	F

29
42

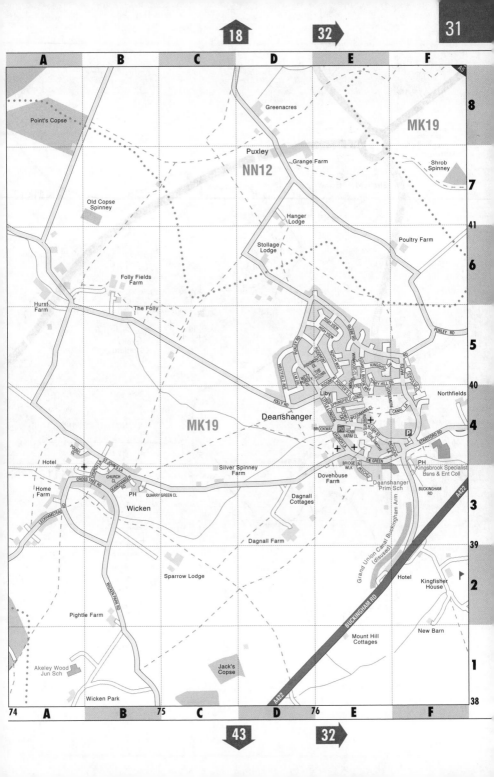

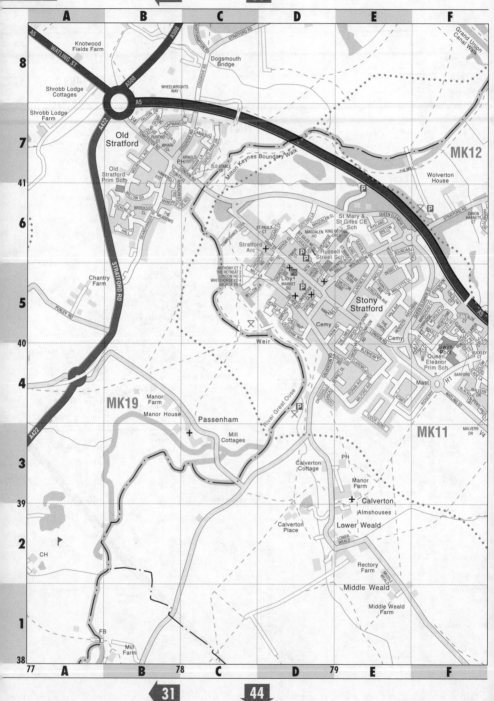

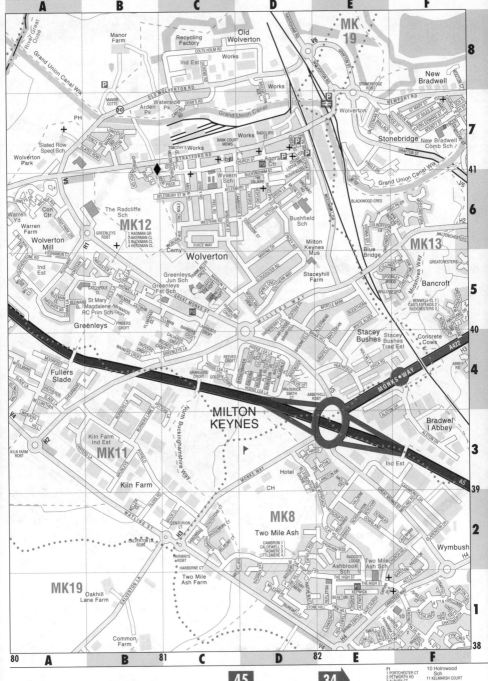

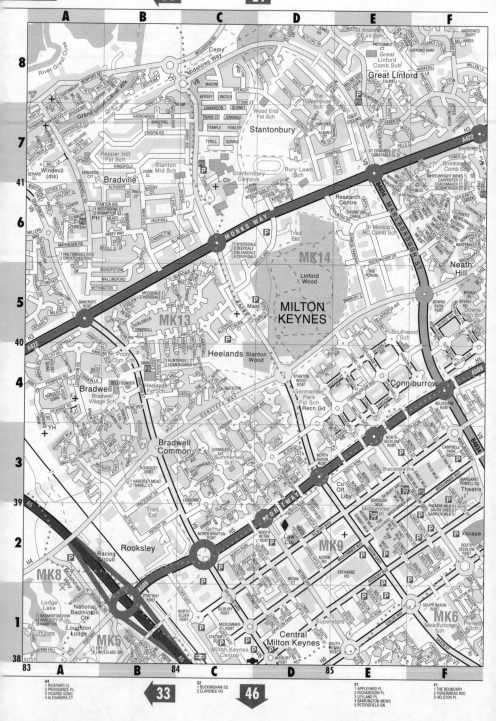

A4
1 RICKYARD CL
2 PROVIDENCE PL
3 VICARAGE GDNS
4 ALEXANDRA CT

C2
1 BUCKINGHAM SQ
2 CLARENCE HO

E1
1 APPLEYARD PL
2 RICHARDSON PL
3 LEYLAND PL
4 BARRINGTON MEWS
5 PETERSFIELD GN

F1
1 THE BOUNDARY
2 FISHERMEAD BVD
3 HELSTON PL

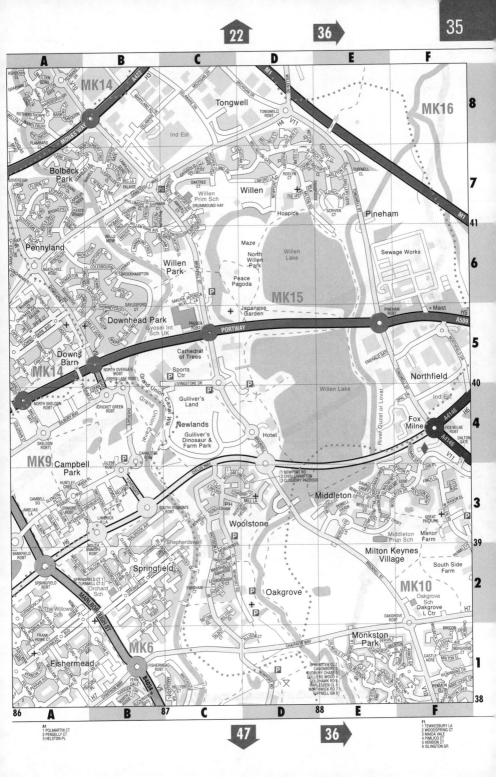

A1
1 PERSHORE CROFT
2 STAVORDALE
3 TYNEMOUTH RISE
4 LEOMINSTER GATE
A3
1 FRESHFIELD AVE
2 PAIGNTON WAY

A4
1 WEYBOURNE RD
2 GOODDRINGTON PL
3 KELLING WAY

B1
1 LAUNDE
2 ST BOTOLPHS
B2
1 MAYPOOL WAY
2 BIGTON CHASE
3 KIDDERMINSTER
WLK

B3
1 BLUE ANCHOR AVE
2 HAWORTH CFT
3 ROPLEY WAY
4 CLIPSTONE BROOK WAY
5 BUTTERFLY GATE
6 RAVENSGLASS
CROFT
7 ARDLEY MEWS

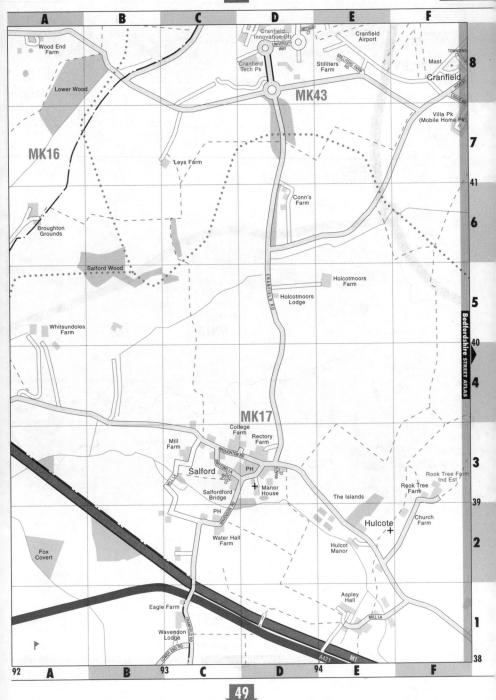

A   B   C   D   E   F

Wood End
Farm

Lower Wood

Cranfield
Innovation Ctr

MEDWAY
CT

UNIVERSITY
WAY

Cranfield
Tech Pk

Cranfield Airport

STILLITERS FARM RD

Stilliters
Farm

MK43

Cranfield

Mast

TOWNSEND CL

HIGH ST

8

Villa Pk
(Mobile Home Pk)

LODGE RD

MK16

Leys Farm

7

41

Conn's
Farm

Broughton
Grounds

Salford Wood

CRANFIELD RD

Holcotmoors
Farm

Holcotmoors
Lodge

6

5

Whitsundoles
Farm

40

4

MK17

College
Farm

Mill
Farm

BROUGHTON RD

COURT LA

Rectory
Farm

MANOR CL

3

Salford

PH

MILL LA

Salfordford
Bridge

Manor
House

PH

NETHERCROFT RD

The Islands

Rook Tree Farm
Ind Est

Rook Tree
Farm

39

Church
Farm

Hulcote

Water Hall
Farm

Hulcot
Manor

Fox
Covert

2

Eagle Farm

CRANFIELD RD

Aspley
Hall

MILL LA

1

Wavendon
Lodge

LOWER END RD

A421

M1

38

92   A   B   93   C   D   94   E   F

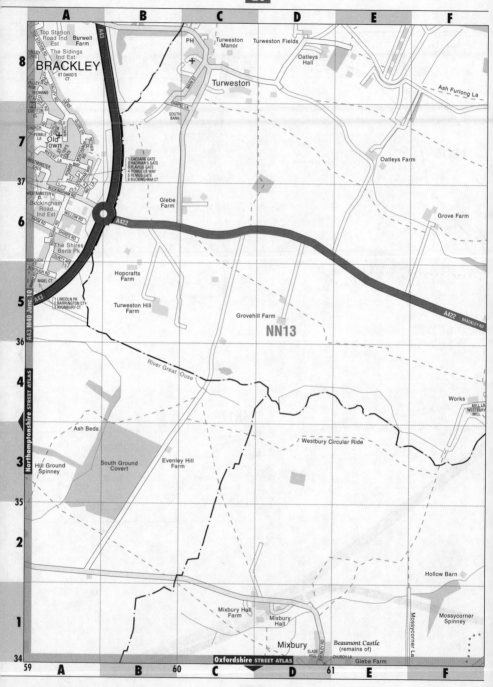

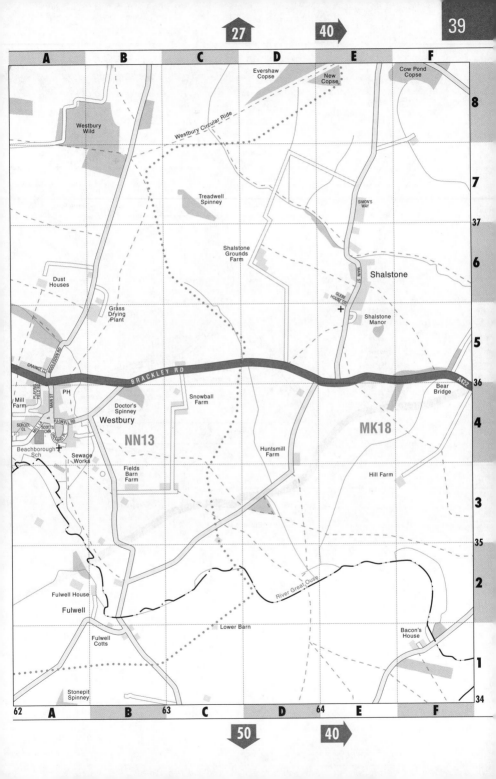

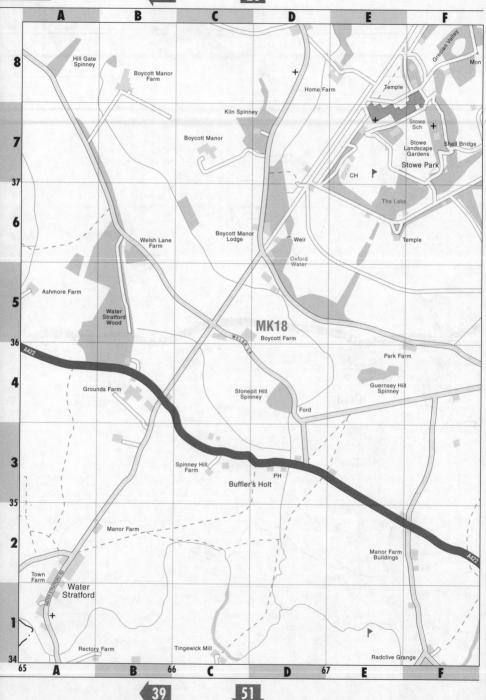

A B C D E F

8

Hill Gate
Spinney

Boycott Manor
Farm

Home Farm

Kiln Spinney

Temple

Stowe
Sch

Grecian Valley

Mon

Boycott Manor

Stowe
Landscape
Gardens

Shell Bridge

7

Stowe Park

37

CH

The Lake

Temple

Welsh Lane
Farm

Boycott Manor
Lodge

Weir

6

Oxford
Water

Ashmore Farm

5

Water
Stratford
Wood

MK18

Boycott Farm

Park Farm

36

A422

WELSH LA

4

Grounds Farm

Stonepit Hill
Spinney

Ford

Guernsey Hill
Spinney

Spinney Hill
Farm

PH

3

Buffler's Holt

35

Manor Farm

Manor Farm
Buildings

2

A422

Town
Farm

Water
Stratford

1

Rectory Farm

Tingewick Mill

Radclive Grange

34

65 A B 66 C D 67 E F

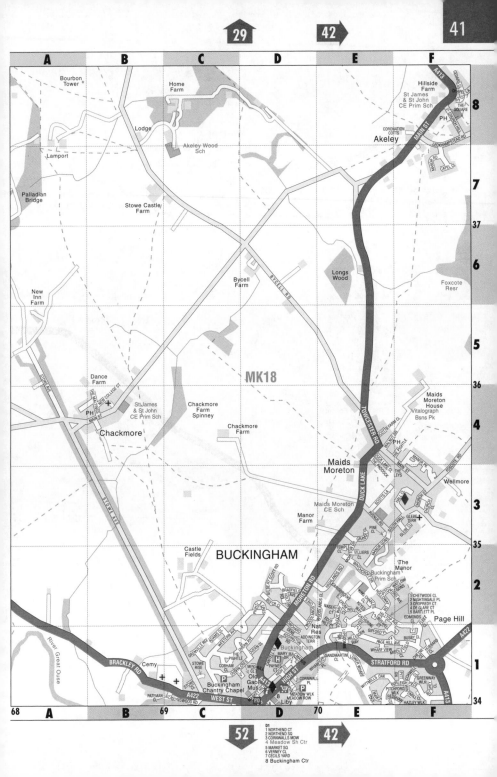

A B C D E F

8
7
37
6
5
36
4
3
35
2
1
34

Bourbon Tower
Home Farm
Hillside Farm
St James & St John CE Prim Sch
Akeley
PH
THE SQUARE
CORONATION COTTS
LEIGHAMSTEAD RD
MAIN ST
GEORGES LA
CHURCH LA
CAPEL CL

Lodge
Akeley Wood Sch

Lamport

Palladian Bridge

Stowe Castle Farm

New Inn Farm

Bycell Farm
BYCELL RD

Longs Wood

Foxcote Resr

MK18

Dance Farm
THE NEW COLLEGE CT
PH
MAIN ST
St James & St John CE Prim Sch
Chackmore

Chackmore Farm Spinney
Chackmore Farm

Maids Moreton House
Vitalograph Bsns Pk

Maids Moreton
Wellmore

TOWCESTER RD
DUCK LAKE
SCOTTS LA
SCOTTS FARM CL
WALNUT DR
PH
THE PADDOCK
THE LEYS
MANOR PK
PRESCOTT RD

Maids Moreton CE Sch

Manor Farm

Castle Fields

BUCKINGHAM

Buckingham Prim Sch
The Manor

Page Hill

1 CHETWODE CL
2 NIGHTINGALE PL
3 CROPREDY CT
4 DE CLARE CT
5 BARTLETT PL

EDMONDS CL

River Great Ouse

BRACKLEY RD
Cemy
A422
WEST ST
PATEMAN CL
GLYNSWOOD RD

Buckingham Chantry Chapel
STOWE RISE
COBHAM

Nat Res
Old Gaol Mus
Buckingham Chantry Chapel
Mary MacArthur
PAYNES
HIGH ST
MORETON RD
STRATFORD RD

Liby
MEADOW ROW
MEADOW WLK

A413
A422

D1
1 NORTHEND CT
2 NORTHEND SQ
3 CORNWALLS MDW
4 Meadow Sh Ctr
5 MARKET SQ
6 VERNEY CL
7 CECILS YARD
8 Buckingham Ctr

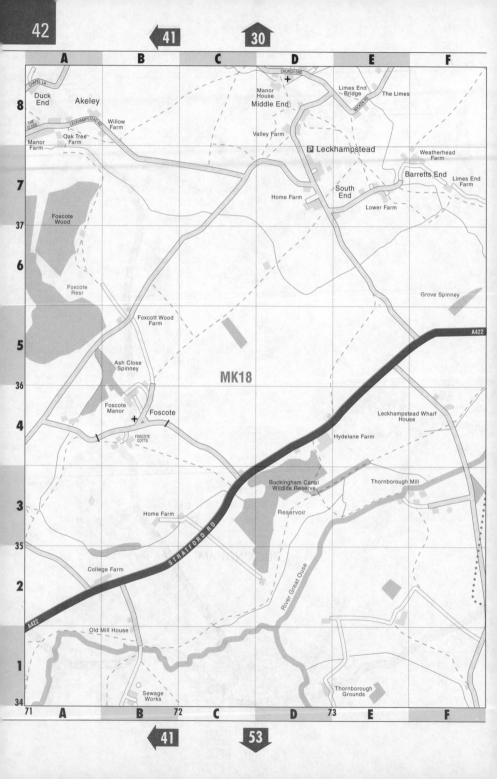

A B C D E F

8

CHURCH END

Duck
End

Akeley

Manor
House

Middle End

Limes End
Bridge

The Limes

WICKEN RD

CHAPEL LA

Willow
Farm

Valley Farm

Leckhampstead

Weatherhead
Farm

THE CLOSE

LECKHAMPSTEAD RD

Oak Tree
Farm

Manor
Farm

7

Foxcote
Wood

Home Farm

South
End

Barretts End

Limes End
Farm

37

Lower Farm

6

Foxcote
Resr

Grove Spinney

Foxcott Wood
Farm

A422

5

Ash Close
Spinney

MK18

36

Foscote
Manor

Foscote

Leckhampstead Wharf
House

4

FOSCOTE
COTTS

Hydelane Farm

Buckingham Canal
Wildlife Reserve

Thornborough Mill

3

Home Farm

Reservoir

35

STRATFORD RD

College Farm

River Great Ouse

2

A422

Old Mill House

1

Thornborough
Grounds

34

Sewage
Works

71 A B 72 C D 73 E F

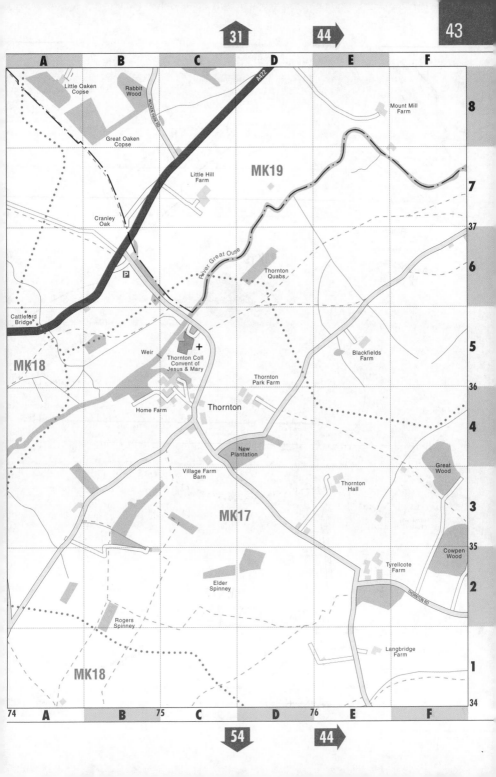

44

43 32

| | A | B | C | D | E | F |

8

River Great Ouse

Blacon Spinney

Upper Weald

Milton Keynes Boundary Walk

7

Beachampton Hall

Manor Farm

Hill Farm

37

Beachampton

PH

Home Farm

MK19

6

WATER LA

ELM ST

MAIN ST

Red House Farm

Grange Farm

Beachampton Grove

Grove Farm

5

School Furze

The Oaks

36

4

Beachampton Bsns Pk

Potash Farm

3

Furzenfield Farm

35

Elm Farm

2

MK17

Yew Tree Farm

Basshill Farm

NASH RD

North Buckinghamshire Way

WHADDON RD

THORNTON RD

Holywell Cottages

The Hill

Town End

Nash

Holywell Farm

1

STRATFORD RD

HIGH ST

WINSLOW RD

34

THORNBOROUGH RD

OLD ENGLISH

Barnhill Farm

77 A 78 B C 79 D E F

43 55

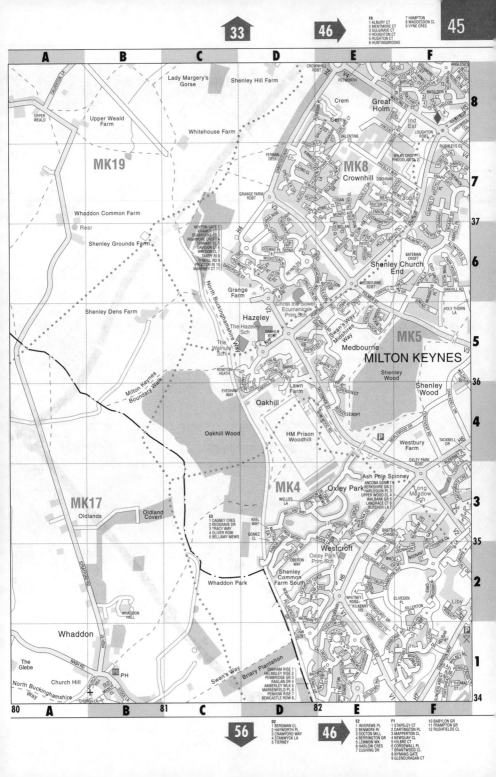

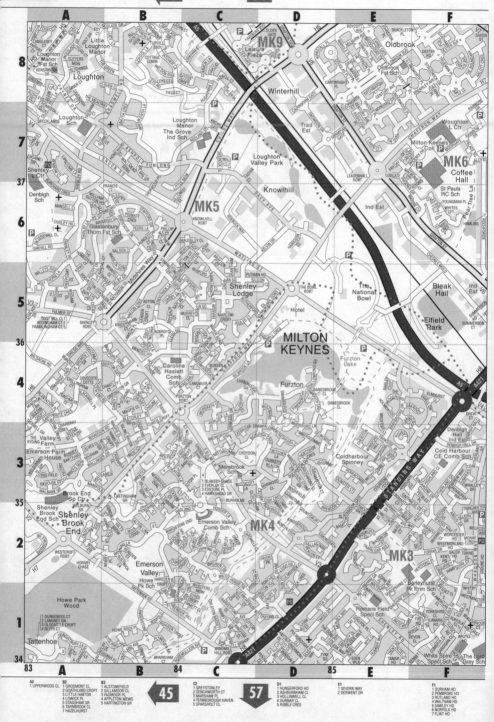

A3
1 UPPERWOOD CL

B2
1 GROSMONT CL
2 GOATHLAND CROFT
3 LITTLE HABTON
4 LOWICK PL
5 STAGSHAW GR
6 TARNBROOK CL
7 HAZELHURST

B3
1 ALSTONEFIELD
2 GILLAMOOR CL
3 FADMOOR PL
4 APPLETON MEWS
5 HARTINGTON GR

C2
1 GREYSTONLEY
2 DENCHWORTH CT
3 MARSHAW PL
4 FERNBOROUGH HAVEN
5 SPARSHOLT CL

D1
1 HUNGERFORD HO
2 ASHBURNHAM CL
3 HOLLINWELL CL
4 DUNBAR CL
5 RIBBLE CRES

E1
1 SEVERN WAY
2 DERWENT DR

F1
1 DURHAM HO
2 PEMBROKE HO
3 RUTLAND HO
4 WALTHAM HO
5 SAWLEY HO
6 NORFOLK HO
7 FLINT HO

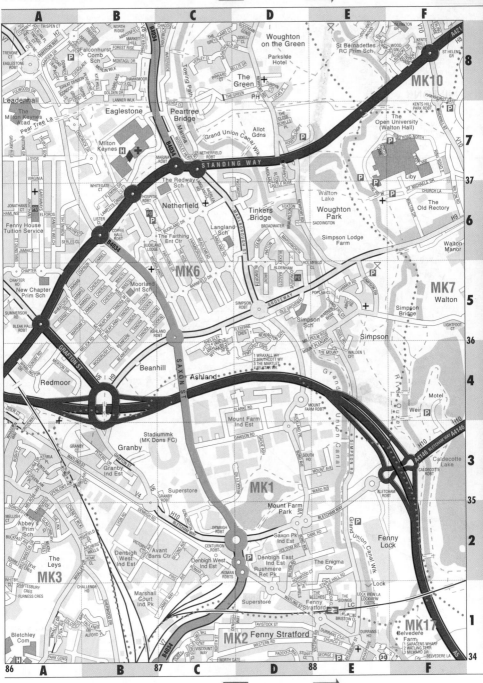

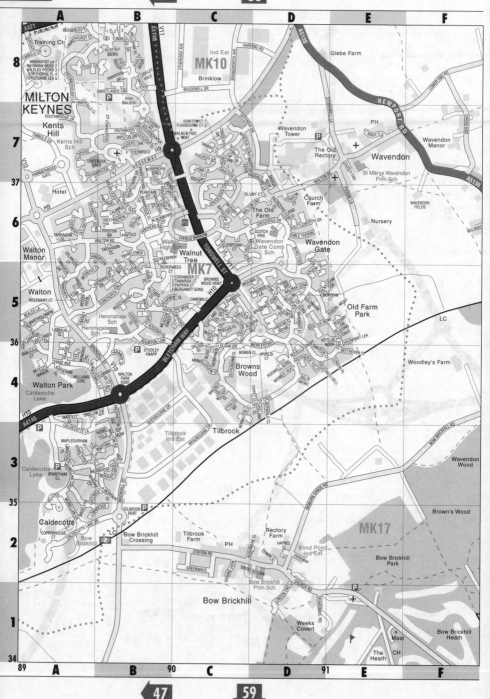

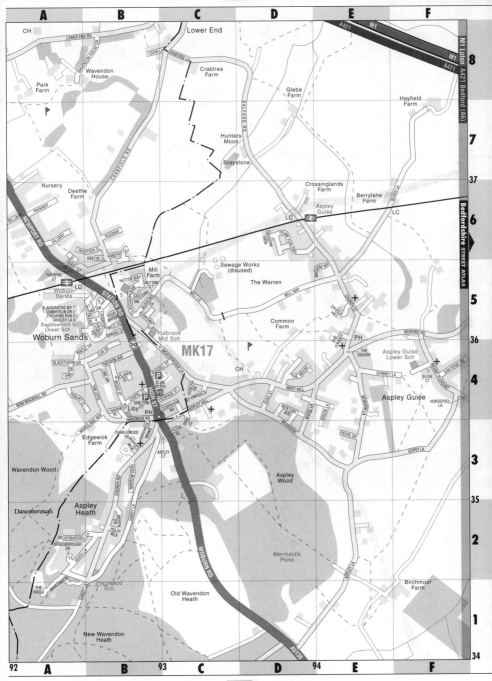

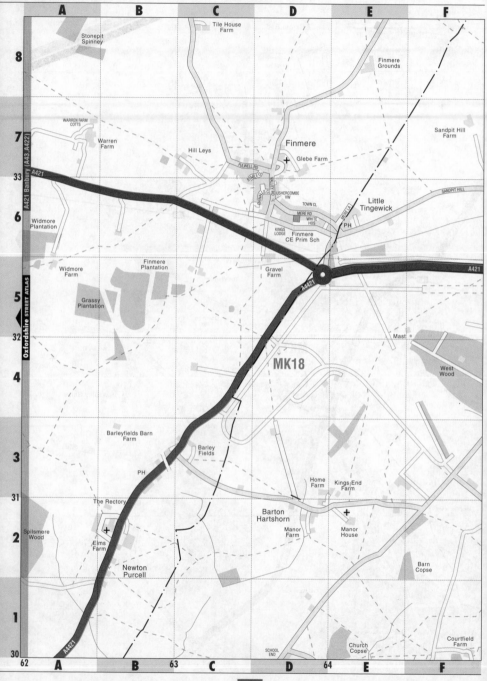

Stonepit Spinney

Tile House Farm

Finmere Grounds

WARREN FARM COTTS

Warren Farm

Hill Leys

Sandpit Hill Farm

Finmere

FULWELL RD

Glebe Farm

A421

A421 Banbury (A43, A421)

Widmore Plantation

USHERCOMBE VW

TOWN CL

Little Tingewick

SANDPIT HILL

Sandpit Hill

MERE RD

WHITE HOS

PH

Widmore Farm

Finmere Plantation

KINGS LODGE

Finmere CE Prim Sch

Gravel Farm

Grassy Plantation

A4421

Mast •

West Wood

Oxfordshire STREET ATLAS

MK18

Barleyfields Barn Farm

Barley Fields

PH

Home Farm

Kings End Farm

The Rectory

Spilsmere Wood

Elms Farm

Barton Hartshorn

Manor House

Barn Copse

Newton Purcell

Manor Farm

A421

SCHOOL END

Church Copse

Courtfield Farm

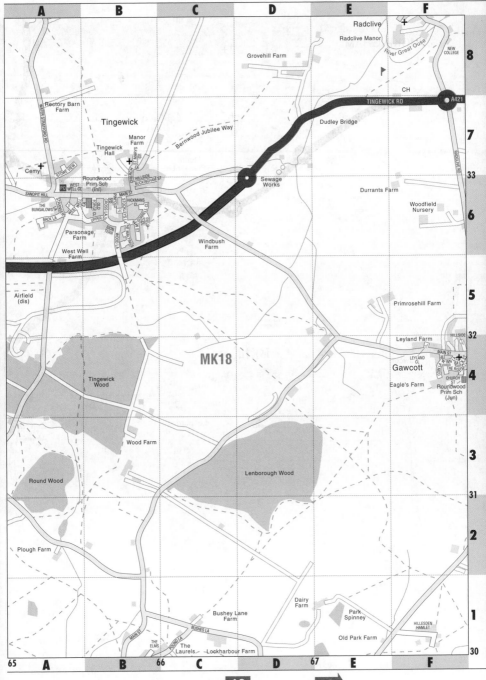

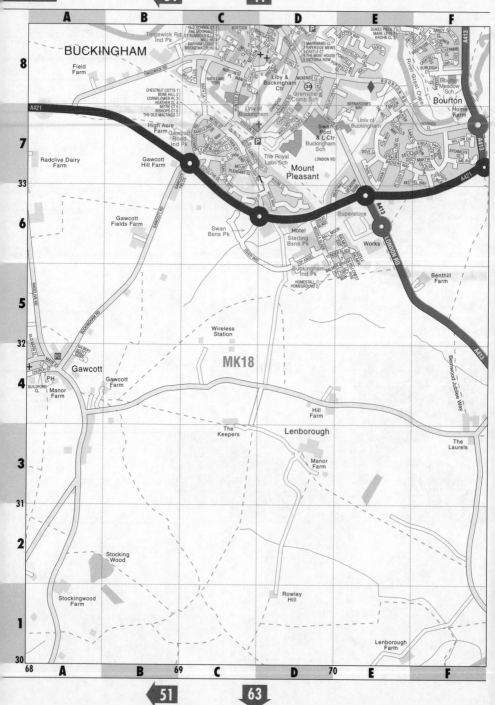

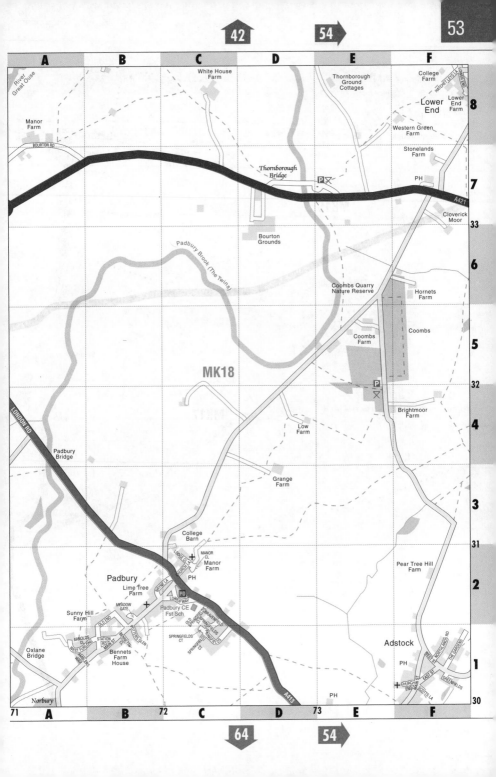

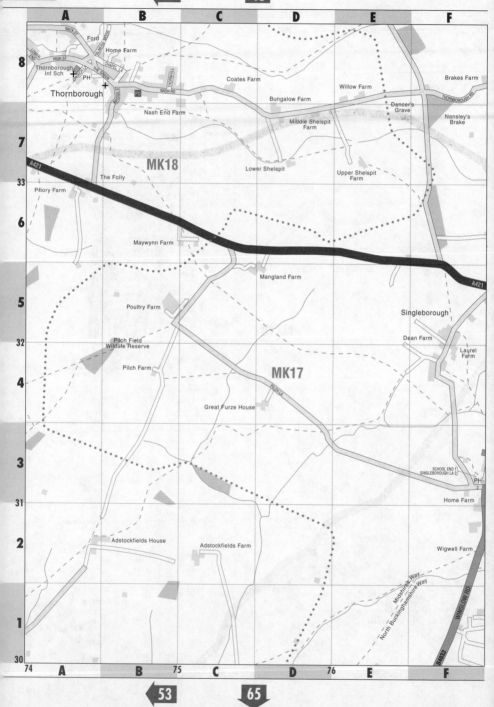

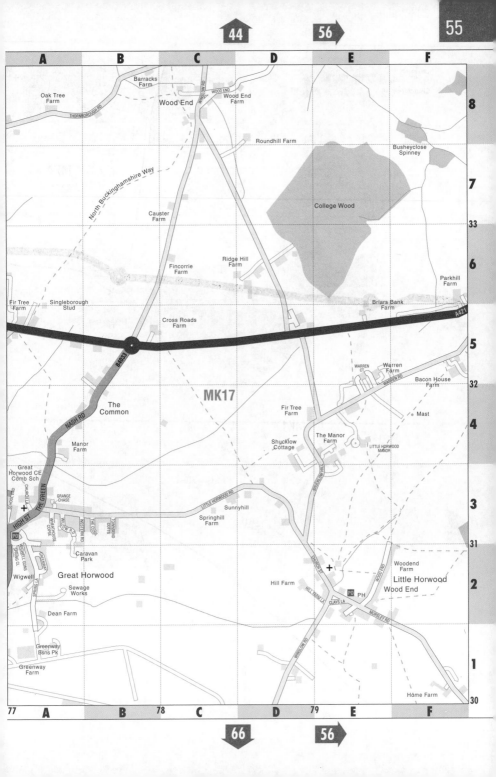

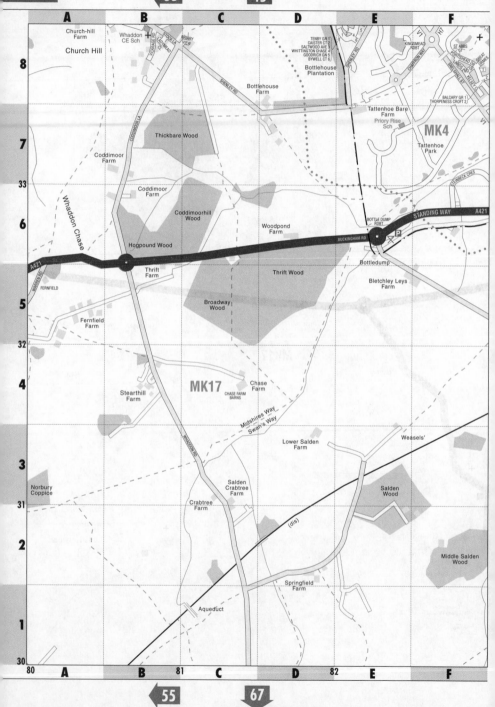

A B C D E F

8

7

33

6

5

32

4

3

31

2

1

30

80 A B 81 C D 82 E F

Church-hill Farm

Church Hill

Whaddon CE Sch

PRIORY VIEW

STOCK LA

CODIMEAD

SHENLEY RD

CODDIMOOR LA

Bottlehouse Farm

Bottlehouse Plantation

TENBY GR 1
CAISTER CT 2
SALTWOOD AVE 3
WHITTINGTON CHASE 4
GOODRICH GN 5
BYWELL CT 6

SHENLEY RD

KINGSMEAD ROBT

CHURCHILL WAY

St ABBS GT

BALCARY GR 1
THORPENESS CROFT 2

Tattenhoe Bare Farm
Priory Rise Sch

MK4

Tattenhoe Park

Thickbare Wood

Coddimoor Farm

Coddimoor Farm

Coddimoorhill Wood

Woodpond Farm

Whaddon Chase

BOTTLE DUMP ROBT

STANDING WAY

A421

Hogpound Wood

Thrift Farm

BUCKINGHAM RD

Bottledump

Thrift Wood

Bletchley Leys Farm

A421

WEBBER RD

FERNFIELD

Broadway Wood

FERNFIELD

Fernfield Farm

Stearthill Farm

MK17

Chase Farm

CHASE FARM BARNS

WHADDON RD

Midshires Way

Swan's Way

Lower Salden Farm

Weasels'

Norbury Coppice

Crabtree Farm

Salden Crabtree Farm

Salden Wood

(dis)

Middle Salden Wood

Springfield Farm

Aqueduct

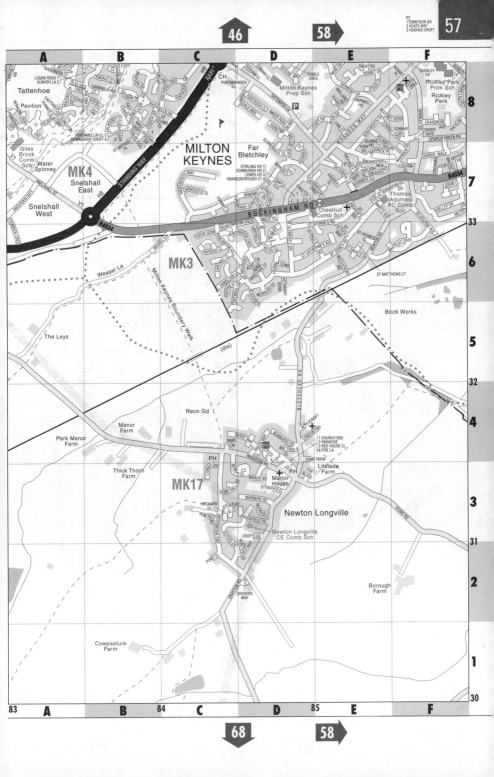

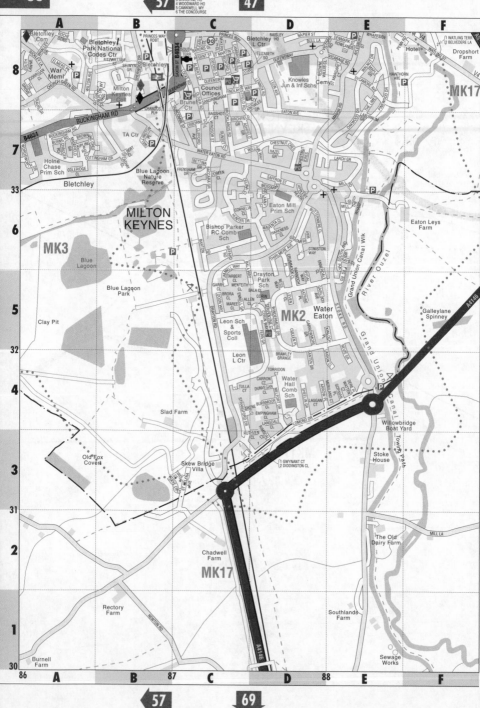

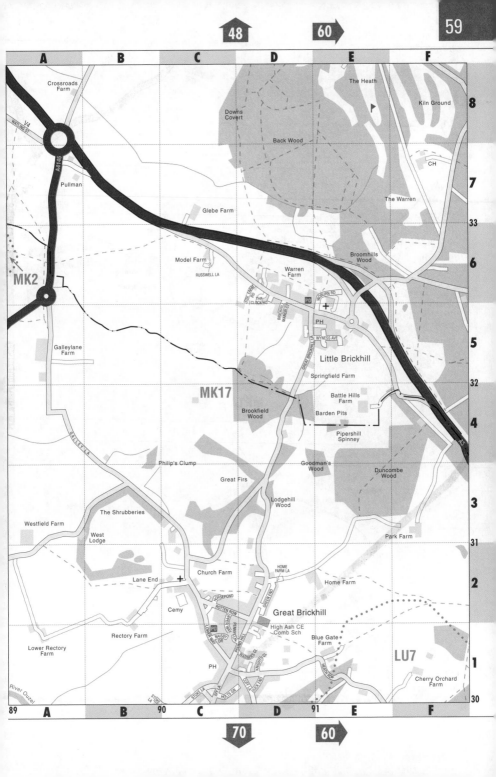

A B C D E F

8

New Wavendon Heath

Bells Copse

7

Tollhouse Grove

Hundreds Farm

Horsemoor Farm

Dolton's Farm

PH

A5130 WOBURN RD

NEWPORT RD

CRAWLEY RD A4012

A5130

BEDFORD ST

STAUNTON HO

Woburn Lower Sch

MARQUIS RD

ELEANOR WLK

Woburn

PO

MARKET

TH

GEORGE ST

33

Little Brickhill Copse

Charle Wood

TIMBER LA

LEIGHTON ST

A4012 Leighton Buzzard

6

Shire Oak

Pinfold Pond

Pinfoldpond

Wayn Close

Crowholt Plantation

Lowe's Wood

Job's Farm

Greensand Ridge Wlk

5

Utcoate Grange

Circuitt's Covert

32

Buttermilk Farm

Buttermilk Wood

MK17

4

Nun Wood

Apesfield Farm

Sheeplane Belt

3

A5

31

Milton Keynes Boundary Walk

2

Rammamere Farm

SHEEPLANE

Sand Pit

PH

Bushycommon Wood

Hill Farm

1

LU7

Rammamere Heath

Bragenham Wood

King's Wood National Nature Reserve

WOBURN RD

A5

LU7

Arnold's Cottages

30

92 A B 93 C 94 E F

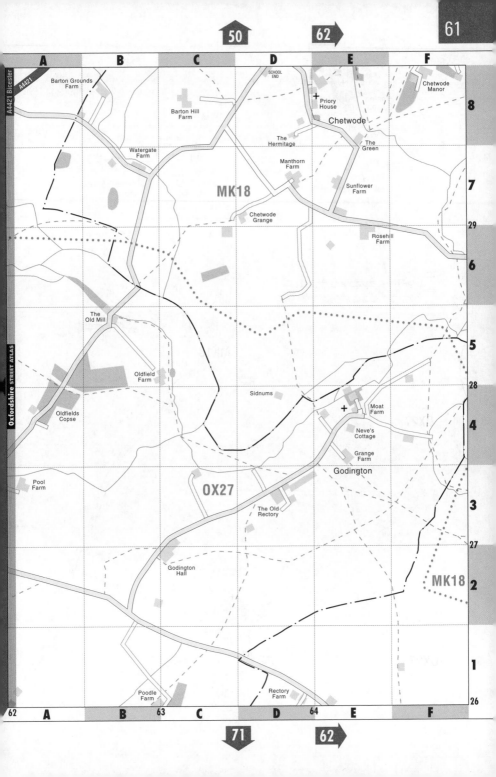

A **B** **C** **D** **E** **F**

8

Church Farm

PO

Preston Bissett

SCHOOL LA

The Laurels

The Common

Jubilee Farm House

Poplars Farm

THE SQUARE

Thorpes Farm

MAIN ST

College Farm

Jubilee Farm

7

Fir Tree Cottage

Copperhouse Farm

Buryfield Spinney

29

6

Casemore Farm

Westfield Farm

Manor Farm

5

MK18

28

Cowley Farm

OX27

4

Cowley Old House

Cowley Lodge

3

Twyford Mill

27

Three Bridge Mill

2

Church View Farm

Twyford CE Fst Sch

MILL LA

MAIN ST

CHURCH ST

GRANGE CL

SCHOOL

BROOK FARM CL

Home Farm

OX27

1

Twyford

PO

Hall

PH

BICESTER RD

Portway Cottages

PORTWAY RD

26

MANOR CT

ROKEHILL CRES

65 **A** **B** 66 **C** **D** 67 **E** **F**

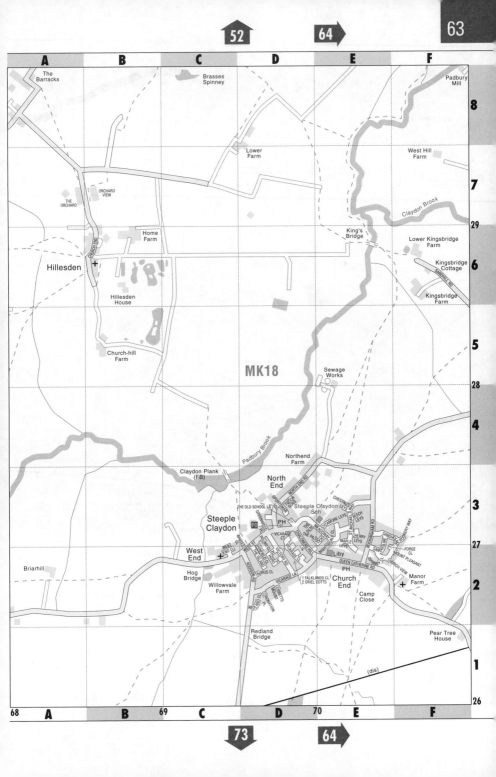

A B C D E F

The Barracks

Padbury Mill

8

Brasses Spinney

Lower Farm

West Hill Farm

7

ORCHARD VIEW

THE ORCHARD

Claydon Brook

29

King's Bridge

Lower Kingsbridge Farm

Home Farm

Kingsbridge Cottage

SANDHILL RD

Hillesden

6

Kingsbridge Farm

Hillesden House

MK18

Church-hill Farm

5

Sewage Works

28

Padbury Brook

4

Claydon Plank (FB)

Northend Farm

North End

THE OLD SCHOOL LA

GREENWAY

SPRING CLOSE

NORTH END RD

Steeple Claydon Sch

CASSORE LEYS

CHESTNUT LEYS

BEECH LEYS

3

Steeple Claydon

PO

PH

VICARAGE CL

THE PADDOCKS

MAPLE LEYS

CHERRY LEYS

OAKENHAM RD

SANDYS CL

COVERTY WAY

MOUNT PLEASANT

27

West End

WEST END

THE ISLAND

ADDISON RD

FORGE CL

CHURCH VIEW

Liby

PH

Manor Farm

Hog Bridge

TAURUS CL

VICARAGE LA

QUEEN CATHERINE RD

Church End

2

Briarhill

Willowvale Farm

CORONATION

REDLAND

1 FALKLANDS CL
2 ORIEL COTTS

Camp Close

Redland Bridge

Pear Tree House

1

(dis)

26

68 A B 69 C D 70 E F

63
53

	A	B	C	D	E	F

8

Wardens Farm

Folly Farm

A413

Adstock Manor Stud

A413

7

Padburyhill Farm

White Bridge

29

Hill Farm Cottages

Hill Farm

6

Claydon Brook

5

MK18

28

Herd's Hill Cottage

Claydon Hill Farm No 6

Claydon Hill Farm

HERD'S HILL

Claydon Hill Farm No 5

SANDHILL RD

Swan's Way

4

Jubilee Bridge

Windmillhill Farm

Verney Junction

PH.

JUBILEE COTTS

3

Littleworth Farm

Verney Junction Bans Pk Littleworth

(dis)

Ashmore Farm House

27

Mount Pleasant Farm

Sandhill

Greenacres

Sandhill

Sandhill Farm

2

RAILWAY COTTS

LC

Rectory Farm

QUEEN CATHERINE RD

North Buckinghamshire Way

1

QUEEN CATHERINE RD

26

71	A		B	72	C		D	73	E		F

63
74

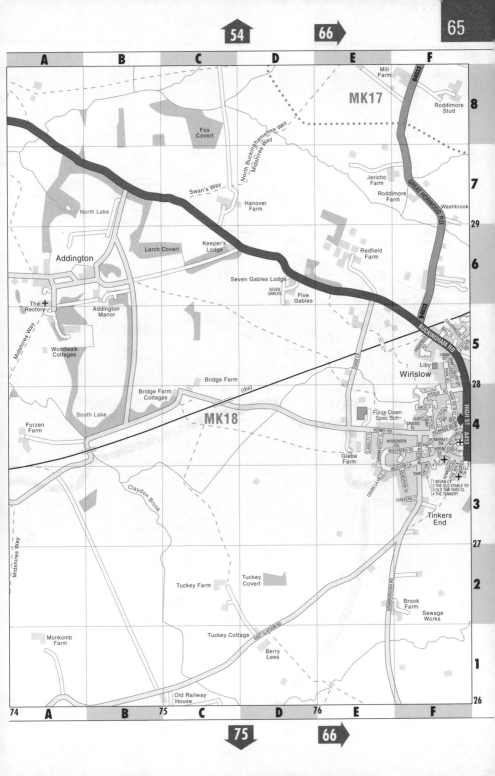

A B C D E F

8

Greenway Farm

Mount Pleasant

The Hollows

Horwood House

7

Fishpond Spinney

Osierbed Spinney

29

The White House

(dis)

Roddimore Covert

Moco Farm

6

Clare Farm

Canada

Foxhole Farm

1 STATION COTTS
2 OLD STATION CL

TANK HOUSE RD

Spring Corner

Dodley Hill Farm

MK17

COMBEFORD WAY

MCLERNON WAY

THE SPINNEY

MAGPIE WAY

RUDDS CL

FLEDGELINGS WAY

SANDWELL LA

OLD MILL FURLONG

Station Rd Ind Est

KEACH CL

LONGLANDS CT

LONGLANDS WAY

5

SCOTT EVANS

DUKES WAY

Winslow CE Comb Sch

LAMB WAY

ELMOT

MEETES CL LA

Redhall Farm

Abovemead Farm

PICCADILLY MEWS

28

P

CRICKETERS WAY

BELL WALK

CHAPEL FIELDS GATE

NORTH CROFT

WINSLOW RD

MK18

Winslow

P

BREWERNON CL

GREYHOUND

PO

ST CLELAND GATE

ELSDALE CL

OVERN CL

OVERS END

4

Ivy Farm

A413

SHEEP ST

Hotel

CLAYCUTTERS

TENNIS LA

FIVE CL

Shipton Mead Farm

Cross Bucks Way

ELD END

CHARLTON CL

Duck End

B4032 WINSLOW RD

B4032

SHIPTON

Rands Farm

Jubilee Cottages

3

Shipton Farm

Swanbourne House Sch

27

Shipton Bridge

2

Haybush Farm

Claydon Brook

BENNETT'S HILL A413

1

Bennett's Hill

Midshires Way

Swan's Way

North Hill Farm

26

77 A B 78 C D 79 E F

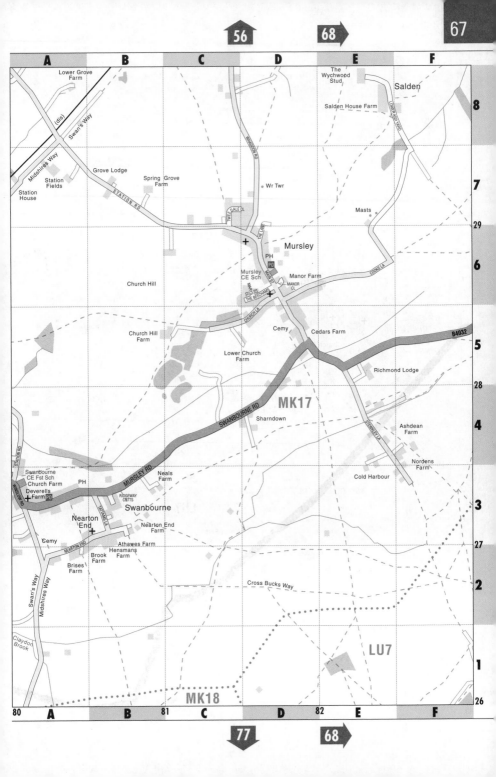

	A	B	C	D	E	F

8

Ash Farm

Highfield

Villiers Farm

NEWTON RD

Drayton Crossroad Farm

7

29

Prospect Farm

MK17

HIGHWAY

NEWMANS END

CARRINGTON

PROSPECT CL

STONES WAY

The Lower Farm

LOVE ROW

Sewage Works

6

Drayton Parslow Village Sch

PO

Chestnut Farm

Drayton Parslow

Manor Farm

PH

BARTLEMAS
MEADOW
BARTON CL
CALDON CL
NORTH CL
SOUTH CL
CHAPEL LA
NEW RD

Kingsland Farm

Bungler's Hall

Church End

Stokeroad Farm

5

B4032

MAIN RD

28

Merrymead

Old Leighton Farm

BLETCHLEY RD

Grange Farm

4

3

27

The Grange

LU7

HEYWOOD PK

GRANGE CL

North End

Heywood House

Lansdowne Farm

Lower Dean Farm

Upper Dean Farm

White Horse Lodge

Laurel Farm

Stewkley House

2

HIGH ST N

STOCKHALL

STOCKHALL
TERR

Stewkley

DEAN RD

Stewkley Dean

Dean Farm

Sycamore Farm

PH

Bonham Farm

St Michael's
CE Comb Sch

FISHMERE
CHAPEL
CRES

Church Farm

1

Dean Tithe Farm

Bury Farm

SCHOOL LA

TYTHE GDNS

SOULBURY RD B4032

ST
MICHAELS

26

83	A	B	84	C	D	85	E	F

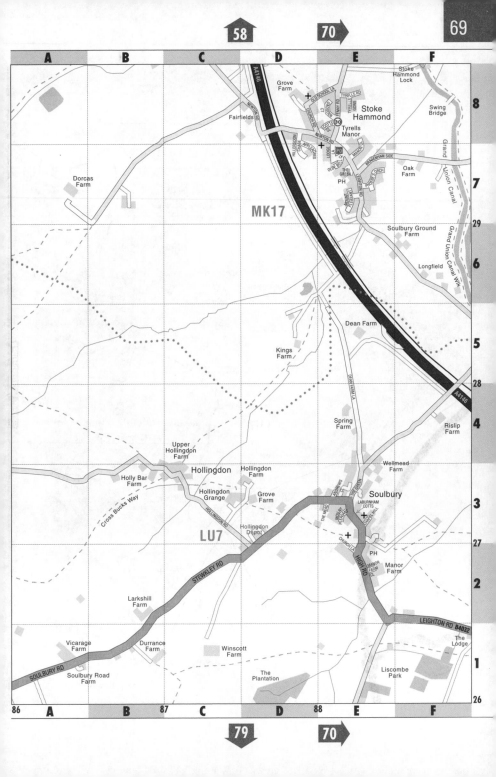

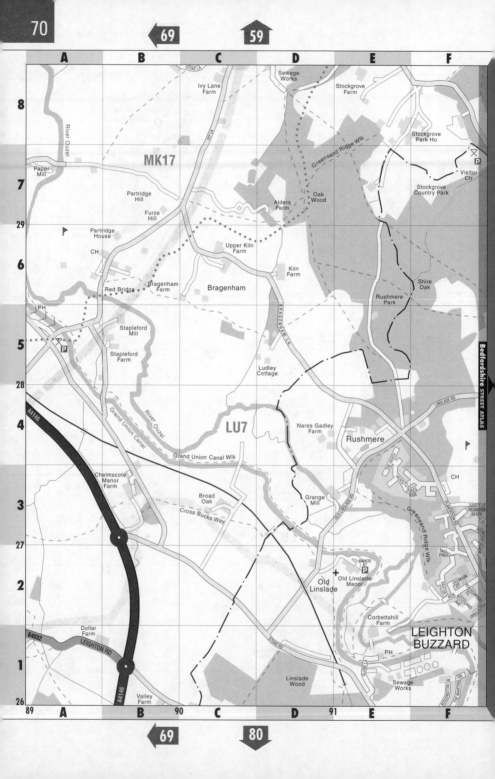

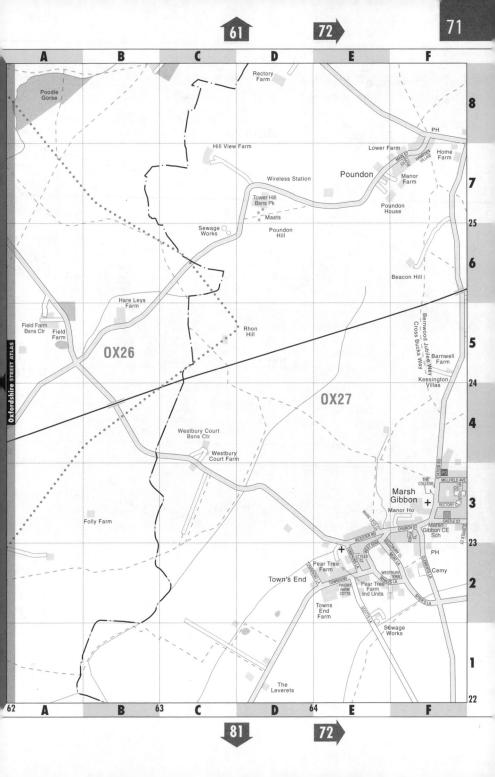

| | A | B | C | D | E | F |

8 Red Furlong Farm

Twyford Lodge

Rosehill Farm

MK18

Portway Farm

PORTWAY RD

7

25

Grebe Lake

Station House

Lawn Farm

CHESHIRE COTTS

SCHOOL HILL

6 Windmill Hill

BARCLAY CL

HAMPDEN HILL

Charndon

WOOTTON GN

BEATRICE CL

Charndon Grounds

MAIN ST

SPENCER GDNS

5

OX27

Middle Farm

Valley Farm

MK18

Hill Farm

24

4

3

LITTLE MARSH RD

Swan Farm

SWAN LA

SCOTTS CL

Little Marsh

Gubbinshole Ditch

CASTLE ST

23

CASTLE CL

Leopold Farm

2

Summerstown

Rectory Farm

ST MICHAEL CL

LEONARDS CL

CROSS

HP18

Edgcott

BUCKINGHAM RD

New Swan Farm

Gubbin's Hole

PO

GREN

LAWN

SHERINGHAM LA

1

Gubbins Hole Farm

Lower Farm

22

65 | A | B | 66 C | D | 67 E | F |

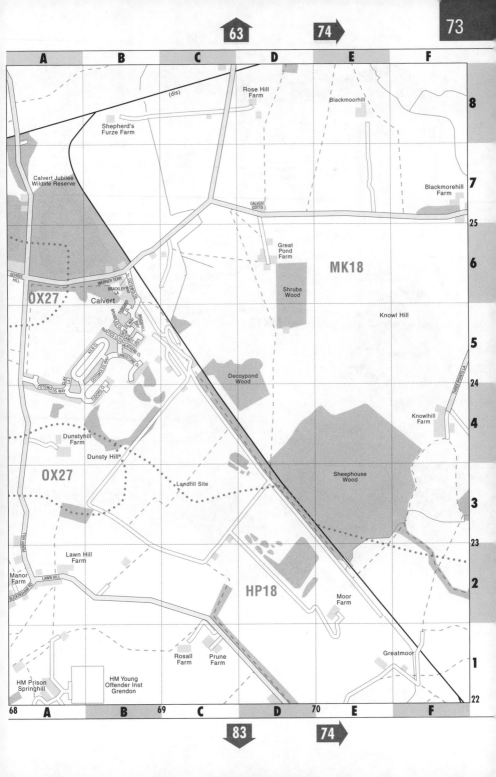

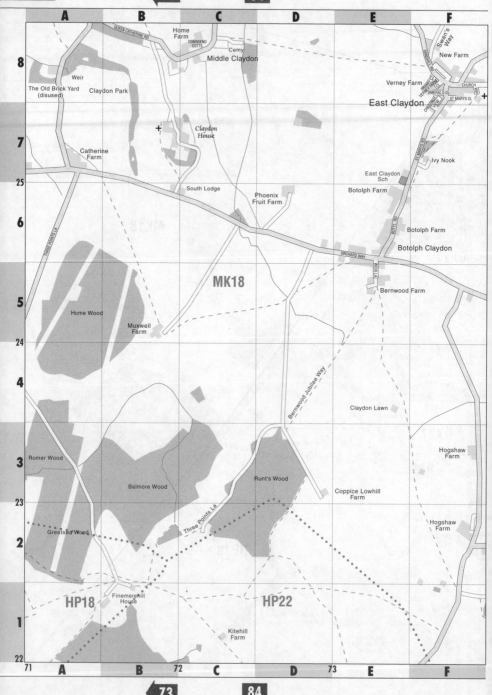

A B C D E F

8

The Old Brick Yard (disused)

Weir

Claydon Park

QUEEN CATHERINE RD

Home Farm

TOWNSEND COTTS

Cemy

Middle Claydon

Swan's Way

New Farm

Verney Farm

East Claydon

VERNEY FARM
EMERALD CL
ST MARYS CL
CHURCH WAY

7

Catherine Farm

Claydon House

East Claydon Sch

Ivy Nook

ST MARYS RD

25

South Lodge

Phoenix Fruit Farm

Botolph Farm

6

THREE POINTS LA

Botolph Farm

ORCHARD WAY

Botolph Claydon

BOTYL RD

MK18

Bernwood Farm

5

Home Wood

Muxwell Farm

24

Bernwood Jubilee Way

Claydon Lawn

4

Hogshaw Farm

3

Romer Wood

Balmore Wood

Runt's Wood

Coppice Lowhill Farm

Hogshaw Farm

23

Greatsea Wood

Three Points La.

2

HP18

Finemerehill House

HP22

Kitehill Farm

1

22

71 A B 72 C D 73 E F

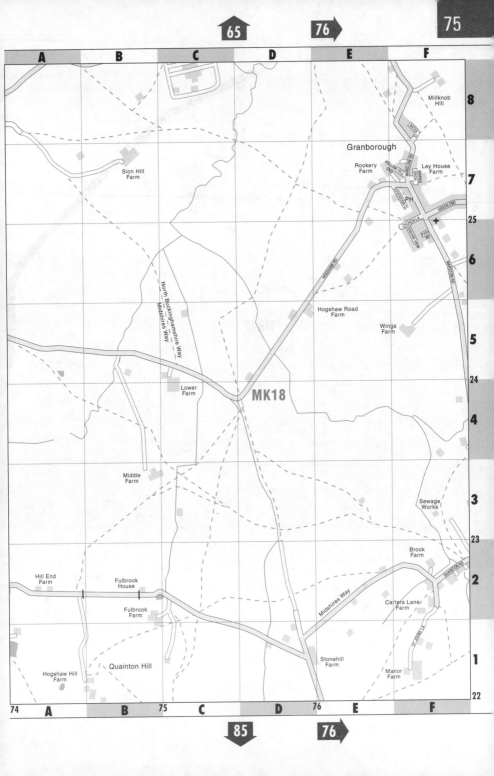

65
76

A　B　C　D　E　F

8

Millknob
Hill

Granborough

Sion Hill
Farm

Rookery
Farm

Ley House
Farm

7

PH

25

North Buckinghamshire Way
Midshires Way

Hogshaw Road
Farm

Wings
Farm

6

5

24

Lower
Farm

MK18

4

Middle
Farm

Sewage
Works

3

23

Brook
Farm

Hill End
Farm

Fulbrook
House

Midshires Way

Carters Lane
Farm

2

Fulbrook
Farm

Hogshaw Hill
Farm

Quainton Hill

Stonehill
Farm

Manor
Farm

1

22

74　A　B　75　C　D　76　E　F

85
76

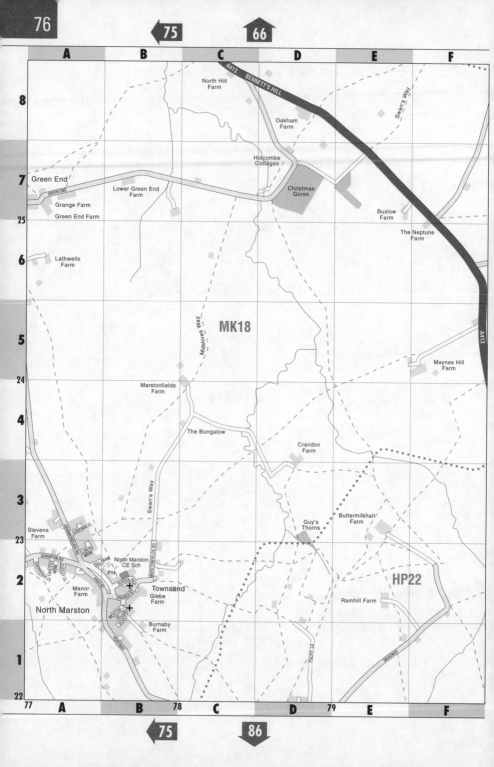

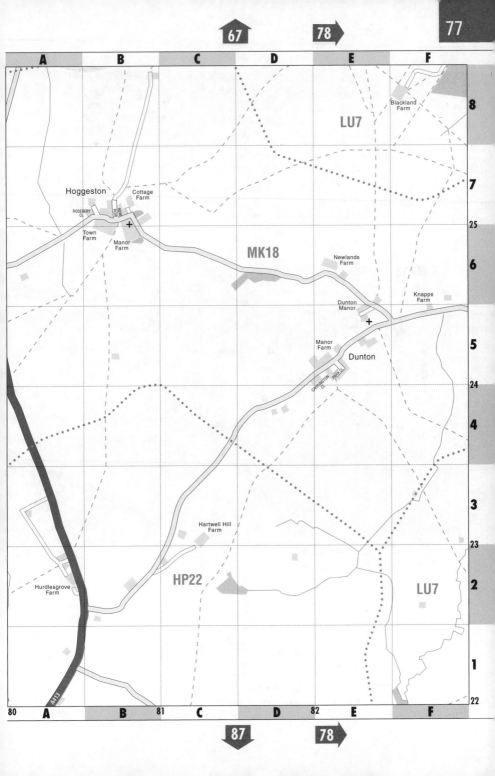

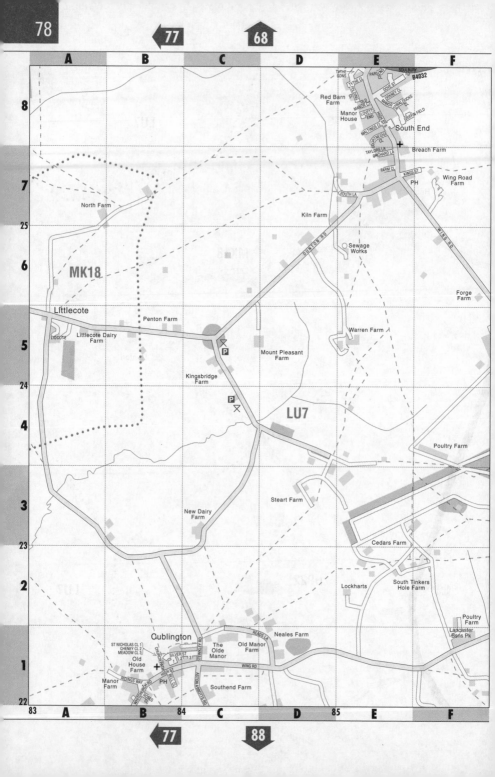

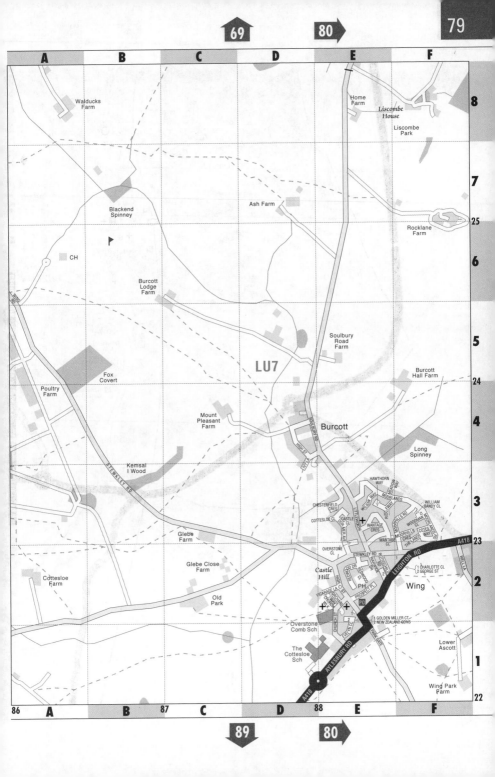

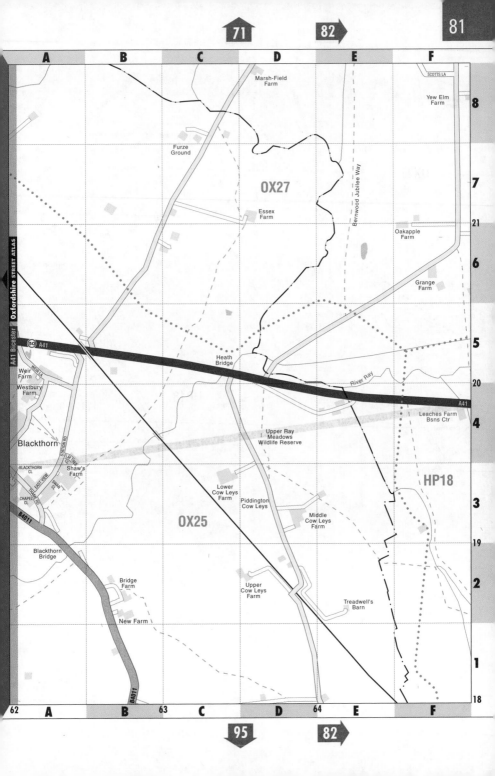

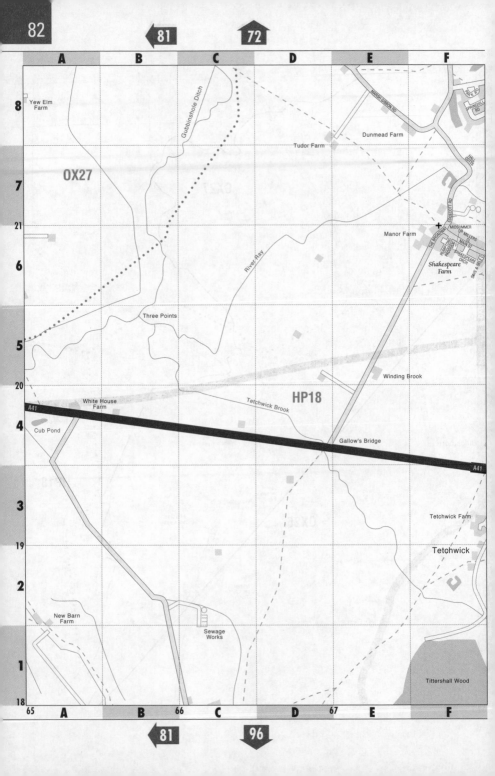

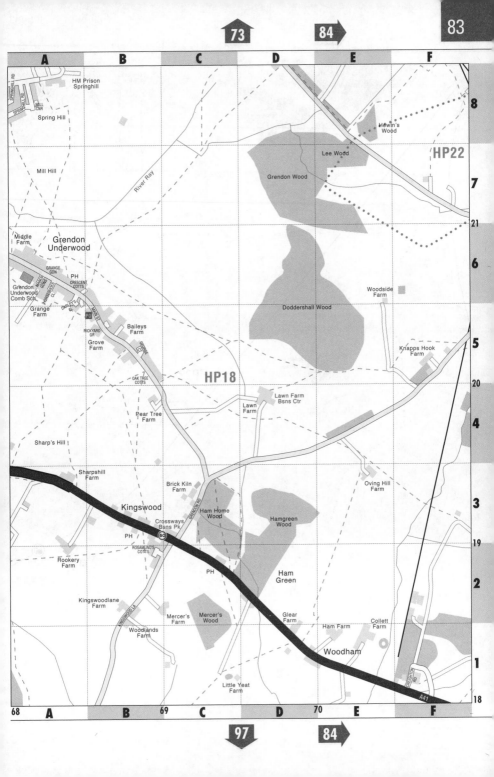

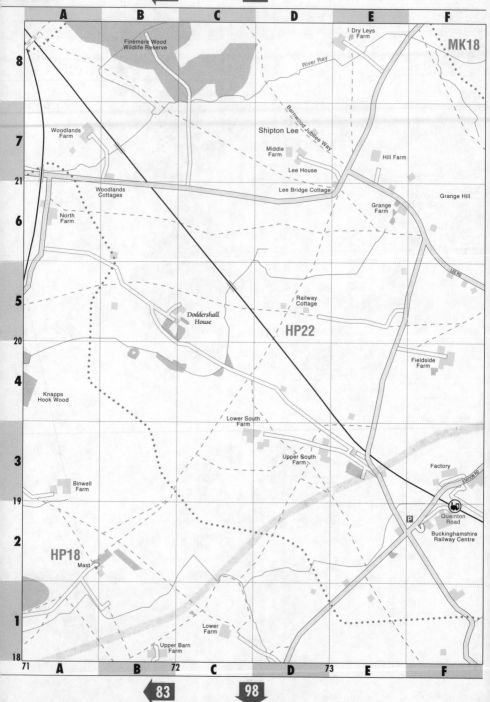

MK18

Finemere Wood
Wildlife Reserve

River Ray

Dry Leys
Farm

Shipton Lee

Bernwood Jubilee Way

Woodlands
Farm

Middle
Farm

Hill Farm

Lee House

Woodlands
Cottages

Lee Bridge Cottage

Grange Hill

North
Farm

Grange
Farm

LEE RD

Railway
Cottage

HP22

Doddershall
House

Fieldside
Farm

Knapps
Hook Wood

Lower South
Farm

Upper South
Farm

Factory

STATION RD

Binwell
Farm

Quainton
Road

P

HP18

Buckinghamshire
Railway Centre

Mast

Lower
Farm

Upper Barn
Farm

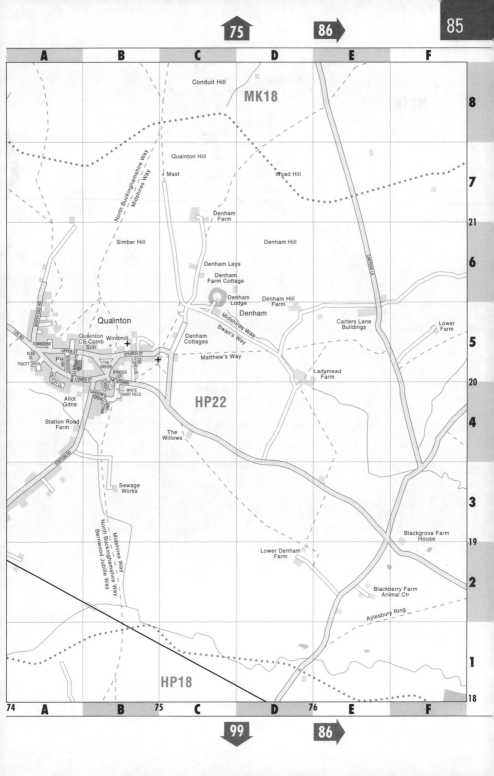

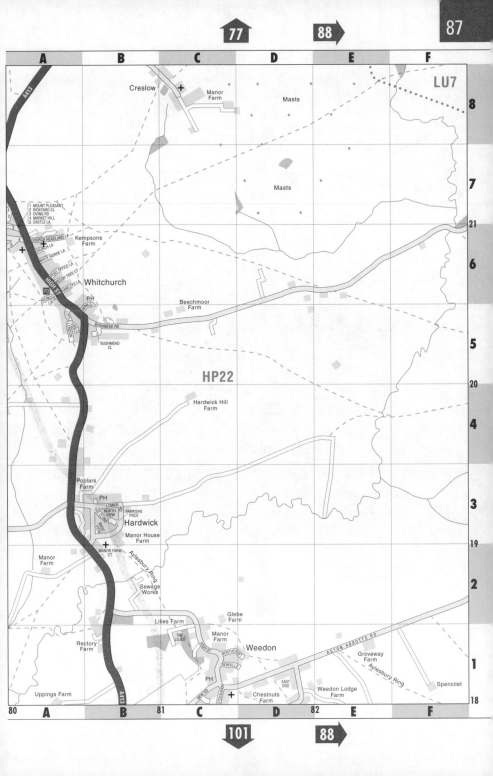

87
78

	A	B	C	D	E	F

Sewage Works

LU7

Red Barn

8

7

21

Willowbrook Farm

Vicarage Farm

Red Barn Farm

The Hay Barn Bsns Pk

6

DUNLINGTON RD

Longmoor Farm

Sewage Works

Freemasons Wood

Church Farm

Aston Abbotts +

5

Norduck Farm

The Abbey

CHARNHAM LEE
CROSS RD
THE OLD BAKERY

HAMBRETS
CL

20

THE GREEN

MOAT LA.

NASHS FARM

PH

New Zealand Cotts

Windmill Hill Farm

WINGRAVE RD

WINGRAVE CROSS RDS

4

THE LIMES

HP22

WINSLOW RD

A418

Windmill Hill

Fox Covert

Barns Farm

3

LIMES HILL

19

Lower Burston Farm

2

Burston Hill Farm

Burston Hill

1

Manor Farm

18

BREWHOUSE LA

Aylesbury Ring MANOR RD

Hale Farm

A418

83	A	B	84	C	D	85	E	F

87
102

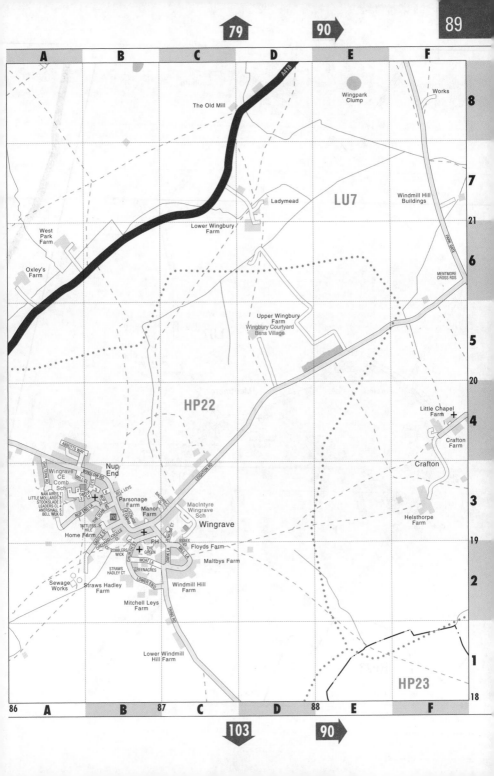

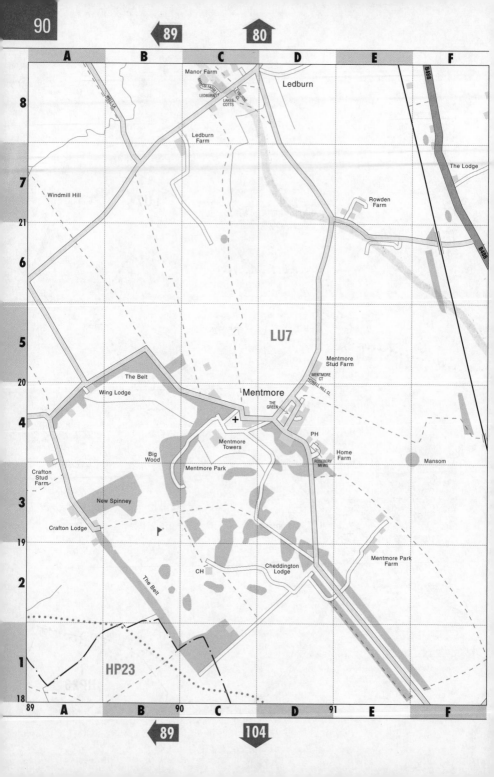

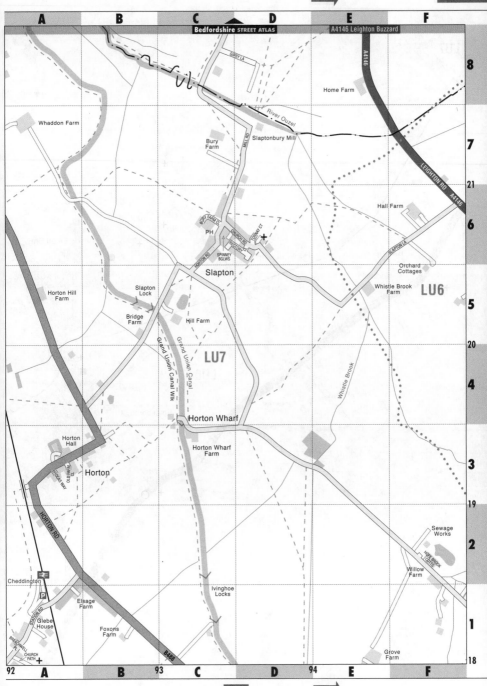

Bedfordshire STREET ATLAS

A4146 Leighton Buzzard

A   B   C   D   E   F

8

Home Farm

A4146

Whaddon Farm

River Ouzel

LEIGHTON RD

7

Bury Farm

MILL RD

Slaptonbury Mill

21

Hall Farm

6

BURY FARM CL

PH

CHURCH RD

RECTORY RD

DORAM CT

SPINNEY BGLWS

HORTON RD

Slapton

SLAPTON LA

A4146

Orchard Cottages

Whistle Brook Farm

LU6

Horton Hill Farm

Slapton Lock

Bridge Farm

Hill Farm

5

20

Grand Union Canal Wlk

Grand Union Canal

LU7

Whistle Brook

4

Horton Wharf

Horton Hall

Horton Wharf Farm

3

THOMAS WAY

Horton

19

HORTON RD

NICHOLAS CL

Sewage Works

2

HOPE BROOK COTTS

Willow Farm

Cheddington

P

SLAPTON RD

Elsage Farm

Glebe House

Ivinghoe Locks

BRIDGEWELL PL

CHURCH PATH

Foxons Farm

B488

Grove Farm

1

18

92   A   B   93   C   D   94   E   F

91

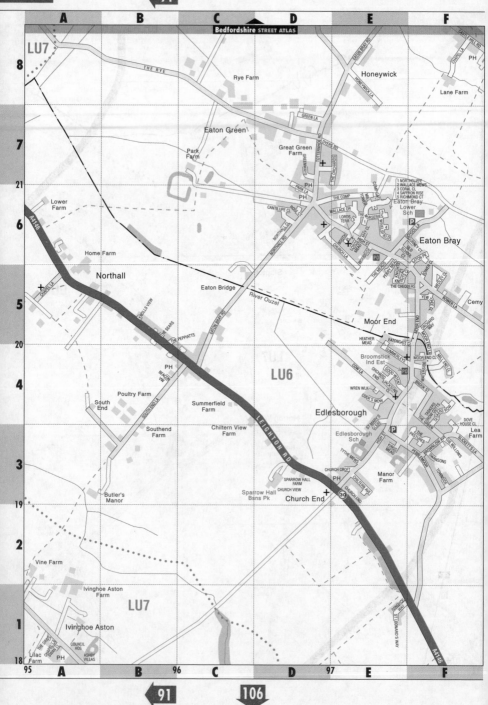

91 106

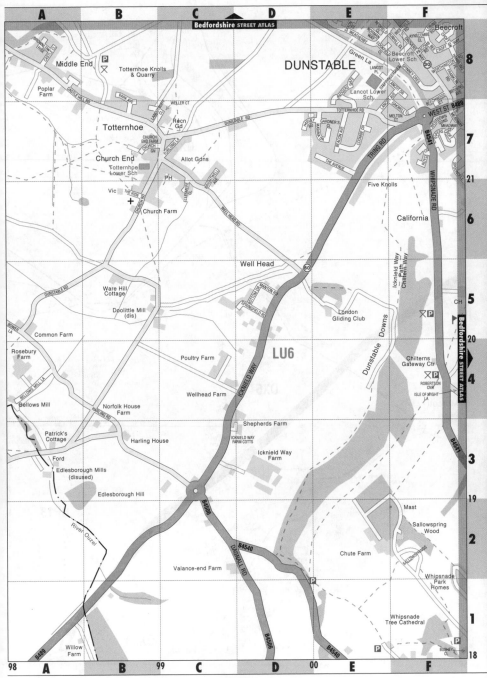

DUNSTABLE

Middle End

Totternhoe Knolls & Quarry

Poplar Farm

Totternhoe

Church End

Totternhoe Lower Sch

Totternhoe Lower Sch

Vic

Church Farm

Recn Gd

Allot Gdns

Dunstable Rd

Green La

Beecroft

Beecroft Lower Sch

Lancot Lower Sch

West St B489

Totternhoe Rd

Gardner's

Tring Rd

Five Knolls

California

Well Head

London Gliding Club

Ware Hill Cottage

Doolittle Mill (dis)

Common Farm

Rosebury Farm

Bellows Mill

Poultry Farm

Wellhead Farm

LU6

Icknield Way Path Chiltern Way

Dunstable Downs

Chilterns Gateway Ctr

Robertson Cnr

Isle of Wight La

Norfolk House Farm

Harling House

Patrick's Cottage

Ford

Edlesborough Mills (disused)

Shepherds Farm

Icknield Way Farm Cotts

Icknield Way Farm

River Ouzel

Edlesborough Hill

B4506

B4540

Dagnall Rd

Valance-end Farm

Chute Farm

Mast

Sallowspring Wood

Sallowsprings

Whipsnade Park Homes

Whipsnade Tree Cathedral

B4541

B4506

B4540

B489

Willow Farm

Bushey Cl

107

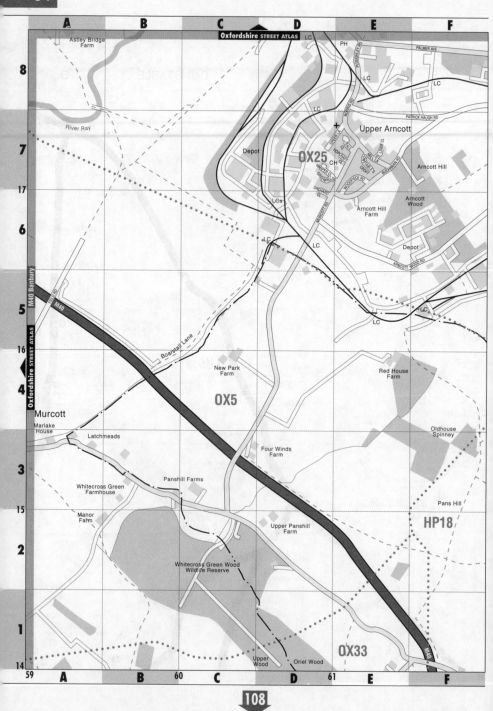

Oxfordshire STREET ATLAS

Astley Bridge Farm

River Ray

Upper Arncott

PALMER AVE

PATRICK HAUGH RD

LC
PH
LC
LC
LC

Depot

OX25

CH

LCs

LC

Arncott Hill

Arncott Wood

Arncott Hill Farm

Depot

ARNCOTT WOOD RD

LC

LC

LC

M40 Banbury

M40

Boarstall Lane

New Park Farm

Red House Farm

Oldhouse Spinney

OX5

Murcott

Marlake House

Latchmeads

Four Winds Farm

Whitecross Green Farmhouse

Panshill Farms

Manor Farm

Upper Panshill Farm

Pans Hill

HP18

Whitecross Green Wood Wildlife Reserve

Upper Wood

Oriel Wood

OX33

M40

59   60   61

A B C D E F

8 7 17 6 5 16 4 3 15 2 1 14

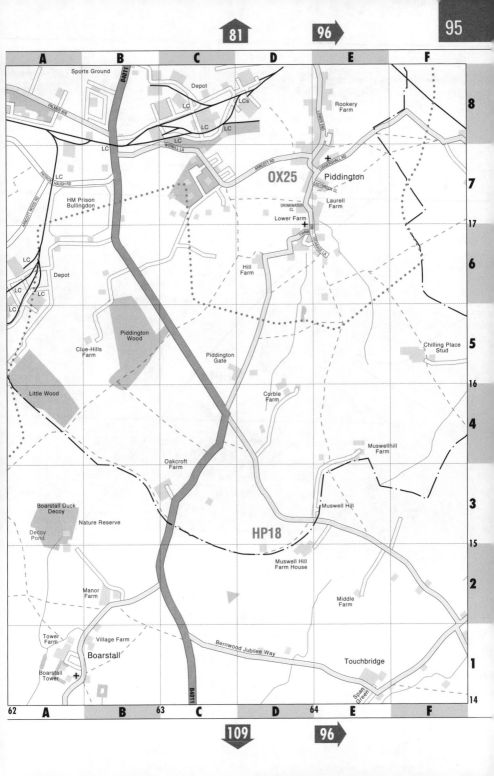

← 95
↑ 82

A B C D E F

8

Nursery

Kings
Farm

POUNDON RD

D'Oyley's
Farm

BICESTER RD

Rookery
Farm

The Green

Bridge
Farm

Ludgershall

PH

CHAPEL LA

SALTERS
CL

SALTERS LA

BROOK
CL

Manor
Farm

WHITE HART

Glebe
Farm

HILL ST

CHURCH LA

BRILL RD

Luggershall
Farm

SPOTTON END

7

17

Eastfield
Farm

KINGSWOOD LA

Tittershall
Wood

6

Clearfields
Farm

The Lake

5

Poletrees
Farm

Lapland
Farm

HP18

Long
Wood

The Warrells

16

Fivearch
Bridge

4

Fivearch
Wood

Rushbeds Wood
Wildlife Reserve

Grenville's
Wood

3

Tramway
Farm

Lawn Farm

15

Brillbury Hall
Farm

Rid's Hill

2

TRAM HILL

Coldharbour
Farm

Dorton Park
Farm

Brill
Common

NORCOTTS KILN
COTTS

NORTH
HILLS

WINDMILL ST

Brill

Chinkwell Wood

Dorton

1

Windmill

SOUTH
HILLS

PH

THE
HILL

HIGH ST

THE
LAWNS

GODFREYS CL

CL

Brill CE
Comb Sch

Brook
Farm

14

65 A B 66 C D 67 E F

← 95
↓ 110

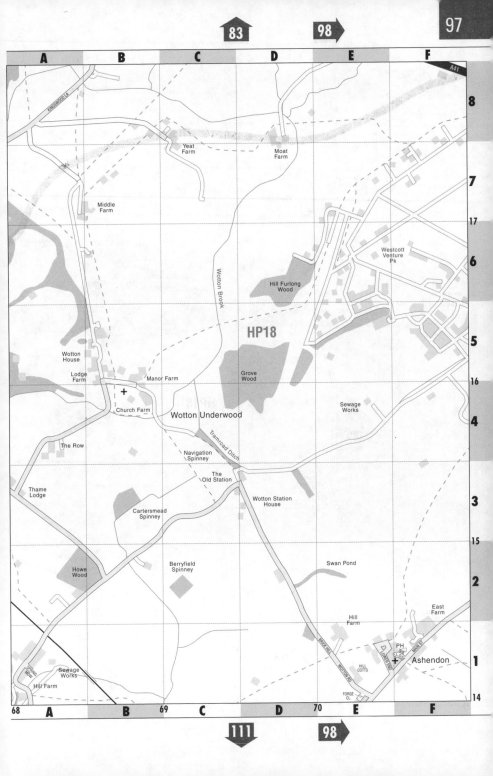

A · B · C · D · E · F

8

KINGSWOOD LA

Yeat Farm

Moat Farm

7

Middle Farm

17

Westcott Venture Pk

6

Wotton Brook

Hill Furlong Wood

HP18

5

Wotton House

Lodge Farm

Manor Farm

Grove Wood

16

Church Farm

Wotton Underwood

Sewage Works

4

The Row

Tramroad Ditch

Navigation Spinney

The Old Station

Thame Lodge

Cartersmead Spinney

Wotton Station House

3

15

Berryfield Spinney

Swan Pond

Howe Wood

2

East Farm

Hill Farm

PH

Ashendon

BRICK HILL

WOTTON RD

LOWER RD

MAIN ST

CLOSE

HILL COTTS

1

Sewage Works

Hill Farm

FORGE CL

14

68 · A · B · 69 · C · D · 70 · E · F

A41

A **B** **C** **D** **E** **F**

8

A41

Newhouse Farm

South View Farm

7

Westcott CE Inf Sch

Westcott

Hall Farm

Littleton Middle Farm

17

Waddesdon Gardens

Waddesdon Farm

Waddesdon Dairy

QUEEN ST

A41 HIGH ST

6

Works

Westcott Farm

Lodge Hill

WADDESDON MANOR FLATS

Waddesdon Manor

Westcott Venture Pk

5

Westcott Field Farm

16

Windmill Plantation

4

Gypsy Bottom

HP18

Windmill Hill Farm

3

Watbridge Farm Cottages

15

2

Grassy Dell

1

Watbridge Farm

Decoy Farm

14

Decoy Wood

71 **A** **B** 72 **C** **D** 73 **E** **F**

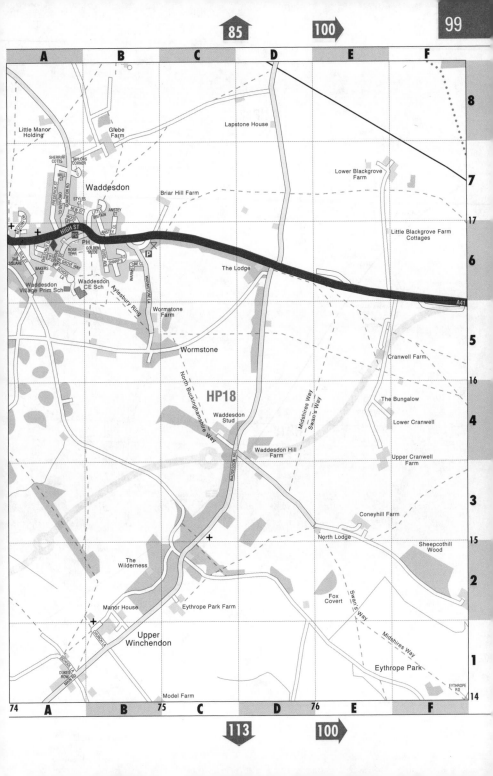

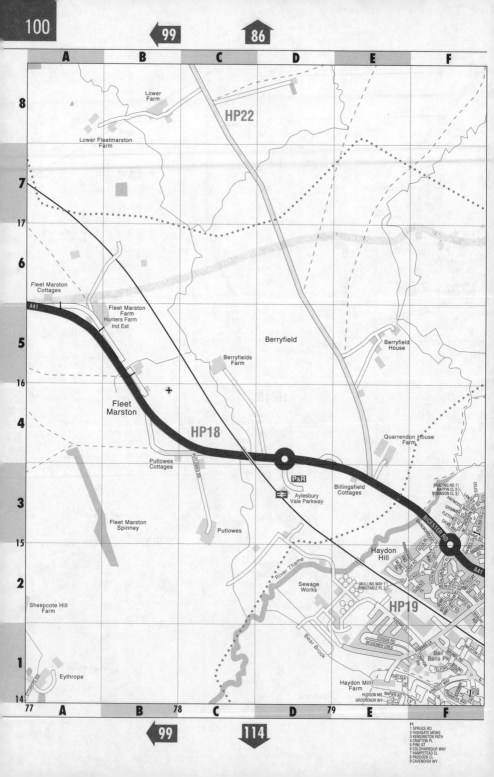

87   102

| A | B | C | D | E | F |

8

7

17

6

HP22

Evelyn's Patch

Weedon Lodge Farm

Uppings Farm

A413

NEW RD

Fields Farm

Grendon Hill Farm

5

17

River Thame

Weedon Hill

HP18

Weedon Hill Farm

St Peter's Church (remains of)

16

Watermead

1 WELL MDW
2 HYTON SQ
3 PLUTO WAY

SKIPPER CL

Holman's Bridge

HP19   AYLESBURY

Quarrendon

Elmhurst

Hotel

15

1 ANGUS RD
2 KERRY CL
3 GUERNSEY CL
4 HEREFORD WAY
5 DEVON RD
6 SUSSEX CL

Manor Park

Alfred Rose Park

ELMHURST RD

BICESTER RD

A41

WEEDON RD

BUCKINGHAM RD

BIERTON RD

A418

A4157

HM Young Offender Inst

HP20

Manor House

Park Sch

Stocklake Ind Est

Aylesbury Ind Ctr

St Andrews Way Ind Est The Courtyard

NEW ST

14

80   A   B   81   C   D   82   E   F

115   102

101
88

	A	B	C	D	E	F

8

Aylesbury Ring

MANOR FARM
Home
Farm

Hale Farm

Ridgeway

BENNETTS LA

Rowsham

Baileys
Farm

Seabrook
Farm

7

Rowsham
Bridge

Aylesbury Ring

17

Crane End
Farm

6

Manor Farm

Church
Farm

Hulcott

CRANE END LA

5

Grove
Farm

HP22

New
Covert

16

GROVE CL

CH

4

ROWSHAM RD

The Green
BROOK ALLEY
Brook Mead

GIB LA

Badricks
Farm

3

Bierton

PH

Church
Farm

Burcott

MARSHALLS LEA

Bierton
CE Comb
Sch

ST JAMES WY

AYLESBURY RD

15

1 OLDHAMS MDW
2 HONOUR CL
3 BIERTON RD
4 LAWRENCE CL
5 SHEPHERD CL

2

A418

POPLAR
CL

GREEN VIEW

BROUGHTON
CROSSING

PH

Round Aylesbury Walk

1

AYLESBURY

HP20

Buckinghamshire
Fire Service HQ

GRASSLANDS

DOUGLAS RD
A4157

WARWICK
ROW

STOCK LANE

Grand Union Canal   Aylesbury Arm

P Grand Union Canal Wlk

Park Street
Ind Est

STOCKLAKE

OAKFIELD RD
A4157

Towing Path

14

Bear Brook

Brook Farm

GIB LA

83	A	B	84	C	D	85	E	F

101
116

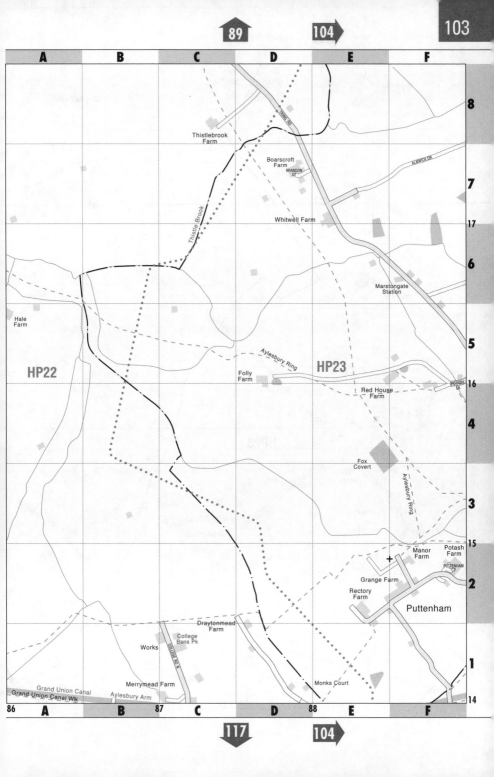

A B C D E F

8

Thistlebrook Farm

TRING RD

Boarscroft Farm
BRANDON CT

7

ALNWICK DR

POTASH

Thistle Brook

Whitwell Farm

17

6

Marstongate Station

Hale Farm

HP22

5

Aylesbury Ring

HP23

Folly Farm

16

POTASH LA

Red House Farm

4

Fox Covert

Aylesbury Ring

3

15

Manor Farm

Potash Farm

PUTTENHAM CT

Grange Farm

2

Rectory Farm

Puttenham

Draytonmead Farm

College Bsns Pk

Works

COLLEGE RD N

1

Merrymead Farm

Monks Court

Grand Union Canal
Grand Union Canal Wlk

Aylesbury Arm

14

A B C D E F

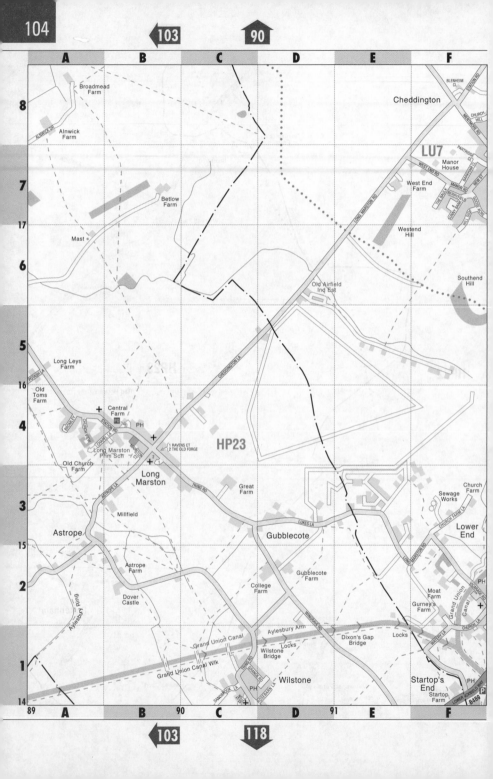

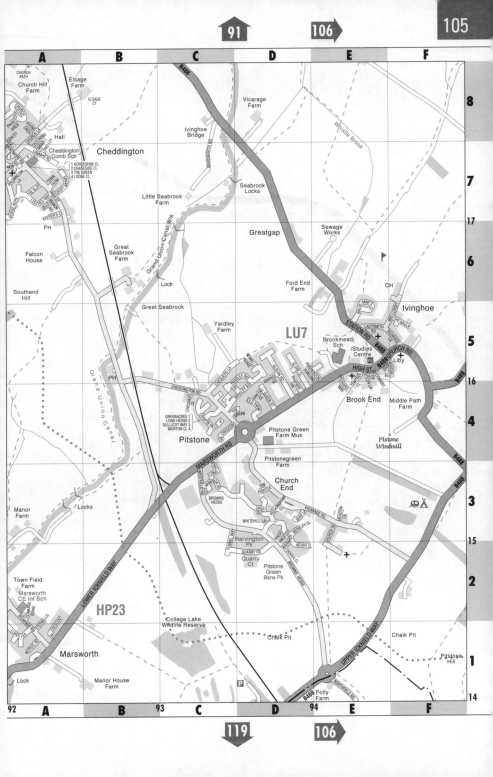

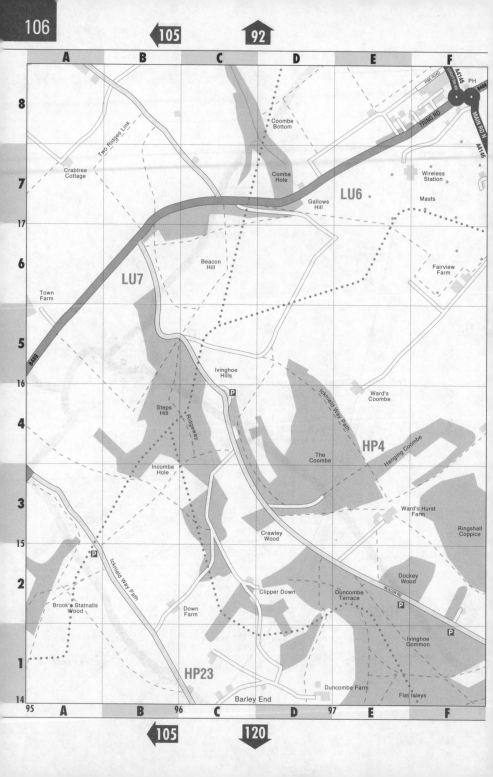

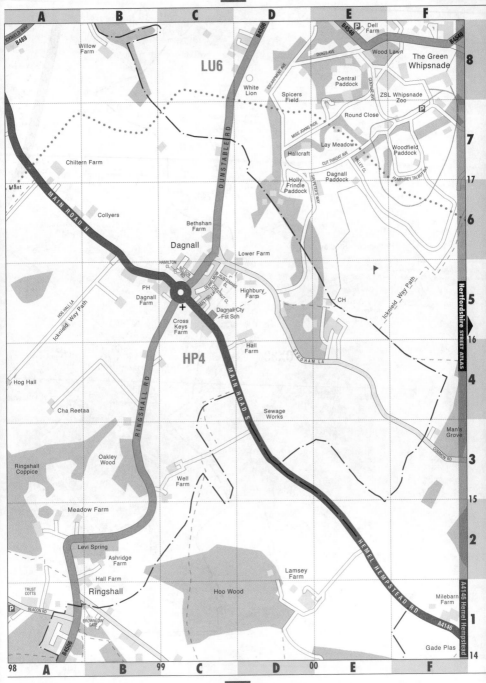

A B C D E F

8

LU6

White Lion

7

17

6

Dagnall

5

16

HP4

4

3

15

2

1

14

98 A B 99 C D 00 E F

B489
ICKNEILD WAY
Willow Farm

Chiltern Farm

Mast

Collyers

HOG HALL LA
Ickneild Way Path

Hog Hall

Cha Reetaa

Ringshall Coppice

Meadow Farm

Levi Spring

Ashridge Farm

Hall Farm

Ringshall

TRUST COTTS

BEACON RD

B506

BROWNLOW GATE

Bethshan Farm

HAMILTON CL

NELSON RD

PH
Dagnall Farm

Cross Keys Farm

RINGSHALL RD

Oakley Wood

Well Farm

DUNSTABLE RD

B506

ESCARPMENT AVE
DUKES AVE

Spicers Field

MISS JOANS RIDE

Hallcraft

Holly Frindle Paddock

Lower Farm

BEECHES VIEW
HUNTSMANS CL
CHESTNUT CL
MALTINGS LA

Dagnall Cty Fst Sch

Highbury Farm

Hall Farm

MAIN ROAD S

Sewage Works

Hoo Wood

Lamsey Farm

Dell Farm
B4540

Wood Lawn

Central Paddock

CENTRAL AVE

Round Close

CUT THROAT AVE
Lay Meadow

SIR PETERS WAY
VALLEY CL

Dagnall Paddock

HUMPHREY TALBOT AVE

CH

SIBDHAM LA

COMMOOR RD

The Green
Whipsnade

ZSL Whipsnade Zoo

Woodfield Paddock

Ickneild Way Path

Man's Grove

Herfordshire STREET ATLAS

HEMEL HEMPSTEAD RD

A4146 Hemel Hempstead

Milebarn Farm

A4146

Gade Plas

MAIN ROAD N

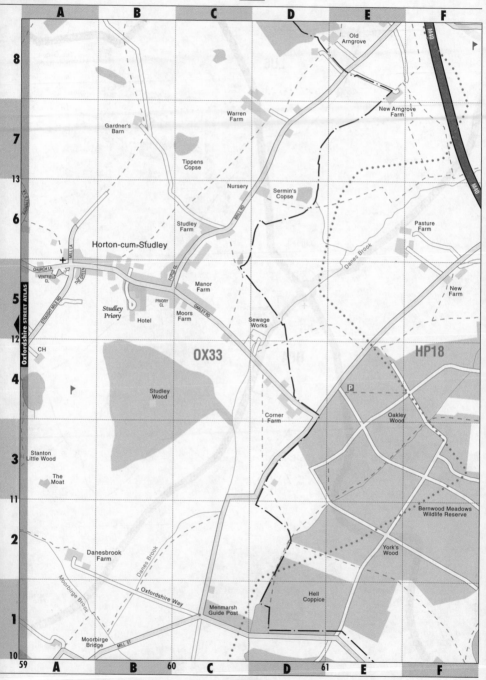

Old Arngrove

New Arngrove Farm

Warren Farm

Gardner's Barn

Tippens Copse

Nursery

Sermin's Copse

Pasture Farm

Studley Farm

Horton-cum-Studley

CHURCH LA

VENTFIELD CL

New Farm

Danes Brook

Manor Farm

PRIORY CL

Studley Priory

Hotel

Moors Farm

Sewage Works

CH

OX33

HP18

Studley Wood

P

Oakley Wood

Corner Farm

Stanton Little Wood

The Moat

Bernwood Meadows Wildlife Reserve

York's Wood

Danesbrook Farm

Danes Brook

Moorbirge Brook

Oxfordshire Way

Hell Coppice

Menmarsh Guide Post

Moorbirge Bridge

MILL ST

59

60

61

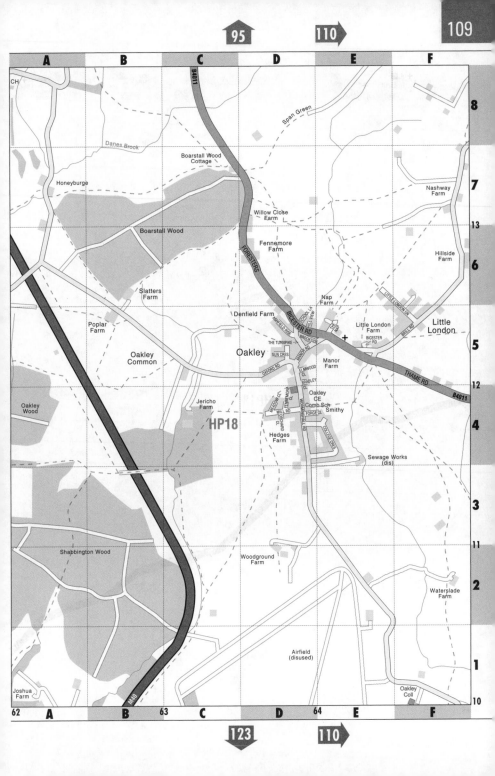

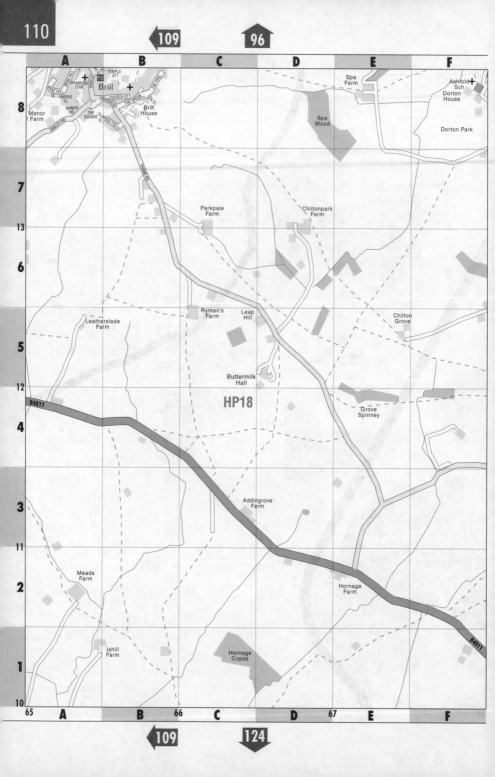

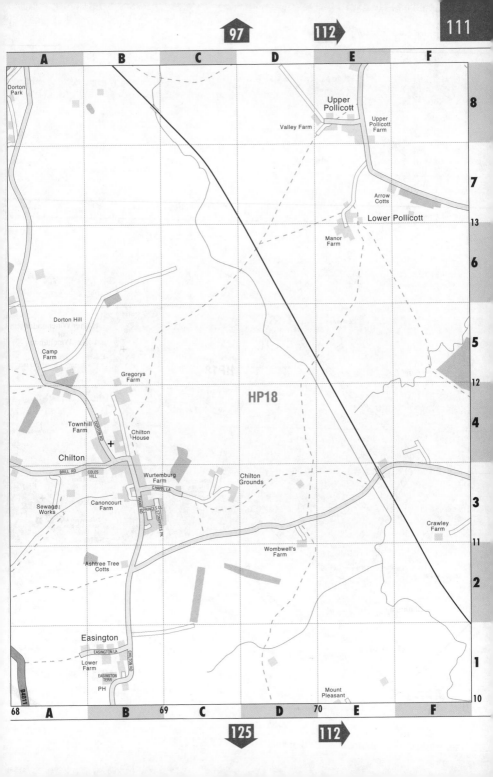

8
7
13
6
5
12
4
3
11
2
1
10

A B C D E F

Dorton
Park

Upper
Pollicott

Valley Farm

Upper
Pollicott
Farm

Arrow
Cotts

Lower Pollicott

Manor
Farm

Dorton Hill

Camp
Farm

Gregorys
Farm

HP18

Townhill
Farm

DORTON RD

Chilton
House

+

Chilton

BRILL RD

COLES
HILL

Wurtemburg
Farm

Chilton
Grounds

CHAPEL LA

THAME RD

PRINCES CL

ST CUTHBERTS PK

Sewage
Works

Canoncourt
Farm

Crawley
Farm

Ashtree Tree
Cotts

Wombwell's
Farm

Easington

EASINGTON LA

CHILTON RD

Lower
Farm

EASINGTON
TERR

PH

Mount
Pleasant

B4011

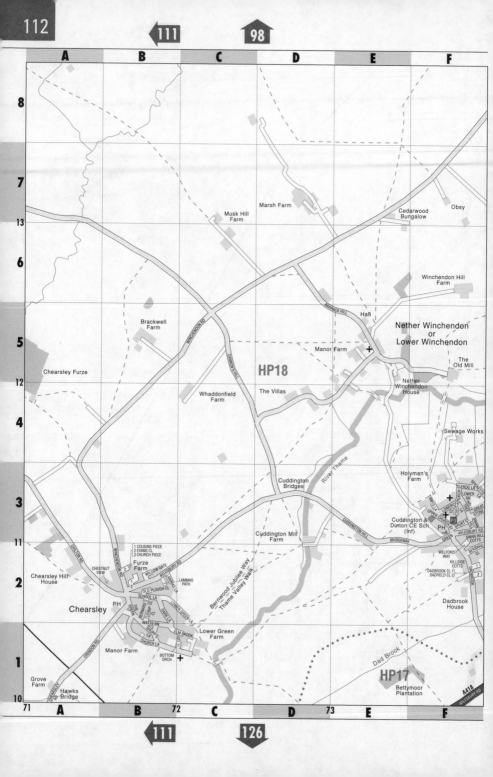

111

98

A B C D E F

8

7

13

6

5

12

4

3

11

2

1

10

71 A B 72 C D 73 E F

Musk Hill Farm

Marsh Farm

Cedarwood Bungalow

Obsy

Winchendon Hill Farm

Brackwell Farm

BARRACK HILL

Hall

Nether Winchendon
or
Lower Winchendon

WINCHENDON RD

CANON'S HILL

Manor Farm

The Old Mill

HP18

Chearsley Furze

Whaddonfield Farm

The Villas

Nether Winchendon House

Sewage Works

River Thame

Holyman's Farm

Cuddington Bridges

FROG LANE

LOWER GN

CHURCH

GREAT STONE

THE SPUR'S

Cuddington & Dinton CE Sch (Inf)

PH

Cuddington Mill Farm

CUDDINGTON HILL

BRIDGEWAY

AYLESBURY RD

SWAN HILL COTTS

WELFORD WAY

HILLSIDE COTTS

Chearsley Hill House

CHILTON RD

WINCHENDON RD

CHESTNUT VIEW

Furze Farm

1 COUSINS PIECE
2 EVANS CL
3 CHURCH PIECE

OLD PLOUGH CL

AYLESBURY RD

WILLOW GATE

LAMMAS LA

LAMMAS PATH

Bernwood Jubilee Way
Thame Valley Walk

DADBROOK CL 1
DADFIELD CL 2

Dadbrook House

Chearsley

PH

SCHOOL LA

LOKLE LEIGH LA

WATTS GN

CHURCH LA

ELM BROOK CL

BOTTOM ORCH

Lower Green Farm

Manor Farm

Grove Farm

CHEARSLEY RD

Hawks Bridge

Dad Brook

HP17

Bettymoor Plantation

AYLESBURY RD
A418

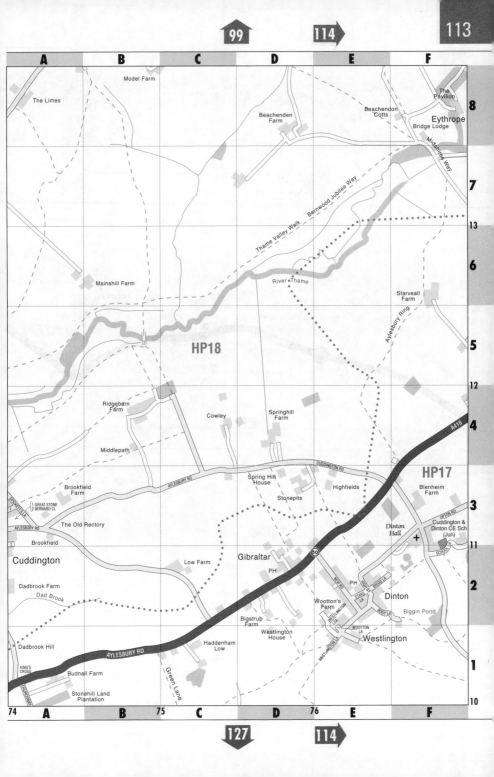

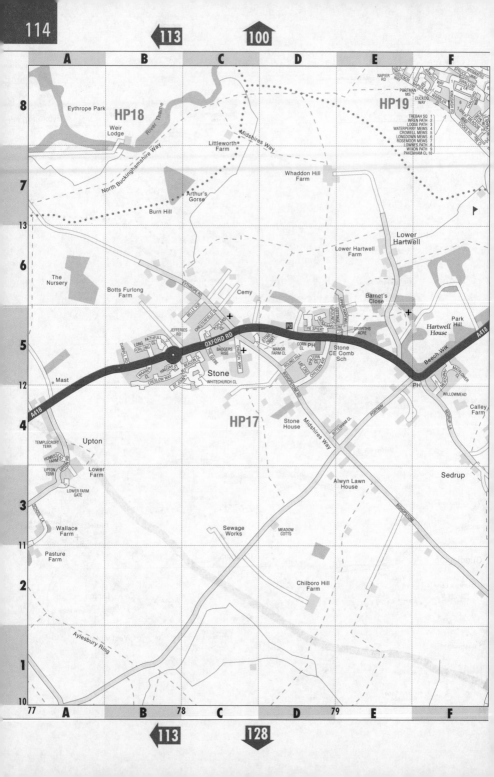

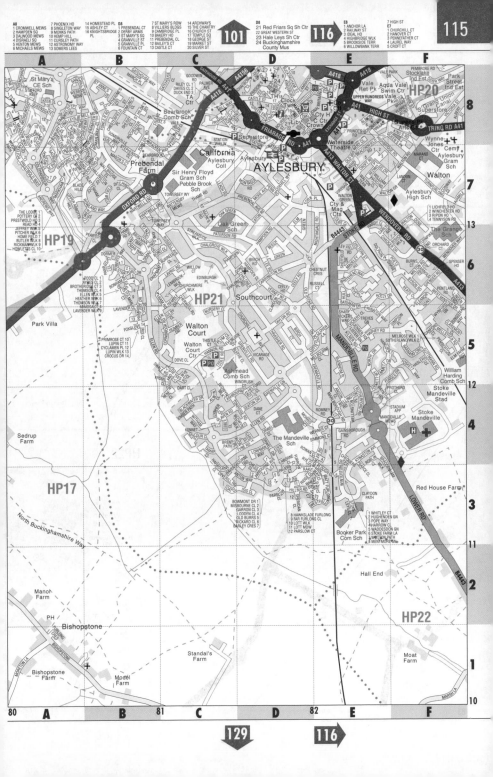

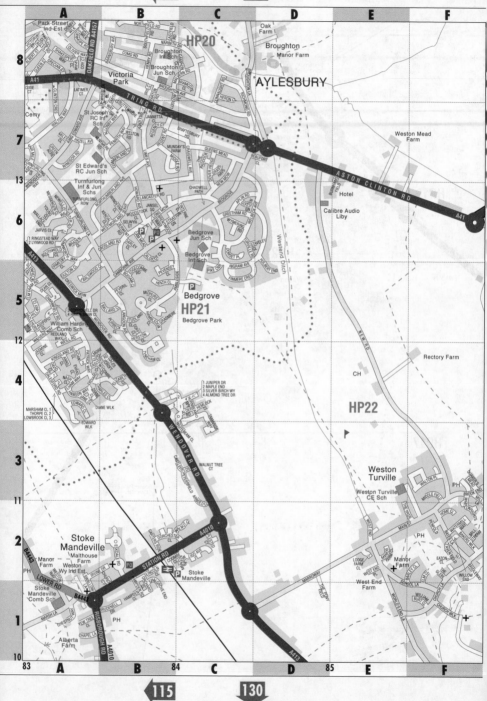

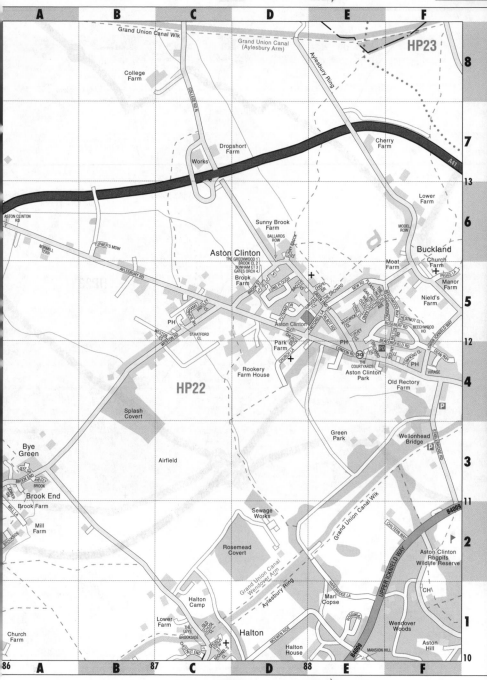

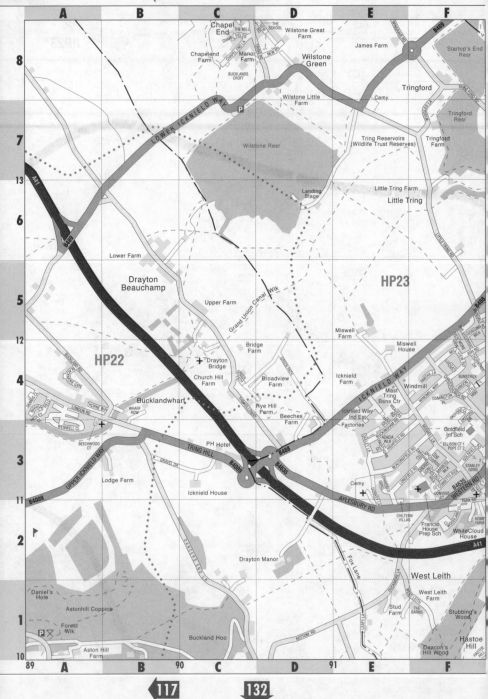

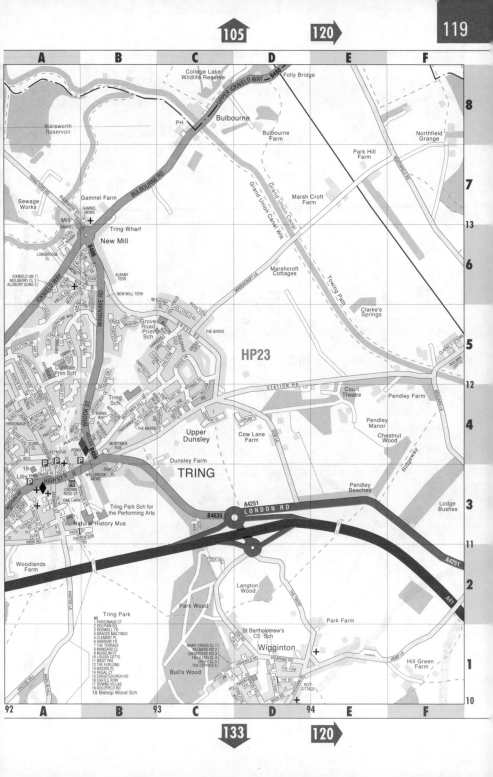

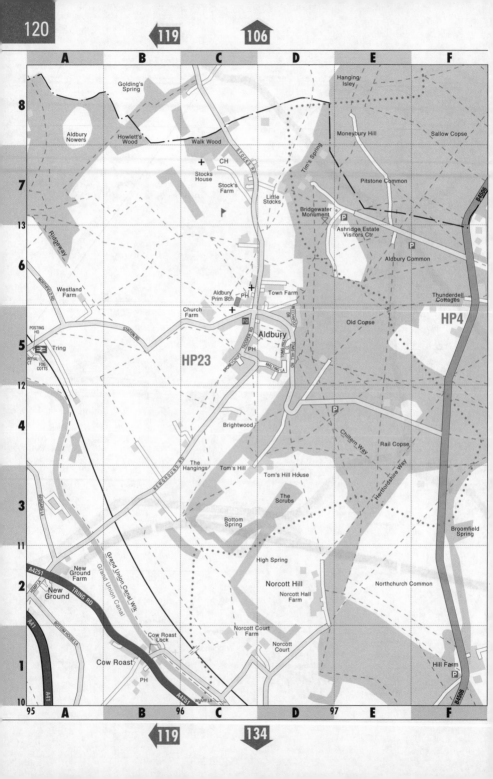

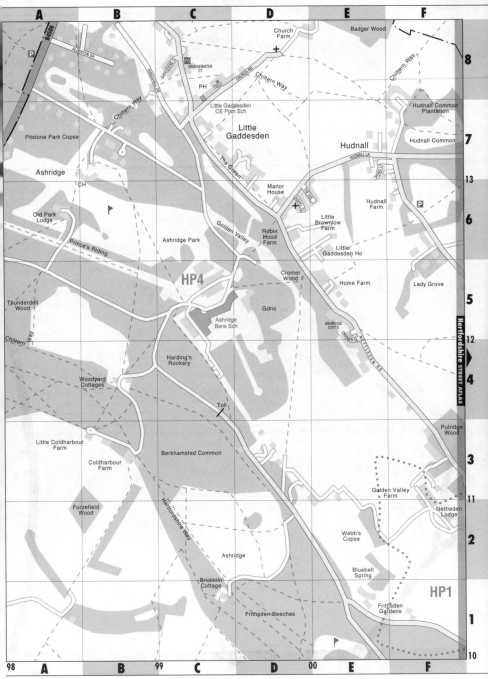

B4506
P
ALDERTON DR

BINGHAMS DR

Chiltern Way

GATESDENE CL
CHURCH RD

PO
BRIDGEWATER CT
PH

Church Farm

Badger Wood

Chiltern Way

Little Gaddesden CE Prim Sch

Little
Gaddesden

Hudnall

Hudnall Common
Plantation

Pitstone Park Copse

Ashridge

Hudnall Common

CH

The Green

Manor
House

HUDNALL LA

DOLLS LA

Hudnall Farm

P

Old Park
Lodge

Prince's Riding

Ashridge Park

Golden Valley

Robin
Hood
Farm

Little Brownlow
Farm

Little
Gaddesden Ho

HP4

Cromer
Wood

Home Farm

Lady Grove

Thunderdell
Wood

Gdns

Ashridge
Bsns Sch

ASHRIDGE
COTTS

NETTLEDEN RD

CHURCH CL

Chiltern Way

Harding's
Rookery

Woodyard
Cottages

Toll

Pulridge
Wood

Little Coldharbour
Farm

Coldharbour
Farm

Berkhamsted Common

Golden Valley
Farm

Nettleden
Lodge

Furzefield
Wood

Hertfordshire Way

Webb's
Copse

Ashridge

Brickkiln
Cottage

Bluebell
Spring

HP1

Frithsden
Gardens

Frithsden Beeches

108

MILL ST

Moorbridge Brook

Wood
Farm

HP18

Clearsafe   Hursthill

Waterperry
Common

Bernwood Forest

Commonleys
Farm

Waterperry Wood

Park Farm
House

Park
Farm

Polecat End

Drunkard's
Corner

Oxfordshire Way

Parson's
Farm

Polecat End
Hollows

Marsh
Copse

Ledall
Cottage

Holton Wood

OX33

Holton Brook

M40

Buryhook
Barn

Keeper's
Cottage

Warren
Farm

Pond
Farm

Warren
Wood

Old Park
Farm

WHEATLEY RD

Lyehill Quarries
(dis)

BURYHOOK
CNR

Cottage
Copse

A40 Oxford

B4027

Warwick Close
Farm

Rech
Gd

Wheatley
Park Sch

Holton

The
Rectory

Holton
Place

Liby

BARNS
CL

Park Sports
Ctr

John
Watson
Sch

Wheatley

Church Farm

Moat

Garden
Copse

WESTFIELD RD

LONDON RD

A40

PARK HILL

Brookes Univ
(Wheatley Campus)

COLLEGE CL

59   A   B   60   C   D   61   E   F

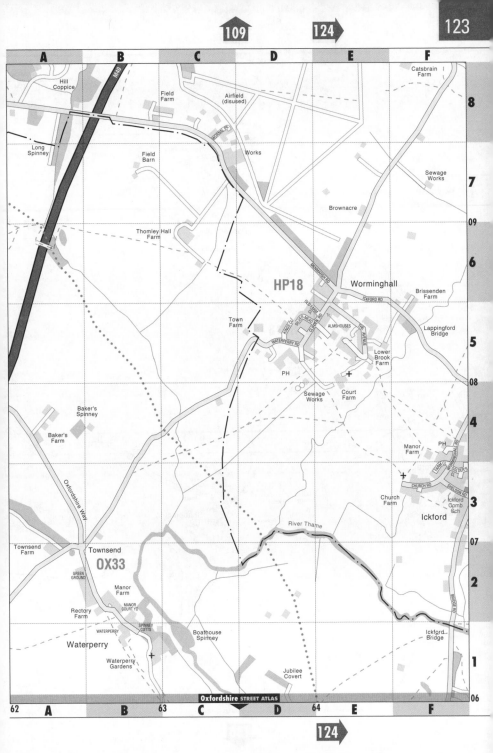

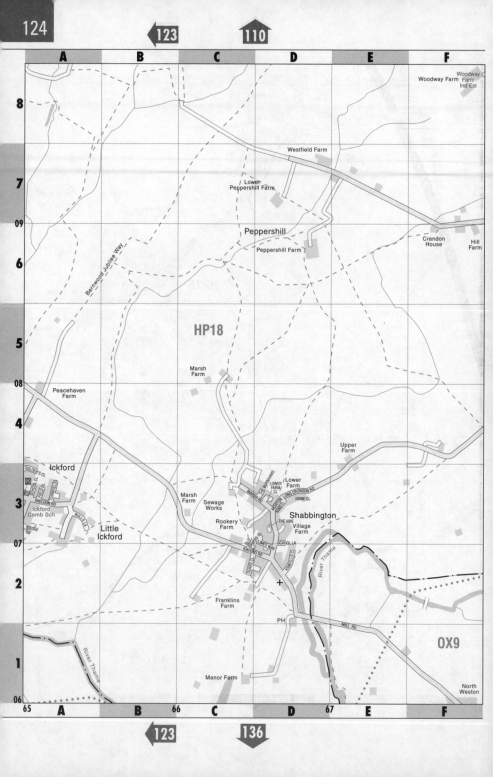

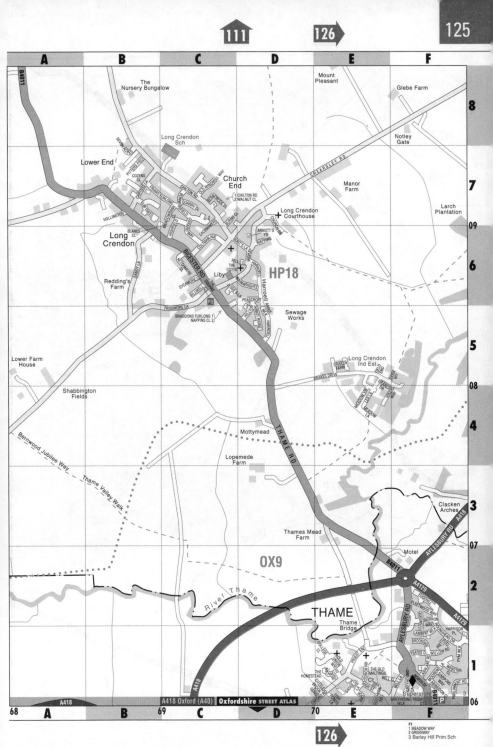

F1
1 MEADOW WAY
2 GREENWAY
3 Barley Hill Prim Sch

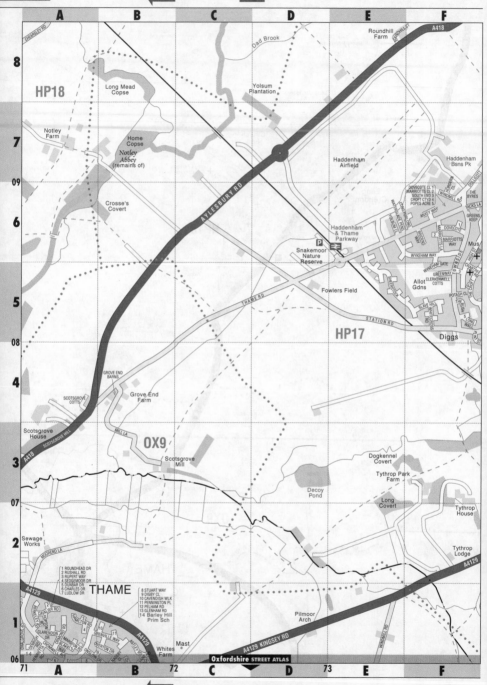

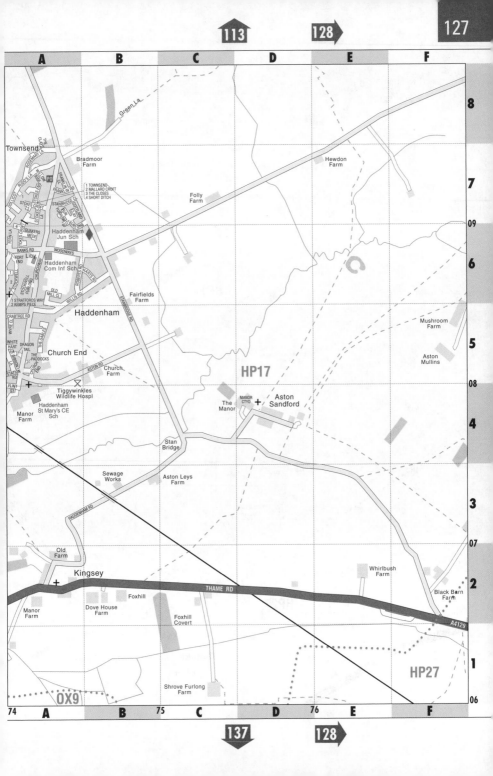

A   B   C   D   E   F

8

BRIDGE FARM BLDGS
Moat Farm
Moreton Village
PH
WATER LA
Ford
Moreton Farm

7

Manor Farm
TRACEY CL
BURGESS LA
Ford Farm
ORMEL RD
INDIA WAY

09

6

Aylesbury Ring

HP17

North Buckinghamshire Way
Midshires Way

5

Lower Waldridge Farm
Fox Covert

08

Pollard Farm

4

Poplar Farm

Waldridge Manor

3

Waldridge Village

Black Barn

07

2

Pasture Farm

Stockwell Lane Farm

Swan's Way
Midshires Way

Hill Ground Farm

HP27

Owlswick Farm

A4129

Midshires Way

STOCKWELL LA

1

THAME RD
Green Lane Farm
GREEN LA
Owlswick

Little Acre Farm
Manor Farm

Ray Farm
A4129

06

77   A   B   78   C   D   79   E   F

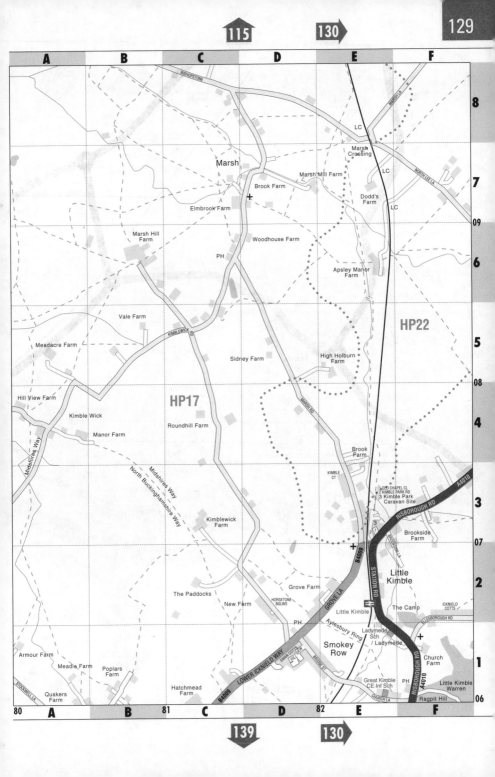

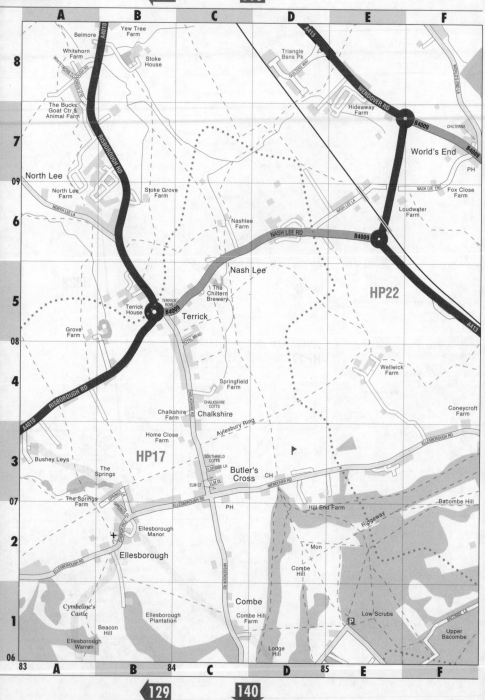

A B C D E F

8

7

09

6

5

08

4

3

07

2

1

06

83 A B 84 C D 85 E F

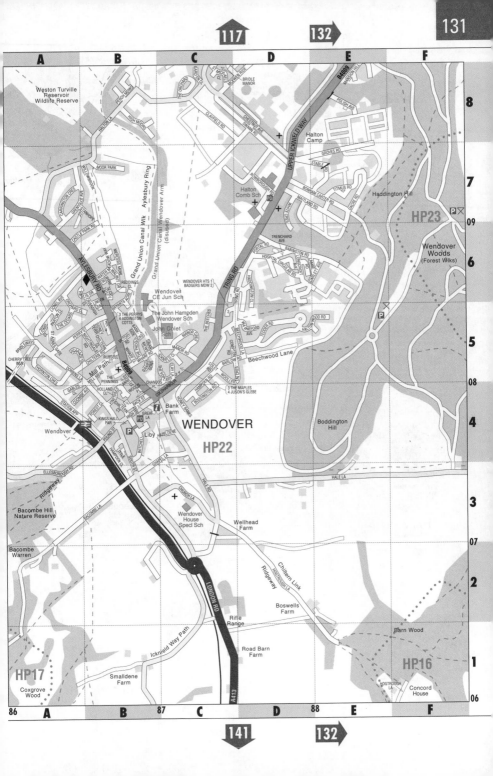

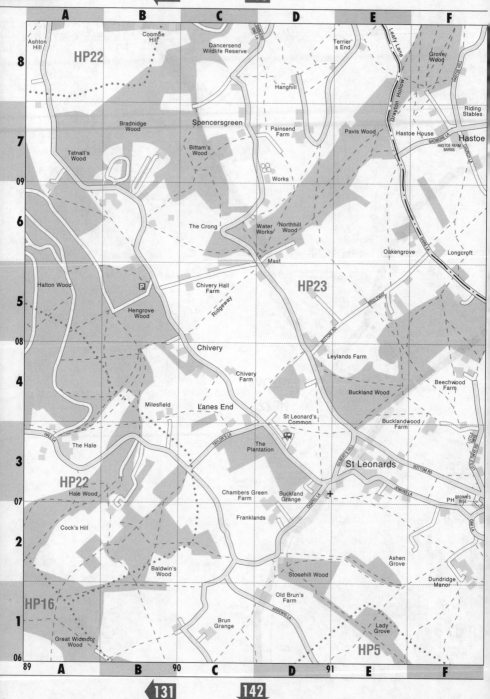

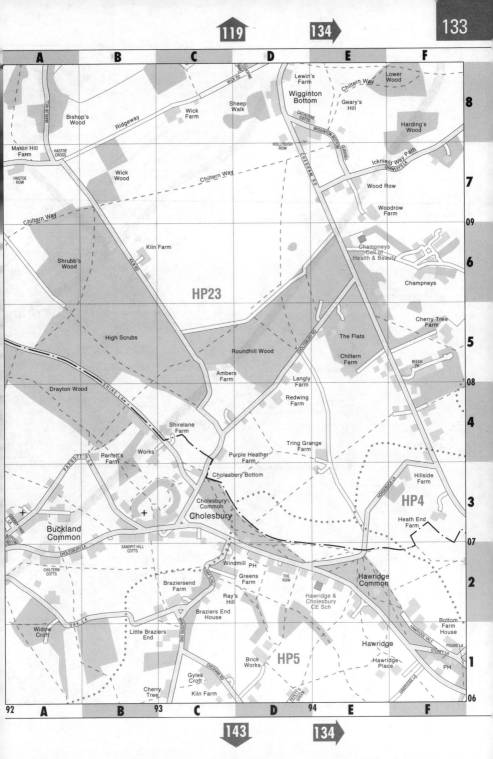

133
120

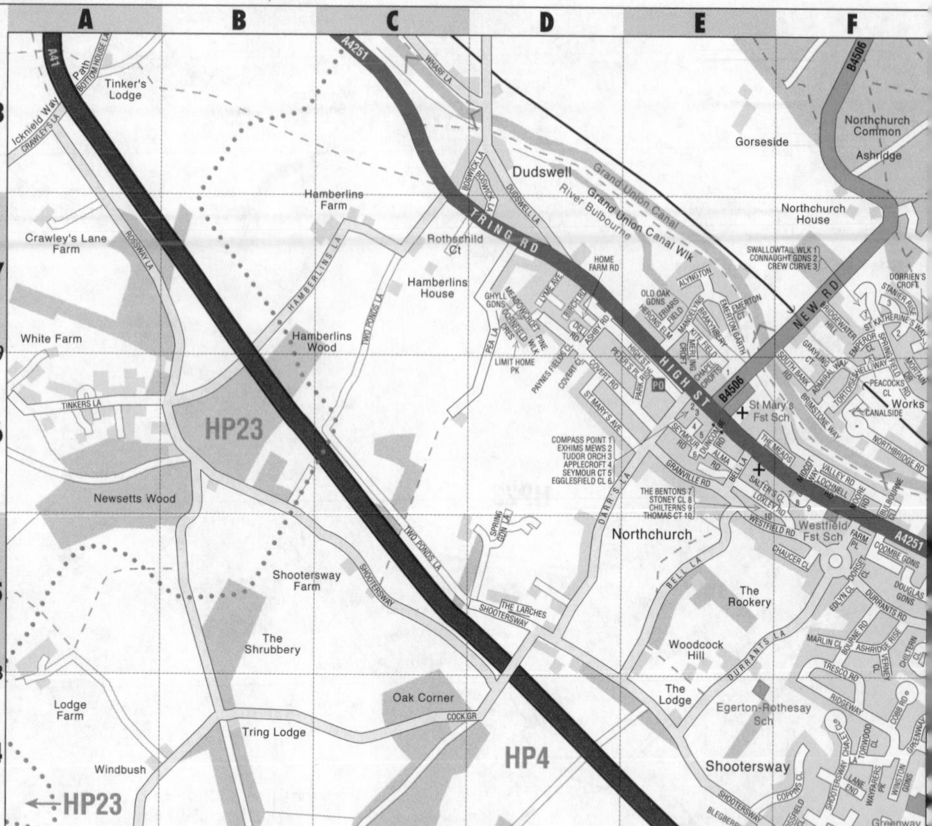
A
B
C
D
E
F
8
7
09
6
5
08
4
3
07
2
1
06
95
96
97
A41
Icknield Way
Path
BOTTOM HOUSE LA
CRAWLEYS LA
Tinker's Lodge
A4251
WHARF LA
B4506
Northchurch Common
Ashridge
Gorseside
Dudswell
Grand Union Canal
River Bulbourne
Grand Union Canal Wlk
BOSWICK LA
DUDSWELL LA
Hamberlins Farm
TRING RD
Rothschild Ct
Northchurch House
SWALLOWTAIL WLK 1
CONNAUGHT GDNS 2
CREW CURVE 3
Crawley's Lane Farm
ROSSWAY LA
HAMBERLINS LA
Hamberlins House
TWO PONDS LA
HOME FARM RD
ALYNGTON
OLD OAK GDNS
EMERTON CT
EMERTON GARTH
NEW RD
DORRIEN'S CROFT
STANIER RISE
ST KATHERINE'S WAY
White Farm
Hamberlins Wood
GHYLL GDNS
LIMIT HOME PK
HIGH ST
PO
SOUTH BANK RD
ADMIRAL WAY
BRIMSTONE WAY
PEACOCKS CL
Works
CANALSIDE
TINKERS LA
HP23
COVERT RD
ST MARY'S AVE
St Mary's Fst Sch
COMPASS POINT 1
EXHIMS MEWS 2
TUDOR ORCH 3
APPLECROFT 4
SEYMOUR CT 5
EGGLESFIELD CL 6
THE MEADS
NORTHBRIDGE RD
VALLEY RD
Newsetts Wood
GRANVILLE RD
THE BENTONS 7
STONEY CL 8
CHILTERNS 9
THOMAS CT 10
SALTER'S CL
LOXLEY RD
WESTFIELD RD
Westfield Fst Sch
SPRING GDN LA
DARR'S LA
Northchurch
A4251
CHAUCER CL
COOMBE GDNS
TWO PONDS LA
SHOOTERSWAY
Shootersway Farm
BELL LA
The Rookery
DOUGLAS GDNS
DURRANTS RD
THE LARCHES
The Shrubbery
Woodcock Hill
MARLIN CL
ASHRIDGE RISE
TRESCO RD
RIDGEWAY
Lodge Farm
Oak Corner
COCK GR
The Lodge
Egerton-Rothesay Sch
Tring Lodge
HP4
Windbush
Shootersway
HP23
Greenway Fst Sch
Cock Grove
Rossway Home Farm
COCK GR
Rossway
CHESHAM RD
Marlin Chapel Farm
OAKWOOD
CROSS OAK RD
HOCKERIDGE VW
DENNY'S LA
Heath End
NORTHCHURCH LA
A41
Glebe Farm
Pancake Wood
HOG LA
HP5
The Old Farm
Hill Farm
JOHNS LA
Hockeridge Wood
Hockeridge Bottom
Woodfield Spring Farm
HP5
Hog Lane Farm
Johns Lane Farm
A416
POUND LA
Hadden's Plantation
CHESHAM RD

133
144

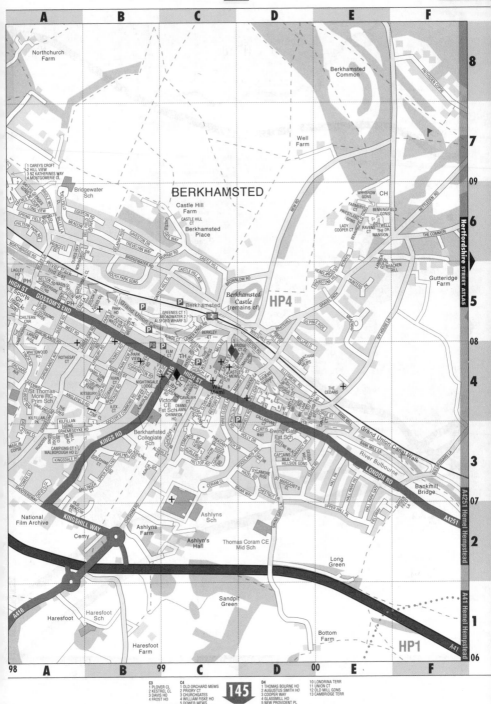

BERKHAMSTED

HP4

HP1

124

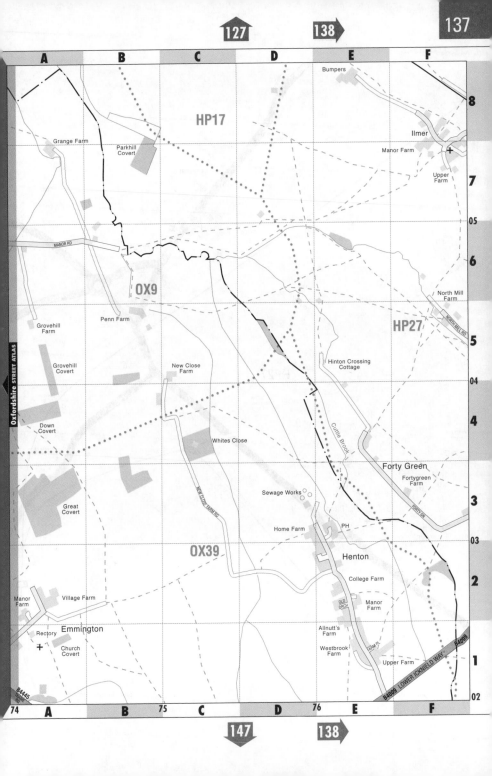

HP17

OX9

HP27

OX39

Grange Farm

Parkhill Covert

Bumpers

Ilmer

Manor Farm

Upper Farm

MANOR RD

Grovehill Farm

Penn Farm

North Mill Farm

NORTH MILL RD

Grovehill Covert

New Close Farm

Hinton Crossing Cottage

Down Covert

Whites Close

Cuttle Brook

Forty Green

Fortygreen Farm

FORTY GM

NEW CLOSE FARM RD

Sewage Works

Great Covert

Home Farm

PH

Henton

College Farm

Manor Farm

OLD ORCH

Manor Farm

Village Farm

Rectory

Emmington

Church Covert

Allnutt's Farm

Westbrook Farm

Upper Farm

B4009 LOWER ICKNIELD WAY

B4009

125M PL

B4445

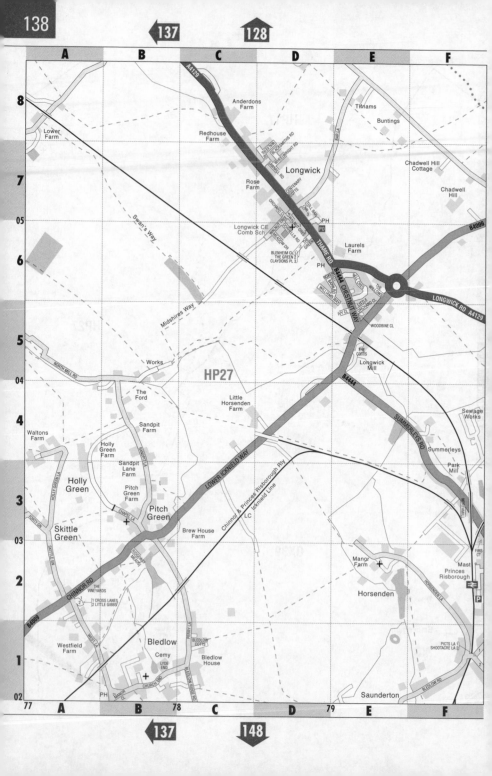

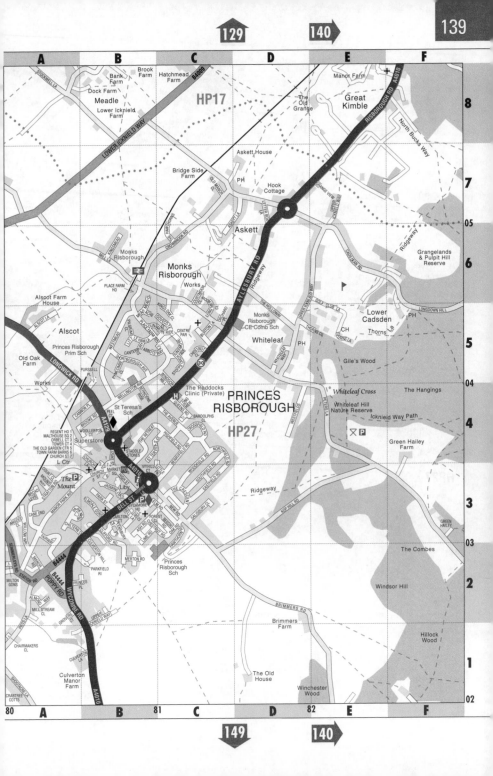

8

The Dene

Lodge
Hill

Lodge Hill
Farm

High
Scrubs

Chequers

Whorley
Wood

Ridgeway

Linton's
Wood

HP22
Fugsdon
Wood

7

Ridgeway

Maple Wood

HP17

Goodmerhill
Wood

05

Pulpit
Hill

LEE
COTTS

Dunsmore
Old Farm

Brockwell
Farm

Chisley
Wood

6

Pulpit
Wood

Pond
Wood

Buckmoorend

P

Little Hampden
Manor

Longdown
Farm

Hengrove
Wood

5

Hobb's
Hill

Little Hampden Common

Weyburn's
Wood

04

Ninn
Wood

Blyth's
Wood

PH

Little
Hampden

4

Sergeant's
Wood

Cross
Coppice

Dirtywood
Farm

Chiltern Way

Little
Hampden
Farm

Solinger
House

HP27

Little Boy's
Heath

Hampden
Bottom
Farm

Warren
Wood

3

Knighton's Hill
Wood

HP16

03

Kingsfield Wood

2

Chiltern Way

*Hampden
House*

Barnes's
Grove

The Glade

1

Hillock
Wood

+

Park
Farm

Oaken
Grove

Redland
End

02

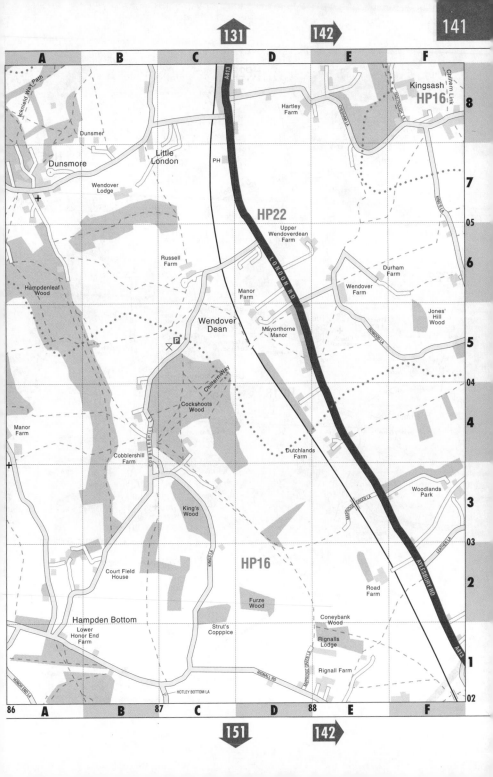

141
132

| | A | B | C | D | E | F |

HP23

Lordling Wood

8

Chiltern Way

SWAN LA

PH

Kingswood

KERRIWIG LA

Erriwig Farm

PH

HP5

Lee Gate

7

Swan Bottom

Kingsgate Farm

Three Gates Farm

05

Gwenfa Farm

Bray's Wood

6

HP22

Lownde's Wood

Chiltern Link

Lee Clump

Home Farm

Lee Clump House

Church Farm

The Lee

Lee Clump

5

Church (restored)

Hawthorn Farm

Lee Common CE Fst Sch

PRINCES LA

PH

OXFORD ST

ST MARY'S

CROCKETS LA

Bassibones Farm

PH

Rushmoor Wood

Lee Common

Lower Bassibones Farm

04

KING'S LA

MARTIN DELL COTTS

CHERRY TREE LA

HP16

Pipers

Hunt's Green

ELY CRS

4

Hunt's Green Farm

Field End Grange

Ballinger Bottom

Chiltern Link

3

LEATHER LA

Ballinger Row

SPRINE LA

CHILTERN RD

Hammonds Hall Farm

P

BLACKFIELD LA

Ballinger Common

03

Springfield Farm

Ballinger Farm

BALLINGER GRANGE

2

Wr Twr

Ballinger Grove

Havenfields

HERBERTS HOLE

POTTER ROW

Ballinger Bottom (South)

1

A 413

MISBOURNE RD

Park Farm

PO

BALLINGER AVE

MEADOW LA

MARRIOTTS AVE

MARRIOTTS AVE

02

Bury Farm

89 | A | B | 90 | C | D | 91 | E | F

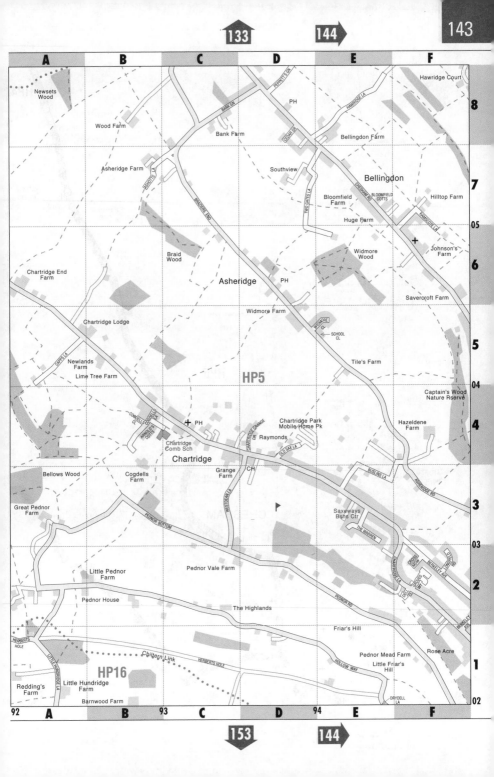

143 134

HP4

A-416

Chesham Rd

Snowhill Farm

PH

Snowhill Cotts

Ashley Green

Old Oak Farm

Nursery

Hog La

Nut Hazel Cross Farm

Woodlands Farm

Wood View Cotts

Flamstead Farm

Thorne Barton Farm

Ramscoat Wood

White Hawridge Bottom

PH

Bower Farm

Chesham Vale

Little Pressmore Farm

Pressmore Farm

The Warren

Woodside

HP5

Ashley Green Rd

Mount Nugent Farm

Broadview Farm

Sloelands Farm

Nashleigh Farm

Lye Green

Little Hivings

Meadow Cl

Gorse Way

Four Oaks

Hollybush Av

Marston Cl

Mount Nugent

Captains Cl

Lye Ridge Cl

Park Greenways

Hivings

Pd

1 WOODCOTE LAWNS
2 LITTLE GREENCROFT
3 REYNOLDS WLK
4 DURRANTS PATH
5 MOUNT NUGENT

Whitethorn's Farm

Amersham & Wycombe Coll

Nashleigh Ho

Dodderoft Rd

Sycamore Dene

Lye Green Cotts

Lycrome Rd

Deer Park Rd

PH

Lye Green Farm

B4505

Great Hivings

Farriers Way

Little Spring Prim Sch

Spring

Greenhill

Vale

Pop Yar Cl

CHESHAM

Nashleigh Hill

Brushwood Jun Sch

Brockhurst Farm

Chiltern Commerce Centre

Ashridge Rd Ind Est

Works

Chesterton Cl

Manor Rd

Upland Ave

Vale Rise

Abbott

PH

Hilltop

Chilton Rd

Russell St

Preston Hill

Cherry Tree Wlk

Birch Way

Hilltop

Crab Tree Cres

Bayman Manor

Codmore

Lye Green Rd

Pond Park

Dellfield

Tom Scott Rd

Alma Rd

Newtown Sch

Britannia

Addison Rd

Berkhampstead Rd

Brockman's La

Severalls Ave

Francis St

Punch Bowl La

Maltees Rd

Mayer View

Heritage House Sped Sch

Elmtree Inf Sch

Acacia Rd

Cemy

Crown's Bsns Est

Masons Rd

Broad St

Upper George St

Buckingham View

Essex Rd

Cameron Rd

Newtown

Escombe Ave

Codmore Cross

Botley Rd

PH

Little Chartridge

Westridge Cl

Willow Chase

Sunnyside Rd

Brushmakers

The Kiln

Broad St

A-416

Townsend Rd

B4505

Harding Rd

White Hill

Cheyne Rd

Chesham High Sch

Hollybush Farm

Chesham Park Com Coll

Webb Cl

B4505

143 154

B1
1 WESLEY HILL
2 UPPER MDW
3 PHOENIX BSNS CTR
B2
1 THE CHASE
2 NIGHTINGALE RD

C1
1 QUEENS RD
2 UPPER GLADSTONE RD
3 FRANCHISE ST
4 TURNERS WLK
5 GEORGE ST
6 CAMERON RD
7 GREATACRE

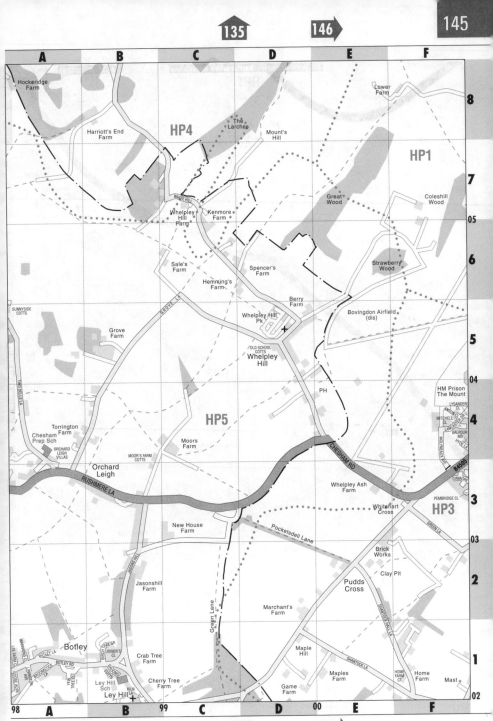

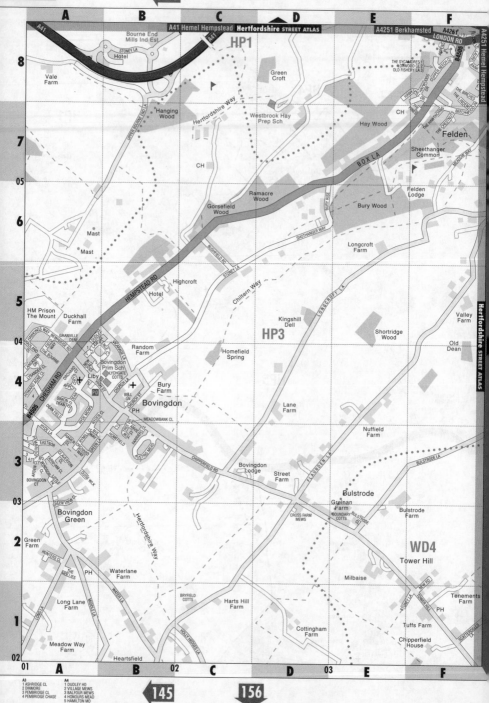

A41 Hemel Hempstead **Hertfordshire** STREET ATLAS   A4251 Berkhamsted

HP1

A41

Bourne End
Mills Ind Est

STONEY LA

Hotel

Vale
Farm

Green
Croft

Hanging
Wood

Herttfordshire Way

Westbrook Hay
Prep Sch

Hay Wood

THE SYCAMORES 1
LORWOOD CL 2
OLD FISHERY LA 3

CH

Felden

Sheethanger
Common

CH

Felden
Lodge

BOX LA

Ramacre
Wood

Gorsefield
Wood

Bury Wood

Mast

BUCHFIELD RD

SHOTHANGER WAY

Longcroft
Farm

HEMPSTEAD RD

Highcroft

STONEY LA

Chiltern Way

Kingshill
Dell

Shortridge
Wood

Valley
Farm

Mast

Hotel

HM Prison
The Mount

Duckhall
Farm

HP3

Random
Farm

Homefield
Spring

Old
Dean

Bovingdon
Prim Sch

Bury
Farm

Lane
Farm

Nuffield
Farm

Liby

CHESHAM RD

B4505

Bovingdon

PH

MEADOWBANK CL

CHIPPERFIELD RD

Bovingdon
Lodge

Street
Farm

Bulstrode

BULSTRODE LA

Bovingdon
Green

Greinan
Farm

CROSS FARM
MEWS

BOUNDARY
COTTS

Bulstrode
Farm

Green
Farm

Hertfordshire Way

WD4

Tower Hill

Waterlane
Farm

PH

Milbaise

Long Lane
Farm

BRYFIELD
COTTS

Harts Hill
Farm

Tuffs Farm

PH

Tenements
Farm

Meadow Way
Farm

Cottingham
Farm

Chipperfield
House

Heartsfield

A3
1 ASHRIDGE CL
2 DINMORE
3 PEMBRIDGE CL
4 PEMBRIDGE CHASE

A4
1 DUDLEY HO
2 VILLAGE MEWS
3 BALFOUR MEWS
4 HONOURS MEAD
5 HAMILTON MD

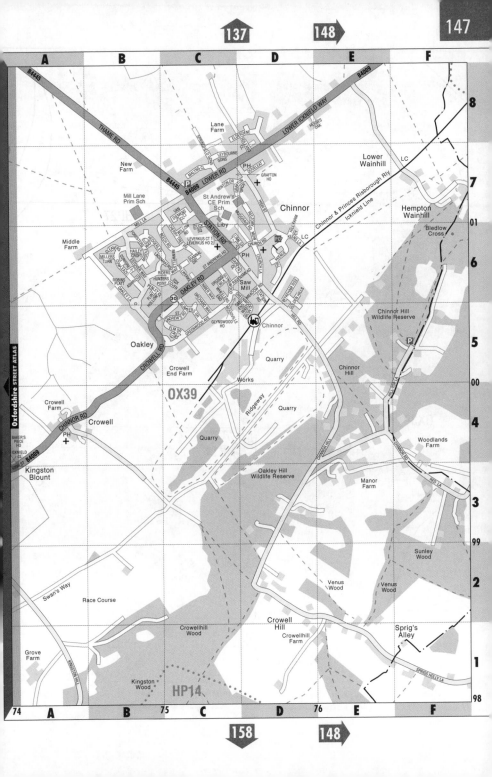

147 138

A **B** **C** **D** **E** **F**

Ickneild Line

8

Frogmore
Farm

TROUT
HOLLOW

ODDLEY LA

Midshires Way

FLEDGLING RD

BLEDLOW RD

Chiltern Way

The
Warren

7

The
Cop

Ickneild Way Path

Church
Farm

UPPER ICKNIELD WAY

Home
Farm

HP27

01

Thickthorne
Wood

Ridgeway

CH

LEE RD

6

Dean
Plantation

Parsonage
Farm

Keeper's
House

Bledlow Cycling Ride

WIGAN'S LA

Lodge
Hill

5

Bledlow
Great Wood

Chiltern Way

Shimmels
Farm

00

4

OX39

Callow Down
Farm

Chiltern Way

Home Wood

HP14

Frenche's Wood

Wigan's
Farm

3

Beechgrove
Farm

CHINNOR RD

Harper's
Farm

Lodge Hill
Farm

99

Hedgerley
Wood

Bledlow Ridge

ROUTE EM

Rout's
Green

BETTER'S

2

Radnage
Bottom Farm

RADNAGE LA

CHAPEL LA

PH

1

Daws Hill
Farm

CHURCH
LA

Studmore
Farm

SPRIGS HOLEN LA

98

A 77 **B** 78 **C** **D** 79 **E** **F**

147 159

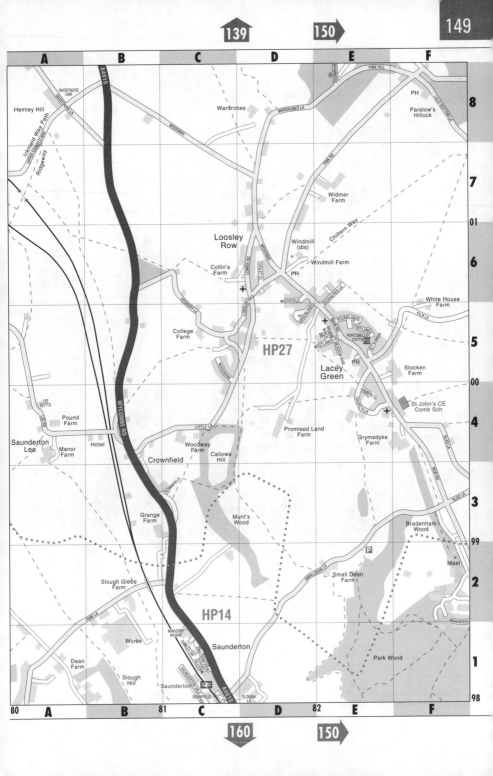

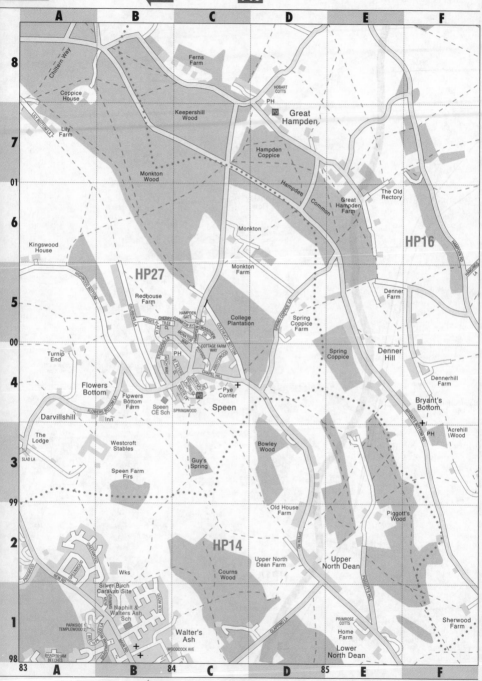

8

7

01

6

5

00

4

3

99

2

98

A B C D E F

Chiltern Way

Coppice House

Lily Farm

LILY BOTTOM LA

Ferns Farm

Keepershill Wood

Monkton Wood

HOBART COTTS

PH
PO
Great Hampden

Hampden Coppice

Hampden Common

Great Hampden Farm

The Old Rectory

HP16

Kingswood House

HP27

Redhouse Farm

Monkton

Monkton Farm

College Plantation

Spring Coppice Farm

Denner Farm

Denner Hill

HIGHWOOD BOTTOM LA

GOLDING LA

Turnip End

Flowers Bottom

MOSES PL
CHERRY TREE CL
HAMPDEN GATE
CONNELL CATS
WINDSOR
COTTAGE FARM WAY
COLLEGE BOTTOM
SPRING COPPICE LA

Spring Coppice

Dennerhill Farm

STUDRIDGE LA
MAIN WAY
PH
KINGS LA

Flowers Bottom Farm

Speen CE Sch
SPRINGWOOD

Pye Corner

Speen

Bryant's Bottom
PH
Acrehill Wood

FLOWERS BOTTOM LA

Inn

Darvillshill

The Lodge

SLAD LA

Westcroft Stables

Guy's Spring

Bowley Wood

BRYANT'S BOTTOM RD

Speen Farm Firs

Old House Farm

Piggott's Wood

HP14

GREENWOOD
NEW RD
PARKWOOD

Wks

Upper North Dean Farm

Upper North Dean

DENNER HILL

Silver Birch Caravan Site

Naphill & Walters Ash Sch

Courns Wood

CLAPPINS LA

PRIMROSE COTTS

Sherwood Farm

PARKSIDE
TEMPLEWOOD

NAPHILL
MAIN RD
WOODCOCK AVE

Walter's Ash

Home Farm

Lower North Dean

PIGGOTT'S HILL

BRADENHAM BEECHES

83 A 84 B C 85 D E F

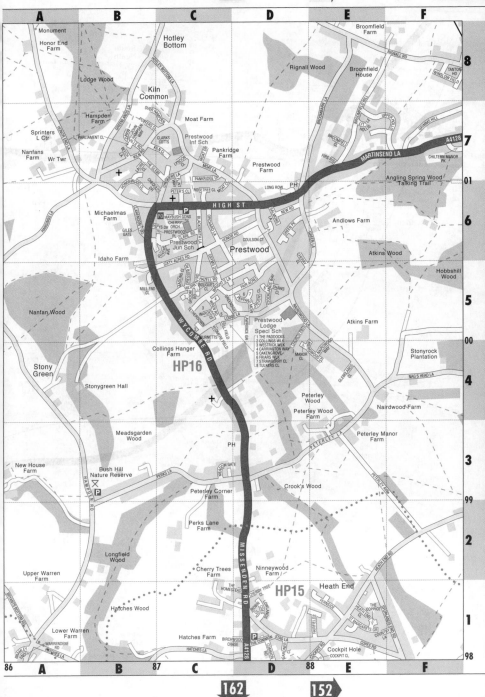

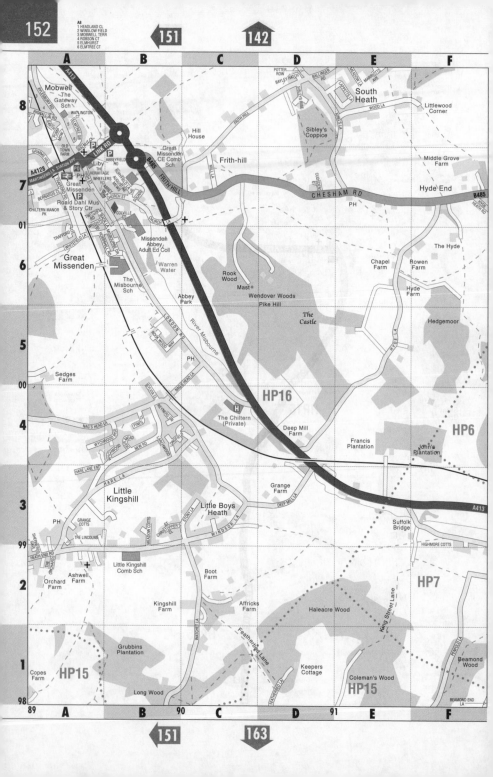

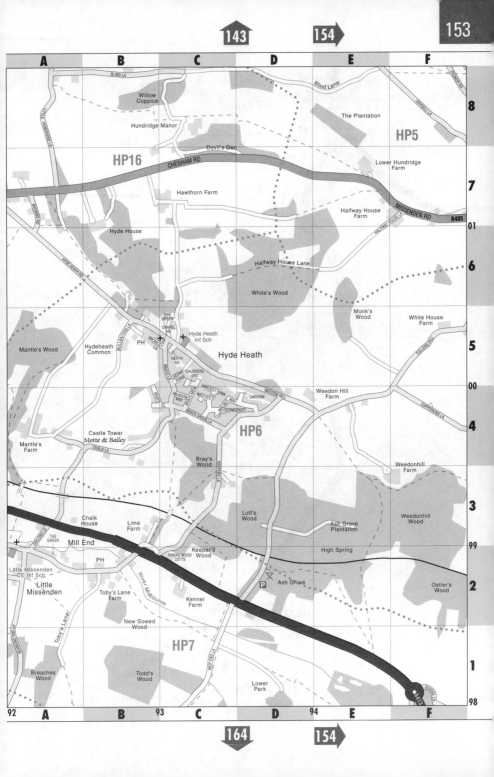

153 144

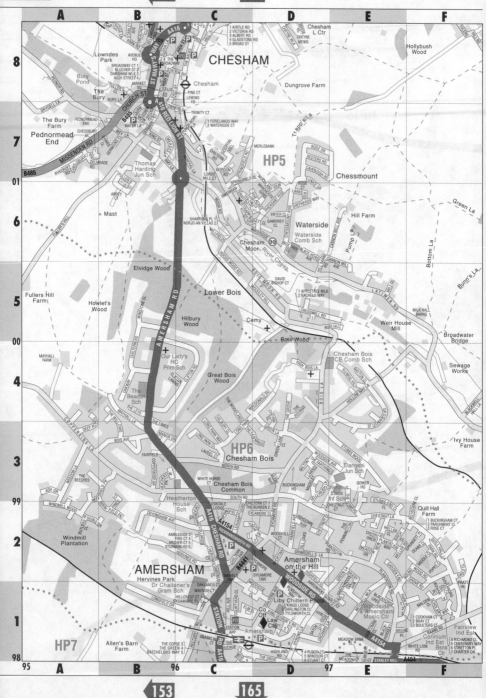

153 165

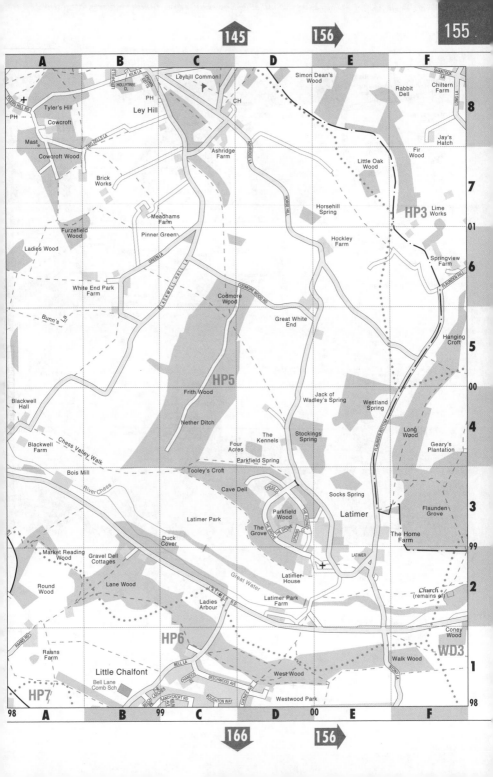

155
146

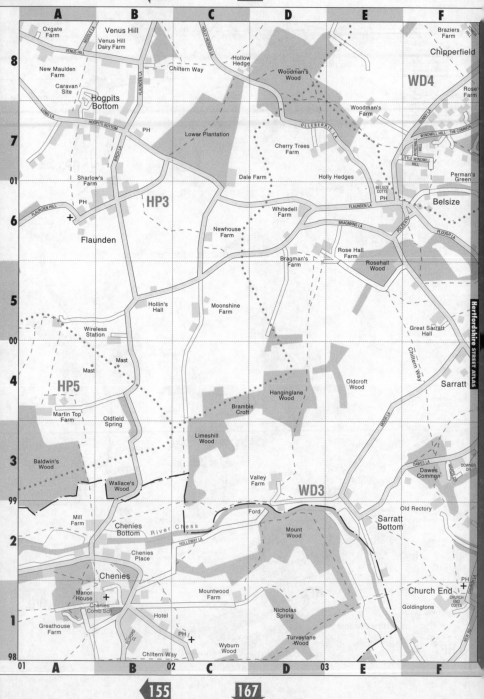

Hertfordshire STREET ATLAS

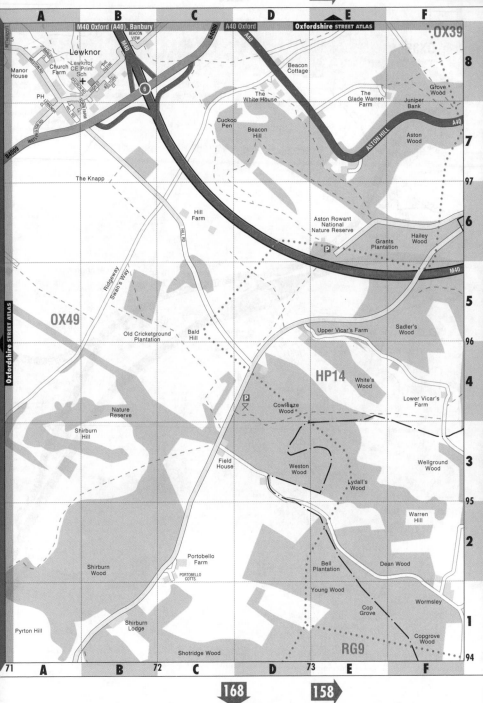

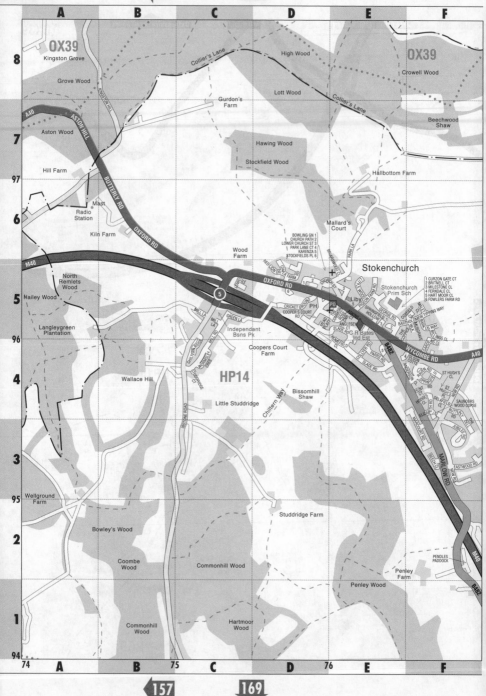

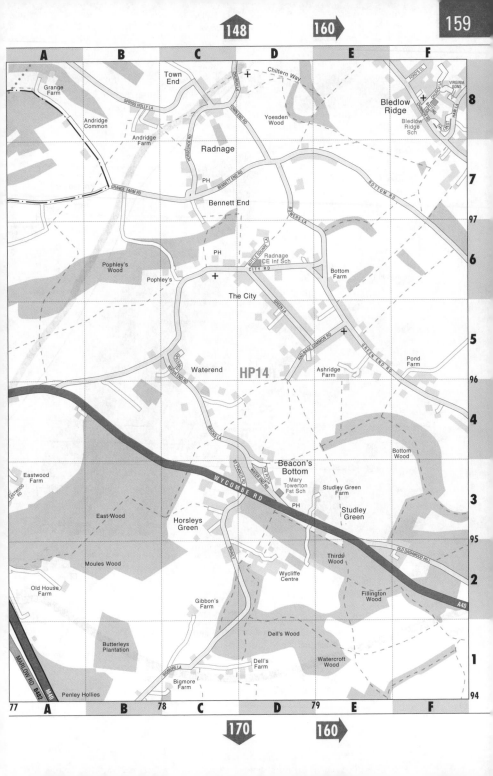

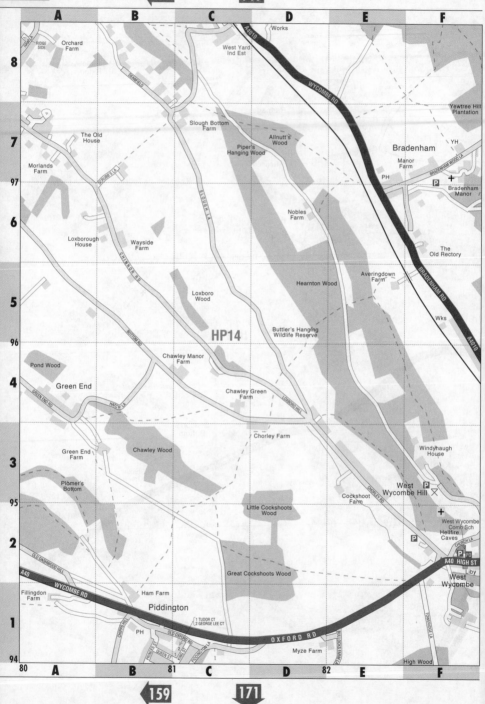

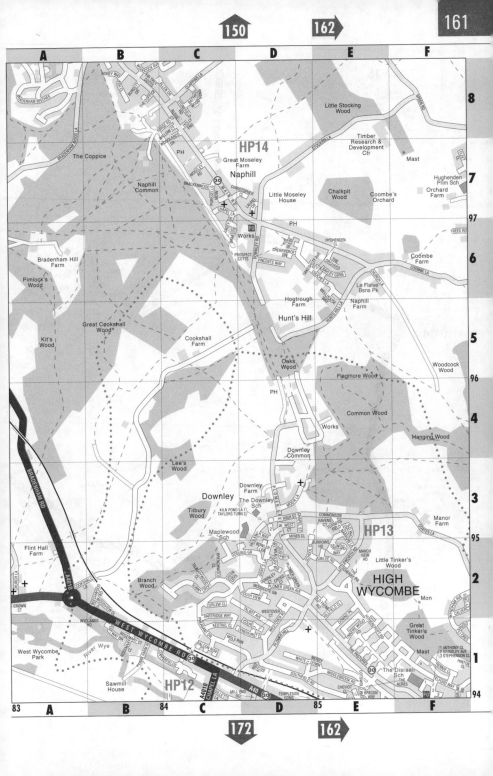

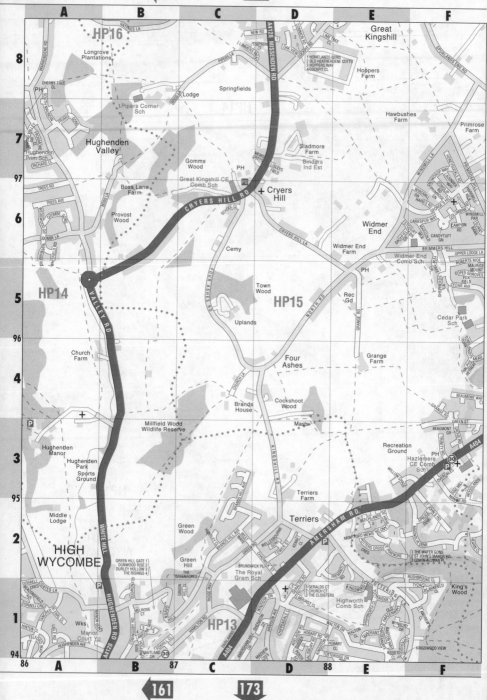

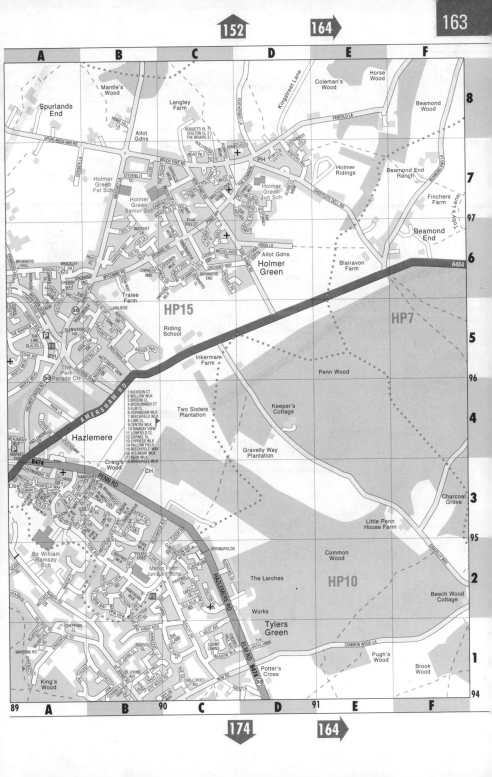

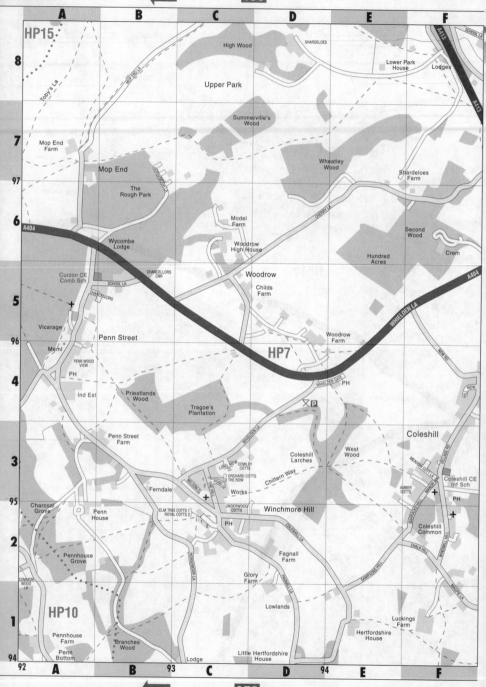

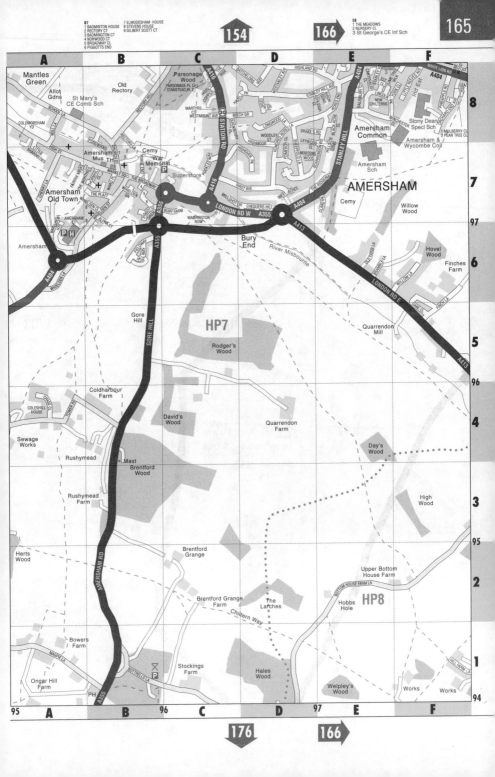

165
155

A B C D E F

A404

8

WHITE LION RD

HP6

AMERSHAM RD

A404

CHILTERN CL
ARBOUR VIEW
Boughton
Bsns Pk
REPTON PL
CHESSFIELD PK
CHESSFIELD PK
WESTWOOD DR
PARK LA
AMERSHAM WAY
OAKINGTON AVE
CHURCH DR
OLD FIELD
OAKFIELD
ST ELIZABETH AVE
RUSSELL CL
STATION APP
BEDFORD AVE
BEDFORD CT
ASHMEAD
P
PO
30

Bendrose
Farm
Works
Dr Challoner's
High Sch
Beel
House
LOUDHAMS RD
HALIFAX
APPLEFIELD
CHALFONT STATION RD
Chalfont & Latimer
Little Chalfont
Prim Sch
CH
Little Chalfont
Prim Sch

7

Little
Chalfont
Snell's
Farm
CHALFONT VILLAGE WAY
Liby
1 NIGHTINGALES CNR
2 NIGHTINGALES CT
3 THE HAWTHORNS
LOUDHAMS WOOD LA
Netherground
Spring
Lodge
Copse

97

APPLETON FIELD
HAZELWOOD RD
BURTON'S RD
Lodge
Farm

6

HP7

Coke's
Farm
DOGGETTS WOOD CL
BOWERY WAY
PARK GR
LONG WLK
LODGE LA
NEW RD
Burton's
Farm
WD3

5

CH
DOGGETTS WOOD LA
LODGERS REACH
BURTON'S LA
Burton's
Wood

96

A413

Crosslane
Wood

4

PH
Pollards Wood
Pollards Park
House
HP8
NIGHTINGALES LA
Roughwood
Park

Harewood
Downs House
Roughwood
Farm

3

BOTTOM HOUSE FARM LA
AMERSHAM RD
River Misbourne
Warren
Farm
ROUGHWOOD LA
Roughwood
Cottages

95

Lower Bottom
House Farm
Bow Wood

2

Chiltern Way
Misbourne
Farm
Chiltern Way
Bailey Wood
Mon
Grovespring
Wood

MISBOURNE
HO

Kilnpond
Wood

1

HILL FARM LA
STRATTON CHASE DR
MILL LA
A413
Chalfont Mill
Ford
Mill Farm
St Giles
Lodge
B4442
VACHE LA
KINGS
GORELANDS LA
The
Vache
CHENIES PARK BSN
BOWSTRIDGE LA
Shortenills
Wood
Newland
Gorse
Chiltern Way

94

98 A B 99 C D 00 E F

165
177

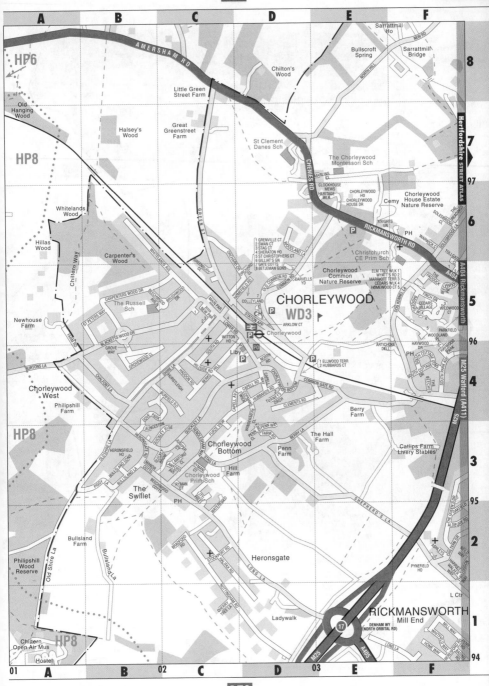

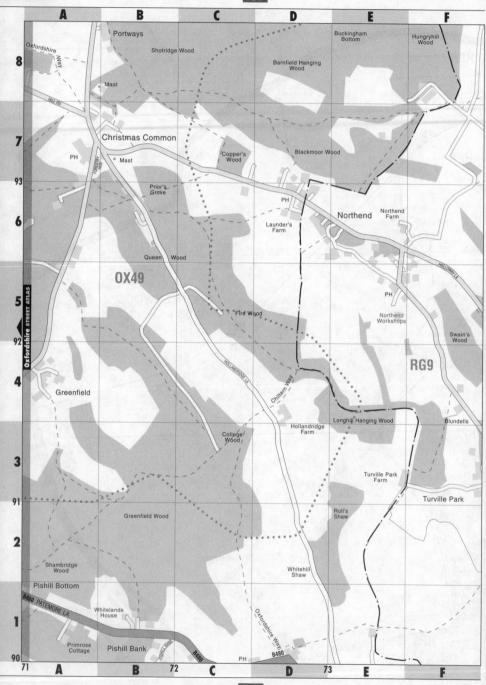

A B C D E F

8

7

93

6

5

92

4

3

91

2

1

90

71 72 73

Oxfordshire Street Atlas

Oxfordshire Way

HILL RD

Portways

Shotridge Wood

Mast

Christmas Common

PH

Mast

FORESTRY RIDE

Prior's Grove

Queen Wood

OX49

Greenfield

College Wood

Greenfield Wood

Shambridge Wood

Pishill Bottom

B480 PATEMORE LA

Whitelands House

Primrose Cottage

Pishill Bank

PISHILL BANK

B480

Copper's Wood

Launder's Farm

Fire Wood

HOLLANDRIDGE LA

Chiltern Way

Hollandridge Farm

Barnfield Hanging Wood

Blackmoor Wood

PH

Roll's Shaw

Whitehill Shaw

Oxfordshire Way

PH

B480

Buckingham Bottom

Northend

PH

Northend Workshops

Longhill Hanging Wood

Turville Park Farm

Northend Farm

RG9

Swain's Wood

Blundells

Turville Park

Hungryhill Wood

HOLLOWAY LA

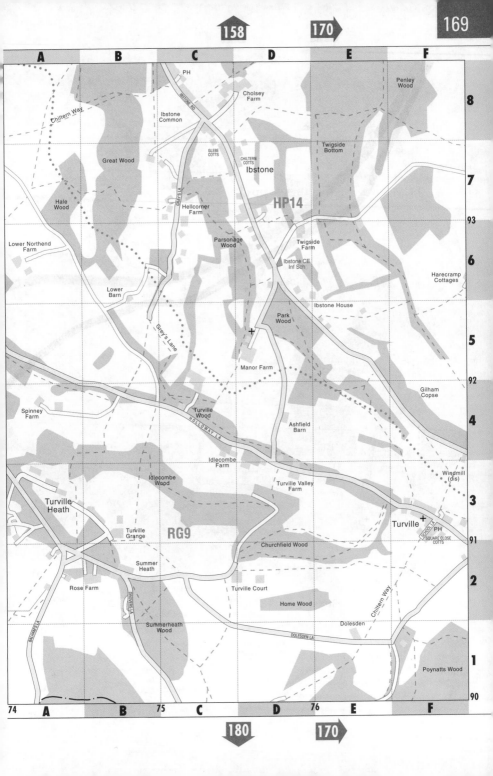

169
159

A B C D E F

8

7

93

6

5

92

4

3

91

2

1

90

B4482
M40

Chequers Manor
Farm

PH

MARLOW RD

Pound
Wood

HP14

Barn
Wood

Leygrove's
Wood

Watercroft
Farm

Huckenden
Farm

Pound
Farm

Pound
Farm

Cadmore End
CE Comb Sch

Cadmore
End

PH

Kensham
Farm

Cadmore End
Common

M40

Bolter
End

NEW RD

PH

BOLTER END LA

FININGS RD B482

Hill
Farm

Rackley's
Farm

Hanger
Wood

Priestley's
Farm

CHEQUERS LA

Gravesend

Manor
Farm

Mill Hanging
Wood

Hanger
Farm

FINGEST LA

Hanover
Hill

Long
Copse

Turville
Hill

Fingest

PH

RG9

Fingest
Wood

Mousells Wood

Dovers
Farm

Murrage
Farm

Chiltern Way

Maiden
House

Spurgrove

PH

DOLESDEN
LA

SPURGROVE LA

Goddard's
Wood

Adam's
Wood

Little
Frieth

PERRIN SPRINGS
LA

Poynatts
Farm

Bottom
Wood

Frieth

PH

ELLERY RD

PH

Colliers
Farm

FININGS
GATE

HATCHET RD

Maiden
Farm

Frieth
CE Comb Sch

Stud
Farm

Lower
Goddards
Farm

SHOGMOOR LA

Upper
Goddards

SHOGMOOR LA

Skirmett

77 A B 78 C D 79 E F

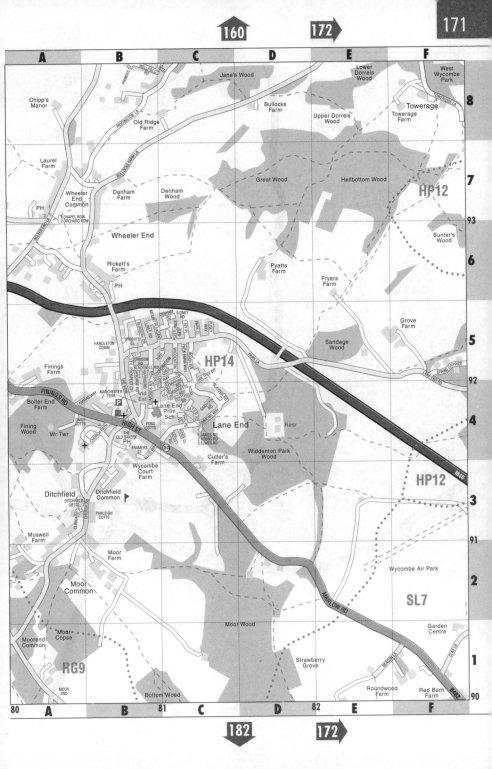

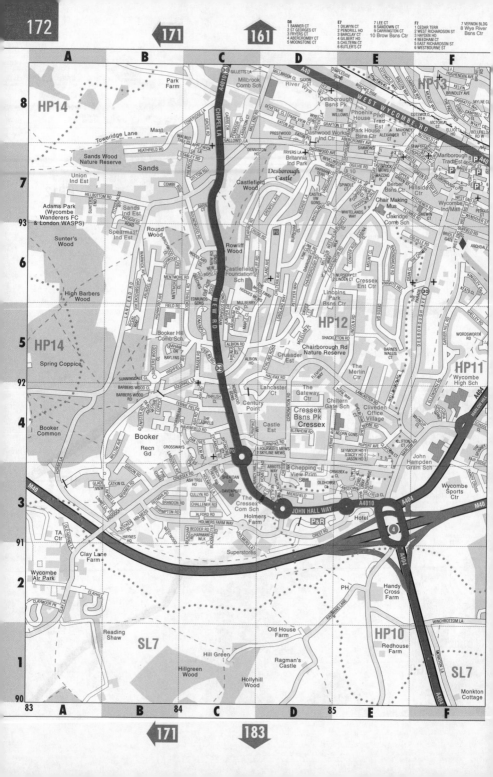

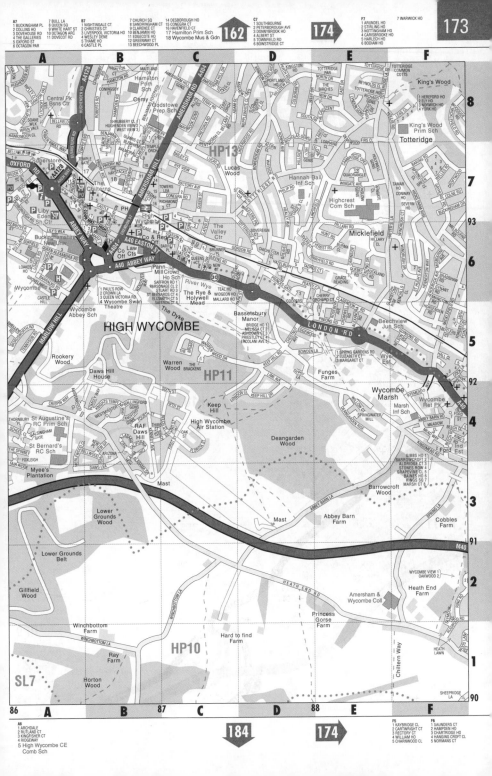

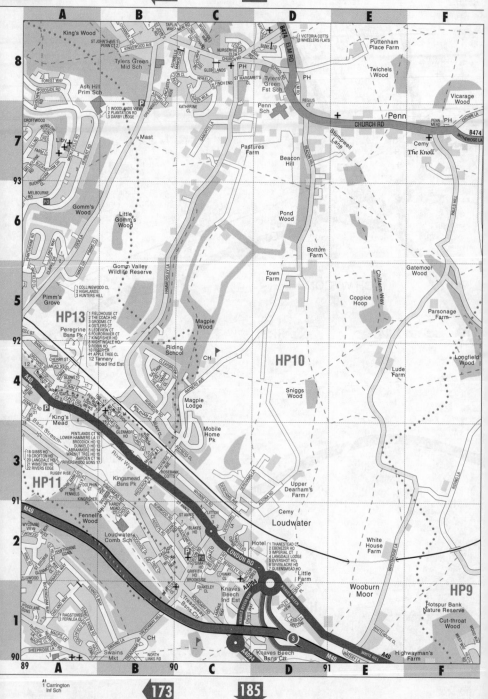

A1
1 Carrington
Inf Sch

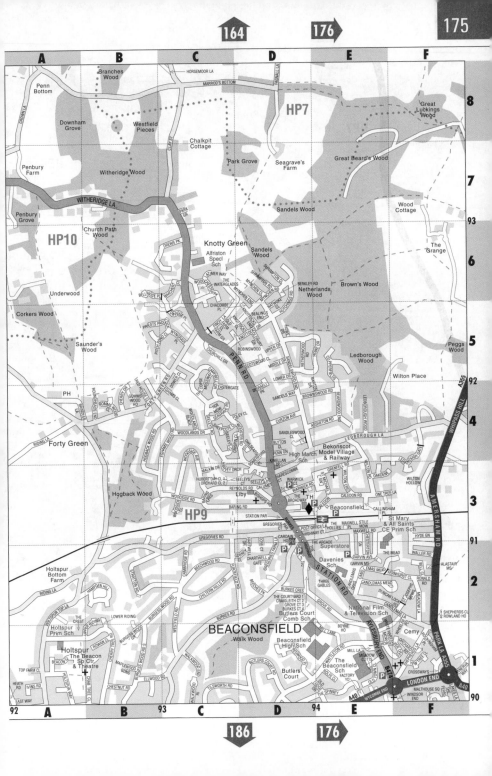

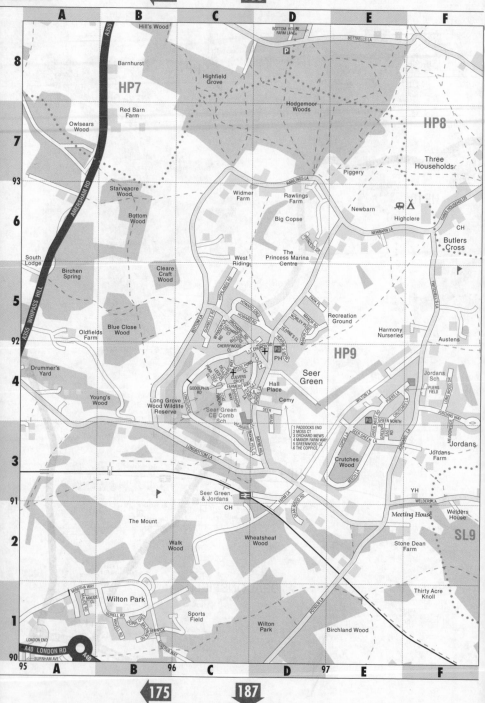

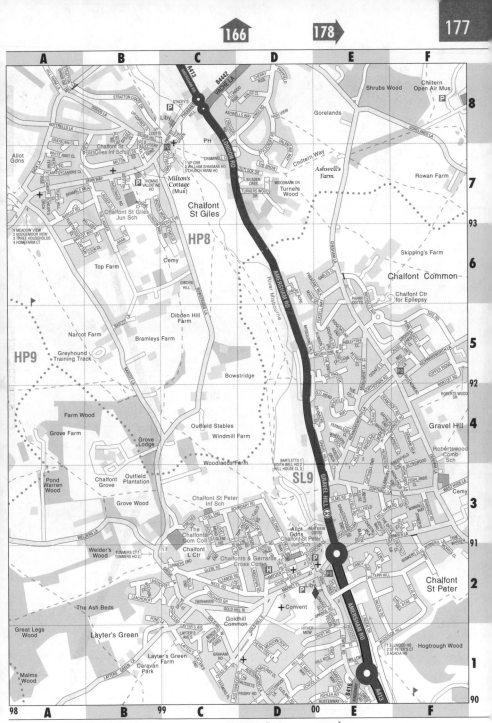

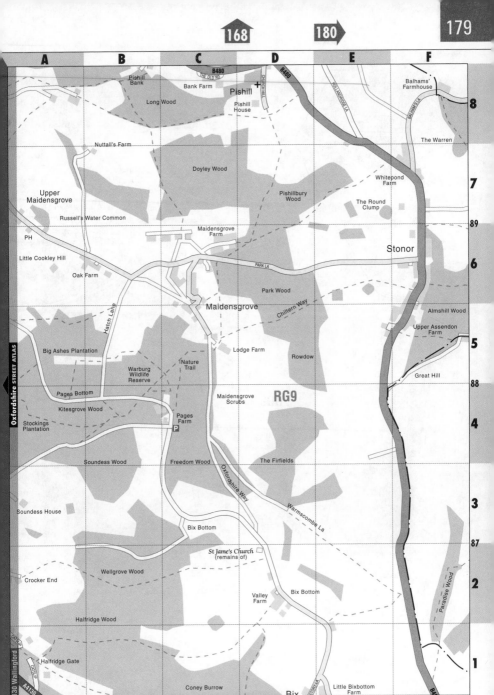

Pishill Bank
Pishill
Bank Farm
Long Wood
Pishill House
+
B480
B480
Balhams' Farmhouse
The Warren
8

Nuttall's Farm
Doyley Wood
Whitepond Farm
HOLLANDRIDGE LA
BALHAMS LA
7

Upper Maidensgrove
Russell's Water Common
Pishillbury Wood
The Round Clump
89

PH
Little Cookley Hill
Maidensgrove Farm
PARK LA
Stonor
6

Oak Farm
Park Wood
Maidensgrove
Chiltern Way
Almshill Wood

Hatch Lane
Big Ashes Plantation
Nature Trail
Lodge Farm
Rowdow
Upper Assendon Farm
Great Hill
5

Warburg Wildlife Reserve
Maidensgrove Scrubs
RG9
88

Pages Bottom
Kitesgrove Wood
Pages Farm
P
4

Stockings Plantation
Soundess Wood
Freedom Wood
The Firfields
Oxfordshire Way

Soundess House
Warmscombe La
3

Bix Bottom
87

St Jame's Church (remains of)
Wellgrove Wood
Paradise Wood

Crocker End
Valley Farm
Bix Bottom
2

Halfridge Wood

Halfridge Gate
1

Coney Burrow
Bix
Little Bixbottom Farm
B480
86

Oxfordshire STREET ATLAS

179
169

A B C D E F

8

Southend

Southend Farm

Drovers

Binfield Bottom

Great Wood

Balhams's Wood

Chiltern Way

7

Stonor House & Gardens

Kimble Farm

Chiltern Valley Winery & Brewery

89

Kildridge Wood

Stonor Park (Deer Park)

Gussetts Wood

Jubilee Plantation

6

Henleyhill Wood

PURLEY LA

5

Coxlease Farmhouse

Upper Woodend Farm

Woodcocks Bill

88

Bosmore Farm

RG9

Hanging Wood

4

Lower Woodend Farm

Jubilee Plantation

Highfield Plantation

3

Roundhouse Farm

87

PH

Great Wood House

Great Wood

Fawley Green Farmhouse

FAWLEY GN

2

Jackson's Farm

Fawley Bottom

Fawley

Red Hill

Fawley Bottom Farm House

Kitchener's Firs

Pallbach Hill

FAWLEY BOTTOM LA

DOBSON'S LA

BENHAM'S LA

1

Eversdown

NEW COTTS

Benhams

86

Brackenhill Stud Farm

74 A B 75 C D 76 E F

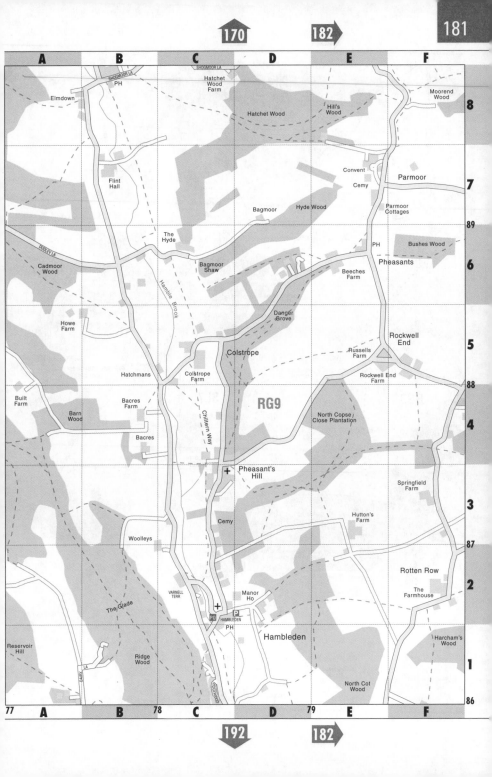

181
171

B482

A B C D E F

8

Moorend
Wood

HP14

Bottom Wood

Beacon
Farm

Finnamore La

Beacon La

7

Finnamore
Wood

Bluey's
Farm

The Roost

89

Chisbridge

Chisbridge
Cross

Copy Green

6

Shillingridge Wood

Woodlands

SHILLINGRIDGE
PK

Denelands
Farm

Holme Wood
Cottage

Holme
Wood

Oaklands
Farm

5

Kent's
Wood

Holme Wood

FRIETH RD

Hawkins
Farm

Mundaydean
Bottom

MUNDAYDEAN LA

88

Bottom House

RG9

Woodend
House

SL7

4

Fountain's

Woodend Farm

Holywick

Arbon

Lower
Woodend

Walnut
Tree
Farm

3

Heath Wood

Homefield Wood
Wildlife Reserve

Lord's
Wood

Marlow
Common

MARLOW COMM

87

Rogues Plantation

2

Chiltern Way

Davenport Wood

Bockmer End
Farm

Pullingshill
Wood

1

Woodland Plain

Bockmer
House

BOCKMER LA

Bockmer End

Hook's Farm

86

Widefield

80 A B 81 C D 82 E F

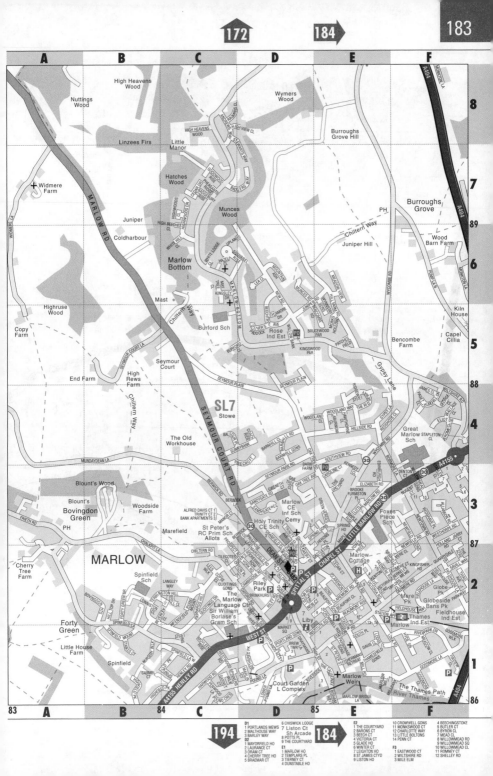

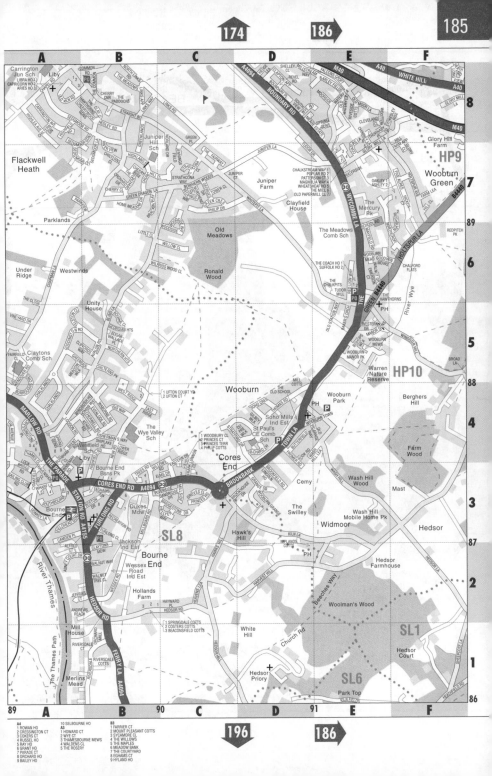

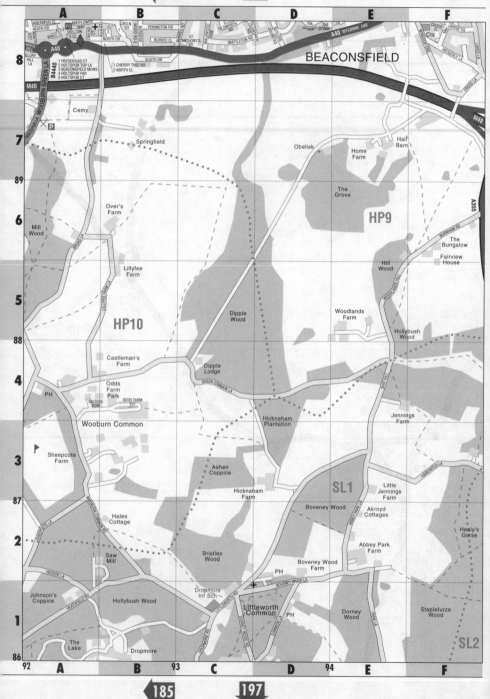

185
175

A **B** **C** **D** **E** **F**

HOLTSPUR
HEATH RD
MAYFLOWER
KINGS CL
WHITE
HILL LA
GLORY
HILL LA

KILN CT
NORTH DR
PENINGTON RD
BURKES CL
ST ANTHONY'S CT
WATTLETON RD
THE SPINNEY
A40 WYCOMBE END
CROSBY CTS
HEDGERLY LA
CROSS LA
LAKES LA
MAXROSE SQ

A40

1 FREDERICKS CT
2 HOLTSPUR TOP LA
3 BEACONSFIELD MEWS
4 HOLTSPUR PAR
5 HOLTSPUR CT

1 CHERRY TREE RD
2 NORTH CL

SOUTH DR

8

BEACONSFIELD

M40

M40

A355

Cemy

7

Springfield

Obelisk

Home Farm

Hall Barn

89

Over's Farm

The Grove

HP9

6

Mill Wood

The Bungalow

Fairview House

Lillyfee Farm

Hill Wood

5

Dipple Wood

Woodlands Farm

Hollybush Wood

HP10

88

Castleman's Farm

Dipple Lodge

4

Odds Farm Park

GREEN COMMON LA

Jennings Farm

PH

SALTERS ROW

ODDS FARM EST

Wooburn Common

Hicknham Plantation

3

Sheepcote Farm

Ashen Coppice

SL1

Little Jennings Farm

Hicknham Farm

87

Hales Cottage

Boveney Wood

Akroyd Cottages

Healy's Gorse

2

Saw Mill

Bristles Wood

Abbey Park Farm

Johnson's Coppice

Boveney Wood Farm

PH

Boveney Wood La

Dropmore Inf Sch

Littleworth Common

Dorney Wood

Staplefurze Wood

1

Hollybush Wood

PH

SL2

86

The Lake

Dropmore

A **B** **C** **D** **E** **F**

92   93   94

185
197

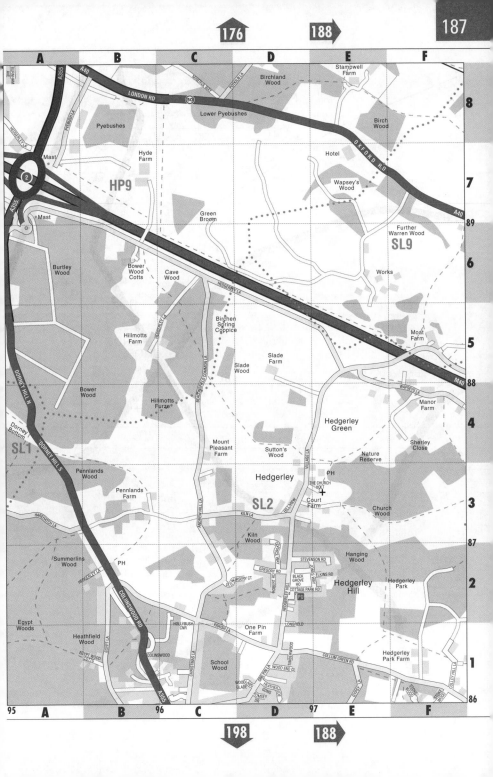

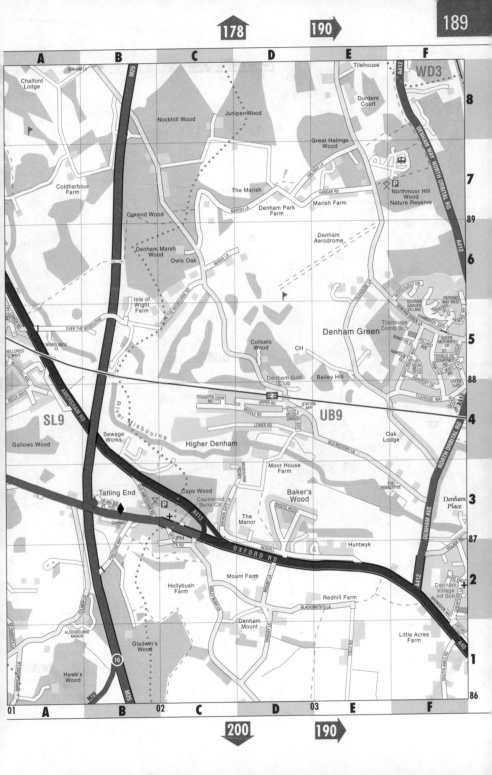

189

Hertfordshire STREET ATLAS

London STREET ATLAS

A B C D E F

8

Langley Farm

Breakspear Path

Bourne Farm

Highbones

BREAKSPEAR RD N

Broadwater Farm

Breakspear House

St Mary's Rd

St Anne Rd

7

Broadwater La

Bearley Dri

Broad Water

Park Lodge Farm Ctr

Bayhurst Wood Country Park

Gore La

Priory Ave

89

Priory Cotts

Presedene Cl

South Harefield

Widewater Pl

Widewater Lock

6

Moorhall Rd

PH

Lower Lodge

Battlesford Wood

A412 NORTH ORBITAL RD

Broadwater Pk

Harefield Moor

UB9

1 SHEEPCOTE GDNS
2 DENHAM GREEN LA

5

Green Bridge

Grand Union Canal Towing Path

Newyears

Linn Way

James Martin Rd

Savay Farm

Newyears Green La

Highway Farm

88

Gloucester

London Loop Grand Union Canal Wk

A412

Station Par

Braemar Farm

Denham

4

Station Cotts

Dews Farm

Newyears Green

Pyghtle Footpath

River Colne

Boot La

Copthall Covert

3

87

South Bucks Way

The White House

Court Farm

Denham Court

CH

CH

Harvil Farm

Copthall Farm

2

Denham

River Misbourne

Denham Court

Denham Country Park Nature Reserve

The Cottages

UB10

St George's Dr

GREENACRES AVE

Priory Covert

Denham Country Park

Ickenham

Campion Cl

SHOREDICHE CL 1
CAMPDEN RD 2

Colne Valley Park Visitor Ctr

Denham Court Rd

Denham Quarry Park Nature Reserve

Fray's River

The Drive

Highfield Dr

Swakeleys Rd

B467

Oxford Rd A40

1

Priory Cl

The Lea

Denham Lock

B467

Three Oaks Cl

B467

86

189 201

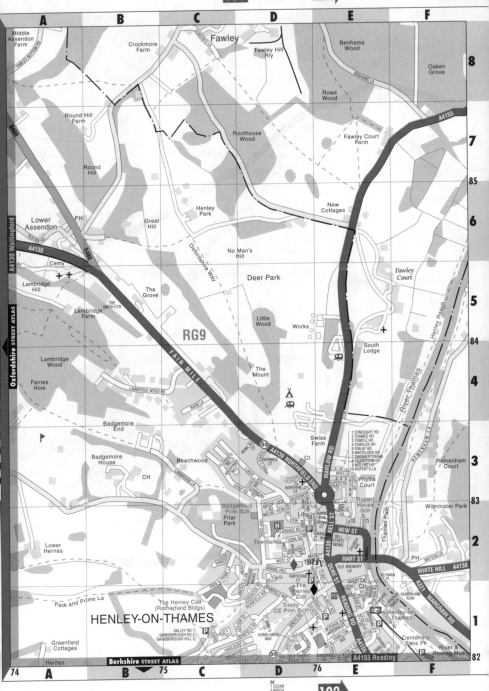

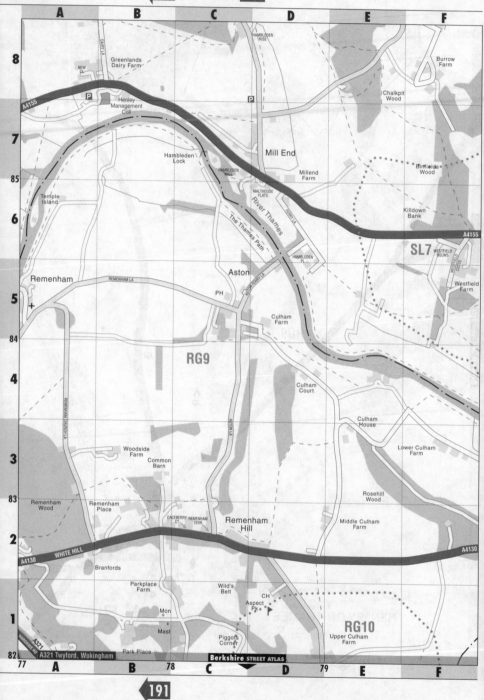

191

181

A B C D E F

8
7
85
6
5
84
4
3
83
2
1
82

Greenlands
Dairy Farm

NEW
PL

Henley
Management
Coll

Hambleden
RISE

Chalkpit
Wood

Burrow
Farm

Mill End

Hambleden
Lock

HAMBLEDEN
MILL

Millend
Farm

Binfields
Wood

MALTHOUSE
FLATS

Temple
Island

River Thames

The Thames Path

Killdown
Bank

SL7

WESTFIELD
BGLWS

WESTFIELD
COTTS

Westfield
Farm

Remenham

REMENHAM LA

HAMBLEDEN
PL

Aston

PH

Culham
Farm

RG9

Culham
Court

Culham
House

Lower Culham
Farm

REMENHAM CHURCH LA

ASTON LA

Woodside
Farm

Common
Barn

Rosehill
Wood

Remenham
Wood

Remenham
Place

DACEBERRY
CT

REMENHAM
TERR

Remenham
Hill

Middle Culham
Farm

WHITE HILL

A4130

A4130

Branfords

Parkplace
Farm

Wild's
Belt

CH

Aspect
Pk

RG10

Mon

Mast

Piggots
Corner

Upper Culham
Farm

Park Place

A321 Twyford, Wokingham

Berkshire STREET ATLAS

191

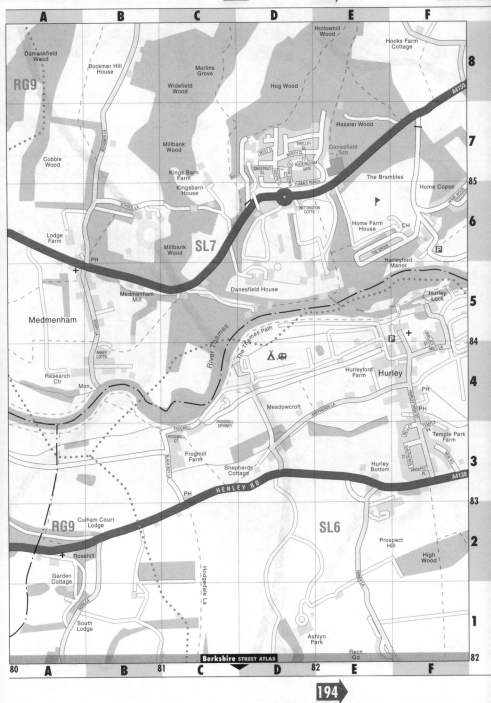

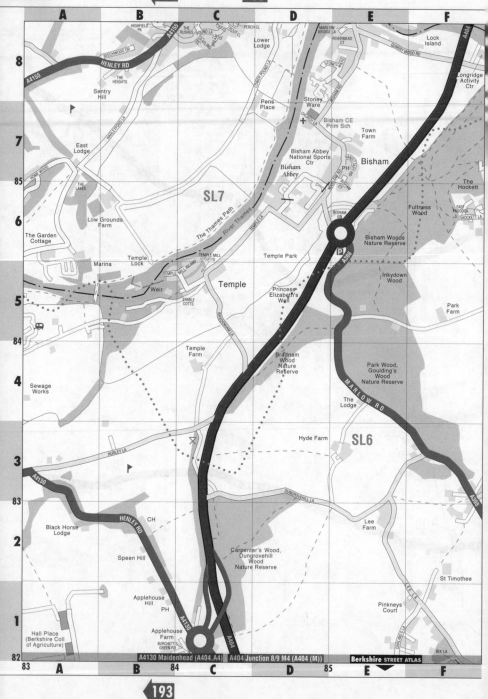

SL7

SL6

A4130 Maidenhead (A404, A4)   A404 Junction 8/9 M4 (A404 (M))   Berkshire STREET ATLAS

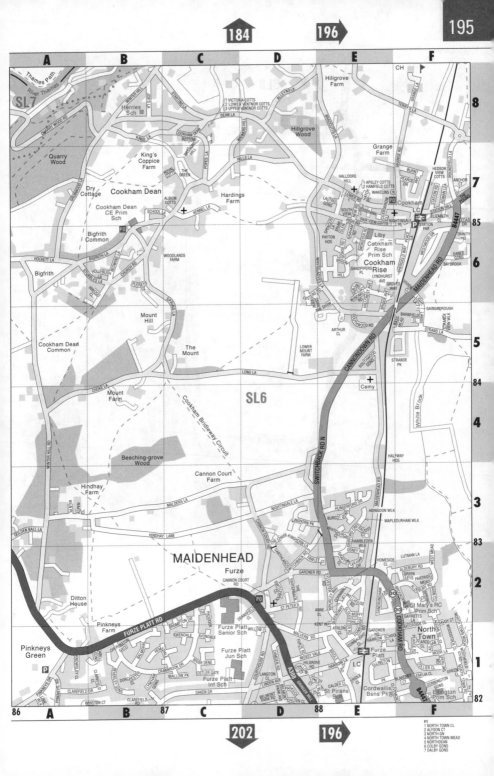

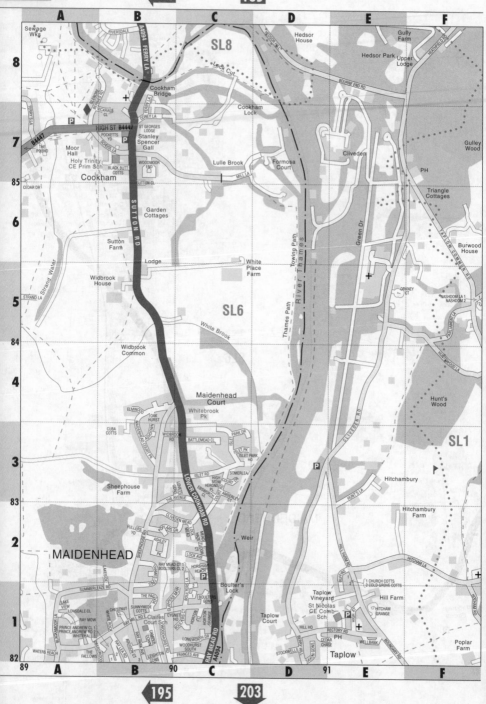

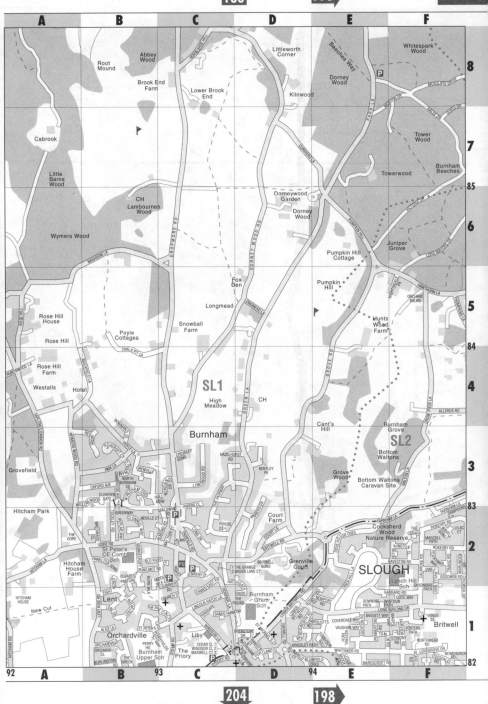

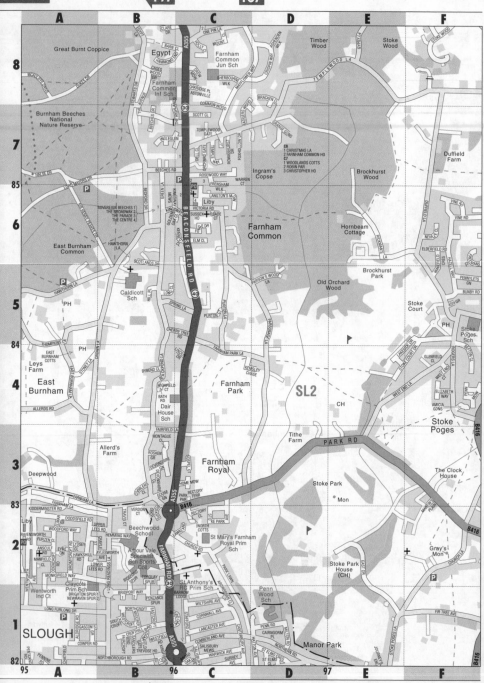

199 189

	A	B	C	D	E	F

HAWKSWOOD LA

M40

8

Alderbourne Arches

SL9

M25

1a

16

Rush Green

SOUTHLANDS RD

M40

New House Farm

WILLETTS LA

7

Brown's Wood

Ways Farm

Gossams Wood

Oldhouse Wood

HOLLYBUSH LA

FIELD RD

FIELD RD

UB9

ALDERBOURNE LA

Alderbourne Farm

Blanchards Farm

Kingcup Farm

WILLETTS LA

A412

85

HAWKSWOOD DR

FULMER COMMON RD

Belle Farm

Sevenhills Farm

Long Coppice

SEVENHILLS RD

Alder Bourne

Southlands Manor

6

Strawberry Wood

The Clump

Dromenagh Farm

LADY YORKE PK

Round Coppice Farm

Black Park Nature Reserve

DENHAM RD

Pinewood Film Studios

SLO

5

BOND CL

PINEWOOD GR

Mansfield Farm

84

PINEWOOD CL

ASHFORD RD

COPSE WOOD

PEACE RD

Park Lodge Farm

CEDARS

THORNBRIDGE RD

HEATHERDEN

LAUREL ST

A4007

4

Park Lodge

RD

AVE PARKWAY

LONGFIELD

Iver Heath

M25

Black Park Country Park

ST DAVID'S PAR

Recn Gd

BIRCH CL

ANSLOW GDNS

Chandlers Hill

3

CHURCH RD

BODLEY

TREWARDEN AVE

LAURELS CL

LAURELS RD

THE WAY

1 ST MARGARET'S GATE
2 ST MARGARETS CT

ROWAN GDNS

Libry

Warren House

HAWTHORN CL

Iver Heath Jun Sch

MEAD HO

LOWER MEAD

POTTERS CROSS

SLOUGH RD

83

A412

Iver Heath Inf Sch

WHITEFIELD

THE CLOSE

SWALLO

SL3

Beeches Way

Home Cottage Farm

Moorwards Farm

2

UXBRIDGE RD

A4007

Five Points

PLEASANT COTTS

PH

WOOD LANE

White Lodge

HARDINGS RO

HARDINGS ROW

BANGORS RD S

Bangors Park Farm

A412

WOOD LA

COOPERS ROW

PH

SWALLOW FIELDS

NORWOOD LA

BANGOR COTTS

1

Langley Park Country Park

BILLET LA

P

MARTINDALE

COPPINS LA

82

01

A

02

B

C

03

D

E

F

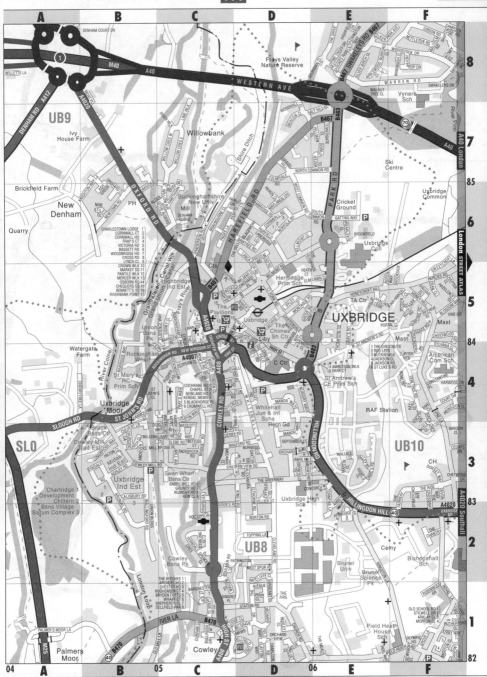

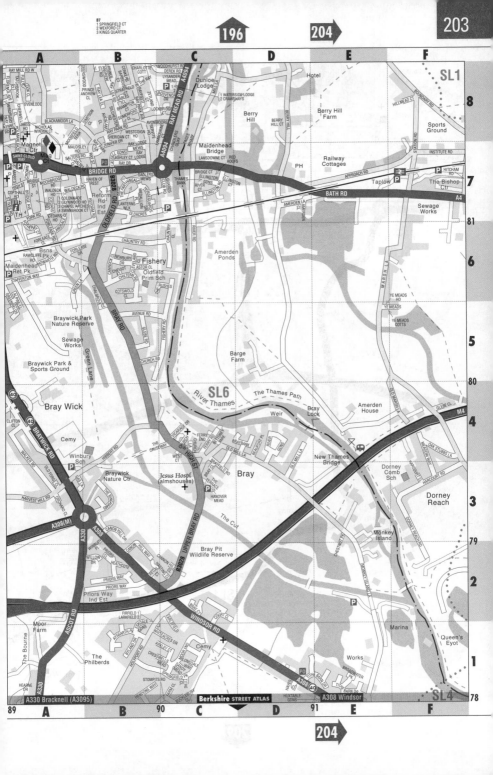

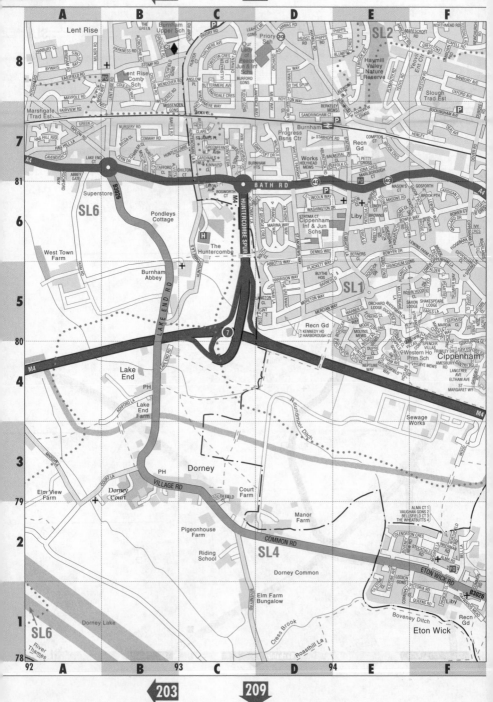

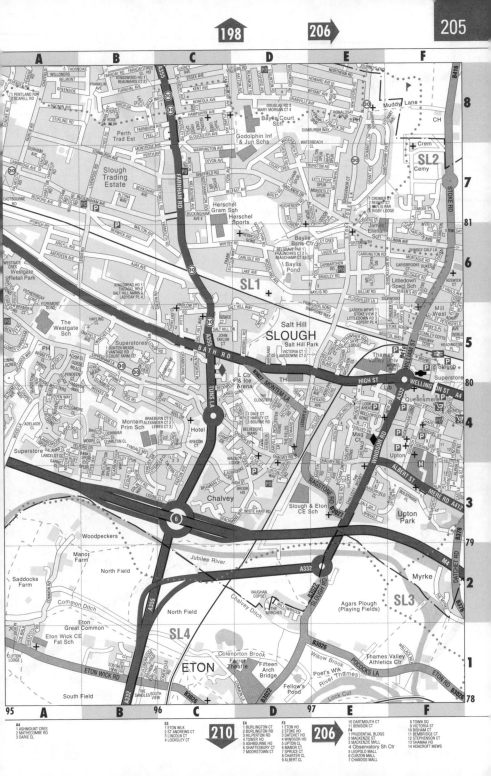

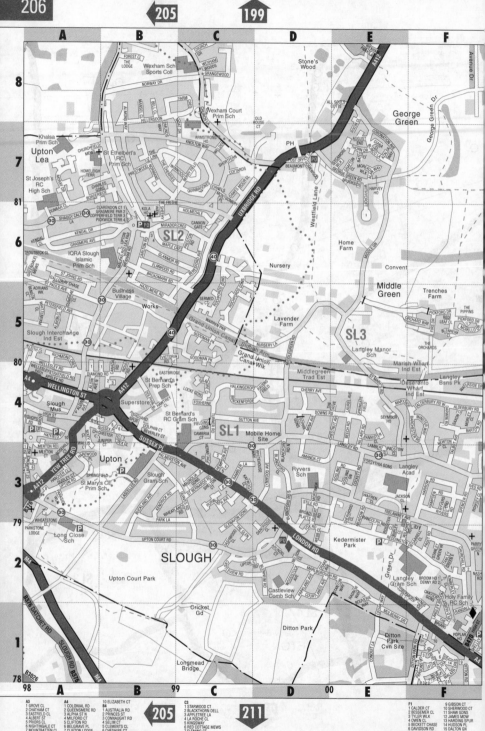

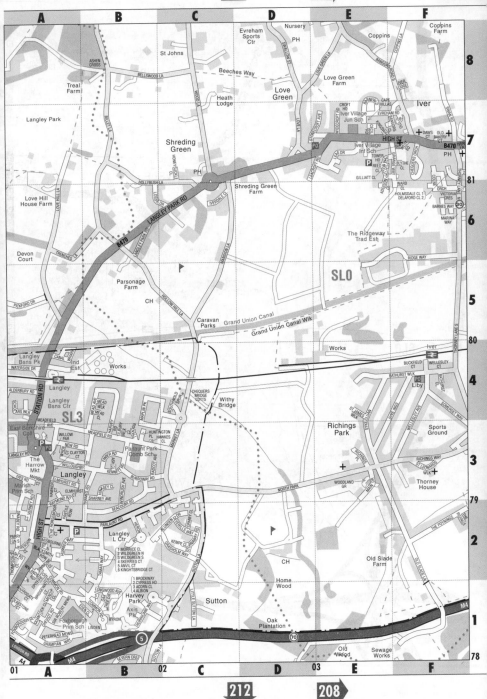

200
208
212
208

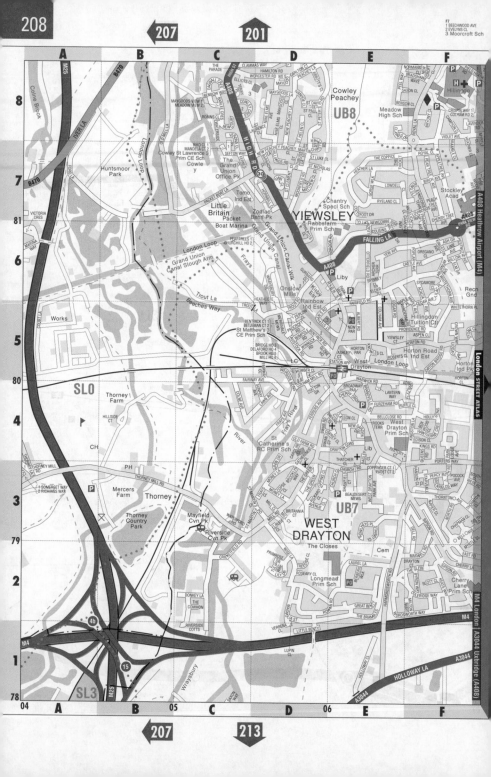

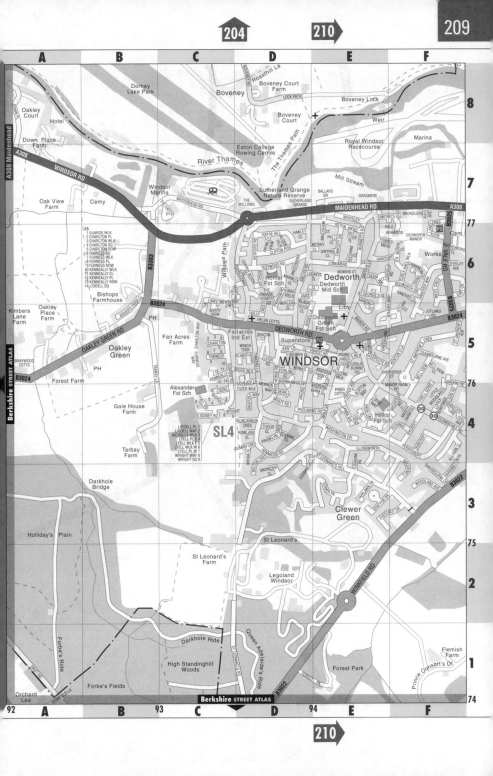

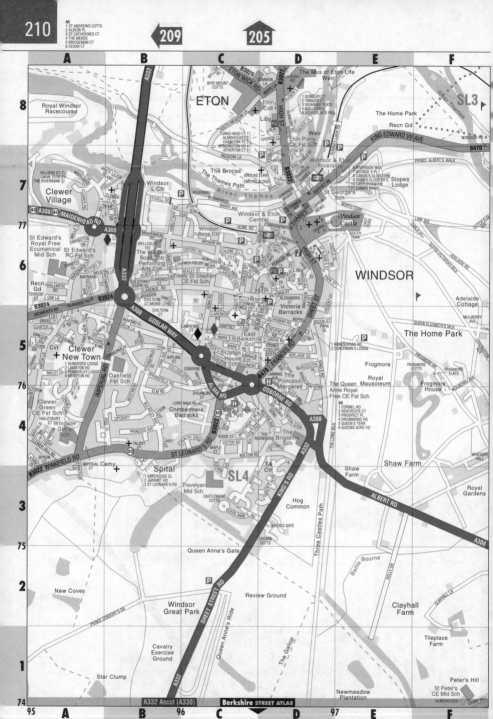

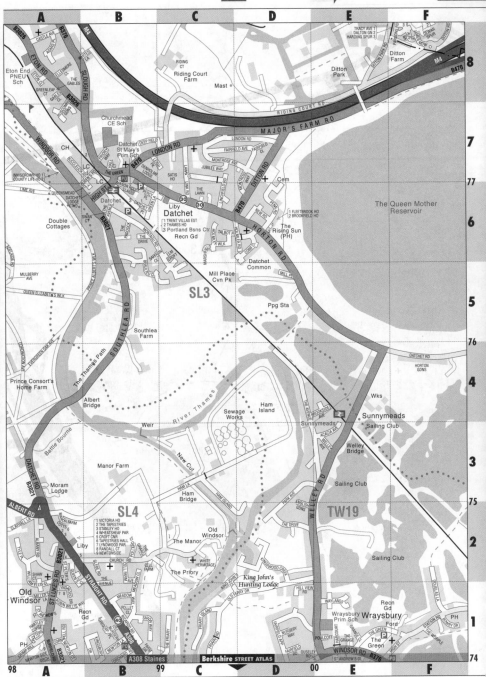

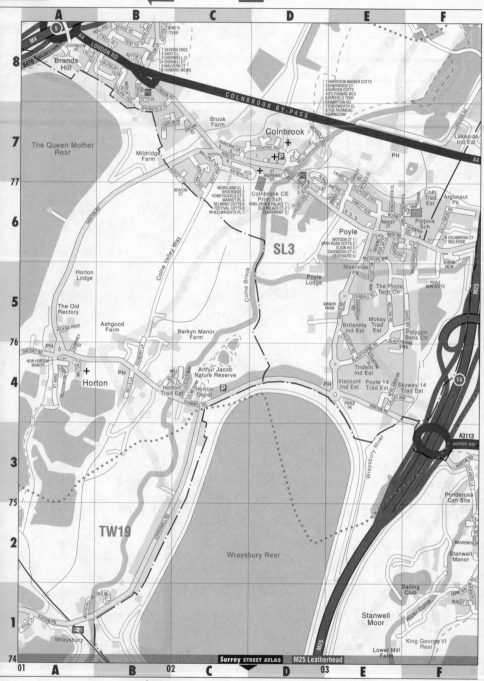

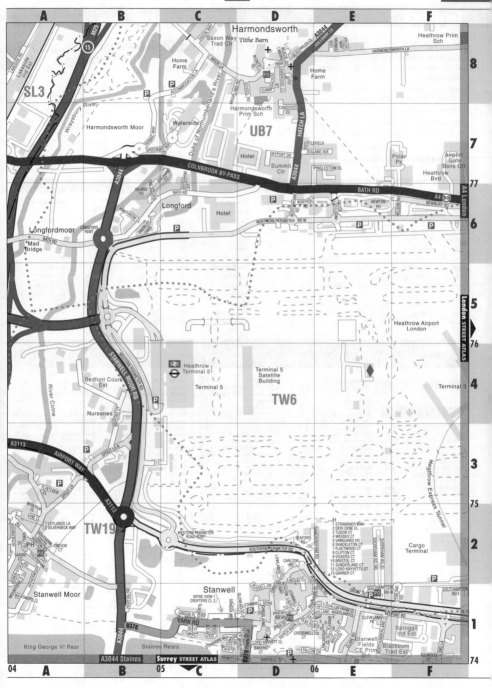

Index

Place name May be abbreviated on the map

Church Rd 6 Beckenham BR2..........**53** C6

Location number Present when a number indicates the place's position in a crowded area of mapping

Locality, town or village Shown when more than one place has the same name

Postcode district District for the indexed place

Page and grid square Page number and grid reference for the standard mapping

Cities, towns and villages are listed in CAPITAL LETTERS

Public and commercial buildings are highlighted in magenta Places of interest are highlighted in blue with a star⭐

Abbreviations used in the index

Acad	Academy	Comm	Common	Gd	Ground	L	Leisure	Prom	Promenade
App	Approach	Cott	Cottage	Gdn	Garden	La	Lane	Rd	Road
Arc	Arcade	Cres	Crescent	Gn	Green	Liby	Library	Recn	Recreation
Ave	Avenue	Cswy	Causeway	Gr	Grove	Mdw	Meadow	Ret	Retail
Bglw	Bungalow	Ct	Court	H	Hall	Meml	Memorial	Sh	Shopping
Bldg	Building	Ctr	Centre	Ho	House	Mkt	Market	Sq	Square
Bsns, Bus	Business	Ctry	Country	Hospl	Hospital	Mus	Museum	St	Street
Bvd	Boulevard	Cty	County	HQ	Headquarters	Orch	Orchard	Sta	Station
Cath	Cathedral	Dr	Drive	Hts	Heights	Pal	Palace	Terr	Terrace
Cir	Circus	Dro	Drove	Ind	Industrial	Par	Parade	TH	Town Hall
Cl	Close	Ed	Education	Inst	Institute	Pas	Passage	Univ	University
Cnr	Corner	Emb	Embankment	Int	International	Pk	Park	Wk, Wlk	Walk
Coll	College	Est	Estate	Intc	Interchange	Pl	Place	Wr	Water
Com	Community	Ex	Exhibition	Junc	Junction	Prec	Precinct	Yd	Yard

Index of towns, villages, streets, hospitals, industrial estates, railway stations, schools, shopping centres, universities and places of interest

Abb–Ale

A

Abbey Barn La HP10 ...173 E3
Abbey Barn Rd HP11 ...173 F4
Abbey Cl SL1............204 E6
Abbey Cotts SL7 ....153 B4
Abbey Ct HP5...........154 B6
Abbey Ctr The HP19...101 B2
Abbeydore Gr MK10....35 F1
Abbeyfield Ho HP16....152 A7
Abbey Gate SL6.........204 A7
Abbeyhill Rdbt MK12....33 E4
Abbey Mead SL8........184 F5
Abbey Park La SL1......186 E2
Abbey Rd
  Aylesbury HP19........101 B2
  Bourne End SL8........184 F5
  Milton Keynes, Bradwell
    MK13.................34 A4
  Milton Keynes, Simpson
    MK6..................47 E5
  Syresham NN13.........27 C2
Abbey's Prim Sch MK3...47 A2
Abbey Sq MK43...........8 E5
Abbey Terr MK16.........22 D4
Abbey Way
  High Wycombe HP11...173 A6
  Milton Keynes MK13....34 B6
  Ravenstone MK46........5 E2
Abbey Wlk HP16.........152 B7
Abbot Ridge HP18.......125 D5
Abbotsbury MK4..........45 E2
Abbots Cl MK13..........34 B6
Abbotsfield MK6.........47 B8
Abbots Way
  High Wycombe HP12...172 D3
  Monks Risborough HP27 139 C5
Abbot's Wlk SL4........209 E5
Abbotswood HP27.......150 C4
Abbotts Cl HP20.........101 E1
Abbotts Cl UB8..........208 D8
Abbotts Rd HP20........101 E1
Abbotts Vale HP5.......144 C3

Abbotts Way
  Slough SL1.............204 D5
  Wingrave HP22.........89 A4
Abbot Wlk HP18.........125 D5
Abell Gdns SL6..........195 B1
Abercromby Ave HP12..172 E8
Abercromby Ct 4
  HP12.................172 D8
Aberdeen Ave SL1......205 A6
Aberdeen Cl MK3........46 F2
Abingdon Cl
  Thame OX9.............125 F1
  Uxbridge UB10.........201 F4
Abingdon Wlk SL6......195 E3
Abington Cl SL0.........196 B1
Abington Rd
  Chesham HP5..........144 C2
  Steeple Claydon MK18...63 D2
Acacia 3 RG9............191 D2
Acacia Ave
  West Drayton UB7......208 F6
  Wraysbury TW19.......211 B3
Acacia Cl HP5...........144 A1
Acacia Gr HP4...........135 B3
Acacia Ho SL9..........177 E2
Acacia Mews UB7.......213 D8
Acacia Wlk HP23........118 E3
Accommodation La
  UB7..................213 C8
Ackerman Cl MK18......52 F8
Ackroyd Pl MK5..........46 B5
Acorn Cl
  High Wycombe HP13...173 D7
  Slough SL3............207 B1
Acorn Gdns HP12.......172 E4
Acorn Ho MK9...........34 D2
Acorn Wlk MK9..........34 E2
Acrefield SL9...........188 D8
Acre Pas SL4...........210 D6
Acres End HP7..........165 E8
Acres The HP13.........161 E1
Acres Way HP19.........101 C4
Acre The SL7...........183 F2
Adam Cl
  High Wycombe HP13...173 D8
  Slough SL3............205 A5
Adam Ct RG9............191 E2
Adams Cl MK18..........41 C1

Adams Ct MK6...........47 C8
Adams Pk (Wycombe
  Wanderers FC & London
  Wasps) HP12..........172 A7
Adams Way HP23........119 B6
Addenbrookes MK16....22 F3
ADDINGTON.............65 A6
Addington Cl SL4.......210 A4
Addington Cotts HP22..131 B5
Addington Rd MK18......41 D1
Addington Terr MK18....41 D1
Addison Cl SL0.........207 E6
Addison Ct SL6.........196 B1
Addison Rd
  Chesham HP5..........144 C2
  Steeple Claydon MK18...63 D2
Adelaide Ct SL1.........205 A4
Adelaide Rd
  High Wycombe HP13...162 D1
  Windsor SL4...........210 F6
Adelaide Sq SL4........210 D5
Adelphi Gdns SL1......205 E4
Adelphi St MK9..........34 F4
Adkins Ct HP19.........100 F3
Adkins Cl HP14.........158 E5
Admiralty Cl UB7.......208 F4
Admiral Way HP4.......134 F6
Adrians Wlk SL2........205 F5
ADSTOCK...............53 F1
Adstock Mews 2 SL9 .177 D2
Adwell Sq RG9..........191 D2
Agars Pl SL3............211 A8
Agora Ctr MK12.........33 D7
Agora Ctr (Sh Ctr) 7
  MK2...................58 C8
Aidan Ct HP21.........116 A4
Ailward Rd HP19........101 A2
Ainsdale Cl MK3.........46 D1
Aintree Cl
  Milton Keynes MK3 ....57 C6
  Poyle SL3.............212 E6
Airport Gate Bsns Ctr
  UB7..................213 F7
Airport Way TW19.......213 A3
Aiston Pl HP20.........101 F2
Ajax Ave SL1...........205 B6
AKELEY................41 E8
Akeley Wood Jun Sch
  MK19.................31 A1

Akeley Wood Lower Sch
  MK18.................29 B4
Akeley Wood Sch MK18 .41 C7
Akeman St HP23........119 A3
Akerlea Cl MK6..........47 C6
Akerman Cl MK12.......33 B5
Akister Cl MK18.........52 E8
Alabama Circ HP11.....173 B4
Alabama Dr HP11.......173 B3
Alan Way SL3...........206 E7
Alaska St HP11.........173 B4
Alastair Mews HP9.....175 F2
Albany Ct MK14..........34 D7
Albany Gate HP5.......144 B1
Albany Pk SL3..........212 D7
Albany Pl HP19.........101 A2
Albany Rd
  Old Windsor SL4......211 A2
  Windsor SL4...........210 D5
Albany Terr HP23.......119 B6
Albert Pl SL4...........205 A1
Albert Rd
  Chesham HP5..........154 C8
  Henley-on-Thames RG9..191 E1
  West Drayton UB7......208 E5
  Windsor SL4...........210 E3
Albert St
  Aylesbury HP20........116 A8
  4 High Wycombe HP13..173 C7
  Maidenhead SL6.......202 F7
  Milton Keynes MK2 ....58 C8
  Slough SL1............205 F3
  Tring HP23.............119 A3
  Windsor SL4...........210 B6
Albion SL3.............207 B1
Albion Cl SL2..........206 A5
Albion Cotts SL6.......195 C7
Albion Cres HP8.......177 B7
Albion Ho HP12.........172 C5
Albion Pl
  Milton Keynes MK9 ....35 A3
  2 Windsor SL4........210 A5
Albion Rd
  Chalfont St Giles HP8..177 B8
  High Wycombe HP12...172 C5
  Pitstone LU7..........105 D5
Albion St HP20.........115 E8
ALBURY................136 B7

Albury Ct 3 MK8 ....33 F1
Albury View OX9........136 A6
Aldborough Spur SL1 ..205 E7
Aldbourne Rd SL1......204 B8
ALDBURY...............120 D5
Aldbury Gdns HP23 ....119 B6
Aldbury Prim Sch
  HP23.................120 C6
Aldbury Rd WD3........167 F2
Aldebury Rd SL6.......195 F2
Aldene Rd MK13........11 B3
Aldenham MK6..........47 D5
Alden View SL4.........209 D6
Alderbourne La SL3....199 E8
Alderbourne Manor
  SL9..................189 A1
Alderbury Rd SL3.......207 A3
Alderbury Road W SL3 .206 F4
Alder Cl SL1............204 F5
Aldergill MK13..........34 C5
Alderley Ct HP4........135 C3
Aldermead MK12.......33 E5
Alderney Pl MK5........45 F4
Alder Rd
  Aylesbury HP22.......116 C4
  Iver Heath SL0........200 D3
  New Denham UB9......201 C6
Alderson Cl 1 HP19 ...101 A2
Alders The UB9.........201 C6
ALDERTON...............9 A2
Alderton Dr HP4........121 B8
Aldin Avenue N SL1....206 A4
Aldin Avenue S SL1....206 A4
Aldrich Dr MK15.........35 C1
Aldridge Ct HP11......173 F4
Aldridge Rd SL2........198 A1
Aldwick Dr SL6.........202 D6
Aldwycks Cl MK5........45 F6
Alexander Ct
  High Wycombe HP12...172 E4
  Slough SL1............205 C4
Alexander Fst Sch SL4 .209 C4
Alexander Ho 1 MK2 ...58 C8
Alexander Rd HP20....101 D1
Alexander St HP5......144 C1
Alexandra Ct
  Leighton Buzzard LU7 ..80 F8
  4 Milton Keynes MK13..34 A4
  Windsor SL4...........210 D5

Alexandra Dr MK16. . . . . 22 C2
Alexandra Pk HP11. . . . . 173 A6
Alexandra Rd
High Wycombe HP13 . . . . 173 E5
Maidenhead SL6 . . . . 202 B8
Slough SL1. . . . . 205 D3
Uxbridge UB8. . . . . 201 D3
Windsor SL4 . . . . 210 D5
Alford Pl MK5. . . . . 47 B1
Alford Rd HP12 . . . . 172 C3
Alfred Ct SL8. . . . . 185 B3
Alfred Davis Ct SL7 . . . . . 183 D3
Alfriston Specl Sch
HP9. . . . . 175 C6
Alham Rd HP21 . . . . 115 C6
Alice Cl HP15 . . . . 163 C7
Alice La SL1 . . . . 197 B1
Aliadale Pl MK12. . . . . 33 D4
Allanson Rd SL7 . . . . 183 F3
Allenby Rd SL6 . . . . 202 B7
Allen Cl MK2. . . . . 58 C5
Allen Dr HP14 . . . . 161 C8
Allerds Rd SL2. . . . . 198 A4
Allerford Ct MK4. . . . . 46 C4
Alleyns La SL6 . . . . 195 D8
Allhusen Gdns SL1. . . . . . 199 E8
Allington Circ MK4. . . . . . . 45 E1
Allington Ct SL2 . . . . 205 F6
Allison Ct SL4 . . . . 35 C1
Alkins Ct SL4 . . . . 210 D5
Allonby Way HP21 . . . . . . 116 B7
All Saints' Ave SL6. . . . . . 202 D7
All Saints CE Controlled
Jun Sch SL6. . . . . 202 C6
All Saints View MK5. . . . . . 46 B8
All Souls Cotts SL3. . . . . . 206 E8
Allyn Cl HP13. . . . . 173 C8
Alma Ct
Burnham SL1. . . . . 197 C2
Eton Wick SL4 . . . . 204 F2
Alma Rd
Berkhamsted HP4 . . . . . . 134 E6
Chesham HP5 . . . . 144 D3
Eton Wick SL4 . . . . 204 F2
Windsor SL4 . . . . 210 C6
Almahouses The MK4. . . . . 21 E1
Almond Cl
Newport Pagnell MK16. . . . 22 B3
Windsor SL4 . . . . 210 B5
Almond Rd SL1. . . . . 197 C2
Almond Tree Dr HP22 . . . 116 C4
Almond Way HP27 . . . . . . 139 A2
Almond Wlk HP15. . . . . . . 163 B3
Almons Way SL2. . . . . 206 B8
Almshouses
Eton SL4. . . . . 210 D7
Old Windsor SL4 . . . . . . 210 F1
Worminghall HP18. . . . . . 123 E5
Almshouses The MK46 . . . . 5 E2
Alnwick Dr HP23. . . . . 103 F7
Alpha Ct HP7 . . . . 165 B7
Alpha Street N SL1 . . . . . 206 A4
Alpha Street S SL1 . . . . . 205 F3
Alpine Cl SL6. . . . . 203 A6
Alpine Croft MK6 . . . . 46 A3
Alsford Wharf HP4 . . . . . . 135 C5
Alscot La HP27. . . . . 139 A5
Alston Dr MK13. . . . . 33 F3
Alstonefield ■ MK4. . . . . . 46 B3
Alston Gdns 202 A8
Althorpe Cres MK13. . . . . . 34 B6
Altona Rd HP10. . . . . 174 D4
Altona Way SL1. . . . . 205 B7
Alton Bsns Pk HP19. . . . . 101 B1
Alton Gate MK4 . . . . 45 F3
Altwood Bailey SL6 . . . . . 202 B5
Altwood CE Sch SL6 . . . . 202 B5
Altwood Cl
Maidenhead SL6 . . . . 202 B5
Slough SL1. . . . . 204 E8
Altwood Dr SL6. . . . . 202 B5
Altwood Rd SL6. . . . . 202 B5
Alverton MK14 . . . . 34 F8
Alvista Ave SL6 . . . . 204 B7
Alvric Way ■ MK12 . . . . . . 33 A6
Alwin Cl HP21 . . . . 115 C4
Alwins Field LU7. . . . . 80 D8
Alwyn Inf Sch SL6. . . . . . . 202 C8
Alwyn Rd SL6. . . . . 202 B8
Alyngton HP4 . . . . 134 E7
Alyson Ct ■ SL1 . . . . 195 F1
Amanda Ct SL3 . . . . 206 D3
Amber Cotts HP7 . . . . 164 F3
Ambergate MK16 . . . . 36 B4
Amberley Ct SL6 . . . . 196 C3
Amberley Pl ■ SL4 . . . . . 210 D6
Amberley Rd SL2 . . . . 204 E8
Amberley Way HP21 . . . . 115 D3
Amberley Wlk MK4. . . . . . . 45 E1
Amblers Way MK18 . . . . . . 53 A1
Ambleside
Amersham HP6 . . . . 154 C2
Slough SL1. . . . . 211 B5
Ambleside Wlk UB8. . . . . . 201 D4
Ambridge Gr MK6. . . . . 35 C1
Ambrose Ct MK15. . . . . 35 C2
Amelias La MK9. . . . . 35 A3
Amerden Cl SL6 . . . . 203 D7

Amerden La SL6 . . . . 203 D7
Amersham La ■ SL1 . . . . 205 A4
American Com Sch
UB10. . . . . 201 F4
AMERSHAM. 165 C8
AMERSHAM COMMON . . 165 E8
Amersham Ct HP7. . . . . . . 165 A7
Amersham Hill HP13 . . . . 173 B7
Amersham Hill Dr
HP13 . . . . 173 C8
Amersham Hill Gdns
HP13 . . . . 173 C8
Amersham Hospl HP7. . . . 165 A6
Amersham Mus ★ HP7. . . 165 B7
AMERSHAM OLD
TOWN. 165 A7
AMERSHAM ON THE
HILL. 154 D2
Amersham Rd
Beaconsfield HP7. . . . . . . 176 A6
Chalfont Common HP8,
SL9 . . . . 177 D6
Chalfont St Giles HP8 . . . 166 B2
Chalfont St Peter SL9 . . . 177 E2
Chesham HP6 . . . . 154 B5
Chorleywood WD3. . . . . . 167 C8
Denham Green SL9 . . . . . 189 A4
Gerrards Cross SL9 . . . . 188 F7
Hazlemere HP15 . . . . . . 162 E2
High Wycombe HP13 . . . . 173 C8
Little Chalfont HP6. . . . . . 166 E8
Amersham Sch HP7. . . . . . 165 C7
Amersham Sta/U Sta
HP6. . . . . 154 C1
Amersham Way HP6. . . . . 154 C1
Amersham & Wycombe Coll
Amersham HP7 . . . . 165 F8
Chesham HP5 . . . . 144 D3
Flackwell Heath HP10 . . . 173 E2
Amesbury Rd SL1. . . . . . . 204 F4
Ames Cl MK6 . . . . 46 F8
Amherst Ct MK15. . . . . 35 C7
Amicia Gdns SL2. . . . . 198 F4
Amos La HP5 . . . . 154 B7
Amy La HP5 . . . . 154 B7
Ancastle Gn RG9. . . . . . . 191 D1
Ancell Rd MK11. . . . . 32 E5
Anchor Ct SL6. . . . . 195 F7
Anchor La ■ HP20. . . . . . 115 E8
Ancona Gdns MK5 . . . . 45 F3
Andermans SL4. . . . . 209 D6
Andersen Gate MK4. . . . . . 57 A7
Anderson Cl HP14. . . . . . . 158 F4
Anding Cl MK46 . . . . 6 E4
Andover Cl UB8. . . . . 201 B3
Andrewes Croft MK14 . . . . 34 F8
Andrew Hill La SL2. . . . . . 187 C3
Andrews Cl LU7. . . . . 69 E3
Andrews Reach SL8. . . . . 185 A2
Andrews Way
Aylesbury HP19 . . . . 115 A7
Marlow Bottom SL7. . . . . 183 C8
Anershall HP22. . . . . 89 B3
Angel Cl MK15 . . . . 35 B7
Angelica Ct UB7 . . . . 208 F7
Angelica MK7 . . . . 48 A5
Angels Cl MK4 . . . . 65 F4
Anglefield Rd HP4 . . . . . . 135 B4
Anglesey Ct
Milton Keynes MK8 . . . . . . 46 A8
Stokenchurch HP14 . . . . . 158 E5
Angling Spring Wood
Talking Trail ★ HP16. . . . 151 F7
Angood Cl HP27. . . . . 139 A3
Angora Cl MK5 . . . . 46 A3
Angstrom Cl MK5 . . . . 46 B5
Angus Dr MK3 . . . . 46 F2
Angus Rd HP19 . . . . 101 A3
Anne Cl SL6 . . . . 195 E2
Annes Gr MK14 . . . . 21 D1
Annesley Rd MK16 . . . . . . 22 B3
Anns Cl
Aylesbury HP21 . . . . 116 A4
Tring HP23 . . . . 118 E3
Anscroft Rd SL2 . . . . 198 A2
Anslow Gdns SL0 . . . . . . 200 D3
Anslow Pl SL1. . . . . 204 C8
Anson Cl
Aylesbury HP21 . . . . 115 C4
Bovingdon HP3 . . . . 145 F4
Anson Rd MK12. . . . . 33 C6
Anstey Brook HP22. . . . . . 117 A3
Anstey Cl HP18 . . . . 99 B6
Anstey Ct HP18 . . . . 99 B7
Anthony Cl HP13. . . . . 161 F1
Anthony Ct MK11. . . . . 32 D5
Anthony Way SL1 . . . . . . 204 D6
Anton Way HP21 . . . . 115 D3
Anvil Cl HP3 . . . . 146 B3
Anvil Ct SL3 . . . . 207 A2
Anxey Way HP17. . . . . 126 F6
Aplin Rd HP21 . . . . 116 C6
Apperknees MK17 . . . . 49 D8
Appleby Heath MK2 . . . . . . 58 D6
Apple Cotts HP3 . . . . 146 A4
Applecroft
Berkhamsted HP4 . . . . . . 134 E6
Maidenhead SL6 . . . . 202 C3

Applecroft continued
Newton Longville MK17. . . . 57 D4
Appledell HP7 . . . . 166 C7
Appleton St HP7. . . . . 166 B7
Appletree Ave UB7, UB8. 208 F7
Apple Tree Cl
Leighton Buzzard LU7. . . . 80 D6
Loudwater HP13 . . . . 174 A4
Appletree La ■ SL3. . . . . 206 C8
Appletree Wlk HP5. . . . . . 154 D5
Applewick La HP12. . . . . . 172 C3
Applewood Cl UB10. . . . . 201 E8
Appleyard Pl ■ MK6. . . . . . 34 E1
Approach Rd SL4 . . . . 203 E2
Approach The MK8. . . . . . . 33 E2
Apsley Cl SL6 . . . . 195 E7
Apsley Ho SL1 . . . . 206 A4
Aqua Vale Swimming &
Fitness Ctr HP20. . . . . . 115 F8
Aran Hts HP9. . . . . 177 B6
Arborfield Cl SL1 . . . . 205 E3
Arbour Vale Specialist Sch
Sports Coll SL2 . . . . 198 B2
Arbour View HP7 . . . . 166 B8
Arbrook Ch MK3 . . . . 46 E3
Arbrook Ave MK13 . . . . 34 D3
Arcade The HP9 . . . . 175 E3
Archdale ■ HP11. . . . . . . 173 A6
Archer Cl HP6 . . . . 202 B8
Archer Ct HP6 . . . . 154 C2
Archer Dr HP20. . . . . 102 A2
Archers Way HP14 . . . . . . 171 B5
Archers Wells MK3. . . . . . . 47 B2
Archer Terr UB7 . . . . 208 E6
Archford Croft MK4 . . . . . . 46 C3
Archive Cl HP22. . . . . 117 D5
Arch Way
High Wycombe HP13 . . . . 173 A7
Speen HP27. . . . . 150 B4
Archways ■ HP20 . . . . . . 115 D8
Arden Cl HP3 . . . . 146 A4
Ardenham La HP19. . . . . . 101 D1
Ardenham St HP19. . . . . . 101 C1
Ardere Park MK12 . . . . 33 B7
Ardley Mews ■ MK10. . . . 36 B3
Ardrossan Cl SL2 . . . . . . 198 C1
Ardwell La MK12 . . . . 33 B5
Ardys Ct MK5. . . . . 46 B8
Argonaut Pk SL3. . . . . 212 F6
Argyle Ave HP19 . . . . 101 B2
Argyll Ave MK15 . . . . 205 A6
Argyll Ho MK3 . . . . 46 D5
Aries Ho HP10 . . . . 185 A8
Aris Way MK18. . . . . 52 D6
Arizona St HP11 . . . . 173 B4
Arklay Cl UB8. . . . . 201 F1
Arkley Ct SL6 . . . . 203 C1
Arklow Ct WD3 . . . . 167 D5
Arkwright Rd SL3 . . . . 212 E5
Arlington Cl SL6 . . . . 202 A8
Arlington St MK4 . . . . 46 E3
Arlott Cres MK6. . . . . 46 F8
Armourer Dr MK14 . . . . 34 F6
Armstrong Cl MK8 . . . . 45 E7
Armstrong Ho SL2 . . . . . . 206 C7
Arncliffe Dr MK13. . . . . 34 B5
Arncott Rd OX25 . . . . 95 D7
Arncott Way HP19 . . . . . . 100 F1
Arncott Wood Rd OX25 . . 94 E6
Arne La MK7. . . . . 48 D5
Arnison Ave HP13. . . . . . . 162 D1
Arnold Cl HP22. . . . . 116 C2
Arnold Cott MK19. . . . . 32 C7
Arnold Ct HP21 . . . . 115 F6
Arnolds Cl MK18 . . . . 53 A1
Arnold's Cotts HP5. . . . . . 143 B4
Arnos Gr MK10 . . . . 35 F1
Arnott's Yd HP18 . . . . 125 D6
Arranmore Ho HP11. . . . . 174 B4
Arrewig La HP5 . . . . 142 E8
Arrow Pl MK2. . . . . 58 D4
Arthur Ct SL6. . . . . 195 E5
Arthur Jacob Nature
Reserve ★ SL3 . . . . 212 C4
Arthur Rd
Slough SL1. . . . . 205 D4
Windsor SL4 . . . . 210 C6
Artichoke Dell WD3. . . . . . 167 E4
Arundel Cl SL6. . . . . 202 A8
Arundel Ct SL3 . . . . 206 D2
Arundel Gn HP20 . . . . . . 101 F2
Arundel Gr MK3. . . . . 57 E7
Arundel Ho
■ High Wycombe
HP13 . . . . 173 F7
Uxbridge UB8. . . . . 201 C1
Arundel Rd
High Wycombe HP12 . . . . 172 B6
Uxbridge UB8. . . . . 201 B1
Ascot Dr LU7 . . . . 80 D6
Ascot Ho MK9 . . . . 34 C2
Ascot Pl SL5 . . . . 57 D7
Ascot Rd SL6 . . . . 203 A1
ASCOTT. 80 A2
Ascott Ct MK10. . . . . 101 E1
Ascott House ★ LU7. . . . . 80 A2
Ascott Rd HP20 . . . . 101 E1
Ascough Cl HP19. . . . . . . 101 D3

Ashbourne End HP21. . . . 115 D4
Ashbourne Gr SL6 . . . . . . 202 C3
Ashbourne Ho ■ SL1 . . . 205 E4
Ashbrook Sch MK8. . . . . . . 33 E1
Ashburnham Cl ■ MK3. . . 46 D1
Ashburnham Cres LU7 . . . 80 E6
Ashby MK6 . . . . 47 A8
Ashby Rd HP4 . . . . 134 D7
Ashby Villas LU7 . . . . 92 A1
Ash Cl
Aylesbury HP20 . . . . 102 A2
Slough SL3. . . . . 207 B3
Walter's Ash HP14 . . . . . 161 B8
Ashcroft Ct SL1. . . . . 197 B3
Ashcroft Dr UB9 . . . . 189 F4
Ashcroft Rd SL6. . . . . 202 C8
Ashcroft Terr HP23 . . . . . 119 A5
Ashdown Cl SL6. . . . . 196 B3
Ashdown Ct MK14. . . . . 35 A8
Ashdown HP13 . . . . 173 D6
Ashdown Rd HP13 . . . . . . 174 A8
Ashdown Way HP6. . . . . . 154 D2
Ashen Cross SL3. . . . . 207 B8
Ashendon Wlk SL2. . . . . . 198 D8
ASHENDON 97 F1
Ashendon Rd HP18. . . . . . 96 C6
ASHERIDGE 143 C6
Asheridge Rd HP5 . . . . . . 144 A2
Asheridge Rd Ind Est
HP5. . . . . 144 A2
Ashfield MK14 . . . . 34 D8
Ashfield Cl HP15. . . . . 163 B2
Ashfield Cotts UB9 . . . . . . 190 A1
Ashfield Gr MK2 . . . . 58 C7
Ashfield Rd HP5 . . . . 144 D2
Ashfield Rise HP18 . . . . . 109 D5
Ashfield Way HP15. . . . . . 163 B3
Ashfold Sch HP18. . . . . . . 110 F8
Ashford Cl HP21 . . . . 116 A5
Ashford Cres MK46. . . . . . . 45 D6
Ashford La SL4 . . . . 204 B4
Ashford Rd SL0 . . . . 200 C4
Ash Gn UB9. . . . . 201 B6
Ash Gr
Amersham HP6 . . . . 154 A3
Aylesbury HP21 . . . . 116 A7
Stoke Poges SL2 . . . . . . 198 F5
West Drayton UB7. . . . . . 208 E5
Ashgrove MK18 . . . . 63 D2
Ashgrove Gdns HP22. . . . . 86 E7
Ash Hill Prim Sch
MK13. . . . . 174 A7
Ash La SL4 . . . . 209 B6
Ashland Rdbt MK1 . . . . 47 C5
Ashlea MK6. . . . . 6 A3
Ashlea Rd SL9 . . . . 177 E1
Ashleigh Cl HP7 . . . . 165 E8
Ashley Cl HP10. . . . . 185 F7
Ashley Cl LU7. . . . . 105 A8
Ashley Ct
■ Aylesbury HP19 . . . . . 115 A8
Maidenhead SL6 . . . . 203 B7
Tylers Green HP10. . . . . . 163 B1
West Drayton UB7. . . . . . 208 E5
Ashley Dr HP10 . . . . 163 C1
ASHLEY GREEN. 144 F7
Ashley Green Rd HP5 . . . 144 E6
Ashley Pk SL6 . . . . 196 B2
Ashley Rd UB8 . . . . 201 B3
Ashley Row HP20 . . . . . . 102 A1
Ashleys WD3 . . . . 167 F2
Ashlyns Ct HP4 . . . . 135 B3
Ashlyns Rd HP4. . . . . 135 B3
Ashlyns Sch HP4. . . . . . . 135 C2
Ashmead Comb Sch
HP21. . . . . 115 C5
Ash Mead Dr UB9 . . . . . . 190 A2
Ashmead La UB9. . . . . . . 190 A2
Ashmead Pl HP7. . . . . 166 C8
Ashmount Cres ■ SL1. . . 205 A4
Ashotts La HP5 . . . . 143 B7
Ashover MK10 . . . . 36 C4
Ash Rd
High Wycombe HP12 . . . . 172 C4
Princes Risborough
HP27. . . . . 139 B3
Tring HP23 . . . . 118 F4
Ashridge Cl HP3 . . . . 146 A3
Ashridge Bsns Sch
HP4. . . . . 121 C5
Ashridge Cl
■ Bovingdon HP3. . . . . . 146 A3
Milton Keynes MK3 . . . . . . 57 D7
Ashridge Coll Gdns ★
HP4. . . . . 120 E6
Ashridge Cotts HP4 . . . . . 121 C5
Ashridge Est Visitor Ctr ★
HP4. . . . . 120 C6
Ashridge La HP5. . . . . 155 D7
Ashridge Rise HP4 . . . . . . 134 F5
ASHTON. 9 E8
Ashton Pl SL6 . . . . 202 D8
Ashton Rd NN12 . . . . 9 D8
Ash Tree Ho HP12 . . . . . . 172 C4
Ashtree Wlk HP15. . . . . . . 163 B2
Ash Vale WD3 . . . . 178 D5
Ashwells HP10. . . . . 174 B8

Ashwells Manor Dr
HP10. . . . . 174 C8
Ashwell St ■ LU7. . . . . 80 F8
Ashwells Way HP8 . . . . . . 177 D8
Ashwood MK13 . . . . 34 A7
Ashwood Dr HP5. . . . . 144 B1
ASKETT 139 D6
Askett La HP27 . . . . 139 D7
Aspen Cl
Aylesbury HP20 . . . . 102 A2
Maidenhead SL6 . . . . 195 A3
Slough SL2. . . . . 205 B8
West Drayton UB7 . . . . . . 208 F5
Aspens Pl HP1 . . . . 146 F8
Aspery Pl SL1. . . . . 205 F5
Asplands Cl MK17. . . . . . . 49 B4
Aspley Ct
Aylesbury HP19 . . . . 101 C1
Woburn Sands MK17 . . . . 49 C3
ASPLEY GUISE 49 E2
Aspley Guise Lower Sch
MK17 . . . . 49 F4
Aspley Guise Sta MK17. . . 49 D6
ASPLEY HEATH 49 A2
Aspley Hill MK17 . . . . 49 D3
Aspley La MK17. . . . . 49 E2
Aspreys MK46. . . . . 6 E4
Assheton Rd HP9 . . . . 175 D4
Astlethorpe MK8. . . . . 33 F2
Astley Rd OX9 . . . . 126 B1
ASTON. 192 B5
ASTON ABBOTTS. 88 D5
Aston Abbotts Rd
Cublington LU7 . . . . 78 C1
Weedon HP22 . . . . 87 E1
Aston Cl
Aylesbury HP19 . . . . 101 A3
Milton Keynes MK5 . . . . . . 46 B5
ASTON CLINTON 117 D6
Aston Clinton Ragpits
Wildlife Reserve ★
HP22. . . . . 117 F2
Aston Clinton Rd HP22. . . 116 E6
Aston Clinton Sch
HP22. . . . . 117 D5
Aston Ferry La RG9 . . . . . 192 D5
Aston Hill OX49. . . . . 157 E7
Aston La RG9 . . . . 192 C3
Aston Mead SL4 . . . . 209 E6
Aston Rd HP17. . . . . 127 B5
Aston Rowant National
Nature Reserve ★
HP14. . . . . 157 E6
ASTON SANDFORD 127 D4
Astonville St SL2 . . . . 198 C8
Astor Cl SL6 . . . . 203 B6
Astronomy Way ■
HP19 . . . . 115 A8
ASTROPE 104 A3
Astrope La HP23 . . . . 104 B3
ASTWOOD 16 A3
Astwood Rd MK43. . . . . 25 C7
Atherstone Ct MK8. . . . . . . 33 C2
Atherton Cl TW19. . . . . . . 213 D1
Atherton Ct SL4. . . . . 210 D7
Athlone Cl SL6. . . . . 195 E1
Athlone Sq SL4. . . . . 210 C5
Atkins Cl MK13. . . . . 34 B3
Atlas Ho HP5 . . . . 144 B1
Atterbrook MK13. . . . . 34 A4
ATTERBURY. 36 A4
Attingham Hill
■ Milton Keynes MK8 . . . 33 F1
Milton Keynes MK8 . . . . . . 33 A1
Atwell Cl MK8 . . . . 45 E7
Auckland Cl SL6 . . . . 203 B8
Auckland Pk MK1. . . . . 47 D4
Auckland Rd HP13 . . . . . . 173 E6
Auden Cl MK16 . . . . 22 A5
Audley Dr SL6 . . . . 202 B6
Audley Mead MK13. . . . . . . 34 B3
August End SL3 . . . . 206 E7
Augustine Cl SL3 . . . . 212 E4
Augustine Mews HP16 . . 152 B7
Augustus Rd MK11 . . . . . . 32 E4
Augustus Smith Ho ■
HP4 . . . . 135 C4
Austen Ave MK46 . . . . 7 A4
Austen Pl HP19 . . . . 100 F2
Austenway SL9 . . . . 188 E8
AUSTENWOOD 188 C8
Austenwood Cl
Chalfont St Peter SL9 . . . 177 C1
High Wycombe HP11 . . . . 173 A4
Austenwood La
Chalfont St Peter SL9 . . . 177 D1
Gerrards Cross SL9 . . . . 188 D8
Austins Mead HP3 . . . . . . 146 B3
Austin Ways SL3. . . . . 211 F8
Austin Waye UB8 . . . . 201 C4
Australia Ave SL6. . . . . . . 202 F8
Australia Rd ■ SL1. . . . . . 206 B4
Austwick La MK4. . . . . 46 B2
Autumn Cl
Aylesbury HP19 . . . . 101 A3
Slough SL1. . . . . 204 F5

Autumn Wlk SL6 . . . . .202 A5
Avalon Rd SL8 . . . . .185 B5
Avant Bsns Ctr MK1 . . .47 C2
Avebury SL1 . . . . .205 A6
Avebury Bvd MK9 . . . . . . .34 E2
Avebury Rdbt MK9 . . . . . .34 D1
Aveling Rd HP13 . . . . . . .173 C6
Avenue CI UB7 . . . . .208 D3
Avenue Dr
  Iver Heath SL3. . . . . . . .199 F1
  Slough SL3. . . . . .206 F8
Avenue Ho HP5 . . . . .154 B8
Avenue Rd
  Buckingham MK18 . . . . .41 E3
  Maidenhead SL6 . . . . . .203 B5
  Winslow MK18. . . . . .65 F4
Avenue The
  Amersham HP7 . . . . . . .154 C1
  Bourne End SL8 . . . . . .184 F4
  Chinnor OX39. . . . . . . .147 D6
  Datchet SL3. . . . . .211 B6
  Dunstable LU6 . . . . .93 E7
  Farnham Common SL2. .198 B8
  Maidenhead SL6 . . . . . .196 C3
  Old Windsor SL4 . . . . .211 B2
  Princes Risborough
    HP27. . . . . .139 C4
  Uxbridge UB8. . . . . . . .201 D1
  Whitfield NN13 . . . . .26 D4
  Worminghall HP18. . . . .123 E5
  Wraysbury TW19. . . . . .211 D4
Averil Ct SL6 . . . . .204 C7
Avery Ave HP13 . . . . .161 D2
Avery Ct MK16 . . . . .22 C2
Avington MK8 . . . . .33 E1
Avocet Way HP19 . . . . . .101 E3
Avonbury Ct NN13 . . . . . .38 A5
Avon CI
  Newport Pagnell MK16 . . .22 D3
  Slough SL1. . . . . .204 E6
Avondale SL6. . . . . .195 C1
Avon Gr MK3 . . . . .57 E8
Avonmoore SL6. . . . . . . .203 B8
Avon PI HP21 . . . . .115 D4
Axis Pk SL3. . . . . .207 B1
AYLESBURY 115 D7
Aylesbury Bsns Ctr
  HP19 . . . . .101 B1
Aylesbury Coll HP21 . . . .115 C7
Aylesbury Cres SL1 . . . .205 D6
Aylesbury End HP9 . . . . .175 E1
Aylesbury Gram Sch
  HP21 . . . . .115 F7
Aylesbury High Sch
  HP21 . . . . .115 F7
Aylesbury Ind Ctr HP19 .101 C1
Aylesbury Rd
  Aston Clinton HP22 . . . .117 B5
  Bierton HP22. . . . . .102 B3
  Chearsley HP18. . . . . . .112 B2
  Cuddington HP18. . . . . .113 A3
  Great Missenden HP16 .141 F2
  Haddenham HP17, OX9 .126 C6
  Monks Risborough HP27 139 D6
  Thame OX9 . . . . .125 F2
  Tring HP23. . . . . .118 E2
  Wendover HP22. . . . . . .131 B6
  Wing LU7 . . . . .79 E1
Aylesbury St
  Milton Keynes, Bletchley
    MK2. . . . . .58 E8
  Milton Keynes, Wolverton
    MK12. . . . . .33 D6
Aylesbury Sta HP20 . . . .115 D7
Aylesbury Street W
  MK12 . . . . .33 C6
Aylesbury Vale Acad
  HP19 . . . . .101 C2
Aylesbury Vale Parkway Sta
  HP18. . . . . .100 D3
Aylesbury Waterside
  Theatre HP20. . . . . . . .115 E8
Aylesford Gr MK10 . . . . . .36 A1
Ayless CI HP18. . . . . .98 B7
Ayleswater HP19. . . . . . .101 E4
Aylesworth Ave HP22 . . .198 B2
Aylward Gdns HP5 . . . . .144 A1
Aynho Ct MK8 . . . . .45 F8
Ayscombe CI LU6. . . . . . .93 F8
Ayres CI HP21 . . . . .115 B6
Ayrshire Ct HP19 . . . . . .101 A3
Ayrton CI MK8 . . . . .45 D6
Ayr Way MK3 . . . . .46 E2
Aysgarth Pk SL6 . . . . . . .203 B1
Azalea CI SL3 . . . . .163 A3
Azalea Way SL3. . . . . . . .206 E7

B

Babington CI MK10. . . . . .36 A3
Babington Rd HP22 . . . . .131 D6
Babylon Gr [10] MK4. . . . .45 F1
Baccara Gr MK2 . . . . .58 C7
Bachelors Acre SL4 . . . .210 D6
Back Dr MK16 . . . . .12 F3

Back La
  Chalfont St Giles HP8 . . . .177 A7
  Great Missenden HP16 . .152 B7
  Tingewick MK18. . . . . . . .51 A6
Back St
  Gawcott MK18. . . . . .51 F4
  Thornborough MK18 . . . .54 A8
  Wendover HP22. . . . . . .131 B4
Backs The HP5 . . . . .154 C8
Bacombe La HP22. . . . . .131 A3
Bacombe Hill Nature
  Reserve* HP22. . . . . . .131 B3
Bacon Hill MK46. . . . . .6 E3
Baconsmead UB9 . . . . . .190 A2
Bader Gdns SL1. . . . . . . .205 A4
Badgebury Rise SL7. . . .183 C7
Badgemore Ct MK8 . . . . .33 C2
Badgemore La RG9 . . . .191 D3
Badgemore Prim Sch
  RG9. . . . . .191 D2
Badger CI SL6 . . . . .202 D4
Badgers Gate LU6. . . . . . .93 E8
Badgers Mdw HP22 . . . .131 C5
Badgers Oak MK7. . . . . . .48 B7
Badgers Rise HP17. . . . .114 C5
Badgers Way
  Buckingham MK18. . . . . .52 E7
  Marlow Bottom SL7. . . .183 D7
Badgers Wlk WD3. . . . . .167 F5
Badgers Wood SL2. . . . .198 C7
Badger Way HP15. . . . . .163 B5
Bad Godesberg Way
  SL6. . . . . .202 F7
Badmington Ct [3] HP7 .165 B7
Badminton Ho HP7 . . . . .165 B7
Badminton Rd SL6 . . . . .202 B6
Badminton View MK8 . . .34 A1
Badrick Rd HP19. . . . . . .100 F2
Bagley CI UB7 . . . . .208 E4
Bagshot Ct MK2. . . . . .58 C7
Bailey CI
  High Wycombe HP13 . . .173 C7
  Maidenhead SL6 . . . . . .202 F7
  Windsor SL4 . . . . .210 A5
Bailey Ho [8] SL8 . . . . . .185 A4
Bailey's Ct [12] HP20. . .115 D8
Baily Ct MK5. . . . . .46 A5
Baines Ho HP11. . . . . . . .173 F4
Baird CI SL1 . . . . .205 B4
Baisley Ho MK2 . . . . .58 D8
Bakers CI
  Stoke Goldington MK16. . .12 B5
  Turvey MK43 . . . . .8 E5
Bakers Ct
  Stanwell TW19. . . . . . . .213 D1
  Waddesdon HP18 . . . . . .99 A6
Bakers La NN12. . . . . .9 A8
Baker's Orch HP10 . . . . .185 E5
Baker's Piece Ho OX39 .147 A4
Baker's Rd UB8 . . . . .201 D5
Baker St
  High Wycombe HP11 . . .172 F7
  Waddesdon HP18 . . . . . .99 A6
Bakers Wlk HP22 . . . . . .116 F2
Bakers Wood UB9. . . . . .189 D3
Bakery CI MK43. . . . . .25 B1
Bakery Ho [10] HP20. . . .115 D8
Bala CI MK2 . . . . .58 D5
Bala Lake Cres MK10. . . .36 B4
Bala Way MK2 . . . . .58 C5
Balcary Gdns HP4. . . . . .134 F3
Balcary Gr MK4 . . . . .56 F8
Baldways CI HP22 . . . . . .89 C3
Baldwin Cres MK16 . . . . .22 C3
Baldwin PI SL6 . . . . .202 C7
Baldwin Rd
  Beaconsfield HP9. . . . . .176 B1
  Burnham SL1 . . . . .197 C2
Baldwin's Shore SL4 . . .210 D8
Balfe Mews MK7 . . . . .48 C4
Balfour Mews [3] HP3 . .146 A4
Balfour PI SL7 . . . . .183 D4
Balfour Way HP10. . . . . .101 E2
Balham's La RG9. . . . . . .179 F8
Ballard CI HP21. . . . . . . .116 B5
Ballard Gn SL4. . . . . .209 E7
Ballards Row HP22 . . . . .177 D6
Ballinger Common. 142 E3
Ballinger Ct HP4. . . . . . .135 B3
Ballinger Grange HP16 .142 E2
Ballinger Rd HP16 . . . . .142 E1
Ballinger Row HP16. . . .142 D3
Ball Moor MK18. . . . . .52 D6
Balmer Bridge MK18. . . .52 E5
Balmer Cut MK18 . . . . . . .52 E6
Balmerino CI MK10. . . . . .36 B2
Balmoral SL6. . . . . .195 B1
Balmoral CI SL1. . . . . . . .204 E7
Balmoral Ct
  High Wycombe HP13 . . .173 B7
  Newport Pagnell MK16 . .22 B3
Balmoral Gdns SL4. . . . .210 D4
Balsam CI MK7. . . . . .48 B6
Bamfords La MK43 . . . . . . .8 E6
Bamfords Yd MK43. . . . . . .8 E6
Bampton CI MK4 . . . . .46 E2
Banburies CI MK3. . . . . . .47 A3

Banbury Ave SL1. . . . . . .204 F8
BANCROFT. 33 F5
Bancroft Rdbt MK13. . . . .34 A5
Bandon CI UB10 . . . . . . .201 F3
Bangor Cotts SL0 . . . . . .200 D1
Bangors CI SL0 . . . . .200 D1
Bangors Road N SL0 . . .200 D3
Bangors Road S SL0 . . .207 E8
Bank Apartments SL7 . .183 D3
Bank Court Mews MK12 . .33 D7
Bankfield Rdbt MK9. . . . .35 A2
Bank Gn HP5 . . . . .143 C8
Bank Mill HP4 . . . . .135 E4
Bank Mill La HP4 . . . . . .135 E3
Bank Rd HP10 . . . . .174 D8
Bankside HP22. . . . . .131 B5
Banks Rd HP17 . . . . .127 A6
Banks Spur SL1. . . . . . . .205 B4
Bank St HP13 . . . . .174 A4
Banktop PI MK4. . . . . .46 C3
Bannard Rd SL6 . . . . . . .202 A5
Banner Ct [1] HP12 . . . .172 D8
Bannister CI SL3. . . . . . .206 E4
Bantock CI MK7. . . . . .48 C5
Bantry Rd SL1 . . . . .204 F4
Barbers Mews MK14 . . . .34 F6
Barbers Wlk HP23. . . . . .118 F3
Barbers Wood CI HP12 .172 B4
Barbers Wood Rd
  HP12 . . . . .172 B4
Barbicus Ct SL6. . . . . . . .203 B8
Barbury Ct MK14. . . . . . . .35 A8
Barchester CI UB8 . . . . .201 C1
Barchester Rd SL3 . . . . .206 F4
Barclay Ct OX27 . . . . .72 E6
Barclay Ct [3] HP12 . . . .172 E7
Bardney CI SL6 . . . . .202 D3
Bardolphs CI HP27 . . . . .139 C4
Bardon Gn HP20 . . . . . . .101 E2
Bardsey Ct MK10. . . . . . . .36 A2
Barford MK11 . . . . .32 F4
Bargeman Rd SL6. . . . . .202 E5
Barham Lodge MK18 . . . .52 C8
Baring Cres HP9 . . . . . . .175 C3
Baring Rd
  Beaconsfield HP9. . . . . .175 D3
  High Wycombe HP13 . . .173 F7
Barkers Croft MK12 . . . . .33 C4
Barkestone CI MK4. . . . . .46 C1
Barkham CI LU7 . . . . . . .104 F7
Barkus Way HP14 . . . . . .158 F5
Bar La HP27 . . . . .138 E7
Barle Cres UB8 . . . . .208 C8
Barley CI
  Hazelmere HP15 . . . . . .163 A3
  Lewknor OX49 . . . . .157 A8
  Weston Turville HP22. . .116 F2
Barley Cres HP21 . . . . . .115 D3
Barleycroft MK4 . . . . .46 E4
Barley Fields HP10 . . . . .185 E8
Barley Hill Prim Sch
  OX9. . . . . .126 A1
Barleyhurst Park Prim Sch
  MK3 . . . . .46 F1
Barley Mead SL6. . . . . . .202 A5
Barley Way [3] SL7 . . . . .183 D1
Barlow Rd HP22 . . . . . . .131 C5
Barnacre CI UB8 . . . . . . .208 D7
Barnard Cres HP21 . . . . .115 F5
Barnards Hill SL7 . . . . . .183 C2
Barn CI
  Farnham Common SL2. .198 B8
  Maidenhead SL6 . . . . . .195 F2
  Taplow SL6. . . . . .203 E7
Barncroft MK43 . . . . .8 E6
Barncroft Rd HP4 . . . . . .134 F3
Barn Ct HP12 . . . . .172 C7
Barn Dr SL6 . . . . .202 A4
Barnes Ave HP5. . . . . . . .144 C1
Barnes PI MK6. . . . . .46 E8
Barnes Wallis Ct HP12. .172 E5
Barnes Way SL0 . . . . . . .207 F6
Barnet CI MK5 . . . . .45 D5
Barnett Way HP22. . . . . .102 B4
Barn Farm SL7 . . . . .183 D3
Barnfield
  Iver SL0. . . . . .207 F1
  Slough SL3. . . . . .204 D5
Barnfield CI SL6 . . . . . . .195 F5
Barnfield Dr MK6 . . . . . . .47 C5
Barnhill CI SL7. . . . . .183 D4
Barnhill Gdns SL7 . . . . .183 D4
Barnhill Rd SL7 . . . . .183 D4
Barn La RG9 . . . . .191 C4
Barn Rd HP27 . . . . .138 E6
Barnsbury Ave HP20 . . .116 B8
Barnsbury Gdns MK16. . .22 C3
Barns CI OX33 . . . . .122 B1
Barnsdale Dr MK4. . . . . . .45 F2
Barnsfield PI UB8. . . . . .201 C5
Barnstable Ct MK4 . . . . . .46 D3
Barns The HP23. . . . . . . .118 F1
Baroma Way RG9 . . . . . .191 E2
Barons CI MK2 . . . . .58 C8
Barons Ct [2] SL7 . . . . . .183 E2
Baronsmead RG9 . . . . . .191 D2
Baronsmead Rd HP12 . .172 E4
Barrack Hill HP18 . . . . . .112 C5
Barrack La SL4 . . . . .210 D6

Barracks Hill HP7. . . . . .164 F2
Barracks Rd HP11. . . . . .173 A6
Barrards Way HP9 . . . . .176 C4
Barrett PI
  High Wycombe HP11. . . .173 C6
  Milton Keynes MK5 . . . . .45 F6
BARRETTS END 42 F7
Barrie CI HP19. . . . . .100 F2
Barrington Ct NN13. . . . .38 A5
Barrington Mews [4]
  MK6 . . . . .34 E1
Barrington Park Gdns
  HP8 . . . . .166 D1
Barrowcroft HP11 . . . . . .173 F4
Barrow Lodge SL2 . . . . .198 C1
Barr Piece MK12 . . . . . . .33 C6
Barr's Rd SL6. . . . . .204 B7
Barry Ave
  Eton SL4. . . . . .210 C7
  Milton Keynes MK14 . . . .34 C7
Barry CI HP12. . . . . .172 C4
Barry View SL1 . . . . .209 C5
Bartelotts Rd SL2 . . . . . .197 E1
Bartholomew CI MK7. . . .48 A5
Bartholomew Tipping Way
  HP14 . . . . .158 F5
Bartlett PI MK18 . . . . .41 E1
Bartletts SL9 . . . . .177 E3
Barton Dr HP9 . . . . .175 E4
BARTON HARTSHORN. . . .50 D2
Barton Rd
  Milton Keynes MK2 . . . . .58 C6
  Slough SL3. . . . . .206 F4
Barton Way HP13 . . . . . .162 E1
Barton Way HP22 . . . . . .116 C1
Bascote MK6 . . . . .47 D5
Base CI [8] HP20 . . . . . .101 F2
Basford Way SL4. . . . . . .209 D4
Basildon Ct
  [1] Leighton Buzzard LU7. .80 F7
  Milton Keynes MK8 . . . . .45 F8
Basing Rd MK9 . . . . .167 F1
Baskerfield Gr MK6 . . . . .47 C8
Basset Rd HP14 . . . . . . .171 C4
Bassetsbury La HP11. . .173 D5
Bassett Ct MK16 . . . . .22 C4
Bassett Rd
  Leighton Buzzard LU7 . . .80 F7
  Uxbridge UB8. . . . . . . .201 C5
Bassett Way SL2 . . . . . . .197 E1
Bass Mead SL6 . . . . .195 F5
Batchelor CI HP20 . . . . .101 F2
Batchelors Way
  Amersham HP7 . . . . . . .165 D8
  Chesham HP5. . . . . . . .144 B2
Bateman Croft MK5. . . . . .45 F6
Bateman Dr HP21 . . . . . .115 E5
Bates CI
  Granborough MK18 . . . . .75 F8
  Milton Keynes MK15 . . . .35 D7
Bates Ct HP20 . . . . .101 F2
Bates Gdns MK17. . . . . . .68 B6
Bates La HP22 . . . . .116 F2
Bath Ct SL6. . . . . .202 C6
Bath La MK18. . . . . .52 C8
Bath Lane Terr MK18. . . .52 C8
Bath Rd
  Harmondsworth UB7. . . .213 C6
  Maidenhead SL6 . . . . . .202 C6
  Poyle SL3. . . . . .212 E6
  Slough SL1, SL6. . . . . .204 D6
  Slough SL2. . . . . .198 B4
  Taplow SL6. . . . . .203 E7
Bath Road Cotts SL3 . . .212 E6
Bathurst CI SL0 . . . . .207 F4
Bathurst Wlk SL0 . . . . . .207 F4
Battersby Mews HP21. . .115 C7
Batt Furlong HP21 . . . . . .115 E3
Batting CI HP14 . . . . .159 F8
Battings Wood Gdns
  HP14 . . . . .161 C8
Battle CI MK46. . . . . .13 F8
Battlemead CI SL6 . . . . .196 C3
Battoney Vare SL6 . . . . .203 C4
Baulk The
  Cheddington LU7 . . . . .104 F7
  Ivinghoe LU7 . . . . .105 F5
Bawtree Rd UB8 . . . . . . .201 D6
Baxter CI
  Milton Keynes MK8 . . . . .45 E7
  Slough SL1. . . . . .205 E3
Baybrook SL6. . . . . .195 F6
Bay Ct HP4 . . . . .135 B4
Bayhurst Wood Ctry Pk*
  UB9. . . . . .190 F6
Bay La MK46. . . . . .5 D2
Bayley Cres SL1 . . . . . . .204 A8
Bayley Gdns HP14. . . . . .161 E6
Bayley Hatch HP16 . . . . .152 D8
Baylis Bsns Ctr SL1 . . . .205 D6
Baylis Court Sch SL1. . .205 D8
Baylis Par SL1. . . . . .205 E7
Baylis Rd SL1. . . . . .205 E6
Bayman Manor HP5 . . . .144 E2
Bayne Hill HP9 . . . . .176 D3
Bayne Hill CI HP9 . . . . . .176 D3
Baynham Mead MK7 . . . .48 B8
Bayntor Rd HP21. . . . . . .115 E4

Baysfarm Ct UB7. . . . . . .213 C6
Bay Tree CI
  Loudwater HP11 . . . . . .174 B2
  Newton Longville MK17. .57 D4
Bay Tree Ct SL1. . . . . . . .197 C2
BEACHAMPTON. 44 B6
Beachampton Bsns Pk
  MK19 . . . . .44 C4
Beacham Rd HP12 . . . . .172 C3
Beachborough Sch
  NN13. . . . . .39 A4
Beacon Ave LU6 . . . . .93 E7
Beacon CI
  Beaconsfield HP9. . . . . .175 A1
  Chalfont St Peter SL9 . .177 E3
  Stone HP17 . . . . .114 C5
  Uxbridge UB8. . . . . . . .201 D7
Beacon Ct
  Colnbrook SL3 . . . . . . .212 C7
  Milton Keynes MK4 . . . . .46 D2
Beacon Hill HP10 . . . . . .174 D7
Beacon La SL7. . . . . .171 E1
Beacon Rd HP4. . . . . . . .106 E2
BEACON'S BOTTOM 159 D3
Beacon Sch The HP6. . .154 B4
BEACONSFIELD. 175 D1
Beaconsfield Ave HP22 .117 C4
Beaconsfield PI MK16. . .22 C4
Beaconsfield Rd
  Aston Clinton HP22 . . . .117 C4
  Aylesbury HP21 . . . . . .115 E8
  Farnham Common SL2. .198 C5
  Tring HP23. . . . . .118 C3
Beaconsfield Sch The
  HP9. . . . . .175 E1
Beaconsfield Sta HP9 . .175 E3
Beacon Sports Ctr &
  Theatre The HP9. . . . . .175 A1
Beacon View
  Dunstable LU6. . . . . . . .92 B4
  Lewknor OX49 . . . . .157 B8
Beacon Way HP23. . . . . .119 C5
Beadlemead MK6. . . . . . .47 C6
Beales La MK7 . . . . .48 A5
Bealings End HP9. . . . . .175 D5
Beamish Way MK18 . . . . .66 B5
Beamond End La HP7,
  HP15 . . . . .163 F7
BEANHILL 47 B4
Beanfare MK6 . . . . .47 B4
Bearbrook CI HP21. . . . .115 C7
Bearbrook Comb Sch
  HP19 . . . . .115 C8
Bearswood End HP9 . . .175 E4
Beatrice CI OX27. . . . . . . .72 E6
Beauchamp CI MK14 . . . .34 E6
Beauchamp Ct SL1. . . . .205 B4
Beaudesert Mews UB7 .208 E4
Beaufort CI
  Aylesbury HP21 . . . . . .116 D7
  Marlow SL7 . . . . .183 E2
Beaufort Dr MK15. . . . . . .35 C7
Beaufort Gdns SL7 . . . . .183 E2
Beaufort PI SL6. . . . . . . .203 D4
Beaulieu CI SL3. . . . . . . .211 B5
Beaumaris CI SL1 . . . . . .205 E8
Beaumaris Gr MK5 . . . . . .46 A6
Beaumont CI SL6 . . . . . .202 A3
Beaumont Cotts [1]
  SL4. . . . . .210 C6
Beaumont Ct SL3 . . . . . .206 D7
Beaumont Gr HP15. . . . .162 F3
Beaumont Rd
  Slough SL2. . . . . .205 D8
  Windsor SL4 . . . . .210 C5
Beaumont Rise SL7 . . . .183 E2
Beaumont Way HP15. . .162 F4
Beaverbrook Ct MK3. . . .46 F1
Beaver CI MK18. . . . . .52 E7
Becketts Sq MK4 . . . . . . .45 A6
Beckett Chase [5] SL3 . .206 F1
Beckings Way HP10. . . .185 C7
Beckinsale Gr MK8. . . . . .45 E7
Beckinson Rise MK10. . . .35 E1
Beckwell Rd SL1 . . . . . . .205 C4
Bec La MK15. . . . . .35 B7
Bedder Rd HP22 . . . . . . .172 C3
Beddoes Croft MK5 . . . . .45 E4
Bede Ct HP4 . . . . .121 C8
Bedford Court Est
  TW19. . . . . .213 B4
Bedford Rd TW19 . . . . . .213 F1
Bedford Ave
  Little Chalfont HP6. . . . .166 D3
  Slough SL1. . . . . .205 A7
Bedford CI
  Chenies WD3 . . . . .156 B1
  Maidenhead SL6 . . . . . .202 A3
Bedford Ct HP6. . . . . . . .166 D8
Bedford Dr SL2 . . . . .198 B6

Bedford Rd
Aspley Guise MK17 . . . . 49 F5
Cold Brayfield MK46 . . . . 8 B5
Cranfield MK43 . . . . . . 25 C2
Sherington MK16 . . . . . 14 A1
Bedford Road E NN7 . . 1 D5
Bedford Road W NN7 . . 1 A6
Bedford St
Berkhamsted HP4 . . . . 135 D4
Milton Keynes, Bletchley
MK2 . . . . 58 C8
Milton Keynes, Wolverton
MK12 . . . . 33 D6
Woburn MK17 . . . . . . 60 F7
Bedgebury Pl MK7 . . . 48 A8
BEDGROVE 116 C5
Bedgrove HP21 . . . . . 116 C6
Bedgrove Inf Sch HP21 116 C5
Bedgrove Jun Sch
HP21 . . . . 116 C5
BEDLAM 14 C1
Bedlam La MK16 . . . . 14 C1
Bedlam Wlk MK16 . . . 14 C1
Bedwins La SL6 . . . . 195 B6
Bedwyn Wlk HP21 . . . 115 D4
Beech 2 RG9 . . . . . . 191 D2
Beechams The MK17 . . 67 D6
Beech Ave
Lane End HP14 . . . . . 171 C5
Olney MK46 . . . . 6 E3
Beech Cl
Bierton HP22 . . . . 102 B3
Buckingham MK18 . . . . 41 D2
Flackwell Heath HP10 . 174 E2
High Wycombe HP11 . . 173 F4
Maidenhead SL6 . . . . 202 B8
Stokenchurch HP14 . . . 158 F3
Beechcroft HP4 . . . . . 135 C3
Beechcroft Rd
Chesham HP5 . . . . . . 144 B1
Milton Keynes MK3 . . . 57 E6
Beech Ct
Berkhamsted HP4 . . . . 135 D4
 3 Marlow SL7 . . . . . 183 E2
Beech Dr HP4 . . . . . . 135 C3
Beechen Wood HP18 . . 178 D5
Beeches Dr SL2 . . . . . 198 B7
Beeches Gr HP10 . . . . 163 A4
Beeches Pk HP9 . . . . 175 D2
Beeches Rd SL2 . . . . . 198 B7
Beeches The
Amersham HP6 . . . . . 154 A3
Chorleywood WD3 . . . 167 F4
Deanshanger MK19 . . . 31 E3
Milton Keynes MK1 . . . 47 E1
Tring HP23 . . . . 119 C4
Uxbridge UB8 . . . . . . 201 C1
Wendover HP22 . . . . . 131 C5
Beeches Way SL1 . . . 199 F5
Beech Fern MK7 . . . . . 48 A5
Beechfield Cl SL6 . . . . 202 C4
Beechfield Way HP15 . 163 B3
Beechfield Wlk HP15 . 163 A3
Beech Gn HP21 . . . . . 115 D6
Beech Gr
Amersham HP6 . . . . . 165 D8
Leighton Buzzard LU7 . 80 E7
Tring HP23 . . . . 119 C4
Beech Hill Ct HP4 . . . 135 D5
Beech House Dr NN12 . 18 F4
Beechingstoke 4 SL7 . 183 F3
Beech La
Prestwood HP16 . . . . 151 B4
Seer Green HP9 . . . . . 176 E3
Beechlands HP15 . . . . 162 E2
Beech Leys MK18 . . . . 63 E3
Beech Pk
Little Chalfont HP6 . . . 155 B5
Naphill HP14 . . . . 150 A1
Wigginton HP23 . . . . . 133 F5
Beech Rd
Aylesbury HP21 . . . . . 115 D6
Chinnor OX39 . . . . . . 147 C6
High Wycombe HP11 . . 173 F4
Newport Pagnell MK16 . 22 B3
Princes Risborough
HP27 . . . . 139 C3
Slough SL3 . . . . 206 E4
Beech St HP11 . . . . . 173 C4
Beechtree Ave SL7 . . . 183 D5
Beech Tree Cl MK19 . . 20 D2
Beech Tree Ct HP22 . . 87 A6
Beech Tree Rd HP15 . . 163 C7
Beech Trees Rd HP12 . 172 C5
Beechview Jun Sch
HP13 . . . . 173 E5
Beech Waye SL9 . . . . 189 A4
Beech Wlk HP23 . . . . 119 B4
Beechwood Ave
Chorleywood WD3 . . . 167 B5
Little Chalfont HP6 . . . 155 C1
 1 Uxbridge UB8 . . . . 208 F7
Beechwood Cl HP6 . . . 166 C8
Beechwood Cotts WD3 167 B3
Beechwood Dr
Aston Clinton HP22 . . . 118 A3
Dunstable LU6 . . . . . . 93 F7
Beechwood Dr
Aldbury HP23 . . . . . . 120 D5

Beechwood Dr *continued*
Maidenhead SL6 . . . . 202 A6
Marlow SL7 . . . . 194 B8
Beechwood Gdns SL1 . 205 E4
Beechwood Ho HP22 . 117 F5
Beechwood La HP22 . . 131 D5
Beechwood Pk
Chorleywood WD3 . . . 167 F5
Felden HP3 . . . . 146 F7
Beechwood Pl 18 HP13 173 B7
Beechwood Rd
Beaconsfield HP9 . . . . 175 C2
High Wycombe HP12 . . 161 B2
Slough SL2 . . . . 205 D8
Beechwood Sch SL2 . . 198 B2
Beechwood Way HP22 . 117 F5
BEECROFT 93 F8
Beecroft Lower Sch LU6 93 F8
Beecroft Way LU6 . . . . 93 F8
Beehive Rd UB10 . . . . 201 F5
Beel Cl HP7 . . . . 166 C8
Beethoven Cl MK7 . . . 48 C4
Beeward Cl MK42 . . . . 33 A5
Beggars La HP23 . . . . 119 F4
Bekonscot Ct MK13 . . 21 F1
Bekonscot Model Village &
Railway★ HP9 . . . . . 175 C4
Belfast Ave SL1 . . . . . 205 D7
Belgrave Mews UB8 . . 201 D1
Belgrave Par SL1 . . . . 205 E6
Belgrave Pl 6 SL1 . . . 206 A4
Belgrave Rd
Aylesbury HP19 . . . . . 101 A3
Slough SL1 . . . . 205 E6
Bellamy Mews 5 MK4 . 45 E3
Bellamy Rd HP13 . . . . 173 C8
Bell Ave UB7 . . . . . . 208 F3
Bell Cl
Beaconsfield HP9 . . . . 175 F2
Cublington LU7 . . . . . 78 B1
Drayton Parslow MK17 . 68 B6
Princes Risborough
HP27 . . . . 139 B3
Slough SL2 . . . . 206 B8
Thame OX9 . . . . 125 E1
Bellclose Rd UB7 . . . . 208 E4
Bell Cres HP27 . . . . . 138 E4
Bell Ct SL6 . . . . 193 F3
Belle Vue HP17 . . . . . 114 C5
Bellfield Rd HP13 . . . . 173 A8
Bellfounder Ho MK13 . 34 B4
Bell Gn HP3 . . . . 146 B4
BELLINGDON 143 E7
Bellingdon Rd HP5 . . . 144 B1
Bellini Cl MK7 . . . . . . 48 D5
Bellis Gr MK6 . . . . . . 47 C8
Bell La
Aylesbury HP19 . . . . . 101 C3
Slough SL2 . . . . 206 C6
Berkhamsted HP4 . . . . 134 C5
Eton Wick SL4 . . . . . . 204 F2
Henley-on-Thames RG9 191 E4
Little Chalfont HP6 . . . 155 C1
Princes Risborough
HP27 . . . . 139 B3
Syresham NN13 . . . . . 27 B8
Thame OX9 . . . . 125 F1
Bell Lane Comb Sch
HP6 . . . . 155 B1
Bell Leys HP22 . . . . . 89 B3
Bellows Mill La LU6 . . 93 A4
Bellridge Pl SL4 . . . . . 175 B6
Bellsfield Ct SL4 . . . . 204 F2
Bells Hill SL2 . . . . . . 199 A4
Bells Hill Gn SL2 . . . . 199 A5
Bells La SL3 . . . . 212 B4
Bells Mdw MK15 . . . . 35 B7
Bell St
Henley-on-Thames RG9 191 E4
Maidenhead SL6 . . . . 202 F6
Princes Risborough
HP27 . . . . 139 B3
Bell Street Mews RG9 . 191 E2
Bellswood La SL0 . . . . 207 B8
Bell View SL4 . . . . . . 209 F5
Bell View Cl SL4 . . . . 209 F5
Bellway MK17 . . . . . . 49 A6
Bellwether HP4 . . . . . 33 A4
Bell Wlk
Wingrave HP22 . . . . . 89 B3
Winslow MK18 . . . . . . 65 F3
Bellwood Rise HP11 . . 173 B4
Belmers Rd HP23 . . . . 119 D1
Belmont SL2 . . . . 205 A8
Belmont Cl HP18 . . . . 201 D6
Belmont Cotts SL3 . . . 212 C7
Belmont Cres SL6 . . . 202 D8
Belmont Dr SL6 . . . . . 33 C2
Belmont Park Ave SL6 . 202 D8
Belmont Park Rd SL6 . 202 D8
Belmont Rd
Chesham HP5 . . . . . . 144 B3
Maidenhead SL6 . . . . 202 D8
Uxbridge UB8 . . . . . . 201 D5
Belmont Vale SL6 . . . 202 D8
Belsham HP5 . . . . . . 144 B3
BELSIZE 156 F6
Belsize Ave MK6 . . . . 35 B1

Belsize Cotts WD3 . . . 156 E6
Belton M HP4 . . . . . . 135 A5
Belvedere Cl HP6 . . . . 154 F7
Belvedere La MK17 . . . 58 F8
Belvedere Mans SL1 . . 205 D4
Belvedere Rdbt MK9 . . 34 F4
Belvoir Ave MK4 . . . . 46 C1
Bembridge Gr 11 SL1 . 205 F4
Benacre Croft MK4 . . . 57 A8
Benbow St MK5 . . . . . 46 A7
Benbow Way SL6 . . . . 208 C8
Bench Manor Cres SL9 177 C1
Bencombe Rd SL7 . . . 183 E5
Benen-Stock Rd TW19 . 213 A3
Benham Cl HP5 . . . . . 144 B1
Benhams La RG9 . . . . 180 D2
Benison Ct 13 SL1 . . . 205 F3
Benjamin Ho 10 HP13 . 173 B7
Benjamin La SL3 . . . . 199 B1
Benjamin Rd HP13 . . . 173 B8
Benjamins Footpath
HP13 . . . . 173 B8
Ben More SL9 . . . . . . 188 F6
Benmore Rise 2 MK4 . 45 E2
Bennet Cl MK11 . . . . . 32 D4
Bennet's Yd UB8 . . . . 201 D5
Bennett Cl
Padbury MK18 . . . . . . 53 B1
Slough SL1 . . . . 205 A5
Bennett's Hill MK18 . . 76 C8
Bennetts La HP22 . . . . 102 E8
Benning Ave LU6 . . . . 93 F8
Benning Cl SL4 . . . . . 209 D4
Benningfield Gdns HP4 135 E6
Bens Cl MK9 . . . . 19 F5
Bensheim Way HP6 . . 154 C4
Benson Cl
Slough SL2 . . . . 206 A5
Uxbridge UB8 . . . . . . 208 E8
Bentall Cl MK15 . . . . . 35 C7
Bentinck Cl SL9 . . . . . 188 D6
Bentinck Cl SL7 . . . . . 208 D5
Bentinck Rd UB7 . . . . 208 D5
Bentley Cl MK10 . . . . 35 E3
Bentley La MK10 . . . . 35 E3
Bergamot Gdns MK7 . . 48 B5
Bergman Cl 1 MK4 . . . 45 D2
Berkeley Ave HP5 . . . 143 F1
Berkeley Cl
Chesham HP5 . . . . . . 144 A1
Stoke Goldington MK16 . 12 B6
Berkeley Mews
Marlow SL7 . . . . 183 F2
Slough SL1 . . . . 204 E7
Berkeley Rd
Loudwater HP10 . . . . . 174 C2
Thame OX9 . . . . 126 A1
Berkeley Rise 1 HP19 . 101 B2
Berkhampstead Rd
HP5 . . . . 144 C2
BERKHAMSTED 135 C6
Berkhamsted Castle★
HP4 . . . . 135 D5
Berkhamsted Collegiate
Sch HP4 . . . . 135 B4
Berkhamsted Sch 8
HP4 . . . . 135 C4
Berkhamsted Sta HP4 . 135 C5
Berkley Cl
Maidenhead SL6 . . . . 202 A8
Pitstone LU7 . . . . 105 D3
Berkley Ct HP4 . . . . . 135 C4
Berkley Rd HP5 . . . . . 175 D6
Berks Hill WD3 . . . . . 167 C4
Berkshire Ave SL1 . . . 205 B7
Berkshire Gn MK5 . . . 45 F3
Berkshire Lodge 1
SL6 . . . . 202 F6
Berling Rd MK8 . . . . . 33 F2
Bernard Cl HP18 . . . . 112 F2
Bernardines Way MK18 52 A7
Bernards Cl HP16 . . . . 152 A7
Bernard's Cl HP18 . . . 112 B2
Bernards Way HP10 . . 174 A2
Bernay Gdns MK15 . . . 35 B7
Berndene Rise HP27 . . 139 B4
Berners Cl SL1 . . . . . 204 E6
Bernewode Cl HP18 . . 125 C7
Bernstein Cl MK7 . . . . 48 C4

Bernwood Mdws Wildlife
Reserve★ HP18 . . . . 108 F2
Berrell's Ct 2 MK46 . . 6 F3
Berries Rd SL6 . . . . . 196 A8
Berrington Gr 4 MK4 . . 45 E2
BERRYFIELD 100 D5
Berryfield LU7 . . . . . . 104 F7
Berry Field SL2 . . . . . 206 C7
Berry Field Pk HP6 . . 154 B2
Berryfield Rd
Aylesbury HP19 . . . . . 101 B3
Princes Risborough
HP27 . . . . 139 C4
Berry Hill SL6 . . . . . . 203 D8
Berry Hill Ct SL6 . . . . 203 D8
Berry La
Aspley Guise MK17 . . . 49 F5
Chorleywood WD3 . . . 167 D3
Berrystead MK7 . . . . . 48 B3
Berry Way MK17 . . . . 57 D4
Bertram Cl MK13 . . . . 34 B8
Berwald Ct MK7 . . . . 48 D4
Berwick Ave SL1 . . . . 205 B6
Berwick Cl
Beaconsfield HP9 . . . . 176 B1
Marlow SL7 . . . . 183 D3
Berwick Dr MK3 . . . . . 46 F2
Berwick La SL7 . . . . . 183 D3
Berwick Rd SL7 . . . . . 183 C3
Bessemer Cl 2 SL3 . . 206 F1
Bessemer Cres HP19 . 100 E1
Bessemer Ct MK14 . . . 22 A1
Bestobell Rd SL1 . . . . 205 C7
Betjaman Ct UB7 . . . . 208 D5
Betjeman Gdns WD3 . . 167 D5
Bettina Gr MK2 . . . . . 58 C7
Bettles Cl 3 UB8 . . . . 201 C3
Bettles Cl SL3 . . . . . . 201 C3
Betty's Cl MK17 . . . . . 57 D3
Betty's La HP23 . . . . . 119 A4
Bevan Cl MK18 . . . . . 65 F4
Bevan Hill HP5 . . . . . 144 B2
Bevelwood Gdns HP12 172 D7
Beverley Cl SL7 . . . . . 183 B2
Beverley Cl SL1 . . . . . 205 B6
Beverley Gdns SL6 . . . 195 B1
Beverley Pl MK6 . . . . . 35 B2
Bewcastle Row MK4 . . 45 E1
Bewdley Dr LU7 . . . . . 80 C7
Bewdley Gr MK10 . . . . 36 A4
Bexley St SL4 . . . . . . 210 C6
Bicester Rd
Aylesbury HP19 . . . . . 101 B2
Long Crendon HP18 . . 125 C6
Ludgershall HP18 . . . . 96 C8
Marsh Gibbon OX27 . . 71 E3
Oakley HP18 . . . . 109 D5
Twyford MK18 . . . . . . 62 C1
Bickleigh Cres MK4 . . 46 D3
Biddles Cl SL1 . . . . . . 204 E5
BIDDLESDEN 27 D5
Biddlesden Rd NN13 . . 39 A5
Bideford Cl SL1 . . . . . 80 C8
Bideford Ct LU7 . . . . . 80 C8
Bideford Spur SL2 . . . 198 B2
BIERTON 102 A3
Bierton Cr Comb Sch
HP22 . . . . 102 B3
Bierton Rd HP20 . . . . 101 F1
Bigfrith La SL6 . . . . . 195 B6
Biggs La HP17 . . . . . 113 C2
Bigmore La
Beacon's Bottom HP14 170 B8
Stokenchurch HP14 . . . 159 C1
Bignell Croft MK5 . . . . 34 B1
Bigton Chase 2 MK10 . 36 B2
Biko Cl UB8 . . . . 208 C7
Bilbrook La MK4 . . . . 46 C4
Billet La
Berkhamsted HP4 . . . . 135 A6
Iver SL0, SL3 . . . . . . 207 B7
Billings Cl HP14 . . . . . 158 F5
Billingwell Pl MK6 . . . 35 B2
Billwell HP18 . . . . 125 C6
Bilton Rd MK1 . . . . . . 47 D2
Binders Ind Est HP15 . 162 D7
Bingham Cl MK4 . . . . 46 C1
Bingham Rd SL1 . . . . 204 A8
Binghams The SL3 . . . 203 B3
Birch Ave UB7 . . . . . 208 F7
Birch Cl
Amersham HP6 . . . . . 154 E2
Bedford MK43 . . . . . . 25 C3
Iver Heath SL0 . . . . . 200 D3
Birch Cres UB10 . . . . 201 F4
Birch Ct HP21 . . . . . . 115 D5
Birchdale SL9 . . . . . . 188 D3
Birch Dr WD3 . . . . . . 178 D5
Birchen Lee MK4 . . . . 46 C2
Birches Rise HP12 . . . 172 E8
Birches The
Felden HP3 . . . . 146 F8
High Wycombe HP13 . . 173 E8
Birchfield Gr MK2 . . . . 58 C7
Birch Gdns HP7 . . . . . 165 E8
Birch Gr
Slough SL2 . . . . 205 B8
Windsor SL4 . . . . 209 D6
Birchington Rd SL4 . . 210 A5

Birch La HP3 . . . . . . 156 B7
Birchmoor Gn MK17 . . 60 F8
BIRCHMOOR GREEN . . 60 E8
Birch Rd HP4 . . . . . . 134 D7
Birch St HP11 . . . . . . 173 B3
Birch Tree Gr HP5 . . . 145 B1
Birch Way
Chesham HP5 . . . . . . 144 D2
Tylers Green HP10 . . . 163 B1
Birchwood Chase
HP15 . . . . 151 D1
Birchwood Cl HP12 . . 172 B6
Birdcage Wlk HP13 . . 173 B6
Birdlip La MK7 . . . . . . 48 B7
Bird Mount Cotts SL4 . 210 C8
Birdwood Rd SL6 . . . . 202 B7
Birfield Rd HP10 . . . . 174 C2
Birinus Ct HP12 . . . . 172 C5
Birkdale Cl MK3 . . . . . 57 D7
Birkett Way HP3 . . . . 166 D6
Birley Rd SL1 . . . . . . 205 D6
Birtchnell Cl HP4 . . . . 135 A5
BISHAM 194 E7
Bisham Abbey National
Sports Ctr SL7 . . . . 194 D7
Bisham CE Prim Sch
SL7 . . . . 194 D7
Bisham Ct
Bisham SL7 . . . . 194 E6
 10 Slough SL1 . . . . . 205 F4
Bisham Gn SL7 . . . . . 194 E6
Bisham Rd
Bisham SL7 . . . . 194 E8
Marlow SL7 . . . . 183 E8
Bisham Woods Nature
Reserve★ SL6 . . . . . 194 E6
Bishop Cl SL6 . . . . . . 202 D6
Bishop Ctr The SL6 . . 203 F7
Bishop Parker RC Comb
Sch MK2 . . . . 58 C6
Bishops Cl MK18 . . . . 52 C7
Bishops Farm Cl SL4 . 209 B6
Bishops Field HP22 . . 118 A4
Bishophalt Sch UB8 . . 201 F2
Bishops Ho 175 D3
Bishops Mdw HP22 . . 102 A3
Bishops Orch SL2 . . . 198 B2
Bishops Rd SL1 . . . . . 206 A4
BISHOPSTONE 115 A1
Bishopstone
Milton Keynes MK13 . . 34 B5
Stone HP17 . . . . 115 A1
Bishopstone Rd HP17 . 114 C5
Bishops Wlk
Aylesbury HP21 . . . . . 115 F6
Woburn Sands MK17 . . 49 B3
Wooburn Green HP10 . . 185 E5
Bishop Wood Sch 19
HP23 . . . . 119 A3
Bissley Dr SL6 . . . . . . 202 A3
Bittenham Cl HP17 . . 114 D4
Bittern Way 4 HP20 . . 101 E3
Bit The HP23 . . . . . . 119 D1
BIX 179 D1
Bix La SL6 . . . . 194 F1
Black Acre Cl HP7 . . . 165 E8
Blackamoor La SL6 . . 196 A1
Blackberry Ct MK7 . . . 48 B6
Black Boy La SL6 . . . . 193 C3
Blackburn Trad Est
TW19 . . . . 213 F1
Black Butt Cotts SL6 . 196 B7
Blackdown MK11 . . . . 32 F4
Blacketts Wood Dr
WD3 . . . . 167 B5
Blackfield La HP16 . . . 142 E3
Blackheath Cres MK13 34 D3
Blackhill Dr MK12 . . . . 33 A6
Black Horse Ave HP5 . 154 D6
Blackhorse Cl HP6 . . . 154 E4
Black Horse Cl SL4 . . 209 D5
Blackhorse Pl UB8 . . . 154 E1
Black Horse Pl UB8 . . 201 C4
Black Horse Pl UB8 . . 201 C4
Blackmoor Gate MK4 . 46 E2
Blackmore Gate HP22 118 A4
Blackmore Way UB8 . . 201 D6
Black Park Ctry Pk★ SL0,
SL3 . . . . 199 F3
Black Park Ctry Pk Visitor
Ctr★ SL3 . . . . 199 F2
Black Park Nature
Reserve★ SL0 . . . . . 200 A5
Black Park Rd SL3 . . . 199 E4
Blackpond La SL2 . . . 198 B4
Blacksmith La HP16 . . 151 C6
Blacksmith's La SL3 . . 207 A2
Blacksmith's La UB9 . . 189 D2
Blacksmiths Way MK17 49 B5
BLACKTHORN 81 A3
Blackthorn Cl OX25 . . 81 A3
Blackthorn Dell SL3 . . 206 C3
Blackthorne Cres SL3 . 212 E5
Blackthorne Ind Pk
SL3 . . . . 212 E5

Blackthorne La HP16 ... 142 E3
Blackthorne Rd SL3 ... 212 E4
Blackthorn Gr MK17 ... 49 A4
Blackwater Dr HP21 ... 115 C4
Blackwell End NN12 ... 18 C3
Blackwell Hall La HP5 .. 155 C6
Blackwell Pl MK5 ... 46 A4
Blackwell Rd HP14 ... 171 B5
Blackwells Yd NN7 ... 1 B6
Blackwood Cres MK13 ... 33 E6
Blaine Cl HP23 ... 119 A6
Blairmont St MK9 ... 34 F4
Blair Rd SL1 ... 205 E5
Blakedown Rd LU7 ... 80 C6
BLAKELANDS ... 22 B1
Blakeney Ct
Maidenhead SL6 ... 195 F1
Milton Keynes MK4 ... 57 B8
Blakes Ho HP10 ... 174 C2
Blake Way OX9 ... 126 A1
Blanchland Circ MK10 ... 36 A1
Blandford Cl SL3 ... 206 D3
Blandford Ho SL6 ... 202 C8
Blandford Road N SL3 .. 206 D3
Blandford Road S SL3 .. 206 D3
Blanes Cl HP18 ... 125 C6
Blansby Chase MK4 ... 46 C3
Blatherwick Ct MK5 ... 45 F7
Blaydon Cl MK3 ... 57 D6
BLEAK HALL ... 46 F5
Bleak Hall Rdbt MK6 ... 47 A5
Bleasdale MK13 ... 34 C5
BLEDLOW ... 138 B1
Bledlow Cotts HP27 ... 138 C1
Bledlow Rd HP27 ... 148 E8
BLEDLOW RIDGE ... 159 F8
Bledlow Ridge Rd
HP14 ... 148 C8
Bledlow Ridge Sch
HP14 ... 159 F8
Blegberry Gdns HP4 ... 134 E4
Blenheim Ave MK11 ... 32 E4
Blenheim Cl
Cheddington LU7 ... 104 F8
Longwick HP27 ... 138 D6
Slough SL3 ... 206 F5
Blenheim Ct HP13 ... 173 B7
Blenheim Pl
Aylesbury HP21 ... 115 E5
Syresham NN13 ... 27 C7
Blenheim Rd
High Wycombe HP12 ... 172 D4
Maidenhead SL6 ... 202 B8
Slough SL3 ... 206 D2
Bletcham Rdbt MK1 ... 47 E3
Bletcham Way
Milton Keynes MK1 ... 47 C2
Milton Keynes MK1 ... 47 E2
Walton Park MK7 ... 48 B4
BLETCHLEY ... 58 A7
Bletchley Com Hospl
MK3 ... 47 A1
Bletchley L Ctr MK2 ... 58 C8
Bletchley Park National
Codes Ctr★ MK3 ... 58 A8
Bletchley Rd
Milton Keynes MK5 ... 46 B4
Newton Longville MK17 ... 57 D4
Stewkley LU7 ... 68 D3
Bletchley Sta MK3 ... 58 B8
Blinco La SL3 ... 206 E7
Blind La
Bourne End HP10, SL8 ... 185 B5
South Heath HP16 ... 153 B8
Blind Pond Ind Est
MK17 ... 48 D2
Bliss Ave MK43 ... 25 C2
Bliss Ct MK7 ... 48 C4
Blisworth MK6 ... 47 D5
Blondell Cl UB7 ... 213 D8
Bloomfield Cotts HP5 ... 143 E7
Bloomfield Rd SL6 ... 202 A5
Bloomsbury Cl MK17 ... 60 F6
Blossom Way UB10 ... 201 F5
Blucher St HP5 ... 154 B8
Blue Anchor Ave 1
MK10 ... 36 B3
Bluebell Cl MK18 ... 52 C7
Bluebell Croft MK7 ... 48 B6
Blue Lagoon Nature
Reserve★ MK3 ... 58 B7
Blumfield Cres SL1 ... 204 E8
Blumfield Ct SL1 ... 197 D1
Blundells Rd MK13 ... 34 C6
Blunden Dr SL3 ... 207 C2
Blyth Ct MK4 ... 57 A8
Blythebridge MK10 ... 36 C3
Blythe Cl
Aylesbury HP21 ... 115 C5
Iver SL0 ... 207 F7
Newport Pagnell MK16 ... 22 D3
Blythe Hos SL1 ... 204 D5
Blyton Cl HP9 ... 175 D4
Boadicea Cl SL1 ... 204 E5
Boarlands Cl SL1 ... 204 F6
BOARSTALL ... 95 B1
Boarstall Duck Decoy★
HP18 ... 95 A3
Boarstall Tower★ HP18 .. 95 A1
Boathouse Reach RG9 .. 191 E1
Bobmore La SL7 ... 183 F3
BOCKMER END ... 182 C1
Bockmer La SL7 ... 193 B7
Boddington Rd HP22 ... 131 C4
Bodenham Cl MK18 ... 52 F8
Bodiam Cl
Aylesbury HP21 ... 116 B5
Milton Keynes MK5 ... 46 A5
Bodiam Ho 6 HP13 ... 173 F7
Bodle Cl MK15 ... 35 A7
Bodley Ho SL0 ... 200 D3
Bodmin Ave SL2 ... 205 A8
Bodnant Ct MK4 ... 45 F2
Bogart Pl MK4 ... 45 D2
Bois Ave HP6 ... 154 B3
Bois Hill HP5 ... 154 E5
Bois La HP6 ... 154 D4
Bois Moor Rd HP5 ... 154 D5
Bolan Ct MK8 ... 45 E6
BOLBECK PK ... 35 A7
Bold's Ct SL2 ... 199 A5
BOLTER END ... 170 F5
Bolter End La HP14 ... 171 A6
Bolton Ave SL4 ... 210 D4
Bolton Cres SL4 ... 210 C4
Bolton Rd SL4 ... 210 C4
Boltwood Gr MK5 ... 45 E5
Bond Ave MK1 ... 47 D3
Bond Cl
Aylesbury HP21 ... 115 B6
Iver Heath SL0 ... 200 B5
West Drayton UB7 ... 208 F7
Bone Hill MK18 ... 52 C7
Bonham Carter Rd
HP22 ... 131 E7
Bonham Cl HP21 ... 115 B6
Bonham Ct HP22 ... 117 D5
Bonnards Rd MK17 ... 57 D4
Bonnersfield HP18 ... 125 C7
BOOKER ... 172 B4
Booker Ave MK13 ... 34 D4
Booker Hill Comb Sch
HP12 ... 172 B5
Bookerhill Rd HP12 ... 172 C6
Booker La HP12 ... 172 D7
Booker Park Com Sch
HP21 ... 115 E3
Booker Pl HP12 ... 172 B3
Booth Pl LU6 ... 92 E6
Boot La HP17 ... 113 E2
Borderside SL2 ... 206 A7
Borodin Ct MK7 ... 48 D5
Boroma Way RG9 ... 191 E2
Borough Ct NN13 ... 38 A5
Borough Rd NN13 ... 38 A5
Borough Wlk MK9 ... 34 E3
Bosanquet Cl UB8 ... 201 D1
Bossiney Pl MK6 ... 34 F1
Bossington La LU7 ... 80 E7
Boss La
Great Kingshill HP15 ... 162 B8
Hughenden Valley HP14 . 162 B6
Bostock Ct MK18 ... 52 C8
Boston Dr SL8 ... 185 B3
Boston Gr SL1 ... 205 C7
Boswell Ct MK18 ... 41 E2
Boswell La MK19 ... 31 E4
Boswick La HP4 ... 134 D8
Bosworth Cl MK3 ... 46 E2
Bosworth Ct SL1 ... 204 C6
Botham Dr SL1 ... 205 E3
BOTLEY ... 145 A1
Botley La HP5 ... 145 A1
Botley Rd HP5 ... 144 E1
BOTOLPH CLAYDON ... 74 F6
Bottesford Cl MK3 ... 46 D1
Bottle Dump Rdbt MK17 . 56 E6
Bottle Square La HP14 . 159 D6
Bottom Dr LU6 ... 93 D5
Bottom House Farm La
HP8 ... 165 E2
Bottom House La HP23 120 A1
Bottom La HP9 ... 176 C5
Bottom Orch HP18 ... 112 C1
Bottom Rd
Bledlow Ridge HP14 ... 160 B5
Buckland Common HP23 . 132 F3
Bottom Waltons Caravan
Site SL2 ... 197 F3
Bottrells La HP8 ... 176 E8
Botyl Rd MK18 ... 74 E6
Boughton Bsns Pk HP6 166 B8
Boughton Way HP6 ... 155 C1
Boulevard The MK9 ... 34 E2
Boulmer Rd UB8 ... 201 C2
Boulters Cl
Maidenhead SL6 ... 196 C1
Slough SL1 ... 205 A4
Boulters Ct
Amersham HP6 ... 154 E1
Maidenhead SL6 ... 196 C1
Boulters Gdns SL6 ... 196 C1
Boulters La SL6 ... 196 C1
Boulters Lock MK14 ... 21 F2
Boundary Cotts WD4 ... 146 E2
Boundary Cres MK11 ... 32 E6
Boundary Pl HP10 ... 185 D8
Boundary Rd
Brackley NN13 ... 38 A6
Chalfont St Peter SL9 ... 177 D3
Loudwater HP10 ... 174 C1
Taplow SL6 ... 203 F8
Wooburn Green HP10 ... 185 D8
Boundary The 1 MK6 ... 34 F1
Bounds Croft MK12 ... 33 C4
Bounty St MK13 ... 33 F7
Bouquet Cl HP16 ... 151 C5
Bourbon St HP20 ... 115 D8
Bourne Ave SL4 ... 210 C3
Bourne Cl SL8 ... 185 B5
BOURNE END ... 185 B2
Bourne End MK43 ... 25 C6
Bourne End Bsns Pk
SL8 ... 185 B3
Bourne End Mills Ind Est
HP1 ... 146 B8
Bourne End Rd
Bourne End SL6, SL8 ... 196 E8
Cranfield MK43 ... 25 C4
Bourne End Sta SL8 ... 185 A3
Bourne Rd
Berkhamsted HP4 ... 134 F5
Slough SL1 ... 205 D4
Bourne The HP3 ... 146 A4
BOURTON ... 52 F8
Bourton Low MK7 ... 48 B5
Bourton Meadow Sch
MK18 ... 52 F8
Bourton Rd MK18 ... 52 E8
Bourtonville MK18 ... 52 D8
Bouverie Way SL3 ... 206 E2
BOVENEY ... 209 D8
Boveney Cl SL1 ... 205 A4
Boveney New Rd SL4 ... 204 E2
Boveney Rd SL4 ... 204 C1
Boveney Wood La SL1 .. 186 D1
BOVINGDON ... 146 B4
Bovingdon Ct HP3 ... 146 A3
BOVINGDON GREEN ... 146 A2
Bovingdon Hts SL7 ... 183 B2
Bovingdon Prim Sch
HP3 ... 146 B4
BOW BRICKHILL ... 48 C1
Bow Brickhill Prim Sch
MK17 ... 48 D2
Bow Brickhill Rd MK17 .. 48 F3
Bow Brickhill Sta MK7 .. 48 B2
Bowden La HP11 ... 173 D5
Bowen Cl MK7 ... 48 C5
Bowerbank Ct HP20 ... 101 F1
Bower Cl LU6 ... 92 F5
Bower Ct SL1 ... 204 F6
Bowerdean Rd HP13 ... 173 D7
Bower La LU6 ... 92 F5
Bowers La HP14 ... 159 D7
Bower Way SL1 ... 204 E6
Bowes Cl MK16 ... 22 C3
Bowes-Lyon Cl 7 SL4 .. 210 C6
Bowland Dr MK4 ... 46 B1
Bowler Lea HP13 ... 161 D2
Bowler Rd HP21 ... 115 E4
Bowler's Orch HP8 ... 177 A7
Bowles Pl MK6 ... 47 D7
Bowling Alley HP22 ... 86 D7
Bowling Cl UB10 ... 201 F4
Bowling Ct RG9 ... 191 D3
Bowling Gn HP14 ... 158 D5
Bowling Green Rd MK43 . 25 C1
Bowling Leys MK10 ... 36 A2
Bowl Rdbt The MK4 ... 46 D5
Bowmans Cl SL1 ... 197 B3
Bowmont Dr HP21 ... 115 D4
Bowood Ct 5 MK8 ... 33 F1
Bowood La HP22 ... 141 E5
Bowry Dr TW19 ... 211 F1
Bowstridge Ct 6 HP13 173 C7
Bowstridge La HP8 ... 177 C5
Bowyer Cres UB9 ... 189 F5
Bowyer Dr SL1 ... 204 E6
Bowyers Mews MK14 ... 34 F6
Boxberry Gdns MK7 ... 48 A6
Boxer Rd HP27 ... 138 E6
Boxgrove Ct MK10 ... 36 A1
Box La HP3 ... 146 E7
Box Tree Cl HP5 ... 154 D6
Boxwell Rd HP4 ... 135 B4
Boxwood Cl UB7 ... 208 F4
Boyce Cres MK7 ... 48 E5
Boycott Ave MK6 ... 34 E1
Boyle Cl UB10 ... 201 F3
Boyndon Rd SL6 ... 202 D7
BOYNE HILL ... 202 D6
Boyne Hill CE Inf Sch
SL6 ... 202 D6
Boyne Ho HP9 ... 175 E1
Boyn Hill Ave SL6 ... 202 D6
Boyn Hill Cl SL6 ... 202 D6
Boyn Hill Rd SL6 ... 202 D6
Boyn Valley Ind Est
SL6 ... 202 E6
Boyn Valley Rd SL6 ... 202 D5
Bozenham Mill La NN7 ... 9 F5
Bracken Cl SL2 ... 198 D8
Brackenforde SL3 ... 206 C4
Bracken Hill HP4 ... 135 E5
Bracken Rd SL6 ... 202 C4
Brackens The HP11 ... 173 C5
Bracken Way
Aylesbury HP21 ... 115 B8
Flackwell Heath HP10 ... 185 B7
Brackenwood HP14 ... 161 C7
BRACKLEY ... 38 A8
Brackley Dr HP15 ... 163 A6
Brackley La MK18 ... 73 B6
Brackley Rd
Chackmore MK18 ... 41 B1
Hazelmere HP15 ... 163 A6
Westbury NN13 ... 39 B5
Bradbery WD3 ... 178 D5
Bradbourne Dr MK7 ... 48 C3
Bradbury Cl MK13 ... 34 A3
Bradbury Gdns SL3 ... 199 D8
Bradcutts La SL6 ... 195 E8
Braddenham Wlk HP21 115 E4
Braddons Furlong
HP18 ... 125 C6
Braden Cl HP21 ... 116 A6
BRADENHAM ... 160 F7
Bradenham Beeches
HP14 ... 161 A8
Bradenham La SL7 ... 194 C5
Bradenham Rd HP14 ... 161 A3
Bradenham Wood La
Naphill HP14 ... 150 B1
Walter's Ash HP14 ... 161 A7
Bradfield Ave MK18 ... 41 D2
Bradford Gdns MK5 ... 46 B4
Bradford Rd
Heronsgate WD3 ... 167 C2
Slough SL1 ... 205 A7
Bradley Cl HP18 ... 109 D5
Bradley Gr MK4 ... 46 B2
Bradley Rd SL1 ... 205 E6
Bradnam Wood Nature
Reserve★ SL6 ... 194 D4
Bradshaw Cl SL4 ... 209 E6
Bradshawe Waye UB8 .. 208 F8
Bradshaw Rd HP13 ... 173 F6
BRADVILLE ... 34 B7
Bradvue Cres MK13 ... 34 B6
BRADWELL ... 34 A4
BRADWELL ABBEY ... 33 F3
BRADWELL COMMON ... 34 B3
Bradwell Common Bvd
MK13 ... 34 C3
Bradwell Rd
Milton Keynes, Bradville
MK13 ... 34 A6
Milton Keynes, Loughton
MK5 ... 46 B8
Milton Keynes MK5, MK8 .. 34 A1
Bradwell Village Sch
MK13 ... 34 B4
Braeburn Ct SL1 ... 205 C4
Brae Hill HP18 ... 110 A8
Brae Hill Cl HP18 ... 110 A8
Braemar Ct 5 SL7 ... 183 D2
Braemar Gdns SL1 ... 205 A4
Braeside HP14 ... 161 C6
Braford Gdns MK5 ... 46 B4
BRAGENHAM ... 70 C6
Bragenham La LU7,
MK17 ... 70 D5
Bragenham Side MK17 .. 69 F7
Bragmans La WD4 ... 156 E6
Brahms Cl MK7 ... 48 C5
Braid The HP5 ... 144 E1
Brakynbery HP4 ... 134 E7
Bramber Cl MK3 ... 57 E7
Bramber Ct SL1 ... 205 A5
Bramble Ave MK14 ... 34 E4
Bramble Cl
Chalfont St Peter SL9 ... 177 E4
Uxbridge UB8 ... 208 F7
Bramble Cres HP15 ... 163 C6
Bramble Dr SL6 ... 202 A4
Bramble La HP7 ... 165 E6
Bramble Mead HP8 ... 177 B7
Brambleside HP11 ... 174 B4
Brambles The UB7 ... 208 E2
Brambling HP19 ... 101 E3
Bramcote Cl HP20 ... 116 C8
Bramley Chase SL6 ... 202 C4
Bramley Cl SL6 ... 202 C3
Bramley Ct MK43 ... 3 F6
Bramley End HP14 ... 151 A1
Bramley Grange MK2 ... 58 D4
Bramley Mdws MK16 ... 22 B3
Bramley Rd MK1 ... 47 D3
Brammas Cl SL1 ... 205 C3
Brampton Ct
Maidenhead SL6 ... 203 B8
Milton Keynes MK13 ... 34 A6
Branch Rd HP10 ... 174 B2
Brandon Ct HP23 ... 103 D7
Brandon Rd HP12 ... 172 B3
BRANDS HILL ... 212 A8
Brands Hill Ave HP13 .. 162 C2
Brands Rd SL3 ... 212 B8
Brandville Rd UB7 ... 208 E4
Bransgill Ct MK13 ... 34 B4
Bransworth Ave MK10 ... 48 C8
Brantham Cl MK7 ... 48 A3
Brantwood Cl 7 MK4 ... 45 F1
Braunston MK6 ... 47 D6
Bravenfield MK18 ... 53 C2
Brawlings La SL9 ... 178 A6
BRAY ... 203 D3
Braybank SL6 ... 203 D4
Braybourne Cl UB8 ... 201 C6
Braybrooke Dr MK4 ... 46 E4
Bray Cl SL6 ... 203 C3
Bray Ct
Amersham HP6 ... 154 E1
Maidenhead SL6 ... 203 C2
Brayfield Ho MK46 ... 8 B5
Brayfield Rd SL6 ... 203 C4
Bray Pit Wildlife Reserve★
SL6 ... 203 C2
Bray Rd SL6 ... 203 B5
Brays Cl HP6 ... 153 C4
Brays Green La HP6 ... 153 C4
Brays La HP6 ... 153 C5
Brays Mdw HP6 ... 153 C4
Brayton Ct MK5 ... 46 C6
BRAY WICK ... 203 A4
Braywick Nature Ctr★
SL6 ... 203 B3
Braywick Park Nature
Reserve★ SL6 ... 203 A5
Braywick Park & Sports Gd
SL6 ... 203 A5
Braywick Rd SL6 ... 203 A4
Braywood Cotts SL4 ... 209 A5
Braziers End HP5 ... 133 C1
Breachwell Pl LU7 ... 91 A1
Breakspear Road N
UB9 ... 190 E8
Breakspear Road S
UB10 ... 190 F2
Bream Cl SL7 ... 194 C8
Breamore Ct MK8 ... 45 F8
Brearley Ave MK6 ... 46 E7
Brearley Cl UB8 ... 201 E6
Breckland MK14 ... 34 D6
Brecon Ct
Milton Keynes MK10 ... 35 F1
Slough SL1 ... 205 C4
Brecon Way HP13 ... 172 E8
Bredward Cl SL1 ... 197 B2
Breezes The SL6 ... 202 E4
Bremen Gr MK5 ... 46 A4
Brenchwood Cl HP13 ... 161 C2
Brendon Ct MK4 ... 46 D2
Brent MK6 ... 47 D5
Brent Path HP21 ... 115 D4
Brent Rd SL8 ... 185 A4
Brentwood Way HP21 ... 116 B6
Bretby Chase MK4 ... 45 F3
Breton MK11 ... 32 E6
Brewhouse La HP22 ... 88 E1
Brewster Cl MK5 ... 45 D5
Brew Twr SL7 ... 183 D1
Briaily HP14 ... 159 C2
Briar Cl SL6 ... 204 B7
Briar Dene SL6 ... 195 C1
Briar Glen SL6 ... 195 E6
Briar Hill MK12 ... 33 E4
Briar Lodge MK12 ... 33 D5
Briars Cl HP19 ... 101 B2
Briars The
High Wycombe HP11 ... 173 C5
Holmer Green HP15 ... 163 C7
Slough SL3 ... 206 F1
Briarswood HP15 ... 163 B3
Briarswood Cl HP14 ... 158 E5
Briar Way
Berkhamsted HP4 ... 135 D3
Slough SL2 ... 205 B8
Briary Ct MK18 ... 74 F8
Briary View MK17 ... 56 C8
Brices Mdw MK5 ... 46 A3
Brick Cl MK11 ... 33 C2
Brickfield La SL1 ... 197 B4
Brickfields Way UB7 ... 208 F3
Brick Hill HP18 ... 97 E1
Brickhill Manor Ct
MK17 ... 59 D5
Brickhill St
Giffard Park MK14 ... 22 A1
Milton Keynes, Monkston Park
MK10 ... 35 E2
Milton Keynes, Willen Park
MK15 ... 35 C6
Walton Park MK7 ... 48 A4
Brickhill Way MK18 ... 73 B5
Brick Kiln La HP22 ... 102 B4
Bricks La HP14 ... 159 C4
Brickwell Wlk HP15 ... 163 B3
Bricstock HP22 ... 88 D4
Bridens Way HP17 ... 126 F6
Bridge Ave
Cookham Rise SL6 ... 195 E6
Maidenhead SL6 ... 203 A7
Bridge Bank Cl HP11 ... 174 A3
Bridge Cl SL1 ... 204 F6
Bridge Ct
Berkhamsted HP4 ... 135 D4
Maidenhead SL6 ... 203 C7
Bridge Farm Bldgs
HP17 ... 128 B8
Bridgeford Ct MK6 ... 46 E8

Bridgegate Bsns Pk
  HP19.........................101 B1
Bridge Ho
  High Wycombe HP13......173 D6
  West Drayton UB7.........208 D5
Bridge Hook Cl 4 MK12..33 A6
Bridgeman Ct 5 SL4....210 A5
Bridgeman Dr SL4.........210 A5
Bridge Pl HP6.............154 F1
Bridge Rd
  Cosgrove MK19...............19 E2
  Ickford HP18................123 F2
  Maidenhead SL6...........203 B7
  Stoke Bruerne NN12.......9 A8
  Uxbridge UB8..............201 C3
Bridge St
  Berkhamsted HP4.........135 D4
  Buckingham MK18.........52 D8
  Colnbrook SL3.............212 D7
  Great Kimble HP17.......129 D1
  High Wycombe HP11......173 A7
  Leighton Buzzard LU7.....80 F7
  Maidenhead SL6...........203 A7
  Milton Keynes MK13.......33 F7
  Olney MK46...................6 F2
  Thornborough MK18......54 B8
  Turvey MK43..................8 D5
Bridgestone Dr SL8.....185 C3
Bridgeturn Ave MK12....33 D8
Bridgewater Ct
  Little Gaddesden HP4....121 C8
  Slough SL3.................207 A2
Bridgewater Hill HP4..134 F7
Bridgewater Ho MK18...52 C8
Bridgewater Monument★
  HP4........................120 E7
Bridgewater Rd HP4.....135 B5
Bridgewater Sch HP4....135 A6
Bridgewater Terr SL4..210 D6
Bridgewater Way SL4..210 D6
Bridgeway
  Cuddington HP18..........112 E3
  Milton Keynes MK13.......34 A7
Bridge Wlk MK19...........31 E4
Bridgnorth Dr MK4........45 E1
Bridle Cl
  Maidenhead SL6...........195 E1
  Milton Keynes MK13.......34 B6
Bridle Gate HP11.........172 F6
Bridle Manor HP22......131 C8
Bridle Rd SL6.............195 E1
Bridleway
  Buckland Common
  HP22........................132 E5
  Weston Turville HP22....116 F2
Bridle Way HP4...........135 A6
Bridleways HP21.........131 A5
Bridlington Cres MK10...36 A1
Bridlington Spur SL1....205 B4
Bridport Way SL2.........198 B1
Briery Way HP6...........154 E1
Brighton Spur SL1........198 B1
Brightwell Ave HP7........93 C7
Brigidine Sch The SL4..210 D4
BRILL.......................96 B1
Brill CE Comb Sch HP18.96 B1
Brill Cl
  Maidenhead SL6...........202 D3
  Marlow SL7................183 C2
Brill Ho SL6...............202 C3
Brill Pl MK13..............34 C3
Brill Rd
  Chilton HP18..............111 A3
  Horton-cum-S OX33......108 C6
  Ludgershall MK18.........96 B7
  Oakley HP18...............109 F5
Brimmers Hill HP15.....162 F6
Brimmers Rd HP27.......139 D2
Brimmers Way HP19.....114 F8
Brimstone La HP19.......101 C4
Brindlebrook MK8.........33 E1
Brindles Cl MK18..........73 B5
Brindles La HP9...........175 A4
Brindley Ave HP13.......173 D6
Brinkburn Chase MK10...36 A1
Brinkhurst SL7...........183 D2
Brinklow Rdbt MK10......36 C1
Briskman Way HP21.....115 B6
Bristle Hill MK18..........52 C8
Bristol Cl TW19..........213 E1
Bristol Ct 10 TW19.....213 E1
Bristol Way SL1...........205 F5
Bristow Cl MK2.............47 E1
Britannia Cl HP18.........123 E1
Britannia Ct 6 HP5.....144 C2
Britannia HP20...........115 E8
Britnell Ct HP14..........158 E5
Britten Gr MK7.............48 D5
Brittens Ct MK46...........7 C3
Brittons La MK17..........37 C3
BRITWELL..................197 F1
Britwell Dr HP4...........135 E6
Britwell Gdns SL1........197 D2
Britwell Rd SL1...........197 D2
Broad Arrow Cl MK14....34 E7

Broad Dean MK6............47 A8
Broadfields HP19.........101 A1
Broadfields Ct HP19.....101 A1
Broadfields Ret Pk
  HP19........................101 A1
Broad Gn MK43.............25 C3
BROAD GREEN..............25 B3
Broad La HP9, HP10......186 A6
Broadlands MK46..........47 C5
Broadlands Ave HP5.....144 C1
Broadleys SL4.............209 F7
Broad Leys HP27..........139 A3
Broadmark Rd SL2......206 B6
Broad Oak SL2.............198 C1
Broad Oak Ct SL2........198 C1
Broadpiece MK15..........35 A7
Broad Platts SL3.........212 A2
Broad Rush Gn LU7.......80 E8
Broad St
  Chesham HP5.............144 C1
  Newport Pagnell MK16....22 C4
  Syresham NN13............27 B8
Broadview MK17...........115 B4
Broadwater
  Berkhamsted HP4.........135 C5
  Milton Keynes MK6........47 D6
Broadwater Gdns UB9...190 C7
Broadwater La UB9......190 C5
Broadwater Pk UB9.....190 A5
Broadwater Pk SL6.....203 E1
Broadway SL6.............202 F7
Broadway Ave MK14.......21 F2
Broadway Cl 5 HP7.....165 B7
Broadway Ct HP5.........154 B8
Broadway Par UB7......208 E4
Broadway The
  Amersham HP7...........165 B7
  Beaconsfield HP9.........175 D3
  3 Chalfont St Peter SL9 177 D2
  Chesham HP5.............154 B8
  Farnham Common SL2...198 C6
  Grendon Underwood HP18 82 F4
Brocas Cl SL4.............210 A7
Brocas Terr SL4..........210 D7
Brocas Way LU7...........91 A3
Brockhampton MK15......35 B6
Brockhurst Rd HP5.......144 C2
Brock La SL6...............202 F7
Brockton Ct SL6..........202 F6
Brockway SL3.............207 B1
Brockwell MK16............22 C4
Broddick Ho HP11........174 B4
Broken Furlong SL4......205 B8
Broken Gate La UB9.....189 C3
Bromham Mill MK14......21 F2
Bromley HP23.............104 A4
Bromley La MK16.........153 C5
Brompton Cl 2 HP19...101 B3
Brompton Cres HP19....101 B3
Brompton Dr SL6.........195 C2
Bromycroft Rd SL2......198 A2
Bronsdon Way UB9......189 F2
Bronte Cl
  Aylesbury HP19...........100 F2
  Slough SL1................205 D8
Brookbank HP10..........185 D3
Brook Bsns Ctr UB8.....201 B3
Brook Cl
  Aston Clinton HP22......117 D5
  Ludgershall MK18..........96 C8
Brook Cres SL1...........204 E7
Brookdene Cl SL6........195 F2
Brooke Cl MK3..............57 F7
Brooke Furmston Pl
  SL7........................183 E3
BROOK END
  Ivinghoe...................105 E4
  North Crawley.............23 F5
  Weston Turville.........117 F3
Brook End
  North Crawley MK16......24 A6
  Weston Turville HP22....117 A3
Brooke Rd MK27.........139 B4
Brookes Univ (Wheatley
  Campus) OX33.........122 C1
Brook Farm Cl MK18......62 C1
Brookfield UB8............201 E6
Brookfield Cl HP23......189 B4
Brookfield Ho SL3........211 D6
Brookfield La MK18.......52 D7
Brookfield Rd
  Haversham MK19..........20 D2
  Newton Longville MK17...57 D3
  Wooburn HP10............185 D3
Brook Ho
  Slough SL1................205 D3
  West Drayton UB7........208 D5
Brookhouse Dr HP10....185 C3
Brook La
  Berkhamsted HP4.........135 B5
  Harrold MK43...............3 F7
  Newton Blossomville MK43. 8 B3
  Thame OX9................125 E1
Brooklands Rd MK2.......58 C7
Brooklyn Way SL7.........208 D3
Brookmead Sch LU7.....105 E5
Brook Path SL1............204 F6
Brooks Ct MK18...........52 D8

Brookside
  Colnbrook SL3............212 C7
  Halton HP22...............117 C1
  Lillingstone Lovell MK18..30 A6
  Loudwater HP10..........174 C2
  Milton Keynes MK12.......33 D4
  Oakley HP18...............109 D5
  Slough SL3................206 E7
  Thame OX9................125 F1
  Uxbridge UB10...........201 F5
  Weston Turville HP22....117 A2
Brookside Ave TW19....211 E4
Brookside Cl
  Old Stratford MK19........32 B6
  Tiddington OX9...........136 A7
Brookside La HP17.......129 E3
Brookside Terr 5
  HP21........................115 E8
Brook St
  Aston Clinton HP22......117 D5
  Edlesborough LU6........92 F4
  High Wycombe HP11......173 A7
  Tring HP23.................119 B4
  Windsor SL4..............210 D5
Brooksward Comb Sch
  MK14........................34 F7
Brookway MK19.............31 E4
Broombarn La HP16......151 E7
Broom Cl HP15............163 A3
Broomfield MK12...........33 D4
Broomfield Cl HP16......151 E7
Broomfield Gate SL2....198 B1
Broomfield Hill HP16....151 E7
Broom Ho
  Cookham Rise SL6........195 E6
  Stoke Poges SL2.........199 A5
Broom La SL3.............206 F2
Broomlee MK13............34 A5
Brooms Ind Est LU6...92 E4
Broomstick La HP5......145 A1
Brora Cl MK2...............58 C5
Brotheridge Ct HP21...115 B6
Brough Cl MK5.............46 A5
BROUGHTON
  Aylesbury.................116 D8
  Milton Keynes.............36 A3
Broughton Ave HP20....116 B8
Broughton Cl HP22......102 B3
Broughton Crossing
  HP22........................102 C2
Broughton Fields Prim Sch
  MK10, MK16...............36 A4
Broughton Grounds Com
  Woodlands★ MK16.......36 C4
Broughton Inf Sch
  HP20........................116 B8
Broughton Jun Sch
  HP20........................116 B8
Broughton La HP20,
  HP22........................116 C8
Broughton Manor Bsns Pk
  MK16........................36 B4
Broughton Manor Prep Sch
  MK10........................36 C4
Broughton Rd
  Milton Keynes MK10......36 B4
  Salford MK17................37 C3
Brow Bsns Ctr 10 HP11 172 E7
Brownbaker Ct MK14......34 F6
Browne Willis Cl MK2....58 D8
Brownfield Gdns SL6....202 E5
Browning Cl MK16..........22 A4
Browning Cres MK3.......58 A7
Brownlow Ave LU6.........92 F3
Brownlow Gate HP4.....107 A1
Brownlow La LU7..........105 A7
Brownlow Rd MK4.........135 C5
Brownlow Rise LU6........93 A8
Browns Ct SL1............204 E6
Brownset Dr MK4..........45 E1
Brownsfield Rd NN12....18 E4
Browns Hedge
  Leighton Buzzard LU7...105 D2
  Pitstone LU7..............105 C3
Brown's Rise HP23......132 F3
Brown's Rise HP23......132 F3
Brow MK17...................49 E5
BROWNS WOOD...........48 C4
Brownswood Dr NN12...18 D3
Brownswood Rd HP9....175 E4
Brow Wood Rdbt MK7....48 C5
Brow The HP8.............177 D7
Bruce Cl SL1..............205 A5
Bruce Wlk SL4............209 D5
Brucewood Par SL7.....183 E5
Bruckner Gdns MK7......48 D5
Brudenell SL4.............209 F3
Brudenell Dr
  Milton Keynes MK10......48 C8
  Stoke Mandeville HP22..116 B1
Brunel Cl SL6..............202 E5
Brunel Ct MK16............22 B3
Brunel Ctr (Sh Ctr) MK2. 58 C8
Brunel Gate HP19........100 F1
Brunel Rd
  Aylesbury HP19...........100 F1

Brunel Rd continued
  High Wycombe HP13......161 F1
  Maidenhead SL6...........202 D5
Brunel Rdbt SL1...........205 F5
Brunel Science Pk UB8 201 E2
Brunel Univ UB8...........201 E2
Brunel Way SL1............205 F5
Bruneleys MK11............33 B3
Brunner PI HP13..........173 C6
Brunswick Cl HP10.......101 B3
Brunswick PI HP13.......162 D2
Brushford Cl MK4..........46 D3
Brush Hill Nature Reserve★
  HP16........................151 B3
Brushmakers Ct HP5...144 B1
Brushwood Dr WD3......167 C3
Brushwood Jun Sch
  HP5........................144 A2
Brushwood Rd HP5......144 B2
Bryans Cres MK16.........24 A6
Bryanston Ave HP20....101 F2
Bryant Ave SL2............205 B4
Bryants Acre HP22......131 B6
BRYANT'S BOTTOM......150 B6
Bryants Bottom Rd
  HP16........................150 F4
Bryden Cotts UB8........201 C1
Bryer PI SL4...............209 D4
Bryfield Cotts HP3.......146 C1
Bryher The SL6............202 A7
Bryne La MK18.............53 B2
Bryony Cl UB8.............208 F8
Bryony PI MK14............34 E5
Buccleuch Rd SL3.......213 A1
Buchanan Rd OX25.......94 E7
Buchan Cl UB8............201 C2
Buckby MK6................47 D6
Buckfast Ave MK3.........47 A2
Buckfield Ct SL0.........207 F4
Buckingham Ave SL1....205 B4
Buckingham Avenue E
  SL1........................205 C7
Buckingham Canal Wildlife
  Reserve★ MK18.........42 D3
Buckingham Chantry
  Chapel MK18...............41 D1
Buckingham Cl HP13...174 E4
Buckingham Ct
  Amersham HP6...........154 E2
  Brackley NN13.............38 A6
  Newport Pagnell MK16....22 B3
Buckingham Ctr 8
  MK18........................41 D1
Buckingham Dr HP13...174 A7
Buckingham Gate
  Medmenham SL7.........193 D7
  Milton Keynes MK3........35 B1
Buckingham Gdns SL1..205 F4
Buckingham Ho
  Amersham HP6...........154 D3
  4 Maidenhead SL6......202 F6
Buckingham Hospl
  MK18........................41 D1
Buckingham Ind Pk
  MK18........................52 D5
Buckingham Par 4
  SL9........................177 D2
Buckingham PI 1
  HP13........................173 A7
Buckingham Prim Sch
  MK18........................41 E2
Buckingham Rd
  Aylesbury HP19, HP20...101 D3
  Brackley NN13.............38 A6
  Deanshanger MK19.......31 E2
  Edgcott HP18..............72 F2
  Gawcott MK18.............52 A5
  Milton Keynes, Church Hill
  MK7.........................56 E6
  Milton Keynes MK3........57 D7
  Steeple Claydon MK18....63 E3
  Tring HP23.................118 E3
  Winslow MK18.............65 F5
Buckingham Road Ind Est
  NN13........................38 A6
Buckingham Sch MK18..52 D7
Buckinghamshire County
  Mus★ HP20..............115 D8
Buckinghamshire New Univ
  Chalfont St Peter HP8...178 A8
  High Wycombe HP11......173 B6
  Uxbridge UB8.............201 C6
Buckinghamshire Railway
  Ctr★ HP22................84 F2
Buckingham Sq 1 MK9. 34 C2
Buckingham St
  8 Aylesbury HP20.......101 D1
  Milton Keynes MK12.......33 D7
  Tingewick MK18...........51 B6
Buckingham View HP5.144 C1
Buckingham Way HP10 174 A1
BUCKLAND..................117 D1
Buckland Ave SL3........206 B3
BUCKLAND COMMON....133 A3
Buckland Cres SL4......209 F6
Buckland Dr MK6..........47 C6
Buckland Gate SL3......199 B2
Buckland Lodge MK6.....47 B6

Buckland Rd HP22.......118 A4
Bucklands Croft HP23..118 C8
BUCKLANDWHARF.......118 B4
Bucklebury Cl SL6.......203 C1
Buckley Cl MK11..........32 F4
Buckman Cl MK12.........33 B5
Buckmaster Rd HP22...172 C3
BUCKMOOREND...........140 D6
Bucks Goat Ctr & Animal
  Farm The★ HP22.......130 A7
Buckthorn MK12...........33 C5
Budge Rd NN12............18 F5
Buffins SL6.................196 C2
BUFFLER'S HALT..........40 C3
BULBOURNE................119 C3
Bulbourne Cl HP4........134 F6
Bulbourne Ct HP23......119 A3
Bulbourne Rd HP23......119 B7
Bulkeley Ave SL4.........210 B4
Bulbaiters La HP6........153 B5
Bullbeggars La HP4......135 F3
Bullfinch Gdns 8 HP19. 101 F3
BULLINGTON END..........20 C7
Bullington End Rd MK19. 20 A6
Bull La
  Gerrards Cross SL9......188 C7
  7 High Wycombe HP11..173 A7
  Milton Keynes MK2........58 D8
Bullocks Farm La HP14 171 B7
Bullrush Gr UB8...........201 C1
Bulls La HP18.............124 A3
Bullsland Gdns WD3....167 B3
Bullsland La WD3.........167 B3
Bulmer Cl MK10............36 B3
BULSTRODE................146 E3
Bulstrode Cl WD4........146 E2
Bulstrode Ct SL9.........188 D5
Bulstrode La WD4........146 E3
Bulstrode Way SL9......188 D6
Bunby Rd SL2..............198 F5
Bunces Cl SL4............205 B1
Bunces Ct MK18..........101 D1
Bungalows The MK18....51 A6
Bunhill Cl LU6..............93 F8
Bunkers La LU7............80 D6
Bunsen PI MK5............46 C4
Bunstrux HP23............119 A4
Bunsty Ct MK11...........32 F5
Bunten Meade SL1.......205 B5
Bunyan Ct MK13..........33 B5
Burano Cl MK7.............48 C6
Burchard Cres MK5......46 A6
Burchett's Green Rd
  SL6........................194 C1
Burcot Gdns SL6.........195 E3
BURCOTT....................79 E4
Burcott Cl HP22..........102 B3
Burcott La HP22..........102 C3
Burdeleys La MK5.........46 A4
Burdett Dr HP14.........161 B8
Burdock Ct MK16.........21 F4
Burewelle MK18............33 C1
Burfield Rd
  Chorleywood WD3......167 C4
  Old Windsor SL4.........211 A1
Burford Cl
  Ickenham UB10..........201 E8
  Marlow Bottom SL7.....183 C5
Burford Gdns SL1........204 C8
Burford Ho 18 SL4.......210 D6
Burford Sch SL7..........183 C5
Burgess Gdns MK16.....22 B2
Burgess La HP17.........128 C3
Burgess Wood Gr HP9. 175 B2
Burgess Wood Rd HP9. 175 B3
Burgess Wood Road S
  HP9........................175 B1
Burgett Rd SL1...........205 B3
Burghley Ct MK8...........45 F8
Burholme MK4.............46 C3
Burke Rd HP22............131 C5
Burkes Cl HP9.............186 B8
Burkes Cres HP9.........175 D2
Burkes Ct HP9............175 D2
Burkes Par HP9...........175 D2
Burkes Rd HP9............175 C3
Burleigh Ct MK18..........52 F8
Burleigh Piece MK18.....41 F1
Burleys Rd MK18...........65 F4
Burlington Ave SL1......205 E4
Burlington Ct 1 SL1....205 E4
Burlington Rd
  Burnham SL1.............197 B1
  2 Slough SL1............205 E4
Burma Cl HP13............173 E6
Burners La MK11..........33 A4
Burners Lane S MK11....33 A4
Burness Cl UB8...........201 D3
Burnet MK14................34 C7
Burnetts Ct HP16.........151 C5
Burnetts Rd SL4..........209 E7
BURNHAM...................197 C3
Burnham Ave HP9........176 A1
Burnham Beeches National
  Nature Reserve★ SL2. 198 A7

Burnham Cl
Bourne End SL8 . . . . .185 A4
High Wycombe HP12 . . . .172 D6
Windsor SL4 . . . . .209 D5
Burnham Ct SL6 . . . . .202 F8
Burnham Dr MK13 . . . . . . .34 C3
Burnham Gram Sch
SL1 .197 D1
Burnham Hts SL1 . . . . .204 C7
Burnham La SL1 . . . . .204 E7
Burnham Pl NN13 . . . . . . .27 B8
Burnham Rd
Beaconsfield HP9 . . . . .186 F6
Hughenden Valley HP14 .162 A6
Westcott HP18 . . . . .98 B7
Burnhams Field HP22 . . .116 C7
Burnham Sta SL1 . . . . .204 D7
Burnhams The
Aston Clinton HP22 . . . . .117 C5
Shabbington HP18 . . . . . . .124 D3
Burnham Upper Sch
SL1 .204 B8
Burnmoor Cl MK2 . . . . . . .58 D4
Burns Cl
Long Crendon HP18 . . . . .125 D7
Newport Pagnell MK16 . . .22 A4
Burns Ct HP21 . . . . .115 F6
Burns Rd MK3 . . . . .58 A7
Burnt Oak SL6 . . . . .195 F7
Burn Wlk SL1 . . . . .197 B1
Burrell Cl HP21 . . . . .115 C6
Burren The HP6 . . . . .154 D2
Burroughs Cres SL8 . . . . .185 A4
Burrow Ash Cl MK19 . . . .10 F2
Burroway Rd SL3 . . . . .207 B3
Burrows Cl
Tylers Green HP10 . . . . . . .163 C2
Woburn Sands MK17 . . . . .49 B5
Burrows Ho HP13 . . . . . . .161 E2
Burton La HP27 . . . . .139 C5
Burtons La WD3 . . . . .167 A4
Burton's La HP8 . . . . .166 E5
Burton's Way HP8 . . . . . . .166 C7
Burton Way SL4 . . . . .209 E4
Burtree Cl MK12 . . . . .33 D5
Burt's La HP18 . . . . .125 D6
Bury Ave MK16 . . . . .22 C4
Bury Cl MK16 . . . . .22 C4
BURY END 165 D6
Bury Farm HP7 . . . . .165 C7
Bury Farm Cl LU7 . . . . . . .91 C6
Buryfield La HP10 . . . . . . .152 B7
Buryhook Cnr OX33 . . . . .122 C2
Bury La HP5 . . . . .154 B8
Bury Lawn Sch MK14 . . . .34 D7
Bury Rise HP3 . . . . .146 D6
Bury St MK16 . . . . .22 C4
Busby Cl MK18 . . . . .41 F1
Buscot Pl MK8 . . . . .45 F8
Bushel Wharf HP23 . . . . . .119 A6
Bushes La MK18 . . . . .51 C1
Bushey Bartrams MK5 . . .46 A3
Bushey Cl
Buckingham MK18 . . . . . . .41 F1
High Wycombe HP12 . . . .172 E7
Whipsnade LU6 . . . . .93 F1
Bushfield Rd HP3 . . . . . . .146 C6
Bushfields MK12 . . . . .33 D6
Bushfield Sch MK12 . . . . .33 D6
Bushmead Cl HP22 . . . . . .87 B5
Bushmead Rd HP22 . . . . . .87 B5
Bushnell Pl 2 SL6 . . . . . . .202 B8
Bush The HP17 . . . . .126 F5
Bushy Cl MK3 . . . . .47 A3
Business Ctr The HP6 . . .154 F1
Business Village SL2 . . . .206 B5
Buslins La HP5 . . . . .143 E3
Butcher La MK5 . . . . .45 F3
Bute Brae MK3 . . . . .46 E2
Butler Ct 5 SL7 . . . . .183 F3
Butlers Cl
Amersham HP6 . . . . .154 A2
Windsor SL4 . . . . .209 D6
Butlers Court Comb Sch
HP9 . . . . .175 D1
Butlers Court Rd HP9 . . .175 D1
BUTLERS CROSS 176 F6
BUTLER'S CROSS 130 C3
Butlers Ct HP13 . . . . .173 F5
Butlers Gr MK14 . . . . .34 D8
Butler Wlk HP19 . . . . .115 A7
Butterfield HP10 . . . . .185 D4
Butterfield CI MK15 . . . . .35 C2
Butterfield Cotts WD3 . .178 E7
Butterfly Gate 5 MK10 . .36 B3
Butterly Rd
High Wycombe HP14 . . . .158 B6
Stokenchurch HP14 . . . . . .158 F4
Buttermere HP21 . . . . .116 B7
Buttermere Ave SL1 . . . . .204 C8
Buttermere Cl MK2 . . . . . .58 D6
Butterton Gdns MK10 . . .36 C3
Buttfurlong HP27 . . . . . . .127 A7
Buttlehide WD3 . . . . .178 D5
**Buttler's Hanging Wildlife
Reserve*** HP14 . . . . . .160 D5

Button Gr MK6 . . . . .47 A7
Buzzacott La MK4 . . . . . . .46 C3
Bybend Cl SL2 . . . . .198 B4
Bycell Rd MK18 . . . . .41 C6
Bye Gn HP22 . . . . .117 A3
BYE GREEN 117 A3
Byerly Ho MK14 . . . . .34 F5
Byerly Pl MK14 . . . . .34 F5
Byford Way MK18 . . . . . . .65 F4
Byland Dr SL6 . . . . .203 B1
Byrd Cres MK7 . . . . .48 D6
Byres The HP17 . . . . .126 F6
Byron SL3 . . . . .207 B1
Byron Cl
6 Marlow SL7 . . . . .183 F3
Milton Keynes MK3 . . . . . .57 F7
Byron Ct SL4 . . . . .210 A4
Byron Dr MK16 . . . . .22 A4
Byron Rd HP21 . . . . .115 F6
Byron Way UB7 . . . . .208 F2
Byward Cl MK14 . . . . .34 E7
Byways
Berkhamsted HP4 . . . . . . .135 C5
Burnham SL1 . . . . .204 A8
Bywell Ct MK4 . . . . .56 E8
By-Wood End SL9 . . . . . . .178 A5

C

Cabair Coll of Air Training
MK43 . . . . .24 E1
Cable Cres MK17 . . . . .49 B5
Cadeby Ct MK10 . . . . .36 B3
Cadman Sq MK5 . . . . .46 C5
CADMORE END 170 C6
Cadmore End CE Comb Sch
HP14 . . . . .170 C6
Cadsdean Rd HP27 . . . . . .139 C6
Cadwell Dr SL6 . . . . .202 D3
Caernarvon Cres MK3 . . .57 E7
Caesars Cl MK3 . . . . .57 E7
Caesars Gate NN13 . . . . . .38 A6
Cages Wood Dr SL2 . . . . .198 B8
Cagney Cres 1 MK4 . . . . .45 E3
Cairngorm Gate MK6 . . . .46 D8
Cairngorm Pl SL2 . . . . . . .198 D1
Cairnside HP13 . . . . .173 E6
Caister Ct MK4 . . . . .56 E8
Caithness Ct MK3 . . . . . . .46 E2
Calamus Ct MK7 . . . . .48 B6
Calbroke Rd SL2 . . . . .197 F2
CALDECOTE 22 E1
Caldecote La MK16 . . . . . .22 F2
Caldecote St MK16 . . . . . .22 C4
CALDECOTTE 48 A3
Caldecotte La MK7 . . . . . .48 A3
Caldecotte Lake Dr MK7 .48 A2
Caldecotte Rdbt MK7 . . . .47 F3
Calder Cl SL6 . . . . .195 E1
Calder Ct
Maidenhead SL6 . . . . .195 D1
1 Slough SL3 . . . . .206 F1
Calder Gdns LU7 . . . . .80 B7
Calder Vale MK3 . . . . .46 E1
Calder Way SL3 . . . . .212 E4
Caldwell MK8 . . . . .33 D1
Caldicot Cl HP21 . . . . .116 B6
Caldicott Sch SL2 . . . . . . .198 B5
Caledon Cl HP9 . . . . .175 E3
Caledon Rd MK13 . . . . . . .33 E7
Caledon Rd HP9 . . . . .175 E3
Calewen MK8 . . . . .33 E1
CALIFORNIA
Aylesbury 115 C7
Dunstable 93 F6
California Circ HP11 . . . . .173 B4
Callaghan Ct HP4 . . . . . . .135 D4
Callingham Pl HP19 . . . . .175 E3
Callis Farm Ct TW19 . . . .213 E1
Calluna Dr MK3 . . . . .47 A3
Calumet HP9 . . . . .175 D3
Calvards Croft MK12 . . . .33 C4
Calverleigh Cres MK4 . . .46 D3
Calverley Cres MK13 . . . .161 F2
CALVERT 73 B6
Calvert Cotts MK18 . . . . .73 D7
**Calvert Jubilee Wildlife
Reserve*** MK18, OX27 .73 A7
CALVERTON 32 E3
Calverton La MK19 . . . . . .33 B1
Calverton Lane Rdbt
MK11 . . . . .33 B2
Calverton Rd MK11 . . . . . .32 D4
Calves Cl MK5 . . . . .46 A3
Calvie Croft MK12 . . . . . . .33 D4
Cambell Sq MK9 . . . . .35 A3
Camber Cl MK3 . . . . .57 E7
Camberton Rd LU7 . . . . . .80 E6
Camborne Ave HP21 . . . .116 B5
Cambria Cl SL3 . . . . .206 C4
Cambridge Ave
Burnham SL1 . . . . .197 B3
Slough SL1 . . . . .205 A7
Cambridge Cl
Aylesbury HP20 . . . . .101 E1
5 Aylesbury HP20 . . . . . .101 E1
Harmondsworth UB7 . . . .213 D8

Cambridge Close Ret Pk 6
HP20 . . . . .101 E1
Cambridge Cres HP13 . . .173 E7
Cambridge Ho 2 SL4 . . .210 C6
Cambridge Pl 9 HP20 . . .115 D8
Cambridge Rd
Beaconsfield HP9 . . . . .175 C2
Marlow SL7 . . . . .183 D2
Uxbridge UB8 . . . . .201 D6
Cambridge St
Aylesbury HP20 . . . . .101 E1
Milton Keynes, Bletchley
MK2 . . . . .58 C8
Milton Keynes, Wolverton
MK12 . . . . .33 C6
Cambridge Terr 13
HP4 . . . . .135 D4
Cambron MK8 . . . . .33 D2
Cam Ct MK3 . . . . .57 E8
Camden Cl HP19 . . . . .101 C1
Camden Pl SL8 . . . . .185 A3
Camden Rd SL6 . . . . .195 D1
Cameron Rd 6 HP5 . . . . .144 C1
Camfield Ct SL6 . . . . .202 A8
Camlet Gr HP4 . . . . .134 D7
Camley Gdns SL6 . . . . . . .202 A8
Camm Ave SL4 . . . . .209 E4
Camomile Cl MK7 . . . . . . .48 C5
Camomile Way UB7 . . . . .208 E6
Campania Cl MK10 . . . . . .36 A2
Campbell Cl
Buckingham MK18 . . . . . . .52 E8
High Wycombe HP13 . . . .172 F8
Campbell Dr HP9 . . . . .175 C5
Campbell Park Rdbt
MK9 . . . . .34 F3
Campbells Ride HP15 . . .163 D7
Campden Rd UB10 . . . . . .190 F1
Camperdown SL6 . . . . . . .196 B1
Camperdown Ho 9
SL4 . . . . .210 C5
Camp Ind Est SL9 . . . . . . .136 B4
Campion MK14 . . . . .21 E2
Campion Cl
Aylesbury HP20 . . . . .116 C8
Denham UB9 . . . . .190 A1
Uxbridge UB8 . . . . .208 F8
Campion Rd HP15 . . . . . . .162 F6
Cane End HP27 . . . . .139 B3
Cane End La HP22 . . . . . . .102 C6
Canford Ct HP21 . . . . .115 F5
Cannock Cl SL6 . . . . .203 B6
Canal Ct HP4 . . . . .135 C4
Canal La MK19 . . . . .31 F4
Canalside
Berkhamsted HP4 . . . . . . .134 F6
Old Stratford MK19 . . . . . .32 C7
Stoke Bruerne NN12 . . . . .9 A8
Canalside Rdbt MK9 . . . . .35 B4
Canal Wharf SL3 . . . . .207 A4
Candlemas La HP9 . . . . . .175 E2
Candlemas Mead HP9 . . .175 E2
Candlemas Oaks HP9 . . .175 E2
Candlewicks MK7 . . . . .48 B6
Candover Cl UB7 . . . . .213 D7
Candy La MK5 . . . . .46 B4
Candytuft Gm HP15 . . . . .162 F6
Cane End HP27 . . . . .139 B3
Cane End La HP22 . . . . . . .102 C6
Canford Ct HP21 . . . . .115 F5
Cannock Cl SL6 . . . . .203 B6
Cannock Rd HP20 . . . . . . .101 C3
Cannon Court Rd SL6 . . .195 D3
Cannon Gate SL2 . . . . . . .206 C6
Cannon Hill Cl SL6 . . . . . .203 C2
Cannon La SL6 . . . . .202 A6
Cannon Mill Ave HP5 . . .154 E5
Cannon Pl HP27 . . . . .139 B4
Cannon's Hill HP18 . . . . .112 C5
Cannon's Orch HP22 . . . .85 B4
Canonbury MK10 . . . . .35 E1
Canon Harnett Ct MK12 .32 F6
Canon Hill Dr SL6 . . . . . . .203 B3
Canon Hill Way SL6 . . . . .203 B2
Canon's Cloisters SL4 . . .210 D7
Canons Rd MK12 . . . . .33 C7
Canons The MK16 . . . . . . .22 E3
Cantell Cl MK18 . . . . .41 D1
Canterbury Ave SL2 . . . . .198 C1
Canterbury Cl
Amersham HP7 . . . . .165 E8
Monks Risborough HP27 .139 B5
Cantilupe Cl LU6 . . . . .92 D6
Cantle Ave MK14 . . . . .35 A5
Cantley Cl HP20 . . . . .101 E2
Capel Cl MK18 . . . . .41 F7
Capel Dr MK14 . . . . .34 F5
Capell Ave WD3 . . . . .167 C4
Capell Rd WD3 . . . . .167 D4
Capell Way MK18 . . . . .66 A4
Cape Villas SL0 . . . . .207 E2
Capian Wlk MK4 . . . . .46 E2
Capps La HP5 . . . . .143 A5
Capricorn Ho HP10 . . . . . .185 A8
Capron MK6 . . . . .47 B5

Capswood Bsns Ctr
UB9 . . . . .189 C3
Captain Cook Cl HP8 . . .177 B6
Captain's Cl HP5 . . . . .144 A4
Captains Wlk HP4 . . . . . . .135 D3
**Captain's Wood Nature
Reserve*** HP5 . . . . . . .143 F4
Caraway Cl MK7 . . . . .48 B4
Cardain Ho HP9 . . . . .175 D3
Cardigan Cl
Milton Keynes MK3 . . . . . .46 F1
Slough SL1 . . . . .204 F6
Cardinals Wlk SL6 . . . . . .204 C7
Cardwell Cl MK4 . . . . .46 C2
Carey Cl
Aylesbury HP21 . . . . .115 D4
Windsor SL4 . . . . .210 B4
Careys Croft HP4 . . . . .135 A7
Careys Rd NN12 . . . . .17 A8
Carey Way MK46 . . . . .7 A4
Carhampton Ct MK4 . . . . .46 D3
Carisbrooke Ave HP12 . .172 B6
Carisbrooke Cl SL6 . . . . .202 C6
Carisbrooke Ct
Buckingham MK18 . . . . . . .41 E2
Slough SL1 . . . . .205 F6
Carisbrooke Ho 4
HP13 . . . . .173 F7
Carisbrooke Way MK4 . . .45 E1
Carleton Gate MK15 . . . . .35 E7
Carlina Pl MK14 . . . . .34 D3
Carlisle Rd SL1 . . . . .205 D6
Carlton Cl
Aylesbury HP19 . . . . .101 A2
Newport Pagnell MK16 . . .22 E4
Carlton Ct HP27 . . . . .139 B3
Carlton Ho TW19 . . . . . . .213 D2
Carlton Rd
Slough SL2 . . . . .206 B6
Turvey MK43 . . . . .8 E7
Carlyle Ave HP21 . . . . . . .115 F7
Carlyle Cl MK16 . . . . .22 A4
Carman Ct HP23 . . . . .118 F3
Carmarthen Rd SL1 . . . . .205 E6
Carmel Ct SL7 . . . . .183 B1
Carnation Way HP21 . . . .115 E5
Carne The MK11 . . . . .32 E5
Carnot Cl MK5 . . . . .46 C4
Carnoustie Cl MK3 . . . . . .57 C7
Carnweather Ct MK4 . . . .57 B8
Caroline Cl UB7 . . . . .208 D4
Caroline Ct SL7 . . . . .183 E3
Caroline Haslett Comb Sch
MK5 . . . . .46 B4
Carolus Creek MK15 . . . .35 A7
Carpenter Ct MK14 . . . . . .34 F6
Carpenters Wood Dr
WD3 . . . . .167 B5
**Carpenter's Wood,
Dungrove Wood Nature
Reserve*** MK5 . . . . . . .194 C2
Carpenters Yd HP23 . . . .119 B3
Carr Cl HP19 . . . . .101 A2
Carrick Rd MK6 . . . . .34 F1
Carriers Cl MK19 . . . . .11 A8
Carrington Ave HP10 . . . .185 A8
Carrington Cl MK18 . . . . .77 E5
Carrington Cres HP22 . . .131 A7
Carrington Ct 5 HP12 . . .172 D7
Carrington Hall Rd
MK17 . . . . .68 C6
Carrington Inf Sch 1
HP10 . . . . .174 A1
Carrington Jun Sch
HP10 . . . . .185 A8
Carrington Pl
Holmer Green HP15 . . . . .163 C7
Tring HP23 . . . . .119 B5
Carrington Rd
Aylesbury HP21 . . . . .115 D6
High Wycombe HP12 . . . .172 D6
Newport Pagnell MK16 . . .22 B3
Slough SL1 . . . . .205 E6
Carrington Way HP16 . . .151 C5
Carroll Cl MK16 . . . . .22 A5
Carron Cl LU7 . . . . .80 B7
Carron Ct MK2 . . . . .58 C4
Carrs Dr HP12 . . . . .172 C8
Carter Cl SL4 . . . . .210 A5
Carteret Cl MK15 . . . . .35 E7
Carters Cl MK14 . . . . .13 F1
Carters La
Long Crendon HP18 . . . . .125 D7
Milton Keynes MK11 . . . . .33 A3
Quainton MK22, MK18 . . .85 E6
Carters Mdw MK18 . . . . . .76 A2
Carters Ride HP22 . . . . . . .116 B2
Carter Wlk HP10 . . . . .174 C8
Cartmel Cl MK3 . . . . .57 C6
Cartwright Ct 2 HP13 . . .173 F5
Cartwright Pl MK6 . . . . . .46 E8
Carver Hill Rd HP11 . . . . .172 F5
Carvers Mews MK14 . . . . .34 F6
Cascadia Cl HP11 . . . . . . .174 B2
Cashmere Cl MK5 . . . . . . .46 A4
Casterton Cl MK13 . . . . . .34 C4
Castle Acre MK10 . . . . .35 F1
Castle Ashby Rd NN7 . . . .1 B7

Castle Ave
Datchet SL3 . . . . .211 A8
West Drayton UB7 . . . . . . .208 F6
Castle Cl
Marsh Gibbon OX6 . . . . . .72 A3
Pitstone LU7 . . . . .105 D3
Totternhoe LU6 . . . . .93 A8
Wing LU7 . . . . .79 E3
Castle Ct
13 Aylesbury HP20 . . . . . .115 D8
Buckingham MK18 . . . . . . .52 D8
Castle Dr SL6 . . . . .202 D7
Castle Est HP12 . . . . .172 D4
Castlefield Foundation Sch
HP12 . . . . .172 C6
Castlefields HP22 . . . . . . .172 C6
Castle Gate Way HP4 . . . .135 C6
Castle Hill
Berkhamsted HP4 . . . . . . .135 C5
High Wycombe HP11 . . . .173 A6
Maidenhead SL6 . . . . .202 E7
Windsor SL4 . . . . .210 D6
Castle Hill Ave HP4 . . . . .135 C5
Castle Hill Cl HP4 . . . . . . .135 C5
Castle Hill Rd HP4 . . . . . .135 C5
Castle Hill Rd LU6 . . . . . . .93 A8
Castle Hill Terr SL6 . . . . .202 E7
Castle Ho 5 LU7 . . . . .80 E7
Castle La HP22 . . . . .86 F6
Castle Lodge SL6 . . . . .202 F7
Castlemead Cotts SL4 . . .210 C3
Castle Meadow Cl MK16 .22 E4
Castle Mews
Berkhamsted HP4 . . . . . . .135 C4
Maidenhead SL6 . . . . .202 E7
Castle Park Rd HP22 . . . .131 B6
Castle Pl 6 HP13 . . . . .173 B7
Castle Rd MK46 . . . . .2 F1
Castle Rose MK6 . . . . .47 D6
Castle Row 16 HP23 . . . .119 A3
Castle St
Aylesbury HP20 . . . . .115 D8
Berkhamsted HP4 . . . . . . .135 C4
Buckingham MK18 . . . . . . .52 D8
High Wycombe HP13 . . . .173 B7
Marsh Gibbon OX27 . . . . .72 A3
Slough SL1 . . . . .205 F3
Wingrave HP22 . . . . .89 B3
CASTLETHORPE 19 E5
Castlethorpe Fst Sch
MK19 . . . . .19 F5
Castlethorpe Rd MK19 . . .11 A2
Castleton Ct SL7 . . . . .183 E2
Castleview Comb Sch
SL3 . . . . .206 D2
Castle View Gdns
HP12 . . . . .172 D7
Castleview Ho SL4 . . . . . .210 D7
Castleview Rd SL3 . . . . . .206 C2
Caswell La MK17 . . . . .60 F7
Catchpole Cl MK12 . . . . . .33 B5
Cater Rd HP14 . . . . .171 C4
Catesby Croft MK5 . . . . . .46 C8
Cathay Cl MK3 . . . . .58 B7
Cathedral of Trees*
MK15 . . . . .35 C5
Catherine Cotts HP23 . . .133 E8
Catherine Ct MK18 . . . . . .41 E2
Catherines Cl UB7 . . . . . .208 D4
Catherines Ct HP22 . . . . .102 B3
Catkin Cl HP12 . . . . .172 B3
Catslip RG9 . . . . .179 A1
Causeway The
Bray SL6 . . . . .203 C4
Marlow SL7 . . . . .183 E1
Causey Arch MK10 . . . . . .36 C3
Cautley Cl HP22 . . . . .85 A5
Cavalier Ct HP4 . . . . .135 C4
Cavalier Rd OX9 . . . . .126 A1
Cavalry Cres SL4 . . . . .210 C4
Cavan Way MK10 . . . . .36 A4
Cavendish Cl
Burnham SL6 . . . . .204 A7
Little Chalfont HP6 . . . . . .166 B8
Wendover HP22 . . . . .131 B6
Cavendish Ct
Milton Keynes MK5 . . . . . .46 A7
Poyle SL3 . . . . .212 E6
Cavendish Rd HP5 . . . . . .154 D7
Cavendish Way 9
HP19 . . . . .100 F1
Cavendish Wlk OX9 . . . . .126 B1
Cavenham MK8 . . . . .33 F2
Caversham Gn 1
HP20 . . . . .101 D9
Cawardon MK14 . . . . .34 C7
Cawcott Dr SL4 . . . . .209 E6
Cawdor Rise MK4 . . . . . . .45 E2
Cawkwell Way MK2 . . . . . .58 C8
Caxton Ct RG9 . . . . .191 E1
Caxton Dr UB8 . . . . .201 D3
Caxton Rd MK12 . . . . .33 B7
Cecil Cl SL0 . . . . .207 E2
Cecils Yd 7 MK18 . . . . . . .41 D1
Cecil Way SL2 . . . . .197 F1
Cecily Ct MK5 . . . . .46 A5
Cedar 1 RG9 . . . . .191 D2

Cedar Ave
Hazelemere HP15 . . . . .163 A5
West Drayton UB7. . . . . . . .208 F6
Cedar Chase SL6. . . . . . . .196 D1
Cedar Cl
Aylesbury HP20 . . . . .102 A2
Burnham SL1. . . . . .197 C1
Chesham HP5 . . . . .144 E1
Iver Heath SL0. . . . . .200 C4
Milton Keynes MK19 . . . . .32 B7
Cedar Ct
Gerrards Cross SL9 . . . . . .188 E7
High Wycombe HP13 . . . . .173 B7
Maidenhead SL6 . . . . .202 D7
Marlow SL7 . . . . .183 E2
⑥ Windsor SL4. . . . . .210 A5
Cedar Dr
Chesham HP5 . . . . .144 A1
Cookham Rise SL6. . . . . . .195 F7
Cookham SL6. . . . . .196 A4
Marlow Bottom SL7 . . . . . .183 C7
Cedar Gr
Amersham HP7 . . . . .165 D8
Bellingdon HP5 . . . . .143 D8
Cedar Lodge Dr MK2. . . . .33 D7
Cedar Park Sch HP15 . . . .162 F5
Cedar Rd HP4 . . . . .135 D3
Cedar Ridge HP6 . . . . .153 C5
Cedars Cl
Akeley MK18 . . . . .41 F8
Chalfont St Peter SL9 . . . . .177 E5
Cedars Com Sch MK16 . .22 C4
Cedars Dr UB10. . . . . .201 F3
Cedars Ho SL6. . . . . .203 A7
Cedars Rd SL6. . . . . .203 A7
Cedars The
Berkhamsted HP4 . . . . . . .135 E4
Slough SL1. . . . . .197 F2
Wendover HP22. . . . . .131 A5
Cedars Upper Sch & Com
Coll LU7. . . . . .80 E5
Cedars Village WD3. . . . . .167 F5
Cedars Way
Leighton Buzzard LU7 . . . .80 E5
Newport Pagnell MK16 . . .22 C4
Cedars Wlk WD3. . . . . .167 F5
Cedar Terr ❶ HP11 . . . . .172 F7
Cedar Way
Berkhamsted HP4 . . . . . . .135 D3
Ceely Ho HP21. . . . . .115 D6
Ceely Rd HP21. . . . . .115 D6
Celandine Ct MK7. . . . . . . .48 A5
Celina Cl MK2 . . . . .58 C7
Cell Farm SL4 . . . . .211 B2
Cell Farm Ave SL4 . . . . . . .211 B2
Centenary Bsns Pk
RG9. . . . . .191 F1
Centenary Cotts HP27. . . .138 D7
Centenary Way HP6. . . . . .154 F1
Central Ave
Cranfield MK43 . . . . .24 E2
Whipsnade LU6 . . . . .107 E8
Central Dr SL1. . . . . .204 F6
Central Est SL6 . . . . .202 E7
Central Est SL6 . . . . .202 E8
CENTRAL MILTON
KEYNES. 34 D1
Central Park Bsns Ctr
HP13. . . . . .173 A8
Centre Par HP27 . . . . .139 C5
Centre The SL2. . . . . .198 C6
Centre Wlk HP15. . . . . . . .163 A3
Centurion Ct MK11. . . . . . .33 C2
Centurion Rdbt MK1 . . . . .47 C2
Century Ave
Milton Keynes MK6 . . . . . .46 E7
Oldbrook MK6 . . . . .46 E8
Century Point HP12. . . . . .172 C4
Cestreham Cres HP5 . . . . .144 D2
CHACKMORE. 41 B4
Chacombe Pl HP5. . . . . . . .175 D5
Chadbone Pl HP20 . . . . . .115 D8
Chadds La MK4 . . . . .47 C8
Chadwell Path HP21. . . . . .116 C6
Chadwick Dr MK6. . . . . . . .47 B7
Chadwick St HP13 . . . . . . .162 D2
Chaffinch HP19 . . . . .101 F4
Chaffron Way
Leadenhall MK6. . . . . .46 F7
Milton Keynes, Oakgrove MK6,
MK10, MK15 . . . . .35 D1
Milton Keynes, Shenley Lodge
MK4, MK5, MK6 . . . . . . .46 C5
Chairborough Rd HP12 .172 D6
Chairborough Rd Nature
Reserve★ HP12. . . . . . .172 C5
Chairmakers Cl HP7. . . . .139 A3
Chalcot Pl MK8 . . . . .45 F8
Chalcott SL1. . . . . .205 E3
Chalet Cl HP4. . . . . .134 F4
Chalfont Ave HP6 . . . . . . .166 D8
Chalfont Cl MK13 . . . . . . .34 A6
CHALFONT COMMON . . .177 F6
Chalfont & Gerrards Cross
Com Hospl SL9 . . . . .177 D2
Chalfont Ho HP7. . . . . .166 D7
Chalfont La
Chorleywood WD3. . . . . . .167 B4

Chalfont La continued
Maple Cross WD3 . . . . . . .178 D3
Chalfont & Latimer Sta/U
Sta HP7. . . . . .166 C8
Chalfont L Ctr SL9 . . . . . . .177 C2
Chalfont Rd
Maple Cross SL9 . . . . .178 D3
Seer Green HP9. . . . . .176 D5
CHALFONT ST GILES. 177 C7
Chalfont St Giles Inf Sch
HP8. . . . . .177 B7
Chalfont St Giles Jun Sch
HP8. . . . . .177 C7
CHALFONT ST PETER. 177 F2
Chalfont St Peter Inf Sch
SL9 . . . . .177 C3
Chalfont St Peter Jun Sch
SL9 . . . . .177 D2
Chalfonts Com Coll The
SL9 . . . . .177 C3
Chalfont Station Rd
HP7. . . . . .166 C7
Chalfont Way HP12 . . . . . .172 D3
Chalford HP10. . . . . .185 F6
Chalford Way HP19 . . . . . .116 F8
Chalgrove Cl SL6 . . . . .203 B6
Chalgrove End HP22 . . . . .116 B1
Chalgrove Rd OX9 . . . . . . .126 A1
Chalgrove Wlk HP21. . . . .115 C6
Chalkdell Dr MK5 . . . . . . .45 F4
Chalk Farm Rd HP14. . . . .158 D5
Chalk Hill
Chesham HP5 . . . . .144 B2
Coleshill HP7 . . . . .164 F2
Windsor SL4. . . . . .210 F6
Chalkhill Blue Cl HP19 .101 C4
Chalk La HP6, HP7. . . . . . .153 B4
Chalklands SL6 . . . . .185 A4
Chalkpit La SL7 . . . . .183 B3
Chalk Pit La SL1 . . . . .197 B4
Chalkpits The HP10 . . . . . .185 E6
CHALKSHIRE 130 C4
Chalkshire Cotts HP17. . .130 C4
Chalkshire Rd HP17 . . . . .130 C4
Chalkstream Way HP10 .185 E7
Challacombe MK4 . . . . . . .46 D2
Challener Rd MK2 . . . . . . .172 C3
Challenge Ho MK3 . . . . . .47 B3
Challow Ct SL6. . . . . .195 D1
Chalmers Ave MK19. . . . . .20 D2
Chaloner Pl HP21. . . . . . . .115 D6
Chaloner Rd HP21. . . . . . .115 D6
Chaloners Hill MK18 . . . .63 D3
CHALVEY 205 C3
Chalvey Gdns SL1. . . . . . .205 E4
Chalvey Gr SL1 . . . . .205 E4
Chalvey Road E SL1. . . . . .205 E4
Chalvey Road W SL1. . . . .205 E4
Chalwell Ridge MK5. . . . .46 B4
Chamberlain Rd HP19 . .101 B1
Champflower HP21. . . . . . .46 D3
Champney Cl SL3 . . . . . . .212 A4
Champneys Coll of Health &
Beauty HP23. . . . . .133 E6
Chancellors HP7. . . . . .164 B5
Chancellors Cnr HP7. . . .164 B5
Chancery Cl MK13. . . . . . .34 A6
Chancery Pl SL4 . . . . .210 D7
Chandlers Ct MK6. . . . . . .47 E5
CHANDLERS HILL 200 E3
Chandlers Quay SL6. . . . .203 C8
Chandos Cl
Buckingham MK18. . . . . . .52 D7
Little Chalfont HP6. . . . . . .155 C1
Chandos Mall ❼ SL1. . . . .205 F4
Chandos Pl
Milton Keynes MK2 . . . . . .58 B8
Wendover HP22. . . . . .131 B4
Chandos Rd MK18. . . . . . .52 D8
Channer Dr HP4 . . . . .163 B1
Channory Cl MK4 . . . . . . .46 A1
Chantry Cl
Windsor SL4. . . . . .210 D7
Woburn Sands MK17. . . . .49 B4
Chantry Rd HP19. . . . . . . .101 C3
Chantry Rise ❽ MK46. . . .6 F3
Chantry Specl Sch UB7 .208 E6
Chantry The
⑱ Aylesbury HP20 . . . . .115 D8
Uxbridge UB8. . . . . .201 F7
Chapel Arches SL6. . . . . . .203 A7
Chapel Cl
Blackthorn OX25 . . . . .81 A3
Little Gaddesden HP4 . . . .121 D6
Chapel Cotts SL2 . . . . .199 B5
Chapel Crofts HP4 . . . . . . .134 E6
Chapel Dr HP22. . . . . .117 E5
CHAPEL END 118 C8
Chapel End La HP23. . . . .118 C8
Chapel Farm NN7 . . . . . . .10 C6
Chapel Fields HP23 . . . . . .118 C8
Chapel Hill
Soulbury LU7. . . . . .69 E3
Speen HP27. . . . . .150 C4
Windsor SL4. . . . . .210 D6
Chapel Ho HP6 . . . . .153 C5

Chapel La
Akeley MK18 . . . . .41 F8
Chilton HP18 . . . . .111 B3
Drayton Parslow MK17 . . .68 B5
High Wycombe HP12 . . . . .172 C8
Ivinghoe Aston LU7 . . . . . .92 A1
Long Marston HP23. . . . . .104 B4
Northall LU6. . . . . .92 A5
Pitch Green HP27 . . . . . . .138 B2
Rout's Green HP14. . . . . . .148 E2
St Leonards HP23 . . . . . . .132 D3
Stoke Bruerne NN12 . . . . .9 A8
Stoke Mandeville MK2. . . .116 A1
Stoke Poges SL2 . . . . .199 B5
Thornborough MK18 . . . . .54 B8
Tottenhoe LU6 . . . . .92 F8
Turweston NN13 . . . . .38 B7
Walter's Ash HP14. . . . . . .161 C7
Wendover HP22. . . . . .131 B4
Whitfield NN13 . . . . .26 D3
Chapel Mdw
Flackwell Heath HP10 . . . .185 A8
Ford HP17. . . . . .128 A7
Chapel Row HP14 . . . . . . .171 A7
Chapels Cl SL1. . . . . .204 E5
Chapel Sq LU7 . . . . .68 E1
Chapel St
Berkhamsted HP4 . . . . . . .135 D4
High Wycombe HP13 . . . . .161 D3
Marlow SL7 . . . . .183 E2
Slough SL1. . . . . .205 F4
Tring HP23 . . . . .118 F3
Uxbridge UB8. . . . . .201 C4
Woburn Sands MK17. . . . .49 B4
Chaplin Gr MK8 . . . . .45 D7
Chaplin Mews ❼ SL3. . . .206 F1
Chapman La MK4 . . . . . . .35 A6
Chapman Cl
Aylesbury HP21. . . . . .115 B6
West Drayton UB7. . . . . . .208 F3
Chapman La HP8, HP10 . .185 A6
Chapmans Cres HP5 . . . . .144 A2
Chapmans Lea HP22 . . . . .88 D5
Chappel Mdw HP23 . . . . . .119 B6
Chapter MK6 . . . . .47 A5
Chapter Ct UB10 . . . . .201 F5
Chapter Ho MK6 . . . . .47 A5
Chapter Mews SL4 . . . . . .210 D7
Charbray Cres MK5. . . . . .46 A4
Chardacre MK8 . . . . .33 E1
Charlbury Rd UB10. . . . . . .190 F1
Charles Cl HP21. . . . . .116 B4
Charles Dr OX9 . . . . .126 A1
Charles Gdns SL2. . . . . . .206 A7
Charles Ho
Henley-on-Thames RG9 . .191 E3
❾ Windsor SL4. . . . . . . .210 C6
Charles Pym Rd HP19 . .101 C1
Charles St
Berkhamsted HP4 . . . . . . .135 B4
Tring HP23 . . . . .119 A3
Windsor SL4. . . . . .210 C6
Charlestown Lodge
UB8 . . . . .201 D6
Charles Way MK16. . . . . . .22 C4
Charlewood Ho MK17 . . . .49 B3
Charlock Ct MK16. . . . . . . .21 F4
Charlotte Ave SL2 . . . . . . .205 F6
Charlotte Cl LU7 . . . . .79 F2
Charlotte Cott SL6. . . . . . .203 B8
Charlotte Way ⑫ SL7 . . . .183 E2
Charlton Cl SL4 . . . . .209 C5
Charlton Ct
Slough SL1. . . . . .205 B4
Swanbourne MK17. . . . . . .66 F3
Charlton Pl ⑧ SL4 . . . . . .209 C5
Charlton Row ❺ SL4. . . . .209 C5
Charlton Way SL4 . . . . . . .209 C5
Charlton Wlk ❸ SL4 . . . . .209 C5
Charmfield Rd HP21 . . . . .116 A5
CHARNDON 72 E6
Charnwood Cl ❺ HP13 .173 F5
Charsley Cl HP6. . . . . .166 C8
Charter Cl ❸ SL1 . . . . . . .205 F3
Charter Dr HP6. . . . . .154 F1
Charter Pl UB8 . . . . .201 D5
Charter Rd SL1. . . . . .204 E6
Chartley Ct MK5 . . . . .46 B4
CHARTRIDGE 143 C4
Chartridge Comb Sch
HP5. . . . . .143 C4
Chartridge Development
UB8. . . . . .201 B3
Chartridge Grange Dr
HP5 . . . . .143 D4
Chartridge Ho ❸ HP3 . .173 F6
Chartridge La HP5 . . . . . . .143 F2
Chartridge Park Mobile
Home Pk HP5 . . . . .143 D4
Chartwell Gate HP9 . . . . . .175 D2
Chartwell Rd MK16. . . . . . .22 E4
Chase Ave MK7. . . . . .48 A4
Chase Cl HP7. . . . . .165 A4
Chase Farm Barns MK17 .56 C4
Chase Park Rd NN7 . . . . . .1 A5
Chaseport Cl MK46. . . . . . .5 D2
Chaseside Cl LU7 . . . . . . .105 A7

Chase The
❶ Chesham HP5. . . . . . .144 B2
Maidenhead SL6 . . . . .195 D3
Marlow SL7 . . . . .184 A3
Tylers Green HP10. . . . . . .163 C1
Chasewater Cres MK10. .36 B3
Chatfield SL2. . . . . .205 A8
Chatham Ct ❷ SL1. . . . . . .206 A3
Chatsworth MK8 . . . . .33 F1
Chatsworth Cl SL6 . . . . . . .202 C5
Chaucer Cl
Berkhamsted HP4 . . . . . . .134 F5
Newport Pagnell MK16 . . .22 A4
Windsor SL4 . . . . .210 D4
Chaucer Dr HP21 . . . . . . .115 F6
Chaucer Rd MK3. . . . . .58 A7
Chaucer Way SL1 . . . . . . .205 F5
Chauntry Cl SL6 . . . . .203 C6
Chauntry Rd SL6. . . . . . . .203 C6
Chawton Cres MK8. . . . . . .33 F1
Cheapside La UB9. . . . . . .189 F2
CHEARSLEY 112 A2
Chearsley Rd HP18. . . . . .125 E7
CHEDDINGTON 105 B7
Cheddington Comb Sch
LU7. . . . . .105 A7
Cheddington La LU7 . . . . .104 C5
Cheddington Rd LU7 . . . . .105 A4
Cheddington Sta LU7 . . . .91 A2
Chelmsford Ct ❽ SL4 . . .210 C5
Chelsea Gn LU7. . . . . .80 D6
Chelsea Ho ❻ LU7 . . . . . .80 D6
Chelsea Rd HP19 . . . . . . .100 E1
Cheltenham Gdns MK3 . .57 D6
Cheney Cl LU7 . . . . .78 B1
Cheneys Wlk MK3. . . . . . . .47 A3
Cheney Way HP20 . . . . . .101 E1
Cheney Wlk ❸ HP20 . . . .101 E1
CHENIES 156 B2
Chenies Ave HP6. . . . . . . .156 D8
CHENIES BOTTOM. 156 B2
Chenies Comb Sch
WD3 . . . . .156 B1
Chenies Manor Ho★
WD3 . . . . .156 A1
Chenies Par HP7. . . . . . . .166 C7
Chenies Rd MK3. . . . . .167 D7
Cheniston Gr SL6 . . . . . . .202 A7
Chepping Cl HP10. . . . . . .163 A1
Chepstow Dr MK3. . . . . . . .57 D6
Chequers Bridge Cotts
SL0. . . . . .207 C4
Chequers Cl LU7 . . . . .105 C4
Chequers Ct HP21. . . . . . .115 E4
Chequers Dr HP16 . . . . . .151 C6
Chequers End MK18. . . . .66 A4
Chequers Hill HP7 . . . . . .165 D7
Chequers La
Ibstone HP14, RG9 . . . . . .170 A5
North Crawley MK16 . . . . .24 B6
Pitstone LU7 . . . . .105 C5
Chequers Orch SL0 . . . . . .207 F7
Chequers Sq MK18 . . . . . .201 C5
Chequers The
Castlethorpe MK19 . . . . . .19 F5
Eaton Bray LU6. . . . . .92 F5
Cherington Gate SL6 . . . .195 B1
Cheriton MK4. . . . . .46 E3
Cherleton MK8. . . . . .33 E1
Cherries The SL2 . . . . .206 B7
Cherry Acre SL9 . . . . .177 D6
Cherry Ave SL3 . . . . .206 D4
Cherry Cl
Flackwell Heath HP10 . . . .185 B7
Prestwood HP16 . . . . .151 D6
Cherry Cnr HP10. . . . . . . .185 B8
Cherrycroft Dr HP14 . . . . .161 D6
Cherry Dr HP9 . . . . .175 B4
Cherry Gdns HP23 . . . . . . .118 F3
Cherry Gr HP15 . . . . .163 C6
Cherry La
Amersham HP7 . . . . .165 A7
West Drayton UB7. . . . . . .208 F2
Woodrow HP7. . . . . .164 D6
Cherry Lane Prim Sch
UB7. . . . . .208 F2
Cherry Leys MK18. . . . . . . .63 C3
Cherry Orch
Amersham HP6 . . . . .154 C2
Olney MK46 . . . . .6 E4
Prestwood HP16 . . . . .151 C6
West Drayton UB7. . . . . . .208 E4
Cherry Orchard Ct
HP13 . . . . .173 E6
Cherry Pit The HP13 . . . . .161 E2
Cherry Rd MK16. . . . . .22 B3
Cherry Rise
Chalfont St Giles HP8 . . . .177 D8
Flackwell Heath HP10 . . . .185 B7
Cherry St HP13 . . . . .174 A4
Cherry Tree Ave HP7 . . . . .208 F7
Cherry Tree Cl
Great Kingshill HP15. . . . .151 D1
Hughenden Valley HP14 . .162 A7
Speen HP27. . . . . .150 B5

Cherry Tree Ho ❹ SL7 .183 D2
Cherrytree La
Chalfont St Peter SL9 . . . .177 D1
Iver Heath SL0. . . . . .201 A4
Cherry Tree La
Buckland Common
HP23. . . . . .133 A3
Fulmer SL3. . . . . .199 F6
Herongate WD3 . . . . .167 C1
Lee Common HP16 . . . . . .142 E4
Cherry Tree Rd
Beaconsfield HP9. . . . . . . .175 B1
Chinnor OX39. . . . . .147 C6
Farnham Common SL2 . . .198 C5
Cherry Tree Way HP10 .163 C1
Cherry Tree Wlk
Chesham HP5 . . . . .144 D2
Leighton Buzzard LU7 . . . .80 E7
Wendover HP22. . . . . .131 A5
Cherry Way
Hazelemere HP15 . . . . . . .163 A6
Horton SL3. . . . . .212 C4
Cherrywood Cl HP9. . . . . .176 D5
Cherrywood Gdns
HP10 . . . . .185 B8
Chervil MK6 . . . . .47 B5
Cherwell Cl
Maidenhead SL6 . . . . .203 A8
Slough SL3. . . . . .212 B8
Cherwell Ho MK3 . . . . .57 E8
Cherwell Rd
Aylesbury HP21. . . . . .115 C6
Bourne End SL8 . . . . .185 B4
CHESHAM 154 C8
Chesham Ave MK13 . . . . .34 C3
CHESHAM BOIS. 154 C3
Chesham Bois CE Comb
Sch HP6. . . . . .154 D4
Chesham High Sch
HP5. . . . . .144 D1
Chesham La
Chalfont St Peter SL9 . . . .177 E6
Wendover HP22, HP16. . .141 E8
Chesham L Ctr HP5. . . . . .154 D8
Chesham Mus★ HP5 . . . . .154 B8
Chesham Park Com Coll
HP5. . . . . .144 A1
Chesham Prep Sch
HP5. . . . . .145 A3
Chesham Rd
Amersham HP6 . . . . .154 C2
Ashley Green PH4, PH5. .144 F8
Bellingdon HP5 . . . . .143 E7
Berkhamsted HP4 . . . . . . .135 B2
Bovingdon HP3, HP5. . . . .145 E4
Hyde Heath HP16 . . . . . . .153 C2
Wigginton HP23. . . . . .133 D7
Chesham U Sta HP5. . . . .154 C8
Cheshire Cotts OX27 . . . .72 F6
Cheshire Ct ❽ SL1 . . . . . .206 B4
Cheshire Rise 46 E1
Cheslyn Gdns MK14 . . . . .35 A8
Chesney Wold MK6 . . . . . .46 F5
Chessbury Cl HP5. . . . . . . .154 A7
Chessbury Rd HP5 . . . . . .154 A7
Chess Cl
Aylesbury HP21. . . . . .115 D3
Latimer HP5. . . . . .155 D3
Chessfield Pk HP6 . . . . . . .166 E8
CHESSMOUNT. 154 E7
Chessmount Rise HP5. .154 D6
Chester Cl MK3 . . . . .57 D7
Chesterfield Cl HP17 . . . .114 C5
Chesterfield Cres HP17 .79 E3
Chesterfield Pl HP19 . . . .115 B8
Chester Ho UB8. . . . . .201 C1
Chesterholm MK13. . . . . . .33 F5
Chester Rd SL1. . . . . .205 D2
Chesterton Cl HP5 . . . . . . .144 B2
Chesterton Gn HP9 . . . . . .175 E2
Chestnut Ave
Chesham HP5 . . . . .144 E2
Halton HP22. . . . . .131 D8
High Wycombe HP11 . . . . .173 D5
Slough SL3. . . . . .206 E4
West Drayton UB7. . . . . . .208 F6
Chestnut Cl
Amersham HP6 . . . . .154 D2
Aston Clinton HP22 . . . . . .117 F5
Chalfont St Peter SL9 . . . .177 F2
Dagnall HP4. . . . . .107 C5
Maidenhead SL6 . . . . .196 B1
Medmenham SL7. . . . . . . .193 D2
Milton Keynes MK11 . . . . .32 D5
Monks Risborough HP27 .139 C5
Newton Longville MK17. . .57 D2
Waddesdon HP18 . . . . . . .99 A6
Chestnut Comb Sch
MK3 . . . . .57 E7
Chestnut Cotts MK18. . . .57 E7
Chestnut Cres
Aylesbury HP21. . . . . .115 D6
Milton Keynes MK2 . . . . . .58 D7
Chestnut Ct HP6 . . . . .154 D2
Chestnut Dr
Berkhamsted HP4 . . . . . . .135 D3

Chestnut Dr continued
Windsor SL4 . . . . 209 F3
Chestnut End HP22 . . . . . . 117 C1
Chestnut Gn NN13 . . . . 26 E4
Chestnut Hill LU7 . . . . 80 D8
Chestnut La
Amersham HP6 . . . . 154 E2
Hazelmere HP15 . . . . 163 B5
Chestnut Leys MK18 . . . . . . 63 E3
Chestnut Pk SL6 . . . . 203 E3
Chestnut Rd
Beaconsfield HP9 . . . . . . 175 B1
Princes Risborough
HP27 . . . . 139 C3
Yardley Gobion NN12 . . . . 18 F6
Chestnut Rise LU7 . . . . 80 D8
Chestnuts The
Castlethorpe MK19 . . . . . . 19 F5
Felden HP3 . . . . 146 F2
Uxbridge UB10 . . . . 201 E5
Chestnut View
Chearsley HP18 . . . . 112 B2
East Claydon MK18 . . . . . 74 F7
Chestnut Way
Longwick HP27 . . . . 138 E6
Stoke Mandeville HP22 . . . 116 A1
Chestnut Wlk SL9 . . . . . . 177 E3
Chestwood Gr UB10 . . . . . 201 F5
Chettle Pl NN12 . . . . 18 E2
CHETWODE 61 E8
Chetwode Ave MK10 . . . . . 36 B1
Chetwode Cl MK18 . . . . . . 41 E2
Chetwynd Dr UB10 . . . . . . 201 F3
Chevalier Gr MK8 . . . . 45 D7
Cheveley Gdns SL1 . . . . . . 197 C3
Cheviot Cl
High Wycombe HP13 . . . . 161 E1
Leighton Buzzard LU7 . . . . 80 C8
Maidenhead SL6 . . . . . . 203 B6
Cheviot Rd SL3 . . . . 207 A1
Cheyne Cl
Amersham HP6 . . . . 154 D3
Buckingham MK18 . . . . . . 41 F1
Gerrards Cross SL9 . . . . . 188 E3
Pitstone LU7 . . . . 105 D4
Cheyne Mews HP5 . . . . . . 154 D8
Cheyne Wlk HP5 . . . . 154 D8
CHICHELEY 23 C8
Chicheley Hall MK16 . . . . . 23 D8
Chicheley Hill MK16 . . . . . . 23 A8
Chicheley Rd MK16 . . . . . . 23 E7
Chicheley St MK16 . . . . . . 22 E4
Chichester Cl HP13 . . . . . 173 C6
Chichester Ct SL1 . . . . . . 206 A2
Chicksands Ave MK10 . . . . 36 A2
Chievely Ct MK4 . . . . 46 C1
Chilcote La HP7 . . . . 166 A8
Childs Way MK4, MK5, MK6,
MK10 . . . . 46 C7
Chillery Leys MK15 . . . . . . 35 E7
Chillingham Ct MK5 . . . . . . 46 A4
Chiltern Ave
Amersham HP6 . . . . 154 D1
Edlesborough LU6 . . . . . . 92 E3
High Wycombe HP12 . . . . 172 D6
Stone HP17 . . . . 114 D5
Chiltern Brewery The★
HP17 . . . . 130 C5
Chiltern Bsns Village
UB8 . . . . 201 B3
Chiltern Cl
Berkhamsted HP4 . . . . . . 134 F5
Princes Risborough
HP27 . . . . 139 A3
Stone HP17 . . . . 114 D5
Wendover HP22 . . . . 131 B5
Chiltern Cnr HP4 . . . . 135 A5
Chiltern Commerce Ctr
HP5 . . . . 144 E2
Chiltern Cotts
Buckland Common
HP23 . . . . 133 A2
Ibstone HP14 . . . . 169 D7
Chiltern Court Mews
SL4 . . . . 210 B6
Chiltern Ct
Amersham HP6 . . . . 154 C2
Chesham HP5 . . . . 154 E4
5 High Wycombe HP12 . 172 E7
Wendover HP22 . . . . 131 B4
Windsor SL4 . . . . 210 B6
Winslow MK18 . . . . 65 F3
Chiltern Dr WD3 . . . . 167 F2
Chiltern Gate Sch
HP12 . . . . 172 E4
Chiltern Gn HP10 . . . . . . 185 A8
Chiltern Hill SL9 . . . . 177 E2
Chiltern Hills Rd HP9 . . . . 175 C2
Chiltern Ho HP12 . . . . . . 172 E5
Chiltern Hospl The (private)
HP16 . . . . 152 C4
Chiltern Hts HP17 . . . . . . 166 A8
Chiltern Manor Pk
HP16 . . . . 152 A7

Chiltern Open Air Mus★
HP8 . . . . 177 F8
Chiltern Par HP6 . . . . 154 C2
Chiltern Park Ave HP4 . . . . 135 A6
Chiltern Pools The
HP6 . . . . 154 D1
Chiltern Rd
Amersham HP6 . . . . 154 B4
Ballinger Common HP16 . . 142 E3
Burnham SL1 . . . . 204 B8
Maidenhead SL6 . . . . . . 203 B6
Marlow SL7 . . . . 183 C2
Wendover HP22 . . . . 131 B5
Wingrave HP22 . . . . 89 A3
Chiltern Ridge HP14 . . . . . 158 C4
Chilterns
Berkhamsted HP4 . . . . . . 134 F6
World's End HP22 . . . . . . 130 F7
Chilterns Cl HP10 . . . . . . 185 B7
Chilterns Gateway Ctr★
LU6 . . . . 93 F4
Chilterns Pk SL8 . . . . 185 B5
Chiltern St HP21 . . . . 115 E6
Chilterns The (Sh Ctr)
HP13 . . . . 173 A7
Chiltern Valley Winery &
Brewery★ RG9 . . . . . . 180 F7
Chiltern View HP14 . . . . . 149 C1
Chiltern View Rd UB8 . . . . 201 D3
Chiltern Villas HP23 . . . . . 118 E2
Chiltern Way
Aston Clinton HP22 . . . . . 117 F2
Tring HP23 . . . . 119 C5
CHILTON 111 A4
Chilton Cl
Holmer Green HP15 . . . . . 163 C7
Tylers Green HP10 . . . . . 163 C2
Chilton Ct SL6 . . . . 204 C7
Chilton Pl HP20 . . . . 101 E1
Chilton Rd
Chearsley HP18 . . . . 112 A2
Chesham HP5 . . . . 144 C2
Long Crendon HP18 . . . . . 125 C7
Chilwick Rd SL2 . . . . 197 F1
Chimes Sh Ctr The
UB8 . . . . 201 D5
Chimes The HP12 . . . . . . 172 E6
Chimney La HP10 . . . . . . 185 E8
Chinalls Cl MK18 . . . . 50 D6
Chingle Croft MK4 . . . . . . 46 C2
Chinneck Ho HP4 . . . . . . 135 C4
CHINNOR 147 D7
Chinnor Hill OX39 . . . . . . 147 E4
Chinnor Hill Wildlife
Reserve★ OX39 . . . . . . 147 F5
Chinnor & Princes
Risborough Rly★
OX39 . . . . 147 C7
Chinnor Rd
Bledlow HP27 . . . . 138 A2
Bledlow Ridge HP14 . . . . 148 C3
Chinnor OX39 . . . . 147 A4
Chinnor Sta★ OX39 . . . . . 147 D5
Chippendale Cl HP13 . . . . 162 D1
Chippendale Waye
UB8 . . . . 201 D5
Chippenham Dr MK10 . . . . 36 C1
CHIPPERFIELD 156 F8
Chipperfield Cl MK13 . . . . 34 A7
Chipperfield Rd HP3 . . . . . 146 C3
Chipping Vale MK4 . . . . . . 46 C2
Chipstead SL7 . . . . 177 C2
Chirbury Cl MK10 . . . . 35 F1
CHISBRIDGE CROSS 182 D6
Chislehampton MK15 . . . . 35 C3
Chiswick Cl MK4 . . . . 46 C1
Chiswick Lodge **6** SL7 . 183 D2
CHIVERY 132 C4
Choke La SL6 . . . . 195 B4
CHOLESBURY 133 C3
Cholesbury La HP23 . . . . . 133 A2
Cholesbury Rd HP23 . . . . 133 D5
Chorley Rd HP14 . . . . 160 E3
CHORLEYWOOD 167 D5
CHORLEYWOOD
BOTTOM 167 C3
Chorleywood Bottom
WD3 . . . . 167 D4
Chorleywood Comm Nature
Reserve★ WD3 . . . . . . 167 E5
Chorleywood Ho WD3 . . . . 167 E6
Chorleywood House Dr
WD3 . . . . 167 E6
Chorleywood House Est
Nature Reserve★
WD3 . . . . 167 F6
Chorleywood Montessori
Sch The WD3 . . . . 167 E7
Chorleywood Prim Sch
WD3 . . . . 167 C3
Chorleywood Sta/U Sta
WD3 . . . . 167 D5
CHORLEYWOOD
WEST 167 A4
Christine Cl TW19 . . . . . . 213 D1
Christchurch CE Prim Sch
WD3 . . . . 167 F6
Christchurch Gr MK12 . . . . 33 B6

Christchurch Ho **15** 119 A3
Christchurch Rd HP23 . . . . 118 F4
Christian Ct MK15 . . . . 35 D7
Christian Smith Ho
SL6 . . . . 202 A1
Christian Sq **4** SL4 . . . 210 C6
Christie Cl MK16 . . . . 22 A5
Christies Ct **2** HP13 . . . 173 B7
Christine Ho **3** MK2 . . . . 58 C8
CHRISTMAS COMMON . . . 168 B7
Christmas La **1** SL2 . . . 198 C8
Christopher Cl HP14 . . . . . 161 D7
Christopher Ho **3** SL2 . . 198 C7
Christ the Sower
Ecumenical Prim Sch
MK8 . . . . 45 D6
Church Ave RG9 . . . . 191 E2
Church Cl
Aston Clinton HP22 . . . . . 117 D5
Cuddington HP18 . . . . . . 112 F3
Eton SL4 . . . . 210 D8
Maidenhead SL6 . . . . . . 202 D6
Maids Moreton MK18 . . . . 41 F3
Uxbridge UB8 . . . . 201 B3
West Drayton UB7 . . . . . . 208 E3
Wicken MK19 . . . . 31 B3
Church Cotts SL6 . . . . . . 196 E2
Church Croft LU6 . . . . 92 E3
Church Ct
Aylesbury HP22 . . . . 116 B2
High Wycombe HP13 . . . . 162 D1
Church Dr SL6 . . . . 203 C4
CHURCH END
Chorley Wood 156 F1
Drayton Parslow 68 B5
Haddenham 127 A5
Hanslope 11 A2
Long Crendon 125 C7
Pitstone 105 D3
Steeple Claydon 63 E2
Totternhoe 93 B7
Church End
Adstock MK18 . . . . 53 F1
Bledlow HP27 . . . . 138 B1
Drayton Parslow MK17 . . . 68 B5
Edlesborough LU6 . . . . . . 92 E3
Haddenham HP17 . . . . . 127 A5
Hillesden MK18 . . . . 63 B6
Leckhampstead MK18 . . . 42 D8
Newton Longville MK17 . . 57 D3
Pottersbury NN12 . . . . . . 18 E3
Sherington MK16 . . . . . . 14 A2
Syresham NN13 . . . . 27 C8
Wavendon MK17 . . . . 48 E7
Church End Cotts WD3 . . . 156 F1
Church End Farm LU6 . . . . 93 B7
Church End Rd MK5 . . . . . 46 A4
Church Farm Cl HP22 . . . . 102 B3
Church Farm Cres MK14 . . 34 E8
Church Farm Ho HP8 . . . . 177 C7
Church Farm La HP23 . . . . 104 F3
Churchfield Mews SL2 . . . 206 A7
Churchfield Rd SL9 . . . . . 177 D2
Churchgates **3** HP4 . . . 135 C4
Church Gn
Long Crendon HP18 . . . . . 125 C7
Totternhoe LU6 . . . . 93 B7
Church Gr
Little Chalfont HP6 . . . . . 166 E8
Slough SL3 . . . . 206 C8
Church Green Rd MK3 . . . . 58 A8
Church Headland La
HP22 . . . . 87 A6
CHURCH HILL 56 A8
Church Hill
Akeley MK18 . . . . 41 F8
Aspley Guise MK17 . . . . . 49 E5
Cheddington LU7 . . . . . . 105 A4
Ellesborough HP17 . . . . . 130 B2
Milton Keynes MK8 . . . . . 33 F2
Pishill RG9 . . . . 179 F7
South Harefield UB9 . . . . 190 C8
Whaddon MK17 . . . . 45 B1
Church Holt The SL2 . . . . 187 E3
Churchill Ave HP21 . . . . . 115 D5
Churchill Cl HP10 . . . . . . 185 B7
Churchill Ct **1** HP21 . . . 115 E7
Churchill Dr
Beaconsfield HP9 . . . . . . 175 C5
Marlow SL7 . . . . 183 E2
Churchill Ho UB7 . . . . . . 208 D6
Churchill Rd SL3 . . . . . . 206 F2
Church La
Alderton NN12 . . . . 9 A2
Aston Clinton HP22 . . . . . 117 D4
Berkhamsted HP4 . . . . . . 135 C4
Bisham SL7 . . . . 194 D7
Bledlow Ridge HP14 . . . . 159 F8
Bovingdon HP3 . . . . 146 B4
Bray SL6 . . . . 203 C4
Chalfont St Peter SL9 . . . 177 D2
Chearsley HP18 . . . . 112 B1
Cheddington LU7 . . . . . . 105 A8
Chinnor OX39 . . . . 147 D6
Clifton Reynes MK46 . . . . 7 C3
Cryers Hill HP15 . . . . . . 162 C4
Deanshanger MK19 . . . . . 31 E4
Eaton Bray LU6 . . . . 92 E6

Church La continued
Edgcott HP18 . . . . 72 F2
Emberton MK46 . . . . 13 F7
Grafton Regis NN12 . . . . . 9 D2
Granborough MK18 . . . . . 75 F6
Great Horwood MK17 . . . . 55 A3
Great Kimble HP17 . . . . . 129 E1
Great Missenden HP16 . . . 152 B7
Hastoe HP23 . . . . 132 F7
Horton-cum-S OX33 . . . . 108 A5
Lacey Green HP27 . . . . . 149 E4
Lillingstone Lovell MK18 . . 30 A6
Ludgershall HP18 . . . . . . 96 C7
Marsworth HP23 . . . . . . 104 F1
Milton Keynes MK5 . . . . . 46 B8
Mixbury NN13 . . . . 38 D1
Mursley MK17 . . . . 67 D5
Newport Pagnell MK16 . . . 22 D7
Oving HP22 . . . . 86 C7
Padbury MK18 . . . . 53 C2
Pottersbury NN12 . . . . . . 18 E3
Princes Risborough
HP27 . . . . 139 B4
Radnage HP14 . . . . 159 D8
Sarratt WD3 . . . . 156 F1
Slough SL2, SL3 . . . . . . 206 C8
Soulbury LU7 . . . . 69 E2
Stoke Bruerne NN12 . . . . 9 A8
Stoke Goldington MK16 . . 12 A7
Stoke Poges SL2 . . . . . . 198 F2
Thornborough MK18 . . . . 54 A8
Tingewick MK18 . . . . 51 B7
Upper Winchendon HP18 . 99 B1
Uxbridge UB8 . . . . 201 B3
Walter's Ash HP14 . . . . . 161 E6
Walton MK7 . . . . 47 F6
Wendover HP22 . . . . 131 C3
Weston Turville HP22 . . . 116 F1
West Wycombe HP14 . . . . 161 A2
Whaddon MK17 . . . . 45 B1
Whitchurch HP22 . . . . . . 87 A6
Wicken MK19 . . . . 31 B3
8 Windsor SL4 . . . . . . 210 D6
Yardley Hastings NN7 . . . . 1 B7
Church Lees MK11 . . . . . . 21 D1
Churchmead CE Sch
SL3 . . . . 211 B7
Churchmere Wlk HP21 . . . 115 C6
Church Pas MK16 . . . . . . 22 D4
Church Path
Cheddington LU7 . . . . . . 91 A1
Cublington LU7 . . . . 78 B1
Lane End HP14 . . . . 171 B4
Prestwood HP16 . . . . . . 151 D5
Stokenchurch HP14 . . . . 158 D5
Church Piece HP18 . . . . . 112 B2
Church Rd
Aspley Heath MK17 . . . . . 49 B3
Bow Brickhill MK17 . . . . . 48 D1
Brackley NN13 . . . . 38 A7
Chinnor OX39 . . . . 147 D6
Cookham Dean SL6 . . . . . 195 B6
Farnham Royal SL2 . . . . . 198 C2
Ickford HP18 . . . . 123 F3
Iver Heath SL0 . . . . 200 C3
Ivinghoe LU7 . . . . 105 F5
Lane End HP14 . . . . 171 B3
Leighton Buzzard LU7 . . . 80 E6
Lewknor OX49 . . . . 157 B8
Little Gaddesden HP4 . . . 121 D8
Little Marlow SL7 . . . . . . 184 C5
Maidenhead SL6 . . . . . . 203 B5
Old Windsor SL4 . . . . . . 211 B2
Penn HP10 . . . . 174 E7
Pitstone LU7 . . . . 105 E3
Seer Green HP9 . . . . . . 176 D4
Sherington MK16 . . . . . . 13 F2
Slapton LU7 . . . . 91 D6
South Harefield UB9 . . . . 190 C8
Stoke Hammond MK17 . . . 69 D8
Stokenchurch HP14 . . . . 158 D5
Thame OX9 . . . . 125 E1
Totternhoe LU6 . . . . 93 B6
Tylers Green HP10 . . . . . 174 C8
Uxbridge UB8 . . . . 201 D1
West Drayton UB7 . . . . . . 208 E3
Church Row SL3 . . . . 199 D8
Churchside HP15 . . . . . . 163 D7
Church Sq
9 High Wycombe
HP11 . . . . 173 B7
Leighton Buzzard LU7 . . . 80 F6
Church St
Amersham HP7 . . . . 165 B7
Aspley Guise MK17 . . . . . 49 E5
16 Aylesbury HP20 . . . . 115 C8
Bovingdon HP3 . . . . 146 B4
Brill HP18 . . . . 110 B8
Buckingham MK18 . . . . . . 52 C8
Burnham SL1 . . . . 197 C1
Chesham HP5 . . . . 154 B7
Gawcott MK18 . . . . 52 A5
Great Missenden HP16 . . . 152 B7
Henley-on-Thames RG9 . . 191 D1
High Wycombe HP11 . . . . 173 B7
Little Horwood MK17 . . . . 55 E2
Maids Moreton MK18 . . . . 41 F3
Marsh Gibbon OX27 . . . . 71 F3

Church St continued
Milton Keynes, Fenny Stratford
MK2 . . . . 47 E1
Milton Keynes, New Bradwell
MK13 . . . . 33 F7
Milton Keynes, Stony Stratford
MK11 . . . . 32 D5
Milton Keynes, Wolverton
MK12 . . . . 33 D7
North Marston MK18 . . . . 76 B2
6 Olney MK46 . . . . 6 F3
Olney MK46 . . . . 7 A3
Princes Risborough
HP27 . . . . 139 B3
Quainton HP22 . . . . 85 B5
Slough, Chalvey SL1 . . . . 205 D4
Slough, Upton Park SL1 . . 205 F4
Stokenchurch HP14 . . . . 158 D5
Twyford MK18 . . . . 62 C2
6 Windsor SL4 . . . . . . 210 D6
Wing LU7 . . . . 79 E2
Wingrave HP22 . . . . 89 B2
Winslow MK18 . . . . 65 F4
Church Terr
Turvey MK43 . . . . 8 E5
Windsor SL4 . . . . 209 E5
Church View
Brackley NN13 . . . . 38 A7
Edlesborough LU6 . . . . . . 92 D3
Halton HP22 . . . . 117 C1
Long Marston HP23 . . . . . 104 A4
Newport Pagnell MK16 . . . 22 D4
9 Slough SL1 . . . . 206 A3
Steeple Claydon MK18 . . . 63 E2
Church View Ct LU7 . . . . . 80 E6
Church Views SL6 . . . . . . 202 F8
Churchway HP17 . . . . . . 127 A6
Church Way
East Claydon MK18 . . . . . 74 F8
Stone HP17 . . . . 114 C5
Church Wlk
Milton Keynes MK3 . . . . . 57 F7
North Crawley MK16 . . . . 24 B6
Weston Turville HP22 . . . 116 F1
Wing LU7 . . . . 79 E2
Winslow MK18 . . . . 65 F4
Church Yd HP23 . . . . 119 A3
Chyne The SL9 . . . . 188 F6
Cinnamon Cl SL4 . . . . . . 209 F6
Cinnamon Gr MK7 . . . . . . 48 A5
CIPPENHAM 204 F4
Cippenham Cl SL1 . . . . . 204 F6
Cippenham Inf Sch
SL1 . . . . 204 D6
Cippenham Jun Sch
SL1 . . . . 204 D6
Cippenham La SL1 . . . . . 205 B5
City Rd HP14 . . . . 159 D6
Clailey Ct MK11 . . . . 32 F5
Claires Court Sch SL6 . . . 196 B1
Clammas Way UB8 . . . . . 208 D8
Clapham Pl MK3 . . . . 34 C2
Clappers Mdw SL6 . . . . . 196 B1
Clappins La
Naphill HP14 . . . . 150 D1
Walter's Ash HP14 . . . . . 161 C8
Clapton App HP10 . . . . . 185 D8
Clare Croft MK10 . . . . 36 A3
Clare Ct SL2 . . . . 198 B8
Clarefield Cl SL6 . . . . . . 195 B1
Clarefield Dr SL6 . . . . . . 195 A1
Clarefield Rd SL6 . . . . . . 195 A1
Claremont SL3 . . . . 212 D6
Claremont Ave MK11 . . . . 32 E4
Claremont Ct HP21 . . . . . 115 F5
Claremont Gdns SL7 . . . . 183 E2
Claremont Rd
Marlow SL7 . . . . 183 E2
Windsor SL4 . . . . 210 A5
Clarence Cres SL4 . . . . . 210 C6
Clarence Ct
9 High Wycombe
HP13 . . . . 173 B7
Maidenhead SL6 . . . . . . 202 E8
Windsor SL4 . . . . 210 B6
Clarence Ho **2** MK9 . . . . 34 C2
Clarence Rd
Berkhamsted HP4 . . . . . . 135 C4
Henley-on-Thames RG9 . . 191 D2
Milton Keynes MK11 . . . . 32 E5
Windsor SL4 . . . . 210 B6
Clarendon Copse SL6 . . . 202 D6
Clarendon Ct
Slough SL2 . . . . 206 B6
Windsor SL4 . . . . 210 B6
Clarendon Dr
Milton Keynes MK8 . . . . . 33 F2
Thame OX9 . . . . 126 A1
Clarendon Rd
High Wycombe HP13 . . . . 173 E5
Prestwood HP16 . . . . . . 151 B6
Clare Park HP27 . . . . 165 E7
Clare Rd
Maidenhead SL6 . . . . . . 202 B6
Prestwood HP16 . . . . . . 151 C6
Slough SL3 . . . . 204 C7
Stanwell TW19 . . . . 213 E1
Claridge Dr MK10 . . . . . . 36 A2
Clarke Ct HP20 . . . . 101 F2

Clarke Dr HP13 . . . . .174 A6
Clarke Rd MK1. . . . . .47 D4
Clarkes Dr U88 . . . . .208 E8
Clarkes Field Cl HP18 . .110 B8
Clarkes Orch MK16. . . . . .12 B5
Clarke's Spring HP23. . .119 F5
Clarke Wlk 2 HP20 . . . .101 F2
Clarks Cotts HP16. . . . . .151 C7
Classon Cl UB7 . . . . .208 E4
Clauds Cl HP15 . . . . .163 A5
Claverton Cl HP3 . . . . . .146 A3
Clay Acre HP5 . . . . .144 D1
Clay Cl HP10. . . . . .185 B8
Claycots Prim Sch S2 . .198 A1
Claycutters MK18 . . . . . . .66 A4
Claydon Cl HP21. . . . . . .115 D6
Claydon Ct HP12. . . . . . .172 C4
Claydon End SL9. . . . . . .188 E8
Claydon Ho★ MK18 . . . .74 C7
Claydon Path HP21. . . . .115 C6
Claydons Pl HP27. . . . . .138 D7
Clayfield Rd HP22. . . . . .131 C6
Clayfields HP10. . . . . . . .163 C2
Clayhall La SL1 . . . . .210 F2
Clayhill
  Marlow Bottom SL7. . . .172 A2
  Wigginton HP23 . . . . . .133 E7
Clay Hill MK8 . . . . .33 E2
Clay La
  Calvert MK18. . . . . .73 A5
  Marlow Bottom SL7. . . .172 A2
  Wendover HP22 . . . . . .131 C5
Claymoor Pk SL7 . . . . . .172 A2
Clay Pit La 9 MK46 . . . . . .6 F3
Clays La MK17 . . . . .55 C2
Clay St HP7, HP9 . . . . . .175 C4
Clays The HP17 . . . . .127 A7
Clayton Cl SL3 . . . . .207 A3
Clayton Gate MK14 . . . . .35 A8
Claytons Comb Sch
  SL8 . . . . .185 A5
Claytons Mdw SL8 . . . . .185 B2
Clayton Way U88 . . . . . .201 D2
Clayton Wlk HP7. . . . . . .166 C8
Clearbrook Cl HP13 . . . .174 B4
Cleares Pasture SL1 . . . .197 B2
Cleavers OX39 . . . . .147 B6
Cleavers Ave MK14. . . . . .34 E3
Cleeve Cres MK3. . . . . . . .47 A2
Clegg Sq MK5 . . . . .46 A5
Clement Ave HP15. . . . . .163 D7
Clement Pl 7 HP23 . . . .119 A3
Clements Cl 5 SL1. . . . .206 B4
Cleland Rd SL9 . . . . .177 D1
Clements Ct MK14 . . . . . .34 F4
Clements Rd
  Chorleywood WD3. . . . .167 D4
  Henley-on-Thames RG9. .191 C3
Clerkenwell Cotts
  HP17 . . . . .126 F5
Clerkenwell Pl MK6 . . . . .35 B2
Clevehurst Cl SL2. . . . . .199 A6
Cleveland Cl
  Maidenhead SL6 . . . . . .203 B6
  Wooburn Green HP10 . .185 E8
Cleveland Dr LU7 . . . . . . .80 C8
Cleveland Pk
  Aylesbury HP20 . . . . . .101 F3
  Stanwell TW19 . . . . . . .213 E1
Cleveland Rd 7 HP20. .101 F3
Cleveland Rd
  Aylesbury HP20 . . . . . .101 F3
  Uxbridge U88. . . . . . . .201 D2
Cleves Cl SL4 . . . . .209 F4
Clewer Ave SL4 . . . . .210 A5
Clewer Court Rd SL4 . . .210 B7
Clewer Fields SL4. . . . . .210 C6
CLEWER GREEN 209 E3
Clewer Green CE Fst Sch
  SL4 . . . . .210 A4
Clewer Hill Rd SL4. . . . .209 F4
CLEWER NEW TOWN . . .210 A5
Clewer New Rd SL4 . . . .210 A5
Clewer Pk SL4 . . . . .210 A7
CLEWER VILLAGE 210 A7
Clicker Yd MK46 . . . . .6 F4
Clifden Rd HP18 . . . . . . .123 E5
Clifford Ave MK2. . . . . . . .58 C7
Clifford Rd HP27 . . . . . .139 B3
Cliffords Way SL8 . . . . . .185 B5
Clifton Bsns Pk HP19. . .101 B1
Clifton Cl SL6. . . . . .203 A4
Clifton Ct
  High Wycombe HP11. . . .172 E4
  Olney MK46 . . . . .7 A3
  8 Stanwell TW19 . . . . .213 E1
Clifton Gn HP19. . . . . . .101 B2
Clifton Lawns HP6 . . . . .154 C4
Clifton Lodge
  Eton Wick SL4 . . . . . . .205 A1
  7 Slough SL1 . . . . .206 A4
Clifton Moor MK5 . . . . . . .45 D5
Clifton Rd
  Amersham HP6 . . . . . . .154 C4
  Newton Blossomville MK43 . .8 A4
  5 Slough SL1 . . . . .206 A4
CLIFTON REYNES 7 C3

Clifton Rise SL4. . . . . . . .209 D6
Cline Ct MK14. . . . . .45 E6
Clinkard Pl HP14. . . . . . .171 A3
Clinton Cres HP21 . . . . .116 A8
Clipstone Brook Way 4
  MK10. . . . . .36 B3
Clive Ct SL1 . . . . .205 D4
Cliveden★ SL6 . . . . .196 E7
Cliveden Gate SL1 . . . . .197 B3
Cliveden Mead SL6. . . . .196 C2
Cliveden Office Village
  HP12. . . . . .172 E4
Cliveden Rd SL6 . . . . . . .196 E4
Clivemont Rd SL6. . . . . .202 F8
Clock Ho The MK17 . . . . .59 D6
Clockhouse Mews
  WD3. . . . . .167 A4
Cloebury Paddock MK15. .35 C3
Cloister Garth HP4 . . . . .135 C4
Cloisters The
  High Wycombe HP13 . . .162 D2
  Slough SL1 . . . . .205 D4
Clonmel Way SL1 . . . . . .197 B2
Closes The HP17 . . . . . . .127 A7
Close The
  Akeley MK18 . . . . .42 A8
  Ashendon HP18. . . . . . . .97 F1
  Bierton HP22. . . . . .102 A4
  Bourne End SL8 . . . . . .185 A6
  Great Horwood MK17 . . .55 B3
  Hardmead MK16 . . . . . . .15 D4
  Hardwick HP22 . . . . .87 B3
  Iver Heath SL0. . . . . . . .200 C2
  Lathbury MK16. . . . . . . .22 D7
  Milton Keynes, Bradwell
    MK13. . . . . .34 A4
  Milton Keynes, The Green
    MK6. . . . . .47 D2
  Newton Blossomville MK43. .7 F3
  Ravenstone MK46 . . . . . .5 E2
  Slough SL1 . . . . .204 D6
  Weston Underwood MK46. .6 A1
Cloudberry MK7 . . . . .48 A6
Cloutsham Cl MK4 . . . . . .46 D3
Clover Cl MK5 . . . . .46 B8
Clover End MK18. . . . . . . .52 C7
Clover La HP21 . . . . .115 E5
Club Cotts MK17 . . . . .49 B4
Cluny Ct MK7 . . . . .48 D6
Clyde Pl MK3 . . . . .46 E1
Clydesdale Dr MK14 . . . . .34 F4
Coach Ho The
  Loudwater HP11 . . . . . .174 A4
  Wooburn Green HP10 . .185 E8
Coachmaker Ct MK14 . . . .34 F6
Coachman's Lodge SL4 .210 D5
Coach Ride SL7. . . . . . . .183 D4
Coach Yd NN12 . . . . .18 E3
Coalmans Way SL1. . . . .204 A8
Coaters La HP10 . . . . . . .185 E7
Coates La HP13. . . . . . . .162 A1
Coat Wicks HP9. . . . . . . .176 C4
Cobb Cl SL3 . . . . .211 D6
Cobbetts Mount MK18. . .63 D2
Cobbetts Ride HP23 . . . .118 F3
Cobb Hall Rd MK17. . . . . .57 C3
Cobblers Cl SL2. . . . . . . .198 B3
Cobblershill La MK18 . . .141 B4
Cobblers Wick HP22 . . . .89 B3
Cobb Rd HP4 . . . . .134 F4
Cobbs Gdn MK46. . . . . . . .6 F4
Cobden Cl U88 . . . . .201 C4
Coberley Cl MK15. . . . . . .35 B6
Cobham Cl
  Buckingham MK18. . . . . .41 C1
  Slough SL1 . . . . .204 F5
Cochran Cl MK8 . . . . .45 E7
Cochrane Ho U88. . . . . . .201 C4
Cockerell Gr MK5. . . . . . .46 C5
Cockett Rd SL3 . . . . .206 E3
Cock Gr HP4. . . . . .134 D4
Cock La HP10 . . . . .174 A6
Cockpit Cl HP15 . . . . . . .151 E1
Cockpit Rd HP15 . . . . . .162 D8
Cockshett Wood Nature
  Reserve★ SL2 . . . . .197 C2
Coddimoor La MK17. . . . .56 B7
CODMORE 144 E1
Codmore Cres HP5. . . . .144 E1
Codmore Cross HP5. . . .144 D1
Codmore Wood Rd
  HP5 . . . . .155 D6
Coe Spur SL1 . . . . .205 B3
COFFEE HALL 47 D2
Coffee Hall Rdbt MK6 . . .47 B6
Cofferidge Cl MK11 . . . . .32 D5
Coftards SL2. . . . . .206 C7
Cogan Cl MK8 . . . . .45 E7
Cogdells Cl HP5 . . . . . . .143 B4
Cogdells La HP5 . . . . . . .143 B4
Coggeshall Gr MK7. . . . . .48 C7
Coin Cl MK10 . . . . .35 F3
Cokers Ct 3 SL8. . . . . . .185 A4
Coke's Farm La HP8. . . .166 B6
Coke's La HP8 . . . . .166 B6
Colborne Rd HP13 . . . . .173 D8
Colby Gdns 1 SL6 . . . . .202 F8
Colchester Ct MK3 . . . . . .57 E7

Colchester Wlk MK3 . . . . .57 E7
COLD BRAYFIELD 8 B5
Coldeaton La MK4 . . . . . .46 B3
Cold Grove Cotts SL6. . .196 E2
Coldharbour HP22 . . . . .131 C4
Cold Harbour CE Comb Sch
  MK3 . . . . .46 A3
Coldharbour Way
  HP19 . . . . .115 A7
Coldmoorholme La
  SL8. . . . . .184 E4
Coldmoreham Yd HP7 . .165 A8
Colehatth Bottom
  HP27 . . . . .150 C5
Colenorton Cres SL4 . . .204 E2
Cole Rd HP21 . . . . .115 C5
Coleridge Cl
  Milton Keynes MK3 . . . . .58 A7
  Newport Pagnell MK16 . .21 F4
Coleridge Cres SL3 . . . .212 E6
Coleridge Way UB7 . . . . .208 F2
Coles Ave MK6. . . . . .46 F6
Colesbourne Dr MK15. . .35 B6
COLESHILL. 164 F3
Coles Hill HP18 . . . . .111 B3
Coleshill CE Inf Sch
  HP7. . . . . .164 F3
Coleshill Ho HP7. . . . . . .165 A4
Coleshill La HP7 . . . . . . .164 D2
Coleshill Pl MK13 . . . . . . .34 C3
Colet Rd HP22 . . . . .131 C5
Colgrain St MK9 . . . . .35 A4
Colham Ave UB7 . . . . . . .208 E5
Colham Mill Rd UB7. . . .208 D5
Colham Rd UB8. . . . . . . .201 F1
Colindale St MK10 . . . . . .35 E1
Colinswood SL2 . . . . . . .187 B1
Colin Way SL1 . . . . .205 B3
College Ave
  Maidenhead SL6 . . . . . .202 F2
  Slough SL1 . . . . .205 E3
College Bsns Pk HP22. .103 C1
College Cres
  Oakley HP18 . . . . .109 E4
  Windsor SL4 . . . . .210 B5
College Glen SL6 . . . . . .202 D7
College Lake Wildlife
  Reserve★ HP23 . . . . . .105 C1
College Rd
  Cranfield MK43 . . . . .24 E2
  Maidenhead SL6 . . . . . .202 E7
  Slough SL1 . . . . .204 F5
College Rise SL6. . . . . . .202 D7
College Road N HP22. . .117 C6
College The OX27 . . . . . . .71 F3
College The (Claires Court
  Schs) SL6 . . . . .202 E7
Colley Hill MK3 . . . . .34 A4
Colley Hill La SL2 . . . . . .187 F1
Colley Ho U88 . . . . .201 D4
Colleyland WD3. . . . . . . .167 D5
Collier Cl SL6. . . . . .195 F1
Colliers Wood MK10 . . . . .35 E8
Collings Walk HP16 . . . .151 C5
Collingwood Cl HP13. . . .174 A6
Collins Ho 2 HP11. . . . .173 A7
Collins Wlk MK16 . . . . . . .22 A4
Collinswood Rd SL2 . . . .187 B2
Collum Green Rd SL2 . .187 E1
Collyer Rd HP14 . . . . . . .158 E4
COLNBROOK 212 D7
Colnbrook By-Pass
  Colnbrook SL3 . . . . .212 D7
  Harmondsworth UB7. . .213 C4
Colnbrook CE Prim Sch
  SL3 . . . . .212 D6
Colnbrook Ct SL3 . . . . . .212 F6
Colndale Rd SL3 . . . . . . .212 E5
Colne MK6 . . . . .47 D6
Colne Ave UB7 . . . . .208 C4
Colnedale Rd UB8. . . . . .201 D7
Colne Orch SL0 . . . . .207 F6
Colne Park Cvn Site
  UB7 . . . . .208 C2
Colne Rd HP13. . . . . . . .173 F7
Colne Reach TW19 . . . . .212 F2
Colne Valley Park Visitor
  Ctr★ UB9. . . . . .190 B1
Coln Trad Est SL3 . . . . . .212 F6
Colonel Grantham Ave
  HP19 . . . . .101 D4
Colonial Rd 1 SL1. . . . .206 A4
Colonnade SL6 . . . . .203 A7
Colossus Way MK3. . . . . .47 A1
Colsons Way MK46. . . . . .6 F5
Colston Bassett MK4 . . . .46 C1
Colston Ct SL3 . . . . .188 E5
COLSTROPE. 181 D5
Coltman Ave HP18 . . . . .125 C6
Coltsfoot Dr HP27. . . . . .208 E2
Coltsfoot Pl MK14. . . . . . .34 D3
Colts Holm Rd MK12 . . . .33 C8
Columbia Pl MK9 . . . . . . .35 A3
Columbine Rd HP15. . . .162 F6

Colville Ct HP16 . . . . . . .152 B7
Colville Rd HP11 . . . . . . .172 F6
COMBE. 130 C1
Combe Martin MK4 . . . . . .46 D3
Combe Rise HP12. . . . . .172 B7
Combermere Cl SL4. . . .210 B5
Combes Cres MK6 . . . . . .46 F6
Comerford Way MK18. . . .66 A5
Comfrey Cl MK7 . . . . .48 A5
Comfrey The 2 HP19 . .101 E4
Common Gate Rd WD3 .167 A4
Common La
  Eton SL4 . . . . .205 D1
  Hedgerley SL1. . . . . . . .186 D1
  Milton Keynes, Bradwell
    MK13. . . . . .34 A4
  Milton Keynes MK5 . . . . .46 C8
Common Rd
  Chorleywood WD3 . . . . .167 D5
  Dagnall LU6 . . . . .107 F3
  Dorney SL4 . . . . .204 D2
  Eton Wick SL4 . . . . . . .205 A2
  Flackwell Heath HP10 . .185 B8
  Great Kingshill HP15 . . .151 D1
  Slough SL3 . . . . .207 A1
Commonside HP13. . . . .161 E3
Common St MK46 . . . . . . .5 D1
COMMON THE 55 B4
Common The
  Berkhamsted HP4 . . . . .135 F6
  Chipperfield WD4. . . . . .156 F7
  Flackwell Heath HP10 . .185 B8
  Great Kingshill HP15 . . .151 D1
  Holmer Green HP15. . . .158 E5
  Stokenchurch HP14 . . . .158 E5
  West Drayton UB7. . . . .208 C2
Common Wood SL2 . . . .198 C8
Common Wood La
  HP10 . . . . .163 E1
Como Rd HP20. . . . . . . .116 B8
Compass Point MK4 . . . . .46 E6
Comp Gate LU6 . . . . .92 E6
Comp The LU6. . . . . .92 E6
Compton Ct
  Moulsoe MK16. . . . . .36 D8
  Slough SL1 . . . . .204 B8
Compton Dr SL6 . . . . . . .202 A8
Compton Rd HP22 . . . . .131 D5
Concorde Cl UB10 . . . . . .201 E3
Concorde Rd SL6 . . . . . .202 D4
Concorde Way SL1. . . . .205 C4
Concourse The 6 MK2. .58 C8
Concra Pk MK17 . . . . .49 C4
Concrete Cows★ MK13. .33 F4
Condor Cl MK9 . . . . .47 A8
Conduit La SL3 . . . . .206 E1
Conegar Ct SL1. . . . . . . .205 E5
Conegra Ct 15 HP13 . .172 F7
Conegra Rd HP13 . . . . .173 C7
Coneygere MK46. . . . . . . .7 A3
Congreve MK5. . . . . .47 D5
Conifer Rise HP12. . . . . .172 E6
Conifers The HP12. . . . . .202 A8
Conigre OX39 . . . . .147 B6
Coningsby Cl SL6 . . . . . .202 D3
Coningsby Ct HP13. . . . .173 B8
Coningsby Rd HP13 . . . .162 B1
Coniston Cres SL3 . . . . .204 C8
Coniston Gn HP20. . . . . .101 D3
Coniston Rd LU7. . . . . . . .80 C7
Coniston Way MK2. . . . . .58 D6
Conkers SL6. . . . . .203 B8
Connaught Cl SL6. . . . . .195 E1
Connaught Gdns HP4 . .134 C7
Connaught Rd
  Aylesbury HP20 . . . . . .116 C8
  3 Slough SL1 . . . . .206 B4
CONNIBURROW 34 E4
Conniburrow Bvd MK14 .34 E4
Conniston Ct SL7 . . . . . .183 B2
Conought Ho RG9. . . . . .191 E3
Constable Cl MK14 . . . . . .34 F7
Constable Pl HP19 . . . . .100 F2
Constable's Croft OX25. .94 E7
Constantine Pl UB10 . . .201 F4
Constantine Way MK13. . .33 F5
Convent Ct HP23. . . . . . .118 F3
Convent Rd SL4 . . . . . . .210 A5
Conway Cl
  Aylesbury HP21 . . . . . .115 F7
  Loudwater HP10 . . . . . .174 C2
  Milton Keynes MK3 . . . . .57 F8
Conway Cres HP13. . . . .173 F7
Conway Ct SL3 . . . . .189 B3
Conway Ho HP13. . . . . .173 F7
Conway Rd SL6 . . . . .204 B7
Cook Cl MK7 . . . . .48 B4
Cookfield Cl LU6. . . . . . . .93 E8
COOKHAM 196 A1
Cookham Ct MK6. . . . . .154 E1
COOKHAM DEAN. 195 B7
Cookham Dean Bottom
  SL6. . . . . .195 C8
Cookham Dean CE Prim
  Sch SL6 . . . . .195 B7
Cookham Lodge 15
  SL6. . . . . .202 F6
Cookham Rd SL6. . . . . .195 F1

COOKHAM RISE. 195 E6
Cookham Rise Prim Sch
  SL6 . . . . .195 E6
Cookham Sta SL6. . . . . .195 F7
Cooks Cl NN7. . . . . .9 F8
Cookshall La HP12 . . . . .161 A2
Cooks La MK17 . . . . .67 E6
Cook's Mdw LU6. . . . . . . .92 E4
Cooks Rd HP19 . . . . .114 B8
Coombe Ave HP22 . . . . .131 B4
Coombe Cl HP22 . . . . . .116 C2
Coombe Dr LU6. . . . . .93 E7
Coombe Gdns
  Berkhamsted HP4 . . . . .134 F5
  Hughenden Valley HP14 .162 A6
Coombe Hill Ct SL4 . . . .209 D4
Coombe La
  Aylesbury HP19 . . . . . .100 F1
  Walter's Ash HP14. . . . .161 F4
Coombes Quarry Nature
  Reserve★ MK18. . . . . . .53 E6
Coombe Vale SL9 . . . . . .188 E3
Cooper Rd RG9 . . . . . . .191 D3
Cooper's Court Rd
  HP14 . . . . .158 D5
Coopers Ct MK16 . . . . . . .22 C4
Coopers Mews MK14. . . .34 F6
Coopers Rise HP13. . . . .173 D5
Coopers Row SL0 . . . . . .200 D1
Cooper's Yd HP20 . . . . .101 D1
Cooper Way
  3 Berkhamsted HP4 . . .135 D4
  Slough SL1 . . . . .205 B3
Coots Cl MK18 . . . . .52 E7
Cope Cl SL6 . . . . .202 C7
Copeland Cl MK7 . . . . . . .48 C5
Copes Rd HP15 . . . . .151 E1
Copes Shroves HP15 . . .162 F5
Copmans Wick WD3 . . . .167 D4
Copners Dr HP15 . . . . . .163 C6
Copners Way HP15. . . . .163 B6
Copper Beech Cl
  Felden HP3 . . . . .146 F8
  Windsor SL4 . . . . .209 D6
Copperfields
  Beaconsfield HP9. . . . . .175 E5
  High Wycombe HP12. . . .161 B1
Copperfield Terr SL2. . . .206 B6
Copperhouse Ct MK7. . . .48 A2
Copperkins Gr HP6 . . . . .154 B3
Copperkins La HP6. . . . .154 A3
Coppermill La SL0 . . . . . .178 F3
Coppermill Rd TW19 . . .212 B2
Copper Ridge SL9. . . . . .177 F5
Coppice Cl HP20 . . . . . .102 A2
Coppice Farm Rd HP10 .163 C2
Coppice The
  Great Kingshill HP15. . . .151 E1
  High Wycombe HP12. . . .172 B4
  Seer Green HP9 . . . . . .176 D4
  Stokenchurch HP14 . . . .158 E5
  Walter's Ash HP14. . . . .161 B8
  West Drayton UB7. . . . .208 E8
  Wigginton HP23 . . . . . .119 C1
Coppice Way
  Aylesbury HP20 . . . . . .102 A2
  Hedgerley SL2. . . . . . . .187 D2
Coppidwell Dr HP21. . . . .116 A5
Coppinger Ct UB7. . . . . .208 E4
Coppin La MK13 . . . . .34 A3
Coppins La SL0 . . . . .207 F8
Copse Cl
  Marlow SL7 . . . . .183 C2
  Slough SL1 . . . . .204 F5
  West Drayton UB7. . . . .208 D7
Copse Gate MK18 . . . . . .66 A4
Copse La HP9 . . . . .176 E3
Copse The
  Amersham HP7 . . . . . . .154 C1
  Beaconsfield HP9. . . . . .175 C4
Copse Way HP15 . . . . . .144 A4
Copse Wood SL0 . . . . . .200 D4
Copthall Cl SL9 . . . . .177 F3
Copthall Cnr SL9. . . . . . .177 E3
Copthall Ho SL0. . . . . . .203 A7
Copthall La SL9 . . . . .177 E3
Copthorn Cl SL6. . . . . . .202 A4
Copthorne Pl MK7 . . . . . .48 B8
Copyground Ct HP12 . . .172 E7
Copyground La HP12. . . .172 E7
Coral Cl LU6. . . . . .92 E6
Coram Ct MK14 . . . . .135 C3
Corbet Side LU7 . . . . .80 D8
Corbet Sq LU7 . . . . .80 D8
Corbett Cl MK15 . . . . .35 D7
Cordons Cl SL9 . . . . .177 D2
Cordwainer Ct MK14 . . . .34 F6
Cordwallis Bsns Pk
  SL6 . . . . .195 E1
Cordwallis Est SL6 . . . . .202 E8
Cordwallis Pk SL6 . . . . . .202 E8
Cordwallis Rd SL6 . . . . .202 F8
Cordwallis St SL6 . . . . . .202 E8
CORES END 185 C4
Cores End Rd SL8. . . . . .185 B3

Corfe Cl HP21 . . . . 116 B5
Corfe Cres MK3 . . . . 57 F8
Corfe Gdns SL1 . . . . 205 A6
Corfe Pl SL6 . . . . 202 C7
Coriander Ct MK7 . . . . 48 B5
Corin Cl MK2 . . . . 58 D5
Corinium Ind Est HP6 . . 154 F1
Corin Way MK2 . . . . 58 D5
Cork Pl MK3 . . . . 46 E2
Cornbrook Rd HP21 . . . . 115 C5
Cornbury Cres MK15 . . . . . 35 A6
Corn Cl HP17 . . . . 114 D5
Corncrake 9 HP19 . . . . . 101 F3
Cornel Cl HP15 . . . . 163 B3
Cornel Ho 1 SL4 . . . . . . 210 D4
Cornelia Cl MK2 . . . . 58 C6
Cornerways HP27 . . . . . . 150 C5
Cornfield Cl UB8 . . . . 201 D3
Cornfield Cres HP4 . . . . . 134 D7
Cornflower Pl MK18 . . . . . 52 C7
Corn Hill MK8 . . . . 33 E1
Corn Mkt HP11 . . . . 173 B7
Cornwall Ave SL2 . . . . . . 198 C1
Cornwall Cl
  Eton Wick SL4 . . . . 204 A1
  Maidenhead SL6 . . . . . . 195 E2
Cornwall Ct UB8 . . . . 201 D6
Cornwall Gr MK3 . . . . 46 F1
Cornwall Lodge 11 SL6 . 202 F6
Cornwall Pl MK18 . . . . 41 D1
Cornwall Rd UB8 . . . . 201 D6
Cornwalls Mdw 3
  MK18 . . . . 41 D1
Cornwell Rd SL4 . . . . . . 211 A1
Coronation Ave
  Slough SL3 . . . . 206 E7
  Windsor SL4 . . . . 211 A4
Coronation Cotts MK18 . . . 41 F8
Coronation Cres HP14 . . 171 C5
Coronation Mews LU7 . . . 80 F8
Coronation Pl MK18 . . . . . 63 D7
Coronation Rd
  Cranfield MK43 . . . . 25 B1
  High Wycombe HP12 . . . 172 D4
  Milton Keynes MK11 . . . 32 E5
Coronation Villas HP21 . 115 E8
Corporation St HP13 . . . . 173 B7
Corrid Ind Pk HP19 . . . . . 101 B1
Corrigan Cl MK3 . . . . 57 E7
Corswall Pl 4 MK4 . . . . . . 45 F1
Corsham Ct 4 MK8 . . . . . 33 F1
COSGROVE 19 D2
Cosgrove Prim Sch
  MK19 . . . . 19 E2
Cosgrove Rd MK19 . . . . . 32 C7
Costers Cotts SL8 . . . . . . 185 B2
Costins Wlk 7 HP4 . . . . 135 D4
Cosway Pl MK4 . . . . 45 D6
Cotes Way LU7 . . . . 79 F3
Cotman Cl MK12 . . . . 33 B5
Cotswold Cl
  Maidenhead SL6 . . . . . . 203 B6
  Slough SL1 . . . . 205 B3
  Uxbridge UB8 . . . . 201 C4
Cotswold Ct HP21 . . . . . . 172 F8
Cotswold Dr LU7 . . . . 80 C8
Cotswold Gn HP20 . . . . . 101 E2
Cotswolds Way MK18 . . . . 73 B5
Cotswold Way HP13 . . . . 172 E8
Cottage Comm MK5 . . . . . 46 B8
Cottage Farm Way
  HP27 . . . . 150 C4
Cottage Grounds HP14 . . 114 D5
Cottage Park Rd SL2 . . . 187 D2
Cottages The
  Ickenham UB10 . . . . . . 190 E2
  Syresham NN13 . . . . . . 27 C5
Cottesbrooke Cl SL3 . . . 212 D6
Cottesloe Cl LU7 . . . . 79 E3
Cottesloe Ct MK11 . . . . . . 32 F5
Cottesloe Rd HP21 . . . . . 115 E5
Cottesloe Sch The LU7 . . 79 D1
Cottingham Gr MK3 . . . . . 58 A7
Cottisford Cres MK14 . . . . 21 F1
Cottland Clay HP17 . . . . . 127 A7
Cotts The
  Long Crendon HP18 . . . . 125 C6
  Longwick HP27 . . . . . . 138 E5
Coulson Ave MK8, MK5 . . . 45 E6
Coulson Ct HP16 . . . . 151 D6
Coulson Way 1 . . . . 204 B8
Council Hos LU7 . . . . 92 A1
Countisbury MK4 . . . . 46 D2
Country La HP15 . . . . 151 F1
Country Life Ho SL3 . . . . 211 B7
County Rd NN13 . . . . 38 A6
Cours La Ville Cl MK18 . . . 65 E3
Court Cl
  Aylesbury HP21 . . . . . . 115 E7
  High Wycombe HP13 . . . 161 D1
  Maidenhead SL6 . . . . . . 203 C2
  Princes Risborough
    HP27 . . . . 139 A3
Court Cnr MK46 . . . . 6 E3
Court Cres SL1 . . . . 205 D7

Court Dr
  Maidenhead SL6 . . . . . . 196 C3
  Uxbridge UB10 . . . . 201 F4
Courteneys Lodge MK4 . . 46 E3
Court Farm Cl SL1 . . . . . 205 B5
Courtfield Dr SL6 . . . . . . 202 C6
Courtfield Gdns UB9 . . . 190 A1
Court Garden L Complex
  SL7 . . . . 183 D1
Courthouse Cl MK18 . . . . 65 F5
Courthouse Jun Sch
  SL6 . . . . 202 B8
Courthouse Mews MK16 . 22 C4
Courthouse Rd SL6 . . . . . 202 C8
Court La
  Burnham SL1 . . . . 197 D2
  Dorney SL4 . . . . 204 B3
  Iver SL0 . . . . 208 A5
Courtlands
  Leighton Buzzard LU7 . . . 80 E6
  14 Maidenhead SL6 . . . . 202 F6
Courtlands Ave SL3 . . . . . 206 D2
Court Lawns HP10 . . . . . 163 C1
Courtmoor Cl HP27 . . . . . 139 C6
Courtneidge Cl LU7 . . . . . 78 E8
Courtney Ho HP9 . . . . . . 189 F5
Court Rd
  Cranfield MK43 . . . . 25 B1
  Maidenhead SL6 . . . . . . 196 C3
Court The MK17 . . . . 37 C3
Courtyard Arts Ctr★
  MK14 . . . . 21 E1
Courtyard 2 MK4 . . . . . . 154 C1
Courtyards The HP22 . . . 117 E4
Courtyard The HP19 . . . 101 C1
Courtyard The
  Beaconsfield HP9 . . . . . 175 D4
  7 Bourne End SL8 . . . . 185 B3
  9 Marlow SL7 . . . . 183 D2
  1 Marlow SL7 . . . . 183 E2
  22 Windsor SL4 . . . . . . 210 D6
Cousins Cl UB8 . . . . 208 E6
Cousins Dr HP20 . . . . . . 101 F2
Cousins Piece HP18 . . . . 112 B2
Coventon Rd HP19 . . . . . 101 C2
Coverack Pl MK4 . . . . 57 B8
Coverdale MK13 . . . . 34 C5
Coverdale Way SL2 . . . . . 197 E1
Covert Cl HP4 . . . . 134 C4
Covert Rd HP4 . . . . 134 D6
Cowdray Cl MK15 . . . . 35 C3
Cow La
  Edlesborough LU6 . . . . . 92 E4
  Gawcott MK18 . . . . 51 F4
  Tring HP23 . . . . 119 D4
Cowleaze OX39 . . . . 147 B6
COWLEY 201 C1
Cowley Bsns Pk UB8 . . . . 201 C2
Cowley Cl HP22 . . . . 102 B3
Cowley Cotts HP7 . . . . . . 164 C3
Cowley Cres UB8 . . . . . . 208 C8
Cowley Mill Rd UB8 . . . . 201 B3
Cowley Mill Trad Est
  UB8 . . . . 201 B3
COWLEY PEACHEY 208 E8
Cowley Rd UB8 . . . . 201 C4
Cowley St Laurence Prim
  CE Sch UB8 . . . . 208 D8
Cowper Cl MK16 . . . . 22 A4
Cowper & Newton Mus
  The★ MK46 . . . . 6 F3
Cowper Rd
  Berkhamsted HP4 . . . . . 135 B4
  Chesham HP5 . . . . 144 B2
  Slough SL2 . . . . 198 A1
Cowpers Orch MK46 . . . . . 6 A1
Cowper St MK46 . . . . 7 A5
COW ROAST 120 B1
Cowslip Ct UB10 . . . . 201 E5
Cowslip Rd HP15 . . . . . . 162 F6
Coxborrow Cl SL6 . . . . . . 195 C4
Coxfield Cl HP14 . . . . 158 F5
COX GREEN 202 C3
Cox Green La SL6 . . . . . . 202 C3
Cox Green L Ctr SL6 . . . 202 A3
Cox Green Rd SL6 . . . . . 202 A3
Cox Green Sch SL6 . . . . . 202 A4
Coxhill Way HP21 . . . . . . 115 D7
Coxwell Cl MK18 . . . . 41 F1
Coy Ct HP20 . . . . 116 A8
Cozens Cl HP18 . . . . 125 B7
Crabbe Cres HP5 . . . . . . 144 D2
Crabs Gr HP22 . . . . 86 F7
Crab Tree Cl
  Beaconsfield HP9 . . . . . 175 B1
  Olney MK46 . . . . 6 E5
Crabtree Cotts HP27 . . . . 139 A1
Crabtree La MK17 . . . . 49 C8
Crabtree Rd HP17 . . . . . . 127 A5
Craddocks Cl MK13 . . . . . 34 B3
Cradley Wlk HP20 . . . . . . 101 E3
CRAFTON 89 F3
Crafton Pl 4 HP19 . . . . . 100 F1
Craigleith Ct HP9 . . . . . . 175 D2
Craigmore Ave MK3 . . . . . 57 F8
Craigwell Ave HP21 . . . . 116 C7
Cranborne Ave MK5 . . . . . 45 E2
Cranbourne Ave SL4 . . . . 209 F5
Cranbourne Cl SL1 . . . . . 205 C5

Cranbourne Rd SL1 . . . . 205 C5
Cranbrook MK7 . . . . 49 B5
Cranbrook Dr SL6 . . . . . 195 C1
Crane Ct MK5 . . . . 34 B1
Cranesbill Pl MK14 . . . . . 34 E4
Cranes Cl MK43 . . . . 8 E5
Crane Way MK43 . . . . 25 C2
CRANFIELD 25 B1
Cranfield Airport MK43 . . 24 F1
Cranfield Innovation Ctr
  MK43 . . . . 37 D8
Cranfield Lower Sch
  MK43 . . . . 25 B1
Cranfield Rd
  Astwood MK16, MK43 . . . 16 B2
  Cranfield MK43 . . . . 25 D2
  Moulsoe MK16 . . . . 36 E8
  Salford MK17 . . . . 37 D5
  Wavendon MK17 . . . . . . 49 B7
Cranfield Tech Pk MK43 . 37 C8
Cranfield Univ MK43 . . . . 24 E2
Cranwell Cl MK5 . . . . 46 B3
Craufurd Ct SL6 . . . . 202 E8
Craufurd Rise SL6 . . . . . 202 E8
Craven The MK3 . . . . 34 C4
Crawford Way 3 MK4 . . . 45 D2
Crawley Rd
  Cranfield MK43 . . . . 25 B3
  Woburn MK17 . . . . 60 F8
Crawley's La HP23 . . . . . 133 F7
Crawshays SL6 . . . . 203 C8
Crayle St SL2 . . . . 198 B2
CR Bates Ind Est HP14 . 158 E5
Creden Cl SL6 . . . . 195 D1
Creed St MK12 . . . . 33 D7
Creighton Rd HP18 . . . . . 83 F1
Crendon Rd HP18 . . . . . . 112 A1
Crendon St HP13 . . . . . . 173 B7
Ceran Wlk LU7 . . . . 80 C7
Crescent Cotts HP18 . . . . 83 A6
Crescent Dale SL6 . . . . . 202 F6
Crescent Dr SL6 . . . . 202 E7
Crescent The
  Cranfield MK43 . . . . 24 E2
  Haversham MK19 . . . . . . 20 E2
  High Wycombe HP13 . . . 173 E8
  Maidenhead SL6 . . . . . . 202 E7
  Marsworth HP23 . . . . . . 105 A1
  Milton Keynes, Fenny Stratford
    MK2 . . . . 47 C1
  Milton Keynes, Giffard Park
    MK14 . . . . 21 E2
  Pitstone LU7 . . . . 105 C4
  Princes Risborough
    HP27 . . . . 139 C3
  Slough SL1 . . . . 205 E4
Crescent Villas 5 SL4 . . 210 C6
CRESLOW 87 B8
Creslow Ct MK11 . . . . 32 F5
Creslow Way HP17 . . . . . 114 B5
CRESSEX 172 C2
Cressex Bsns Pk HP12 . . 172 D3
Cressex Cl HP12 . . . . 172 D3
Cressex Com Sch The
  HP12 . . . . 172 C2
Cressex Ent Ctr HP12 . . 172 E6
Cressex Link HP11 . . . . . 172 D3
Cressex Rd HP12 . . . . . . 172 C3
Cressey Ave MK5 . . . . 46 B4
Cressington Ct 2 SL8 . . 185 A4
Cressington Pl SL8 . . . . . 185 A4
Cress Rd SL1 . . . . 205 B4
Cresswell Ct TW19 . . . . . 213 D1
Cresswell Rd HP15 . . . . . 163 D7
Cresswells Mead SL6 . . . 203 C1
Cresswell Way HP15 . . . . 163 D7
Crest Rd HP11 . . . . 172 D3
Crest The
  Beaconsfield HP9 . . . . . 175 A1
  Bledlow Ridge HP14 . . . 159 F8
Creswell Row SL7 . . . . . . 183 D2
Creswick Mdr HP21 . . . . 116 A5
Crew Curve HP4 . . . . 134 F7
Cricketers Row MK18 . . . . 66 A4
Cricketfield Rd UB7 . . . . 208 C2
Cricket Field Rd HP21 . . 115 C5
Cricket Green Rdbt MK9 . 35 B4
Cricket Ground HP14 . . . 158 D5
Cricklebeck MK13 . . . . . . 34 B5
Crimp Hill SL4 . . . . 211 A1
Crispin Cl HP9 . . . . 175 C4
Crispin Ct HP17 . . . . 105 C4
Crispin Rd MK13 . . . . 34 B7
Crispin Way
  Farnham Common SL2 . . 198 D8
  High Wycombe HP11 . . . 173 A4
  Uxbridge UB8 . . . . 208 F8
Crisp Rd RG9 . . . . 191 C3
Criss Gr SL9 . . . . 177 C1
Crocketts La HP16 . . . . . 142 D5
Crocus Dr HP21 . . . . 115 B5
Croft Cnr SL4 . . . . 211 A2
Croft Ct 5 HP21 . . . . . . 115 E7
Croft Ctyd HP17 . . . . 126 F6
Crofters SL4 . . . . 211 A1
Crofters Cl TW19 . . . . . . 213 D1
Croft Gn LU6 . . . . 93 F8
Crofthill Rd SL2 . . . . 198 B1
Croft Ho SL0 . . . . 207 E7

Croft Mdws LU7 . . . . 105 A7
Crofton Ho HP11 . . . . 174 A4
Croft Rd
  Aylesbury HP21 . . . . . . 115 E7
  Chalfont St Peter SL9 . . 177 E1
CROFTS END 14 A1
Crofts End MK16 . . . . 14 A1
Crofts La MK17 . . . . 57 D3
Croft The
  Haddenham HP17 . . . . . 126 F5
  Maidenhead SL6 . . . . . . 202 B7
  Marlow SL7 . . . . 184 A3
Croftwood HP13 . . . . 173 F7
Cromarty Ct MK3 . . . . 46 E3
Cromer Cl HP4 . . . . 121 E5
Cromer Ct SL1 . . . . 205 E7
Cromhamstone HP17 . . . 114 D5
Cromwell Ave
  Aylesbury HP19 . . . . . . 101 C2
  Newport Pagnell MK16 . . 22 A3
  Thame OX9 . . . . 126 A1
Cromwell Cl HP8 . . . . 177 C7
Cromwell Ct MK18 . . . . . . 41 E2
Cromwell Dr SL1 . . . . . . 205 E7
Cromwell Gdns 10 SL7 . 183 E2
Cromwell Ho
  Chesham HP5 . . . . 144 B1
  Uxbridge UB8 . . . . 201 C4
Cromwell Mews 1
  HP19 . . . . 115 A8
Cromwell Rd
  High Wycombe HP13 . . . 173 E5
  Maidenhead SL6 . . . . . . 202 D7
  Marlow SL7 . . . . 183 E2
Cropredy Ct MK18, MK12 . 172 E5
Cropton Rise MK4 . . . . . . 46 A2
Cropwell Bishop MK4 . . . . 46 C1
Crosby Cl HP9 . . . . 186 F8
Crosby Ct MK8 . . . . 45 E6
Crosland Rd HP21 . . . . . 116 B6
Cross Ct HP13 . . . . 161 D2
Cross End MK17 . . . . 48 F7
Cross Farm Mews MK3 . . 146 D2
Crossfield Cl HP4 . . . . . . 134 F4
Crossfield Rd HP27 . . . . 139 C4
Crosshills MK11 . . . . 32 D4
Cross La
  Beaconsfield HP9 . . . . . 186 F8
  Tingewick MK18 . . . . . . 51 B6
  Weston Underwood MK46 . 6 B2
Crosslands MK14 . . . . 34 E8
Cross Lanes
  Bledlow HP27 . . . . 138 A2
  Chalfont St Peter SL9 . . 177 F5
Cross Lanes Cl SL9 . . . . 177 F5
Crossleys HP5 . . . . 177 C7
Crosslow Bank MK4 . . . . . 46 C3
Cross Mdw HP5 . . . . 143 F2
Cross Oak SL4 . . . . 210 A5
Cross Oak Rd HP4 . . . . . 135 A4
Cross Rd
  High Wycombe HP12 . . . 172 C6
  Uxbridge UB8 . . . . 201 C5
Cross St
  Newport Pagnell MK16 . . 22 C4
  Uxbridge UB8 . . . . 201 C5
Cross Tree Rd MK19 . . . . 31 B3
Crossway HP5 . . . . 144 E1
Crossways
  Beaconsfield HP9 . . . . . 175 F1
  Berkhamsted HP4 . . . . . 134 F3
  High Wycombe HP12 . . . 172 C4
Crossways Bsns Pk
  HP18 . . . . 83 C3
Crossways Ct 4 SL4 . . . 210 C5
Crossway The UB10 . . . . 201 F3
Crosthwaite Way SL1 . . . 204 D8
Crowborough La MK7 . . . . 48 A8
Crowbrook Rd HP27 . . . . 139 C6
CROWELL 147 B4
CROWELL HILL 147 D2
Crowell Mews HP19 . . . . 114 F8
Crowell Rd OX39 . . . . . . 147 B5
CROWFIELD 26 F8
Crow La MK17 . . . . 49 B8
Crown Bsns Est HP5 . . . 144 C1
Crown Cl SL3 . . . . 212 C7
Crown Cotts
  Botley HP5 . . . . 155 B8
  Windsor SL4 . . . . 210 D3
Crown Ct HP14 . . . . 161 A2
CROWNFIELD 149 B4
Crownfield HP27 . . . . . . 149 B4
CROWNHILL 45 E7
Crownhill Rdbt MK8 . . . . 45 E8
Crown House Sch
  HP11 . . . . 173 C6
Crown La
  East Burnham SL2 . . . . . 198 A4
  High Wycombe HP11 . . . 173 B6
  Maidenhead SL6 . . . . . . 203 A3
  Marlow SL7 . . . . 183 D2
  Penn HP10 . . . . 174 F7
Crown Leys HP20 . . . . . . 101 E1
Crown Mdw SL3 . . . . 212 B7
Crown Rd SL1 . . . . 205 D7
Crown Rose Ct HP23 . . . 119 A3
Crown Way UB7 . . . . 208 F5

Crown Wlk
  Milton Keynes MK9 . . . . . 34 E3
  Uxbridge UB8 . . . . 201 C5
Crow Piece La SL2 . . . . . 197 F4
Crowther Ct MK5 . . . . 46 C5
Croxley Ct 3 LU7 . . . . . . 80 F8
Croxley Rise SL6 . . . . . . 202 D6
Croydon Cl MK4 . . . . 45 E7
Cruickshank Gr MK8 . . . . 45 E7
Crummock Cl SL1 . . . . . . 204 C7
Crummock Pl MK2 . . . . . . 58 D6
Crusader Est HP22 . . . . . 172 D5
Crutches La HP9 . . . . . . 176 E4
CRYERS HILL 162 D6
Cryers Hill La HP15 . . . . 162 D6
Cryers Hill Rd HP15 . . . . 162 C6
Cuba Cotts SL6 . . . . 196 B3
Cubb Field HP17 . . . . . . 115 B7
CUBLINGTON 78 B1
Cublington Rd HP22 . . . . . 88 D6
Cuckoo Hill Rise MK19 . . . 10 F2
Cuckoo Way HP19 . . . . . 114 F8
CUDDINGTON 113 A2
Cuddington & Dinton CE
  Sch (Inf) HP18 . . . . . . 112 F3
Cuddington & Dinton CE
  Sch (Jun) HP17 . . . . . . 113 A3
Cuddington Hill HP18 . . 112 F3
Cuddington Rd HP17,
  HP18 . . . . 113 E3
Cudsdens Ct HP16 . . . . . 152 D7
Cuff La MK17 . . . . 59 D1
Culbertson La MK13 . . . . . 33 E6
Culham Dr SL6 . . . . 195 E2
Culham Rd MK2 . . . . 58 D5
Cullern's Pass SL6 . . . . . 202 F6
Culley Way SL6 . . . . 202 A4
Cullyn Rd HP12 . . . . 172 C3
Culmstock Ct MK4 . . . . . . 46 D2
Culrain Pl MK12 . . . . 33 D4
Culross Gr MK10 . . . . 36 A2
Culvers Croft HP9 . . . . . 176 C4
Culvert La UB8 . . . . 201 B3
Culverton Hill HP27 . . . . 139 B1
Culverton La HP27 . . . . . 139 B1
Cumberland Ave SL2 . . . 198 C1
Cumberland Cl
  Aylesbury HP21 . . . . . . 116 B7
  Little Chalfont HP7 . . . . 166 B8
Cumbrae Cl SL2 . . . . 206 A5
Cumbria Cl
  Maidenhead SL6 . . . . . . 202 C4
  Milton Keynes MK3 . . . . 46 F1
Cumbrian Way
  High Wycombe HP13 . . . 172 F8
  Slough SL1 . . . . 201 C5
Curfew Yd The 2 SL4 . . 210 D6
Curlew HP19 . . . . 101 F3
Curlew Cl
  Berkhamsted HP4 . . . . . 135 C3
  High Wycombe HP13 . . . 161 C2
Curls La SL6 . . . . 202 E4
Curls Rd SL6 . . . . 202 D4
Curran Cl UB8 . . . . 201 C1
Currier Dr MK14 . . . . 34 F6
Curriers La SL1 . . . . 197 D7
Cursley Path 11 HP19 . . 115 A8
Curtis Cotts HP5 . . . . . . 144 F7
Curtis Croft MK5 . . . . 46 B3
Curtis Way HP4 . . . . 135 D3
Curzon Ave
  Beaconsfield HP9 . . . . . 175 D4
  Tylers Green HP15 . . . . 163 C2
Curzon CE Comb Sch
  HP7 . . . . 164 A5
Curzon Cl HP15 . . . . 163 C2
Curzon Gate Ct HP14 . . 158 E5
Curzon Mall 6 SL1 . . . . 205 F4
Curzon Pl MK7 . . . . 48 C4
Cushing Dr 7 MK4 . . . . . 45 E2
Cutler's Cl 6 HP12 . . . . 172 E7
Cutlers Mews MK14 . . . . . 34 F6
Cut Throat Ave HP4 . . . . 107 E7
Cuttle Brook Gdns OX9 . 125 F1
Cyclamen HP21 . . . . 115 B5
Cygnet Ho SL6 . . . . 196 C1
Cypress MK16 . . . . 22 A3
Cypress Ho SL3 . . . . 207 B1
Cypress Wlk HP15 . . . . . 163 B3

D

Daceberry Ct RG9 . . . . . 192 C2
Dacre Rd HP22 . . . . 131 E7
Dadbrook HP18 . . . . 112 F2
Dadbrook Cl HP18 . . . . . 112 F2
Dadfield Cl HP18 . . . . . . 112 F2
DADFORD 28 D1
Dadford Rd MK18 . . . . 28 D5
Dag La MK16 . . . . 12 A7
Dagmar Rd SL4 . . . . 210 D5
DAGNALL 107 C6
Dagnall Cres UB8 . . . . . 208 C8
Dagnall Cty Fst Sch
  HP4 . . . . 107 C5
Dagnall Rd
  Olney MK46 . . . . 6 E3
  Whipsnade LU6 . . . . 93 D2

Dair House Sch SL2 198 B4
Dairy La RG9 192 B8
Dairymede HP27 150 C4
Daisy Cotts HP14 171 B4
Dalby Gdns [7] SL6 195 F1
Dale Cl NN13 38 A7
Dale Ct SL1 205 C4
Dalegarth Way MK10 36 C3
Dalesford Rd HP21 116 A4
Dale Side SL9 188 E2
Dalgin Pl MK9 35 A3
Dalston Cl HP20 101 F2
Dalston End MK10 35 E1
Dalton Gate MK10 35 F4
Dalton Gn [15] SL3 206 F1
Dalvina Pl MK12 33 D4
Dalwood Mews [3] HP19 115 A8
Daly Way HP20 116 B7
Damask Cl HP23 119 C4
Damson Gr SL1 205 C4
Danbury Ct MK14 34 E5
Dancers End La HP22, HP23 118 C2
Dancersend Wildlife Reserve★ HP23 132 C8
Dandridge Cl SL3 206 D2
Dandridge Ct MK8 45 C6
Dandridge Dr SL8 185 C3
Dane Cl HP7 165 F6
Dane Ct HP21 115 D4
Dane Rd MK1 47 E2
Danesborough Dr MK17 49 A2
Danesbrook Cl MK4 46 D4
Danes Ct SL6 202 D7
Danesfield Sch SL7 193 E7
Danes Gdns SL6 195 F6
Daneswood MK17 49 A1
Daniels Welch MK6 47 A6
Dansteed Way
  Milton Keynes, Bradwell Common MK8, MK13, MK14, MK15 34 C4
  Milton Keynes, Crownhill MK8 45 D7
Danvers Croft HP23 119 C5
Darby Cl
  Milton Keynes MK5 46 B5
  Milton Keynes MK13 34 C2
Darby Lodge HP13 174 A7
Darie Cl [3] SL1 205 A4
Darin Ct MK8 45 F8
Dark La
  Chearsley HP18 112 B2
  Oving HP22 86 C7
  Wingrave HP22 89 C2
Darley Cl HP21 116 B6
Darley Gate MK14 35 A5
Darley's Cl HP18 83 A6
Darling's La SL6 194 E1
Darlington Cl HP6 154 D1
Darnel Cl MK6 47 A5
Darrell Cl SL3 206 F2
Darr's La HP4 134 D6
Darsham Wlk HP5 154 B8
Dart Cl
  Aylesbury HP21 115 C5
  Newport Pagnell MK16 22 D4
  Slough SL3 212 B8
Dartington Pl [2] MK4 45 F1
Dartmouth Ct [10] SL1 205 F3
Dartmouth Rd MK46 6 F4
Darvell Dr HP5 144 A2
Darvells Yd WD3 167 D5
Darville Ho [19] SL4 210 D6
Darvill Rd HP17 114 B5
DARVILLSHILL 150 A4
Darvill's La SL1 205 D4
Darvills Mdw HP15 163 C7
Darwin Cl MK5 45 E5
Darwin Rd SL3 206 F4
Dashfield Gr HP15 162 F6
Dashwood Ave HP12 172 D7
Dashwood Cl SL3 206 C2
Dashwood Works Ind Est HP12 172 D7
DATCHET 211 C6
Datchet Ho [3] SL1 205 F3
Datchet Lodge Ctyd SL3 211 B6
Datchet Pl SL3 211 B6
Datchet Rd
  Eton SL4 205 F2
  Horton SL3 211 F4
  Old Windsor SL4 211 A3
  Windsor SL4 210 D7
Datchet St Mary's CE Prim Sch SL3 211 B6
Datchet Sta SL3 211 B6
Daubeney Gate MK5 45 F6
Davenies Sch HP9 175 E2
Davenport Lea MK7 48 E5
Davenport Rd HP12 172 C3
Daventry Cl SL3 212 F6
David Bishop Ct HP5 154 D5
David Cl HP21 116 A4
Davidge Pl HP9 175 C5
David Rd SL3 212 F5
Davidson Rd [6] SL3 206 F1
Davies Cl HP20 115 D8
Davies Ct HP12 172 D5
Davies Way HP10 174 C1
Davis Cl SL7 183 E1
Davis Gr MK4 45 E3
Davis Ho [3] HP4 135 C3
Davison Ct MK8 45 D6
Davy Ave MK5 46 D6
Dawes Cl HP5 154 B7
Dawe's Cl UB10 201 E3
Dawes East Rd SL1 197 C2
Dawes La WD3 156 F3
Dawes Moor Cl SL2 206 C7
Dawe's Rd UB10 201 E3
Dawley Ride SL3 212 E6
Dawney Cl HP19 101 C2
Dawn Redwood Cl SL3 212 A4
Daws Ct SL0 207 F7
Daws Hill La HP11 173 A4
Daws Lea HP11 173 B3
Dawson Cl SL4 210 A5
Dawson Rd MK1 47 D3
Daylesford Ct MK15 35 B5
Daylesford Gr SL1 204 F4
Deacon Cl HP12 172 B4
Deacon Ct SL4 209 D5
Deacon Pl MK10 35 F3
Deadhearn La HP8 166 E1
Deal Ave SL1 204 F7
Deanacre Cl SL9 177 E4
Dean Cl
  Aylesbury HP21 116 A5
  High Wycombe HP12 172 E6
  Uxbridge UB10 201 F5
  Windsor SL4 209 D4
Deancroft Rd SL9 177 E4
Dean Farm La LU7 69 E4
Deanfield HP14 160 B8
Dean Field HP3 146 A4
Deanfield Ave RG9 191 D1
Deanfield Cl
  Marlow SL7 183 D2
  Saunderton HP14 149 C1
Deanfield Rd RG9 191 D1
Dean Forest Way MK10 36 A5
Deangarden Rise HP11 173 E4
Dean La SL6 195 C8
Dean Rd LU7 68 B2
Deans Cl
  Amersham HP6 154 F2
  Tring HP23 119 A4
  Wexham Street SL2 199 B4
Dean's Cloisters SL4 210 D7
Deansfield Cl SL6 195 D2
Deans Furlong HP23 119 A4
DEANSHANGER 31 D4
Deanshanger Dr NN12 17 F1
Deanshanger Prim Sch MK19 31 E3
Deanshanger Rd
  Old Stratford MK19 32 B6
  Wicken MK19 31 B3
Deans Lawn HP4 135 C4
Deans Mdw HP4 107 C5
Dean's Rd MK12 33 C7
Dean St SL7 183 D2
Deansway HP5 144 B2
Dean The HP22 89 B3
Dean View SL6 195 D6
Dean Way
  Aston Clinton HP22 117 F4
  Chalfont St Giles HP8 177 B7
  Holmer Green HP15 163 B6
Dean Wood Rd HP9 176 D2
Dearing Cl [11] HP20 101 F2
Debbs Cl MK11 32 E5
Deben Cl MK16 22 E3
Decies Way SL2 199 A4
De Clare Ct MK18 41 E1
Dedmere Ct SL7 183 F2
Dedmere Rd SL7 183 F2
Dedmere Rise SL7 183 E2
DEDWORTH 209 E6
Dedworth Dr SL4 209 F6
Dedworth Green Fst Sch SL4 209 E5
Dedworth Manor SL4 209 F6
Dedworth Mid Sch SL4 209 E6
Dedworth Rd SL4 209 D5
Deeds Gr HP12 172 E5
Deena Cl SL1 204 E6
Deep Acres HP6 154 A3
Deepdale MK13 34 C5
Deep Field SL3 211 B7
Deep Mill La HP16 152 D3
Deerfern Cl MK14 21 E1
Deerfield Cl MK18 52 E7
Deermead HP16 152 B4
Deer Park Wlk HP5 144 E3
Deerswood SL6 196 A1
Deer Wlk MK9 34 F3
Deethe Cl MK17 49 B6
De Havilland Dr HP15 162 E2
De Havilland Way TW19 213 E1
Delafield Cl HP14 158 F4
Delaford Cl SL0 207 F7
Delaford Ho UB7 208 D5
Delahay Rise HP4 135 B6
Delamere Cl HP20 101 F2
Delamere Gdns LU7 80 C7
Delaware Dr
  Milton Keynes MK15 35 B8
  Tongwell MK15, MK16 22 B1
Delius Cl MK7 48 C4
Dell Cl
  Chesham HP5 143 F2
  Farnham Common SL2 198 C7
Dellfield HP5 144 A2
Dell Field HP16 151 C5
Dell Field Ave HP4 135 B6
Dellfield Cl HP4 135 A6
Dellfield Cres UB8 201 C1
Dellfield Par UB8 201 C1
Dell Lees HP9 176 C4
Dell Rd
  Berkhamsted HP4 134 D7
  West Drayton UB7 208 F3
Dells MK46 6 F4
Dellside UB9 190 C6
Dell The
  Aylesbury HP20 102 A2
  Chalfont St Peter SL9 177 E4
  Maidenhead SL6 202 A2
  Stokenchurch HP14 158 F3
  Tylers Green HP10 163 C1
  Uxbridge UB8 201 C6
Delmeade Rd HP5 154 A7
Deltic Ave MK13 34 B2
Demoram Cl MK18 65 F3
Denbigh East Ind Est MK1 47 D2
Denbigh Hall MK3 46 F3
Denbigh Hall Dr MK3 46 F3
Denbigh Hall Ind Est MK3 46 F3
Denbigh Rd
  Milton Keynes MK1 47 B2
  Thame OX9 126 A1
Denbigh Rdbt MK1 47 C2
Denbigh Sch MK5 46 A6
Denbigh Way MK2 47 C1
Denbigh West Ind Est MK1 47 B2
Denby Walk HP20 116 A8
Denchworth Ct [2] MK4 46 C2
Dene Cl
  Winslow MK18 66 A3
  Woburn Sands MK17 49 C4
Dene The MK18 63 D3
Denewood HP13 173 E8
DENHAM
  Denham Green 190 A2
  Quainton 85 D5
Denham Aerodrome UB9 189 E6
Denham Ave UB9 189 F3
Denham Cl
  Denham UB9 190 A1
  Maidenhead SL6 202 C6
  Milton Keynes MK3 57 D8
Denham Court Dr UB9 190 B1
Denham Ctry Park Nature Reserve★ UB9 190 B2
Denham Ctry Pk★ UB9 190 B2
Denham Garden Village UB9 189 F5
Denham Golf Club Sta UB9 189 D4
DENHAM GREEN 189 E5
Denham Green Cl UB9 190 A4
Denham Green La UB9 189 F5
Denham La SL9 178 A2
Denham Lodge UB9 201 C6
Denham Quarry Park Nature Reserve★ UB9 190 C1
Denham Rd
  Iver Heath SL0 200 E5
  Lane End HP14 171 C5
Denham Sta UB9 190 A4
Denham View MK18 75 F6
Denham Village Inf Sch UB9 189 F2
Denham Way UB9 190 A1
Denham Way (North Orbital Rd)
  Denham Green UB9 189 F7
  Maple Cross WD3 178 E4
Denham Wlk SL9 177 F4
Denholme Lodge SL3 211 B7
Denison Ct MK7 48 D6
Denmark St
  Maidenhead SL6 202 E8
  Milton Keynes MK2 58 E8
Denmead MK8 33 E2
Denmead Cl SL9 188 E4
DENNER HILL 150 E4
Dennis Cl HP22 118 A4
Denniston Ho HP12 172 C8
Dennis Way SL1 204 D6
Denny Rd SL3 206 F2
Denny's La HP4 134 F2
Denton Ct SL7 183 F3
De Pirenore HP15 162 E2
Depot Rd SL6 203 A6
Derby Arms [2] HP20 115 D8
Derby Rd UB8 201 D3
Derehams Ave HP10 174 C3
Derehams La HP10 174 C2
Derek Rd SL6 203 C8
Dere Pl MK2 58 E4
Deri Dene Cl [2] TW19 213 E1
Derwent Cl
  Little Chalfont HP7 166 B8
  Newport Pagnell MK16 22 D4
Derwent Dr
  Maidenhead SL6 202 D8
  Milton Keynes MK3 57 E8
  Slough SL1 204 C8
Derwent Rd
  Aylesbury HP21 116 B6
  Leighton Buzzard LU7 80 B7
Desborough Ave HP11 172 F6
Desborough Bsns Pk HP12 172 E8
Desborough Cres SL6 202 D5
Desborough Gn [1] HP20 101 D2
Desborough Ho [14] HP13 173 B7
Desborough Park Rd HP12 172 E8
Desborough Rd HP11 172 F7
Desborough Sch SL6 202 E5
Desborough St HP11 172 F7
Deseronto Wharf Ind Est SL3 206 E4
Develin Cl MK14 34 F7
Devereux Pl
  Aylesbury HP19 101 A2
  Milton Keynes MK6 46 F7
Devereux Rd SL4 210 D5
Deverill Rd HP21 115 C3
Deverills Way SL3 207 C2
Devon Ave SL1 205 C7
Devon Cl MK3 46 F1
Devon Rd HP19 101 A3
Devonshire Ave HP6 154 B2
Devonshire Cl
  Amersham HP6 154 C2
  Farnham Royal SL2 198 B3
Devonshire Gn SL2 198 B3
Devonshire Lodge [10] SL6 202 F6
Devon Way UB10 201 F3
Dewar Spur SL3 211 F8
Dexter Ave MK6 46 F8
Dexter Ho MK6 46 F8
Dhoon Rise SL6 202 F6
Diamond Rd SL1 206 A4
Diana Cl SL3 206 E7
Diane Cl HP21 116 A4
Diane Wlk HP21 116 A4
Dibden Hill HP8 177 C6
Dickens Cl MK43 3 F6
Dickens Dr MK19 32 B6
Dickens Pl SL3 212 E6
Dickens Rd MK12 33 C8
Dickens Spinney MK46 6 E4
Dickens Way HP19 100 F2
Dickins Pl SL3 212 E6
Dicks Way HP19 100 F3
Diddington Cl MK2 58 C3
Digby Cl OX9 126 B1
Digby Croft MK10 35 E3
DIGGS 126 F5
Dilwyn Ct [1] HP12 172 E7
Dingle Dell LU7 70 F2
Dingledery MK46 6 F4
Dinmore [2] HP3 145 F3
DINTON 113 F2
Disraeli Cres HP13 161 F1
Disraeli Ct SL3 212 B8
Disraeli Pk HP9 175 D4
Disraeli Sch The HP13 161 F1
Disraeli Sq [4] HP19 115 A8
Diswell Brook Way MK19 31 E5
DITCHFIELD 171 A3
Ditchfield Cotts HP14 171 A3
Ditchingham Cl HP19 115 B7
Ditton Park Cvn Site SL3 206 F1
Ditton Park Rd SL3 211 E8
Ditton Rd
  Datchet SL3 211 D7
  Slough SL3 211 F8
Dixie Ct HP20 116 A8
Dixie La MK7 48 C6
Dixon Cl HP21 115 B6
Dobbins La HP22 131 B5
Dobson's La RG9 191 C8
Docton Mill [3] MK4 45 E2
Doctor's Commons Rd HP4 135 B4
Doddsfield Rd SL2 198 A2
Dodds La HP8 177 B8
Dodkin MK6 47 B5
Dodman Gn MK4 57 B8
Doggetts Farm Rd UB9 189 C4
Doggetts Wood Cl HP8 166 B6
Doggetts Wood La HP8 166 B5
Dog Kennel La WD3 167 F5
Dolben Ct MK15 35 D8
Dolesden La RG9 169 D1
Dollicot HP17 126 F6
Dolphin Ct
  Loudwater HP11 174 A3
  Slough SL1 206 B4
Dolphin Pl HP21 115 E6
Dolphin Rd SL1 206 B4
Dolphin Sq [2] HP23 119 A3
Donkey Dr SL8 185 A3
Donkey La
  Bourne End SL8 185 A3
  Tring HP23 118 E2
  West Drayton UB7 208 C2
Donnay Cl SL9 188 D5
Donnington MK13 34 B6
Donnington Gdns SL6 195 F1
Donnybrook Ho [3] HP13 173 C7
Don The MK3 46 D1
Doon Way MK2 58 C5
Dorchester Ave MK3 47 A2
Dorchester Cl
  Maidenhead SL6 195 B1
  Stoke Mandeville HP22 116 B2
Dorchester Ho SL9 188 F6
Doreen Cl MK2 58 C7
Dorian Cl HP23 119 D4
Dorking Pl MK5 46 B4
Dormans Cl MK10 36 A2
Dormer Ave LU7 79 E3
Dormer Cl HP21 115 B6
Dormer Ct [4] HP20 101 F2
Dormer La HP15 163 B7
Dornels SL2 206 C7
DORNEY 204 C3
Dorney Comb Sch SL6 203 F3
Dorney Court★ SL4 204 B3
Dorney End HP5 144 A1
Dorney Hill N SL1, HP9 187 A4
Dorney Hill S SL2 187 A4
Dorney Lake Pk★ SL4 209 B8
Dorney Pl MK13 34 C3
DORNEY REACH 203 F3
Dorney Reach Rd SL6 203 F3
Dorneywood Gdn★ SL1 197 D6
Dorney Wood Rd
  Burnham SL1 197 D6
  Littleworth Common SL1 186 C1
Dorrells Rd HP27 138 D6
Dorrien's Croft HP4 134 F7
Dorset Cl
  Berkhamsted HP4 134 F5
  Milton Keynes MK3 46 F1
Dorset Lodge [9] SL6 202 F6
Dorset Pl HP21 116 C6
Dorset Rd SL4 210 C6
Dorset Way UB10 201 F3
Dorsey Cl MK8 45 E6
DORTON 96 F1
Dorton Cl MK8 33 F1
Dorton Rd HP18 111 B4
Douglas Ct SL7 184 A3
Douglas Gdns HP4 135 A5
Douglas La TW19 211 F1
Douglas Pl MK6 46 E8
Douglas Rd
  Aylesbury HP20 102 A1
  Slough SL2 205 D8
  Stanwell TW19 213 D1
Doune Ho MK3 46 F2
Dove Cl
  Aylesbury HP21 115 C5
  Buckingham MK18 52 E7
  Newport Pagnell MK16 22 D4
Dovecote
  Haddenham HP17 126 F6
  Newport Pagnell MK16 22 C4
Dovecote Cft MK14 21 E1
Dovecote Cl
  Haddenham HP17 126 F6
  Monks Risborough HP27 139 C5
Dovecote Cotts MK5 46 A4
Dovecot Rd [11] HP13 173 A7
Dove Ct HP9 175 D3
Dove Ho HP19 101 F4
Dove House Cl
  Edlesborough LU6 92 F4
  Winslow MK18 66 A4
Dove House Cres SL2 197 E2
Dovehouse Mews MK16 12 B6
Dovehouse Rd [3] HP11 173 A7
Doveleat OX39 147 D7
Dove Pk WD3 167 B4
Dover Cl LU7 105 D2
Dover Gate MK3 57 F8
Dover Hedge HP21 116 C7
Dover Rd SL1 204 F7
Dove St LU7 78 E8
Dovetail Cl HP12 172 D8
Dowding Rd UB10 201 F5
Dower Cl HP9 175 C5
Dower Mews [5] HP4 135 C4
Dower Pk SL4 209 E3
Downdean MK6 47 A8
Downderry Croft MK4 57 B8
Downer Cl MK18 52 F8
Downer Dr WD3 156 F3

Downham Rd MK17 ....49 C4
DOWNHEAD PARK 35 B5
Downing Cl MK3 ....58 B8
Downing Path SL2 .....197 E1
Downings Wood WD3 ..178 D5
Downland 33 E2
DOWNLEY 161 C3
Downley Ave MK13 .....34 C3
Downley Ct HP13 .....161 D2
Downley Rd HP14 ....161 D6
Downley Sch The
  HP13............161 D3
DOWNS BARN 35 A5
Downs Barn Bvd MK14 .34 F5
Downs Barn Rdbt MK14 .34 F5
Downs Barn Sch MK14 .34 F5
Downs Field MK16 .....22 F3
Downs Pk HP13 ......161 E2
Downs Rd SL3 ....206 D4
Downs View 48 C2
Downs Villas HP23 ...119 A3
Dragon Tail HP17 ....127 A5
Drake Ave SL3 ......206 D2
Drake Cl HP21 ......115 B6
Drakeloe Ct MK17 .....60 F8
Drakes Dr HP18 .....125 E5
Drakes Farm HP18 ...125 E5
Drakes Mews MK8 .....45 F7
Drake's Rd HP7 .....165 E8
Drakewell Rd MK17 ...48 D1
Draymans La SL7 ....183 D1
DRAYTON
BEAUCHAMP 118 B5
Drayton Ct SL8 .....208 F2
Drayton Gdns UB7 ...208 E4
Drayton Park Sch MK2 .58 D5
DRAYTON PARSLOW 68 C6
Drayton Parslow Village
  Sch MK17 ....68 C6
Drayton Rd
  Aylesbury HP20 .....101 D2
  Milton Keynes MK2 ...58 C5
  Newton Longville MK17 .57 C2
Dr Challoner's Gram Sch
  HP6.............154 C1
Dr Challoner's High Sch
  HP7 ....166 B7
Dresser Rd HP16 ....151 C5
Drew Ct MK3 ....47 A4
Drew Mdw SL2 ......198 C8
Drews Pk HP9 ......175 C6
Drey The SL9 ....177 E5
Drift Rd SL4 ....209 A1
Drift Way
  Colnbrook SL3 ......212 C7
  Olney MK46 ....6 F5
Drinkwater Cl OX25 ...95 D7
Drive The
  Amersham HP7 ......154 D1
  Bourne End SL8 .....184 F4
  Chalfont St Peter SL9 .177 F3
  Cranfield MK43 ......24 D2
  Datchet SL3 ....211 B6
  Ickenham UB10 .....190 E1
  Ivinghoe Aston LU7 ...92 A1
  Slough SL3 ....206 E4
  Wraysbury TW19 ....211 D2
Dropmore Inf Sch SL1 .186 C1
Dropmore Rd
  Burnham SL1 ....197 C5
  Littleworth Common SL1 186 C1
Drovers Croft MK12 ...33 B4
Drovers La RG9 .....169 B2
Drovers Way
  Dunstable LU6 ....93 F8
  Newton Longville MK17 .57 D2
  Seer Green HP9 .....176 C4
Druce Rd NN12 ......18 E6
Druids Wlk OX39 ....147 C6
Drummond Rd ⓱ SL4 .210 D4
Drummond Ride HP23 .119 A5
Drummound Hay MK15 .35 C7
Drydell La HP5 .....153 F8
Dryden Cl
  Aylesbury HP20 .....101 E2
  Newport Pagnell MK16 .22 A4
Duchess Gdns NN12 ...18 D3
Duchess Gr MK7 .....48 C7
Duchess St SL1 ....204 E5
DUCK END
  Akeley 42 A8
  Swanbourne.........66 F4
Duck End
  Aylesbury HP20 .....115 C8
  Great Brickhill MK17 ..59 D1
Duck La
  Ludgershall HP18.....96 C8
  Woburn MK17 ....60 F7
Duck Lake MK18 ......41 E3
Duck Lake MK18......41 E4
Duckmore La HP23 ...118 E2
Duck Sq OX39 ......147 C6
Duckworth Ct MK6 ....46 E7
Dudley Ct MK18......76 A2
Dudley Ct SL1 .....206 A3

Dudley Hill MK5 ......46 A6
Dudley Ho ① HP3.....146 A4
Dudley La RG9 ......181 A6
DUDSWELL 134 D8
Dudswell La HP4.....134 D7
Duffield La SL3 .....198 F6
Duffield Pk SL2 .....199 A2
Dukes Ave LU6 .....107 E8
Dukes Cl
  Gerrards Cross SL9 ..188 E3
  Shabbington HP18 ...124 C2
Dukes Dr
  Farnham Common SL2 .198 A8
  Milton Keynes MK2 ...47 C1
Dukes Kiln Dr SL9 ...188 E3
Dukes La SL9 ......188 E4
Dukes Mdw SL8 .....185 B3
Dukes Piece MK18 ....52 F8
Dukes Pl
  Marlow SL7 ....183 D2
  Slough SL1 ....205 F6
Dukes Ride
  Gerrards Cross SL9 ..188 E3
  Ickenham UB10 .....201 E8
  Leighton Buzzard LU7 .70 F3
Dukes Row HP18......99 A1
Duke St
  Aspley Guise MK17 ...49 D4
  Eton SL4...........210 C7
  Henley-on-Thames RG9 .191 E2
  High Wycombe HP13 ..173 C4
  Princes Risborough
    HP27............139 B4
Dukes Valley SL9 ....188 B2
Dukes Way
  Berkhamsted HP4 ....135 A6
  Uxbridge UB8.......201 C4
Dukes Wood Ave SL9 .188 E3
Dukes Wood Dr SL9...188 D3
Dulverton Ct LU7 ....80 C8
Dulverton Dr MK4 ....46 D1
Dulwich Cl MK16.....22 C2
Dumbletons WD3 ....178 E6
Dumfries Cl MK3.....46 F3
Dunbar Cl
  Milton Keynes MK3 ...57 D8
  Slough SL2.........206 A6
Dunbar Dr OX9 .....126 A1
Duncan Gr MK5 ......45 F6
Duncan Lock Ho HP4 ..135 B5
Duncannon Cres SL4 .209 D4
Duncan Rd MK43......24 E2
Dunchurch Dale MK7 ..48 B5
Duncombe Cl HP6 ....154 E1
Duncombe Rd MK2 ...58 C7
Duncroft SL4 ....209 F4
Dundale Prim Sch
  HP23............119 A5
Dundale Rd HP23 ...119 A4
Dundee Rd SL1 .....205 A8
Dungeness Ct MK4 ...46 A1
Dungrovehill La SL7 ..194 D3
Dunholme End SL6 ...202 D3
Dunkeld Ho HP11 ...174 B4
Dunkery Beacon MK4 ..46 D3
Dunnet Cl MK4 ......57 A8
Dunny La WD4 ......156 F7
Dunoon Rd MK6 .....47 A4
Dunsham La HP20 ...101 E2
Dunsley Pl HP23 ....119 B3
DUNSMORE 141 A7
Dunsmore Ave HP27 .139 C5
Dunsmore Ride HP27..139 C5
DUNSTABLE 93 E8
Dunstable Downs★ LU6 .93 E4
Dunstable Ho ④ SL7 .183 E1
Dunstable Rd
  Dagnall HP4........107 C7
  Eaton Bray LU6 ......93 A5
  Totternhoe LU6 ......93 D7
Dunster Ct MK4 .....46 E3
Dunster Gdns SL1 ...205 A6
Dunston Hill HP23 ...119 A4
Dunthorne Way MK8 ..45 D6
DUNTON.............77 E5
Dunton Rd LU7 ......78 D6
Dunvedin Pl MK12 ....33 D4
Dunvegan Cl MK2....58 D4
Dunwood Cl SL6 ....202 C5
Dunwood Rise HP13..162 B1
Duparc Cl MK7......48 C5
Dupre Cl SL1 ....204 E4
Dupre Cres HP9 .....176 B1
Du Pre Wlk HP10 ...185 D4
Durgate MK7 ....48 A8
Durham Ave SL1 ....205 A7
Durham Ho ① MK3...46 F1
Durley Hollow HP11 .162 B1
Durlston End MK4.....57 A8
Durrans Cl MK2......47 E1
Durrans Ho MK2.....47 E1
Durrants La HP4 ....134 F5
Durrants Path HP5 ..144 A4
Durrants Rd HP4 ....134 F5
Durrell Cl LU7 ......80 E7
Dutch Barn Cl TW19..213 D1
Dutch Elm Ave SL4..210 F7
Dutton Way SL0.....207 E7

Dyersdale MK13 ......34 C5
Dyers Mews MK14 ....34 F6
Dyers Rd LU6 ....92 D7
Dymock Ct HP22......85 B4
Dyson Cl SL4 ....210 B4

E

Eagle Cl HP6 ....154 F2
Eagles Rd HP20 ....116 A8
EAGLESTONE.........47 B7
Eaglestone Rdbt MK6 ..47 A8
Eagle Way MK43 ......3 F6
Eagle Wlk MK9 ......34 F3
EAKLEY LANES 4 D2
Ealing Chase MK10....47 F8
Eames Ct MK20 .....101 F3
Eardley Pl MK8 ......45 D6
Earl Cl HP13 ....162 A1
Earl Howe Rd HP15 .163 D6
Earl Cl MK2.........58 C8
Earls Field SL6 .....203 C2
Earls La SL1 ....204 F5
Earls Willow MK13 ....34 A8
Earlswood Cl HP21...116 A5
Easby Gr MK10......36 A1
Eascote Rd HP21 ...116 B4
EASINGTON.........111 B1
Easington La HP18 ..111 B1
Easington Terr HP18 .111 B1
East Berkshire Coll
  Slough SL3.........207 A3
  Windsor SL4 ....210 C5
Eastbourne Rd SL1...205 A7
Eastbridge SL2 .....206 B5
Eastbrook Cl OX25 ...95 E7
EAST BURNHAM 198 A4
East Burnham Cotts
  SL2..............198 A4
East Burnham La SL2 .198 A4
Eastbury Ct MK4 ....46 D1
East Chapel MK4.....57 B8
EAST CLAYDON.......74 E7
East Claydon Rd MK18..65 D2
East Claydon Sch MK18 .74 E7
East Comm SL9 ....188 E5
East Cres SL4 ......209 F6
Eastcroft SL2 ......198 B1
East Dales MK13 ....34 C5
East Dr
  High Wycombe HP13 ..173 C8
  Stoke Poges SL2 ....198 E2
EAST END
  Cranfield 25 C1
  North Crawley 24 F6
East End HP22 ......87 D1
Eastergate HP9 ....175 C4
Eastern Dene HP15 ..163 B5
Eastern Dr SL8 .....185 C4
Eastern St HP20 ....101 E1
Eastfield Ct ③ SL1 ..206 A3
Eastfield Cres NN12...18 F5
Eastfield Dr MK19 ....11 A3
Eastfield Rd
  Aylesbury HP20 ....116 B8
  Burnham SL1 ......204 A8
  Princes Risborough
    HP27............139 C3
East Green Cl MK5....45 F6
East Hills MK43 ......25 B1
East La MK7 ....47 F7
Eastlands HP27 ....149 E5
Eastnor HP3........146 A3
Eastoke Pl MK4 .....57 A8
Easton St HP11 ....173 B6
Easton Terr HP11 ...173 C6
East Paddock SL6 ..194 F6
East Rd
  Cranfield MK43 ......24 E2
  Maidenhead SL6 ....202 E7
  West Drayton UB7 ..208 F2
East Richardson St ⑤
  HP11.............172 F7
East Ridge SL8 .....185 B4
East Spur MK7 ......47 F7
East St
  Adstock MK18 ....53 F1
  Chesham HP5 ......154 B8
  Olney MK46 ....7 A4
East Terr SL4.......210 E7
East View OX25 .....96 A8
East Walk N MK9 ....34 E2
East Walk S MK9 ....34 E2
East Way HP9.......175 A1
Eastwick Cres WD3 ..178 F8
Eastwood Ct ① SL7 .183 F3
Eastwood Rd HP14 ..158 F3
Eaton Ave
  High Wycombe HP12 ..172 D8
  Milton Keynes MK2 ...58 D7
  Slough SL1.........204 C6
EATON BRAY........92 F6
Eaton Bray Lower Sch
  LU6..............92 F6
Eaton Bray Rd
  Edlesborough LU6 ...92 C5
  Honeywick LU6 ......92 E8
Eaton Cl HP22 ......116 F2

Eatongate Cl LU6 ....92 E5
EATON GREEN.......92 C7
Eaton Mill Prim Sch
  MK2..............58 D6
Eaton Pk LU6 ....92 F6
Eaton Pl HP12 .....172 D8
Eaton Rd HP21......115 D7
Ebble Cl HP21 ......115 C4
Ebbsgrove MK5 ......34 B1
Ebenezer Ho HP10 ..174 C2
Ebsworth Cl SL6 ....196 C3
Eddington St MK4.....46 D1
Eddy St HP14 ......135 A5
Eden Cl
  Aylesbury HP21 .....115 D4
  Slough SL3.........207 A1
Eden Sh Ctr HP11 ..173 A7
Eden Wlk MK1 ......46 E1
Edgar Rd HP21......208 E5
Edgar Wallace Pl SL3 .185 B5
EDGCOTT...........72 F2
Edgecombe Rd HP21 .116 B5
Edgecote MK8 ....46 A8
Edgecote Rd HP11 ...173 B7
Edgecott Rd HP18....82 F7
Edgehill OX9 ....125 F2
Edge Hill Ct MK18....41 E2
Edgewood HP11 ....173 D5
Edinburgh Ave SL1 ..205 B7
Edinburgh Gate UB9 .189 F5
Edinburgh Gdns SL4 .210 D5
Edinburgh Ho MK3 ...57 D7
Edinburgh Pl HP21 ..115 C6
Edinburgh Rd
  Maidenhead SL6 ....195 E1
  Marlow SL7 ....183 E3
Edison Cl HP12 ....172 C5
Edison Rd HP19 ....100 E1
Edison Sq MK5.......46 C5
Edith Bell Ho SL9 ...177 F4
Edith Rd SL6.......202 A7
Edlesborough 92 E4
EDLESBOROUGH......92 E4
Edlesborough Sch LU6..92 E3
Edlyn Cl HP4.......134 F5
Edmonds Cl MK18....41 F1
Edmonds Rd HP14 ..171 B4
Edmund Ct
  Beaconsfield HP9 ...186 A8
  Milton Keynes MK5 ...45 B7
Edmunds Cl HP12 ...172 C5
Edmunds Gdns HP22 .172 C5
Edmunds Way SL2 ..206 B7
Edstone Pl MK4......46 C8
Edward Cl HP21.....116 A4
Edwards Croft MK13 ..34 A7
Edward Wlk HP21 ...116 A4
Edwin Allman Pl HP15 .162 E2
Edwin Cl MK17 ......48 D2
Edy Ct MK5.........34 A1
Edzell Cres MK4 ....46 B1
Eelbrook Ave MK13 ..34 C2
Eeles Cl HP19 ......100 F3
Egerton Gate MK5....46 B4
Egerton Rd
  Berkhamsted HP4 ...135 B6
  Slough SL1.........197 E1
Egerton-Rothesay Sch
  HP4.............134 C4
Egglesfield Cl MK18 ..134 E6
Eggleton Dr HP23 ...119 A5
Egham Cl HP9 ......175 C4
Eghams Cl HP9 .....175 C4
Eghams Ct SL8 .....185 B3
Eghams Wood Rd HP9 .175 C4
Egmont Ave MK11....32 E4
Egremont Gdns SL1 .205 A5
EGYPT.............198 B8
Egypt La SL2 ....187 B1
Egypt Way HP19 ....115 A8
Egypt Wood Cotts SL2 .187 B1
Eider Cl MK18 ....52 E8
Eight Acres
  Burnham SL1 ....197 B1
  Tring HP23 ....119 A4
Elangeni Jun Sch HP6 .154 E3
Elbow Mdw SL3 .....212 F6
Elder Cl
  Loudwater HP11 ....174 D1
  West Drayton UB7 ..208 E6
Elderdene OX39 ....147 D8
Elderfield Rd SL2 ...198 F6
Elder Gate
  Milton Keynes, Rooksley
    MK9..............34 C1
  Milton Keynes, Winterhill
    MK9..............46 C8
Elder Way HP15.....163 B3
Eldridge La HP17 ...130 C3
Eleanor Cl MK17 .....60 F7
Eleanor Gdns HP21 .115 F6
Eleanor Rd SL3 ....177 C2
Eleanor Wlk MK17 ...60 F7
Elford's MK6........47 A6
Elgar Gr MK7 ....48 C4
Elgin Ho SL3.......212 E6
Elgiva La HP5 ......154 B8
Elham Way HP21....116 A4

Eliot Cl
  Aylesbury HP19 .....100 F2
  Newport Pagnell MK16 ..21 F5
Eliot Dr SL7 ....183 F4
Elizabeth Ave HP6 ..166 C8
Elizabeth Cl
  Aylesbury HP21 .....116 B4
  Cookham Rise SL6 ..195 F7
Elizabeth Ct
  High Wycombe HP13 ..173 C6
  High Wycombe, Wycombe
    Marsh HP13 ......173 E5
  ⑩ Slough SL1 .....206 A4
  ③ Windsor SL4 ....210 C5
Elizabeth Dr HP23 ..119 B6
Elizabeth Rd
  Marlow SL7 ....183 E3
  Stokenchurch HP14 ..158 F4
Elizabeth Sq MK2 ....58 C8
Elizabeth Way SL2 ..198 F4
Elkins Rd SL2 ......187 E2
Ellen Pl HP21 ......115 C5
Ellen Rd HP21 .....115 C5
Ellenstow MK13......34 A4
Ellen Wlk HP21 ....115 B6
Ellerburn Pl MK4.....46 B3
Ellery Rise RG9 ....170 F1
ELLESBOROUGH.....130 B2
Ellesborough Gr MK8..33 D3
Ellesborough Rd
  Butler's Cross HP17 .130 C2
  Ellesborough HP17 ..130 A2
  Wendover HP22 ....131 A3
Ellesmere Cl
  Datchet SL3 ....211 A8
  Totternhoe LU6 ......93 C6
Ellesmere Rd HP4...135 D4
Elliman Ave SL2 ....205 F6
Ellington Cl SL6 ....203 C7
Ellington Gdns SL6 .203 C7
Ellington Pk SL6 ...195 E1
Ellington Prim Sch SL6 .195 F1
Ellington Rd SL6 ...203 C7
Elliots Cl UB8 ......208 C8
Elliott Ho HP11 ....172 F8
Ellis Ave
  Chalfont St Peter SL9 .177 F2
  Slough SL1.........205 E4
Ellisgill Ct MK13 .....34 B4
Ellison Cl SL4 ......209 F4
Ellison Ct HP23 ....118 F3
Ellison Ho ⑭ SL4 ..210 D6
Ells Way HP11......171 B4
Ellwood Ho SL9 ....177 E2
Ellwood Ho HP9 ....175 B1
Ellwood Rise SL9 ...177 C8
Ellwood Terr WD3 ..167 C4
Elmar Gn SL2.......198 A2
Elm Brook Cl HP18 ..112 C1
Elm Cl
  Amersham HP6 .....154 C1
  Butler's Cross HP17 .130 C3
  Chinnor OX39.......147 C5
  Farnham Common SL2 .198 C6
  Hazelmere HP15 ...163 A3
  Newton Longville MK17 .57 C2
  Weston Turville HP22 .116 F2
Elm Croft SL3.......211 C6
Elm Ct
  Berkhamsted HP4 ...135 B4
  Butler's Cross HP17 .130 C3
Elmdale Gdns HP27 .139 B3
Elm Dr
  Chinnor OX39.......147 C5
  Deanshanger MK19 ..31 D5
Elmers Cl HP19......44 A6
Elmers Mdw MK18 ...76 A2
Elmers Pk MK3 ......58 A8
Elm Farm Rd HP21 ..116 A5
Elmfield Cl NN12.....18 D3
Elmfields Gate MK18 ..66 A4
Elm Gn HP21 ......115 D7
Elm Gr
  Berkhamsted HP4 ...135 C4
  Maidenhead SL6 ....202 E7
  West Drayton UB7 ..208 A2
  Woburn Sands MK17...49 B4
ELMHURST..........101 C3
Elmhurst ⑤ HP11 ...152 A8
Elmhurst Cl
  High Wycombe HP13 ..162 D1
  Milton Keynes MK4 ...46 F4
Elmhurst Cl SL3 ....207 A3
Elmhurst Rd
  Aylesbury HP20 ....101 C2
  Slough SL3.........207 A3
Elmhurst Sch HP20 .101 C2
Elm La SL8 ....184 F5
Elm Lawn Cl UB8 ..201 E5
Elmlea Dr MK46 ......6 E3
Elmodesham Ho ⑦
  HP7 ....165 B7
Elm Rd
  High Wycombe HP12 ..172 C4
  Princes Risborough
    HP27............139 C3
  Tylers Green HP10 ..174 D8
  Windsor SL4 ....210 B4

Elmridge Ct MK4.....46 C2
Elms Dr SL8.....185 C3
Elmshott Cl HP10.....163 A1
Elmshott La SL1.....204 E6
Elmside MK18.....66 A4
Elmslie Ct SL6.....202 E7
Elms Rd SL9.....177 E3
Elm St MK18.....52 D8
Elms The
  Leighton Buzzard LU7.....80 E7
  Milton Keynes MK3.....57 F8
  Preston Bissett MK18.....51 B1
Elm Tree Cl OX25.....81 A4
Elm Tree Cotts HP7.....164 C2
Elmtree Ct 6 HP16.....152 A8
Elmtree Gn HP16.....152 A8
Elmtree Hill HP5.....144 B1
Elmtree Inf Sch HP5.....144 B1
Elm Trees HP18.....125 B7
Elm Tree Wlk
  Chorleywood WD3.....167 F5
  Tring HP23.....119 A5
Elmwood
  Maidenhead SL6.....196 B4
  Turvey MK43.....8 E6
Elmwood Cl HP18.....109 C5
Elmwood Pk SL9.....188 E3
Elmwood Rd SL2.....206 B6
Elora Rd HP13.....173 E7
Elruge Cl UB7.....208 D3
Elsage Ct LU7.....105 B8
Elsmere Cl HP21.....116 A7
Eltham Ave SL1.....204 E4
Elthorne Rd UB8.....201 D3
Elthorne Way MK16.....22 C2
Elton MK6.....47 D7
Elton Dr SL6.....202 D6
Elwes Rd HP14.....171 C4
Ely Ave SL1.....205 C8
Ely Cl HP7.....165 E8
Ely Ho HP13.....173 E8
Ember Path HP21.....115 C4
Ember Rd SL3.....207 B3
EMBERTON.....36 F5
Emberton Ctry Pk★ MK46 6 E1
Emberton Fst Sch MK46.....13 F8
Embleton Wlk MK18.....52 C7
Emerald Cl MK4.....74 F8
Emerald Ct SL1.....205 E4
Emerald Gate MK15.....35 E5
Emerald Gn HP10.....185 E6
EMERSON VALLEY.....46 B2
Emerson Valley Comb Sch
  MK4.....46 C2
Emerton Ct HP4.....134 E7
Emerton Garth HP4.....134 E7
Emerton Gdns MK11.....32 E5
Emilia Cl SL6.....195 C1
Emlyns Bldgs SL4.....210 D7
Emma Rothschild Ct
  HP23.....119 A5
Emmett Cl MK4.....46 C1
Emmett Dr HP21.....115 E5
EMMINGTON.....137 A1
Emperor Cl HP4.....134 F7
Empingham Cl MK2.....58 D4
Empstead Ct RG9.....191 D2
Enborne Cl HP21.....115 D4
Enders Ct MK5.....45 E5
Endfield Pl SL6.....202 B6
Enfield Chase MK14.....34 D5
Enfield Cl UB8.....201 D3
Engaine Dr MK5.....45 F7
English Gdns TW19.....211 D2
Enigma Ctr The MK1.....47 F2
Enmore Gate MK9.....35 A3
Enmore Rdbt MK9.....35 A3
Ennell Gr MK2.....58 C5
Ennerdale Cl MK2.....58 D6
Ennerdale Cres SL1.....204 D5
Ensbury Path HP20.....101 E2
Enstone Rd UB10.....190 F1
Enterprise La MK9.....35 A3
Epsom Cl LU7.....80 D6
Epsom Gr MK3.....57 D6
Ercolani Ave HP13.....173 D6
Eriboll Cl LU7.....80 B6
Erica Cl SL1.....204 E6
Erica Rd MK12.....33 E4
Eridge Gn MK7.....48 A8
Errington Dr SL4.....210 A6
Escarpment Ave LU6.....107 D8
Eskan Ct MK9.....35 A4
Eskdale Ave HP5.....144 D1
Eskdale Gdns SL6.....203 B2
Eskdale Lodge HP6.....154 C2
Eskdale Rd
  Stoke Mandeville HP22.....116 B2
  Uxbridge UB8.....201 B3
Eskdale Way MK10.....36 B3
Esk Way MK3.....46 E1
Essenden Ct MK11.....32 F5
Essex Ave SL2.....205 C8
Essex Cl MK3.....46 F1
Essex Ho 5 HP20.....101 D1
Essex Pl HP19.....101 A3
Essex Rd HP5.....144 C2
Essex Yd HP22.....89 C2
Estcourt Dr HP15.....162 F6

Esther Cl MK13.....34 A6
Eston Ct MK13.....34 A5
Estover Way OX39.....147 B6
Etheridge Ave MK10.....48 C8
Ethorpe MK8.....33 E1
Ethorpe Cl SL9.....188 E6
Ethorpe Cres SL9.....188 E6
Ethorpe Ho SL9.....188 E6
ETON.....210 C8
Eton Cl SL3.....211 A8
Eton Coll SL4.....210 D8
Eton College Rowing Ctr★
  SL4.....204 D7
Eton Cres SL4.....33 C6
Eton Ct SL4.....210 D7
Eton End PNEU Sch
  SL3.....211 A8
Eton Ho 1 SL1.....205 F3
Eton Porny CE Fst Sch
  SL4.....210 D8
Eton Rd SL3.....211 A8
Eton Riverside SL4.....210 D7
Eton Sq SL4.....210 D7
ETON WICK.....204 F1
Eton Wick CE Fst Sch
  SL4.....205 A1
Eton Wick Rd SL4.....205 B1
Eton Wlk 1 SL1.....205 E3
Eunice Gr HP5.....154 D7
Europa Bsns Pk MK10.....36 C2
Europa Ho SL9.....188 E6
Evans Cl
  Aylesbury HP21.....116 A4
  Chearsley HP18.....112 B2
Evans Gate MK6.....46 E8
Evans Way MK23.....119 B4
Evelyn Cl LU7.....79 E1
Evelyn Pl MK13.....34 A7
Evelyns 2 UB8.....208 F7
Evenley La MK18.....54 C6
Evenlode SL6.....202 F8
Evenlode Cl HP21.....115 C5
Evenlode Rd SL8.....185 B4
Everard Ave SL1.....205 E4
Everest Cl SL3.....173 D6
Everest Rd HP13.....173 E6
Everglade HP4.....47 A8
Evergreen Oak Ave
  SL4.....211 A4
Everley Cl MK4.....46 C3
Evesham Gn HP19.....101 C3
Evesham Way MK5.....45 D5
Evreham Rd SL0.....207 E7
Evreham Sp Ctr SL0.....207 D8
Exbury La MK4.....45 F1
Exchange Ho MK9.....34 E2
Exchange St HP20.....115 E8
Exebridge MK4.....46 C3
Exhims Mews HP4.....134 E6
Exmoor Gate MK4.....46 E2
Eynsford Terr UB7.....208 F7
Eynsham Ct MK15.....35 C2
Eyre Cl HP19.....114 F8
Eyre Gn SL2.....198 A2
EYTHROPE.....113 F8
Eythrope Rd
  Eythrope HP18.....100 A1
  Stone HP17.....114 C6

F

Factory Yd HP9.....175 E1
Fadmoor Pl 3 MK4.....46 B3
Fagnall La HP7.....164 D2
Fairacre SL6.....202 C6
Fair Acres SL6.....202 C6
Fairacres Ind Est SL4.....209 D5
Faircroft SL2.....198 B1
Fairfax MK13.....34 C6
Fairfax Cres HP20.....101 E2
Fairfax Mews HP7.....165 A7
Fairfield HP6.....154 B3
Fairfield App TW19.....211 E1
Fairfield Ave SL3.....211 D7
Fairfield Cl
  Bourne End SL8.....185 A5
  Datchet SL3.....211 D7
  Olney MK46.....7 A3
Fairfield La SL2.....198 B3
Fairfield Rd
  Burnham SL1.....197 C2
  Paulerspury NN12.....17 B7
  Uxbridge UB8.....201 D6
  West Drayton UB7.....208 E6
  Wraysbury TW19.....211 D1
Fairfields HP15.....151 E1
Fairford Cres MK15.....35 B6
Fairford Leys Way
  HP19.....115 A7
Fairford Rd SL6.....202 F8
Fairhaven SL9.....177 C2
Fairlawn Pk SL4.....209 E3
Fairlawns HP13.....162 C1
Fairlea SL6.....202 F7
Fair Leas HP5.....144 A2
Fairlie Rd SL1.....205 A8
Fairlight Ave SL4.....210 D5

Fairlight Dr UB8.....201 D6
Fair Mdw MK10.....48 A4
Fairmead The SL3.....212 B7
Fair Mile
  Aylesbury HP21.....116 A7
  Henley-on-Thames RG9.....191 C4
Fairmile Ct RG9.....191 D3
Fair Ridge HP11.....172 F4
Fairthorn Cl HP23.....118 E3
Fair View Cotts
  Chalfont St Peter SL9.....177 E3
  Cookham Rise SL6.....195 E7
Fairview Ind Est
  Amersham HP6.....154 F1
  High Wycombe HP11.....173 F4
Fairview La HP10.....174 A1
Fairview Rd
  Burnham SL6.....204 A7
  Slough SL2.....197 F1
Fairway MK27.....139 A3
Fairway Ave UB7.....208 D5
Fairway Cl UB7.....208 D5
Fairways MK8.....33 C2
Fairways Rdbt MK8.....33 C2
Fairway The
  Burnham SL1.....197 C3
  Flackwell Heath HP10.....185 C7
  Maidenhead SL6.....202 B3
  Uxbridge UB10.....201 F3
Faithfull Cl HP17.....114 B5
Faithorn Cl HP5.....144 A1
Faith Terr MK11.....11 A2
Falaise MK15.....35 B7
Falcon Ave MK6.....35 B2
Falcon Dr
  Milton Keynes MK19.....32 B7
  Stanwell TW19.....213 E1
Falconhurst Comb Sch
  MK6.....47 B8
Falcon Ridge HP4.....135 C3
Falcon Rise HP13.....161 C1
Falcons Croft HP10.....185 E8
Falcon The HP19.....101 F4
Falkland Ho SL1.....205 C6
Falklands Cl MK18.....63 D2
Fall Cl HP19.....101 D3
Falling La UB7.....208 E6
Fallow Field HP15.....163 B3
Fallows The SL6.....196 A1
Falmouth Pl MK6.....34 F1
Falmouth Rd SL1.....205 C7
Fane Way SL6.....202 D5
Fantail La HP23.....118 F4
Faraday Cl SL2.....205 B8
Faraday Dr MK5.....46 C5
Faraday Rd
  Aylesbury HP19.....101 A1
  Slough SL2.....205 B8
FAR BLETCHLEY.....57 D7
Far Furlong Cl HP21.....115 D3
Farinton MK8.....33 F2
Farjeon Ct MK7.....48 D4
Farmborough MK6.....47 C6
Farmbrough Cl HP20.....102 A1
Farm Cl
  High Wycombe HP13.....174 A7
  Ickford HP18.....123 F3
  Little Chalfont HP6.....166 D8
  Maidenhead, Highway
    SL6.....202 A7
  Maidenhead SL6.....203 C1
  Stewkley LU7.....78 C7
Farm Cres SL2.....206 C8
Farm Ct SL1.....211 B1
Farmers Cl SL6.....202 A4
Farmers Pl SL9.....177 C1
Farmers Way
  Maidenhead SL6.....202 A4
  Seer Green HP9.....176 C4
Farmery Ct HP4.....135 E6
Farm Gr HP9.....175 C5
Farm La HP9.....176 D3
Farm Lea HP10.....185 F7
Farm Pl
  Berkhamsted HP4.....134 F5
  Henton OX39.....137 E1
Farm Rd
  Bourne End SL8.....184 F4
  Brackley NN13.....38 A6
  Burnham SL6.....204 A5
  Chorleywood WD3.....167 A5
  Maidenhead SL6.....202 A7
Farm Way TW19.....212 F1
Farm Yd SL4.....210 D7
Farnburn Ave SL1.....205 B8
Farndale Gdns HP15.....163 A6
Farnell Ct MK5.....46 C8
Farnham Cl HP21.....146 A3
FARNHAM COMMON.....198 D6
Farnham Common Ho 2
  SL2.....198 C8
Farnham Common Inf Sch
  SL2.....198 B8
Farnham Common Jun Sch
  SL2.....198 C8
Farnham La MK8.....33 F1
Farnham La SL2.....198 A2
FARNHAM PARK.....198 C4
Farnham Park La SL2.....198 C4

Farnham Rd SL1, SL2.....205 C7
FARNHAM ROYAL.....198 C3
Farnley Rd HP20.....101 E2
Farrer Cl NN13.....26 D4
Farrer Theatre Eton★
  SL4.....205 C1
Farrier Ct 1 SL8.....185 B3
Farrier Pl MK14.....35 A5
Farriers Cl HP13.....146 B3
Farriers Way HP5.....144 A3
Farringdon St MK10.....35 F1
Farthingales The SL6.....203 B7
Farthing Ent Ctr The
  MK6.....47 C6
Farthing Gr MK6.....47 C6
Farthing Green La SL2.....199 C4
Farthings The HP6.....154 A3
Fassets Rd HP10.....174 B2
Faulkner Dr MK5.....47 B1
Faulkner's Way LU7.....80 E7
Faulkner Way HP13.....161 D3
Favell Dr MK4.....46 F4
Faversham Cl HP22.....119 A4
Fawcett Rd SL4.....210 B6
Fawley.....191 C8
FAWLEY BOTTOM.....180 B2
Fawley Bottom La RG9.....180 A4
Fawley Cl SL6.....195 D2
Fawley Court★ RG9.....191 E5
Fawley Gn RG9.....180 D2
Fawley Hill Rly★ RG9.....191 D8
Fawley Rd SL1.....205 C6
Fawsley Cl SL3.....212 E7
Featherbed La HP15.....163 D8
Featherstone Rd MK12.....33 A5
Fedden Ho MK43.....24 D3
Fegans Ct MK11.....32 C6
Felbridge MK7.....48 A7
FELDEN.....146 F7
Felden La HP3.....146 F8
Fells Cl HP18.....125 D6
Fellstead Ct SL6.....202 C6
Felstar Wlk MK6.....47 C4
Felsted MK7.....48 A3
Fences La MK16.....13 A2
Fennel Dr MK14.....34 E4
Fennels Farm Rd HP10.....174 A1
Fennels Rd HP11.....174 A4
Fennels The HP11.....174 A4
Fennels Way HP10.....174 A1
Fennemore Cl HP18.....109 D4
Fennings The HP6.....154 D3
Fenny House Tuition
  Service MK6.....47 A6
FENNY LOCK.....47 E2
Fennymere MK8.....33 D1
Fenny Rd MK17.....69 E8
FENNY STRATFORD.....47 D1
Fenny Stratford Sta
  MK1.....47 E1
Fen St MK17.....36 F1
Fenton Ct MK8.....45 F8
FERN.....184 E5
Fernan Dell MK8.....45 F8
Fernborough Haven 4
  MK4.....46 C2
Fern Cotts SL7.....184 E5
Fern Ct HP4.....135 B4
Ferndale MK8.....35 B1
Ferndale Cl HP14.....158 F4
Ferndale Cres UB8.....201 C2
Fern Dr SL6.....204 B7
Ferne Furlong MK46.....6 F7
Fernes Cl UB8.....208 C7
Fernfield MK17.....56 A5
Fern Gr MK2.....58 D5
Fernhill Cl OX9.....136 A6
Fernhurst Cl HP9.....175 F2
Fernie Fields HP12.....172 C4
Fern La
  Fern SL7.....184 E5
  Haddenham HP17.....127 A3
Fernlea Cl HP10.....174 A1
Fernley Ct SL2.....195 C1
Fernside
  Great Kingshill HP15.....151 E1
  Hazlemere HP15.....163 A6
Fernsleigh Cl SL9.....177 E4
Ferns The HP9.....175 F1
Fern Wlk HP15.....163 B3
Fernwood Sch MK17.....49 B2
Ferrers Ave SL4.....208 D4
Ferrers Cl SL1.....204 E5
Ferry End SL6.....203 C4
Ferry La
  Bourne End SL8.....196 B8
  Medmenham SL7.....193 B5
  Mill End RG9.....190 D8
Ferry Mdws MK10.....36 A4
Ferry Rd SL6.....203 C4
Festival Cotts SL3.....212 C7
Fetty Pl SL6.....202 D4
Field Cl
  Aylesbury HP20.....102 A2
  Buckingham MK18.....51 B6
  Chesham HP5.....144 E3
  Ickford HP18.....124 A3
  Sherington MK16.....14 A2
Field Ct MK5.....46 B8
Field End HP18.....125 F5

Field End Cl HP23.....119 D1
Fieldfare HP19.....101 E4
Field Farm Bsns Ctr
  OX26.....71 A5
Fieldhead Gdns SL8.....185 A3
Fieldhouse Ct HP13.....174 A4
Fieldhouse Ind Est SL7.....183 F2
Fieldhouse La SL7.....183 F2
Fieldhouse Way SL7.....183 F2
Field Hurst SL3.....206 F1
Fielding Gdns SL3.....206 C4
Fielding Rd SL6.....202 B8
Field La MK12.....33 B5
Field Rd
  Denham, Rush Green
    UB9.....200 E8
  Denham UB9.....189 E1
  High Wycombe HP12.....172 B5
  Murcott OX5.....94 A5
Fields End HP23.....119 E8
Fields The SL1.....205 D4
Fieldway
  Amersham HP7.....165 B6
  Berkhamsted HP4.....135 E2
  Chalfont St Peter SL9.....177 D3
  Wigginton HP23.....119 D1
Field Way
  Aylesbury HP20.....102 A2
  Bovingdon HP3.....146 A4
  Chalfont St Peter SL9.....177 D2
  Uxbridge UB10.....201 D1
Field Wlk MK9.....34 F3
Fife Ct MK4.....57 A8
Fife Ho MK3.....46 F1
Fifth St HP11.....173 C4
Filey Spur SL1.....205 B4
FILGRAVE.....13 C5
Filgrave Sch MK16.....13 C5
Filmer Rd SL4.....209 D5
Finch Cl MK10.....35 F3
Finch Cres LU7.....80 E5
Finch Ct SL6.....202 D5
Finch End HP10.....174 C8
Finch Gn WD3.....167 F5
Finch La
  Amersham HP7.....165 F5
  Beaconsfield HP9.....175 C5
  Little Chalfont HP7.....166 B7
Finch Rd HP4.....135 A4
Findlay Way MK2.....58 C8
Finemere Wood Wildlife
  Reserve★ HP22.....84 B8
Fingest La RG9.....170 D4
Fingle Dr MK13.....33 E7
Finians Cl UB10.....201 F5
Finings Rd HP14.....171 A4
Finlay Dr RG9.....191 E2
Finlay Ho RG9.....191 E3
FINMERE.....50 D7
Finmere CE Prim Sch
  MK18.....50 D6
Finmere Cres HP21.....116 C5
Finsbury Chase MK10.....47 F8
Fircroft Cl SL2.....199 A6
Fircroft Ct SL2.....199 A6
Firecrest Way HP19.....100 F1
Fire La MK17.....57 D4
Firemans Run MK17.....49 B5
Firfield SL6.....203 B1
Firs Ave SL4.....209 F4
Firs Cl
  Hazlemere HP15.....163 B2
  High Wycombe HP15.....173 E8
  Iver Heath SL0.....200 C5
  Lane End HP14.....171 C5
  Whitchurch HP22.....87 A5
Firs Ct
  Amersham HP6.....154 C2
  Bierton HP22.....102 C4
  Princes Risborough
    HP27.....138 F3
Firs Dr SL3.....206 F8
Firs End SL9.....188 E8
Firs Rise HP16.....151 E7
First Ave
  Amersham HP6.....165 D7
  Marlow SL7.....184 A2
  Milton Keynes MK1.....47 C1
First Cres SL1.....205 C8
Firs The
  Bierton HP22.....102 C4
  Brill HP18.....110 B8
  Maidenhead SL6.....202 F2
  Uxbridge UB8.....201 D1
  Wigginton HP23.....119 D1
First St HP11.....173 C3
Firs View Rd HP15.....163 B8
Firs Wlk HP15.....163 B2
Fir Tree Ave SL2.....198 F1
Fir Tree Cotts HP14.....161 B8
Firview Cl SL2.....183 F1
Fishermans Cl MK46.....6 E4
Fishermans Retreat
  SL7.....183 E1
Fisherman's Way SL8.....185 B4
FISHERMEAD.....35 A1

Fishermead Bvd 2 MK6. 34 F1
Fishermead Rdbt MK1.. 47 B2
Fishers Field MK18..... 52 C8
Fishery Rd SL6........ 203 C5
Fishguard Spur SL1.... 206 B4
Fishweir LU7........... 68 D1
Fitzgeralds Way HP12.. 172 B7
Fitzhamon Ct MK12.... 33 A5
Fitzwilliam St MK3..... 58 B8
Five Acres
  Chesham HP5 .... 154 D6
  Wooburn Green HP10 .185 F7
Five Acre Wood HP12 .172 C6
Five Points SL0 .... 200 C2
FLACKWELL HEATH ... 185 A7
Flaggs Mdw MK46...... 6 E4
Flambard Cl MK15 ..... 35 A7
Flamborough Spur SL1 205 A4
Flamstead Gate MK5 .. 45 E1
FLAUNDEN............ 156 A6
Flaunden Bottom HP5.. 155 E4
Flaunden Hill HP3 ..... 156 A6
Flaunden La
  Bovingdon HP3 .... 146 D3
  Chipperfield WD3. ....156 E6
Flavius Gate NN13 .... 38 A7
Flaxbourne Ct MK7.... 48 C7
Flaxen Field HP22..... 116 F2
Flaxley Gate MK10 .... 36 A2
Fledgelings Wlk MK18.. 66 A5
Fleetbrook Ho SL3 .... 211 D6
Fleet Cl
  Buckingham MK18..... 41 F2
  Walter's Ash HP14..... 161 F7
FLEET MARSTON...... 100 B4
Fleet St HP20 .... 101 D1
Fleet The MK6 .... 35 B2
Fleetwood Cl HP8...... 177 A6
Fleetwood Ct 7 TW19 .213 E1
Fleetwood Rd SL2 .... 205 F6
Fleetwood Way OX9.... 125 F2
Fleming Ct 3 SL3..... 206 C3
Fleming Dr MK6 .... 47 B6
Fleming Way HP12..... 172 D5
Fletcher Cl HP19...... 100 F3
Fletchers Mews MK14 .. 34 F6
Flexerne Cres MK6..... 47 D5
Flintergill Ct MK13 .... 34 B4
Flint Ho 7 MK4........ 45 E3
Flint Hollow OX39..... 147 B6
Flintlock Ct TW19..... 213 A3
Flint St HP17 .... 127 A5
Flint Way HP16 .... 151 C7
Flitcroft Lea HP13..... 173 A8
Flitt Leys Cl MK43..... 25 B2
Flitton Ct MK11....... 32 F5
Flora Thompson Dr
  MK16................ 21 F6
Florence Ave SL6 ..... 203 A8
Florence Ct HP19 ..... 101 D1
Florence Way SL8 ..... 201 C5
Florey Gdns HP20..... 115 F8
Florida St HP11....... 173 C4
Florin Cl MK15........ 35 A7
FLOWERS BOTTOM.... 150 A4
Flowers Bottom La
  HP27................ 150 B4
Flynn Croft MK4 ...... 45 D1
Fog Cotts HP23 .... 120 A5
Folding Cl LU7........ 78 E8
Foley Cl HP9.......... 175 C4
Foliejohn Way SL6..... 202 A1
Folkestone Ct SL3 .... 207 A1
Follet Cl SL4.......... 211 B1
Folleys Pl HP10 .... 174 C1
Folly La
  Hartwell NN7 .... 10 C8
  North Crawley MK16 .. 24 B5
Folly Rd MK19 .... 31 D4
Fonda Mdws MK4 ..... 45 D3
Fontwell Cl SL6....... 202 A8
Fontwell Dr MK3...... 57 C6
Forbes Pl MK5 .... 45 E4
Forches Cl MK4....... 46 D2
FORD................ 128 B7
Fordcombe Lea MK7... 48 B8
Ford End UB9......... 189 F2
Ford La SL0 .... 208 A7
Ford's Cl HP14....... 159 F8
Ford St
  Buckingham MK18..... 52 D8
  High Wycombe HP11... 173 F4
Ford Way HP13 .... 161 E3
Forelands Way HP5 ... 154 C7
Forest Cl
  Princes Risborough
    HP27.............. 139 B3
  Slough SL2........... 206 B8
  Wendover HP22....... 131 B4
Foresters
  Beacon's Bottom HP14 .159 C5
  Chinnor OX39........ 147 B6
  Oakley HP18 .... 109 D6
Forest Pk SL4......... 209 E1
Forest Point HP13 .... 173 F5

Forest Rd
  Hanslope MK19 .... 10 F5
  Piddington (Northants) NN7 4 A8
  Windsor SL4 .... 209 E5
Forest Rise MK6 ...... 47 B8
Forestry Hos OX49 .... 168 A7
Forest Way HP13...... 174 A8
Forfar Dr MK3 .... 46 F2
Forge Cl
  Ashendon HP18....... 97 E1
  Holmer Green HP15... 163 C6
  Horton-cum-S OX33... 108 B5
  Marsh Gibbon OX27... 71 F3
  Oakley HP18 .... 109 D4
  Steeple Claydon MK18.. 63 E2
Forge Dr SL2 .... 198 C6
Forge End HP7 .... 165 B7
Forge Rd HP14........ 161 C8
Forge The MK46 ..... 13 F8
Forgetts Rd HP14..... 171 C4
Forlease Cl SL6....... 203 A6
Forlease Dr SL6....... 203 A6
Forlease Rd SL6....... 203 A6
Formby Cl
  Milton Keynes MK3.... 57 C7
  Slough SL3........... 207 C2
Forrabury Ave MK13 .. 34 C3
Forsythia Gdns SL3 ... 206 E3
Fort End HP17 .... 127 A6
Forthill Pl MK5 .... 45 F7
Fortuna Ct MK7 ...... 48 C6
Forty Gn HP27 .... 137 F3
FORTY GREEN
  Beaconsfield 175 A4
  Princes Risborough ... 137 F3
Forty Green Dr SL7 ... 183 B2
Forty Green Rd HP9... 175 C4
Forum The MK14...... 34 E5
FOSCOTE 42 B4
Foscote Cotts MK18... 42 B4
Foscote Rd MK18 ..... 41 F3
Foscot Way MK18 .... 41 E2
Foskett Way HP21..... 115 E5
Fossey Cl MK5 .... 45 F3
Foster Ave SL4........ 209 E4
Foster Cl HP20........ 101 F3
Fosters La MK13 ..... 34 A3
Fosters Path MK13.... 197 F1
Fotherby Ct SL6....... 203 A6
Fotheringay Gdns SL1.. 205 A6
Fotherley Rd WD3 .... 178 F8
Founders Mews MK14.. 34 F6
Foundry La
  Horton SL3........... 212 B4
  Lacey Green HP27.... 149 C5
Fountain Ct
  6 Aylesbury HP20.... 115 D8
  1 Olney MK46 ...... 6 F3
Fountaine Cl MK14 .... 34 E7
Fountain Gdns SL4.... 210 D4
FOUR ASHES......... 162 D4
Four Ashes Rd HP15 .. 162 C5
Fourdrinier Ct HP11.... 174 A4
Four Oaks HP5........ 144 A4
Fourth Ave SL7 .... 184 A2
Fourth St HP11 .... 173 B4
Fourways Mews HP12 .172 C4
Fowler MK14 .... 34 C7
Fowler Rd HP19....... 115 B8
Fowlers Farm Rd HP14 158 E4
Foxborough Cl SL3.... 207 A1
Foxborough Ct SL6 ... 202 E4
Foxborough Prim Sch
  SL3................. 207 A1
Fox Cl HP23 .... 119 D1
Fox Cover OX39....... 147 C6
Fox Covert La MK19 .. 20 A5
Foxcovert Rd MK5 .... 45 F4
Foxdell Way SL9 ...... 177 E5
Foxes Piece SL7 ...... 183 E2
Foxes Piece Sch SL7.. 183 E3
Fox Farm Rd MK17.... 59 D6
Foxfield MK10 .... 36 B3
Fox Field HP15........ 162 F5
Foxgate MK10 .... 22 B4
Foxglove HP21........ 115 B5
Foxglove Cl MK18..... 52 C7
Foxglove Ct MK16..... 21 F4
Foxgoles Cl MK19..... 31 F5
Foxherne SL3......... 206 C4
Foxhill MK16 .... 6 E5
Foxhill Cl HP13 .... 162 B1
Foxhollow Dr SL2 .... 198 C7
Foxhunter Dr MK14 .. 34 E6
Fox La HP15 .... 163 B6
Foxleigh HP11 .... 173 A4
Foxley Pl MK5 .... 46 C8
FOX MILNE........... 35 F4
Fox Milne Rdbt MK10.. 35 F4
Foxmoor Ct UB9 ..... 190 A5
Fox Rd
  Holmer Green HP15... 163 B6
  Slough SL3........... 206 D2
  Wigginton HP23...... 119 C2
Foxton MK6 .... 47 D6
Fox Way MK18........ 52 E7
Fraderica Cotts MK16 . 22 C3
Framers Ct HP14...... 171 B4

Framewood Manor
  SL2................. 199 C6
Framewood Rd
  Slough SL3........... 188 C1
  Wexham Street SL2, SL3 199 C6
Framlingham Ct MK5.. 45 A5
Frampton Gr 11 MK4 .. 45 F1
France Furlong MK14 . 34 F8
Frances Ave SL6....... 196 C1
Frances Ct LU7 .... 80 E7
Frances Rd SL4....... 210 D5
Frances St HP5........ 144 C2
Franchise St 3 HP5... 144 C1
Francis Ct MK5 .... 46 B6
Francis House Prep Sch
  HP23................ 118 F3
Francis Way SL1...... 204 D6
Frank Atter Croft MK12.. 33 C5
Frank Howe Ct MK6... 35 A1
Franklin Ave SL2...... 205 B8
Franklin Cl HP17...... 127 A7
Franklin Ct HP7....... 154 C1
Franklin Rd
  Dunstable LU6........ 93 F8
  Haddenham HP17..... 127 A7
Franklins Croft MK12.. 33 C5
FRANKLIN'S SPRING... 178 D5
Frank Lunnon Cl SL8.. 185 C3
Franklyn Cres SL4 .... 209 D4
Frankston Ave MK11 .. 32 E5
Frank Sutton Way SL1.. 205 D6
Frankswood Ave UB7 . 208 F7
Frantons The SL6..... 202 A7
Frascati Way SL6 ..... 202 F7
Fraser Rd HP14....... 172 C5
Fraucup Cl HP17...... 128 B7
Fraunchies Ct SL1.... 205 E6
Frays Ave UB7 .... 208 D4
Frays Cl UB7.......... 208 D3
Fray's Ct UB8......... 201 C5
Frayslea UB8 .... 201 C3
Frays Valley Nature
  Reserve* UB10...... 201 D8
Fray's Waye UB8...... 201 C4
Frederick Pl HP11..... 174 B3
Fredericks Ct HP9 .... 186 A8
Frederick Smith Ct
  MK12................ 33 D4
Frederick St HP18 .... 99 A7
Freeman Cl MK12..... 33 B5
Freeman Ct HP5 ..... 144 C1
Freemans Cl SL2...... 199 A6
Freemans Gdns MK46.. 7 A3
Freemans Wlk 2 SL4.. 210 C2
Fremantle Rd
  Aylesbury HP21...... 115 E5
  High Wycombe HP13.. 162 E2
Frenchum Gdns SL1... 204 E5
Frensham Dr MK2..... 58 C7
Frensham Rd SL2..... 198 C6
Freshfield Ave 1 MK10.. 36 A3
Friariage Rd HP20.... 115 D8
Friarscroft Way HP20 . 115 C8
Friars Field HP4 ...... 134 E7
Friars Furlong HP18... 125 B7
Friars Gdns HP14 .... 162 A7
Friars Wlk HP10 ..... 151 D5
Friars Wlk HP23 ..... 119 A4
Friary Gdns MK16 .... 22 C2
Friary Island TW19 ... 211 C1
Friary Rd TW19 ...... 211 C1
Friary The SL4 .... 211 C1
Friday St
  Henley-on-Thames RG9 .191 E2
  Leighton Buzzard LU7 .. 80 E7
FRIETH 170 F1
Frieth CE Comb Sch
  RG9................. 170 F1
Frieth Rd SL7 .... 182 E5
Frimley Dr SL1........ 204 F4
Fripp Gdns MK8....... 45 D6
Frithe The SL2........ 206 B7
FRITH-HILL........... 152 C7
Frith Hill
  Great Missenden HP16 .152 B7
  South Heath HP16..... 152 C8
Frithsden Copse HP4.. 135 F8
Frithwood Cres MK7... 48 B7
Froggy La UB9........ 189 D1
Frog La HP18 .... 112 F3
Frogmill SL6.......... 193 C3
Frogmill Cl HP17...... 127 A5
Frogmill Spinney SL6 .. 193 C4
Frogmoor HP13....... 173 A7
Frogmore Cl
  Hughenden Valley
    HP14.............. 162 A7
  Slough SL3........... 206 D3
Frogmore Cotts SL4... 210 E5
Frogmore Ct 4 SL6... 202 F7
Frogmore Dr SL4 .... 210 F5
Frogmore Flats SL4 .. 210 E5
Frogmore Ho* SL4 ... 210 F5
Frogmore La HP18.... 125 C5
Frogmore St HP23 ... 119 A3
Frome Cl HP21........ 115 C5
Fromer Rd HP10 ..... 185 D4
Frost Ho 4 HP4....... 135 C3

Froxfield Ct MK4....... 46 C1
Fryday St MK6 .... 46 E7
Fryer Cl HP5.......... 154 D6
Fryers Ct 3 HP12 .... 172 D8
Fryers La HP12 .... 172 D8
Frymley View SL4..... 209 D6
Fuggle Dr HP21....... 115 E5
Fulbrook Mid Sch MK17 .49 B5
Fullbrook Cl SL6...... 203 A8
Fuller's Cl HP5........ 154 B6
Fuller's Hill HP5, HP6.. 154 A6
FULLERS SLADE 33 A4
Fullers Yd SL6 .... 196 B2
Fulmar Pl 1 HP19 .... 101 F3
FULMER.............. 199 C8
Fulmer Chase SL3 .... 199 C8
Fulmer Common Rd SL3,
  SL0................. 199 E6
Fulmer Dr SL9 .... 188 D2
Fulmer Inf Sch SL3 ... 199 E8
Fulmer La SL9 .... 189 A2
Fulmer Rd SL3........ 188 F2
Fulmer St
  Milton Keynes, Emerson
    Valley MK4......... 46 C3
  Milton Keynes, Medbourne MK8,
    MK5.............. 45 E6
Fulmer Way SL9 ...... 188 E5
Fulton Cl HP13........ 173 A8
FULWELL............. 39 A2
Fulwell Ct MK14 ..... 34 E8
Fulwell Rd
  Finmere MK18....... 50 C7
  Westbury NN13....... 39 A4
Fulwood Ct TW19..... 213 F1
Fulwoods Dr MK6..... 47 A8
Furlong Cl SL8........ 185 B3
Furlong Cres HP17.... 115 A1
Furlong La LU6 .... 93 C7
Furlong Rd SL8....... 185 B3
Furlong The 12 HP23.. 119 A3
Furness SL4 .... 209 C5
Furness Cres MK3..... 47 A1
Furness Pl 8 SL4..... 209 C5
Furness Row 9 SL4... 209 C5
Furness Sq 6 SL4 ... 209 C5
Furness Way SL4 .... 209 C5
Furness Wlk 7 SL4... 209 C5
Furnival Ave SL2..... 205 B8
Furrow Cl HP21....... 115 D4
Furrows The UB9..... 190 C6
Furrow Way SL6 ..... 202 A4
FURTHO 19 A3
Furtho Ct MK19....... 32 B7
Furtho La NN12...... 18 E3
Fury Ct MK8.......... 45 E7
Furze Down Specl Sch
  MK18................ 65 E4
Furze Field La HP16... 142 B8
Furzefield Rd HP9 .... 175 C2
Furzeham Rd UB7.... 208 E4
Furze La MK18........ 65 E5
Furzen Cl SL2......... 198 A2
FURZE PLATT........ 195 C2
Furze Platt Inf Sch SL6 195 C1
Furze Platt Jun Sch
  SL6................. 195 C1
Furze Platt Rd SL6... 195 B1
Furze Platt Senior Sch
  SL6................. 195 C2
Furze Platt Sta SL6... 195 E1
Furze Rd SL6......... 195 D1
Furze View WD3 ..... 167 C4
Furze Way MK12...... 33 C6
FURZTON............ 46 A2
Furzton Rdbt MK4.... 46 C4
Fuzzens Wlk SL4..... 209 E5
Fyfield Barrow MK7... 48 C6
Fyne Dr LU7.......... 80 C8

G

Gables Cl
  Chalfont St Peter SL9 .177 E6
  Datchet SL3.......... 211 A8
  Maidenhead SL6...... 203 B8
  Wendover HP22....... 131 A4
Gables Dr HP14....... 149 C1
Gables Mdw HP15.... 163 C6
Gables The
  Datchet SL3.......... 211 A8
  Haddenham HP17..... 127 A5
  Leighton Buzzard LU7 .. 80 E6
Gable Thorne MK7 ... 48 D6
Gabriel Cl MK7 .... 48 C5
Gaddesden Cres MK7 . 48 C6
Gadge Cl OX9......... 125 E1
Gadmore La HP23..... 132 F7
Gadsden Cl MK43..... 25 D3
Gadsden Cl MK17..... 69 E8
Gage Cl SL6.......... 202 E4
Gainsborough
  Gainsborough SL6.... 195 F5
Gainsborough Cl MK8.. 45 D6
Gainsborough Dr SL6 . 202 D8
Gainsborough Hill RG9 191 D1
Gainsborough Pl HP19 . 100 F3
Gainsborough Rd
  Aylesbury HP21...... 115 E4

Gainsborough Rd continued
  Henley-on-Thames RG9 ..191 D1
Gairloch Ave MK2..... 58 D5
Galahad Cl SL1....... 205 A4
Gallagher Cl MK8..... 45 E8
Galleries The 4 HP13 .173 A7
Galley Hill MK11 ..... 32 F5
Galley La MK17 ...... 59 A4
Galleymead Rd SL3 .. 212 F6
Galloway HP19........ 101 A3
Galloway Chase SL4.. 206 A6
Galloway Cl MK3..... 46 E2
Galloway La HP12.... 172 C8
Gallows La HP12...... 172 C8
Gallys Rd SL4......... 209 D6
Galsworthy Pl HP19... 100 F2
Galvin Rd SL1........ 205 C6
Gamnel HP23......... 119 B7
Gamnel Mews HP23 .. 119 B7
Gamnel Terr HP23 ... 119 A6
Gandon Vale HP13 ... 173 A8
Ganton Cl MK3....... 46 D1
Garamonde Dr MK8... 33 F2
Garbo Cl MK8........ 45 D7
Garden Cl
  Halton HP22.......... 131 C8
  Maidenhead SL6...... 202 A5
Garden Cotts SL3 .... 212 D7
Garden Ct HP11...... 174 B3
Garden End HP6...... 154 C2
Gardener Wlk HP15... 163 C6
Garden Field La HP4 . 135 F2
Garden Mews SL1.... 205 F5
Garden Reach HP8.... 166 D6
Gardens Cl HP14..... 158 F4
Gardens The MK18.... 53 F1
Gardiner Ct MK13.... 33 E6
Gardner Cl
  Aylesbury HP19...... 101 A3
  Great Kingshill HP15.. 151 D1
Gardner Ho SL6...... 195 E1
Gardner Rd SL6...... 195 D2
Gardner's Cl LU6..... 93 E7
Garfield Pl 1 SL4..... 210 C5
Garland Ct MK8...... 45 E8
Garland Way HP22.... 117 C5
Garner Ct 13 TW19 .. 213 E1
Garners Cl SL9....... 177 F4
Garners End SL9..... 177 E4
Garners Rd SL9...... 177 F4
Garnet Cl SL1........ 205 A4
Garnet Ct SL7........ 183 C1
Garrard Rd SL2...... 197 F1
Garraways MK6...... 47 A6
Garretts La SL6...... 195 F2
Garrick Wlk MK9..... 34 F3
Garron Cl HP21...... 115 D3
Garrowmore Gr MK2. 58 D5
Garry Cl MK2 .... 58 C5
Garside Way HP20.... 102 A1
Garson Gr HP5....... 144 A2
Garston MK8......... 33 F1
Garthlands SL6...... 195 D2
Garth The HP16...... 152 A8
Garthwaite Cres MK5.. 46 A4
Garvin Ave HP9...... 175 E2
Garvin Mews HP9.... 175 E2
Garwood Cres MK8... 45 C6
Gascon's Gr SL2..... 198 A1
Gaskin Ct MK14...... 35 A5
Gas La SL6........... 203 A3
Gatcombe MK8....... 33 F1
Gate Cotts WD3...... 167 D5
Gatehouse Cl
  Aylesbury HP19...... 115 C8
  Windsor SL4......... 210 B4
Gatehouse Sch The
  MK14................ 34 D7
Gatehouse Way HP19 . 101 B1
Gatensbury Pl HP27 .. 139 B3
Gatesdene Cl HP4..... 121 C8
Gates Orch HP27..... 117 D5
Gateway Ctr The HP12.. 172 C4
Gateway Sch The HP16 152 E8
Gatewick Cl SL1...... 205 E5
Gatewick La MK7..... 48 A3
Gatting Way UB8..... 201 E6
Gatward Ave SL6..... 202 A3
Gaveston Dr HP4..... 135 B6
Gaveston Rd SL2..... 197 F2
Gaviots Cl SL9....... 188 F3
Gaviots Gn SL9...... 188 F3
Gaviots Way SL9..... 188 E3
GAWCOTT............ 51 F4
Gawcott Fields MK18.. 52 B7
Gawcott Rd MK18.... 52 B6
Gawcott Road Ind Pk
  MK18................ 52 B7
Gawdrey Cl HP5...... 154 D6
Gayal Croft MK5..... 46 B4
GAYHURST........... 12 D2
Gayhurst Ho MK16.... 12 D1
Gayhurst Rd HP13.... 173 F7
Gayhurst Sch SL9.... 188 C7
Gayton Cl HP6....... 154 E4
Gees Farm Cl NN7... 1 A5
Gell Cl UB10......... 190 F1
George Cl SL7........ 183 F4
George St HP18....... 83 B5

GEORGE GREEN. 206 E8
George Green Dr SL3 . . . 206 F7
George Green Rd SL3 . . . 206 E7
George Inn Pl MK16 . . . . 12 B6
George Lee Ct HP14 . . . . 160 C1
George Rd MK14 . . . . . . 158 E5
Georges Dr HP10 . . . . . . 185 F2
George's Hill HP15 . . . . . 162 F6
George St
18 Aylesbury HP20 . . . . 115 D8
Berkhamsted HP4 . . . . 135 D4
5 Chesham HP5 . . . . . . 144 C1
High Wycombe HP11 . . 172 F7
Milton Keynes MK2 . . . . 47 E1
Uxbridge UB8 . . . . 201 D5
Wing LU7 . . . . 79 E2
Woburn MK17 . . . . 60 F7
George V Pl SL4 . . . . . . 210 D7
George Yd MK11 . . . . 32 D5
Georgian Cl UB10 . . . . . 201 E8
Georgian Hts SL8 . . . . . 185 B5
Geralds Ct HP13 . . . . . . 162 D1
Geralds Rd HP13 . . . . . . 162 D2
Gerard Cl MK13 . . . . 34 A7
Germains Cl HP5 . . . . . . 154 B7
Germain St HP5 . . . . 154 B7
Germander Park First Sch
MK14 . . . . 34 D4
GERRARDS CROSS 188 E5
Gerrards Cross CE Sch The
SL9 . . . . 188 E2
Gerrards Cross Rd SL2 . 199 A6
Gerrards Cross Sta SL9 188 E6
Gershwin Ct MK7 . . . . . . 48 C5
Gervaise Cl SL1 . . . . . . 204 F5
Ghyll Gdns HP4 . . . . 134 D7
Gibbings Cl MK18 . . . . . . 76 A3
Gibbs Cl HP13 . . . . 172 F8
Gibbs Ho HP11 . . . . 173 F4
Gibbwin MK14 . . . . 34 E8
Gib La HP22 . . . . 102 D4
GIBRALTAR 113 D2
Gibraltar La SL4 . . . . . . 184 C1
Gibson Ct 8 SL3 . . . . . . 206 F1
Gibson La HP17 . . . . 127 A5
Gibson Pl TW19 . . . . . . 213 D1
Gibson Rd
High Wycombe HP12 . . 172 B3
Ickenham UB10 . . . . . . 201 F8
Gibsons Gn MK13 . . . . . . 34 C4
Gibsons Green MK13 . . . 34 C4
GIFFARD PARK 22 A2
Giffard Park Prim Sch
MK14 . . . . 22 A2
Giffard Park Rdbt MK14 . 21 F3
Giffard Rd MK2 . . . . 58 C6
Giffard Way HP18 . . . . . 125 C7
Gifford Gate MK14 . . . . . 34 E7
Gifford Pl MK18 . . . . 41 E1
Gilbert Cl MK3 . . . . 58 B7
Gilbert Ho 4 HP11 . . . . . 172 E7
Gilbert Scott Ct 9 HP7 165 B7
Gilbert Scott Gdns
MK18 . . . . 52 A4
Gilbert Scott Rd MK18 . . 41 D2
Gilbert's Hill HP23 . . . . 132 E3
Gilbert Way
Berkhamsted HP4 . . . . 135 A4
Slough SL3 . . . . 206 F1
Gilbey Wlk HP10 . . . . . . 185 D4
Gilders Mews MK14 . . . . 34 F6
Giles Brook Comb Sch
MK4 . . . . 57 A7
Gilgal 2 MK4 . . . . 46 B3
Gilletts La HP12 . . . . . . 161 C1
Gillfield Cl HP11 . . . . . . 172 E3
Gilliat Rd SL1 . . . . 205 E6
Gilliat's Gn WD3 . . . . . . 167 D5
Gilliatt Cl SL1 . . . . 207 E2
Gillions Pl HP21 . . . . . . 116 B7
Gillott Cl SL4 . . . . 202 F8
Gilman Cres SL4 . . . . . . 209 C4
Gilmore Cl SL3 . . . . 206 C4
Gilmore Rd HP20 . . . . . . 101 D3
Gilpin's Ride HP4 . . . . . 135 D5
Gilpin Way MK46 . . . . . . 7 A4
Gingers Cl HP22 . . . . . . 117 E5
Gipsy La MK11 . . . . 91 D8
Girton Way MK3 . . . . 58 B8
Gisburn Cl MK13 . . . . . . 34 B5
Glade Ho 5 SL7 . . . . . . 183 E2
Glade Rd SL7 . . . . 183 E2
Glade The
Gerrards Cross SL9 . . . 188 D2
Tylers Green HP10 . . . . 163 C1
Glade View HP12 . . . . . 172 A3
Gladstone Cl MK16 . . . . 22 D3
Gladstone Ind Est 1
SL6 . . . . 202 E8
Gladstone Rd HP5 . . . . . 144 C1
Gladstone Rise HP13 . . . 173 F6
Gladstone Way SL1 . . . . 205 A5
Glaisyer Way SL1 . . . . . 200 D3
Glamis Cl HP13 . . . . 173 B8
Glamis Ho MK3 . . . . 57 E7
Glamorgan Cl MK3 . . . . . 46 F1
Glanmor Rd SL2 . . . . . . 206 B6

Glassmill Ho 4 HP4 . . . 135 D4
Glastonbury Cl MK3 . . . . 47 A2
Glastonbury Thorn Fst Sch
MK5 . . . . 46 B6
Glaven Rd HP21 . . . . . . 115 C4
Glazier Dr MK14 . . . . 34 F6
Glebe Cl
Chalfont St Peter SL9 . . 177 D3
Dorney SL6 . . . . 203 F4
Holmer Green HP15 . . . 163 B7
Maids Moreton MK18 . . . 41 F3
Milton Keynes MK5 . . . . 46 A8
Pitstone LU7 . . . . 105 D5
Glebe Cotts HP14 . . . . . 169 C7
Glebe Dr NN13 . . . . 38 A7
Glebe Ho SL9 . . . . 177 D3
Glebe House Dr MK18 . . 39 E6
Glebe La MK19 . . . . 10 E5
Glebelands Cl MK12 . . . . 33 A5
Glebelands Cl HP16 . . . . 151 E4
Glebe Rd
Chalfont St Peter SL9 . . 177 C2
Deanshanger MK19 . . . . 31 E5
Maidenhead SL6 . . . . . 202 D7
Old Windsor SL4 . . . . . . 211 B2
Uxbridge UB8 . . . . 201 C3
Glebe Rdbt MK9 . . . . 35 B4
Glebe Terr MK18 . . . . . . 41 F3
Glebe The
Lavendon MK46 . . . . . . 7 F8
Lewknor OX49 . . . . 157 B8
Prestwood HP16 . . . . . 151 C7
Stone HP17 . . . . 114 C5
Walter's Ash HP14 . . . . 161 D6
West Drayton UB7 . . . . 208 F2
Weston Turville HP22 . . 116 F2
Glebe Way HP6 . . . . 154 D3
Gledfield Pl MK12 . . . . . . 33 D4
Gleeman Cl MK12 . . . . . . 33 A5
Glenavon Gdns SL3 . . . 206 C3
Glenduragan Ct 9 MK4 . 45 F1
Gleneagles Cl
Milton Keynes MK3 . . . . 57 D7
Stanwell TW19 . . . . 213 D1
Glenfield Mews SL6 . . . . 22 D1
Glenfield Cl
Aylesbury HP21 . . . . . . 116 A5
Stoke Poges SL2 . . . . . 198 F4
Glenham Rd OX9 . . . . . . 126 B1
Glenister Rd
Chesham HP5 . . . . 144 C3
High Wycombe HP12 . . 172 B4
Glenisters Rd HP13 . . . . 173 A8
Glenmore Cl HP10 . . . . . 174 A2
Glenmore Ho HP11 . . . . 174 B3
Glenore SL6 . . . . 196 A8
Glenstal Pl MK9 . . . . 35 A3
Glen The SL3 . . . . 206 C2
Glentworth Cl SL1 . . . . . 205 C5
Glenwater Ho HP15 . . . . 163 A5
Glenwoods MK16 . . . . . . 22 C3
Globe Ho UB7 . . . . 208 D5
Globe La LU7 . . . . 70 E1
Globe Pk (Bsns Ctr)
SL7 . . . . 183 F2
Globeside Bsns Pk SL7 183 F2
Glory Cl HP10 . . . . 185 F7
Glory Mill La
Beaconsfield HP9 . . . . . 185 F8
Wooburn Green HP10 . . 185 E2
Gloucester Ave SL1 . . . . 205 C8
Gloucester Ct UB9 . . . . . 190 A4
Gloucester Pl SL4 . . . . . 210 D5
Gloucester Rd
Maidenhead SL6 . . . . . 195 E2
Milton Keynes MK12 . . . 33 D5
Glovers Ct 2 HP20 . . . . 101 E1
Glovers La MK13 . . . . 34 A4
Glyn Sq MK13 . . . . 33 D7
Glyn St MK13 . . . . 34 A7
Glynswood
Chalfont St Peter SL9 . . 177 F3
Chinnor OX39 . . . . 147 C6
High Wycombe HP13 . . 162 B1
Glynswood Ho OX39 . . . 147 C6
Glynswood Rd MK18 . . . . 41 C1
Glynwood Ho SL4 . . . . . 203 A7
Goathland Croft 2 MK4 . 46 B2
Goddards Croft MK12 . . . 33 C5
Goddington Rd SL8 . . . . 185 A5
Godfreys Cl HP18 . . . . . . 96 B1
GODLINGTON 61 E3
Godolphin Inf Sch SL1 205 C7
Godolphin Jun Sch
SL1 . . . . 205 D7
Godolphin Rd
Seer Green HP9 . . . . . . 176 C4
Slough SL1 . . . . 205 D6
Godrevy Gr MK4 . . . . 57 B8
Godstowe Prep Sch
HP13 . . . . 173 B8
Godwin Cl MK7 . . . . 48 C7
Gogh Rd HP19 . . . . 100 F2
Gold Crest HP19 . . . . . . 101 F4
Golden Ball La SL6 . . . . 195 A3
Golden Dr MK6 . . . . 47 B8
Golden Hills OX39 . . . . . 147 D6
Golden Mede HP18 . . . . . 99 B6

Golden Miller Ct LU7. . . . 79 E2
Golden Oak Cl SL2 . . . . 198 C6
Golden Riddy LU7 . . . . . . 80 E8
Golder's Cl HP18 . . . . . . 123 F3
Goldfield Inf Sch HP23 118 F3
Goldfield Rd HP23 . . . . . 118 F3
Goldhawk Rd MK10 . . . . . 47 E8
Gold Hill E SL9 . . . . 177 C2
Gold Hill N SL9 . . . . 177 C2
Gold Hill W SL9 . . . . 177 C1
Goldilocks MK7 . . . . 48 B6
Goldmark Cl MK7 . . . . . . 48 D5
Gold Oak Wlk MK9 . . . . . 34 F3
Goldsmith Dr MK16 . . . . 21 F4
Gold St MK11 . . . . 11 A2
Goldsworthy Way SL1 . . 204 C5
Golf Club La HP27 . . . . . 139 E5
Golspie Croft MK12 . . . . . 33 C4
Gomez Cl MK4 . . . . 45 D3
Gomm Pl HP13 . . . . 174 A1
Gomm Rd HP13 . . . . 174 A1
Gomms Wood Cl HP9 . . 175 B4
Gomms Wood Ho HP9 . . 175 B4
Gomm Valley Wildlife
Reserve* HP13 . . . . . . 174 B5
Goodacres La HP27 . . . . 149 E6
Goodall Cl RG9 . . . . 191 E1
Good Intent Lo MK1 . . . . 92 E4
Goodlake Ct UB9 . . . . . . 189 F4
Goodman Gdns MK6 . . . . 47 D8
Goodman Pk SL2 . . . . . 206 C5
Goodrich Gn MK4 . . . . . . 56 E8
Goodrington Pl 2 MK6 . 36 A4
Goodwick Gr MK4 . . . . . . 57 B8
Goodwin Mdws HP10. . . 185 E6
Goodwin Rd
Aylesbury HP19 . . . . . . 115 C8
Slough SL1 . . . . 205 C7
Goodwins Mead LU7 . . . 105 A7
Goodwin Villas SL1 . . . . 204 F5
Goodwood MK8 . . . . 45 F8
Goodwood Rise SL1 . . . 173 D6
Goose Acre
Botley HP5 . . . . 145 A1
Cheddington LU7 . . . . . 105 A7
Goose Gn SL2 . . . . 198 B3
Goosemere MK19 . . . . . . 31 E4
Goosen Gn HP21 . . . . . . 116 C6
Goran Ave MK11 . . . . 32 C4
Gordale MK13 . . . . 34 C5
Gordon Rd
Chesham HP5 . . . . 154 C7
High Wycombe HP13 . . 173 D6
Maidenhead SL6 . . . . . 202 D7
West Drayton UB7 . . . . 208 E6
Windsor SL4 . . . . 209 F5
Gordon Way HP8 . . . . . . 177 B7
Gore Cl SL9 . . . . 190 C7
Gore Hill HP7 . . . . 165 B5
Gorelands La HP8 . . . . . 177 F8
Gorell Rd HP9 . . . . 176 B1
Gore Rd SL1 . . . . 197 B2
Gore The SL1 . . . . 197 A2
Gorman Pl MK2 . . . . 58 E4
Gorrell Cl MK18 . . . . 51 B6
Gorrell La MK18 . . . . 51 B6
Gorricks MK11 . . . . 32 D4
Gorse Meade SL1 . . . . . 205 B5
Gorse Rd SL6 . . . . 195 E6
Gorse Wlk
Hazlemere HP15 . . . . . 163 A3
West Drayton UB7 . . . . 208 A3
Gosforth Pl SL1 . . . . . . 204 F6
Goslar Way SL4 . . . . . . 210 B5
Gosling Gn SL3 . . . . . . 206 E3
Gosling Gr HP13 . . . . . . 161 D2
Gosling Rd SL3 . . . . . . 206 E3
Gossage Rd UB10 . . . . . 201 F5
GOSSARD'S GREEN. . . . 25 C4
Goss Ave HP18 . . . . 99 B6
Gossmore Cl SL7 . . . . . 183 F1
Gossmore La SL7 . . . . . 183 F1
Gossmore Wlk SL7 . . . . 183 F1
Gossom's End HP4 . . . . 135 A5
Gossoms Ryde HP4 . . . . 135 A5
Goswell Hill SL4 . . . . . . 210 D6
Goswell Rd SL4 . . . . . . 210 D6
Goudhurst Cl MK7 . . . . . 48 B7
Governors Cl HP6 . . . . . 154 F1
Gower Ho HP6 . . . . 154 E3
Gowers Field HP19,
HP20 . . . . 101 D1
Gowers The HP6 . . . . . . 154 E3
Gowings Gn SL1 . . . . . . 204 E4
Goya Pl HP19 . . . . 100 F2
Grable Ave MK4 . . . . 45 E1
Grace Ave MK6 . . . . 46 E8
Grace Ct SL1 . . . . 205 C5
Grace Reading HP13 . . . 173 E6
Grace Reading Cl HP13 173 E6
Graces Cl MK43 . . . . 25 C3
Graces Maltings 4
HP23 . . . . 119 A3
Graeme Ave MK15 . . . . . 151 A3
Grafham Cl MK14 . . . . . . 35 A8
Grafton Cl
Maidenhead SL6 . . . . . 195 E2
Pottersbury NN12 . . . . . 18 E3

Grafton Cl continued
Slough SL3 . . . . 206 E7
Grafton Ct NN7 . . . . 4 A8
Grafton Gate MK9 . . . . . . 34 C1
Grafton Ho OX9 . . . . 147 C7
Grafton Orch OX39 . . . . 147 D7
Grafton Park MK9 . . . . . . 34 D1
Grafton Rd
Aylesbury HP19 . . . . . . 101 A2
Yardley Gobion NN12 . . . 18 F6
GRAFTON REGIS 9 D2
Grafton St
High Wycombe HP12 . . 172 D8
Milton Keynes, Bradwell
MK13 . . . . 34 B4
Milton Keynes, Granby
MK1 . . . . 47 B3
Milton Keynes, New Bradwell
MK12, MK13, MK14 . . 33 E8
Milton Keynes, Winterhill
MK6 . . . . 46 F7
Graham Cl SL6 . . . . 202 C5
Graham Dr HP12 . . . . . . 172 B5
Graham Ho SL9 . . . . 177 F2
Graham Rd SL6 . . . . 195 E6
Grainge Chase MK7 . . . . 55 A3
Grainge Cl NN13 . . . . 39 A5
Grampian Gate MK6 . . . . 46 E7
Grampian Way SL3 . . . . 207 A1
Gramwell MK5 . . . . 45 F7
Granary Cl MK19 . . . . . . 21 A3
GRANBOROUGH 75 E7
Granby Ct MK1 . . . . 47 A3
Granby Ind Est MK1 . . . . 47 B3
Granby Rdbt MK1 . . . . . . 47 C3
Grandison Ho RG9 . . . . 191 E3
Grand Union Office Pk The
UB8 . . . . 208 C2
Granes End MK14 . . . . . . 34 E8
Grange Chase MK7 . . . . 55 A3
Grange Cl
Chalfont St Peter SL9 . . 177 E2
Leighton Buzzard LU7 . . 80 D6
Maids Moreton MK18 . . . 41 E3
Twyford MK18 . . . . 62 D2
Wraysbury TW19 . . . . . 211 E1
Grange Cotts HP16 . . . . 152 A3
Grange Farm Rd HP4 . . 159 B7
Grange Farm Rdbt MK8 . 45 D7
Grange Fields SL9 . . . . . 177 E2
Grange Gdns HP18 . . . . . 83 A6
Grange Gdns
Farnham Common SL2 . 198 D2
Wendover HP22 . . . . . . 131 B5
Grange La SL6 . . . . 195 E8
Grange Rd
Chalfont St Peter SL9 . . 177 E2
Cookham Rise SL6 . . . . 195 F7
Hazlemere HP15 . . . . . 162 F4
Hazlemere, Widmer End
HP15 . . . . 162 E5
Henley-on-Thames RG9 191 E1
Milton Keynes MK3 . . . . 57 F7
Pitstone LU7 . . . . 105 D5
Tring HP23 . . . . 119 C4
Wilstone HP23 . . . . 104 D1
Grangers Croft MK12 . . . 33 C4
Grange Sch The HP21 . . 115 C4
Grange The
Burnham SL1 . . . . 197 C2
Gerrards Cross SL9 . . . 188 E6
Old Windsor SL4 . . . . . . 211 B2
Wraysbury TW19 . . . . . 211 E1
Grange View HP27 . . . . . 139 E7
Grange Way SL6 . . . . . . 207 F7
Grangewood SL3 . . . . . 206 C8
Grant Ave SL1 . . . . 205 E7
Grantham Ct MK5 . . . . . . 46 C5
Grantham Mews HP4 . . 135 D4
Grant Ho 6 SL8 . . . . . . 185 A4
Granville Ave SL1 . . . . . 205 D8
Granville Dene HP3 . . . . 146 A4
Granville Pl 5 HP20 . . . 115 D8
Granville Rd HP4 . . . . . . 134 E6
Granville Sq MK15 . . . . . 35 C7
Granville St 4 HP20 . . . 115 D8
Grapevine Cl HP11 . . . . 173 F4
Grasholm Way SL3 . . . . 207 C2
Grasmere
Aylesbury HP21 . . . . . . 116 B5
Windsor SL4 . . . . 209 E7
Grasmere Ave SL2 . . . . 206 A6
Grasmere Par SL2 . . . . 206 B6
Grasmere Way
Leighton Buzzard LU7 . . 80 D7
Milton Keynes MK2 . . . . 58 D6
Grasscroft MK6 . . . . 46 E4
Grass Hays HP21 . . . . . 116 C7
Grassingham End SL9 . 177 E3
Grassingham Rd SL9 . . 177 E3
Grassington MK13 . . . . . 34 A5
Grasslands HP20 . . . . . 102 A1

Grassy La SL6 . . . . 202 E7
Grattan Ct SL7 . . . . 184 A3
Gratton Cl MK4 . . . . 46 C3
Gratton Dr SL4 . . . . 209 E3
Gravel Dr HP23 . . . . 118 B3
GRAVEL HILL 177 F4
Gravel Hill
Chalfont St Peter SL9 . . 177 E3
Henley-on-Thames RG9 . 191 D2
Uxbridge UB8 . . . . 201 D7
Gravelly Way HP10 . . . . 163 F2
Gravel Path HP4 . . . . . . 135 E5
Gravel Wlk MK46 . . . . 13 F7
Graveney Pl MK6 . . . . . . 35 B2
Grayburn Cl HP8 . . . . . . 177 A8
Graylands Cl SL1 . . . . . 204 F5
Grayling Cl SL7 . . . . 194 C8
Grayling Ct HP4 . . . . . . 134 F6
Grays Cl NN12 . . . . 17 D8
Grays La
Paulersbury NN12 . . . . . 17 D8
Yardley Gobion NN12. . . 18 E6
Gray's La
High Wycombe HP13 . . 161 D2
Ibstone HP14 . . . . 169 C7
Gray's Mon* SL9 . . . . . 198 F2
Grays Park Rd SL2 . . . . 199 A3
Gray's Pl SL2 . . . . 205 F5
Gray's Rd
Slough SL1 . . . . 205 F5
Uxbridge UB10 . . . . . . 201 E5
Grays Wlk HP5 . . . . 144 B2
Greamesdyke Rd HP4 . 135 A3
Greatacre 7 MK4 . . . . . 144 C1
Great Benty UB7 . . . . . . 208 E2
Great Brickhill 59 D2
Great Brickhill La MK17 . 59 D5
Greatchesters MK13 . . . . 33 F5
Great Denson MK6 . . . . . 47 A8
GREATGAP 105 D6
Great Ground MK14 . . . . 34 E7
GREAT HAMPDEN 150 D7
Greatheed Dell MK7 . . . . 48 D4
Great Hill Cres SL6 . . . . 202 C6
GREAT HIVINGS 144 A3
Great Hivings HP5 . . . . . 144 A4
GREAT HOLM 45 E8
GREAT HORWOOD 55 A1
Great Horwood CE Comb
Sch MK17 . . . . 55 A3
Great Horwood Rd MK18 55 B8
GREAT KIMBLE 139 E8
Great Kimble CE Inf Sch
HP17 . . . . 129 E1
GREAT KINGSHILL 162 E8
Great Kingshill CE Comb
Sch HP15 . . . . 162 C6
Great La
Bierton HP22 . . . . 102 A4
Wendover HP22 . . . . . . 131 B4
Great Linch MK10 . . . . . . 36 A2
GREAT LINFORD 34 E8
Great Linford Comb Sch
MK14 . . . . 34 E8
Great Linford Lakes*
MK14 . . . . 21 D3
Great Marlow Sch SL7 . 183 F4
Great Meadow Way
HP19 . . . . 114 F8
GREAT MISSENDEN . . 152 A6
Great Missenden CE Comb
Sch HP16 . . . . 152 B7
Great Missenden Sta
HP16 . . . . 152 A7
Great Monks St
Milton Keynes, Wolverton
MK12 . . . . 33 C5
Milton Keynes, Wymbush
MK8 . . . . 33 E2
Great Ormes MK4 . . . . . . 56 F8
Great Pasture MK10 . . . . 35 F3
Great Slade MK18 . . . . . 52 C6
Great Stone HP18 . . . . . 112 F3
Great Western St 22
HP20 . . . . 115 D8
Greaves Rd HP13 . . . . . 173 D6
Grebe Cl HP19 . . . . 101 F3
Grecian St HP20 . . . . . . 116 A8
Greenacre SL4 . . . . 209 E5
Green Acre HP21 . . . . . 116 A7
Greenacres
Aylesbury HP22 . . . . . . 89 B2
Pitstone LU7 . . . . 105 C4
Greenacres Ave UB10 . 190 F1
Green Acres Cl HP22 . . . 86 E7
Greenacres La HP10 . . . 163 A1
Greenacres The HP13 . . 162 C1
Greenbury Cl WD3 . . . . . 167 C5
Green Cl
Burnham SL6 . . . . 204 A7
High Wycombe HP13 . . 173 F7
Maidenhead SL6 . . . . . 195 F1
Green Common La HP10, HP9,
SL1 . . . . 186 C4
Green Cres HP10 . . . . . 185 C7
Greendale Mews SL2 . . 206 A6

Green Dragon La HP10 . .185 B7
Green East Rd MK7 . . . . .176 E3
Greene Field Rd HP4. . .135 C4
GREEN END
Granborough 76 A7
High Wycombe 160 A4
Green End
Aylesbury HP20 . . . . . . .115 D8
Granborough MK18. . . . . .76 A7
Great Brickhill MK17 . . . .59 D2
Green End La MK19 . . . . .11 A3
Green End Rd HP14 . . . .159 E5
Green End St HP22. . . . .117 E5
Greenes Ct HP4 . . . . . . .135 C5
Greene Wlk HP4 . . . . . . .135 D3
Green Farm Rd MK16. . . .22 C4
Greenfern Ave SL1 . . . . .204 C7
GREENFIELD 161 A4
Greenfield End SL9 . . . .177 F3
Greenfield Rd MK16. . . . .22 A4
Greenfields
Adstock MK18 . . . . .53 F1
Maidenhead SL6 . . . . . . .203 A5
Upper Arncott OX6 . . . . .94 D7
Green Ground OX33. . . .123 A2
Green Hailey HP27 . . . .139 F3
Green Hill HP13. . . . . . .162 B1
Greenhill Cl MK15. . . . . .46 A8
Green Hill Cl HP13 . . . .162 C1
Green Hill Gate HP13. . .162 B1
Green La
Amersham HP6 . . . . . . .154 E2
Aspley Guise MK17 . . . . .49 E4
Botley HP5. . . . . .155 B6
Bovingdon HP3 . . . . . . .146 A3
Burnham SL1 . . . . .197 D4
Chesham Bois HP6 . . . .154 D3
Datchet SL3 . . . . .211 B6
Eaton Bray LU6 . . . . .92 D7
Farnham Common SL2. .198 B6
Ivinghoe LU7 . . . . .105 E5
Maidenhead SL6 . . . . . .203 A6
Milton Keynes MK12 . . . .33 D6
Owlswick HP27 . . . . . . .128 B1
Prestwood HP16 . . . . . .151 E6
Radnage HP14 . . . . . . .159 D5
Stokenchurch HP14 . . . .158 C5
Upper Arncott OX6 . . . . .94 D7
Windsor SL4 . . . . .210 B5
Greenlands
Flackwell Heath HP10 . .185 B8
Lacey Green HP27 . . . . .149 D5
Greenlands Cl MK16. . . .22 A3
Greenlands Ct SL6. . . . .202 B8
Greenlands La MK16. . .151 B7
Green Lane Cl HP6 . . . .154 D3
Green Lane Ct SL1 . . . .197 C2
Green Lane Rdbt MK9 . .35 B5
Greenlaw Pl MK3 . . . . . .47 A3
Greenleaf Ct SL3. . . . . .211 A8
Greenleas Lower Sch
LU7 . . . . .80 C7
GREENLEYS 33 B5
Green Leys
High Wycombe HP13 . . .161 C2
Maidenhead SL6 . . . . . .195 F2
Greenleys Fst Sch MK12. .33 C5
Greenleys Jun Sch
MK12. . . . . .33 C5
Greenleys La MK12. . . . .33 C4
Greenleys Rdbt MK12 . . .33 B6
Green North Rd MK7 . . .176 E4
Greenock Rd SL1 . . . . .205 A7
Green Park Dr MK16. . . .22 C3
Green Park Sch MK16. . .22 B3
Green Path HP22, HP23 .118 C4
Green Pk HP16 . . . . . . .151 D6
Green Rd HP13 . . . . . . .162 C2
Greenridge HP10 . . . . .174 B8
Greensand View MK17 . .49 B5
Greenside
Bourne End SL8 . . . . . . .185 A5
Prestwood HP16 . . . . . .151 C5
Slough SL2 . . . . .205 A8
Greenside Hill MK4 . . . .46 B1
Greens Keep HP17 . . . .126 F6
Green St
Chorleywood WD3 . . . . .167 C6
Hazlemere HP15 . . . . . .162 F4
High Wycombe HP11. . . .172 F7
Green The
Amersham HP7 . . . . . . .154 C4
Aston Abbotts HP22 . . . .88 D4
Brill HP18. . . . . .110 B8
Burnham SL1 . . . . .197 B1
Chalfont St Giles HP8 . .177 C8
Chearsley HP18. . . . . . .112 B2
Cheddington LU7 . . . . . .105 A4
Cosgrove MK19 . . . . .19 F2
Cranfield MK43 . . . . .24 E2
Cuddington HP18 . . . . .112 F3
Deanshanger MK19 . . . . .31 E4
Edlesborough LU6 . . . . . .92 F4
Great Horwood MK17 . . .55 A3
Hanslope MK19 . . . . .11 A2

Green The continued
Horton-cum-S OX33. . . .108 A5
Hyde Heath HP6 . . . . . .153 C5
Little Missenden HP7. . .153 A2
Longwick HP27 . . . . . . .138 D6
Maidenhead SL6 . . . . . .195 C7
Mentmore LU7. . . . . .90 D4
Milton Keynes, Loughton
MK5. . . . . .46 A8
Milton Keynes, The Green
MK6. . . . . .47 C8
Newport Pagnell MK16 . .22 C4
Paulerspury NN12 . . . . .17 B7
Pitstone LU7 . . . . .105 D4
Quainton HP22. . . . . .85 B5
Slough SL1 . . . . .205 D4
Soulbury LU7 . . . . .69 E3
Stoke Hammond MK17 . .69 E7
Thornborough MK18 . . . .54 A8
Turvey MK43 . . . . .8 E5
West Drayton UB7. . . . .208 D3
Wingrave HP22 . . . . .89 B2
Wooburn Green HP10 . .185 E5
Wraysbury TW19. . . . . .211 E1
Green Tiles UB9 . . . . . .189 F4
Green Tiles La UB9. . . .189 F5
Green Verges SL7 . . . . .183 E3
Green View HP20 . . . . .102 A2
Green View Cl HP13. . . .146 A2
Greenway
Berkhamsted HP4 . . . . .135 A4
Burnham SL1 . . . . .197 B3
Chesham HP5 . . . . .144 B3
Great Horwood MK17 . . .55 A2
Haddenham HP17 . . . . .126 F5
Milton Keynes MK10 . . . .36 C3
Thame OX9 . . . . .125 F1
Green Way MK17. . . . . . .57 D4
Greenway Bsns Pk
MK17 . . . . .55 A1
Greenway Ct HP13 . . . .173 B7
Greenway Fst Sch HP4 .134 F4
Greenway Par HP5 . . . .144 B3
Greenways
Bow Brickhill MK17 . . . . .48 C2
Eaton Bray LU6 . . . . . . .92 D7
Greenways Dr SL6 . . . .202 A8
Greenway The
Gerrards Cross SL9. . . .188 D8
High Wycombe HP13 . . .173 B7
Slough SL1. . . . . .204 D5
Tring HP23 . . . . .118 F5
Tylers Green HP10. . . . .163 B1
Uxbridge UB8. . . . . .201 D3
Green Wlk MK18 . . . . . . .41 F1
Green West Rd HP9 . . .176 E3
Greenwich Gdns MK16 . .22 C2
Greenwood HP14 . . . . .150 A2
Greenwood Cl
Amersham HP6 . . . . . . .154 E1
Seer Green HP9. . . . . . .176 D4
Greenwood Mdw OX39 .147 D6
Greenwood Pk MK18 . . .63 D3
Greenyard The NN7 . . . . .1 B7
Greetham Rd HP21. . . . .116 C6
Gregories Ct HP9 . . . . .175 D3
Gregories Dr MK7. . . . . .48 D6
Gregories Farm La
HP9 . . . . .175 D2
Gregories Rd HP9. . . . .175 C3
Gregory Dr SL4 . . . . . . .211 B1
Gregory Rd SL2 . . . . . . .187 D2
Grenadine Way HP23 . .119 A5
Grendon Rd
Edgcott HP18 . . . . .72 F1
Kingswood HP18 . . . . . . .83 C3
GRENDON
UNDERWOOD 83 A6
Grendon Underwood Comb
Sch HP18. . . . . .83 A6
Grendon Way HP22 . . . .102 A4
Grenfell Ave
High Wycombe HP12 . . .172 D7
Maidenhead SL6 . . . . . .202 F6
Grenfell Pl SL6 . . . . . . .202 F6
Grenfell Rd
Beaconsfield HP9. . . . . .175 E3
Maidenhead SL6 . . . . . .202 E6
Grenville Ave HP22. . . . .131 A7
Grenville Cl SL1. . . . . . .197 B3
Grenville Comb Sch
MK18. . . . . .52 D7
Grenville Ct WD3 . . . . . .167 C5
Grenville Gn HP21 . . . . .115 D4
Grenville Rd
Aylesbury HP21. . . . . . . .115 D5
Buckingham MK18 . . . . .41 C1
Grenville Way OX9 . . . . .126 B1
Gresham Ct HP4 . . . . . .135 B3
Gresham Rd SL1 . . . . . .205 A7
Greyfriars Ct MK10. . . . .36 B2
Greyhound Cl MK18. . . . .66 A4
Greyhound La
Thame OX9 . . . . .125 F1
Winslow MK18. . . . . .66 A4
Greyhound Wlk OX9. . . .125 F1
Greys Hill RG9 . . . . .191 D1

Greys Rd RG9. . . . . .191 D1
Greys The MK6 . . . . .47 C8
Greystoke Cl HP4 . . . . .135 A3
Greystoke Rd SL2 . . . . .204 F8
Greystonley 1 MK4 . . . .46 C2
Griffin Cl
Maidenhead SL6 . . . . . .202 E5
Slough SL1. . . . . .205 C4
Griffin Field LU7 . . . . . . .78 E8
Griffin Ind Mall HP19. . .101 B1
Griffin La HP19 . . . . . . .101 B1
Griffin Lane Ind Est
HP19. . . . . .101 B1
Griffith Gate MK10. . . . . .36 A3
Griffith Gate Rdbt MK10 .36 A2
Griffith Ho HP10 . . . . . .174 C2
Griffiths Acre HP17 . . . .114 E5
Griffiths Yd HP5 . . . . . . .144 B1
Griffon Cl MK6 . . . . .47 A7
Grigby Rise MK6 . . . . . . .47 A7
Griggs Orch MK16. . . . . .14 A2
Grimbold Ct MK15 . . . . . .35 C7
Grimmer Cl HP19 . . . . .100 F3
Grimms Hill HP16. . . . . .151 F7
Grimms Mdw HP14. . . . .150 B1
Grimsby Rd SL1. . . . . . .204 F4
Grimsdell's La HP6. . . . .154 D2
Grimsdyke Rd HP23 . . .119 D1
Gringer Hill SL6 . . . . . . .202 E8
Grizedale MK13 . . . . .34 B5
Groombridge MK7 . . . . . .48 A7
Groom Rd HP16 . . . . . . .151 C5
Groomsby Dr LU7 . . . . .105 E5
Grooms Cotts HP5 . . . . .145 B1
Grooms Ct HP11 . . . . . .174 A4
Grosmont Cl 1 MK4 . . . .46 B2
Grosvenor Cl SL0 . . . . .200 D2
Grosvenor Ct SL1 . . . . .205 E2
Grosvenor Dr SL6. . . . . .203 C8
Grosvenor Way HP19. . .114 E8
Groundsel Cl MK7. . . . . .48 B6
Grove Ash MK1 . . . . .47 D3
Grovebury Rd LU7 . . . . . .80 F4
Grove Cl
Chalfont St Peter SL9 . .177 C2
1 Slough SL1. . . . . . . .206 A3
Grove Cotts UB9 . . . . . .190 C8
Grove Ct
Beaconsfield HP9. . . . . .175 D2
Bierton HP22. . . . . .102 C5
Maidenhead SL6 . . . . . .202 D7
Turvey MK43 . . . . .8 E6
Grove End SL7 . . . . .183 D2
Grove End Barns OX9 . .126 B4
Grove Gdns HP23 . . . . .119 B5
Grove Hill SL9 . . . . .177 C3
Grove Ind Sch The MK5. .46 C7
Grove La
Ashley Green HP5 . . . . .145 C5
Chalfont St Peter SL9 . .177 C2
Little Kimble HP17. . . . . .129 E2
Uxbridge UB8. . . . . .201 F1
Grovelands HP11 . . . . . .173 A6
Grove Leys SL3 . . . . . . .119 C5
Grove Pk HP23. . . . . . . .119 C5
Grove Rd
Amersham HP6 . . . . . . .154 F1
Beaconsfield HP9. . . . . .175 E2
Burnham SL1, SL2 . . . . .197 E4
Hazlemere HP15 . . . . . .162 F3
High Wycombe HP12 . . .172 C8
Maidenhead SL6 . . . . . .202 D7
Tring HP23. . . . . .119 C5
Turvey MK43 . . . . .8 E6
Uxbridge UB8. . . . . .201 D5
Windsor SL4 . . . . .210 D5
Grove Road Prim Sch
HP23. . . . . .119 C5
Grovers Ct HP27 . . . . . .139 A2
Grovesbrook MK17. . . . . .48 D2
Groves Cl SL8 . . . . .185 C3
Groves Rd HP22 . . . . . .131 E7
Groves Way
Chesham HP5 . . . . .143 F2
Cookham Rise SL6 . . . . .195 E6
Grove The
Amersham HP6 . . . . . . .154 D4
Latimer HP5 . . . . .155 D3
Medmenham SL7 . . . . . .193 E6
Milton Keynes, Bradwell
MK13. . . . . .34 A3
Milton Keynes, Rickley Park
MK3. . . . . .58 A3
Newport Pagnell MK16 . .22 B8
Slough SL1. . . . . .206 A4
Tring HP23. . . . . .119 C5
Waddesdon HP18 . . . . . .99 A6
Groveway
Bow Brickhill MK7 . . . . . .48 B7
Milton Keynes, Redmoor
MK3. . . . . .47 A3
Milton Keynes, Simpson
MK6. . . . . .47 E4
Grove Way
Chorleywood WD3 . . . . .167 B4
Uxbridge UB8. . . . . .201 D5
Waddesdon HP18 . . . . . .99 A6
Grovewood Cl WD3 . . . .167 B4
Grubbins La HP27. . . . . .150 B5

Grubbs Cl LU7 . . . . .68 D2
Grubwood La SL6 . . . . .195 A7
Grundy Ho SL8 . . . . . . .201 D3
Grundy Rd MK12 . . . . . . .33 C4
Gryms Dyke HP16 . . . . .151 D6
Guards Club Rd SL6. . . .203 C7
Guards Rd SL4 . . . . .209 C5
Guards View SL4. . . . . . .210 D6
Guards Wlk 1 SL4 . . . . .209 C5
GUBBLECOTE. 104 D3
Guensey Cl HP19. . . . . .101 A3
Guest Gdns MK13 . . . . . .34 B8
Guildford Ave MK4 . . . . .45 E1
Guildford Cl MK18 . . . . . .52 A4
Guillemot Way HP17 . . .116 C6
Guinea Orch MK46 . . . . . .6 E4
Guinions Rd HP13 . . . . .173 F5
Guise Ct MK17 . . . . .49 F4
Gullet Nature Reserve
The★ SL6 . . . . .202 E5
Gullicot Way LU7 . . . . . .105 C4
Gulliford Ave MK4 . . . . . .45 E1
Gulliver's SL4. . . . . .210 D8
Gulliver's Dinosaur & Farm
Park★ MK15. . . . . .35 C4
Gulliver's Land★ SL3. . . .35 C4
Gull Way 4 HP19 . . . . .101 F3
Gundale Ct MK4 . . . . . . .46 B2
Gun La MK16 . . . . .14 A2
Gunmaker Ct MK14 . . . . .34 F6
Gunthorpe Rd SL7 . . . . .184 A3
Gunver La MK4 . . . . .57 B8
Guppy's Orch LU7 . . . . .208 D6
Gurnards Ave MK6 . . . . .35 A2
Gurnells Rd HP9 . . . . . .176 C5
Gurney Cl
10 Aylesbury HP20 . . . .101 F2
Beaconsfield HP9. . . . . .175 D2
Milton Keynes MK5 . . . . .46 A7
Gurney Ct LU6. . . . . .92 F6
Gurneys Mdw HP15 . . . .163 D7
Guttmann Rd HP21. . . . .115 F5
Gwendale SL6 . . . . .195 C1
Gweneth Ct SL7. . . . . . .183 D3
Gwent Cl SL6 . . . . .202 B4
Gwynant Dr MK2. . . . . . .58 C3
Gwynne Cl
Tring HP23 . . . . .119 A5
Windsor SL4 . . . . .209 E6
Gynant Rd HP13 . . . . . .173 F6
Gyosei International Sch UK
MK15 . . . . .35 C5
Gypsy La
Aspley Guise MK17 . . . . .49 F3
High Wycombe HP11. . . .173 D5
Marlow SL7 . . . . .183 E4
Stoke Poges SL2 . . . . . .187 E1

H

Haberley Mead MK13. . . .34 B3
Hackett Pl MK16 . . . . . . .24 A6
HADDENHAM. 127 B5
Haddenham Airfield
HP17 . . . . .126 E7
Haddenham Bsns Pk
HP17 . . . . .126 F7
Haddenham Com Inf Sch
HP17. . . . . .127 A6
Haddenham Jun Sch
HP17. . . . . .127 A6
Haddenham Mus★
HP17. . . . . .126 F6
Haddenham Rd HP17. . .127 A3
Haddenham St Mary's CE
Sch HP17. . . . . .127 A6
Haddenham & Thame
Parkway Sta HP17 . . . .126 E6
Haddington Cl
Milton Keynes MK3 . . . . .46 E2
Wendover HP22 . . . . . . .131 D6
Haddington Way HP20 . .102 A1
Haddon MK8. . . . . .45 F8
Haddon Rd
Chorleywood WD3 . . . . .167 C4
Maidenhead SL6 . . . . . .202 C5
Hadfield Rd TW19. . . . . .213 D1
Hadland Cl HP3 . . . . . . .146 A4
Hadley Cl SL3 . . . . .212 E6
Hadley Pl MK13 . . . . . . .214 C3
Hadlow Ct SL1. . . . . . . .205 C5
Hadrians Dr MK13. . . . . .34 A5
Hadrian's Gate NN13. . . .38 A7
Haggar St HP17. . . . . . . .114 B5
Hag Hill La SL6 . . . . . . .204 A7
Hag Hill Rise SL6 . . . . . .204 A7
Haglis Dr HP22 . . . . . . .131 B6
Haig Dr SL1 . . . . .205 B4
Haileybury Ct SL4 . . . . .210 A4
Hailey Croft OX39 . . . . .147 B6
Hailey Ct SL6 . . . . .202 F5
Hainault Ave MK14 . . . . .22 A1
Haines Cl HP19 . . . . . . .100 F2
Haines Rd HP15 . . . . . . .162 F6
Haithewaite MK8 . . . . . .33 D1
Haldene MK8 . . . . .33 E2
Hale SL4 . . . . .209 F6
Hale Ave MK11. . . . . .32 E5
Hale Ct MK12 . . . . .33 E3

Hale Leys Sh Ctr 23
HP20. . . . . .115 D8
Hale Rd HP22. . . . . .131 C3
Hales Croft HP21. . . . . . .116 B4
Hale St HP20 . . . . .115 E8
Halfacre Hill SL9. . . . . . .177 F2
Halfway Hos
Hanslope MK19 . . . . .10 F4
Maidenhead SL6 . . . . . .195 E4
Halfway House La HP5 . .153 F7
Halifax Cl SL6. . . . . .202 A8
Halifax Ho HP7 . . . . .166 C8
Halifax Rd
Heronsgate WD3 . . . . . .167 C2
High Wycombe HP12 . . .172 D5
Maidenhead SL6 . . . . . .202 A8
Halifax Way SL6 . . . . . . .202 A8
Halings La UB9 . . . . . . .189 E7
Halkingcroft SL3. . . . . . .206 C4
Hall Cl
High Wycombe HP13 . . .173 F5
Maids Moreton MK18 . . .41 F3
Old Stratford MK19 . . . . .32 B6
Hall Cotts HP18. . . . . . . .82 F7
Hall Ct SL3 . . . . .211 B7
Halldore Hill SL6. . . . . . .195 E3
Hall La MK16 . . . . .23 C8
Hall Mdw SL1. . . . . .197 C3
Hall Park Gate HP4 . . . .135 E3
Hall Park Hill HP4. . . . . .135 E3
Hall Pk HP4 . . . . .135 E3
Hall Place (Berkshire Coll
of Agriculture) SL6 . . .194 A1
Halls Cnr HP10. . . . . . . .174 A1
Halse Dr SL1 . . . . .197 F7
Halswell Pl MK10 . . . . . .36 A3
HALTON. 117 D1
Haltonchesters MK13 . . .33 F6
Halton Comb Sch
HP22. . . . . .131 D7
Halton La HP22. . . . . . . .131 B8
Halton Wood Forest Wlks★
HP23. . . . . .132 A3
Halton Wood Rd HP22. .131 D1
Haly Cl MK13 . . . . .34 B4
Hamberlins La HP4,
HP23 . . . . .134 B7
HAMBLEDEN 181 D1
Hambleden RG9 . . . . . .181 C2
Hambleden Mill RG9 . . .192 C7
Hambleden Rd HP14 . . .160 C7
Hambleden Rise RG9. . .192 D6
Hambleden Wlk SL6 . . .195 E3
Hambleden Cl HP21. . . .116 B5
Hamble Dr HP21 . . . . . .115 C6
Hambleton Gr MK4. . . . . .46 B2
Hambling Pl LU6. . . . . . .93 F8
Hamburg Croft MK5. . . . .46 B3
Hambye Cl HP27 . . . . . .149 E4
Hamer Cl HP3 . . . . .146 A3
Hamfield Cotts SL6 . . . .195 F2
HAM GREEN. 83 D2
Hamilton Ave RG9 . . . . .191 E1
Hamilton Cl HP4 . . . . . .107 C5
Hamilton Ct
Aylesbury HP19 . . . . . . .101 D1
High Wycombe HP13 . . .173 B8
Hamilton La MK3 . . . . . . .57 C6
Hamilton Mead 5 HP3 .146 A4
Hamilton Pk SL6. . . . . . .202 A6
Hamilton Pl SL9 . . . . . . .188 E6
Hamilton Prim Sch 17
HP13. . . . . .173 B7
Hamilton Prim Sch
(Annexe) HP13 . . . . . .173 B8
Hamilton Rd
Berkhamsted HP4 . . . . .135 B4
High Wycombe HP13 . . .162 C5
Slough SL1. . . . . .205 A7
Thame OX9 . . . . .126 A1
Uxbridge UB8. . . . . .201 D1
Ham Island SL4 . . . . . . .211 C3
Ham La SL4 . . . . .211 C3
Hamlins MK6 . . . . .47 A6
Hammersley La HP10,
HP11 . . . . .174 B5
Hammerwood Gate MK7. .48 A7
Hammond Cres MK15 . . .35 B6
Hammond End SL2. . . . .198 B8
Hamon Way 2 MK12. . . .33 A6
Hampden Ave HP5 . . . . .144 A1
HAMPDEN BOTTOM. . . .141 B2
Hampden Cl
Aylesbury HP21. . . . . . . .115 D6
Aylesbury HP22. . . . . . . .116 B1
Stoke Mandeville HP22 . .116 B1
Stoke Poges SL2 . . . . . .199 A2
Hampden Gate HP27 . . .150 C5
Hampden Gdns HP21 . . .115 D6
Hampden Hill
Beaconsfield HP9. . . . . .175 B2
Charndon OX27 . . . . . . .72 E6
High Wycombe HP13 . . .173 B8
Hughenden Valley HP16 .151 B3

Hampden Rd continued
Maidenhead SL6 . . . . .202 B8
Slough SL3 . . . . .206 F3
Speen HP27 . . . . .150 C5
Stoke Mandeville HP22 . .116 B1
Wendover HP22 . . . . .131 C5
Hampden Sq HP19 . . . . . .115 A8
Hampden Villas OX27 . . .71 F7
Hampshire Ave SL1 . . . . .205 C8
Hampshire Cl MK3 . . . . . .46 F2
Hampshire Lodge 8
SL6 .202 F6
Hampson Cl MK13 . . . . . . .34 A5
Hampstead Cl 7 HP19 .100 F1
Hampstead Gate MK13 . .34 C3
Hampton 7 MK8 . . . . .45 F8
Hampton Ho SL3 . . . . .212 D7
Hanbury Cl SL1 . . . . .204 A8
Hancock Cl MK17 . . . . . . .116 E5
Handel Mead MK7 . . . . . . .48 E5
Handleton Comm HP14 171 B5
Handley Page Cl MK43 . .24 E2
Handy Cross HP11 . . . . . .172 F3
Hangar Rd U89 . . . . .189 E7
Hanging Croft Cl 4
HP13 . . . . .173 F6
Hangings La HP16 . . . . . .151 A6
Hanley Cl SL4 . . . . .209 D6
Hanmer Rd MK6 . . . . .47 E5
Hannah Ball Inf Sch
HP13 . . . . .173 D7
Hannon Rd HP21 . . . . . . .115 C5
Hanover Cl
3 Aylesbury HP19 . . . . .101 A2
Slough SL1 . . . . .206 A3
Windsor SL4 . . . . .209 F6
Hanover Ct
2 Aylesbury HP21 . . . .115 E7
Hazelmere HP15 . . . . . . .163 B3
Milton Keynes MK14 . . . . .34 D7
Hanover Mead SL6 . . . . .203 C3
Hanover Way SL4 . . . . . . .209 F6
Hanscomb Cl MK15 . . . . .35 C2
Hansen Cl MK5 . . . . .46 B5
HANSLOPE 11 B3
Hanslope Comb Sch
MK19 . . . . .11 A3
Hanslope Rd MK19 . . . . . .19 F6
Hanson Cl U87 . . . . .208 F3
Hanson Way HP21 . . . . . .114 A6
Harborne Ct MK8 . . . . . . .33 C2
Harborough Cl SL1 . . . . .204 D5
Harbourne Cl HP21 . . . . .115 C3
Harby Cl MK4 . . . . .46 C1
Harcourt
Milton Keynes MK13 . . . . .34 A3
Wraysbury TW19 . . . . .211 E1
Harcourt Cl
Dorney SL6 . . . . .203 F3
Henley-on-Thames RG9 .191 C1
Leighton Buzzard LU7 . . . .80 E7
Harcourt Gn HP19 . . . . . .101 B2
Harcourt Rd
Dorney SL6 . . . . .203 F3
Tring HP23 . . . . .119 C4
Windsor SL4 . . . . .209 F6
Hardenwaye HP13 . . . . . .162 E1
Harding Rd
Chesham HP5 . . . . .144 D1
Milton Keynes MK10 . . . . .48 C8
Hardings Cl SL0 . . . . .200 C2
Hardings Spur 13 SL3 . .206 F1
Hardings Row SL0 . . . . . .200 D2
HARDMEAD 15 D3
Hardmead Rd MK43 . . . . .8 A3
HARDWICK 87 B3
Hardwick Cl SL6 . . . . . . .202 A8
Hardwick Gdns HP6. . . . .154 E1
Hardwick Mews MK17. . . .49 B3
Hardwich Pl MK17 . . . . . .49 B4
Hardwick Rd MK17. . . . . .49 B4
Hardy Cl
Aylesbury HP21 . . . . .115 E7
Slough SL1 . . . . .205 D4
Hardy Mead Ct HP11 . . .174 B2
Hardy Mews U88. . . . . . . .201 C3
Harebell Cl MK7 . . . . .48 B5
Harebell Wlk HP15 . . . . .162 F6
Harebridge La HP22. . . . .117 E1
Hare Cl MK18 . . . . .52 E7
Hareden Croft MK4 . . . . .46 B2
Harefield Rd
Maidenhead SL6 . . . . . . .202 A7
Uxbridge U88. . . . . .201 D6
Harehatch La SL1 . . . . . .186 F3
Hare La HP10 . . . . .152 B3
Hare Lane End HP10 . . . .152 A3
Harescombe Ct HP9 . . . .175 D3
Haresfoot Sch HP4. . . . . .135 B1
Hare Shoots SL6 . . . . . . .202 E5
Harewood Pl SL1 . . . . . . .206 A3
Harewood Rd HP8 . . . . . .166 C6
Hargrave Rd SL6 . . . . . . .202 D8
Hargreaves Nook MK14. .22 B2
Harkness Cl MK2. . . . . . . .58 D6
Harkness Rd MK4 . . . . . .204 B8
Harlans Cl MK6 . . . . .47 B8
Harlech Ho 5 HP13 . . . . .173 F7

Harlech Pl MK3 . . . . .57 E7
Harlequin Pl MK5 . . . . . . .45 F3
Harlesden Cl MK10. . . . . .35 E1
Harle Stone Ct MK14 . . .22 A1
Harley Ct SL1. . . . . .205 C4
Harleyford La SL7. . . . . . .194 B7
Harling Rd LU6 . . . . .93 B4
Harlow Cres 6 MK4 . . . . .45 E2
Harlow Rd HP13 . . . . .173 C6
Harmans Cross MK10. . . .36 B3
Harman Terr HP12 . . . . . .172 D7
Harman Wlk HP12 . . . . . .172 C3
HARMONDSWORTH 213 D8
Harmondsworth La
U87 . . . . .213 D8
Harmondsworth Prim Sch
U87 . . . . .213 D8
Harmondsworth Rd
U87 . . . . .208 C2
Harnett Dr MK12. . . . . . . .32 F6
Harper Cl OX25 . . . . .94 D7
Harpers La MK14. . . . . . . .34 F8
Harrier Cl HP20 . . . . .101 F3
Harrier Dr MK6 . . . . .47 A8
Harries Cl HP5 . . . . .144 B1
Harries Way HP15. . . . . . .163 B6
Harriet Walker Way
WD3. . . . . .167 F2
Harrington Cl SL4. . . . . . .209 F3
Harris Cl HP18 . . . . .110 A8
Harris Ct 7 HP20 . . . . . . .101 F2
Harris Gdns SL1 . . . . . . .205 C4
Harrison Barber Cotts
SL3. . . . . .212 D7
Harrison Cl MK5 . . . . .46 D6
Harrison Pl OX9 . . . . .125 F1
Harrison Way SL1 . . . . . .204 D5
Harris Rd HP14 . . . . .171 B5
Harroell
Long Crendon, Church End
HP18. . . . . .125 D6
Long Crendon HP18. . . . .125 D5
Harrogate Ct SL3 . . . . . .207 A1
HARROLD. 3 F6
Harrold Lower Sch MK43. .3 F6
Harrold Priory Mid Sch
MK43 . . . . .3 F6
Harrold Rd MK46. . . . . . . .3 B1
Harrow Cl
Aylesbury HP21 . . . . .115 E4
Maidenhead SL6 . . . . . . .195 E1
Harrowden MK13 . . . . . . .34 B7
Harrow La SL6. . . . . .195 E1
Harrow Mkt The SL3 . . . .207 A3
Harrow Rd SL3 . . . . .206 F3
Harrow Yd 6 HP23 . . . . . .119 A3
Hartdames MK5. . . . . .46 A3
Hatfield Cl MK7 . . . . .48 B5
Hartington Gr 5 MK4 . . . .46 B3
Hartland Ave MK4 . . . . . .57 B8
Hartland Cl SL1 . . . . .205 D5
Hartley MK14 . . . . .34 E8
Hartley Cl SL3 . . . . .199 C4
Hartley Copse SL4 . . . . . .211 A1
Hart Moor Cl HP14 . . . . .158 E4
Hart Rd HP17 . . . . .127 B6
Hart St RG9 . . . . .191 E2
Hartley MK14 . . . . .34 E8
HARTWELL 10 D8
Hartwell Cl HP10. . . . . . . .163 C2
Hartwell Dr HP9 . . . . .175 D3
Hartwell End HP21 . . . . . .115 A7
Hartwell Rd
Ashton NN7 . . . . .9 F8
Hanslope MK19 . . . . .10 E5
Hartwort Cl MK7. . . . . . . .48 B5
Harvard Cl MK14 . . . . . . .21 F2
Harvest Bank HP6 . . . . . .153 C4
Harvester Cl MK12 . . . . . .33 B5
Harvest Hill HP10 . . . . . .185 D2
Harvest Hill Rd SL6 . . . . .202 F3
Harvey Dr MK46. . . . . .6 F1
Harvey Ho SL3. . . . . .206 F7
Harvey Orch HP9 . . . . . . .175 C3
Harvey Rd
Aylesbury HP21 . . . . .115 E5
Dunstable LU6 . . . . .93 D7
Slough SL3 . . . . .207 B4
Harvil Rd U89, U810 . . . .190 E4
Harvington Pk LU7 . . . . .105 D3
Harwich Rd SL1 . . . . .205 A7
Harwood Dr U810 . . . . . .201 F4
Harwood Rd SL7. . . . . . . .183 C1
Harwood St MK13 . . . . . .34 A7
Hasgill Ct MK13. . . . . .34 B4
Haslemere Rd SL4 . . . . .210 A6
Haslerig Cl HP21 . . . . . . .115 C6
Haslow Cl MK8 . . . . .33 E3
Hasting Cl SL6 . . . . .203 C2
Hastings MK11. . . . . .32 E5
Hastings Mdw SL2 . . . . .199 A4
HASTOE. 132 F7
Hastoe Cross HP23. . . . . .133 A7
Hastoe Farm Barns
HP23 . . . . .132 F7
Hastoe Hill HP23. . . . . . . .132 F8
Hastoe La HP23. . . . . .119 A2
Hastoe Pk HP20. . . . . .101 F2

Hastoe Row HP23 . . . . . .133 A7
Hatches La
Great Kingshill HP15 . . . .151 C1
Naphill Valley HP15 . . . . .162 B8
Hatchet Leys La MK18 . . .53 F8
Hatchgate Gdns SL11 . .197 D1
Hatch La
Harmondsworth U87. . . .213 D7
Radnage HP14 . . . . .160 B4
Windsor SL4 . . . . .210 A5
Hatchlands MK8 . . . . .33 F1
Hatch Pl SL6. . . . . .195 E7
Hatch The SL4 . . . . .209 C7
Hatfield Cl SL6 . . . . .202 C6
Hatfield Rd SL1 . . . . .206 A4
Hathaway Ct MK8 . . . . . . .45 E8
Hatter's La HP13 . . . . . . .173 C6
Hatton MK6 . . . . .47 D6
Hatton Ave SL2 . . . . .198 D1
Hatton Cl SL4 . . . . .210 C5
Hatton Gr U87 . . . . .208 D6
Hauksbee Gdns MK5. . . .46 D5
Havelock Bsns Pk SL6. .202 C7
Havelock Cres SL6 . . . . .202 B7
Havelock Ct HP20 . . . . . .101 D1
Havelock Rd SL6 . . . . . . .202 B7
Havelock St HP20 . . . . . .101 D1
Havenfield Ct 16 HP13 . .173 F6
Havenfield Rd HP12 . . . .172 C4
Haven of Rest SL6 . . . . . .203 B7
Haven Shaw Cl HP21 . . .116 A5
Havensfield HP3 . . . . . . .146 F8
Haw St MK10. . . . . .36 C3
HAVERSHAM 20 E2
Haversham Rd MK19 . . . .20 D1
Haversham Village Sch
MK19 . . . . .20 E2
Hawfinch 1 HP19 . . . . . .101 E3
Hawker Ct SL3. . . . . .207 A3
Hawkes Cl SL3 . . . . .207 B3
Hawkhurst Gate MK7. . . .47 F7
Hawkins Way HP3 . . . . . .146 A5
Hawkins Cl MK11 . . . . . . .32 C5
Hawkmoor Cl MK6 . . . . . .47 B8
Hawkmoor Dr MK4 . . . . . .46 C3
Hawkshead Dr MK4 . . . . .46 C3
Hawks Hill SL6 . . . . .185 C3
Hawkshill Dr HP3 . . . . . . .146 F8
Hawkshill Rd SL2 . . . . . .198 D3
Hawkslade Furlong
HP21 . . . . .115 D3
Hawksmoor Cl HP13 . . . .173 A8
Hawkswood MK46 . . . . . .6 F5
Hawkswood Gr SL3 . . . . .199 F6
Hawkswood La SL3, SL9. .199 F8
Hawkwell Dr HP23 . . . . . .119 C4
Hawkwell Est MK19 . . . . .32 B7
Haw La HP14 . . . . .149 A2
Hawley's La HP22. . . . . . . .87 A6
Haworth Croft 2 MK10. . .36 B3
HAWRIDGE 133 E1
Hawridge View HP15 . . .163 B5
Hawridge & Cholesbury CE
Sch HP5. . . . . .133 E2
Hawridge Common. 133 E2
Hawridge Vale HP5 . . . . .133 F1
Hawthorn Ave MK2 . . . . . .58 E8
Hawthorn Cl
Aylesbury HP20 . . . . .116 A7
Iver Heath SL0. . . . . .200 C2
Turvey MK43 . . . . .8 E6
Hawthorn Cres HP15 . . .163 B2
Hawthorn Dr U89 . . . . . .201 C6
Hawthorn Cl
Leighton Buzzard LU7 . . .80 E8
Marlow SL7 . . . . .183 E4
Hawthorne Cres
Slough SL1 . . . . .205 F7
West Drayton U87 . . . . . .208 F4
Hawthorne Gdns HP20 .174 A2
Hawthorne Rd HP13. . . . .174 A6
Hawthorn Gdns SL6. . . . .202 E5
Hawthorn La SL2 . . . . . . .198 A5
Hawthorn Pl HP10 . . . . . .174 C8
Hawthorn Rd HP27 . . . . .139 C3
Hawthorns The
Berkhamsted HP4 . . . . . .135 A5
Cranfield MK43 . . . . .25 B1
Felden HP3 . . . . .146 F7
Little Chalfont HP8. . . . . .166 C7
Maple Cross WD3 . . . . . .178 D5
Monks Risborough HP27 .139 C6
Poyle SL3. . . . . .212 F6
Wooburn Green HP10 . . .185 E6
Hawthorn Way
Chesham HP5 . . . . .144 D2
Wing LU7 . . . . .79 E3
Hawthorn Wlk HP15. . . . .163 B2
Hawtrey Cl SL1 . . . . .206 B4
Hawtrey Rd SL4 . . . . .210 C5
Hay Barn Bsns Pk The
HP22. . . . . .88 C6
Hayden Ho 3 HP11 . . . . .172 F7
Haydock Cl MK3 . . . . .57 C6
Haydon Abbey Comb Sch
HP19. . . . . .101 D1
Haydon Ct SL6 . . . . .202 E6
HAYDON HILL. 100 E2
Haydon Ind Sch 9
HP20. . . . . .101 D1

Haydon Rd HP19 . . . . . . .101 C2
Hayes Cl SL6 . . . . .203 D1
Hayes Pl SL7 . . . . .183 D1
Hayes Rd MK10 . . . . .31 F5
Hayfield Dr HP15 . . . . . . .163 B2
Hay La SL3 . . . . .199 D8
Hayles Field RG9 . . . . . . .170 E1
Hayling Cl SL1 . . . . .205 B5
Haymaker Cl U810 . . . . .201 F5
Hayman Rise MK8 . . . . . .45 D6
Haymill Rd SL1, SL2 . . . .197 D1
Haymill Valley Nature
Reserve★ SL2 . . . . .204 E8
Haynes Cl
Bow Brickhill MK17 . . . . . .48 D2
Slough SL3 . . . . .206 F1
Haynes Ho HP12 . . . . . . .172 B3
Haynes Mead HP4 . . . . . .135 A6
Hayse Hill SL4 . . . . .209 D6
Haystacks The HP13. . . . .173 B7
Haythrop Cl MK15. . . . . . .35 B6
Hayward Dr HP18 . . . . . .133 B7
Haywards Cl RG9 . . . . . . .191 C1
Haywards Croft MK12 . . .33 B5
Haywards Mead SL4 . . . .204 F1
Haywood Dr WD3. . . . . . .167 F4
Haywood Pk
Chorleywood WD3 . . . . . .167 F4
Stewkley LU7 . . . . .68 C3
Haywoods Dr HP3. . . . . . .146 F8
Haywood Way HP19 . . . .100 F3
Hayworth Pl 2 MK4. . . . . .45 D2
Hazelbury Rd HP13 . . . . .173 D6
Hazel Cl SL7 . . . . .183 C6
Hazelcroft Cl UB10. . . . . .201 F5
Hazel Ct WD3. . . . . .178 E5
Hazeldene HP22 . . . . . . .131 C4
HAZELEY 45 D5
Hazeley Sch The MK8 . . .45 D5
Hazel Gr MK2 . . . . .58 D7
Hazelhurst Rd MK4 . . . . .46 B2
Hazelhurst Rd SL1 . . . . .197 D3
Hazell Ave HP21 . . . . . . .116 A7
Hazell Cl SL6 . . . . .202 F8
Hazell Pk HP7 . . . . .165 D8
Hazell Rd HP16 . . . . .151 C5
Hazell Way SL2 . . . . .198 F6
HAZELMERE 163 B4
Hazel Rd HP4 . . . . .135 D3
Hazelwood MK14 . . . . . . .34 F8
Hazelwood Cl HP5 . . . . .144 D2
Hazely HP23 . . . . .119 C4
Hazlehurst Dr HP21 . . . .116 A5
Hazlemere CE Comb Sch
HP15. . . . . .162 F3
Hazlemere Ct HP15 . . . .163 A4
Hazlemere Rd
Slough SL2 . . . . .206 B5
Tylers Green HP10 . . . . . .163 C2
Hazley Wlk MK18 . . . . . . .41 F1
Headington Cl SL6 . . . . .202 A7
Headington Pl SL2 . . . . .205 F5
Headington Rd SL6 . . . .202 A7
Headland Cl 1 HP16 . . . .152 A8
Headlands Dr HP4 . . . . . .135 E5
Healey Ave HP13 . . . . . . .173 D7
Heaney Cl MK16 . . . . .22 A5
Hearn Cl HP10 . . . . .162 F2
Hearne Ct HP8 . . . . .177 B7
Hearne Dr SL6 . . . . .203 A1
Hearne Pl MK6. . . . . .46 F8
Hearnes Mdw HP9. . . . . .176 D5
Heathacre SL3 . . . . .212 E6
Heath Cl
Aylesbury HP21 . . . . .116 B5
Holmer Green HP15. . . . .163 B6
Stanwell TW19 . . . . .213 C1
Woburn Sands MK17 . . . .49 C3
Heathcote SL6 . . . . .202 A4
Heathcote Ct 2 SL4. . . . .210 D4
Heathcote Rd U87 . . . . . .208 D5
Heath Ct
Leighton Buzzard LU7 . . .70 E3
Uxbridge U88. . . . . .201 D5
HEATH END 134 A2
Cholesbury. 134 A2
Prestwood 151 E1
Heath End Cl HP15 . . . . .151 E1
Heath End Rd
Flackwell Heath HP10 . . .174 A1
Great Kingshill HP15,
HP16. . . . . .151 E2
Little Marlow HP10 . . . . . .173 D2
Heather Cl
Buckingham MK18. . . . . . .52 C7
Uxbridge U88. . . . . .208 F8
Heathercroft MK14 . . . . . .34 E7
Heatherden Gn SL0 . . . .200 D4
Heather La U87. . . . . .208 E7
Heather Mead LU6 . . . . . .92 E5
Heathers Cl MK18. . . . . . .73 B5
Heatherside Sch SL2. . . .187 D1
Heatherton House Sch
HP6. . . . . .154 C3
Heatherton Pk HP6 . . . . .154 B3
Heather Wlk
Aylesbury HP21 . . . . .115 B6

Heather Wlk continued
Hazelmere HP15 . . . . . . .163 A3
Heathfield MK12 . . . . .33 E4
Heathfield Rd
High Wycombe HP12 . . . .172 B7
Taplow SL1. . . . . .186 A1
Heath La MK17. . . . . .49 A2
Heathlands Dr SL6 . . . . .202 A6
Heath Lawn HP10 . . . . . .173 F1
Heath Rd
Beaconsfield HP9. . . . . . .186 A8
Great Brickhill MK17, LU7 .59 E1
Hyde Heath HP6 . . . . . . .153 C5
Heathrow Bvd U87 . . . . .213 F7
Heathrow Cl U87 . . . . . . .213 B6
Heathrow Prim Sch
U87. . . . . .213 F8
Heathrow T5 Sta/U Sta
TW6 . . . . .213 C4
Heath The LU7 . . . . .70 E4
Heath Way SL0 . . . . .200 D3
Heavens Lea SL8 . . . . . . .185 C2
Hedge Lea HP10 . . . . . . .185 D8
HEDGERLEY 187 D3
Hedgerley OX39 . . . . .147 B6
HEDGERLEY GREEN 187 E4
HEDGERLEY HILL 187 E2
Hedgerley Hill 3 SL2. . .187 D2
Hedgerley La
Beaconsfield HP9. . . . . . .186 F8
Gerrards Cross SL9 . . . . .188 B4
Hedgerley SL2 . . . . .187 D6
Hedgerow SL9. . . . . .177 E4
Hedgerows The MK4 . . . .46 E4
Hedges Ct MK5 . . . . .46 B6
Hedingham Ct MK5. . . . . .46 A5
Hedingham Mews SL6. .202 D8
Hedley Cl HP22 . . . . .118 A4
Hedley Rd HP10 . . . . .185 B8
Hedley View HP10 . . . . . .174 D1
HEDSOR. 185 F3
Hedsor Hill SL8 . . . . .185 C1
Hedsor La
Hedsor HP10 . . . . .185 F2
Taplow SL1. . . . . .186 A2
Hedsor Rd SL8 . . . . .185 C1
Hedsor View Cotts SL6 .195 F7
HEELANDS 34 C4
Heelands Fst Sch MK13 .34 B4
Heights The SL7 . . . . . . .194 B8
Hele Ct MK7 . . . . .48 B3
Helena Rd SL4 . . . . .210 D5
Helen Cotts SL4 . . . . .209 D1
Helford Cl HP21 . . . . .115 C4
Helford Pl MK6 . . . . .35 A1
Heligan Pl MK4 . . . . .45 F1
Hellfire Caves★ HP14 . .160 F2
Hellyer Way SL8 . . . . .185 C3
Helmsley Rise MK4 . . . . .45 E1
Helston Cl SL4. . . . . .210 B6
Helston Pl 3 MK6 . . . . . .34 F1
Hemel Hempstead Rd
HP4 . . . . .107 F1
Hemingway Cl MK16 . . . .21 F5
Hemingway Rd HP19 . . .100 F2
Hemlock Cl HP22 . . . . . . .116 C4
Hemmings The HP4. . . . .134 F3
Hemming Way SL2 . . . . .198 B2
Hemp Hill 10 HP19 . . . . .115 A8
Hemp La HP23 . . . . .119 F1
Hempson Ave SL3 . . . . . .206 C3
Hempstead Rd HP3 . . . . .146 B5
HEMPTON WAINHILL. . . .147 F7
Hemsdale SL6 . . . . .195 B1
Hemwood Rd SL4 . . . . . .209 D4
Hencroft Mews 14 SL1 . .205 F4
Hencroft Street N SL1. . .205 F4
Hencroft Street S SL1. . .205 F3
Henden Mews SL6 . . . . .202 A6
Henders MK11. . . . . .32 E5
Hendon Ct 5 MK10 . . . . .35 F1
Hendons Way SL6 . . . . . .203 B1
Hendon Way TW19 . . . . .213 D1
Hendrix Dr MK8. . . . . .45 D7
Hengistbury La MK4. . . . .46 A1
Henley Coll The RG9 . . .191 D1
Henley Coll The
(Rotherfield Bldgs)
RG9. . . . . .191 C1
Henley Lodge 12 SL6. . .202 F6
Henley Management Coll
RG9. . . . . .192 B7
HENLEY-ON-THAMES . . .191 B1
Henley-on-Thames Sta
RG9. . . . . .191 E1
Henley Rd
Hurley SL6. . . . . .193 D3
Maidenhead SL6, SL7 . . .194 B2
Marlow SL7 . . . . .194 B8
Slough SL1. . . . . .204 F7
Hennerton Way HP13 . . .173 F6
Henrietta Ct OX9 . . . . . . .126 A1
Henry III Tower 17 SL4 .210 D6
Henry Rd
Aylesbury HP20 . . . . .116 B8
Slough SL1. . . . . .205 D4

Henry St HP23 . . . 119 A3
Hensman Gate MK10 . . . 35 F4
Henson Cl MK43 . . . 24 E3
HENTON . . . 137 E2
Henton Mews 5 HP19 . . 115 A8
Hepburn Cres MK4 . . . 45 E3
Hepleswell MK8 . . . 33 E1
Hepplewhite Cl HP13 . . . 173 D8
Herbert Rd HP13 . . . 174 A7
Herberts Hole
Chesham HP5 . . . 143 C1
South Heath HP5, HP16 . . 142 F1
Hercies Rd UB10 . . . 201 F5
Herdman Cl MK12 . . . 33 B5
Herd's Hill MK18 . . . 64 A4
Hereford Ho HP13 . . . 173 F8
Hereford Way HP19 . . . 101 A3
Heritage Cl UB8 . . . 201 C1
Heritage Gate SL9 . . . 188 E7
Heritage House Specl Sch
HP5 . . . 144 D1
Heritage Wlk WD3 . . . 167 E6
Hermitage Cl SL3 . . . 206 C3
Hermitage La SL4 . . . 210 A4
Hermitage Prim Sch
UB8 . . . 201 D5
Hermitage The
Great Missenden HP16 . . 152 A7
Uxbridge UB8 . . . 201 D6
Hernes Oak OX39 . . . 147 D8
Heron Cl
Aylesbury HP20 . . . 116 C8
Uxbridge UB8 . . . 201 D6
Heron Dr SL3 . . . 207 B2
Heron Lodge MK14 . . . 34 C6
Herons Elm HP4 . . . 134 E7
Heronsfield Ho WD3 . . . 167 B3
HERONSGATE . . . 167 D2
Heronsgate Rd WD3 . . . 167 B3
Heronsgate Sch MK7 . . . 48 B5
Heronshaw Sch MK7 . . . 48 B5
Herons Pl
Maidenhead SL6 . . . 196 C3
Marlow SL7 . . . 183 E3
Heron The HP19 . . . 101 E4
Herries Sch SL6 . . . 195 B8
Herriot Cl MK16 . . . 22 A5
Herschel Gram Sch
SL1 . . . 205 C7
Herschel Sports SL1 . . . 205 C7
Herschel St SL1 . . . 205 F4
Herston Cl HP21 . . . 116 B5
Hertford Pl MK3 . . . 46 F2
Hervines Ct HP6 . . . 154 C2
Hervines Rd HP6 . . . 154 C2
Hesketh Rd NN12 . . . 18 E6
Hetherington Cl SL2 . . . 197 F2
Hetherington Way
UB10 . . . 201 E8
Het's Orch HP27 . . . 149 E5
Hetton Cl MK13 . . . 34 C4
Heusden Way SL9 . . . 188 F3
Hever Cl
Maidenhead SL6 . . . 202 C6
Pitstone LU7 . . . 105 D2
Hewgate Ct RG9 . . . 191 E1
Hexham Gdns MK3 . . . 57 D6
Heybridge Cres MK7 . . . 48 B3
Heydon Ct MK13 . . . 34 A7
Heynes Gn SL6 . . . 202 B3
Heythrop Dr UB10 . . . 201 F8
Heyward Gate MK6 . . . 47 C5
Heywood Ave SL6 . . . 202 A1
Heywood Court Cl SL6 . 202 A2
Heywood Gdns SL6 . . . 202 A1
Hibbert Rd SL6 . . . 203 B4
Hibbert's Alley 16 SL4 . . 210 D6
Hibberts Way SL9 . . . 188 E8
Hickmans Cl MK18 . . . 51 B6
Hickman St HP19 . . . 114 F8
Hickox Ct HP10 . . . 185 F7
Hicks Farm Rise HP13 . . 173 F7
Hidcote Dr MK4 . . . 45 F1
Hide The MK6 . . . 47 C6
Higgs Ct MK5 . . . 46 A8
HIGHAM CROSS . . . 10 D3
Higham Cross Rd MK19 . . 10 E4
Higham Mead HP5 . . . 144 C1
Higham Rd HP5 . . . 144 C1
High Ash CE Comb Sch
MK17 . . . 59 D2
High Beeches
Gerrards Cross SL9 . . . 188 D2
High Wycombe HP12 . . . 172 C6
High Beeches Cl SL7 . . . 183 C7
High Bois La HP6 . . . 154 D4
Highbridge Ind Est
UB8 . . . 201 C5
Highbridge Rd HP21 . . . 115 E8
Highbridge Wlk 4
HP21 . . . 115 E8
Highbury La MK9 . . . 35 B3
High Coppice HP7 . . . 165 C8
Highcrest Com Sch
HP13 . . . 173 E7
Highcroft Cl NN12 . . . 18 E6
HIGHER DENHAM . . . 189 C4
Highfield
Chalfont St Giles HP8 . . . 177 D8
Long Crendon HP18 . . . 125 C7
Highfield Ave HP12 . . . 172 B5
Highfield Cl
Amersham HP6 . . . 154 D2
Milton Keynes MK3 . . . 47 B2
Newport Pagnell MK16 . . . 22 E4
Highfield Ct
Farnham Royal SL2 . . . 198 B4
Hazelmere HP15 . . . 163 A3
Highfield Dr UB10 . . . 190 E1
Highfield La SL6 . . . 202 A4
Highfield Pk SL7 . . . 183 B1
Highfield Rd
Berkhamsted HP4 . . . 135 D4
Bourne End SL8 . . . 185 B4
Chesham HP5 . . . 144 B2
Flackwell Heath HP10 . . . 185 A8
Maidenhead SL6 . . . 202 B8
Princes Risborough
HP27 . . . 139 C4
Tring HP23 . . . 118 E3
Wigginton HP23 . . . 119 D1
Windsor SL4 . . . 209 F4
Winslow MK18 . . . 65 F5
Highfield Sch SL6 . . . 202 E7
Highfield Way
Hazelmere HP15 . . . 163 A3
Yardley Hastings NN7 . . . 1 B6
Highgate Mews 2
HP19 . . . 100 F1
Highgate Over MK7 . . . 48 B6
Highgrove Hill MK8 . . . 45 F8
Highgrove Pk SL6 . . . 202 E8
High Halden MK7 . . . 48 B8
High Heavens Wood
SL7 . . . 183 C8
Highland Cl MK3 . . . 46 F3
High Land Cl HP18 . . . 96 A1
Highland Rd HP7 . . . 165 D8
Highlands
Flackwell Heath HP10 . . . 185 B7
High Wycombe HP13 . . . 174 A5
Highlands Cl SL9 . . . 177 F3
Highlands End SL9 . . . 177 F3
Highlands La SL9 . . . 177 F3
Highlands Rd
Buckingham MK18 . . . 41 E2
Seer Green HP9 . . . 176 C5
Highlands The SL2 . . . 198 C7
Highlea Ave HP10 . . . 185 A8
Highley Gr MK10 . . . 36 B3
High March Sch HP9 . . . 175 D4
High Mdw SL6 . . . 196 C3
Highmoor HP7 . . . 165 D8
High Moors HP22 . . . 131 B8
Highmore Cotts HP7 . . . 152 F3
Highmore Croft MK8 . . . 45 D6
Highover Pk HP7 . . . 165 D7
High Park Dr MK12 . . . 33 A6
High Rd
Cookham Rise SL6 . . . 195 E7
Soulbury LU7 . . . 69 E2
Uxbridge UB8 . . . 208 C7
High St The MK8 . . . 33 E1
High St
Amersham HP7 . . . 165 A7
Aylesbury HP20 . . . 115 E8
Berkhamsted HP4 . . . 135 C4
Berkhamsted, Northchurch
HP4 . . . 134 E6
Bovingdon HP3 . . . 146 A4
Bray SL6 . . . 203 C4
Brill HP18 . . . 110 A8
Buckingham MK18 . . . 28 D1
Buckingham MK18 . . . 41 D1
Burcott LU7 . . . 79 D4
Burnham SL1 . . . 197 C2
Chalfont St Giles HP8 . . . 177 C8
Chalfont St Peter SL9 . . . 177 E2
Chalvey SL1 . . . 205 D3
Cheddington LU7 . . . 105 A7
Chesham HP5 . . . 154 B8
Chinnor, Kingston Blount
OX39 . . . 147 A4
Chinnor OX39 . . . 147 D7
Colnbrook SL3 . . . 212 C7
Cookham SL6 . . . 196 B7
Cranfield MK43 . . . 25 B1
Cublington LU7 . . . 78 B1
Datchet SL3 . . . 211 B6
Deanshanger MK19 . . . 31 E4
Dinton HP17 . . . 113 E2
Downley HP13 . . . 161 D3
Eaton Bray LU6 . . . 92 E6
Edlesborough LU6 . . . 92 E3
Emberton MK46 . . . 13 F7
Eton SL4 . . . 210 D8
Great Horwood MK17 . . . 55 A3
Great Missenden HP16 . . 152 A7
Haddenham HP17 . . . 126 F6
Hanslope MK19 . . . 11 A2
Harmondsworth UB7 . . . 213 D8
Harrold MK43 . . . 3 F6
Haversham MK19 . . . 21 A3
High Wycombe HP11 . . . 173 B6
Iver SL0 . . . 207 F7
High St *continued*
Ivinghoe LU7 . . . 105 E5
Lane End HP14 . . . 171 B4
Lavendon MK46 . . . 7 F8
Leighton Buzzard LU7 . . . 80 F6
Lewknor OX49 . . . 157 B8
Long Crendon HP18 . . . 125 D6
Ludgershall HP18 . . . 96 B8
14 Maidenhead SL6 . . . 202 F7
Marlow SL7 . . . 183 E1
Milton Keynes, Great Linford
MK14 . . . 21 E1
Milton Keynes MK2 . . . 47 E1
Milton Keynes, New Bradwell
MK13 . . . 34 A7
Milton Keynes, Stony Stratford
MK11 . . . 32 D6
Nash MK17 . . . 44 C1
Newport Pagnell MK16 . . . 22 D4
North Crawley MK16 . . . 24 B6
North Marston MK18 . . . 76 A2
Olney MK46 . . . 6 F3
Paulerspury NN12 . . . 17 C8
Potterspury NN12 . . . 18 D3
Prestwood HP16 . . . 151 D6
Princes Risborough
HP27 . . . 139 B3
Sherington MK16 . . . 13 F2
Slough SL3 . . . 207 A2
Slough, Upton SL1 . . . 205 F4
Stanwell TW19 . . . 213 D1
Stoke Goldington MK16 . . . 12 B6
Syresham NN13 . . . 27 B7
Taplow SL6 . . . 196 E1
Thame OX9 . . . 125 E1
Thornborough MK18 . . . 54 A8
Tring HP23 . . . 119 A3
Turvey MK43 . . . 8 E5
Uxbridge, Cowley UB8 . . . 201 C1
Uxbridge UB8 . . . 201 D5
Waddesdon HP18 . . . 99 A6
Weedon HP22 . . . 87 C1
Wendover HP22 . . . 131 B4
Westcott HP18 . . . 98 B7
West Drayton UB7 . . . 208 E6
Weston Underwood MK46 . . 6 B2
West Wycombe HP14 . . . 160 F2
Whaddon MK17 . . . 45 B1
Whitchurch HP22 . . . 87 A6
Windsor SL4 . . . 210 D6
Wing LU7 . . . 79 E2
Winslow MK18 . . . 65 F4
Woburn Sands MK17 . . . 49 B4
Wraysbury TW19 . . . 211 F1
Yardley Gobion NN12 . . . 18 F6
Yardley Hastings NN7 . . . 1 B6
High Street N LU7 . . . 68 D2
High Street S
Olney MK46 . . . 6 F3
Stewkley LU7 . . . 78 E8
High Town Rd SL6 . . . 202 F7
High Trees MK6 . . . 47 B8
Highveer Croft MK4 . . . 46 B1
High View
Chalfont St Giles HP8 . . . 177 D8
Deanshanger MK19 . . . 31 E5
High View Cl SL7 . . . 183 C8
HIGHWAY . . . 202 B7
Highway MK17 . . . 68 C6
Highway Ave SL6 . . . 202 A6
Highway Ct
Beaconsfield HP9 . . . 175 D3
Chesham HP5 . . . 144 D1
Highway Rd SL6 . . . 202 B6
Highway The HP9 . . . 175 D2
Highwood Ave HP12 . . . 172 B5
Highwood Bottom
HP27 . . . 150 A5
Highwood Cres HP12 . . . 172 B6
Highwoods Cl SL7 . . . 183 C7
Highwoods Dr SL7 . . . 183 C7
Highworth Cl HP13 . . . 162 E1
Highworth Comb Sch
HP13 . . . 162 E1
HIGH WYCOMBE . . . 173 B5
High Wycombe CE Comb
Sch 5 HP11 . . . 173 A6
High Wycombe Sta
HP13 . . . 173 B7
Hikers Way HP18 . . . 125 F4
Hilbre Ct 5 MK4 . . . 45 F1
Hilbury Cl HP6 . . . 154 C3
Hilda Wharf HP20 . . . 115 F8
Hildreth Rd HP16 . . . 151 C5
Hilgrove Ho SL6 . . . 195 D1
Hiljon Cres SL9 . . . 177 E2
Hillary Cl
Aylesbury HP21 . . . 116 A5
High Wycombe HP13 . . . 173 E6
Hillary Rd
High Wycombe HP13 . . . 173 E6
Slough SL3 . . . 206 E4
Hill Ave
Amersham HP6 . . . 154 C1
Hazelmere HP15 . . . 163 B5
Hillbeck Gr MK10 . . . 35 E3
Hillbottom Rd HP12 . . . 172 B7
Hill Cl HP10 . . . 185 F7
Hill Cotts HP18 . . . 97 E1
Hillcrest MK43 . . . 25 C2
Hillcrest Ave SL6 . . . 195 E6
Hillcrest Cl MK5 . . . 46 B6
Hillcrest Ct HP6 . . . 154 C1
Hillcrest Rise MK18 . . . 52 E6
Hillcrest Way MK18 . . . 52 E5
Hillcrest Waye SL9 . . . 188 F5
Hillcroft Rd
Chesham HP5 . . . 144 D2
Tylers Green HP10 . . . 163 C1
Hillersdon SL2 . . . 206 B8
Hillersdon Chase MK17 . . 69 D8
HILLESDEN . . . 63 A6
HILLESDEN HAMLET . . . 51 F1
Hillesden Hamlet MK18 . . 51 F1
Hillesden Way MK18 . . . 41 E1
Hill Farm MK18 . . . 76 A2
Hill Farm App HP10 . . . 185 F7
Hill Farm Ct OX39 . . . 147 D6
Hill Farm La
Chalfont St Giles HP8 . . . 166 A1
Little Horwood MK17 . . . 55 E2
Hill Farm Rd
Chalfont St Peter SL9 . . . 177 E3
Chesham HP5 . . . 154 D5
Marlow Bottom SL7 . . . 183 E5
Taplow SL6 . . . 196 E2
Hill Farm Way HP15 . . . 163 B2
Hillfield Cl HP13 . . . 161 E2
Hillfield Rd SL9 . . . 177 E3
Hillfield Sq SL9 . . . 177 E3
Hill Gr SL9 . . . 177 E3
Hill Ho SL6 . . . 196 D1
Hill House Cl SL9 . . . 177 E3
Hilliard Dr MK13 . . . 34 A3
Hilliards Rd UB8 . . . 208 D7
Hillier Rd HP21 . . . 115 D3
Hillingdon Hill UB10 . . . 201 E2
Hillingdon Hospl UB8 . . 208 F8
Hillingdon Rd UB10 . . . 201 E3
Hillingdon Tuition Ctr
UB7 . . . 208 E5
Hillington Cl HP19 . . . 115 B7
Hillman Cl UB8 . . . 201 E7
Hill Mdw HP7 . . . 164 F4
Hill Mead HP4 . . . 135 A3
Hillmead Ct SL6 . . . 203 F8
Hill Pl SL2 . . . 198 B5
Hill Rd
Chinnor OX39 . . . 147 D5
Christmas Common
OX49 . . . 168 A8
Lewknor OX49 . . . 157 C6
Hillrise SL3 . . . 212 A8
Hill Rise SL9 . . . 177 D1
Hill Rise Cres SL9 . . . 177 E1
Hills Cl MK14 . . . 34 E7
Hillside
Chesham HP5 . . . 144 A3
Gawcott MK18 . . . 51 F4
High Wycombe HP13 . . . 173 D7
Maidenhead SL6 . . . 202 D5
Slough SL1 . . . 205 E4
South Harefield UB9 . . . 190 C6
Tingewick MK18 . . . 51 B6
Hill Side LU7 . . . 104 F7
Hillside Cl
Chalfont St Giles HP8 . . . 177 B7
Chalfont St Peter SL9 . . . 177 E4
Upper Arncott OX25 . . . 94 E7
Hillside Cotts HP18 . . . 112 F2
Hillside Ct SL0 . . . 208 B4
Hillside Ctr HP11 . . . 172 F7
Hillside Gdns
Amersham HP7 . . . 165 E7
Berkhamsted HP4 . . . 135 D3
High Wycombe HP13 . . . 173 D7
Hillside Rd
Chorleywood WD3 . . . 167 C4
Marlow SL7 . . . 183 E4
Tylers Green HP10 . . . 163 A2
Hills La SL6 . . . 195 D7
Hill St HP13 . . . 174 A5
Hill The
Syresham NN13 . . . 27 B8
Winchmore Hill HP7 . . . 164 C3
HILLTOP . . . 144 D2
Hilltop HP18 . . . 125 D5
Hilltop Ave MK18 . . . 41 E2
Hill Top Dr SL7 . . . 183 B2
Hilltop Fst Sch SL4 . . . 209 E4
Hill Top La OX39 . . . 147 F4
Hilltop Rd HP4 . . . 135 C3
Hillview
Saunderton HP14 . . . 149 C1
Sherington MK16 . . . 14 A1
Hill View
Berkhamsted HP4 . . . 135 A6
Great Kimble HP17 . . . 129 D1
Hedgerley SL2 . . . 187 D3
Newport Pagnell MK16 . . . 22 A3
Oakley HP18 . . . 109 D5
Hillview Rd HP13 . . . 173 D8
Hill View Rd TW19 . . . 211 D1
Hillway MK17 . . . 49 A6
Hill Way HP7 . . . 165 B6
Hill Waye SL9 . . . 188 F4
Hillwerke OX39 . . . 147 C6
Hillyer Ct MK6 . . . 35 C1
Hilperton Rd 3 SL1 . . . 205 E4
Hilton Ave HP20 . . . 101 E2
Hilton Cl UB8 . . . 201 B3
Himley Gn LU7 . . . 80 D6
Hindemith Gdns MK7 . . . 48 D5
Hindhay La SL6 . . . 195 B3
Hindhead Knoll MK7 . . . 48 B6
Hinds Way HP21 . . . 115 B6
Hinkley Cl UB9 . . . 190 C7
Hinksey Cl SL3 . . . 207 B3
Hinton Cl HP13 . . . 162 A1
Hinton Ct MK3 . . . 46 F1
Hinton Rd
Slough SL1 . . . 204 E6
Uxbridge UB8 . . . 201 C4
Hipwell Ct MK46 . . . 6 F3
Hitcham Grange SL6 . . . 196 E1
Hitcham House SL1 . . . 197 A1
Hitcham La SL6, SL1 . . . 196 F2
Hitcham Rd SL1, SL6 . . . 204 A8
Hithercroft Rd HP13 . . . 161 E1
Hither Mdw SL9 . . . 177 E1
Hithermoor Rd TW19 . . . 213 A2
Hiving's Hill HP5 . . . 144 A2
Hivings Pk HP5 . . . 144 B4
Hoathly Mews MK7 . . . 48 B8
Hobart Cl HP13 . . . 162 E1
Hobart Cotts HP16 . . . 150 D8
Hobart Cres MK15 . . . 35 B7
Hobart Ct SL7 . . . 184 A3
Hobart Rd HP13 . . . 162 D1
Hobbis Dr SL6 . . . 202 A6
Hobbshill Rd HP16 . . . 152 B6
Hobbs Rd HP14 . . . 171 C4
Hobsons Wlk HP23 . . . 118 F5
Hockeridge View HP4 . . 134 F3
Hockett La SL6 . . . 195 A6
Hockley La SL2 . . . 199 B4
Hockliffe Brae MK7 . . . 48 C5
Hodder La MK4 . . . 46 C2
Hodds Wood Rd HP5 . . . 154 C6
Hodge Lea La MK12 . . . 33 D4
Hodgemoor View HP8 . . 177 A7
Hodgemore Ct MK14 . . . 21 F2
Hodges Cl HP14 . . . 158 F4
Hodges Mews HP12 . . . 172 C6
Hoe Mdw HP9 . . . 175 C4
Hogarth Cl
Slough SL1 . . . 204 E6
Uxbridge UB8 . . . 201 C2
Hogarths Ct 9 MK8 . . . 33 F1
Hogback Wood Rd
HP9 . . . 175 B4
Hogfair La SL1 . . . 197 C1
HOGGESTON . . . 77 B7
Hogg La HP15 . . . 163 D6
Hog Hall La HP4 . . . 107 A5
Hog La
Ashley Green HP5 . . . 144 D8
Berkhamsted HP5 . . . 134 C2
HOGPITS BOTTOM . . . 156 B7
Hogpits Bottom HP3 . . . 156 B7
Hogshaw Rd MK18 . . . 75 E6
Hogtrough La
Great Missenden HP16 . . 141 F8
Wendover HP22 . . . 131 D2
Holborn Cres MK4 . . . 57 A8
Holdom Ave MK1 . . . 47 D2
Holes La MK46 . . . 6 F4
Holiday La MK19 . . . 10 F4
Holland Cl
Chinnor OX39 . . . 147 D7
Wendover HP22 . . . 131 B4
Holland Rd
Aylesbury HP19 . . . 101 B2
Marlow SL7 . . . 183 F3
Hollandridge La OX49,
RG9 . . . 168 D4
Holland Way MK16 . . . 22 C3
Holliday Cl MK8 . . . 45 E7
Holliday St HP4 . . . 135 D4
Hollies Ct LU7 . . . 80 E7
Hollies The
Beaconsfield HP9 . . . 175 E3
Bovingdon HP3 . . . 146 A2
Tring HP23 . . . 119 D1
HOLLINGDON . . . 69 C3
Hollingdon Depot LU7 . . 69 D3
Hollingdon Rd LU7 . . . 69 C3
Hollington HP18 . . . 125 B7
Hollin La MK12 . . . 33 E4
Hollinwell Cl 3 MK4 . . . 46 D1
Hollis Rd HP13 . . . 173 F8
Hollister Chase MK5 . . . 46 B4
Holloway Cl UB7 . . . 208 E1
Holloway Dr MK18 . . . 41 E2
Holloway La
Chenies WD3 . . . 156 C2
Turville Heath RG9 . . . 169 C4
West Drayton UB7 . . . 208 F1
Holloway The
Monks Risborough
HP27 . . . 139 D5
Tring HP22, HP23 . . . 118 C4
Hollow Hill End MK18 . . . 75 F7
Hollow Hill La SL0 . . . 207 C5
Hollow Rise HP13 . . . 162 B1
Hollow Way HP5 . . . 143 E1

Hollow Way La HP5, HP6 ....154 E4
Hollow Wood MK46 ....6 E2
Hollyberry Ct HP15 ....163 C7
Hollybush Cnr SL2 ....187 C2
Hollybush Hill SL2 ....199 B5
Hollybush La
  Amersham HP6 ....154 L3
  Cookham Dean SL6 ....195 B6
  Denham UB9 ....200 E8
  Iver SL0, SL3 ....207 B7
Hollybush Rd HP5 ....144 A4
Hollybush Row HP23 ....133 D8
Holly Cl
  Farnham Common SL2 ....198 C8
  Milton Keynes MK8 ....45 E6
Holly Cres SL4 ....209 D5
Holly Dr
  Aylesbury HP21 ....115 E6
  Berkhamsted HP4 ....135 D3
  Maidenhead SL6 ....202 F8
  Windsor SL4 ....161 C8
Holly End HP14 ....161 C8
Hollyfield HP23 ....119 C5
Hollyfield Cl HP23 ....119 C5
Holly Gdns UB7 ....208 F4
HOLLY GREEN 138 A3
Holly Green La HP27 ....138 A3
Holly Hedges La HP3 ....156 C8
Holly Pl HP11 ....174 A3
Hollytree Cl
  Botley HP5 ....155 B8
  Chalfont St Peter SL9 ....177 E5
Holly Tree La HP18 ....112 F3
Holly Wlk MK17 ....49 B2
Holmanleaze SL6 ....203 A8
Holman St HP19 ....101 C2
Holmedale SL2 ....206 C6
HOLMER GREEN 163 D6
Holmer Green Fst Sch HP15 ....163 B7
Holmer Green Jun Sch HP15 ....163 D7
Holmer Green Rd HP15 ....163 A4
Holmer Green Senior Sch HP15 ....163 B7
Holmer Pl HP15 ....163 C7
Holmers Ct HP12 ....172 B3
Holmers Farm Way HP12 ....172 C3
Holmewood MK4 ....46 E4
Holmfield Cl MK6 ....47 D5
Holm Gate MK5 ....46 A8
Holmlea Rd SL3 ....211 D6
Holmlea Wlk SL3 ....211 C6
Holmoak Wlk HP15 ....163 B3
Holmsdale Cl SL0 ....207 F7
Holmwood Cl SL6 ....202 B5
Holmwood Sch 10 MK8 ....33 F1
Holne Chase Prim Sch MK3 ....58 A7
Holst Cres MK7 ....48 D4
Holt Gr MK5 ....46 A8
HOLTON 122 C2
Holton Hill MK4 ....46 C2
Holton Rd MK18 ....41 D2
Holts Gn MK17 ....59 C1
HOLTSPUR 175 A1
Holtspur Ave HP10 ....185 F7
Holtspur Cl HP9 ....186 A8
Holtspur La HP9 ....186 A8
Holtspur La HP10 ....185 F6
Holtspur Par HP9 ....186 A8
Holtspur Prim Sch HP9 ....175 A1
Holtspur Top La HP9 ....175 A2
Holtspur Way HP9 ....175 A1
Holt The MK18 ....52 E7
Holy Family RC Sch SL3 ....206 F1
Holyhead Cres MK3 ....57 C8
Holyhead Mews SL1 ....204 D7
Holyport Rd SL6 ....203 B1
Holyrood MK8 ....45 E8
Holy Thorn La MK5 ....46 A5
Holy Trinity CE Prim Sch SL6 ....196 B7
Holy Trinity CE Sch SL7 ....183 D3
Holywell Gdns HP13 ....173 E7
Holywell Rd MK5 ....35 C2
Holywell Rd MK43 ....25 C1
Holywell Sch MK43 ....25 B1
Home Cl
  Milton Keynes MK3 ....47 B2
  Shabbington HP18 ....124 D3
  Weston Turville HP22 ....116 F2
Home Ct MK10 ....36 A3
Home Farm
  Newton Longville MK17 ....57 D4
  Tring HP23 ....118 F2
Home Farm Cl MK19 ....31 E4
Homefarm Ct HP8 ....177 A7
Home Farm Ct
  Bovingdon HP3 ....145 F1
  Emberton MK46 ....13 E8
Home Farm La MK17 ....59 D2

Home Farm Rd HP4 ....134 D7
Home Farm Way SL3 ....199 C4
Homefield HP3 ....146 B3
Home Field
  Aylesbury HP19 ....115 A7
  Bow Brickhill MK7 ....48 B3
Homefield Ct HP14 ....158 E4
Homefield Rd WD3 ....167 D5
Homefield Wood Wildlife Reserve★ SL7 ....182 E2
Homeground MK8 ....46 E4
Homelands Gdns HP15 ....162 D8
Homelands Way HP15 ....191 D1
Homeleigh Terr SL2 ....206 A7
Home Mdw SL2 ....206 A7
Home Meadow Dr HP10 ....185 B7
Homer Fst Sch SL4 ....209 D8
Homeridings Ho MK13 ....34 B4
Homers Rd SL4 ....209 D8
Homeside Cl SL6 ....195 E2
Homestall MK1 ....52 D6
Homestall Cl MK5 ....46 A7
Homestead Cl HP17 ....114 A4
Homestead Pl 14 HP19 ....115 A8
Homestead Rd SL6 ....202 D4
Homestead The
  Great Kingshill HP15 ....151 D1
  High Wycombe HP12 ....172 D3
  Milton Keynes MK5 ....46 A6
  Thame OX9 ....125 E1
Homestead Way NN12 ....18 E3
Homeward Ct MK5 ....46 B7
Home Way WD3 ....167 F1
Homewood SL3 ....206 D7
Home Wood SL7 ....193 F6
Homewood Ct WD3 ....167 F5
Honey Banks HP22 ....151 A4
Honeycroft Hill UB10 ....201 E5
Honey Hill
  Emberton MK46 ....13 F7
  Uxbridge UB10 ....201 F5
Honey Hill Dr MK19 ....31 E5
Honey La SL6 ....193 E2
Honeypot Cl MK13 ....34 B4
Honeysuckle Cl SL0 ....207 C7
Honeysuckle Cl SL3 ....212 C7
Honeysuckle Field HP5 ....144 C2
Honeysuckle Rd HP15 ....162 F7
Honey Way HP14 ....161 B8
HONEYWICK 92 E8
Honeywick La LU6 ....92 E8
Honiton St MK7 ....48 C7
Honor End La HP14 ....151 A7
Honor Rd HP16 ....151 D6
Honorwood Cl HP16 ....151 B6
Honour Cl HP20 ....102 A2
Honours Mead 4 HP3 ....146 A4
Hoods Farm Cl HP22 ....102 C4
Hooke The MK15 ....35 D7
Hooper Gate MK15 ....35 C7
Hopcraft Cl OX25 ....94 E7
Hope Brook Cotts LU7 ....91 F2
Hop Gdns RG9 ....191 D2
Hopkins Cl MK10 ....36 A2
Hopkins Ct HP20 ....101 F2
Hoppers Hill MK46 ....6 F5
Hoppers Mdw MK5 ....46 A8
Hoppers Way HP15 ....162 D8
Hopton Gr MK16 ....22 F3
Hopton Rd OX9 ....126 A1
Hordern Cl HP17 ....126 F6
Hornbeam MK16 ....22 A3
Hornbeam Cl HP22 ....172 B4
Hornbeam Gdns 8 SL1 ....206 A3
Hornbeam Way HP22 ....116 C4
Hornbeam Wlk HP15 ....163 A3
Hornbill Cl UB8 ....206 D3
Hornby Chase MK4 ....46 B2
Horners Croft MK12 ....33 C5
HORN HILL 178 B6
Hornhill Rd WD3 ....178 D5
Horn La MK11 ....33 D5
Horns La
  High Wycombe HP12 ....172 A3
  Princes Risborough HP27 ....139 B3
Horn St MK18 ....65 F4
Horsebuck La HP23 ....133 E3
Horsefair Gn MK11 ....32 D5
Horseguards Dr SL6 ....203 B7
Horse Hill HP5 ....155 D7
Horsemoor Cl SL3 ....207 A2
Horsemoor La HP7 ....146 C2
HORSENDEN 138 E2
Horsenden La HP27 ....138 F2
Horsenden Rd HP13 ....173 F5
Horsepond Cl MK17 ....59 C2
Horsepool La MK17 ....49 F4
Horseshoe Cl LU7 ....105 C3
Horseshoe Cloisters 3 SL4 ....210 D6
Horseshoe Cres HP9 ....175 F1
Horseshoe Hill SL1 ....197 C8
Horseshoe Rd HP14 ....159 C7
Horseshoes Cl HP18 ....83 A6
Horsetone Bglws HP17 ....129 D2
Horsham Reach SL6 ....196 C2

Horsleys WD3 ....178 D5
HORSLEYS GREEN 159 C3
HORTON
  Cheddington 91 B3
  Wraysbury 212 A4
Horton Bridge Rd UB7 ....208 F5
Horton Cl
  Aylesbury HP19 ....115 A7
  Maidenhead SL6 ....196 C1
  West Drayton UB7 ....208 F5
HORTON-CUM-STUDLEY 108 B6
Horton Depot SL3 ....212 C4
Horton Gate MK14 ....21 F2
Horton Gdns SL3 ....211 F4
Horton Grange SL6 ....196 C1
Horton Par UB7 ....208 F5
Horton Rd UB7 ....208 F5
Horton Rd
  Datchet SL3 ....211 D6
  Horton SL3 ....212 A6
  Ivinghoe LU7 ....91 A6
  Poyle SL3 ....212 E4
  Slapton LU7 ....91 C6
  Stanwell TW19 ....213 A2
  West Drayton UB7 ....208 F5
Horton Road Ind Est UB7 ....208 F5
Hortonsfield Rd NN12 ....18 F5
Horton Trad Est SL3 ....212 B4
HORTON WHARF 91 C4
Horwood Ct MK1 ....47 D2
Hospital Circular Rd HP22 ....131 D6
Hospital Hill HP5 ....154 C7
Hospital Rdbt MK6 ....47 B6
Hotch Croft MK43 ....25 C3
HOTLEY BOTTOM 151 C8
Hotley Bottom La HP16 ....151 C8
Hotspur Bank Nature Reserve★ HP9 ....174 F1
Houghton Ct 8 MK8 ....45 F8
Housman Cl MK15 ....22 A5
Houston Ct 6 SL4 ....210 C5
Howard Ave
  Aylesbury HP21 ....116 B6
  Slough SL2 ....205 B8
Howard Cres HP9 ....176 D5
Howard Ct MK10 ....36 A3
Howard Dr HP9 ....175 E5
Howard Ind Est HP5 ....144 C2
Howard Mews SL3 ....212 B8
Howard Rd
  Chesham HP5 ....144 B3
  Seer Green HP9 ....176 D5
Howards Thicket SL9 ....188 C2
Howards Wood Dr SL9 ....188 D2
Howard Way MK16 ....23 A3
Howarth Rd SL6 ....203 A6
Howe Cl MK10 ....36 A3
Howe Dr HP9 ....175 E6
Howe Hill La HP15 ....163 B8
Howell Hill Cl LU7 ....90 D5
Howe Park Sch MK4 ....46 B1
Howe Rock Pl MK4 ....46 B1
Howitt Dr MK13 ....34 B8
Hownall Pl MK17 ....60 F7
Howletts Cl HP19 ....115 A7
How's Cl UB8 ....201 C4
How's Rd UB8 ....201 C4
Hoylake Cl
  Milton Keynes MK3 ....57 D7
  Slough SL3 ....204 E4
Hoyton Gate MK8 ....45 D6
Hubbard Cl MK18 ....41 F1
Hubbards Ct WD3 ....167 D4
Hubbards Rd WD3 ....167 D4
Hubert Day Cl HP9 ....175 D3
Hubert Rd SL3 ....206 D3
Huckleberry Cl MK7 ....48 B6
Hudnall La HP4 ....121 E7
Hudson La MK8 ....45 D7
Hudson Pl 14 SL3 ....206 F1
Hughenden Ave HP13 ....173 A8
Hughenden Cl SL6 ....202 C6
Hughenden Ct UB8 ....201 C1
Hughenden Gn HP21 ....115 C4
Hughenden Manor★ HP14 ....162 A3
Hughenden Prim Sch HP14 ....162 A7
Hughenden Rd
  High Wycombe HP13 ....162 B1
  Slough SL1 ....205 D7
HUGHENDEN VALLEY 162 B7
Hughenden View HP13 ....173 B8
Hughes Croft 3 MK3 ....57 F7
Hughes Ct HP6 ....154 E1
Hugo Cl MK5 ....46 C8
Hulbert End HP21 ....116 C6
Hulcombe Wlk HP20 ....101 E2
HULCOTE 37 E2
HULCOTT 102 E6
Hull Cl
  Aylesbury HP21 ....115 A6
  Slough SL1 ....205 C4
Hulton Dr MK46 ....13 F8
Humber Cl UB7 ....208 D5
Humber Dr HP21 ....115 C5

Humber Way
  Milton Keynes MK3 ....46 E1
  Slough SL3 ....207 B2
Hume Cl MK13 ....34 B7
Humphreys Cl HP22 ....88 D5
Humphrey Talbot Ave LU6 ....107 F7
Hundred Acres La HP7 ....165 D8
Hungerford Ave SL2 ....205 E8
Hungerford Dr SL6 ....195 E3
Hungerford Ho 1 MK4 ....46 D1
Hunsbury Chase MK10 ....36 A3
Hunsdon Cl MK14 ....34 D6
Hunsford Lodge SL4 ....210 A4
Hunstanton Cl SL3 ....57 C8
Hunstanton Way MK3 ....57 D8
Hunt Ct HP14 ....158 F4
Huntercombe Cl SL1 ....204 C7
Huntercombe Hospl The SL6 ....204 C6
Huntercombe Lane N SL6 ....204 C7
Huntercombe Lane S SL6 ....204 C6
Huntercombe Spur SL6 ....204 C6
Hunter Ct SL1 ....204 C8
Hunter Dr MK2 ....58 C6
Hunters Cl
  Bovingdon HP3 ....146 A2
  Chesham HP5 ....144 A1
Hunters Farm Ind Est HP18 ....100 B5
Hunters Hill HP13 ....173 F5
Hunters Mews SL4 ....210 C6
Hunters Pk SL4 ....135 E5
Hunters Point OX39 ....147 A3
Hunters Reach MK13 ....34 A3
Hunter St MK18 ....52 C8
Hunters Way SL1 ....204 E4
HUNTGATE END 10 D2
Huntingbrooke 8 MK8 ....45 F8
Huntingdon Cres MK3 ....57 D6
Huntington Pl SL3 ....207 B3
Huntley Cl HP13 ....162 C2
Huntley Cres MK9 ....35 A3
Hunt Rd HP13 ....173 E6
Hunts Hill La MK4 ....161 E5
Hunt's La SL6 ....196 F4
Huntsman Gr MK14 ....22 A2
Huntsmans Cl MK4 ....107 C5
Huntswood La SL6, SL1 ....196 F4
HURLEY 193 E4
Hurley Croft MK10 ....36 B1
Hurley High St SL6 ....193 F4
Hurley La SL7 ....194 B3
Hurlstone Gr MK4 ....46 D3
Hurricane Way SL3 ....207 A2
HURST END 24 A3
Hurstfield Dr SL6 ....204 B7
Hurstleigh WD3 ....167 C4
Hurst Rd SL1 ....204 D8
Hurworth Ave SL3 ....206 C3
Hutchings Cl MK5 ....45 A8
Hutchings Rd HP9 ....175 D5
Hutton Ave MK4 ....34 F1
Hutton Cl MK17 ....49 B5
Hutton Way MK17 ....49 B5
Huxley Cl
  Newport Pagnell MK16 ....21 F4
  Slough SL3 ....199 B1
  Uxbridge UB8 ....201 D1
Huxtable Gdns SL6 ....203 E1
Hyacinth Dr UB10 ....201 E5
Hychenden Cl HP14 ....161 E6
Hyde Cl MK16 ....22 C2
HYDE END 152 F7
Hyde Gn
  Beaconsfield HP9 ....175 F3
  Marlow SL7 ....183 F1
HYDE HEATH 153 C5
Hyde Heath Inf Sch HP6 ....153 C5
Hyde Heath Rd HP6, HP10 ....153 A6
Hyde La
  Bovingdon HP3 ....146 A3
  South Heath HP16 ....152 A5
Hyde Mdws HP3 ....146 A4
Hyde The HP22 ....116 F2
Hyland Ho 9 SL8 ....185 B3
Hylle Cl SL4 ....209 E6
Hylton Rd HP12 ....172 C2
Hyrons Cl HP6 ....154 E1
Hyrons Ct HP6 ....154 E1
Hyrons La HP6 ....154 D1
Hythe The MK8 ....33 E3
Hyton Sq HP19 ....101 D4

I

Ibotson Ct SL3 ....212 E6
IBSTONE 158 F8
Ibstone Ave MK13 ....34 D4
Ibstone CE Inf Sch HP14 ....169 D6
Ibstone Rd HP14 ....158 C3
ICKENHAM 190 F1
ICKFORD 124 A3
Ickford Comb Sch HP18 ....124 A3
Ickford Rd
  Shabbington HP18 ....124 C2
  Worminghall HP18 ....123 D8
Icknield Cl
  Chinnor OX39 ....147 A4
  Wendover HP22 ....131 C5
Icknield Cotts HP17 ....129 F2
Icknield Gn HP23 ....119 A6
Icknield Way
  Dunstable LU6 ....93 D4
  Tring HP23 ....118 E4
Icknield Way Farm Cotts LU6 ....93 C3
Icknield Way Ind Est HP23 ....118 E4
Ideal Ho 8 HP18 ....115 E8
Iffley Cl SL8 ....201 D5
Ilchester Cl SL6 ....202 C5
Ilex Cl HP15 ....163 B3
Ilex Wlk HP14 ....135 B4
Illingworth SL4 ....209 E4
Illingworth Pl MK6 ....46 F8
ILMER 137 F8
Imperial Ct
  Henley-on-Thames RG9 ....191 E1
  Loudwater HP10 ....174 C2
  Windsor SL4 ....210 A4
Imperial Rd SL4 ....210 A5
Independent Bsns Pk HP14 ....158 C5
India Rd SL1 ....206 B4
Ingleglen SL2 ....198 B7
Ingleside SL3 ....212 F6
Ingleton Cl MK13 ....34 C4
Ingram Ave HP21 ....116 C5
Inkerman Dr HP15 ....163 B5
Inkerman Rd SL4 ....204 F2
Inkerman Terr HP5 ....154 C6
Innes Ct MK8 ....45 D6
Inn Farm Ct MK16 ....22 D7
Innholder Ct MK14 ....34 F6
Innings Gate RG9 ....170 E1
Inniscrown Ho SL3 ....211 B7
Institute Rd
  Marlow SL7 ....183 E1
  Taplow SL6 ....203 F7
Intalbury Ave HP19 ....101 A2
In the Ray SL6 ....203 B8
Invereve Pl 1 MK4 ....45 E2
Inverness Cl MK3 ....46 F2
Inwood Cl SL6 ....195 B6
Iona Cres SL1 ....204 E7
Ipswich Rd SL1 ....204 D7
IQRA Slough Islamic Prim Sch SL2 ....206 B6
Ireland Cl MK7 ....48 D4
Ireton Cl OX9 ....125 F1
Iris Cl HP21 ....115 B5
Iris Ct HP20 ....116 B8
Ironmonger Ct MK14 ....34 F6
Irvine Dr HP22 ....116 A2
Irvine Ho SL4 ....209 E5
Irving Cres LU7 ....105 A8
Irving Dale MK7 ....48 E5
Isaacson Dr MK7 ....48 C7
Isis Cl HP21 ....115 D3
Isis Way SL8 ....185 B4
Isis Wlk MK3 ....46 E1
Island Ho UB7 ....213 B6
Island The MK18 ....63 D2
Isle of Wight La LU6 ....93 F4
Islet Park Dr SL6 ....196 C3
Islet The MK18 ....63 D2
Islet Park Rd SL6 ....196 C3
Islet Pk SL6 ....196 C3
Islet Rd SL6 ....196 C3
Isling Brook MK5 ....46 B3
Islington Gr 6 MK10 ....35 F1
Ivanhoe Cl UB8 ....208 D8
IVER 207 F7
Iverdale Cl SL0 ....207 C6
IVER HEATH 200 D4
Iver Heath Inf Sch SL0 ....200 D2
Iver Heath Jun Sch SL0 ....200 D3
Iver La SL0 ....208 A8
Iver Lodge SL0 ....207 F8
Iver Sta SL0 ....207 F4
Iver Village Inf Sch SL0 ....207 F7
Iver Village Jun Sch SL0 ....207 E7
Ives Rd SL3 ....207 A3
Ivester Ct LU7 ....80 E6
IVINGHOE 105 F5
IVINGHOE ASTON 92 A3
Ivinghoe View HP20 ....101 F1
Ivinghoe Way LU6 ....92 E1
Ivins Rd HP9 ....175 A1
Ivybridge Cl UB8 ....201 E2
Ivy Cl
  Buckingham MK18 ....41 F8

Ivy Cl continued
Longwick HP27 . . . .**138** E5
Newport Pagnell MK16 . . .**22** E4
Ivy Cotts HP6 . . . .**177** B8
Ivy Cres SL1 . . . .**204** F6
Ivyhill Cl HP27 . . . .**139** B3
Ivy House La HP4 . . . .**135** E5
Ivy La
Bierton HP22 . . . .**102** D1
Burcott LU7 . . . .**79** D4
Great Brickhill MK17 . . . .**70** C8
Newton Longville MK17 . .**57** C3
Stewkley LU7 . . . .**68** E1
Ivy Pl HP14 . . . .**171** C5

J

Jacks Cl MK46 . . . .**7** E7
Jack's La MK43 . . . .**8** E5
Jackson Cl
Slough SL3 . . . .**206** E3
Uxbridge UB10 . . . .**201** E5
Jackson Ct HP15 . . . .**163** A3
Jackson Ind Est SL8 . . . .**185** B2
Jackson Rd
Aylesbury HP19 . . . .**101** A3
Uxbridge UB10 . . . .**201** E5
Jacksons Cl LU6 . . . .**92** E4
Jacob Cl SL4 . . . .**209** E6
Jacobs Cl MK14 . . . .**34** D7
Jakeman Way HP21 . . . . .**115** B6
Jakes Ho SL6 . . . .**203** A8
Jamaica MK6 . . . .**47** A6
James Cl
Hazelmere HP15 . . . .**163** A6
Marlow SL7 . . . .**183** F4
James Elliman Sch SL2 **205** E6
James Martin Cl UB9 . . .**190** A5
James Mdw SL3 . . . .**211** F6
James Rd HP14 . . . .**171** B4
James St SL4 . . . .**210** D6
James Way MK1 . . . .**47** B1
Jane Cl HP21 . . . .**116** A4
Jannetta Cl HP20 . . . .**116** B7
Jansel Sq HP21 . . . .**116** B6
Japonica La MK15 . . . .**35** C6
Jardine Cotts SL2 . . . . . .**199** A8
Jarman Cl MK18 . . . .**52** F8
Jarratt Ho SL4 . . . .**210** B4
Jarry Ct SL7 . . . .**183** F3
Jarvis Cl HP21 . . . .**116** A6
Jasmine Cl HP21 . . . .**116** A4
Jasmine Cres HP27 . . . . .**139** B3
Jasmine Wlk HP5 . . . .**144** A1
Jason Ho HP12 . . . .**172** E4
Jasons Hill HP5 . . . .**145** B2
Jeeves Cl MK6 . . . .**47** C7
Jefferies Rd HP17 . . . .**114** B5
Jefferson Cl SL3 . . . .**207** A2
Jeffrey Wlk HP19 . . . .**115** A7
Jeffries Ct SL8 . . . .**185** B2
Jellicoe Cl SL1 . . . .**205** B4
Jenkins Cl MK5 . . . .**45** F5
Jenkins Ct HP22 . . . .**89** C3
Jenkins La HP23 . . . .**132** E3
Jenna Way MK16 . . . .**23** A3
Jenner Rd HP21 . . . .**115** E5
Jennery La SL1 . . . .**197** C2
Jennings Field HP10 . . . .**185** C2
Jennings Wharf SL4 . . . .**210** D7
Jerome Cl SL7 . . . .**183** F4
Jersey Rd MK12 . . . .**33** C6
Jesse's La HP18 . . . .**125** D6
Job's La SL6 . . . .**195** B8
John Colet Sch HP22 . . .**131** C5
John Hall Way HP11 . . . .**172** D3
John Hampden Gram Sch
HP11 . . . .**172** F4
John Hampden Way
HP16 . . . .**151** B7
John Hampden Wendover
Sch The HP22 . . . .**131** B5
John Hellins Prim Sch
NN12 . . . .**18** D3
Johns La HP5 . . . .**134** E1
Johnson Rd HP14 . . . .**171** B5
Johnsons Field MK46 . . . . .**6** E4
Johnston Pl MK6 . . . .**46** E8
John Taylor Cl SL1 . . . . . .**205** C5
John Watson Sch OX33 **122** B1
Joiner's Cl
Botley HP5 . . . .**145** B1
Chalfont St Peter SL9 . .**177** F3
Joiners La SL9 . . . .**177** F3
Joiner's La SL9 . . . .**177** E3
Joiners Way
Chalfont St Peter SL9 . .**177** E3
Lavendon MK46 . . . .**7** F8
Jonathan Cl SL6 . . . .**202** E7
Jonathans MK6 . . . .**47** A6
Jonathans Ct MK6 . . . .**47** A6
Jones Way SL2 . . . .**187** E2
Joplin Ct MK8 . . . .**45** F7
JORDANS **176** F3

Jordans La HP9 . . . .**176** E3
Jordans Sch HP9 . . . .**176** F4
Jordans Way HP9 . . . .**176** F4
Joules Cl MK45 . . . .**46** C5
Jourdelay's Pass SL4 . . .**210** D8
Journeys End SL2 . . . . . .**205** E8
Jubilee Cotts MK18 . . . . . .**64** F3
Jubilee Rd
High Wycombe, Downley
HP13 . . . .**161** E2
High Wycombe HP11 . . .**172** E7
Stokenchurch HP14 . . . . .**158** F3
Jubilee Terr MK11 . . . .**32** E5
Jubilee Way SL3 . . . .**211** C2
Judge's La LU7 . . . .**80** F6
Juniper Cl HP15 . . . .**163** B3
Juniper Ct
Flackwell Heath HP10 . .**185** C7
Rickmansworth WD3 . . . .**167** F1
Slough SL1 . . . .**204** E6
Slough SL1 . . . .**206** B4
Juniper Dr
Aylesbury HP22 . . . .**116** C4
High Wycombe HP12 . . .**172** C5
Maidenhead SL6 . . . .**203** B8
Juniper Gdns MK7 . . . .**48** B7
Juniper Hill Sch HP10 . .**185** B7
Juniper La HP10 . . . .**185** D7
Juniper Rd SL7 . . . .**183** D5
Jupiter Hts UB10 . . . .**201** F4
Juson's Glebe HP22 . . . . .**131** C5
Jutland Ho SL4 . . . .**209** F5

K

Kalman Gdns MK7 . . . .**48** D5
Kaplan Cl MK5 . . . .**46** B5
Karenza HP14 . . . .**158** E3
Katherine Cl
Tylers Green HP10 . . . . .**174** C8
Walton MK7 . . . .**48** A4
Katrine Pl MK2 . . . .**58** D5
Kaybridge Cl [1] SL3 . . . .**173** F5
Kay Cl HP23 . . . .**119** A5
Kaywood Cl SL3 . . . .**206** C3
Keach Cl MK18 . . . .**66** A5
Keasden Ct MK4 . . . .**46** B2
Keaton Cl MK8 . . . .**45** D7
Keats Cl
Aylesbury HP21 . . . .**115** F6
High Wycombe HP11 . . .**172** F6
Newport Pagnell MK16 . .**22** A4
Keats La SL4 . . . .**210** C8
Keats Way
[2] Milton Keynes MK3 . . .**57** F7
West Drayton UB7 . . . . . .**208** F2
Keble Cl HP19 . . . .**115** B8
Keble Rd SL6 . . . .**202** E8
Keel Dr SL1 . . . .**205** C4
Keeler Cl SL4 . . . .**209** E4
Keel Way MK4 . . . .**45** D3
Keeler Cl HP19 . . . .**115** A8
Keensacre SL0 . . . .**200** D3
Keen's Cl HP13 . . . .**162** E1
Keens La OX39 . . . .**147** D6
Keepers Cl LU7 . . . .**105** A7
Keepers Farm Cl SL4 . . . .**209** E6
Keepers La HP6, HP7 . . . .**153** C3
Keep Hill Dr HP11 . . . .**173** D4
Keep Hill Rd HP11 . . . .**173** D5
Keinches La HP22 . . . .**129** A6
Keith Park Rd UB10 . . . . . .**201** F5
Kellan Dr MK6 . . . .**35** A1
Keller Cl MK11 . . . .**33** B2
Kelling Way [3] MK10 . . . . .**36** A4
Kelmarsh Cl [1] MK8 . . . . . .**33** F1
Kelpatrick Rd SL1 . . . .**204** D7
Kelsey Cl
Maidenhead SL6 . . . .**202** D3
Milton Keynes MK4 . . . . . .**56** F8
Kelso Cl MK3 . . . .**57** D6
Kelton Cl SL8 . . . .**185** C6
Kelvin Ct HP13 . . . .**172** F8
Kelvin Dr MK5 . . . .**36** B6
Kemble Ct MK15 . . . .**35** B6
Kempe Cl SL3 . . . .**207** C2
Kempson Cl HP19 . . . .**101** B1
Kemps Piece HP17 . . . . . .**127** A6
Kempton Gdns MK3 . . . . . .**57** D6
Kemsley Chase SL2 . . . . .**198** D4
Kemsley Cres MK10 . . . . . .**36** A4
Kenchester MK13 . . . .**33** F5
Kendal Cl
Aylesbury HP21 . . . .**116** B6
Slough SL2 . . . .**206** A6
Kendal Dr SL2 . . . .**206** A6
Kendal Gdns LU7 . . . .**80** C7
Kendall Pl
Maidenhead SL6 . . . .**202** C4
Milton Keynes MK5 . . . . . .**45** E5
Kendall Rd HP13 . . . .**173** F6
Kendal Mews UB8 . . . .**201** E2
Kendrick Rd SL3 . . . .**206** B3
Kenilworth Cl SL1 . . . .**205** F3
Kenilworth Dr
Aylesbury HP19 . . . .**101** D2
Milton Keynes MK3 . . . . . .**57** E8
Kenneally Cl SL4 . . . .**209** C5
Kenneally Cl [11] SL4 . . . .**209** C5

Kenneally Pl [12] SL4 . . . .**209** C5
Kenneally Row [13] SL4 . .**209** C5
Kenneally Wlk [10] SL4 . .**209** C5
Kennedy Ave HP11 . . . . . .**173** B4
Kennedy Cl
Farnham Common SL2 . .**198** C6
Maidenhead SL6 . . . .**202** C6
Marlow SL7 . . . .**183** E3
Kennedy Ho SL1 . . . .**204** D5
Kennel La SL6 . . . .**195** C7
Kennels Dr NN12 . . . .**17** D3
Kennet Cl
Aylesbury HP21 . . . .**115** C4
High Wycombe HP13 . . .**162** D2
Kennet Dr MK3 . . . .**57** E8
Kennet Pl MK3 . . . .**57** F8
Kennett Ct
Bourne End SL8 . . . .**185** B4
Maidenhead SL6 . . . .**202** F8
Kennett Rd SL3 . . . .**207** B3
Kennington Cl MK16 . . . . .**22** C3
Kennish Wlk MK18 . . . .**65** F4
Kensal Gn MK10 . . . .**35** E1
Kensington Dr
Great Holm MK8 . . . .**46** A8
Milton Keynes MK8 . . . . . .**33** F1
Kensington Path [3]
HP19 . . . .**100** F1
Kensington Pl MK46 . . . . . .**6** F1
Kent Ave SL1 . . . .**205** C8
Kent Cl UB8 . . . .**201** C6
Kent Ho MK3 . . . .**46** F2
Kent Lodge [6] SL6 . . . . . .**202** F6
Kentmere Rd HP21 . . . . . .**116** B7
Kenton Cl SL7 . . . .**183** E2
Kenton Ct HP19 . . . .**101** C2
Kenton's La SL4 . . . .**209** F5
KENTS HILL **48** A7
Kents Hill Park Rdbt
MK10 . . . .**47** E8
Kents Hill Rdbt MK10 . . . .**47** E8
Kents Hill Sch MK7 . . . .**48** A7
Kents Rd MK14 . . . .**34** D8
Kent Way SL6 . . . .**195** C7
Kenway Dr HP7 . . . .**166** B8
Kenwell Cl MK15 . . . .**35** C3
Kenwood Cl SL6 . . . .**202** A7
Kenwood Dr WD3 . . . .**178** F8
Kenwood Gate MK6 . . . . . .**35** B2
Keppel Ave MK19 . . . .**20** D2
Keppel St SL4 . . . .**210** D5
Kepwick MK8 . . . .**33** E1
Kercroft MK8 . . . .**33** E2
Kernow Cres MK6 . . . .**35** A1
Kerria Pl MK5 . . . .**47** A3
Kerr Pl HP21 . . . .**115** E7
Kerry Cl HP19 . . . .**101** A3
Kersey MK14 . . . .**34** C8
Kesters Rd HP5 . . . .**154** D7
Kestrel Cl
[2] Berkhamsted HP4 . . .**135** C3
High Wycombe HP13 . . .**161** C1
Kestrel Dr HP15 . . . .**163** B5
Kestrel Path SL2 . . . .**197** E1
Kestrel Way
Aylesbury HP19 . . . .**101** E4
Buckingham MK18 . . . . . .**52** F7
Keswick Cl SL2 . . . .**205** F6
Keswick Rd MK19 . . . .**11** B2
Ketchmere Cl MK18 . . . . . .**125** C6
Ketelbey Nook MK7 . . . . . .**48** E5
Ketton Cl MK15 . . . .**35** D7
Kew Cl UB8 . . . .**201** D3
Kew Gdns MK8 . . . .**33** F1
Kew Gr HP11 . . . .**173** B4
Kew Pl HP11 . . . .**173** B4
Keyes Way MK18 . . . .**41** E2
Keynes Cl MK16 . . . .**22** E4
Keys Pl SL6 . . . .**202** F6
Khalsa Prim Sch SL2 . . . .**206** A7
Khasiaberry MK7 . . . .**48** B5
Kidderminster Rd SL2 . .**198** A2
Kidderminster Wlk [3]
MK10 . . . .**36** B2
Kidwells Cl SL6 . . . .**202** F8
Kidwells Park Dr SL6 . . . .**202** F7
Kildonan Pl MK12 . . . .**33** D4
Kilfillan Gdns HP4 . . . . . .**135** A4
Kilfillan Pk HP4 . . . .**135** A3
Kilgour Ct [2] LU7 . . . .**80** F7
Kilkenny Ho MK4 . . . .**45** E2
Killarney Dr SL6 . . . .**202** E7
Killerton Cl MK4 . . . .**45** F7
Kiln Ave HP6 . . . .**155** C1
Kiln Cl
Calvert MK18 . . . .**73** B5
Prestwood HP16 . . . .**151** C7
KILN COMMON **151** B8
Kiln Croft Cl SL7 . . . .**184** A3
Kiln Ct HP9 . . . .**186** B8
Kilner Rd HP15 . . . .**163** C6
KILN FARM **33** B3
Kiln Farm Ind Est MK11 . .**33** B3
Kiln Fields SL6 . . . .**185** E1
Kiln La
Botley HP5 . . . .**155** B8
Cores End SL8, HP10 . . .**185** C3

Kiln La continued
Hedgerley SL2 . . . .**187** D3
Lacey Green HP27 . . . . . .**149** F5
Kiln Pl SL6 . . . .**195** A3
Kiln Pond La HP13 . . . . . .**161** D3
Kiln Rd
Hastoe HP23 . . . .**133** B6
Prestwood HP16 . . . .**151** B7
Kiln The HP5 . . . .**144** C1
Kilnwood HP14 . . . .**150** B1
Kilpin Gn MK16 . . . .**24** B6
Kilwinning Dr MK10 . . . . . .**35** F1
Kimbells Cl HP18 . . . .**124** D2
Kimber Cl SL4 . . . .**210** A4
Kimberley Cl SL3 . . . .**206** F2
Kimbers Dr SL1 . . . .**197** D2
Kimber's La SL6 . . . .**202** E3
Kimble Cl HP22 . . . .**129** E3
Kimble Park Rd HP17 . . . .**129** E3
Kimblewick Rd HP17 . . . .**129** C5
Kimbolton Cl MK14 . . . .**35** A8
Kincardine Dr MK3 . . . .**46** F3
Kindermann Ct MK5 . . . . . .**46** B5
Kindleton MK14 . . . .**34** F8
Kinellan Cl HP9 . . . .**175** D3
King Charles Cl MK18 . . . .**41** E2
King Edward Ave HP21 . .**116** A7
King Edward Ct [5] SL4 . .**210** D6
King Edward St
Milton Keynes MK13 . . . .**33** F7
Slough SL1 . . . .**205** D4
King Edward VII Ave
SL4 . . . .**210** E8
King Edward VII Hospl
SL4 . . . .**210** C4
Kingfisher HP19 . . . .**101** E4
Kingfisher Ct
[3] High Wycombe
HP11 . . . .**173** A6
Slough SL2 . . . .**198** B1
Kingfisher Ctr The
MK16 . . . .**22** C3
Kingfisher Ho
Loudwater HP11 . . . .**174** A4
Marlow SL7 . . . .**183** F2
Kingfisher Pl HP11 . . . . . .**174** B3
Kingfisher Rd MK18 . . . . . .**52** F7
King George Cres MK11 . .**32** E6
King George V Rd HP6 .**154** D1
Kinghorn La SL6 . . . .**195** D5
Kinghorn Pk SL6 . . . .**195** D3
King John's Cl TW19 . . . .**211** C2
King Johns Palace SL3 .**212** D6
Kingsash Rd HP19 . . . . . .**114** F8
Kingsbridge MK4 . . . .**46** D2
**Kingsbrook Specialist Bsns
& Ent Coll** MK19 . . . . . .**31** F4
Kingsbury HP20 . . . .**115** D8
Kingsbury Dr SL4 . . . .**211** B1
Kings Chase SL6 . . . .**202** F6
Kings Cl
Beaconsfield HP9 . . . . . .**186** A8
Chalfont St Giles HP8 . . .**177** D8
Henley-on-Thames RG9 .**191** D2
Westcott HP18 . . . .**98** C6
Wormingball HP18 . . . . .**123** D5
Kingscote Pre Prep Sch
SL9 . . . .**188** E8
King's Cross HP18 . . . . . .**113** A1
Kings Ct HP4 . . . .**135** C5
Kingsdale Rd MK4 . . . .**135** A3
KINGSEY **127** B2
Kingsey Rd OX9 . . . .**126** D3
Kings Farm Rd WD3 . . . . .**167** D3
Kingsfield SL4 . . . .**209** D6
Kingsfold MK13 . . . .**34** B7
Kingsgate HP19 . . . .**115** B8
King's Gr SL6 . . . .**202** E6
King's Grove Ind Est
SL6 . . . .**202** E6
Kings Hall Par HP22 . . . .**131** B4
Kingshill Dr MK19 . . . .**31** E5
Kingshill Rd HP13,
HP15 . . . .**162** D3
Kingshill Way HP4 . . . . . .**135** B2
Kings La SL6 . . . .**195** B8
King's La
Great Missenden HP16 . .**141** C2
Lee Common HP16, HP22 **141** F7
South Heath HP16 . . . . . .**152** E8
Kingsland Rd HP21 . . . . . .**116** A4
Kingsley Cl MK16 . . . .**21** F4
Kingsley Cres HP11 . . . . .**172** F6
Kingsley Dr SL7 . . . .**183** C6
Kingsley Path SL2 . . . . . .**197** D1
Kingsley Wlk HP23 . . . . . .**119** A4
Kings Lodge
Amersham HP6 . . . .**154** C3
Finmere MK18 . . . .**50** D6
Kingsmead HP27 . . . .**139** B6
Kings Mead LU6 . . . .**92** E3
Kingsmead Bsns Pk
HP11 . . . .**174** B3
Kingsmead Ho SL3 . . . . . .**205** C8
Kingsmead Rd HP11 . . . . .**174** B3
Kingsmead Rdbt MK4 . . . .**56** F8
Kings Oak Cl HP27 . . . . . .**139** C5
Kingsoe Leys MK10 . . . . . .**36** A2

Kings Quarter [3] SL6 . . .**203** B7
Kings Rd
Berkhamsted HP4 . . . . . .**135** B3
Chalfont St Giles HP8 . . .**177** D8
Henley-on-Thames RG9 .**191** D2
West Drayton UB7 . . . . . .**208** F4
King's Rd
Aylesbury HP21 . . . .**115** F8
Henley-on-Thames RG9 .**191** D2
High Wycombe HP11 . . .**173** F4
Loudwater HP11 . . . .**174** A4
Slough SL1 . . . .**205** E3
Uxbridge UB8 . . . .**201** D3
Windsor SL4 . . . .**210** D3
Windsor SL4 . . . .**210** D5
Kings Ride HP10 . . . .**163** B1
King's Road Ho SL4 . . . . .**210** D5
Kings Sq HP11 . . . .**173** F4
Kings St LU7 . . . .**78** E7
King St
Chesham HP5 . . . .**154** B7
Maidenhead SL6 . . . .**202** F6
Maidenhead SL6 . . . .**202** F7
Milton Keynes MK11 . . . . .**32** E6
King Stable St SL4 . . . . . .**210** D7
King's Terr SL3 . . . .**212** B8
KINGSTON **36** C2
Kingston Ave
Milton Keynes MK11 . . . . .**32** E5
West Drayton UB7 . . . . . .**208** F6
KINGSTON BLOUNT **147** A3
**Kingston Gymnastics &
Fitness Ctr** MK10 . . . . . .**36** C1
Kingston Hill OX39,
HP14 . . . .**158** B8
Kingston La
Uxbridge UB8 . . . .**201** E2
West Drayton UB7 . . . . . .**208** F4
Kingston Rd HP13 . . . .**162** D1
Kingston Rdbt MK10 . . . . .**36** C1
Kingsway
Farnham Common SL2 . .**198** C6
Gerrards Cross SL9 . . . .**188** E8
Iver SL0 . . . .**207** E7
[5] Slough SL3 . . . .**206** C3
Kingsway Ho [6] SL6 . . . .**202** F7
Kingsway Mews SL2 . . . .**198** C6
Kingswear Dr MK10 . . . . . .**36** B4
Kings Wlk RG9 . . . .**191** D2
KINGSWOOD **83** B3
Kings Wood SL7 . . . .**193** D7
Kingswood Ave HP10 . . . .**174** B8
Kingswood Creek
TW19 . . . .**211** D2
Kingswood Cl SL6 . . . .**202** F5
Kingswood Ho SL2 . . . . . .**205** C8
Kingswood La
Kingswood HP18 . . . .**83** B2
Ludgershall HP18 . . . .**96** F6
**Kings Wood National
Nature Reserve**★
MK17 . . . .**60** B1
Kingswood Par SL7 . . . . . .**183** D5
Kingswood Pl HP13 . . . . . .**162** E1
King's Wood Prim Sch
HP13 . . . .**173** F8
Kingswood Rd HP10 . . . . .**163** A1
Kingswood View HP13 . . .**162** E1
Kinloch Pl MK2 . . . .**58** E5
Kinnaird Cl SL1 . . . .**204** C7
Kinnear Cl MK8 . . . .**45** C7
Kinross Dr MK3 . . . .**46** E2
Kinson Gn HP20 . . . .**101** E3
Kipling Cl SL4 . . . .**210** B5
Kipling Dr MK16 . . . .**21** F4
Kipling Rd MK3 . . . .**58** A7
Kippell Hill MK46 . . . .**6** F5
Kirby Est UB7 . . . .**208** D6
Kirby Way UB8 . . . .**201** F1
Kirkeby Cl MK14 . . . .**34** D6
Kirke Cl MK5 . . . .**46** A5
Kirkham Ct MK5 . . . .**46** C8
Kirkstall Pl MK6 . . . .**46** C8
Kirkwall Spur SL1, SL2 . .**205** E8
Kirkwood Gr MK5 . . . .**45** D5
Kirtle Rd HP5 . . . .**144** C1
Kirtlington MK15 . . . .**35** B5
Kitchener Cl MK46 . . . .**7** A3
Kitchener Rd HP11 . . . . . .**172** E7
Kite Field HP4 . . . .**134** C7
Kite Ho MK46 . . . .**47** B8
Kitelee Cl MK19 . . . .**11** A3
Kite Wood Rd HP10 . . . . . .**163** B1
Kitsbury Ct HP4 . . . .**135** B4
Kitsbury Rd HP4 . . . .**135** B4
Kitsbury Terr HP4 . . . .**135** B4
Kittiwake HP19 . . . .**101** E4
Klee Cl HP22 . . . .**85** A5
Klondyke SL7 . . . .**183** D2
Knapp Gate MK5 . . . .**45** F7
Knaresborough Ct MK3 . .**57** D7
Knaves Beech HP10 . . . . .**174** D1
Knaves Beech Bsns Ctr
HP10 . . . .**174** D1
Knaves Beech Ind Est
HP10 . . . .**174** C1

Knaves Beech Way
HP10 . . . . .174 C1
Knaves Hill LU7 . . . . .80 D8
Knaves Hollow HP10 . . .174 D1
Knebworth Gate MK14 . . .22 A1
Knighton-Way La UB9 . .201 B6
Knightsbridge Ct SL3 . .207 A2
Knightsbridge PI 16
HP19 . . . . .115 A8
Knights CI
Eaton Bray LU6 . . . . .92 E5
Great Brickhill MK17 . . . .59 D1
Windsor SL4 . . . . .209 D6
Knights Ct LU6 . . . . .92 E5
Knights Gn WD3 . . . . . . .167 E6
Knights Hill HP12 . . . . . .172 E6
Knights PI 5 SL4 . . . . . .210 C5
Knights Templar Way
HP11 . . . . .173 B4
Knoll CI MK16 . . . . .13 F2
Knolls CI HP22 . . . . .89 B3
Knolls View LU6 . . . . .92 B5
Knoll The
Aspley Heath MK17 . . . . .49 A1
Sherington MK16 . . . . . . .13 F2
Knolton Way SL2 . . . . . .206 C7
Knottocks CI HP10 . . . . .175 D5
Knottocks Dr HP9 . . . . . .175 D5
Knottocks End HP9 . . . . .175 D5
KNOTTY GREEN 175 C6
Knowles CI UB7 . . . . . . .208 E5
Knowles Gn MK2 . . . . . . .58 C8
Knowles Inf Sch MK2 . . .58 C8
Knowles Jun Sch MK2 . .58 D8
Knowl Gate MK5 . . . . . . .46 C7
KNOWLHILL 46 D6
Knowlhill Rdbt MK5 . . . . .46 C6
Knowsley CI SL6 . . . . . . .195 A1
Knox Bridge MK7 . . . . . . .48 B8
Kola Ho SL2 . . . . .206 B6
Kop Hill Rd HP27 . . . . . .139 D3
Kramer Ct MK8 . . . . .45 D6
Krohn CI MK18 . . . . .52 F8
Krypton CI MK5 . . . . .46 C6
Kynaston Ave HP21 . . . .115 E4

L

Laburnham Cotts LU7 . . .69 E3
Laburnham Rd SL6 . . . . .202 E6
Laburnum Ave UB7 . . . . .208 F6
Laburnum CI SL7 . . . . . .183 E4
Laburnum Gr
Milton Keynes MK2 . . . . .58 E2
Slough SL3 . . . . .212 B8
Laburnum Rd HP12 . . . .172 C5
Lacemakers
Chinnor OX39 . . . . .147 C6
Long Crendon HP18 . . . .125 C7
Lace Mews MK46 . . . . .7 A4
Lacey Dr HP14 . . . . .161 C7
LACEY GREEN 149 E5
Laceys Dr HP15 . . . . . . .163 B5
Ladbroke Ct HP20 . . . . .101 E2
Ladbroke Gr MK10 . . . . . .47 F8
Ladbroke Rd SL1 . . . . . .205 D3
Ladybridge Terr MK43 . . .8 E5
Lady Cooper Ct HP4 . . .135 E6
Ladyday PI SL1 . . . . .205 C5
Lady Dr MK15 . . . . .35 A8
Ladymead CI MK17 . . . . .56 B8
Ladymeadow MK10 . . . . .35 E3
Ladymede Sch HP17 . . .129 E1
Ladysmith Rd LU7 . . . . .105 E5
Lady Verney CI HP13 . . .173 B8
Ladywalk WD3 . . . . .178 E6
Lady Yorke Pk SL0 . . . . .200 D6
Laggan Ct MK2 . . . . .58 D4
Laggan Rd SL6 . . . . .195 F1
Laggan Sq SL6 . . . . .195 F1
Lagger CI HP8 . . . . .177 B7
Lagger The HP8 . . . . . . .177 B7
Lagley Ho HP4 . . . . .135 A5
Lagonda CI MK16 . . . . . . .22 E4
Laidon CI MK2 . . . . .58 D4
Lake Ave SL1 . . . . .205 D6
Lake CI MK18 . . . . .66 B6
LAKE END 204 B4
Lake End Ct SL6 . . . . . . .204 A7
Lake End Rd SL4, SL6 . .204 B5
Laker Ct MK6 . . . . .46 E7
Lakes Cotts LU7 . . . . .90 C8
Lakeside
Aylesbury HP19 . . . . . . .101 E4
Maidenhead SL6 . . . . . .196 B1
Tring HP23 . . . . .119 A5
Lakeside Dr SL2 . . . . . . .198 F4
Lakeside Est SL3 . . . . . .212 F7
Lakeside Rd SL3 . . . . . .212 F7
Lakes La
Beaconsfield HP9 . . . . . .186 F8
Newport Pagnell MK16 . .22 B5
Lakes The SL7 . . . . .194 A6
Lake View SL6 . . . . .196 A1
Lamb CI MK16 . . . . .22 A4
Lambe Rd HP14 . . . . . . .131 C5
Lamberhurst Gr MK7 . . . .48 A8
Lambert Ave SL3 . . . . . .206 E3

Lamberts Croft MK12 . . . .33 C5
Lambert Wlk OX9 . . . . . .125 F1
Lamb La MK7 . . . . .48 C7
Lambourn Ct MK4 . . . . . .46 D2
Lambourne Ave HP21 . .115 D3
Lambourne Ct
Maidenhead SL6 . . . . . .203 C8
Uxbridge UB8 . . . . .201 B4
Lambourne Dr SL6 . . . . .202 C3
Lambridge La RG9 . . . . .191 C5
Lambridge Wood Rd
RG9 . . . . .191 B4
Lambscroft Way SL9 . . .177 E1
Lambton Ho SL4 . . . . . . .210 A4
Lambtons Way MK18 . . . .66 B5
Lamesley Ho SL6 . . . . . .202 E6
Lammas Ave SL4 . . . . . .210 D5
Lammas Ct SL4 . . . . . . .210 C5
Lammas La HP18 . . . . . .112 B2
Lammas Path HP18 . . . .112 B2
Lammas Rd
Cheddington LU7 . . . . . .105 A7
Slough SL1 . . . . .204 D8
Lammas Way
Lane End HP14 . . . . .171 A4
Loudwater HP10 . . . . . . .174 C1
Lampitts Cross MK6 . . . .47 B6
Lamport Ct MK8 . . . . .46 A8
Lamva Ct MK11 . . . . .32 F5
Lanark Ho MK3 . . . . .46 F1
Lancaster Ave SL2 . . . . .198 C1
Lancaster Bsns Park
LU7 . . . . .78 F1
Lancaster CI TW19 . . . . .213 E1
Lancaster Ct HP21 . . . . .172 D4
Lancaster Dr HP3 . . . . . .145 F4
Lancaster Gate MK3 . . . .57 E7
Lancaster Rd
Aylesbury HP21 . . . . . . .116 B6
High Wycombe HP12 . . .172 E4
Maidenhead SL6 . . . . . .202 B8
Uxbridge UB8 . . . . .201 D5
Lancaster Ride HP10 . . .174 B8
Lancastria Mews SL6 . .202 D7
Lancelot CI SL1 . . . . . . .205 A4
Lance Way HP13 . . . . . . .174 A6
Lanchester Rd MK43 . . . .93 F8
Lancot Ave LU6 . . . . .93 F8
Lancotbury CI LU6 . . . . . .93 C7
Lancot Dr LU6 . . . . .93 F8
Lancot Lower Sch LU6 . .93 E8
Lancot PI LU6 . . . . .93 E8
Lancresse CI UB8 . . . . . .201 D6
Lander Rd HP19 . . . . . . .100 F3
Landon Ct HP21 . . . . . . .115 F7
Landrace Ct MK5 . . . . . . .45 F3
Landsborough Gate
MK15 . . . . .35 B7
Lands End Gr MK4 . . . . . .56 F8
Lands The LU7 . . . . .79 F3
Lane End HP4 . . . . .134 C6
Lane End Ind Est HP14 .171 B4
Lane End Prim Sch
HP14. . . . . .171 B4
Lane End Rd HP12 . . . . .172 B6
Lanercost Cres MK10 . . . .36 B1
LANES END 132 C4
Lane The
Grafton Regis NN12 . . . . .9 D2
Mursley MK17 . . . . .67 D6
Lane Wood CI HP7 . . . . .165 F8
Lanfranc Gdns MK15 . . . .35 B7
Langcliffe Dr MK13 . . . . . .34 C5
Langdale CI
Maidenhead SL6 . . . . . .203 A6
Milton Keynes MK2 . . . . .58 D4
Langdale Ho HP11 . . . . .174 A4
Langdale Lodge HP10 . .174 C2
Langdon Ct MK11 . . . . . .116 B5
Langdon St HP23 . . . . . .119 A3
Langdown Way SL6 . . . .202 D5
Langerstone La MK4 . . . .46 F1
Langford PI MK7 . . . . .48 A3
Langham Way MK6 . . . . . .47 C4
Langland Ho MK6 . . . . . . .47 C6
Langland Rd MK6 . . . . . . .47 C6
Langlands MK46 . . . . .7 E7
Langland Sch MK6 . . . . . .47 C6
LANGLEY 207 A3
Langley Acad SL3 . . . . .206 E3
Langley Broom SL3 . . . .206 F1
Langley Bsns Ctr SL3 . .207 A4
Langley Bsns Pk SL3 . .207 A4
Langley CI HP18 . . . . .65 E4
Langley Cnr SL3 . . . . . . .199 F6
Langley Gram Sch SL3 .206 F2
Langley L Ctr SL3 . . . . . .207 B2
Langley Manor Sch
SL3 . . . . .206 E5
Langley Park Ctry Pk★ SL0,
SL3 . . . . .200 A1
Langley Park Rd SL3 . . .207 B6
Langley Rd SL3 . . . . . . .206 E3
Langley Sta SL3 . . . . . . .207 A4
Langley Way SL7 . . . . . .183 C2
Langmuir Ct MK5 . . . . . . .46 C4
Langney Gn MK4 . . . . . . .57 A8

Langport Cres MK5 . . . . .45 D5
Langport Ct HP22 . . . . . .172 C8
Langstone CI HP20 . . . . .101 F3
Langstone Ct MK4 . . . . . .46 D2
Langstone Ct 11 HP20 . .101 F3
Langton CI
Maidenhead SL6 . . . . . .202 D8
Slough SL1 . . . . .204 D8
Langton Dr SL6 . . . . . . .202 C3
Langton's Mdw SL2 . . . . .59 C6
Langtree Ave SL1 . . . . . .204 F4
Lanner Wlk MK6 . . . . .47 B8
Lanrick Copse HP4 . . . .135 E5
Lansdell Ave HP12 . . . . .172 B3
Lansdowne Ave SL1 . . . .205 E5
Lansdowne Ct
Maidenhead SL6 . . . . . .203 C7
Slough SL1 . . . . .205 E5
Lansdowne Rd
Aylesbury HP20 . . . . . . .101 D2
Chesham HP5 . . . . .144 C2
Lansdowne Rd SL9 . . . .177 D2
Lanterns Wlk SL6 . . . . . .203 B7
Lantern Way UB7 . . . . . .208 E4
Lanthorn CI MK14 . . . . . . .34 E6
Lappetts La HP16 . . . . . .152 E8
Larch CI
Aylesbury HP21 . . . . . . .102 A2
Slough SL2 . . . . .205 B8
Tylers Green HP10 . . . . .163 C2
Larches The
Berkhamsted HP4 . . . . .134 D5
Holmer Green HP15. . . .163 D7
Little Chalfont HP6 . . . . .155 B1
Larchfield Prim Sch
SL6 . . . . .202 E4
Larchfield Rd SL6 . . . . . .202 E5
Larch Gr MK2 . . . . .58 E2
Larchlands The HP10 . . .163 D1
Larchmoor Pk SL2 . . . . .199 A7
Larch Rise HP4 . . . . .135 A5
Larchwood HP16 . . . . . . .152 B4
Lark CI MK18 . . . . .52 E7
Larkfield SL6 . . . . .203 B1
Larkfield HP13 . . . . .162 F1
Larkin CI MK16 . . . . .22 A5
Larkings La SL2 . . . . . . .199 B4
Lark Rise HP15 . . . . .163 B5
Larkspur Ave MK14 . . . . .34 E5
Larkspur Way HP15 . . . .162 F6
Larks Rise HP5 . . . . .154 D6
Lark Vale HP19 . . . . .101 E3
La Roche CI SL3 . . . . . . .206 C3
Larwood PI MK6 . . . . .34 F1
Lasborough Rd MK10 . . .36 C1
Lascelles CI MK15 . . . . . .35 B7
Lascelles Rd 8 SL1 . . . .206 A4
Lascelles Rd SL3 . . . . . .206 B3
Laser CI MK5 . . . . .46 C6
Lashlake La OX9 . . . . . . .125 F1
Lassell Gdns SL6 . . . . . .203 B7
Lastingham Gr MK4 . . . . .46 B2
Latchmoor Ave SL9 . . . .188 D7
Latchmoor Gr SL9 . . . . .188 D7
Latchmoor Way SL9 . . . .188 D7
LATHBURY 22 C7
LATIMER 155 E3
Latimer
Latimer HP5 . . . . .155 E2
Milton Keynes MK11 . . . .32 E4
Latimer CI HP6 . . . . .166 C8
Latimer CI HP20 . . . . . . .116 A8
Latimer Rd
Chesham HP5 . . . . .154 E5
Little Chalfont HP5. . . . .155 C2
Latimer Way HP9 . . . . . .175 C6
Laud's CI RG9 . . . . .191 C1
Launceston WD3 . . . . . .167 B3
Launceston Ct MK5 . . . . .46 B6
Launde 1 MK10 . . . . .36 B1
Laurance Ct 2 SL7 . . . .183 D2
Laurel Ave SL3 . . . . .206 E4
Laurel Bank HP23 . . . . .146 F8
Laurel CI
Milton Keynes MK8 . . . . .45 D7
Poyle SL3 . . . . .212 E7
Prestwood HP16 . . . . . .151 B7
Speen HP27 . . . . .150 C4
Laurel Ct
Amersham HP6 . . . . . . .154 C3
Iver Heath SL0. . . . . . . .200 D5
Laurel Dr
Loudwater HP11 . . . . . .174 B3
Walter's Ash HP14 . . . . .161 D7
Laurel La UB7 . . . . .208 E2
Laurel Rd SL9 . . . . .177 D2
Laurels Rd SL0 . . . . .200 D3
Laurels The
High Wycombe HP12 . . .172 C4
Milton Keynes MK1 . . . . .47 D1
Laurel Way 4 HP21 . . . .115 E7
Lautree Gdns SL6 . . . . .195 E7
Lavender CI HP21 . . . . . .115 D5
Lavender Gr MK7 . . . . . . .48 A5
Lavender Rd UB8 . . . . . .208 F8
Lavender Way HP15. . . .162 F7
Lavender Wlk HP21 . . . .115 B6
LAVENDON 7 F7

Lavenden Comb Sch
MK46 . . . . .7 F8
Lavendon Rd MK46 . . . . . .7 A5
Lavric Rd HP21 . . . . .115 C6
Lawford Ave WD3 . . . . . .167 C3
Lawford CI WD3 . . . . . . .167 C3
Lawkland SL2 . . . . .198 C2
Lawn Ave UB7 . . . . .208 D2
Lawn CI SL3 . . . . .211 C7
Lawn Farm Bsns Ctr
HP18. . . . . .83 D4
Lawn Hill HP18 . . . . .73 A2
Lawn House La HP18 . . . .72 F1
Lawn Rd UB8 . . . . .201 C5
Lawnsmead Gdns MK16 .22 D5
Lawns The
Brill HP18 . . . . .96 B1
Tylers Green HP10 . . . . .163 B1
Lawn The SL3 . . . . .211 C6
Lawrence CI
14 Aylesbury HP20 . . . .101 F2
Aylesbury HP20 . . . . . . .102 A3
Lawrence Ct SL4 . . . . . . .210 C5
Lawrence Gr HP16 . . . . .151 D5
Lawrence Way SL1 . . . . .204 B8
Lawrence Wlk MK16 . . . .21 F5
Laws CI MK43 . . . . .8 E6
Lawson Rise HP13 . . . . .162 B1
Lawson PI MK5 . . . . .46 B5
Laxfield Dr MK10 . . . . . . .36 A4
Laxton Gn SL6 . . . . .202 C3
Layburn Cres SL3 . . . . . .212 B8
Lay Ad HP19 . . . . .101 B2
Layter's Ave SL9 . . . . . .177 C1
Layter's Avenue S SL9 .177 C1
Layter's CI SL9 . . . . .177 C1
Layter's End SL9 . . . . . .177 C1
LAYTER'S GREEN 177 B1
Layters Green La SL9 . . .177 B1
Layters Way SL9 . . . . . .188 D6
Leaberry MK13 . . . . .34 A8
Leachcroft SL9 . . . . .177 B2
Leaches Farm Bsns Ctr
HP18. . . . . .81 F4
Leach Rd HP21 . . . . .115 C7
Lea CI SL7 . . . . .183 D6
Leacroft CI UB7 . . . . . . .208 E6
Leacroft Rd SL0 . . . . . . .207 E7
Lea Ct HP7 . . . . .165 F8
LEADENHALL 47 A8
Leadenhall Rdbt MK6 . . .46 F7
Leaders CI MK12 . . . . . . .22 E4
Leafield Rise MK8 . . . . . .33 D2
Leafy La HP23 . . . . .118 C3
Leaholme Gdns SL1 . . . .205 B8
Lea La HP18 . . . . .125 F4
Leapingwell La MK18. . . .66 B5
Leary Cres MK16 . . . . . . .22 E4
Leas CI HP13 . . . . .173 F8
Leas Dr SL0 . . . . .207 F2
Leaside MK16 . . . . .12 B6
Leasowe PI MK13 . . . . . . .34 C3
Leather La HP16 . . . . . . .142 A3
Leaver Rd RG9 . . . . .191 C1
LECKHAMPSTEAD 42 E7
Leckhampstead Rd
MK18 . . . . .42 A8
Leckhampstead Rd MK19 .31 A3
Ledborough Gate HP9. . .175 F4
Ledborough La HP9 . . . .175 E4
Ledborough Wood
HP9 . . . . .175 E4
LEDBURN 90 D8
Ledburn LU7 . . . . .90 C8
Ledburn Gr LU7 . . . . .80 E6
Ledbury MK14 . . . . .21 E1
Ledeview Ct HP11 . . . . . .174 A4
Ledger's Rd SL1 . . . . . . .205 D4
Leeches Way LU7 . . . . . .105 A7
Lee Common CE Fst Sch
HP16. . . . . .142 D5
Lee Cotts
Buckmoorend HP17 . . . .140 D6
Lacey Green HP27 . . . . .149 A4
Lee Ct 7 HP12 . . . . .172 E7
Leeds Rd SL1 . . . . .205 E6
Lee Farm CI HP5 . . . . . .145 A1
LEE GATE 142 A7
Lee Ho 2 MK2 . . . . .58 C8
Lee La 5 . . . . .194 C1
Lee Rd
Aylesbury HP21 . . . . . . .115 D6
Quainton HP22 . . . . .84 F5
Saunderton HP27 . . . . . .148 F6
Lees CI SL6 . . . . .202 B5
Leeson Gdns SL4 . . . . . .204 E2
Lees Wlk SL7 . . . . .183 C1
Le Flaive Bsns Pk HP11 .161 E6
Legoland Windsor★
SL4 . . . . .209 D2
Leicester Ct RG9 . . . . . .191 D3
Leigh Hill MK4 . . . . .46 D2
Leigh Pk SL3 . . . . .211 B7
Leigh Rd SL3 . . . . .205 B6
Leigh Sq SL4 . . . . .209 D5
Leigh St HP11 . . . . .172 F7

LEIGHTON BUZZARD . . .80 F6
Leighton Buzzard Sta
LU7 . . . . .80 E7
Leighton Gdns SL6 . . . .196 B1
Leighton Ho 7 SL7 . . . .183 E2
Leighton Mid Sch LU7 . .80 F6
Leighton Rd
Edlesborough LU6 . . . . .92 D4
Leighton Buzzard LU7 . . .80 F7
Soulbury LU7 . . . . .70 B1
Stoke Hammond MK17 . .69 E7
Wing LU7 . . . . .80 A3
Wingrave HP22 . . . . .89 C3
Leighton St MK17 . . . . . .60 E6
Leiston Spur SL1 . . . . . .205 E7
Leisure Plaza★ MK2 . . . .46 C8
Leith CI SL1 . . . . .206 A5
Leith Rd HP19 . . . . .115 A8
Lembrook Wlk HP21 . . . .115 C6
Lemmon Wlk 5 MK4 . . . .45 E2
LENBOROUGH 52 D3
Lenborough CI MK18 . . . .52 C7
Lenborough Rd MK18 . . .52 C7
Lennon Dr MK8 . . . . .45 E7
Lennox Rd MK2 . . . . .58 C6
LENT. 197 B1
Lent Gn SL1 . . . . .197 B1
Lent Green La SL1 . . . . .197 B1
Lenthall MK13 . . . . .34 A5
LENT RISE 204 A8
Lent Rise Comb Sch
SL1 . . . . .204 B8
Lent Rise Rd SL1 . . . . . .204 B8
Leominster Gate 4
MK10 . . . . .36 A1
Leonards CI HP18 . . . . . .72 F2
Leonardslee MK4 . . . . . . .45 F2
Leon Ave MK2 . . . . .58 D8
Leon L Ctr MK2 . . . . .58 C4
Leon Sch & Sports Coll
MK2 . . . . .58 C5
Leopard Dr MK15 . . . . . . .35 A7
Leopold Mall 5 SL1 . . . .205 F4
Leopold Rd SL0 . . . . .07 D7
Lerwick Dr SL1 . . . . .205 E8
Leslie Dunne Ho SL4 . . .209 E5
Lester Gr HP15 . . . . .163 A4
Lesters Rd SL6 . . . . .195 D6
Letchfield HP5 . . . . .155 B8
Letter Box La HP27 . . . .139 C7
Leven CI
Leighton Buzzard LU7 . . .80 B7
Milton Keynes MK2 . . . . .58 D5
Levens Hall Dr MK4 . . . . .45 F1
Leverkus Ct OX39 . . . . . .147 C6
Leverkus Ho OX39 . . . . .147 C6
Levings CI HP19 . . . . . . .101 A3
Lewens Croft MK16 . . . . .16 A3
Lewes CI SL1 . . . . .205 C4
Lewes Ho MK3 . . . . .57 D7
Lewins Farm Ct SL1 . . . .204 F6
Lewins Rd SL9 . . . . .188 D8
Lewins Way SL1 . . . . . . .204 F6
Lewins Yd HP5 . . . . .154 B8
Lewis CI MK16 . . . . .21 F5
Lewis La SL9 . . . . .177 E2
LEWKNOR 157 B8
Lewknor CE Prim Sch
OX49. . . . . .157 B8
Lewknor CI OX49 . . . . . .157 A7
Lexham Gdns HP6 . . . . .154 C2
Lexington Ave SL6 . . . . .202 D5
Leybourne Gdns OX39 . .147 C6
Leyburn Ct MK13 . . . . . . .34 C5
Leyburne CI LU7 . . . . .90 C8
Ley Field Rd HP21 . . . . .115 E6
LEY HILL 145 B3
Ley Hill Sch HP5 . . . . . . .145 B1
Leyland CI MK18 . . . . . . .51 F4
Leyland PI 3 MK6 . . . . . .34 E1
Leylands La TW19 . . . . . .213 A2
Leys CI HP19 . . . . .101 C4
Leys Ct MK5 . . . . .46 B8
Leys La MK18 . . . . .62 B8
Leys Rd MK5 . . . . .46 B8
Leys The
Amersham HP6 . . . . . . .154 B4
Buckingham MK18 . . . . .41 F3
Halton HP22. . . . . .117 C1
Tring HP23 . . . . .119 B4
Woburn Sands MK17 . . .49 B4
Yardley Hastings NN7 . . .1 A6
Leys View MK16 . . . . .13 F1
Leywood CI HP7 . . . . . . .165 E7
Libra Ho HP10 . . . . .185 A8
Lichfield Down MK7 . . . . .48 B5
Lichfield Ho HP21 . . . . . .115 F6
Lidcote LU7 . . . . .78 A5
Liddall Way UB7 . . . . . . .208 F5
Liddell SL4 . . . . .209 C4
Liddell Gn MK16 . . . . . . .209 C4
Liddell Sq 16 SL4 . . . . . .209 C5
Liddell Way SL4 . . . . . . .209 C4
Liffre Dr HP22 . . . . .131 B6
Lightfoot Ct MK7 . . . . . . .47 F5

Lightlands La SL6 . . . . **195** F5
Ligo Ave HP22 . . . . **116** C2
Lilac Cl MK17 . . . . **57** C3
Lilac Ct SL2 . . . . **197** F2
Lilac Pl UB7 . . . . **208** F6
Lilies The HP22 . . . . **87** C1
Lilleshall Ave MK10 . . . **35** F1
Lilley Way SL1 . . . . . . **204** E5
Lillibrooke Cres SL6 . . **202** A3
LILLINGSTONE
 DAYRELL **29** F4
LILLINGSTONE LOVELL . . **30** B5
Lillyfee Farm La HP16 . **186** B5
Lilly Hill MK46 . . . . **6** F5
Lily Bottom La HP27 . . **150** A7
Lily Dr UB7 . . . . **208** D2
Lily's Wlk HP11 . . . . . **173** A6
Limbaud Cl MK7 . . . . . **48** A5
Lime Ave
 Buckingham MK18 . . . . **52** F7
 High Wycombe HP11 . . **173** D5
 West Drayton UB7 . . . **208** F6
 Windsor SL4 . . . . . . **210** F7
Lime Cl
 Hazelmere HP15 . . . . **163** A3
 Newport Pagnell MK16 . **22** B3
Lime Gr
 Chinnor OX39 . . . . . **147** D6
 Leighton Buzzard LU7 . **80** E8
 Woburn Sands MK17 . . **49** B4
Lime Rd
 Princes Risborough
 HP27 . . . . **139** B3
 Yardley Gobion NN12 . **18** E6
Limerick La MK9 . . . . . **35** B3
Limes Ave HP21 . . . . . **116** B7
Lime St MK46 . . . . **6** F3
Limes The
 Amersham HP6 . . . . . **154** B3
 Milton Keynes, Fenny Stratford
 MK2 . . . . **58** E8
 Milton Keynes MK11 . . **32** E5
 Windsor SL4 . . . . . **209** C6
Limes Way HP18 . . . . . **124** D2
Lime Tree Cl HP15 . . . . **162** D8
Lime Tree Wlk HP7 . . . **165** F8
Lime Wlk
 Maidenhead SL6 . . . . **202** A8
 New Denham UB9 . . . **201** C7
Limit Home Pk HP4 . . . **134** D7
Limmer La HP12 . . . . . **172** B3
Limmers Mead HP15 . . **162** D8
Linceslade Gr MK5 . . . . **34** B1
Linchfield HP13 . . . . . **173** E7
Linchfield Rd SL3 . . . . **211** C6
Lincoln MK14 . . . . **34** C8
Lincoln Cl HP22 . . . . . **116** B2
Lincoln Rd
 Berkhamsted HP4 . . . **135** B4
 3 Slough SL1 . . . . **205** E3
Lincoln Hatch La SL1 . . **197** C1
Lincoln Ho HP10 . . . . . **185** D3
Lincoln Park Bsns Ctr
 HP12 . . . . **172** D6
Lincoln Pk
 Amersham HP7 . . . . . **165** E8
 Brackley NN13 . . . . . **38** A5
Lincoln Rd
 Chalfont St Peter SL9 . **177** E2
 High Wycombe HP12 . . **172** E5
 Maidenhead SL6 . . . . **202** B8
Lincolnshire Cl MK3 . . . **46** E1
Lincolns The HP16 . . . . **152** A3
Lincoln Way SL1 . . . . **204** D6
Lincombe Slade LU7 . . . **80** E8
Lincroft MK43 . . . . **25** B1
Linden SL3 . . . . **207** B1
Linden Ave SL6 . . . . . **195** D1
Linden Cl SL0 . . . . . . **200** D3
Linden Ct HP12 . . . . . **172** D6
Linden Dr
 Chalfont St Peter SL9 . **177** E1
 Farnham Royal SL2 . . **198** C4
Linden End HP21 . . . . . **115** F6
Linden Gr MK14 . . . . . **34** C8
Linden Lea HP22 . . . . . **131** B6
Lindens The HP5 . . . . . **146** F8
Linden Way HP17 . . . . **128** B7
Linden Wlk HP15 . . . . **163** B3
Lindisfarne Dr MK10 . . **36** A1
Lindo Cl HP5 . . . . **144** B1
Lindores Croft MK10 . . **36** B1
Lindsay Ave HP12 . . . . **172** E7
Lindsay Cl TW19 . . . . . **213** D2
Lindsey Rd UB9 . . . . . **190** A1
Lines Hill HP22 . . . . . . **88** B3
Lines Rd HP14 . . . . . . **171** B5
Lines The HP22 . . . . . **88** C4
Linfields HP7 . . . . . . **166** C7
Linford Ave MK16 . . . . **22** A4
Linford La
 Milton Keynes, Willen
 MK15 . . . . **35** D7
 Milton Keynes, Woolstone
 MK15 . . . . **35** C3
Lingfield MK12 . . . . . . **33** E4

Lingfield Cl HP13 . . . . **174** A5
Lingholm Cl SL6 . . . . . **202** C6
Linington Ave HP5 . . . **145** A3
Link Cl HP12 . . . . **172** D6
Link Rd
 Datchet SL3 . . . . . **211** C6
 Great Missenden HP16 . **152** A3
 High Wycombe HP12 . . **172** D6
Links App HP10 . . . . . **185** B8
Links Rd HP10 . . . . . . **185** C8
Links Way HP10 . . . . . **185** B8
Linkswood Rd SL1 . . . . **197** C3
Link The
 Hazelmere HP15 . . . . **163** A5
 Slough SL2 . . . . . . **206** B7
Link Way UB9 . . . . . . **190** A5
Linnet Cl HP21 . . . . . . **172** B3
Linnet Dr HP18 . . . . . . **98** C5
Linney Ct MK4 . . . . . . **46** A1
LINSLADE **80** D7
Linslade Lower Sch LU7 . **80** F4
Linslade Mid Sch LU7 . . **80** E5
Linslade Rd LU7 . . . . . **70** F4
Lintlaw Pl MK3 . . . . . . **47** A3
Linton Cl MK13 . . . . . **34** C4
Lintott Ct TW19 . . . . . **213** D1
Linx The MK3 . . . . . . **47** A2
Lionel Ave HP22 . . . . . **131** A6
Lionel Cl HP22 . . . . . . **131** A5
Lipscombe Dr MK18 . . . **41** E1
Lipscomb La MK5 . . . . **46** A7
Lisburn Path ⑪ HP20 . . **101** F2
Lisle Rd HP13 . . . . . . **162** A1
Lisleys Field HP15 . . . **162** D7
Lismore Pk SL2 . . . . . **205** F7
Lissel Rd MK6 . . . . . . **47** E5
Lisset Rd SL6 . . . . . . **203** A6
Lister Cl MK6 . . . . . . **47** B6
Lister Gn HP21 . . . . . . **115** E5
Liston Ct (Sh Arcade) **7**
 SL7 . . . . **183** D2
Liston Ho **9** SL7 . . . . **183** E2
Liston Rd SL7 . . . . . . **183** D2
Litcham Spur SL1 . . . . **205** D7
Little Balmer MK18 . . . **52** E6
Little Benty SL4 . . . . . **208** D1
Little Boltons **15** SL7 . . **183** E2
Little Boltons **15** SL7 . . **183** E2
LITTLE BOYS HEATH . . . **152** C3
LITTLE BRICKHILL **59** E5
Little Bridge Rd HP4 . . **135** D4
LITTLE BRITAIN **208** C7
Little Britain HP18 . . . . **99** B7
Littlebrook Ave SL2 . . . **204** E8
Little Buntings SL4 . . . **209** F4
LITTLE CHALFONT **155** B1
Little Chalfont Prim Sch
 HP6 . . . . **166** E8
Little Chapels Way SL1 . **205** A4
Little Chartridge Ct
 HP5 . . . . **144** A1
Little Cl
 Aylesbury HP20 . . . . **101** D1
 Flackwell Heath HP10 . **185** B6
 High Wycombe HP12 . . **172** E3
LITTLECOTE **78** A5
Littlecote MK8 . . . . . . **34** A1
Littledown Rd SL1 . . . . **205** F5
Littledown Specl Sch
 SL1 . . . . **205** F6
Little Dunmow MK10 . . **36** A1
LITTLE END **23** B8
Littlefield Ct UB7 . . . . **213** D7
LITTLE FRIETH **170** E2
LITTLE GADDESDEN . . . **121** D7
Little Gaddesden CE Prim
 Sch HP4 . . . . . **121** D7
Little Gaddesden Ho
 HP4 . . . . **121** E5
Little Gibbs HP27 . . . . **138** A2
Little Greencroft HP5 . . **144** A4
Little Habton **3** MK4 . . **46** B2
Little Ham MK10 . . . . . **35** F3
Little Ham La HP27 . . . **139** B5
LITTLE HAMPDEN **140** F4
Little Hampden Cl
 HP22 . . . . **131** B4
Little Hill WD3 . . . . . . **167** C3
Little Hivings HP5 . . . . **144** A4
Little Hollis HP16 . . . . **151** E7
Little Hoo HP23 . . . . . **118** F4
LITTLE HORWOOD **55** F2
Little Horwood Manor
 MK17 . . . . **55** C3
Little Horwood Rd MK17 . **55** C3
Little Hundridge La
 HP16 . . . . **153** A8
LITTLE KIMBLE **129** E2
Little Kimble Sta HP17 . **129** E2
LITTLE KINGSHILL **152** B3
Little Kingshill Comb Sch
 HP16 . . . . **152** B2
Little La
 Lacey Green HP27 . . . **149** C4
 Yardley Hastings NN7 . **1** A7
LITTLE LINFORD **21** C5
Little Linford La MK16,
 MK19 . . . . **21** E4
Little Linford Wood Wildlife
 Reserve * MK16 . . . **21** B8

LITTLE LONDON
 Oakley **109** F5
 Wendover **141** C7
Little London
 Deanshanger MK19 . . **31** E4
 Whitchurch HP22 . . . . **87** A5
Little London Gn HP18 . **109** F5
LITTLE MARLOW **184** D5
Little Marlow CE Inf Sch
 SL7 . . . . **184** C5
Little Marlow Rd SL7 . . **183** E3
LITTLE MARSH **72** A3
Littlemarsh MK7 . . . . . **48** B4
Little Marsh Rd OX27 . . **72** A3
Little Mdw MK5 . . . . . **46** C7
Littlemere MK8 . . . . . . **33** D1
LITTLE MISSENDEN . . . **153** A2
Little Missenden CE Inf Sch
 HP7 . . . . **153** A2
Little Mollards HP22 . . **89** A3
Little Orchard Cl HP27 . **138** E5
Little Orchs HP20 . . . . **101** F3
Little Pk
 Bovingdon HP3 . . . . **146** A3
 Princes Risborough
 HP27 . . . . **139** C3
Littleport Spur SL1 . . . **205** E7
Little Reeves Ave HP7 . **165** F8
LITTLE ROW **202** A5
Little Shardeloes HP7 . . **165** A8
Little Spinney MK43 . . . **25** C3
Little Spring HP5 . . . . **144** B3
Little Spring Prim Sch
 HP5 . . . . **144** B3
Little St NN7 . . . . **1** B6
Little Stanton MK14 . . . **34** D8
Little Stocking MK5 . . . **46** A3
Littlestone Gate MK10 . . **36** B3
Little Sutton La SL3 . . . **207** C1
LITTLE TINGEWICK . . . **50** E6
Little Tring Rd HP23 . . **118** F6
Little Tring Rd HP23 . . **118** F6
Little Twye HP23 . . . . **132** F3
Little Twye Rd HP23 . . **132** F3
Little Windmill Hill
 WD4 . . . . **156** F7
Little Wood HP14 . . . . **158** E5
Little Woodlands SL4 . . **209** F4
Littleworth LU7 . . . . . . **79** E3
LITTLEWORTH
 COMMON **186** D1
Littleworth Rd
 Hedgerley SL1 . . . . . **186** C1
 High Wycombe HP13 . . **161** E2
Litton Ct HP10 . . . . . . **174** C2
Liverpool Rd SL1 . . . . **205** B7
Liverpool Victoria Ho **3**
 HP13 . . . . **173** B7
Livesey Hill MK5 . . . . **46** B5
Living Furniture Making
 Mus * HP11 . . . . . **172** F7
Livingstone Dr MK15 . . **35** C5
Llanbury Cl SL9 . . . . . **177** E3
Lloyds MK6 . . . . **47** A7
Loakes Ho HP11 . . . . . **173** A6
Loakes Rd HP11 . . . . . **173** A6
Lochinvar Cl SL1 . . . . **205** B4
Lochnell Rd HP4 . . . . . **134** F6
Lochy Dr LU7 . . . . . . **80** C7
Lock Ave SL6 . . . . . . **196** C2
Lockbridge Ct SL6 . . . **203** C8
Lock Bridge Rd SL8 . . . **185** A3
Locke Cl HP19 . . . . . **101** A2
Locke Gdns SL3 . . . . . **206** C4
Locke Rd MK2 . . . . . . **58** C8
Lockets Ct SL4 . . . . . **209** D6
Lockhart Ave MK4 . . . . **45** D2
Lock La
 Cosgrove MK19 . . . . **19** E2
 Maidenhead SL6 . . . . **202** C4
Lock Mead SL6 . . . . . **196** C2
Lock Path SL4 . . . . . . **209** D8
Lock Rd SL7 . . . . **183** F1
Locksley Ct **4** SL1 . . . **205** E3
Lockton St MK4 . . . . . **46** B3
Lockview Cotts MK1 . . . **47** E1
Lock View La MK1 . . . . **47** E1
Lockwood Chase MK4 . . **45** D2
Loddon HP21 . . . . **115** D3
Loddon Dr SL6 . . . . . . **202** D8
Loddon Rd SL8 . . . . . . **185** A4
Loddon Spur SL1 . . . . **205** E7
Lodge Cl
 Cheddington LU7 . . . . **105** A7
 Marlow SL7 . . . . . . **183** E1
 Padbury MK18 . . . . . **53** C2
 Slough SL3 . . . . . . **205** C4
 Uxbridge UB8 . . . . . **201** C1
Lodge Farm Bsns Ctr
 MK19 . . . . **20** C3
Lodge Farm Cl HP22 . . **116** E2
Lodge Farm Ct MK19 . . **19** F6
Lodge Gate MK14 . . . . **34** E7
Lodge La
 Little Chalfont HP8 . . . **166** F6
 Prestwood HP16 . . . . **151** D5
 Stoke Hammond MK17 . **69** E7
Lodge Park The MK6 . . **22** C4
Lodge Rd MK43 . . . . . **37** F8

Lodge The
 Aylesbury HP19 . . . . **115** A7
 Slough SL2 . . . . . . **206** B8
Lodge Way SL4 . . . . . **209** E4
Lodgings of the Military
 Knights **4** SL4 . . . **210** D6
Lodore Rd GU18 . . . . . **190** E1
Logan Rock MK4 . . . . . **57** B8
Lollards Cl HP6 . . . . . **154** C2
Lombardy Dr HP4 . . . . **135** D3
Lomond Dr
 Leighton Buzzard LU7 . **80** C7
 Milton Keynes MK2 . . **58** D4
London End
 Beaconsfield HP9 . . . **175** F1
 Newton Longville MK17 . **57** D4
 Woburn MK17 . . . . . **60** F6
London End La MK17 . . **48** D1
London Ho MK11 . . . . . **32** D5
London Rd
 Aston Clinton HP22 . . **117** E4
 Beaconsfield HP9 . . . **187** B8
 Berkhamsted HP4 . . . **135** E3
 Buckingham MK18 . . . **52** E6
 Chalfont St Giles HP8 . **177** C7
 Datchet SL3 . . . . . **211** C7
 Felden HP3 . . . . . . **146** A4
 High Wycombe HP11 . **173** E5
 Little Kingshill HP16 . **152** B5
 Loughton MK5 . . . . **46** B7
 Milton Common OX9 . . **136** B3
 Milton Keynes MK16 . . **36** B5
 Milton Keynes, Stony Stratford
 MK11 . . . . **32** E5
 Newport Pagnell MK16 . **22** F3
 Old Stratford MK19 . . **32** C7
 Slough, Brands Hill SL3 . **212** B8
 Slough, Langley SL3 . . **206** D2
 Slough SL3 . . . . . . **212** B8
 Tring HP23 . . . . . . **119** C3
 Wendover HP22 . . . . **141** D6
 Wheatley OX33 . . . . **122** B1
London Road E HP7 . . . **165** C4
London Road W HP7 . . . **165** C1
Londrina Ct **9** HP4 . . . **135** D4
Londrina Terr **10** HP4 . **135** D4
Long Ayres MK7 . . . . . **48** A3
Longborns MK43 . . . . . **25** C2
Longbottom La HP9 . . . **176** C5
Long Bridge La SL9 . . . **210** A4
Longbridge Cl HP23 . . . **119** A6
Longbridge Way UB8 . . **201** B3
Long Cl SL2 . . . . **198** B5
Long Close Sch SL3 . . . **206** A2
LONG CRENDON **125** B6
Long Crendon
 Courthouse * . . . .
 HP18 . . . . **125** D7
Long Crendon Ind Est
 HP18 . . . . **125** E5
Long Crendon Rd
 HP18 . . . . **124** D3
Long Crendon Sch
 HP18 . . . . **125** C7
Longcroft HP22 . . . . . **117** F5
Longcroft Ave
 Bovingdon HP3 . . . . **146** D5
 Paulerspury NN12 . . . **17** C8
Long Croft Rd WD3 . . . **178** D5
Longcross MK15 . . . . . **35** A6
Longdown Hill HP27 . . **139** F5
Longdown Mews HP19 . **114** F8
Long Dr SL1 . . . . **197** C2
Longfellow Dr MK16 . . **22** A4
Longfield
 Hedgerley SL2 . . . . . **187** D1
 Little Kingshill HP16 . **152** B4
Longfield Dr HP6 . . . . **154** B3
Longfield Gdns HP23 . . **118** E3
Longfield Rd
 Chesham HP5 . . . . . **143** F2
 Tring HP23 . . . . . . **118** F3
LONGFORD **213** C6
LONGFORDMOOR **213** A6
Longford Rdbt UB7 . . . **213** B6
Long Furlong
 Haddenham HP17 . . . **126** F6
 Stone HP17 . . . . . . **114** B5
Long Furlong Dr SL2 . . **197** E1
Long Gr HP9 . . . . **176** C4
Long Grove Wood Wildlife
 Reserve * HP9 . . . . **176** C4
Long Hale LU7 . . . . . . **105** C3
Longhedge MK7 . . . . . **48** A2
Long Hedge LU7 . . . . . **105** C4
Long Hide HP27 . . . . . **139** C4
Long La
 Bovingdon HP3 . . . . **146** D5
 Cookham Rise SL6 . . . **195** D5
 Heronsgate WD3 . . . **167** D2
 Olney MK46 . . . . . . **6** F4
 Rickmansworth WD3 . . **167** F1
 Stanwell TW19 . . . . **213** F1
Longlands Ct MK18 . . . **66** A5
Longlands Wlk MK18 . . **66** A5
Longland Way HP12 . . . **172** D5
Longleat **7** MK8 . . . . . **33** F1
Longleat Gdns SL6 . . . **202** D6

Longlees WD3 . . . . . . **178** D5
Long Ley LU7 . . . . . . **105** A7
Long Leys HP19 . . . . . **115** A8
Long Lional HP20 . . . . **115** D8
LONG MARSTON **104** B3
Long Marston Prim Sch
 HP23 . . . . **104** B4
Long Marston Rd
 Cheddington LU7 . . . . **104** E7
 Marsworth LU7 . . . . **104** F2
Long Massey MK46 . . . . **6** E5
Long Mdw
 Aylesbury HP21 . . . . **116** B6
 Chesham HP5 . . . . . **144** C3
Longmead SL4 . . . . . . **209** E6
Longmead La SL1 . . . . **197** D5
Long Meadow Cl
 Amersham HP7 . . . . **164** C3
 Monks Risborough HP27 . **139** C5
Long Meadow Sch MK5 . **45** F3
Longmead Prim Sch
 UB7 . . . . **208** E2
Longmire MK46 . . . . . . **7** F8
Longmore Cl WD3 . . . . **178** F6
Long Orchard Dr HP10 . **174** C8
Long Park Cl HP6 . . . . **154** C3
Long Park Way HP6 . . . **154** C3
Longpeak Cl MK4 . . . . **46** B1
Long Pk HP6 . . . . **154** C3
Long Plough HP22 . . . . **117** D5
Long Readings La SL2 . **198** B2
Long Ride HP27 . . . . . **139** C3
Longridge (Activity Ctr) *
 SL7 . . . . **194** F8
Long Row
 Leckhampstead MK18 . . **30** E1
 Prestwood HP16 . . . . **151** D6
Longstone Rd SL0 . . . . **200** C4
LONG STREET **10** F4
Longview HP9 . . . . . . **185** F8
Long View HP4 . . . . . **135** A6
Longville MK12 . . . . . . **33** B7
Long Walk The * SL4 . . **210** D4
Long Wall HP17 . . . . . **126** F5
LONGWICK **138** D7
Longwick CE Comb Sch
 HP27 . . . . **138** D6
Longwick Rd
 Longwick HP27 . . . . **138** F6
 Monks Risborough HP27 . **139** A5
Long Wlk HP8 . . . . . . **166** E6
Longwood Ave SL3 . . . **207** B1
Long Wood Dr HP9 . . . **176** F4
Longwood La HP7 . . . . **165** D8
Longworth Dr SL6 . . . **196** C1
Lonsdale Cl SL6 . . . . . **196** A1
Lonsdale Way SL6 . . . . **203** C1
Look Ahead SL1 . . . . . **205** E4
Loosen Dr SL6 . . . . . . **202** A3
Loose Path HP19 . . . . **114** F8
Loosley Hill HP27 . . . . **149** D6
LOOSLEY ROW **149** C6
Lord Grey Sch The MK3 . **46** F1
Lord Knyvett Cl TW19 . . **213** D3
Lord Knyvetts Ct **12**
 TW19 . . . . **213** E1
Lord Mayors Dr SL2 . . **198** A2
Lord Raglan Ho SL4 . . . **210** C4
Lords Cl MK2 . . . . **47** C1
Lordsmead MK43 . . . . **25** C2
Lords Mead LU6 . . . . . **92** E6
Lords Mill Ct HP5 . . . . **154** C7
Lords Terr LU6 . . . . . . **92** E6
Loriner Pl MK14 . . . . . **35** A6
Loring Rd
 Berkhamsted HP4 . . . **135** C3
 Dunstable LU6 . . . . . **93** F8
 Windsor SL4 . . . . . **209** F6
Lorne Cl SL1 . . . . **205** C3
Lorraine Cl HP13 . . . . **173** E8
Lorne Mews MK4 . . . . **45** C3
Loseley Cl MK8 . . . . . **33** F1
Losfield Rd SL4 . . . . . **209** E6
Lossie Dr SL3 . . . . . . **207** B6
Lothersdale MK13 . . . . **34** B5
Lott La MK3 . . . . **46** E2
Lott Mdw HP21 . . . . . **115** D3
Lott Wlk HP21 . . . . . . **115** D3
Louches La HP14 . . . . **161** E6
Loudhams Rd HP7 . . . . **166** C8
Loudhams Wood La
 HP8 . . . . **166** D8
LOUDWATER **174** D2
Loudwater Comb Sch
 HP11 . . . . **174** B2
Loughborough Dr MK10 . **36** C4
LOUGHTON **46** A8
Loughton Manor First Sch
 MK5 . . . . **46** A8
Loughton Rd MK13 . . . **34** A3
Loughton Rdbt MK5 . . . **45** F8
Loughton Sch MK5 . . . **46** A7
Loughton Valley Pk * . . . .
 MK5 . . . . **46** D7
Louisa Cotts **10** HP23 . **119** A3
Louise Wlk HP3 . . . . . **146** A3
Lovat Meadow Cl MK16 . **22** E4
Lovat St MK16 . . . . . . **22** D4
Lovatt Dr MK3 . . . . . . **57** E8

LOVE GREEN 207 D8
Love Green La SL0 . . . . 207 E8
Lovegrove Dr SL2 . . . . 197 F1
Love Hill La SL3 . . . . . . 207 A6
Lovel La SL4 . . . . 209 D5
Love La SL0 . . . . 207 D7
Lovelace CI SL6 . . . . . . 193 F4
Lovel End SL9 . . . . 177 C3
Lovel Mead SL9 . . . . . . 177 C3
Lovel Rd SL9 . . . . 177 C2
Love Row MK17 . . . . 68 D6
Lovett Gdns SL6 . . . . . . 196 C3
Lovett Rd UB9 . . . . 190 C8
Lovetts End LU7 . . . . 78 E8
Lovibonds Ave UB7 . . . 208 F7
Lowbrook CI HP21 . . . . 116 A4
Lowbrook Dr SL6 . . . . . 202 A3
Lowbrook Prim Sch
  SL6 . . . . 202 A3
Lowdell CI UB7 . . . . . . 208 E7
Lowdon CI HP11 . . . . . . 173 D4
LOWER ASCOTT 79 F1
Lower Ash Yard MK17 . . 67 F8
LOWER ASSENDON 191 A6
LOWER BOIS 154 C5
Lower Boyndon Rd SL6 202 E6
Lower Britwell Rd SL2 . 197 D1
LOWER CADSDEN 139 E5
Lower Church St
  Cuddington HP18 . . . . . 112 F3
  Stokenchurch HP14 . . . 158 E5
Lower Cippenham La
  SL1 . . . . 204 F6
Lower CI HP19 . . . . 115 B7
Lower Cookham Rd
  SL6 . . . . 196 C3
Lower Dr HP9 . . . . 175 D5
Lower Eighth St MK9 . . 34 E2
LOWER END
  Long Crendon 125 B7
  Marsworth 104 F3
  Thornborough 53 F8
  Woburn Sands 49 C8
Lower End
  Ashendon HP18 . . . . 97 E1
  Lower End MK18 . . . . . . 53 F8
  Newton Longville MK17 . 57 C3
  Piddington OX25 . . . . . . 95 E8
  Wingrave HP22 . . . . 89 B2
Lower End Rd MK17 . . . . 49 A8
Lower Farm CI HP18 . . 124 D3
Lower Farm Gate HP17 114 A3
Lower Fourth St MK9 . . 34 D1
Lower Furney CI HP13 . 173 D8
Lower Gn
  Cuddington HP18 . . . . . 112 F3
  Westcott HP18 . . . . 98 C7
  Weston Turville HP22 . . 117 A3
Lower Green La HP18 . . 112 C2
Lower Hammersley La
  HP13 . . . . 174 B4
Lower Icknield Way
  Chinnor OX39 . . . . 147 D8
  Great Kimble HP17 . . . 129 D1
  Marsworth HP23 . . . . . . 105 B1
  Monks Risborough HP17 139 B8
  Pitch Green HP27 . . . . . 138 C3
  Wilstone HP22, HP23 . . 118 C7
Lower Kings Rd HP4 . . 135 C5
Lower Lees Rd SL2 . . . 198 B2
Lower Lodge La HP15 . 163 A5
Lower Mead SL0 . . . . . 200 D2
Lower Mount Farm
  SL6 . . . . 195 D5
Lower Ninth St MK9 . . . 34 E2
LOWER NORTH DEAN . . 150 E1
LOWER POLLICOTT 111 F7
Lower Pound La SL7 . . 194 D8
Lower Rd
  Aylesbury HP21, HP22 . 115 F3
  Blackthorn OX25 . . . . . . 81 A4
  Chinnor OX39 . . . . 147 C7
  Chorleywood WD3 . . . . 167 D5
  Cookham Rise SL6 . . . . 195 F7
  Denham UB9 . . . . 189 D4
  Gerrards Cross SL9 . . . 188 F7
  Hardwick HP22 . . . . 87 B3
  Lacey Green HP27 . . . . 149 D6
Lower Ridge SL8 . . . . . 185 B4
Lower Riding HP9 . . . . 175 B2
Lower Second St MK9 . . 34 D1
Lower St
  Pury End NN12 . . . . 17 A7
  Quainton HP22 . . . . 85 A5
Lower Stonehayes MK14 34 F7
Lower Tenth St MK9 . . . 34 F2
Lower Third St MK9 . . . 34 D1
Lower Twelfth St MK9 . . 34 D1
Lower Ventnor Cotts
  SL6 . . . . 195 C8
LOWER WAINHILL 147 E7
Lower Ward SL4 . . . . . 210 D7
Lower Way
  Great Brickhill MK17 . . . 59 C1
  Padbury MK18 . . . . 53 C2
LOWER WEALD 32 E2
Lower Weald MK19 . . . . 32 E2
Lower Wharf MK18 . . . . 41 E1

Lower Woodend 182 D4
Lowes CI HP14 . . . . 158 C5
Lowestoft Dr SL1 . . . . . 204 D7
Lowfield CI HP15 . . . . . 163 B3
Lowfield Way HP15 . . . 163 B3
Lowick PI 4 MK4 . . . . . . 46 B2
Lowland Rd MK3 . . . . . . 57 C8
Lowlands Cres HP15 . . 151 D1
Lowlands Dr TW19 . . . . 213 D2
Lowlands Rd TW19 . . . . 213 D2
Lowman Way HP21 . . . 115 D4
Lowndes Ave HP5 . . . . 144 B1
Lowndes Gr MK5 . . . . . . 45 F7
Lowndes Way MK18 . . . 66 A5
Lownes Path HP19 . . . . 114 F8
Loxbeare Dr MK4 . . . . . . 46 C4
Loxboro Hill HP14 . . . . 160 D4
Loxley Rd HP4 . . . . 134 F6
Loxwood CI HP3 . . . . . . 146 F8
Loyne CI LU7 . . . . 80 C8
Lucas CI MK6 . . . . 47 D8
Lucas Rd HP13 . . . . 173 C7
Luccombe MK4 . . . . 46 C1
Lucky La or Cock La
  HP20 . . . . 101 D1
Lucy La MK5 . . . . 46 B8
Ludgate
  Milton Keynes MK6 . . . . 46 E7
  Tring HP23 . . . . 118 F4
LUDGERSHALL 96 D8
Ludlow CI MK3 . . . . 57 F7
Ludlow Dr OX9 . . . . 126 A1
Ludlow Ho SL6 . . . . 202 E6
Ludlow Mews HP11 . . . 174 A4
Ludlow PI HP20 . . . . . . 116 B8
Ludlow Rd SL6 . . . . 202 E6
Luff CI SL4 . . . . 209 E4
Lufford Pk MK14 . . . . . . 34 F8
Luggershall Rd OX25 . . 95 E7
Luke PI MK10 . . . . 35 F3
Luker Ave RG9 . . . . 191 D3
Lukes La HP23 . . . . 105 A1
Lullingstone Dr MK13 . 33 F5
Lumber La NN12 . . . . . . 17 B7
Lundholme MK13 . . . . . . 34 B5
Lundy Ct SL1 . . . . 204 E6
Lupin CI UB7 . . . . 208 D1
Lupin Ct HP21 . . . . 115 B5
Lupin Wlk HP21 . . . . . . 115 B5
Lutman La SL6 . . . . 195 F2
Lutyens Gr MK7 . . . . 48 C5
Luxborough Gr MK4 . . . . 46 C4
Lychgate Cotts HP3 . . . 146 B4
Lycrome La HP5 . . . . . . 144 D3
Lycrome Rd HP5 . . . . . . 144 E3
Lydbrook La HP17 . . . . . 49 B5
Lyde End HP27 . . . . 138 B1
Lydford Ave SL2 . . . . . . 205 D8
Lydiard MK8 . . . . 33 E1
Lydiard CI HP21 . . . . . . 116 A4
Lydsey CI SL2 . . . . 198 A2
LYE GREEN 144 F4
Lye Green Cotts HP5 . . 144 E2
Lye Green Rd HP5 . . . . 144 E2
Lyell Place E SL4 . . . . . 209 C4
Lyell Place W SL4 . . . . 209 C4
Lyell Rd SL4 . . . . 209 C4
Lyell Walk E SL4 . . . . . 209 C4
Lyell Walk W SL4 . . . . . 209 C4
Lye The HP4 . . . . 121 D6
Lyme Ave HP4 . . . . 134 D7
Lynch CI UB8 . . . . 201 C5
Lynch Hill La SL2 . . . . . 197 E2
Lynch Hill Sch SL2 . . . . 197 F2
Lynch The UB8 . . . . 201 C5
Lyndhurst Ave SL6 . . . . 195 E6
Lyndhurst CI HP13 . . . . 161 D1
Lyndhurst Rd HP5 . . . . 144 B2
Lyndon CI HP15 . . . . . . 151 C7
Lyndon Gdns HP13 . . . 173 E8
Lyndwood Dr SL4 . . . . . 211 A1
Lyndwood Par SL4 . . . . 211 A2
Lyneham Gdns SL6 . . . 195 B1
Lynher CI HP21 . . . . . . 115 C4
Lynmouth Cres MK4 . . . 46 C4
Lynott CI MK8 . . . . 45 E6
Lynton Gn SL6 . . . . 202 E7
Lynton Rd HP5 . . . . 144 C3
Lynwood Ave SL3 . . . . 206 D3
Lynwood Rd HP21 . . . . 116 A5
Lyon Rd MK1 . . . . 47 B2
Lysander CI HP3 . . . . . 146 A4
Lysander Mead SL6 . . . 203 C8

McArdle Way SL3 . . . . . 212 D7
McAuliffe Dr SL1, SL2 . 197 F8
McConnell Dr SL2 . . . . 197 F8
McCorquodale Rd
  MK12 . . . . 33 C7
MacDonald CI HP6 . . . . 154 D4
McDougall Rd 8 HP4 . . 135 D4
McEwen Ride HP27 . . . 117 D1
MacIntyre Wingrave Sch
  HP22 . . . . 89 C3
McKay Trad Est SL3 . . . 212 E5

McKenzie CI MK18 . . . . . 52 D8
Mackenzie Mall 3 SL1 . 205 F4
Mackenzie St 2 SL1 . . . 205 F4
McLellan PI HP21 . . . . . 172 D5
McLernon Way MK18 . . . 66 A5
Maconi Croft MK5 . . . . . 46 C5
Madeira Wlk SL4 . . . . . . 210 D6
Madeley CI HP6 . . . . . . 154 D3
Madeley Rd HP21 . . . . . 115 E6
Magdalen CI
  Milton Keynes MK11 . . . 32 D6
  Syresham NN13 . . . . . . 27 C8
Magdalen Ho MK11 . . . . 32 D6
Magdalen Rd MK2 . . . . . 58 D6
Magenta CI SL4 . . . . . . 211 A1
Magnet L Ctr SL6 . . . . . 203 A8
Magnolia Dene HP15 . . 162 F2
Magnolia Gdns SL3 . . . 206 C3
Magnolia St UB7 . . . . . 208 D2
Magnolia Way HP10 . . . 185 E7
Magpie CI
  Flackwell Heath HP10 . 174 A1
  Milton Keynes MK5 . . . . 46 B3
Magpie La
  Coleshill HP7 . . . . 165 A1
  Flackwell Heath HP10 . 174 A1
  Loudwater HP13 . . . . . . 174 B3
Magpie Way
  Slough SL2 . . . . 197 F1
  Winslow MK18 . . . . 66 B6
Mahler CI MK7 . . . . 48 C5
Mahoney Ct
  High Wycombe HP11 . . 172 F8
  Milton Keynes MK8 . . . . 45 D6
Maida Vale 3 MK10 . . . . 35 F1
MAIDENHEAD 202 F4
Maidenhead Ave MK3 . . 34 C3
Maidenhead Ct Pk
  Cookham Rise SL6 . . . . 195 F6
  Windsor SL4 . . . . 209 E7
Maidenhead Ret Pk
  SL6 . . . . 203 A6
Maidenhead Sta SL6 . . 202 F6
MAIDENSGROVE 179 C5
MAIDS MORETON 41 E4
Maids Moreton CE Sch
  MK18 . . . . 41 E3
Maidstone Rd MK10 . . . . 36 C2
Maigno Way 1 MK12 . . . 33 A6
Main Dr
  Gerrards Cross SL9 . . . 188 C6
  Iver SL0 . . . . 207 E3
  Pottersbury NN12 . . . . . 18 B2
Main Par WD3 . . . . 167 C5
Main Rd
  Astwood MK16 . . . . 16 B3
  Drayton Parslow MK17 . 68 B5
  Lacey Green MK27 . . . . 149 E5
  Syresham NN13 . . . . 27 C7
  Upper Winchendon HP18 99 A1
  Walter's Ash HP14 . . . . 161 C7
Main Road N HP4 . . . . . 107 A6
Main Road S HP4 . . . . . 107 D4
Main St
  Adstock MK18 . . . . 53 F1
  Akeley MK18 . . . . 41 F8
  Ashendon HP18 . . . . 97 F1
  Beachampton MK19 . . . . 44 A6
  Buckingham MK18 . . . . . 41 F3
  Chackmore MK18 . . . . . . 41 B4
  Charndon OX27 . . . . 72 E5
  Cosgrove MK19 . . . . 19 E2
  Gawcott MK18 . . . . 51 F4
  Grendon Underwood HP18 83 B5
  Mursley MK17 . . . . 67 D6
  Padbury MK18 . . . . 53 B1
  Poundon OX27 . . . . 71 F7
  Preston Bissett MK18 . . 62 B8
  Shalstone MK18 . . . . 39 E6
  Tingewick MK18 . . . . 51 B6
  Turweston NN13 . . . . . . 38 C8
  Twyford MK18 . . . . 62 C1
  Westbury NN13 . . . . 39 A4
  Weston Turville HP22 . . 116 C2
Maitland Dr HP13 . . . . . 173 B8
Maitland Rd HP22 . . . . 131 D7
Major's Farm Rd
  Datchet SL3 . . . . 211 E8
  Slough SL3 . . . . 212 A8
Malbons Ct MK6 . . . . 46 F7
Malborough Ho HP4 . . 135 A3
Malborough Way NN12 . 18 F5
Malcolm Rd UB10 . . . . . 201 F8
Malden CI HP6 . . . . 154 F1
Malders La SL6 . . . . . . 195 C3
Malet CI HP14 . . . . 158 F5
Malins Gate MK14 . . . . . 34 E8
Malkin Dr HP9 . . . . 175 C3
Mallard CI HP19 . . . . . . 101 E4
Mallard Croft HP17 . . . 127 A7
Mallard Dr
  Buckingham MK18 . . . . . 52 E8
  Slough SL1 . . . . 204 F6
Mallard Ho HP11 . . . . . 173 C6
Mallard PI HP11 . . . . . . 174 B3

Mallets End HP22 . . . . . 85 B4
Malletts CI MK11 . . . . . . 32 E5
Mallow Gate MK14 . . . . . 34 E4
Mallow Pk SL6 . . . . 195 C1
Malmers Well Rd HP13 173 B7
Malpas Rd SL2 . . . . 206 B6
Malthouse Flats RG9 . . 192 D6
Malthouse Sq
  Beaconsfield HP9 . . . . . 186 F8
  Princes Risborough
    HP27 . . . . 139 B4
Malthouse Way 2 SL7 . 183 D1
Malting CI MK16 . . . . 12 B6
Malting La
  Aldbury HP23 . . . . 120 D5
  Dagnall HP4 . . . . 107 C5
Maltings CI
  Cranfield MK43 . . . . 25 A1
  Stewkley LU7 . . . . 78 E8
Maltings Field MK19 . . . 19 F5
Maltings The
  Chackmore MK18 . . . . . . 41 B4
  Olney MK46 . . . . 7 A3
  Tingewick MK18 . . . . 51 B6
Maltmans Green Sch
  SL9 . . . . 188 C8
Maltmans La SL9 . . . . . 188 C8
Malton Ave SL1 . . . . . . 205 B6
Malton CI MK10 . . . . 35 F1
Malvern CI HP13 . . . . . 172 E8
Malvern Ct SL3 . . . . . . 212 A7
Malvern Dr
  Leighton Buzzard LU7 . . 80 C8
  Milton Keynes MK11 . . . 33 A4
Malvern Rd
  Aylesbury HP20 . . . . . . 116 C3
  Maidenhead SL6 . . . . . 195 D1
Malyns CI OX39 . . . . . . 147 C7
Manchester Terr HP14 . 171 B4
Mandela Ct UB8 . . . . . . 208 C7
Mandelyns HP4 . . . . . . 134 E7
Mandeville Dr MK10 . . . 36 C2
Mandeville Mews HP21 115 E4
Mandeville Rd
  Aylesbury HP21 . . . . . . 115 E5
  Prestwood HP16 . . . . . . 151 B7
Mandeville Sch The
  HP21 . . . . 115 D4
Manfield CI SL2 . . . . . . 198 A2
Manifold La MK4, MK5 . 46 B3
Manor CI
  Berkhamsted HP4 . . . . 135 C4
  Bledlow HP27 . . . . 138 B1
  Buckingham MK18 . . . . . 53 C2
  Cosgrove MK19 . . . . 19 E2
  Hanslope MK19 . . . . 11 A2
  Milton Keynes MK10 . . . 35 F3
  Prestwood HP16 . . . . . . 151 B7
  Salford MK17 . . . . 37 D3
  Stoke Hammond MK17 . . 69 E7
  Tylers Green HP10 . . . . 163 A2
Manor Cotts
  Chorleywood WD3 . . . . 167 B3
  Milton Keynes MK12 . . . 33 B7
Manor Court Yd HP13 . 162 A1
Manor Court Yd OX33 . 123 B2
Manor Cres
  Seer Green HP9 . . . . . . 176 D5
  Wendover HP22 . . . . . . 131 C5
Manor Ct
  Emberton MK46 . . . . 13 F8
  Leighton Buzzard LU7 . . 70 E2
  Marlow SL7 . . . . 183 C3
  Slough, Cippenham SL1 . 204 F5
  6 Slough, Upton Park
    SL1 . . . . 205 F3
  Twyford MK18 . . . . 62 C1
Manor Ctyd
  Haddenham HP17 . . . . . 127 D4
  Sherington MK16 . . . . . . 13 F1
Manor Dr
  Amersham HP6 . . . . 154 B3
  Aylesbury HP20 . . . . . . 101 F2
  Haversham MK19 . . . . . . 20 E2
  Stewkley LU7 . . . . 78 E8
Manor Farm SL3 . . . . . 212 E5
Manor Farm CI
  Soulbury LU7 . . . . 69 E2
  Stone HP17 . . . . 114 E6
  Weston Turville HP22 . . 116 E2
  Windsor SL4 . . . . 209 B4
Manor Farm Cotts SL4 . 211 A2
Manor Farm Ct HP22 . . 87 E2
Manor Farm Ctyd
  HP22 . . . . 102 D8
Manor Farm Ho SL4 . . . 209 F4
Manor Farm Inf Sch
  HP15 . . . . 163 B2
Manor Farm Jun Sch
  HP15 . . . . 163 B2
Manor Farm La LU7 . . . . 90 C8
Manor Farm Way HP9 . 176 D4
Manorfields Rd MK19 . . 32 B6
Manor Gdns
  Grendon Underwood
    HP18 . . . . 83 A6
  High Wycombe HP13 . . 162 A1

LOV–Mar 237

Manor Gdns continued
  Maids Moreton MK18 . . . 41 E2
  Woburn Green HP10 . . . 185 E5
Manor Ho
  Brill HP18 . . . . 110 A8
  Hambleden RG9 . . . . . . 181 D2
Manor House CI HP20 . 101 F1
Manor House Hospl
  HP20 . . . . 101 F1
Manor House La SL3 . . 211 B6
Manor La
  Gerrards Cross SL9 . . . 188 D4
  Maidenhead SL6 . . . . . 202 E4
MANOR PARK
  Aylesbury 101 E2
  Slough 198 D1
Manor Park Ave HP27 . 139 A3
Manor Pk MK16 . . . . 41 F4
Manor Pound Rd LU7 . 105 A7
Manor Rd
  Akeley MK18 . . . . 41 F7
  Aylesbury HP20 . . . . . . 101 E1
  Cheddington LU7 . . . . . 104 F7
  Chesham HP5 . . . . 144 C2
  Emmington OX9 . . . . . . 137 B6
  Maidenhead SL6 . . . . . 202 E4
  Milton Keynes, Bletchley
    MK2 . . . . 58 E8
  Milton Keynes, Wolverton
    MK12 . . . . 33 B7
  Newport Pagnell MK16 . 22 A4
  Newton Longville MK17 . 57 D3
  Oakley HP18 . . . . 109 D5
  Oving HP22 . . . . 86 C7
  Princes Risborough
    HP27 . . . . 139 A2
  Rowsham HP22 . . . . . . 102 D8
  Seer Green HP9 . . . . . . 176 D5
  Tring HP23 . . . . 119 A5
  Tylers Green HP10 . . . . 163 A2
  Wendover HP22 . . . . . . 131 C5
  Windsor SL4 . . . . 209 C5
Manor St
  Berkhamsted HP4 . . . . 135 D4
  Buckingham MK18 . . . . . 52 C8
Manor View HP15 . . . . . 163 B2
Manor View Ho HP13 . . 161 E2
Manor Way
  Chesham HP5 . . . . 144 D1
  Coleshill HP7 . . . . 164 F3
  Yardley Gobion NN12 . . 18 E6
Manor Waye UB8 . . . . . 201 D4
Mansard Ct 8 HP23 . . . 119 A3
Manse CI MK11 . . . . 32 D6
Mansel CI
  Cosgrove MK19 . . . . 19 E2
  Slough SL2 . . . . 206 B8
Mansell CI
  Milton Keynes MK5 . . . . 46 A6
  Windsor SL4 . . . . 209 E6
Manshead CI MK11 . . . . 32 F5
Mansion Dr HP23 . . . . . 119 B3
Mansion Hill HP22 . . . . 131 E8
Mansion La
  Harrold MK43 . . . . 3 F6
  Iver SL0 . . . . 207 C5
Mansion The HP4 . . . . . 135 E6
MANTLES GN 165 A8
Manton Rd LU6 . . . . 93 D5
Maple Ave UB7 . . . . 208 F5
Maple CI
  Hazlemere HP15 . . . . . 163 A3
  High Wycombe HP15 . . 172 C5
  Maidenhead SL6 . . . . . 202 A5
Maple Cres SL2 . . . . . . 206 B6
MAPLE CROSS 178 C6
Maple Cross JMI Sch
  WD3 . . . . 178 C5
Maple Ct
  Gerrards Cross SL9 . . . 188 C6
  Marlow SL7 . . . . 183 C3
  Windsor SL4 . . . . 210 C4
Mapledean MK12 . . . . . . 33 E4
Mapledurham MK4 . . . . . 46 B3
Mapledurham Wlk SL6 . 195 E3
Maple End HP22 . . . . . . 116 C4
Maplefield La HP8 . . . . 166 B6
Maple Gr
  Milton Keynes MK2 . . . . 58 E8
  Woburn Sands MK17 . . . 49 B4
Maple Leys MK18 . . . . . . 63 E2
Maple Lodge CI WD3 . . 178 E6
Maple PI UB7 . . . . 208 F5
Maple Rise SL7 . . . . . . 183 E3
Maples The
  6 Bourne End SL8 . . . . 185 B3
  Wendover HP22 . . . . . . 131 C5
Maplewood Gdns HP9 . 175 B1
Maplewood Sch HP13 . 161 D3
Maplin Pk SL3 . . . . 207 B4
Mapperton CI 3 MK4 . . . 45 F1
Mapridge Green La
  HP16 . . . . 141 D1
Marand Ct HP21 . . . . . . 115 F8
Mara PI MK9 . . . . 35 A3
Marbeck CI SL4 . . . . . . 209 D6

Marchant Ct SL7 . . . . 184 A3
March Edge MK18 . . . . . . 41 E1
Marches The SL4 . . . . . 205 D2
March Mdw MK7 . . . . . . 48 D7
March Pl HP19 . . . . 115 B8
Marcia Ct SL1 . . . . 204 F5
Marcourt Rd HP14 . . . . 158 F3
Mardle Rd LU7 . . . . 80 E6
Maree Cl
  Leighton Buzzard LU7 . . . . 80 C7
  Milton Keynes MK2 . . . . 58 C5
Marefield Rd SL7 . . . . . 183 D2
Mare Leys MK18 . . . . . . 52 F8
Marescroft Rd SL2 . . . . 197 E1
Margam Cres MK10 . . . . 36 A1
Margaret Ct HP13 . . . . . 173 E5
Margaret Powell Sq
  MK9 . . . . 34 F3
Margaret Smythe Ho
  SL9 . . . . 188 F5
Marigold Hl MK14 . . . . . 34 E4
Marigold Wlk HP15 . . . 162 F6
Marina Dr
  Dunstable LU6 . . . . 93 E7
  Milton Keynes MK12 . . . . 33 D6
Marina Rdbt MK6 . . . . . . 47 C7
Marina Way
  Iver SL0 . . . . 208 A6
  Slough SL1 . . . . 204 D6
Marine Ct MK6 . . . . 46 F6
Marish Ct SL3 . . . . 207 A3
Marish La SL9 . . . . 189 D7
Marish Prim Sch SL3 . . . 207 A3
Marish Wharf Ind Est
  SL3 . . . . 206 E4
Marjoram Pl MK14 . . . . 34 E4
Mark Dr SL9 . . . . 177 E6
Markenfield Pl MK4 . . . 45 E1
Market Hill
  Buckingham MK18 . . . . . 41 D1
  Milton Keynes MK6 . . . . 47 B8
  Whitchurch HP22 . . . . . . 86 F6
Market Ho [5] SL9 . . . . 177 D2
Market La SL3 . . . . 207 C3
Market Par HP15 . . . . . 163 A4
Market Pl
  Chalfont St Peter SL9 . . . 177 D2
  Colnbrook SL3 . . . . 212 C7
  Henley-on-Thames RG9 . . 191 D2
  [4] Olney MK46 . . . . 6 F3
  Woburn MK17 . . . . 60 F7
Market Place Mews [5]
  RG9 . . . . 191 D2
Market Sq
  Amersham HP7 . . . . 165 B7
  Aylesbury HP20 . . . . . . 115 D8
  [5] Buckingham MK18 . . 41 D1
  Chesham HP5 . . . . 154 B8
  Hanslope MK19 . . . . 11 A2
  Marlow SL7 . . . . 183 D2
  Milton Keynes MK11 . . . 32 C5
  Princes Risborough
   HP27 . . . . 139 B3
  Uxbridge UB8 . . . . 201 C5
  Winslow MK18 . . . . 65 F4
Market St
  [10] Aylesbury HP20 . . . . 115 D8
  Maidenhead SL6 . . . . . . 202 F7
  [9] Windsor SL4 . . . . . . 210 D6
Markham Cl HP19 . . . . . 115 A7
Marks Orch MK18 . . . . . . 52 D8
Marks Cl HP4 . . . . 75 F7
Marlborough Cl SL6 . . . 202 A6
Marlborough Ct SL1 . . . 204 E7
Marlborough Gate MK9 . 34 F3
Marlborough Ho [5]
  SL6 . . . . 202 F6
Marlborough Rd
  Aylesbury HP21 . . . . . . 115 E4
  Maidenhead SL6 . . . . . . 202 A6
  Slough SL3 . . . . 206 D2
Marlborough St
  Milton Keynes, Neath Hill
   MK14 . . . . 34 E6
  Milton Keynes, Tinkers Bridge
   MK6 . . . . 47 C4
Marlborough Trad Est
  HP11 . . . . 172 F7
Marley Gr MK8 . . . . 45 E7
Marlin Cl HP4 . . . . 134 F5
Marlin Copse HP4 . . . . 135 A3
Marlin Ct SL7 . . . . 183 D1
Marlin Hill HP23 . . . . . 133 A8
Marlins Cl WD3 . . . . . . 167 E7
Marlins End HP4 . . . . . 134 F3
MARLOW 183 B2
MARLOW BOTTOM 183 C6
Marlow Bottom SL7 . . . 183 D6
Marlow Bridge La SL7 . . 194 E8
Marlow CE Inf Sch SL7 183 D3
Marlow Comm SL7 . . . . 182 F3
MARLOW COMMON 182 F3
Marlow Cottage Hospl
  SL7 . . . . 183 E2
Marlow Dr MK16 . . . . . . 22 A4

Marlow Hill HP11 . . . . . . 173 A5
Marlow Ho [1] SL7 . . . 183 E1
Marlow Language Ctr The
  SL7 . . . . 183 D2
Marlow Lodge [13] SL6 . 202 F6
Marlow Mill SL7 . . . . . . 183 E1
Marlow Rd
  Bisham SL7 . . . . 194 E7
  Henley-on-Thames RG9 . . 191 E3
  High Wycombe HP11 . . . 172 E4
  Lane End HP14, SL7 . . . 171 E2
  Little Marlow SL7 . . . . . 184 C5
  Maidenhead, Furze Platt
   SL6 . . . . 194 E4
  Maidenhead SL6 . . . . . . 202 F7
  Stokenchurch HP14 . . . 170 B6
Marlow Sta SL7 . . . . . . 183 F2
Marquis Ct MK17 . . . . . . 60 F7
Marram Cl MK6 . . . . 47 A5
Marriotts Ave HP16 . . . 142 E1
Marriott's Cl HP17 . . . . 126 F6
Marriott's La HP17 . . . . 126 F6
Marriott's Way HP17 . . 126 F6
Marriott Terr WD3 . . . . 167 F5
Marrod's Bottom HP7 . . 175 C8
Marron Cl MK12 . . . . 33 C5
Marroway HP22 . . . . 116 D2
MARSH 129 C7
Marshall Court Ind Pk
  MK1 . . . . 47 B1
Marshalls La MK15 . . . . 35 C2
Marshalls Lea HP22 . . 102 C3
Marsham Cl HP21 . . . . 116 A4
Marsham La SL9 . . . . . . 188 E5
Marsham Lodge SL9 . . . 188 E5
Marsham Way SL9 . . . . 188 F5
Marshaw Pl [3] MK4 . . 46 C2
Marshcroft La HP23 . . . 119 D6
Marsh Ct HP11 . . . . 173 F4
Marsh Dr MK14 . . . . 21 E1
Marsh End Rd MK16 . . . 22 D3
Marshfield SL3 . . . . 211 C6
Marshgate Trad Est
  SL6 . . . . 204 A7
MARSH GIBBON 71 F3
Marsh Gibbon CE Sch
  OX27 . . . . 71 F3
Marsh Gibbon Rd HP18 . . 82 E8
Marsh Inf Sch HP11 . . . 173 F4
Marsh La
  Stoke Mandeville HP22 . . 129 F8
  Taplow SL6 . . . . 203 E6
Marshment HP22 . . . . . 117 D5
Marsh Rd
  Great Kimble HP22 . . . 129 D4
  Shabbington HP18 . . . . 124 D3
Marshworth MK6 . . . . . . 47 D6
Marston Cl HP5 . . . . . . 144 A4
Marston Ct HP23 . . . . . 103 A4
Marstonfields Rd MK18 . . 76 B2
Marston Hill
  Cranfield MK43 . . . . . . 25 F2
  Oving HP22 . . . . 86 C8
Marston Rd
  Granborough MK18 . . . . 75 F6
  Thame OX9 . . . . 126 A1
MARSWORTH 105 A1
Marsworth CE Inf Sch
  HP23 . . . . 105 A2
Marsworth Rd LU7 . . . . 105 D4
Marsworth Reservoir★
  HP23 . . . . 119 A8
Martell Cl MK7 . . . . 48 A3
Martin Cl
  Buckingham MK18 . . . . . 52 F7
  Milton Keynes MK14 . . . 34 E6
  Uxbridge UB10 . . . . 201 E3
  Windsor SL4 . . . . 209 D6
Martindale SL0 . . . . 200 D1
Martin Dell Cotts HP16 142 E4
Martingale Pl MK14 . . . 34 F5
Martin Rd
  Maidenhead SL6 . . . . . . 202 F8
  Slough SL1 . . . . 205 E3
Martins Dr The LU7 . . . . 80 F8
Martinsend La HP16 . . . 151 E7
Martin's Plain SL2 . . . . 198 F3
Martlet The MK6 . . . . . . 47 C4
Martyrs Ct HP7 . . . . . . 165 C8
Marunden Gn SL2 . . . . . 197 F2
Marwood Cl MK4 . . . . . . 46 D3
Mary Bassett Lower Sch
  The LU7 . . . . 80 F7
Mary Cross Cl HP23 . . 119 D1
Marygold Wlk HP6 . . . 166 C8
Maryland Rd MK15 . . . . 35 B8
Mary MacManus Dr
  MK18 . . . . 41 D1
Mary Morgan Ct SL2 . . 205 D8
Maryot Cl MK16 . . . . . . 13 F2
Maryside SL3 . . . . 206 E4
Marys Mead HP15 . . . . 163 A5
Mary Towerton Fst Sch
  HP14 . . . . 159 D3
Mascoll Path SL2 . . . . . 197 F2
Masefield Cl
  Chesham HP5 . . . . 144 B3
  Newport Pagnell MK16 . . 22 A4
Masefield Gr MK3 . . . . . 58 A7

Maslin Dr MK6 . . . . 47 B5
Mason MK4 . . . . 34 C8
Masons Cl HP16 . . . . . . 151 C5
Masons Ct HP5 . . . . 144 C1
Mason's Ct
  Aylesbury HP19 . . . . . . 115 B7
  Slough SL1 . . . . 204 E6
Masons Rd SL1 . . . . 204 E6
Masons Yd HP4 . . . . 135 D4
Massie Cl MK15 . . . . 35 B6
Mathecombe Rd [2]
  SL1 . . . . 205 A4
Mathiesen Rd MK13 . . . 34 A6
Mathisen Way SL3 . . . . 212 E6
Matilda Gdns MK5 . . . . . 46 B5
Matlock Rd HP20 . . . . . 101 F2
Matson Dr RG9 . . . . 191 F2
Matthau La MK4 . . . . . . 45 D3
Matthew Ct MK5 . . . . . . 46 B6
Matthews Cl [12] HP20 . . 101 F2
Maude Cl HP9 . . . . 176 A1
Maude Rd HP9 . . . . 176 A1
Maud Jane's Cl LU7 . . . 105 E5
Maudsley Cl MK5 . . . . . 46 C6
Maudsley Ho SL6 . . . . . 203 A7
Mauduit St MK19 . . . . . 11 A3
Maulden Gdns MK14 . . . 35 A8
Maurice Mount HP15 . . 162 F5
Mavoncliff Dr MK4 . . . . 57 A8
Maxham MK5 . . . . 46 A3
Maxwell Ct SL1 . . . . 197 C1
Maxwell Dr HP15 . . . . . 163 B5
Maxwell Pl HP9 . . . . . . 175 E3
Maxwell Rd
  Beaconsfield HP9 . . . . . 175 E3
  West Drayton UB7 . . . . 208 F2
Maybach Ct MK5 . . . . . . 46 B5
Maybrook Gdns HP13 . . 173 C8
Maybury Cl SL1 . . . . . . 204 D7
Maybush Gdns HP16 . . 151 C6
Maybush Wlk MK46 . . . . 6 C5
May Cl LU6 . . . . 92 E6
Mayditch Pl MK13 . . . . 34 C3
Mayer Gdns MK5 . . . . . . 46 C5
Mayfield Dr SL4 . . . . . . 210 A4
Mayfield Rd HP10 . . . . 185 E6
Mayflower Cl HP17 . . . 114 F5
Mayflower Way
  Beaconsfield HP9 . . . . . 186 A8
  Farnham Common SL2 . . 198 C8
Maygoods Cl UB8 . . . . . 208 D8
Maygoods Gn UB8 . . . . 208 D8
Maygoods La UB8 . . . . . 208 D8
Maygoods View UB8 . . 208 C8
Mayhall Farm HP6 . . . . 154 A4
Mayhall La HP4 . . . . 154 B4
Mayhew Cres HP13 . . . 173 D8
Maylands Dr UB8 . . . . . 201 D6
Maynard Cl MK13 . . . . . 34 A3
Maynard Ct SL4 . . . . . . 210 A6
Mayorfield Ho [1] SL7 183 D2
Maypole Rd SL6 . . . . . . 204 A8
Maypool Way [1] MK10 . . 36 B2
May Rd MK43 . . . . 34 C8
Mays Way NN12 . . . . . . 18 D3
May Tree Cl SL7 . . . . . . 183 C6
Mead Acre HP27 . . . . . 139 B5
Mead Ave SL3 . . . . 207 B4
Mead Cl
  Denham UB9 . . . . 190 A2
  Slough SL1 . . . . 205 B3
Meades La HP5 . . . . . . 154 B7
Meadfield Ave SL3 . . . . 207 A3
Meadfield Rd SL3 . . . . . 207 B3
Meadfurlong Sch MK6 . . 34 F1
Mead Haze SL6 . . . . 196 C2
Mead Ho SL0 . . . . 200 D2
MEADLE 139 B8
Meadow
  Steeple Claydon MK18 . . 63 D3
  Stone HP17 . . . . 114 F5
Meadow Bank [6] SL8 . . 185 B3
Meadowbank Cl
  Bovingdon HP3 . . . . 146 B3
  Long Crendon HP18 . . . 125 C7
Meadow Bank Cl HP7 . . 154 E1
Meadowbrook HP13 . . . 119 B6
Meadowbrook Cl SL3 . . 212 F6
Meadow Cl
  Aylesbury HP20 . . . . . . 102 A1
  Chesham HP5 . . . . 144 A4
  Cublington LU7 . . . . 78 C1
  High Wycombe HP11 . . . 173 F4
  Marlow SL7 . . . . 183 F1
  Oakley HP18 . . . . 109 D4
  Old Windsor SL4 . . . . . 211 B2
  Tring HP23 . . . . 119 A4
Meadowcourt La HP7 . . 164 F3
Meadow Cotts
  Beaconsfield HP9 . . . . . 175 E1
  Little Kingshill HP16 . . 152 B3
  Stone HP17 . . . . 114 D3
Meadowcroft
  Aylesbury HP19 . . . . . . 101 B3
  Berkhamsted HP4 . . . . 134 D7
  Chalfont St Peter SL9 . . 177 D1

Meadow Ct MK46 . . . . . . 5 D2
Meadow Dr
  Amersham HP6 . . . . 154 E2
  Longwick HP27 . . . . . . 138 D6
Meadow Farm Rd MK43 . . 16 F1
Meadow Gate
  Padbury MK18 . . . . 53 B2
  Prestwood HP16 . . . . . 151 C3
Meadow Gdns MK18 . . . . 52 E6
Meadow High Sch UB8 208 E8
Meadow La
  Beaconsfield HP9 . . . . . 175 F2
  Eton SL4 . . . . 210 C7
  Long Crendon HP18 . . . 125 E4
  Milton Keynes MK10 . . . 36 A3
  Pitstone LU7 . . . . 105 E3
  South Heath HP16 . . . 152 E8
Meadowlea Cl UB7 . . . . 213 D8
Meadow Pk HP22 . . . . . 116 C2
Meadow Rd
  Berkhamsted HP4 . . . . 135 B6
  Chinnor OX39 . . . . 147 D6
  Henley-on-Thames RG9 . . 191 E1
  Slough SL3 . . . . 206 E3
Meadow Rise HP27 . . . 149 E5
Meadow Row MK18 . . . 41 D1
Meadow Sh Ctr [4] MK18 41 D1
Meadows Sch The
  HP10 . . . . 185 E7
Meadows The
  [1] Amersham HP7 . . . 154 E1
  Flackwell Heath HP10 . . 185 B8
  Old Stratford MK19 . . . 32 B6
  Whitchurch HP22 . . . . . 86 F7
Meadowsweet MK7 . . . . 48 B5
Meadowview TW19 . . . . 212 F2
Meadow View
  Aspley Guise MK17 . . . . 49 D6
  Chalfont St Giles HP8 . . 177 A7
  Long Crendon HP18 . . . 125 E4
  Marlow Bottom SL7 . . . 183 E6
  Pottersbury NN12 . . . . . 18 D3
  Stanwell TW19 . . . . 213 A2
  Uxbridge UB8 . . . . 208 C8
Meadow Wlk
  Bourne End SL8 . . . . . . 185 A5
  Buckingham MK18 . . . . . 41 D1
  Tylers Green HP10 . . . . 163 C1
Mead Pk HP15 . . . . 163 C7
Mead Platt HP14 . . . . . 158 D5
Mead Rd UB8 . . . . 201 D5
Meads Cl MK13 . . . . 34 B8
Mead St HP13 . . . . 174 A4
Meads The
  Berkhamsted HP4 . . . . 134 F6
  Eaton Bray LU6 . . . . . . 92 E5
  Stoke Poges SL2 . . . . . 199 A2
  Tring HP23 . . . . 119 B4
  Uxbridge UB8 . . . . 201 E1
  [4] Windsor SL4 . . . . . 210 A5
Mead Way
  Beaconsfield HP9 . . . . . 175 E2
  Soulbury LU7 . . . . 69 E3
Meadway
  Berkhamsted HP4 . . . . 135 E5
  Buckingham MK18 . . . . . 52 D6
  Dunstable LU6 . . . . 93 F7
  Oving HP22 . . . . 76 E1
Mead Way
  High Wycombe HP11 . . . 173 F4
  Slough SL1 . . . . 204 D8
Meadway Ct LU6 . . . . . . 93 F7
Meadway Pk SL9 . . . . . 188 D3
Meadway The MK5 . . . . . 46 A7
Mead Wlk SL3 . . . . 207 B4
Meare Estate HP10 . . . 188 E8
Meavy Cl HP13 . . . . 174 B3
Medale Rd MK6 . . . . 47 B5
Medallion St MK6 . . . . 203 B7
MEDBOURNE 45 E5
Medbourne Rdbt MK8 . . 45 E6
Medeswell MK4 . . . . 46 E3
Medhurst MK8 . . . . 33 E2
Medland MK6 . . . . 47 D7
Medley Cl LU6 . . . . 92 F5
Medman Cl UB8 . . . . 201 D5
MEDMENHAM 193 A5
Medway Cl MK16 . . . . . . 22 E3
Medway Ct MK43 . . . . . . 37 D8
Meeting Oak La MK18 . . 66 B5
Megdale Pl HP20 . . . . . 101 D2
Melbourne Ave SL1 . . . 205 C7
Melbourne Pl HP13 . . . 115 E5
Melbourne Rd HP13 . . . 174 A7
Melbourne Terr MK13 . . 34 A7
Melford Gn HP19 . . . . . 101 C3
Melfort Dr
  Leighton Buzzard LU7 . . 80 B6
  Milton Keynes MK2 . . . . 58 D4
Melick Rd MK6 . . . . 47 B4

Melissa Ct HP13 . . . . . . 173 D6
Mellish Ct MK3 . . . . 47 A2
Mellstock Rd HP21 . . . 115 F5
Melrose Ave MK3 . . . . . 47 A3
Melrose Ct HP13 . . . . . 162 B1
Melrose Wlk HP21 . . . . 115 F5
Melton MK14 . . . . 34 C8
Melton Ct
  Dunstable LU6 . . . . 93 F7
  Maidenhead SL6 . . . . . 202 F6
Mendelssohn Gr MK7 . . 48 C4
Mendip Cl SL3 . . . . 207 A1
Mendip Way HP13 . . . . 172 F8
Mendy St HP11 . . . . . . 173 A7
Menmarsh Rd HP18 . . 123 E6
Menteith Cl MK2 . . . . . . 58 C5
MENTMORE 90 D4
Mentmore Cl HP12 . . . 172 B6
Mentmore Cross Rds
  LU7 . . . . 89 F6
Mentmore Ct
  Mentmore LU7 . . . . 90 D5
  [2] Milton Keynes MK5 . . 45 F8
Mentmore Gdns LU7 . . . 80 E5
Mentmore Gn HP21 . . . 115 E3
Mentmore Rd
  Cheddington LU7 . . . . . 104 F8
  High Wycombe HP12 . . . 172 B6
  Leighton Buzzard LU7 . . 80 E5
Mentmore Towers★
  LU7 . . . . 90 C4
Mentmore View HP23 . . 118 F5
Mentone Ave MK17 . . . . 49 D4
Menzies Ct MK5 . . . . . . 46 B4
Mercers Dr MK13 . . . . . 34 B6
Mercers Mdw HP22 . . 131 B6
Mercer Wlk UB8 . . . . . 201 C5
Merchant La
  Cranfield MK43 . . . . 25 A1
  Cranfield, Wharley End
   MK43 . . . . 24 F2
Merchant Pl MK10 . . . . 35 E3
Mercian Way SL1 . . . . 204 D5
Mercia Rd SL6 . . . . 202 C4
Mercury Gr MK8 . . . . . . 45 E7
Mercury Pk The HP10 185 E7
Merebrook Sch MK4 . . 46 C3
Mere Cl SL7 . . . . 183 F2
Meredith Dr HP19 . . . . 100 F2
Mere La MK18 . . . . 50 E6
Mere Pk SL7 . . . . 183 F2
Mere Rd
  Finmere MK18 . . . . 50 D6
  Slough SL3 . . . . 205 F3
Meriland Ct MK4 . . . . . . 58 E4
Merlebank HP5 . . . . 154 C7
Merlewood Cl HP11 . . . 173 A4
Merlewood Dr MK5 . . . 45 F4
Merlin Cl SL3 . . . . 212 B8
Merlin Ctr SL6 . . . . 202 B8
Merlin Ctr HP19 . . . . . . 101 C1
Merlin Ctr The HP12 . . 172 E5
Merling Croft HP4 . . . . 134 E7
Merlin Wlk MK6 . . . . . . 47 B8
Merman Rise MK4 . . . . 45 D2
Merrivale Mews MK7 . . 208 D5
Merrydown HP13 . . . . . 161 D1
Merryfields UB8 . . . . . 201 D3
Mersey Cl MK3 . . . . 46 E1
Mersey Way MK3 . . . . . 46 E1
Merthen Gr MK4 . . . . . . 57 B8
Merton Cl SL6 . . . . 202 C3
Merton Ct SL1 . . . . 206 A3
Merton Dr MK6 . . . . 47 A4
Merton Rd
  Princes Risborough
   HP27 . . . . 139 B2
  Slough SL1 . . . . 206 A3
Merwin Way SL4 . . . . . 209 D4
Meryton Ho SL4 . . . . . . 210 A4
Messenger Cl HP21 . . . 116 A6
Metcalfe Gr MK14 . . . . . 22 B2
Mews Cotts HP15 . . . . . 162 D7
Mews Gamnel HP23 . . . 119 B6
Mews The HP6 . . . . 154 D3
Michael Cl SL6 . . . . 202 C5
Michaelis Rd OX9 . . . . 125 C1
Michaels Mews [6]
  HP19 . . . . 115 A8
Michigan Dr
  Milton Keynes MK15 . . . 35 C8
  Newport Pagnell MK15 . . 22 C1
Nicholls Ave SL9 . . . . . 177 E5
MICKLEFIELD 173 E6
Micklefield Rd HP13 . . 174 A7
Mickleton MK15 . . . . . . 35 A4
Midas Ind Est UB8 . . . 201 B3
Midbrook Cl MK14 . . . . 22 A2
Midcot Way HP4 . . . . . 134 F6
Midcroft SL2 . . . . 198 B1
Mid Cross La SL9 . . . . . 177 E5
Middlebrook Rd HP13 . . 161 E4
Middle Cl HP6 . . . . 154 F2
Middle Cres UB9 . . . . . 189 D4
Middle Dr HP9 . . . . 175 D5
MIDDLE END
  Leckhampstead 42 D8
  Totternhoe 93 A8

Middle Field HP22 ... 116 F3
Middlefield Cl MK18 ... 41 F1
Middle Gn SL3 ... 206 E6
MIDDLE GREEN ... 206 E5
Middlegreen Rd SL3 ... 206 D5
Middlegreen Trad Est
SL3 ... 206 D4
Middle La HP3 ... 146 A1
Middle Mdw HP8 ... 177 C7
Middle Rd
Aylesbury HP21 ... 116 B7
Berkhamsted HP4 ... 135 B4
Denham UB9 ... 189 D4
Middlesex Dr MK3 ... 46 F1
Middle Slade MK18 ... 52 D6
MIDDLETON ... 35 E3
Middleton MK14 ... 34 E7
Middleton Prim Sch
MK10 ... 35 E3
Middleton Swimming Pool
MK16 ... 22 E3
Middle Way OX39 ... 147 B6
Middleway The HP12 ... 172 C6
MIDDLE WEALD ... 32 E1
Middle Weald MK19 ... 32 E2
Middle Wlk SL1 ... 197 C2
Midhurst Cl HP21 ... 116 B5
Midland Dr MK10 ... 36 C3
Midland Rd MK46 ... 7 A5
Midshires Bsns Pk
HP19 ... 101 A1
Midsumer Ct HP15 ... 163 A3
Midsummer Arc MK9 ... 34 E3
Midsummer Bvd MK9 ... 34 E2
Midsummer Dr HP18 ... 82 F6
Midsummer Pl (Sh Ctr)
MK9 ... 34 E2
Midsummer Rdbt MK9 ... 34 C1
Miersfield HP11 ... 172 D3
Mikern Cl MK2 ... 58 C8
Milburn Ave MK6 ... 46 E8
Milburn Dr UB7 ... 208 E6
Mildenhall Rd SL1 ... 205 E7
Milebush LU7 ... 80 C8
Milecastle MK13 ... 34 A5
Mile Elm SL7 ... 184 A3
Miles Cl
Aylesbury HP21 ... 116 A7
Milton Keynes MK14 ... 22 A3
Miles Ct HP22 ... 102 B3
Miles End HP21 ... 115 B6
Milesmere MK8 ... 33 D1
Milestone Cl HP14 ... 158 E5
Milfoil Ave MK14 ... 34 E4
Milford Ave MK11 ... 32 E4
Milford Ct 4 SL1 ... 206 A4
Milk Hall Barns HP5 ... 154 F5
Milland Way MK4 ... 45 D3
Millards Cl MK43 ... 25 C2
Millards Pl MK43 ... 25 C2
Mill Ave UB8 ... 201 C3
Millbank
Leighton Buzzard LU7 ... 80 F8
Marlow SL7 ... 183 F1
Millbank Pl MK7 ... 48 B8
Millboard Rd SL8 ... 185 B3
Mill Bridge Pl UB8 ... 201 C3
Millbrook Cl HP12 ... 172 D8
Millbrook Comb Sch
HP12 ... 172 D8
Millbrook Way SL3 ... 212 E5
Mill Cl
Buckingham MK18 ... 65 F5
Chesham HP5 ... 154 E5
West Drayton UB7 ... 208 D3
Wingrave HP22 ... 89 A3
Mill Cnr HP18 ... 83 A8
Mill Cotts HP10 ... 185 D4
Mill Ct
Horton SL3 ... 212 C3
Milton Keynes MK12 ... 33 A5
Waddesdon HP18 ... 99 A7
West Drayton UB7 ... 208 D3
Milldun Way HP12 ... 172 D6
MILL END
Henley-on-Thames ... 192 D7
Little Missenden ... 153 A3
Rickmansworth ... 167 F1
Mill End Cl
Edlesborough LU6 ... 92 F4
Prestwood HP16 ... 151 B5
Mill End Rd HP12 ... 172 C8
Millennium Cl UB8 ... 201 C3
Millennium Point HP19 101 A1
Miller Pl SL9 ... 188 D6
Millers Cl HP18 ... 82 F6
Miller's La SL4 ... 211 A1
Millers Turn OX39 ... 147 B6
Millers Way
Aylesbury HP19 ... 115 A8
Milton Keynes MK12 ... 33 D5
Millfield HP4 ... 135 D5
Millfield Ave OX27 ... 71 F3
Millfield Cl
Cranfield MK43 ... 25 B2
Marsh Gibbon OX27 ... 71 F3
Millfields HP5 ... 154 C6
Millfield Wood Wildlife
Reserve★ HP14 ... 162 B3
Mill Gdns HP23 ... 119 B4
Mill Gn MK43 ... 8 D5
Millhayes MK14 ... 34 F8
Mill Ho
Buckingham MK18 ... 52 C8
West Drayton UB7 ... 208 D5
Millholm Rise MK6 ... 47 E5
Milliners The 1 HP20 ... 101 E1
Millington Gate MK15 ... 35 D7
Mill La
Amersham HP7 ... 165 A8
Aspley Guise MK17 ... 49 C5
Beaconsfield HP9 ... 175 E1
Brackley NN13 ... 38 A6
Buckingham MK18 ... 52 C8
Chalfont St Giles HP8 ... 166 B1
Chinnor OX39 ... 147 B7
Cookham SL6 ... 196 C7
Gerrards Cross SL9 ... 188 F5
Great Brickhill MK17 ... 58 F2
Horton-cum-S OX33 ... 108 A6
Horton SL3 ... 212 C4
Hulcote MK17 ... 37 E1
Hurley SL6 ... 193 F4
Milton Keynes, Bradville
MK13 ... 34 A7
Milton Keynes, Stony Stratford
MK11 ... 32 C5
Milton Keynes, Woolstone
MK15 ... 35 C3
Monks Risborough HP27 139 B6
Salford MK17 ... 37 C3
South Heath HP16 ... 152 C7
Stokenchurch HP14 ... 158 C5
Taplow SL6 ... 203 C8
Thame OX9 ... 126 B3
Turvey MK43 ... 8 D5
Twyford MK18 ... 62 C1
Upper Arncott OX25 ... 94 E7
Westbury NN13 ... 39 A4
Weston Turville HP22 ... 117 A2
Windsor SL4 ... 210 A7
Wingrave HP22 ... 89 C2
Mill Lane Prim Sch
OX39 ... 147 B7
Mill Mdw HP19 ... 115 B8
Mill Mead HP22 ... 131 B5
Mill Pl SL3 ... 211 D5
Mill Rd
Cranfield MK43 ... 25 C2
2 Leighton Buzzard LU7 ... 80 F8
Marlow SL7 ... 183 E1
Milton Keynes MK2 ... 58 E7
Milton Keynes MK19 ... 21 B4
Oakley HP18 ... 109 D4
Slapton LU7 ... 91 D7
Stokenchurch HP14 ... 158 C5
Thame OX9 ... 124 E1
West Drayton UB7 ... 208 D3
Whitfield NN13 ... 26 E3
Millshot Dr HP7 ... 165 D7
Millside SL8 ... 185 C3
Mill Sq MK12 ... 33 A5
Mill St
Aylesbury HP20 ... 101 E1
Berkhamsted HP4 ... 135 C4
Colnbrook SL3 ... 212 D7
High Wycombe HP11 ... 172 F7
Newport Pagnell MK16 ... 22 D5
Oxford OX33 ... 108 B1
Slough SL2 ... 205 F5
Millstream HP22 ... 116 F2
Mill Stream Cl HP27 ... 139 A2
Millstream La SL1 ... 204 E5
Millstream Way
Leighton Buzzard LU7 ... 80 F7
Wooburn Green HP10 ... 185 E8
Mill Terr MK12 ... 33 A6
Mill The
Milton Keynes MK12 ... 32 E7
Tring HP23 ... 104 C1
Wooburn Green HP10 ... 185 E8
Mill Tower LU6 ... 92 E6
Mill View Rd HP23 ... 118 F4
Mill Way
Aspley Guise MK17 ... 49 D5
Aylesbury HP20 ... 115 C8
Rickmansworth WD3 ... 167 F1
Mill West SL2 ... 205 F5
Milner Rd SL1 ... 204 A8
Milton Ave SL9 ... 188 D8
Milton Cl
Henley-on-Thames
RG9 ... 191 D2
Horton SL3 ... 212 A4
MILTON COMMON ... 136 B3
Milton Dr MK16 ... 22 E4
Milton Fields HP8 ... 177 B7
Milton Gdns HP27 ... 139 A2
Milton Gr MK3 ... 57 F7
MILTON KEYNES ... 34 D5
Milton Keynes Acad The
MK6 ... 47 A7
Milton Keynes Central Sta
MK9 ... 34 C1
Milton Keynes Coll MK6 ... 46 F7
Milton Keynes Coll
(Bletchley Ctr) MK3 ... 58 B8
Milton Keynes Hospl
MK6 ... 47 B7
Milton Keynes Materials
Recycling Factory★
MK12 ... 33 C8
Milton Keynes Mus★
MK12 ... 33 D5
Milton Keynes Prep Sch
MK3 ... 57 D8
Milton Keynes Theatre★
MK9 ... 34 F3
MILTON KEYNES
VILLAGE ... 35 E2
Milton Lawns HP6 ... 154 D3
Milton Rd
Aston Clinton HP22 ... 117 F5
Aylesbury HP21 ... 115 F6
Chesham HP5 ... 144 B2
Milton Keynes, Broughton
MK10 ... 36 B3
Milton Keynes, Willen
MK15 ... 35 D7
Slough SL2 ... 198 D1
Walton MK7 ... 47 F6
Milton's Cottage (Mus)★
HP8 ... 177 B7
Milton Way UB7 ... 208 F2
Milverton Cl SL6 ... 202 B3
Milward Dr MK2 ... 47 E1
Mimosa Ct HP21 ... 115 B6
Mina Ave SL3 ... 206 D4
Minall Cl HP23 ... 119 A4
Mineral La HP5 ... 154 C7
Minerva Cl TW19 ... 213 A2
Minerva Gdns MK7 ... 48 C7
Minerva Way HP9 ... 176 A1
Mines Cl HP13 ... 161 D3
Ministry Wharf HP14 ... 149 C1
Minniecroft Rd SL1 ... 197 B2
Minorca Gr MK5 ... 46 A4
Minshull Cl MK18 ... 41 D1
Minster Way SL3 ... 206 F4
Minstrel Ct MK13 ... 34 B7
Minton Cl MK14 ... 22 A1
Minton Rise SL6 ... 204 B7
Mirador Cres SL2 ... 206 B6
Mirrie La UB9 ... 189 C6
Misbourne Ave
Chalfont St Peter SL9 ... 177 E5
High Wycombe HP13 ... 173 F6
Misbourne Cl
Aylesbury HP21 ... 115 D3
Chalfont St Peter SL9 ... 177 E5
Misbourne Ct SL3 ... 207 A2
Misbourne Dr HP16 ... 152 B6
Misbourne Ho HP8 ... 166 C1
Misbourne Mdws UB9 ... 189 D3
Misbourne Sch The
HP16 ... 152 B6
Misbourne Vale SL9 ... 177 D5
Miserden Cres MK4 ... 45 F1
Missenden Abbey Adult Ed
Coll HP16 ... 152 B6
Missenden Cl MK18 ... 65 F4
Missenden Gdns SL1 ... 204 B7
Missenden Rd
Chesham HP5 ... 154 A7
Ellesborough HP17 ... 130 C2
Great Kingshill HP15 ... 151 D2
Winslow MK18 ... 65 F4
Miss Joans Ride HP4 ... 107 D7
Miswell La HP23 ... 118 F3
Mitcham Pl MK13 ... 34 D3
Mitcham Wlk HP19 ... 101 A2
Mitchell Cl
Bovingdon HP3 ... 145 F4
Slough SL1 ... 205 A4
Mitchell Rd MK43 ... 24 E2
Mitchell Wlk HP6 ... 154 E1
Mithras Gdns MK7 ... 48 C6
Mitre Ct MK18 ... 52 C7
Mitre St MK18 ... 52 C7
MIXBURY ... 38 D1
Moat Cl
Prestwood HP16 ... 151 C6
Wendover HP22 ... 131 B6
Moat Dr
Prestwood HP16 ... 151 C7
Slough SL2 ... 206 C8
Moat End HP22 ... 102 B4
Moat House The MK18 ... 52 D8
Moat La
Aston Abbotts HP22 ... 88 D4
Marsh Gibbon OX27 ... 71 F2
Prestwood HP16 ... 151 C7
Wingrave HP22 ... 89 B2
Moat Pl UB9 ... 201 B8
MOBWELL ... 152 A8
Mobwell Terr 3 HP16 ... 152 A8
Model Row HP22 ... 117 F6
Moeran Cl MK7 ... 48 C5
Moffy Hill SL6 ... 195 E2
Mole Run HP13 ... 161 C1
Molyneaux Ave HP3 ... 145 F4
Molyns Ho RG9 ... 191 E3
Molyns Mews SL1 ... 204 E5
Monellan Cres MK7 ... 48 A3
Monellan Gr MK7 ... 48 A2
Monet Pl HP19 ... 100 E2
Money La UB7 ... 208 D3
Monkey Island La SL6 ... 203 E2
Monksfield Way SL2 ... 198 A2
Monks Hollow SL7 ... 183 E5
Monks Path 9 HP19 ... 115 A8
Monks Rd SL4 ... 209 D5
MONKS RISBOROUGH ... 139 C6
Monks Risborough CE
Comb Sch HP27 ... 139 D5
Monks Risborough Sta
HP27 ... 139 B6
MONKSTON ... 36 A1
Monkston Comb Sch
MK10 ... 36 B1
MONKSTON PARK ... 35 E1
Monkston Rdbt MK10 ... 36 B2
Monks Way
Harmondsworth UB7 ... 213 E8
Milton Keynes MK12, MK13,
MK14, MK15 ... 34 C6
Monkswood Ct 11 SL7 ... 183 E2
Monkton La SL7 ... 172 F1
Monkton Way HP27 ... 150 C5
Monmouth Cl HP19 ... 101 A2
Monmouth Gr MK4 ... 45 E1
Monro Ave MK8 ... 45 E7
Montabaur Rd NN13 ... 38 A7
Montagu Dr MK6 ... 47 B8
Montague Cl SL2 ... 198 B3
Montague Rd
Aylesbury HP21 ... 115 D7
Berkhamsted HP4 ... 135 B4
Slough SL1 ... 205 F6
Uxbridge UB8 ... 201 D5
Montagu Rd SL3 ... 211 B6
Montem La SL1 ... 205 D4
Montem L Ctr SL1 ... 205 D4
Montem Prim Sch SL1 ... 205 B4
Montford Mews HP15 ... 162 E2
Montgomerie Cl HP4 ... 135 A6
Montgomery Cres MK15 ... 35 B7
Montgomery Pl SL2 ... 206 C7
Montpellier Ct SL4 ... 210 C5
Montrose Ave
Datchet SL3 ... 211 C7
Slough SL1 ... 205 B7
Montrose Dr SL6 ... 202 A6
Montrose Way SL3 ... 211 C7
Monument La SL9 ... 177 E5
Monycrower Dr SL6 ... 202 E7
Moon St MK12 ... 33 D6
Moonstone Ct 5 HP12 ... 172 D8
Moorbridge Rd SL6 ... 203 A7
MOOR COMMON ... 171 A2
Moorcroft Sch 3 UB8 ... 208 F7
Moore Cl SL1 ... 205 B4
MOOR END
Eaton Bray ... 92 E5
Yardley Gobion ... 18 D6
Moor End
Eaton Bray LU6 ... 92 F5
Frieth RG9 ... 171 A1
Maidenhead SL6 ... 203 C1
Moor End Cl LU6 ... 92 F4
Moorend La OX9 ... 125 F1
Moor End La LU6 ... 92 F5
Moorend Rd NN12 ... 18 E6
Moore Rd HP4 ... 134 F6
Moores Hill MK46 ... 6 F5
Moores La SL4 ... 204 F2
Moorfield MK17 ... 57 D3
Moorfield Rd
Denham Green UB9 ... 190 A5
Uxbridge UB8 ... 208 D7
Moorfield Terr SL6 ... 203 A8
Moorfoot MK11 ... 33 A4
Moor Furlong SL1 ... 204 E5
Moorgate MK6 ... 46 F7
Moorhall Rd UB9 ... 190 B6
Moorhen Ct 2 HP20 ... 101 E3
Moorhen Way MK18 ... 52 E8
Moorhills Cres LU7 ... 79 F3
Moorhills Rd LU7 ... 79 F3
Moorings The
Buckingham MK18 ... 52 C8
Windsor SL4 ... 210 A7
Moor La
Harmondsworth UB7 ... 213 C8
High Wycombe HP13 ... 161 D3
Maidenhead SL6 ... 195 F1
Sarratt WD3 ... 156 E3
Moorland Inf Sch MK6 ... 47 B5
Moorland Rd UB7 ... 213 C8
Moorlands LU7 ... 79 E3
Moorlands Rd LU7 ... 79 F3
Moor Pk
Milton Keynes MK3 ... 57 D8
Wendover HP22 ... 131 B7
Moor Rd HP5 ... 154 C6
Moors Cl MK19 ... 31 E5
Moor's Farm Cotts HP5 145 B4
Moorside HP10 ... 185 E8
Moorside Cl SL6 ... 195 F1
Moorstown Ct 7 SL1 ... 205 E4
Moor The SL7 ... 184 C4
MOP END ... 164 B7
Mop End La HP7 ... 164 B7
Morar Cl LU7 ... 80 C7
Moray Dr SL2 ... 206 A7
Moray Pl MK3 ... 46 F2
Mordaunt Cl MK43 ... 8 E6
Mordaunts Ct MK15 ... 35 C2
Moreau Wlk SL3 ... 206 E7
More Ave HP21 ... 115 D7
Morebath Gr MK4 ... 46 C4
Morefields HP23 ... 119 A6
Moreland Ave SL3 ... 212 C7
Moreland Cl SL3 ... 212 C7
Moreland Dr SL9 ... 188 F4
Morello Dr SL3 ... 206 F5
Moreton Dr MK18 ... 41 E2
Moreton La HP17 ... 115 A1
Moreton Rd MK18 ... 41 D2
Moreton Way SL1 ... 204 D5
Morland Dr MK8 ... 45 D6
Morley Cl SL3 ... 206 F4
Morley Cres MK7 ... 48 D4
Morrell Cl MK5 ... 46 B5
Morrice Cl SL3 ... 207 A2
Morris Cl SL9 ... 177 F2
Morris Ct
Aylesbury HP21 ... 115 D4
Windsor SL4 ... 209 E6
Morrison Ct MK8 ... 45 E6
Morris Wlk MK16 ... 22 A4
Mortain Cl MK7 ... 48 B3
Mortain Dr HP4 ... 134 F6
Morten Gdns UB9 ... 190 A4
Mortens Wood HP7 ... 165 E7
Mortimer Hill HP23 ... 119 B4
Mortimer Rd SL3 ... 206 D3
Mortimer Rise HP23 ... 119 B4
Morton Cl
North Marston MK18 ... 76 B2
Pitstone LU7 ... 105 C4
Uxbridge UB8 ... 201 F1
Morton Dr SL1 ... 197 E8
Morton King Cl HP18 ... 124 D3
Mortons Fork MK13 ... 33 F6
Moseley Rd HP14 ... 161 C7
Moses Plat La HP27 ... 150 B5
Moss Ct HP9 ... 176 D4
Mossdale MK13 ... 34 B5
Mossmans Cl MK2 ... 58 D7
Mossway HP9 ... 175 C5
Mossy Vale SL6 ... 195 D1
MOULSOE ... 36 D8
Moundsfield Way SL1 ... 204 E4
Mountain Ash SL7 ... 183 D6
Mount Ave MK1 ... 47 E3
Mountbatten Cl 7 SL1 ... 206 A3
Mountbatten Sq 8
SL4 ... 210 C6
Mount Cl
Aston Clinton HP22 ... 117 F4
Farnham Common SL2 ... 198 C8
High Wycombe HP12 ... 172 E6
Mount Farm Ind Est
MK1 ... 47 D4
Mount Farm Rdbt MK1 ... 47 D4
Mounthill Ave MK19 ... 32 B7
Mount Hill La SL9 ... 188 B2
Mount La UB9 ... 189 D2
Mount Nugent HP5 ... 144 A4
MOUNT PLEASANT
Buckingham ... 52 D7
Stoke Goldington ... 12 B7
Mount Pleasant
Aspley Guise MK17 ... 49 F4
Aylesbury HP19 ... 101 D1
Lane End HP14 ... 171 B5
Milton Keynes MK6 ... 47 E4
Soulbury LU7 ... 69 E3
Steeple Claydon MK18 ... 63 F2
Stoke Goldington MK16 ... 12 B7
Stoke Hammond MK17 ... 69 E7
Whitchurch HP22 ... 86 F7
Yardley Gobion NN12 ... 18 F6
Mount Pleasant Cl
MK18 ... 52 C7
Mount Pleasant Cotts 2
SL8 ... 185 B3
Mountsfield Cl
Newport Pagnell MK16 ... 22 C3
Stanwell TW19 ... 213 A2
Mount St HP20 ... 115 D8
Mount The
Aspley Guise MK17 ... 49 D4
Milton Keynes MK6 ... 47 E4
Mount View RG9 ... 191 D2
Mount View Ct 4 RG9 ... 191 D2
Mount Way HP27 ... 139 A3
Mowbray Dr LU7 ... 80 D7
Mowbray Rd HP20 ... 101 D2
Mowhills MK43 ... 3 F6
Mow Mead MK46 ... 6 F5
Moyleen Rise SL7 ... 183 C1
Mozart Cl MK7 ... 48 C4
Muddiford La MK4 ... 46 D4
Muirfield Dr MK3 ... 46 D1
Mulberry Ave SL4 ... 210 F5
Mulberry Cl
Amersham HP7 ... 165 F8
High Wycombe HP12 ... 172 C5
Tring HP23 ... 119 A5

Mulberry Ct HP15......163 D7
Mulberry Dr SL3......206 E1
Mulberry Wlk SL6......202 C8
Mullen Ave MK14......34 F4
Mullins Way HP19......100 E2
Mullion Pl MK6......35 A1
Mumfords La SL9......188 A7
Munces Rd SL7......183 D6
MUNDAYDEAN
BOTTOM......182 E5
Mundaydean La SL7...183 B4
Munday's Farm HP21...116 B7
Mundesley Spur SL1...205 E7
MURCOTT......94 A4
Murcott Rd OX6......94 D6
Murray Rd HP4......135 C6
Murrey Cl MK5......46 C5
Murrin Rd SL6......202 C8
MURSLEY......67 D6
Mursley CE Sch MK17...67 D6
Mursley CMK11......32 F5
Mursley Rd
  Little Horwood MK17...55 E2
  Swanbourne MK17......67 B3
Museum St ☉ HP23...119 A3
Musgrave Rd OX39...147 D7
Musgrave Wlk HP14...158 F5
Musgrove Pl MK5......45 F6
Mus of Eton Life The★
  SL4......210 D8
Myddleton Rd UB8...201 C4
Mylne Cl HP13......172 F8
Mynchen Cl HP9......175 D6
Mynchen End HP9...175 D6
Mynchen Rd HP9......175 D6
MYRKE......205 F2
Myrke The SL3......205 F2
Myrtle Bank MK12......33 E5
Myrtle Cl
  Poyle SL3......212 E6
  Uxbridge UB8......208 F8
  West Drayton UB7......208 F3
Myrtle Cres SL2......205 F6

N

Nag's Head La HP16...152 A4
Nailzee Cl SL9......188 E4
Nairdwood Cl HP16...151 E4
Nairdwood La HP16...151 D5
Nairdwood Way HP16..151 E4
Nairn Ct MK3......46 E2
Naisby Dr MK17......59 C1
Nalders Rd HP5......144 D2
Nan Aires HP22......89 A3
Nancy Hall Ct HP12...172 D3
Nans Gdn MK17......57 C4
NAPHILL......161 D7
Naphill Pl MK13......33 F6
Naphill & Walters Ash Sch
  HP14......150 B1
Napier Cl UB7......208 F3
Napier Rd
  Aylesbury HP19......114 F8
  Harmondsworth TW6...213 D6
  Maidenhead SL6......202 B6
Napier St MK2......58 D8
Nappin Cl HP19......101 A3
Nappins Cl HP18......125 D5
Nap The HP18......109 E5
Narbeth Dr HP20......116 B8
Narcot La HP8......177 B5
Narcot Rd HP8......177 A7
Narcot Way HP8......177 B6
Narrow La HP13......161 E3
Narrow Path MK17......49 B3
Naseby Cl
  Newport Pagnell MK16...22 A3
  Thame OX9......126 B1
Naseby Ct
  Buckingham MK18......41 E2
  Milton Keynes MK13...34 B6
NASH......44 C1
Nash Cl
  Aylesbury HP21......116 A4
  Berkhamsted HP4...135 A5
Nash Croft MK4......52 F7
Nashdom SL1......196 F5
Nashdom La SL1......197 B6
NASH LEE......130 C5
Nash Lee End HP22......130 F6
Nash Lee La HP22......130 E6
Nash Lee Rd
  Nash Lee HP17......130 D6
  World's End HP22......130 F7
Nashleigh Hill HP5...144 D3
Nashleigh Ho HP5......144 E3
Nash Pl HP10......163 B1
Nash Rd
  Great Horwood MK17...55 A4
  Slough SL3......207 A2
  Thornborough MK18......54 B8
  Whaddon MK17......45 A1
Nashs Farm HP22......88 D4
Nathanial Cl MK5......46 B5

Nathaniel Wlk HP23...119 A5
National Badminton Ctr
  MK8......34 A1
National Bowl The★
  MK6......46 E5
National Film & Television
  Sch HP9......175 C1
National Waterways Mus★
  NN12......9 A8
Natural History Mus at
  Tring★ HP23......119 A3
Natwoke Ct HP9......175 D5
Neal Cl SL9......189 B3
Neale Cl HP12......172 D3
Neapland MK6......47 B5
NEARTON END......67 A3
Nearton End MK17......67 A3
Near Town MK46......7 A3
Near Town Gdns MK46...7 A3
Neath Cres MK3......47 A2
NEATH HILL......34 F6
Neath Hill Rdbt MK15...35 A6
Needham Cl SL4......209 E6
Needham Ct ⬛ HP11...172 F7
Neild Way WD3......167 F2
Neilson Ct MK7......48 C5
Nelson Cl
  High Wycombe HP13...173 F5
  Milton Keynes MK8......45 E6
  Slough SL3......206 D2
  Winchmore Hill HP7...164 C3
Nelson Ct MK14......52 C8
Nelson Rd
  Dagnall HP4......107 C5
  Harmondsworth TW6...213 F6
  Windsor SL4......209 F4
Nelson St MK18......52 C8
Nelson Terr HP20......115 D8
Nene Cl
  Aylesbury HP21......115 C4
  Newport Pagnell MK16...22 D3
Nene Dr MK3......57 E8
Neptune Way SL1......204 E4
Ness Way MK2......58 D5
Netherby Cl HP13......119 C6
Nether Cl NN13......38 A7
Nethercote La OX49...157 A8
NETHERFIELD......47 C6
Netherfield Rdbt MK6...47 C7
Nether Winchendon Ho★
  HP18......112 E5
Netherwood Rd HP9...175 D5
Netley Ct MK10......36 A1
Nettlecombe MK4......46 C3
Nettleden Rd
  Berkhamsted HP4......121 F6
  Little Gaddesden HP4...121 E4
Nettleton Rd UB10...201 F8
Neve Ho SL6......202 F8
Nevill Cl MK19......11 B2
Neville Cl SL2......198 F6
Neville Ct SL1......197 C2
Nevis Cl LU7......80 C7
Nevis Gr MK2......58 E4
Newark Ct MK7......48 A3
Newbarn La HP9......176 E6
Newberry Cres SL4...209 D5
Newbery Way SL1......205 D4
Newbolt Cl
  Newport Pagnell MK16...21 F5
  Paulersbury NN12......17 B8
NEW BRADWELL......33 F8
New Bradwell Comb Sch
  MK13......33 F7
Newbridge Oval MK4...46 B3
Newbury Cl MK3......57 D6
Newbury Dr SL6......203 B6
Newbury Rd UB7......213 F6
Newby Pl MK4......46 B2
New Chapter Prim sch
  MK6......47 A5
New Chilterns HP7...165 E8
Newchurch Rd SL2...204 F8
New Cl RG9......192 A8
New Cl Farm Rd OX39..137 C3
New College Ho HP18...51 F8
New College Ct MK18...41 A4
New Coll Rd HP19...101 C4
Newcombe Rise UB7...208 E7
New Cotts RG5......180 C1
Newcourt UB8......208 C8
Newcroft Cl UB8......208 F8
New Ct
  High Wycombe HP13...173 C6
  Marlow SL7......183 D2
NEW DENHAM......201 A6
New Dr HP13......173 E8
Newell Cl HP21......116 A6
Newells Hedge LU7...105 D5
Newfield Gdns SL7...183 F3
Newfield Rd SL7......183 F3
Newfield Way SL7...183 F2
New Garden Dr UB7...208 E4
NEW GROUND......120 A2
Newground Rd HP23...120 B3
New Hall Cl HP3......146 A4
Newhaven Spur SL3...198 B1

New Horton Manor
  SL3......212 A4
Newhouse Rd HP3...146 A4
Newington Gate MK6...47 D5
New Inn La MK18......51 F4
Newland Ho UB8......201 C4
NEWLAND PARK......178 A7
Newlands Dr
  Maidenhead SL6......202 A7
  Poyle SL3......212 E4
Newlands Girls Sch
  SL6......202 A7
Newlyn Pl MK6......35 A2
Newmans Cl MK14......21 E1
Newmans Ctyd MK17...68 C6
Newmarket Ct MK10...36 C2
New Mdw HP21......116 C7
Newmer Rd HP12......172 B3
NEW MILL......119 B6
New Mill Terr HP23...119 B6
New Par
  Chorleywood WD3...167 C5
  West Drayton UB7......208 F4
New Peachey La UB8...208 D4
New Pond Rd HP5......163 C7
NEWPORT PAGNELL......22 B5
Newport Pagnell Rd
  MK43......16 C4
Newport Rd
  Astwood MK16......15 C2
  Emberton MK46......13 F6
  Hanslope MK19......11 B2
  Milton Keynes MK10...36 D1
  Milton Keynes, New Bradwell
    MK13......34 A8
  Milton Keynes, Oakgrove
    MK15......35 C2
  Milton Keynes, Willen
    MK15......35 D7
  Milton Keynes, Woughton on
    the Green MK6......35 D1
  Moulsoe MK16......36 C7
  Slough SL2......197 E1
  Wavendon MK17......48 E7
  Woburn MK17......60 F8
  Woughton on the Green
    MK6......47 D8
  Woughton Park MK6...47 D6
Newport Way MK19...11 C3
New Provident Pl ⬛
  HP4......135 D4
Newquay Cl ⬛ MK4...45 F1
New Rd
  Amersham HP6......154 E2
  Aston Clinton HP22...117 E5
  Berkhamsted HP4...135 D6
  Berkhamsted, Northchurch
    HP4......134 F7
  Bolter End HP14......170 F6
  Bourne End SL8......185 B4
  Castlethorpe MK19...19 F5
  Chipperfield WD4......146 F1
  Coleshill HP7......164 F4
  Cookham Rise SL6......195 E7
  Datchet SL3......211 D6
  Dinton HP17......113 E2
  Drayton Parslow MK17...68 C5
  Great Kingshill HP15...162 D8
  Harrold MK43......3 E6
  High Wycombe HP12...172 C5
  Hurley SL6......193 F3
  Leighton Buzzard LU7...80 E7
  Little Chalfont HP8......166 F6
  Little Kingshill HP16...152 B4
  Marlow Bottom SL7...183 D6
  Naphill HP14......150 A2
  Prestwood HP16......151 D6
  Princes Risborough
    HP27......139 C3
  Sarratt HP8......156 F1
  Slough SL3......207 A3
  Stokenchurch HP14...158 F4
  Tring HP23......119 B6
  Tylers Green HP10......163 C1
  Weedon HP22......101 B8
  Weston Turville HP22...116 E5
  Wilstone HP23......118 D8
New Road Cl HP22......116 C6
New Road Gdns HP12...172 C6
New Row
  Hoggeston MK18......77 B7
  Lavendon MK46......7 B8
New Sq SL1......205 F4
New St
  Aylesbury HP20......101 D1
  Berkhamsted HP4......135 D4
  Cheddington LU7......104 F7
  Henley-on-Thames RG9...191 E2
  Milton Keynes MK11...32 D5
  Tingewick MK18......51 B6
  Waddesdon HP18......99 A7
NEWTON......144 C1
NEWTON
  BLOSSOMVILLE......8 A4
Newton Blossomville CE
  Sch MK43......8 B4
Newton Cl SL3......206 F4
Newton Ct SL4......211 A1
Newton Ct SL4......211 B1

NEWTON LONGVILLE......57 D3
Newton Longville CE Comb
  Sch MK17......57 D3
NEWTON PURCELL......50 B2
Newton Rd
  Drayton Parslow MK17...68 D8
  Milton Keynes MK3......57 E6
  Stoke Hammond MK17...69 D8
  Turvey MK43......8 E5
  West Drayton UB7......213 F6
Newtonside SL4......211 A1
Newton Side Orch SL4..211 A1
Newton St MK46......7 A4
Newtown Rd
  Marlow SL7......183 F3
  New Denham UB9......201 B6
Newtown Sch HP5......144 C2
Newville HP22......87 C1
New Windsor St UB8...201 C4
NEWYEARS GREEN......190 F5
Newyears Green La
  UB9......190 F5
New Zealand Cotts
  HP22......88 E4
New Zealand Gdns LU7...79 E2
Neyland Dr HP19......101 D3
Nicholas Gdns
  High Wycombe HP13...173 D8
  Slough SL1......204 E5
Nicholas Mead MK14...34 F8
Nicholas Winton Ct
  SL6......203 A8
Nicholls SL4......209 C4
Nicholls Wlk SL4......209 C4
Nicholson Gr MK8......45 E6
Nicholsons La SL6......202 F7
Nicholsons Sh Ctr ☉
  SL6......202 F7
Nickson Ct HP15......163 A3
Nicol Cl SL9......177 C2
Nicol End SL9......177 C2
Nicol Rd SL9......177 C2
Nielson Ct MK7......48 D5
Nigel Ct NN13......38 A5
Nightingale Cl
  Hazelmere HP15......163 B5
  Steeple Claydon MK18...63 E3
Nightingale Cres SL4...34 A7
Nightingale Ct
  ☐ High Wycombe
    HP13......173 B7
  ☑ Slough SL1......206 A3
Nightingale Ho HP11...174 A4
Nightingale La SL6...195 D3
Nightingale Lodge HP4 135 B4
Nightingale Pk SL2...197 F5
Nightingale Pl
  Buckingham MK18......41 E1
  Cookham Rise SL6......195 F7
Nightingale Rd
  Aylesbury HP21......115 E6
  ☑ Chesham HP5......144 B2
  Wendover HP22......131 B5
Nightingales Cnr HP7...166 C7
Nightingales Ct HP8...166 C7
Nightingales La HP8...166 D4
Nightingale Way UB9...189 F5
Nightingale Wlk SL4...210 C4
Nightingale Wood MK18...63 E3
Nine Acres SL1......204 F5
Nine Elms Ave UB8...208 D8
Nine Elms Cl UB8......208 D8
Nine Stiles Cl UB9...201 B6
Ninnings Rd SL9......177 F3
Ninnings Way SL9......177 F3
Niplands Cotts HP10...185 D2
Niven La MK9......45 E3
Nixey Cl SL1......206 A4
Nixons Cl MK6......46 E6
Noble Cl MK15......35 A7
Noble Ct SL2......205 F5
Noon Layer Dr MK10...35 E3
Norbrek MK8......33 E2
NORCOTT HILL......120 D2
Norcotts Kiln Cotts
  HP18......96 A1
Norden Cl SL4......202 C4
Norden Mdws SL6......202 C5
Norden Rd SL6......202 C5
Norelands Dr SL1......197 C3
Norfolk Ave SL1......205 C8
Norfolk Ho ⬛ MK3......46 F1
Norfolk Park Cotts SL6...202 F8
Norfolk Rd
  Maidenhead SL6......202 F8
  Turvey MK43......8 E6
  Uxbridge UB8......201 D6
Norfolk Terr HP20......101 E1
Norgrove Pk SL9......188 E7
Norjo-An Villas HP5...154 C6
Norland Dr HP10......185 C8
Norman Ave RG9......191 E1
Norman Cres MK10...35 E3
Normandy Dr HP4......135 B6
Normandy Way MK3...46 E2
Normans Cl UB8......208 F8
Normans Ct ⬛ HP13...173 F6
Normanstead RG9......191 D1
Normans The SL2......206 B7

Norman Way LU6......93 E8
Normill Terr HP22......117 A6
Norreys Dr SL6......202 D4
Norrington MK8......33 E2
Norris Ho SL6......202 E7
Norris Rd OX6......94 E8
NORTHALL......92 B5
Northall Cl LU6......92 D6
Northall La LU6......92 D6
Northampton Ave SL1...205 D7
Northampton Rd
  Brackley NN13......26 A1
  Cosgrove MK19......19 C1
  Cosgrove MK19......32 C8
  Grafton Regis NN12......9 C3
  Lathbury MK16......22 D6
  Lavendon MK46......7 F8
  Yardley Hastings NN7...1 A6
Northborough Rd SL2...198 B1
Northbridge Rd HP4...135 A6
North Burnham Cl SL1...197 B3
NORTHCHURCH......134 E5
Northchurch La HP5...134 D2
North Cl
  Beaconsfield HP9......186 B8
  Drayton Parslow MK17...68 C5
  Medmenham SL7......193 D7
  Windsor SL4......209 F6
Northcliffe LU6......92 E6
North Common Rd
  UB8......201 D7
North Cotts SL2......198 C2
NORTH CRAWLEY......24 A6
North Crawley CE Sch
  MK16......24 B6
North Crawley Rd MK16...23 C4
Northcroft
  Milton Keynes MK5......46 C5
  Slough SL2......198 B1
  Weedon HP22......87 C1
  Wooburn Green HP10...185 F6
North Croft MK18......66 A4
Northdean ⬛ SL6......195 F1
Northdown Rd SL9...177 E4
North Dr
  Aylesbury HP21......115 C5
  Beaconsfield HP9......186 B8
  High Wycombe HP13...173 E8
North Eastern Rd HP19 101 C2
North Eighth St MK9...34 E3
North Elder Rdbt MK9...34 C1
North Eleventh St MK9...34 E3
NORTHEND......168 E6
  Stagsden......16 B8
  Steeple Claydon......63 D3
  Stewkley......68 D3
Northend MK46......5 E3
Northend Cl HP10......185 C7
Northend Ct ⬛ MK18...41 D1
North End Rd
  Quainton MK18......85 A5
  Steeple Claydon MK18...63 D3
Northend Sq ☑ MK18...41 D1
Northend Workshops
  RG9......168 E5
Northern Hts SL8......185 B5
Northern Perimeter Rd (W)
  TW6......213 D6
Northern Rd
  Aylesbury HP19......101 C2
  Slough SL2......198 D2
Northern Woods HP10...185 C7
NORTHFIELD......35 F5
Northfield Ct RG9......191 D3
Northfield Dr MK15......35 F5
Northfield End RG9...191 D3
Northfield Rd
  Aylesbury HP20......116 B3
  Eton Wick SL4......204 F2
  Maidenhead SL6......195 F1
  Princes Risborough
    HP27......139 C4
  Tring HP23......119 F7
Northfield Rdbt MK10...36 A5
North Fifth St MK9......34 D2
North Fourteenth St
  MK9......34 F4
North Fourth St MK9...34 D2
North Gate MK2......47 C1
North Gn
  ☑ Maidenhead SL6...195 F1
  Slough SL1......205 E6
North Grafton Rdbt
  MK13......34 C2
North Hill
  Buckingham MK18......28 D2
  Dadford MK18......28 D2
  Sarratt WD3......167 E8
North Hills HP18......96 A1
North La MK7......47 E7
Northlands Rd SL7......53 F1
NORTH LEE......130 A7
North Lee La
  Lee HP22......130 A6
  Stoke Mandeville HP22...129 F7
Northleigh MK4......46 D2
North Links Rd HP10...174 B1
NORTH MARSTON......76 A2

North Marston CE Sch
MK18 . . . . 76 B2
North Marston La HP22 . . 86 E7
Northmead Rd SL2 . . . . . . 204 F8
Northmill HP27 . . . . 138 F3
North Mill Rd HP27 . . . . . 138 A5
Northmoor Hill Wood
Nature Reserve★
UB9 . . . . 189 F7
North Ninth St MK9 . . . . . 34 E3
Northolt Rd TW6 . . . . 213 E6
North Orbital Rd
Denham Green UB9 . . . . . 189 F4
Rickmansworth WD3 . . . . 178 E7
North Overgate Rdbt
MK15 . . . . 35 B5
North Pk
Gerrards Cross SL9 . . . . . 188 E8
Iver SL0 . . . . 207 D3
North Rd
Amersham HP6 . . . . 154 C3
Berkhamsted HP4 . . . . . . 135 B4
Chorleywood WD3 . . . . . 167 F4
Cryers Hill HP15 . . . . 162 D5
Maidenhead SL6 . . . . . . 202 E7
West Drayton UB7 . . . . . . 208 F3
North Ridge MK6 . . . . 35 B1
North Row
Fulmer SL3 . . . . 199 E8
Milton Keynes MK9 . . . . . 34 C2
North Saxon Rdbt MK14 . 34 D3
North Secklow Rdbt
MK14 . . . . 34 E3
North Second St MK9 . . . 34 C2
North Seventh St MK9 . . . 34 D2
North Sixth St MK9 . . . . . 34 C2
North Skeldon Rdbt
MK9 . . . . 35 A4
North Sq MK16 . . . . 22 D5
North St
Castlethorpe MK19 . . . . . 19 F5
Milton Keynes, Bradville
MK13 . . . . 34 A7
Milton Keynes, Fenny Stratford
MK2 . . . . 47 C1
Thame OX9 . . . . 125 F1
North Star La SL6 . . . . 202 C6
North Tenth St MK9 . . . . . 34 E3
North Terr SL4 . . . . 210 E7
North Third St MK9 . . . . . 34 C2
North Thirteenth St MK9 34 F3
NORTH TOWN 195 F1
North Town Cl 1 SL6 . . . 195 F1
North Town Mead 4
SL6 . . . . 195 F1
North Town Moor SL6 . . . 195 F1
North Town Rd SL6 . . . . . 195 F1
North Twelfth St MK9 . . . 34 F3
Northumberland Ave
HP21 . . . . 116 B6
Northumberland Cl
TW19 . . . . 213 E1
Northumbria Rd SL6 . . . . 202 B4
North View HP22 . . . . 87 B3
North Way
Deanshanger NN12 . . . . . 31 E5
Pottersgrove NN12 . . . . . 14 E2
Uxbridge UB10 . . . . 201 E5
NORTH WESTON 136 F8
Northwich MK6 . . . . 47 D7
Northwick MK10 . . . . 35 F1
North Witan Rdbt MK10 . 34 D2
Northwood Rd TW6 . . . . . 213 D6
Nortoft Rd SL9 . . . . 177 F5
Norton Leys MK7 . . . . 48 C7
Norton Rd UB8 . . . . 201 D2
Norton's Pl MK18 . . . . 52 C8
Nortons The MK7 . . . . 48 B3
Norvic Rd HP23 . . . . 105 A1
Norway Dr SL2 . . . . 206 B8
Norwich Ho
High Wycombe HP13 . . . . 173 F8
Maidenhead SL6 . . . . . . 202 E8
Norwood Cl HP20 . . . . . . 101 F2
Norwood Cl 4 HP7 . . . . . 165 B7
Norwood La
Newport Pagnell MK16 . . 22 C3
Uxbridge SL0 . . . . 200 D1
Norwood Rd HP10 . . . . . . 174 B2
Notley Farm HP18 . . . . . . 126 A3
Nottingham Ave MK3 . . . . 46 E2
Nottingham Ho 3
HP13 . . . . 173 F7
Nottingham Rd WD3 . . . . 167 C1
Nova Lodge MK4 . . . . 46 B2
Novello Croft MK7 . . . . . . 48 D4
Nugent Cl HP19 . . . . 101 D4
Nugent Ct
Chesham HP5 . . . . 144 A3
Marlow SL7 . . . . 183 F3
Nuneham Gr MK4 . . . . 45 F3
NUP END 89 B3
Nup End Cl HP22 . . . . 89 B3
Nup End La HP22 . . . . 89 B3
Nurseries The LU6 . . . . . . 92 E6
Nursery Cl
2 Amersham HP7 . . . . . 165 E8
Aylesbury HP21 . . . . 115 C5
Tylers Green HP10 . . . . . 174 C4

Nursery Ct HP12 . . . . 172 D6
Nursery Dr HP14 . . . . 171 B5
Nursery Gdns
Milton Keynes MK13 . . . . 34 A4
Tring HP23 . . . . 119 B4
Nursery La
Slough SL3 . . . . 206 D5
Tylers Green HP10 . . . . . 174 C8
Nursery Pl SL4 . . . . 211 B1
Nursery Rd SL6 . . . . 204 B7
Nursery Way TW19 . . . . . 211 D1
Nursery Waye UB8 . . . . . 201 D4
Nursery Wlk SL7 . . . . 183 B1
Nutfield La HP11 . . . . 172 F8
Nuthatch 10 HP19 . . . . . 101 F3
Nutkins Way HP5 . . . . . . 144 C2
Nutkin Wlk UB10 . . . . . . 201 E5
Nutmeg Cl MK7 . . . . 48 B5
Nye Way HP3 . . . . 146 A3
Nymans Gate 8 MK4 . . . 45 F1

O

Oak Barn Cl MK43 . . . . . . 25 A1
Oak Cres HP12 . . . . 172 C4
Oak Ct MK9 . . . . 34 E2
Oakdene HP9 . . . . 175 E3
Oakdown Cres MK46 . . . . . 6 F3
Oak Dr HP4 . . . . 135 D3
Oakend Dr SL0 . . . . 200 C3
Oak End Way
Chinnor OX39 . . . . 147 D5
Gerrards Cross SL9 . . . . . 188 F6
Oaken Gr SL6 . . . . 195 C1
Oakengrove Cl HP15 . . . . 163 C6
Oakengrove La HP15 . . . . 163 B3
Oakengrove Rd HP15 . . . . 163 A3
Oaken Head MK4 . . . . 46 C2
Oakeshott Ave HP14 . . . . 161 D6
Oakfield WD3 . . . . 167 F2
Oak Field HP5 . . . . 144 B1
Oakfield Ave SL1 . . . . 205 B5
Oakfield Cl HP6 . . . . 154 C2
Oakfield Cnr HP6 . . . . 154 C2
Oakfield Fst Sch SL4 . . . . 210 B5
Oakfield Rd
Aylesbury HP20 . . . . 116 A8
Bourne End SL8 . . . . 185 A3
Oak Gn HP21 . . . . 115 C7
Oak Green Sch HP21 . . . . 115 C7
OAKGROVE 35 D2
Oakgrove L Ctr MK10 . . . 35 F2
Oakgrove Rdbt MK10 . . . 35 F2
Oakgrove Sch MK10 . . . . 35 F2
Oakham Rise MK4 . . . . . . 45 E1
OAKHILL 45 D4
Oakhill Cl
Maple Cross WD3 . . . . . . 178 E6
Milton Keynes MK5 . . . . . 45 E6
Oakhill Rd
Maple Cross WD3 . . . . . . 178 D6
Milton Keynes, Hazeley
MK5 . . . . 45 D5
Milton Keynes, Shenley Church
End MK5 . . . . 45 D5
Oakhill Rdbt MK5 . . . . . . 45 D5
Oakhurst SL6 . . . . 196 B4
Oakington Ave HP6 . . . . . 166 E8
Oak La
Buckland Common
HP23 . . . . 133 A2
Windsor SL4 . . . . 210 A6
Oaklands HP4 . . . . 135 A4
Oaklands St HP4 . . . . 154 C1
Oakland Way HP10 . . . . . 174 A1
Oak Lawn HP23 . . . . 119 A3
OAKLEY
Brill 109 D5
Chinnor 147 B5
Oakley HP10 . . . . 185 F7
Oakley CE Comb Sch
HP18 . . . . 109 D4
Oakley Coll HP18 . . . . . . 109 F1
Oakley Cres SL1 . . . . 205 E6
Oakley Gdns MK15 . . . . . 35 B5
OAKLEY GREEN 209 B5
Oakley Green Rd SL4 . . . . 209 B5
Oakley Hill Wildlife
Reserve★ OX39 . . . . . . 147 D4
Oakley La OX39 . . . . 147 B6
Oakley Rd
Brill HP18 . . . . 110 A8
Chinnor OX39 . . . . 147 C6
Horton-cum-S OX33 . . . . 108 C5
Oak Rd HP27 . . . . 139 C3
Oakridge MK4 . . . . 46 E4
Oakridge Combined Sch
HP11 . . . . 172 E7
Oakridge Ct HP12 . . . . . . 172 D6
Oakridge Pl SL22 . . . . . . 198 C8
Oakridge Rd HP11 . . . . . . 172 E7
Oakside UB9 . . . . 201 B6
Oaks Rd TW19 . . . . 213 D2
Oak St HP11 . . . . 173 C4
Oaks The HP4 . . . . 135 A4
Oak Stubbs La SL6 . . . . . 203 F4
Oak Tree Ave SL7 . . . . . . 183 D3

Oaktree Cl HP10 . . . . 163 B2
Oak Tree La SL7 . . . . 183 D3
Oak Tree Cotts HP18 . . . . 83 B5
Oaktree Ct MK15 . . . . 35 C7
Oak Tree Dr
Lane End HP14 . . . . 171 C5
Slough SL3 . . . . 207 B1
Oak Tree Rd SL7 . . . . 183 D4
Oakview HP6 . . . . 153 D4
Oak View
Great Kingshill HP15 . . . . 162 D8
Towcester NN12 . . . . 18 D3
Oakview Gdns SL3 . . . . . . 206 F2
Oakway
Amersham HP6 . . . . 154 B4
Winslow MK18 . . . . 66 A4
Oakwell Cl LU6 . . . . 93 F7
Oakwood HP10 . . . . 174 A2
Oak wood HP4 . . . . 134 F3
Oakwood Dr MK2 . . . . 58 E7
Oakworth Ave MK10 . . . . 36 A4
Oat Cl HP21 . . . . 115 C3
Oatlands Dr SL1 . . . . 205 D7
Oban Ct SL1 . . . . 205 D4
Oberon Way MK4 . . . . 45 D2
Observatory Sh Ctr 4
SL1 . . . . 205 F4
Ockells Nature Reserve★
SL6 . . . . 202 E2
Ockwells Rd SL6 . . . . 202 C2
Octagon Arc 10 HP11 . . . 173 A7
Octagon Par 6 HP11 . . . . 173 A7
Octavian Dr MK13 . . . . . . 33 F5
Octavian Way NN13 . . . . . 38 A7
Oddley La HP27 . . . . 148 D8
Odds Farm Est HP10 . . . . 186 B4
Odds Farm Park★
HP10 . . . . 186 B4
Oddy Hill
Tring HP23 . . . . 119 C3
Wigginton HP23 . . . . . . 119 C2
Odell Cl MK6 . . . . 47 C8
Odencroft Rd SL2 . . . . . . 198 A2
Odney La SL6 . . . . 196 B7
Offas La MK18 . . . . 66 B5
Ogilvie Rd HP12 . . . . 172 E7
O'Grady Way HP19 . . . . . 101 A3
Okeford Cl HP23 . . . . 118 F4
Okeford Dr HP23 . . . . 118 F4
Okeley La HP23 . . . . 118 E3
Oldacres SL6 . . . . 203 B7
Old Airfield Ind Est
HP23 . . . . 104 D6
Old Amersham Rd SL9 . . 189 B3
Old Bakery Est SL0 . . . . . 207 F7
Old Bakery The
Aston Abbotts HP22 . . . . 88 D5
Lane End HP14 . . . . 171 B4
Old Barn Cl MK18 . . . . . . 52 A4
Old Bix Rd RG9 . . . . 191 A6
Old Brewery Cl HP21 . . . . 115 E7
Old Brewery La RG9 . . . . 191 E2
Old English Cl MK17 . . . . 44 C1
Oldershaw Mews SL6 . . . 202 B8
Old Farm LU7 . . . . 105 D4
Old Farm Cl
Beaconsfield HP9 . . . . . . 175 C5
Slapton LU7 . . . . 91 A3
Worminghall HP18 . . . . . 123 C5
Old Farm La HP7 . . . . 165 E6
OLD FARM PARK 48 E5
Old Farm Rd
High Wycombe HP13 . . . . 161 E2
West Drayton SL1 . . . . . . 208 D4
Old Ferry Dr TW19 . . . . . 211 D1
Old Field Cl HP6 . . . . 166 E8
Oldfield Prim Sch SL6 . . . 203 B6
Oldfield Rd SL6 . . . . 203 B7
Old Fishery La HP1 . . . . . 146 F8
Old Fives Ct SL1 . . . . 197 C2
Old Forge Cl
Maidenhead SL6 . . . . . . 203 A3
Tingewick MK18 . . . . 51 B6
Old Forge Gdns HP22 . . . 102 B4
Old Forge Rd HP10 . . . . . 174 C2
Old Forge The HP23 . . . . 104 B4
Old Gaol Mus★ MK18 . . . 41 D1
Old Garden Ctr The
HP27 . . . . 139 B3
Old Groveway MK6 . . . . . 47 D5
Oldham Rise MK5 . . . . . . 45 E6
Oldhams Mdw 9 HP20 . . 101 F2

Old Hardenway HP13 . . . 162 E1
Old Heatherdene Cotts
HP15 . . . . 162 D8
Old Horns La SL7 . . . . . . 172 A3
Oldhouse Cl HP11 . . . . . . 172 E3
Old House Ct SL3 . . . . . . 206 D7
Old Kiln Rd
Flackwell Heath HP10 . . . 185 A8
Tylers Green HP10 . . . . . 163 C2
Old Linslade Rd LU7 . . . . 70 D2
Old Lodge Dr HP9 . . . . . . 175 E1
Old Maltings The
Buckingham MK18 . . . . . 52 C7
Thame OX9 . . . . 125 E1
Old Manor Cl
Askett HP27 . . . . 139 C7
Whaddon MK17 . . . . 45 B1
Old Manor Ct LU7 . . . . . . 78 E8
Old Marsh La SL6 . . . . . . 203 F4
Old Mead SL9 . . . . 177 E4
Old Meadow Cl HP4 . . . . 135 A2
Old Mews The MK46 . . . . 6 F4
Old Mill Cl HP17 . . . . 127 A6
Old Mill Furlong SL1 . . . . 66 A5
Old Mill La HP4 . . . . 135 D4
Old Mill Pl TW19 . . . . . . 212 B1
Old Mill Rd UB9 . . . . 190 A1
Old Moor La HP10 . . . . . . 185 E8
Old Nursery Ct SL2 . . . . . 187 C2
Old Oak Gdns HP4 . . . . . 134 E7
Old Orch
Henton OX39 . . . . 137 E2
Iver SL0 . . . . 207 F7
Old Orchard Mews 1
HP4 . . . . 135 C4
Old Orchard Rd HP22 . . . 102 A3
Old Oxford Rd HP14 . . . . 160 C1
Old Palace Ct SL3 . . . . . . 212 D6
Old Papermill Cl HP10 . . 185 E8
Old Plough Cl HP18 . . . . 112 B2
Old Post Office La 11
SL6 . . . . 202 F7
Old Rd LU7 . . . . 80 E7
Old Rd The RG9 . . . . 179 C8
Old Rectory La UB9 . . . . . 189 E4
Old Risborough Rd
HP22 . . . . 130 A8
Old Sax La HP5 . . . . 143 D4
Old School Cl HP22 . . . . . 117 C5
Old School Cotts HP5 . . . 145 D5
Old School Ct
Buckingham MK18 . . . . . 52 C8
Eaton Bray LU6 . . . . 92 E6
Old School La HP22 . . . . . 117 E8
Old School Rd UB8 . . . . . 201 F1
Old School The HP10 . . . . 174 D8
Old Shire La WD3 . . . . . . 167 B3
Old Slade La SL3 . . . . 207 F2
Old Springfields MK18 . . 53 C2
Old Stable Yd MK9 . . . . . . 32 C7
Old Stable Yd The MK18 . 65 F4
Old Station Cl MK18 . . . . 66 A5
Old Station La TW19 . . . . 213 A1
Old Station Way HP10 . . . 185 E5
Old Stoke Rd HP21 . . . . . 115 D6
OLD STRATFORD 32 B7
Old Stratford Prim Sch
MK19 . . . . 32 B6
Old Tan Yard Cl MK18 . . . 65 F4
OLD TOWN 38 A7
Old Town NN13 . . . . 38 A7
Old Town Cl HP9 . . . . 175 E1
Old Town Farm HP16 . . . 152 A7
Old Union Way OX9 . . . . . 125 E1
Old Uxbridge Rd WD3 . . . 178 E3
Old Vicarage Way
HP10 . . . . 185 D4
Old Watery La HP10 . . . . 185 E8
Oldway La SL1 . . . . 204 D5
Old Windmill Way
HP18 . . . . 125 C2
OLD WINDSOR 211 A1
OLD WOLVERTON 33 D8
Old Wolverton Rd MK12 . 33 C8
Oliffe Cl HP20 . . . . 101 D3
Oliffe Way HP20 . . . . 101 D3
Oliver Rd MK2 . . . . 58 C8
Oliver Row 4 MK4 . . . . . . 45 E3
Oliver's Paddock SL7 . . . . 183 D5
Olivia Dr SL3 . . . . 206 F1
Olivier Way HP20 . . . . . . 116 A8
Olleberrie La WD4 . . . . . . 156 D7
OLNEY 6 E4
Olney Ind Est MK46 . . . . . 6 F6
Olney Inf Sch MK46 . . . . . 6 E3
Olney Mid Sch MK46 . . . . 6 F5
Olney Rd
Emberton MK46 . . . . . . 13 F8
Lavendon MK46 . . . . 7 E7
Olson Cotts HP14 . . . . . . 158 F4
Olympic Ho UB8 . . . . 201 F1
O'Neill Rd MK8 . . . . 45 D6
One Pin La SL2 . . . . 187 D1
One Tree La HP9 . . . . 175 E3

Onslow Ct MK7 . . . . 48 A4
Onslow Dr OX9 . . . . 126 B1
Onslow Gdns HP13 . . . . . 173 E7
Onslow Mills UB7 . . . . . . 208 D6
Opal Cl SL3 . . . . 199 C1
Opal Dr MK15 . . . . 35 F4
Opecks Cl SL3 . . . . 199 B1
Opendale Rd SL1 . . . . . . 204 B8
Open University (Walton
Hall) The MK7 . . . . 47 F7
Oram Ct 3 SL7 . . . . 183 D2
Orbell Ct HP27 . . . . 139 B3
Orbison Ct MK8 . . . . 45 D7
Orchard Ave
Berkhamsted HP4 . . . . . . 135 A4
Slough SL1 . . . . 204 D8
Windsor SL4 . . . . 210 A6
Orchard Bglws SL2 . . . . . 197 F5
Orchard Cl
15 Aylesbury HP20 . . . . 101 F3
Beaconsfield HP9 . . . . . . 175 D3
Chorleywood WD3 . . . . . 167 D5
Cranfield MK43 . . . . 25 A1
Hughenden Valley HP14 . 162 A7
Longwick HP27 . . . . 138 D7
Maidenhead SL6 . . . . . . 203 A3
Milton Keynes MK3 . . . . . 57 F7
New Denham UB9 . . . . . 201 B6
Newton Longville MK17 . . 57 C3
Oakley HP18 . . . . 109 D4
Slough SL1 . . . . 197 B1
Stoke Mandeville HP22 . . 116 B1
Upper Arncott OX25 . . . . 94 D6
Waddesdon HP18 . . . . . . 99 A7
Wendover HP22 . . . . 131 A5
Wingrave HP22 . . . . 89 B3
Yardley Gobion NN12 . . . 18 F6
Orchard Ct
Aylesbury HP21 . . . . 115 F6
Bovingdon HP23 . . . . . . 146 A4
Harmondsworth TW6 . . . 213 C7
Seer Green HP9 . . . . 176 C5
Orchard Dene MK18 . . . . 41 D6
Orchard Dr
Aston Clinton HP22 . . . . 117 A4
Chorleywood WD3 . . . . . 167 D5
Hazelmere HP15 . . . . . . 163 A3
Leighton Buzzard LU7 . . . 80 D6
Uxbridge UB8 . . . . 201 D1
Wooburn HP10 . . . . 185 D4
Orchard End
Edlesborough LU6 . . . . . . 92 E4
Hazelmere HP15 . . . . . . 163 B6
Orchard End Ave HP7 . . . 165 F8
Orchard Gate SL2 . . . . . . 198 C7
Orchard Gr
Chalfont St Peter SL9 . . . 177 C2
Flackwell Heath HP10 . . . 185 B7
Hazelmere HP15 . . . . . . 202 C7
Orchard Ho
8 Bourne End SL8 . . . . . 185 A4
Milton Keynes MK12 . . . . 33 D6
Orchard La
Amersham HP6 . . . . 154 D1
Harrold MK43 . . . . 3 F7
Prestwood HP16 . . . . . . 151 C6
Stewkley LU7 . . . . 78 E7
ORCHARD LEIGH 145 B3
Orchard Leigh Villas
HP5 . . . . 145 A4
Orchard Lodge SL1 . . . . . 204 E5
Orchard Mews HP9 . . . . . 176 D4
Orchard Mill SL8 . . . . 185 B1
Orchard Pk SL15 . . . . 163 C6
Orchard Pl
Monks Risborough
HP27 . . . . 139 C5
Uxbridge UB8 . . . . 201 D5
Westbury MK13 . . . . 39 A4
Orchard Rd
Beaconsfield HP9 . . . . . . 175 F1
Chalfont St Giles HP8 . . . 177 C8
Loudwater HP13 . . . . . . 174 A4
Old Windsor SL4 . . . . . . 211 B1
Seer Green HP9 . . . . 176 C5
Orchard Rise HP14 . . . . . . 6 F3
Orchard Row HP14 . . . . . 171 A7
Orchard Sch MK6 . . . . . . 35 B2
Orchards The
Eaton Bray LU6 . . . . 92 F4
Little Kingshill HP15 . . . . 152 A2
Slough SL3 . . . . 206 F5
Tring HP23 . . . . 118 F3
Orchard The
Aston Clinton HP22 . . . . 117 C5
Flackwell Heath HP10 . . . 185 B7
Halton HP22 . . . . 131 C8
Hazelmere HP15 . . . . . . 163 A6
Hillesden MK18 . . . . 63 A7
Marlow SL7 . . . . 183 B3
Pottersbury NN12 . . . . . 18 C3
Walter's Ash HP14 . . . . . 161 A7
Orchard View
Hillesden MK18 . . . . 63 B7
Uxbridge UB8 . . . . 201 D1
ORCHARDVILLE 197 B1

Orchardville SL1 . . . .**197** B1
Orchard Way
Aylesbury HP20 . . . .**101** F2
Bovingdon HP3 . . . .**146** A3
Chinnor OX39 . . . .**147** C5
Cranfield MK43 . . . .**25** A1
East Claydon MK18 . . . . . .**74** E6
Eaton Bray LU6 . . . .**92** F5
Holmer Green HP15 . . . . .**163** C6
North Crawley MK16 . . . . .**24** A6
Pitstone LU7 . . . .**105** E4
Slough SL3 . . . .**206** F5
Stoke Goldington MK16 . . .**12** B7
Wing LU7 . . . .**79** E2
Orchard Waye UB8 . . . . .**201** D3
Orchard Wlk MK46 . . . .**7** F7
Orchehill Ave SL9 . . . . . .**188** D7
Orchehill Ct SL9 . . . .**188** E6
Orchehill Rise SL9 . . . . .**188** E6
Oregano Cl MK7 . . . .**46** B6
Orford Ct MK5 . . . .**46** B6
Oriel Cl MK12 . . . .**33** B6
Oriel Cotts MK18 . . . .**63** D2
Orkney Cl
Milton Keynes MK3 . . . . . .**46** F2
Stewkley LU7 . . . .**78** E8
Orkney Ct SL6 . . . .**196** E5
Ormesby Cl HP21 . . . . . .**116** A5
Ormonde MK4 . . . .**34** D7
Ormond Rd OX9 . . . .**126** A1
Ormsgill Ct MK13 . . . . . .**34** B5
Orne Gdns MK15 . . . .**35** A7
Orpington Gr MK5 . . . . . .**46** B4
Ortensia Dr MK7 . . . .**48** C7
Orwell Cl
Aylesbury HP21 . . . .**115** D4
Newport Pagnell MK16 . . . .**21** F5
Windsor SL4 . . . .**210** D4
Orwell Dr HP21 . . . .**115** D4
Osborne Cl SL4 . . . .**210** C5
Osborne Mews SL4 . . . .**210** C5
Osborne Rd SL4 . . . .**210** D4
Osborne St
Milton Keynes MK2 . . . . . .**58** C7
Slough SL1 . . . .**205** F4
Osborne Way HP23 . . . . .**119** D1
Osborn Rd UB8 . . . .**201** C5
Osborn's Ct **5** MK46 . . . . .**6** F3
Osbourne St MK12 . . . . . .**33** D6
Osier La MK5 . . . .**46** B4
Osier Way
Aylesbury HP20 . . . .**115** F8
Buckingham MK18 . . . . . .**52** C6
Osmington Pl HP23 . . . . .**118** F4
Osney Rd SL6 . . . .**195** E2
Osprey Cl
Milton Keynes MK6 . . . . . .**47** B8
West Drayton UB7 . . . . . .**208** E4
Osprey The HP19 . . . . . .**101** E4
Osprey Wlk
Aylesbury HP19 . . . .**101** E4
Buckingham MK18 . . . .**52** F7
Osterley Cl MK16 . . . .**22** C3
Ostler Gate SL6 . . . .**195** C1
Ostlers Ct HP11 . . . .**174** A4
Ostlers La MK11 . . . .**32** D6
Otterburn Cres MK5 . . . . .**45** D5
Otter Cl MK3 . . . .**46** D1
Otterfield Rd UB7 . . . . . .**208** E6
Otters Brook MK18 . . . . .**52** E7
Otway Cl HP21 . . . .**115** E3
Oulton Cl HP21 . . . .**116** A5
Our Lady of Peace RC Inf
Sch SL1 . . . .**204** C8
Our Lady of Peace RC Jun
Sch SL1 . . . .**204** C8
Our Lady's RC Prim Sch
HP6 . . . .**154** B4
Ousebank Sch MK16 . . . . .**22** D5
Ousebank Way MK11 . . . . .**32** D5
Ousedale Sch
Newport Pagnell MK16 . . . .**22** B3
Olney MK46 . . . .**6** E4
Ouseley Rd TW19 . . . . . .**211** D1
Outfield Rd SL9 . . . .**177** D3
Outlook Dr HP8 . . . .**177** D7
Ouzel Cl MK3 . . . .**46** E1
Oval The MK6 . . . .**46** E7
Oval Way SL9 . . . .**188** E2
Overdale Rd HP5 . . . .**144** B3
Overdales HP15 . . . .**162** F3
Overgate MK6, MK9, MK14 .**35** B4
Over Hampden HP16 . . . .**151** C7
Overhills MK46 . . . .**6** E4
Overn Ave MK18 . . . .**41** C1
Overn Cl MK18 . . . .**41** D1
Overn Cres MK18 . . . .**41** C1
Overshot Ho HP10 . . . . . .**174** C2
Overstey Ct MK14 . . . .**22** A1
Overstone Cl LU7 . . . .**79** E2
Overstone Comb Sch
LU7 . . . .**79** E2
Overstrand HP22 . . . .**117** E5
Overstreet MK15 . . . .**35** A6
Over the Misbourne
UB9 . . . .**189** B5

Over the Misbourne Rd
UB9 . . . .**189** C5
Overton Dr OX9 . . . .**126** B1
Oville Ct MK1 . . . .**46** B5
OVING **86** D8
Oving Rd HP22 . . . .**86** E7
Ovitts Cl MK18 . . . .**66** A5
Owen Cl **4** SL3 . . . .**206** F1
Owl Cl **5** HP19 . . . .**101** F3
Owlsears Cl HP9 . . . .**175** D4
OWLSWICK **128** D1
Oxendon Ct LU7 . . . .**70** F2
Oxenhope Way MK10 . . . . .**36** A4
Oxfield Cl HP4 . . . .**135** A3
Oxfield Park Dr MK19 . . . .**32** C7
Oxford Ave
Burnham SL1 . . . .**197** B3
Slough SL1 . . . .**204** F8
Oxford Gdns UB9 . . . . . .**190** A1
Oxford Rd
Aylesbury HP17, HP21 . . .**115** B7
Denham UB9 . . . .**189** D2
Gerrards Cross SL9 . . . . .**188** D5
High Wycombe HP11 . . . . .**173** A7
Marlow SL7 . . . .**183** D2
Oakley HP18 . . . .**109** D5
Piddington HP14 . . . .**160** D1
Stokenchurch HP14 . . . . .**158** D5
Stone HP17 . . . .**114** C5
Thame OX9 . . . .**125** E1
Uxbridge UB8, UB9 . . . . .**201** B6
Windsor SL4 . . . .**210** A3
Oxford Road E SL4 . . . . .**210** C6
Oxford St
5 High Wycombe
HP11 . . . .**173** A7
Lee Common HP16 . . . . . .**142** D5
Milton Keynes, Fenny Stratford
MK2 . . . .**58** C8
Milton Keynes, Stony Stratford
MK11 . . . .**32** D5
Milton Keynes, Wolverton
MK12 . . . .**33** D6
Oxhouse Ct MK5 . . . .**46** A3
OXLEY PARK **45** E3
Oxley Park Rdbt MK5 . . . . .**45** F3
Oxleys MK46 . . . .**6** E4
Oxman La MK12 . . . .**33** A5
Oxwich Gr MK4 . . . .**57** B8

P

Pace Ctr The HP19 . . . . .**101** B2
Packet Boat La UB8 . . . . .**208** C7
Packhorse Rd SL9 . . . . . .**188** E6
Pack & Prime La RG9 . . .**191** C2
PADBURY **53** B2
Padbury CE Fst Sch
MK18 . . . .**53** C2
Padbury Oaks UB7 . . . . .**213** B6
Padcroft Rd UB7 . . . .**208** D5
Paddock Cl
8 Aylesbury HP19 . . . . . .**100** F1
Maidenhead SL6 . . . .**202** A2
Milton Keynes MK14 . . . . .**34** E8
Paddock Cotts SL6 . . . . . .**202** A1
Paddocks Clinic The
(private) HP27 . . . .**139** C4
Paddocks End HP9 . . . . .**176** C4
Paddocks The
Chorleywood WD3 . . . . . .**167** F5
Flackwell Heath HP10 . . . .**185** B8
Haddenham HP17 . . . . . .**127** A5
High Wycombe HP12 . . . . .**172** B3
Prestwood HP16 . . . .**151** C5
Steeple Claydon MK18 . . . .**63** E3
Wendover HP22 . . . .**131** B5
Paddock The
Aylesbury HP21 . . . .**116** C7
Chalfont St Peter SL9 . . . .**177** E5
Datchet SL3 . . . .**211** B6
Emberton MK46 . . . .**13** E8
Maidenhead SL6 . . . .**195** C2
Maids Moreton MK18 . . . . .**41** E4
Paddock Way MK2 . . . .**47** F1
Padstow Ave MK6 . . . .**34** F1
Padstow Cl
Aylesbury HP20 . . . .**101** F1
Slough SL3 . . . .**206** E3
PAGE HILL **41** F2
Page Hill Ave MK18 . . . . . .**41** E1
Pages Croft HP4 . . . .**135** A6
Pages La UB8 . . . .**201** C6
Pages Wharf SL6 . . . .**203** C8
Paget Cl SL7 . . . .**183** F4
Paget Ct UB7 . . . .**208** E4
Paget Dr SL6 . . . .**202** A4
Paget Rd SL3 . . . .**206** F2
Pagg's Ct MK16 . . . .**22** D4
Pagoda Rdbt MK15 . . . . . .**35** C5
Pagoda The SL6 . . . .**196** B1
Paignton Way **2** MK10 . . .**36** A3
Paines Orch LU7 . . . .**105** A8
Pakenham Ct HP14 . . . . . .**58** F5
Palace Cl SL1 . . . .**204** F5
Palace Sq MK6 . . . .**46** F7
Palfreyman St HP19 . . . . .**101** D4

Palliser Rd HP8 . . . .**177** B6
Palmer Ave
Aylesbury HP19 . . . .**115** C8
Upper Arncott OX25 . . . . . .**94** F8
Palmers Cl SL6 . . . .**202** A3
PALMERS MOOR **201** A1
Palmers Moor MK18 . . . . .**54** A8
Palmer's Moor La SL0 . . .**201** A1
Palmers Rd MK46 . . . .**7** A3
Palmerston Ave SL3 . . . .**206** B3
Pankridge Dr HP16 . . . . .**151** C7
Panleigh Cotts HP14 . . . .**171** B3
Pannier Pl MK14 . . . .**35** A5
Pann Mill HP13 . . . .**173** C6
Panters Cl MK17 . . . .**44** C1
Pantile Row SL3 . . . .**207** A2
Pantile Wlk UB8 . . . .**201** C5
Paprika Ct MK7 . . . .**48** B5
Papworth Cl MK16 . . . .**22** F3
Parade Ct **7** SL8 . . . .**185** A4
Parade The
Bourne End SL8 . . . .**185** A3
Farnham Common SL2 . . .**198** C6
High Wycombe HP11 . . . . .**172** F6
Uxbridge UB8 . . . .**208** C8
Windsor SL4 . . . .**209** D6
Paradise MK17 . . . .**57** D4
Paradise Mews RG9 . . . .**191** D2
Paradise Rd RG9 . . . .**191** C1
Parchment Cl HP6 . . . . . .**154** E2
Parish La SL2 . . . .**187** C1
Parish Piece HP15 . . . . . .**163** C7
Park Ave
Newport Pagnell MK16 . . . .**22** B4
Totternhoe LU6 . . . .**93** B8
Wraysbury TW19 . . . .**211** D3
Park Cl
Cosgrove MK19 . . . .**19** F2
Dunton MK18 . . . .**77** E5
Lane End HP14 . . . .**171** C5
Windsor SL4 . . . .**210** D5
Park Cnr SL4 . . . .**209** E4
Park Ct UB8 . . . .**201** D4
Parker Cl MK13 . . . .**34** A6
Parker Knoll Way
HP13 . . . .**173** A7
Parker Wlk HP19 . . . .**101** D3
Park Farm Rd HP12 . . . . .**161** B1
Park Farm Way HP14 . . . .**171** C5
Parkfield WD3 . . . .**167** F5
Parkfield Ave HP6 . . . . . .**154** D2
Parkfield Rise HP27 . . . . .**139** B2
Parkgate SL1 . . . .**197** C1
Park Gate LU7 . . . .**79** E1
Park Gdns MK3 . . . .**47** A1
Park Gr
Beaconsfield HP9 . . . .**175** C7
Little Chalfont HP8 . . . . . .**166** D6
Park Hill OX33 . . . .**122** B1
Park Ho
Berkhamsted HP4 . . . . . .**135** B5
Gerrards Cross SL9 . . . . .**188** E7
Maidenhead SL6 . . . .**202** E6
Park House Bsns Ctr
HP12 . . . .**172** E8
Park House Dr MK5 . . . . . .**45** F6
Park La
Beaconsfield HP9 . . . .**175** F1
Burnham SL1 . . . .**197** E7
Eaton Bray LU6 . . . .**92** D6
Hazelmere HP15 . . . .**163** A4
Horton SL3 . . . .**212** A4
Lane End HP14 . . . .**171** D5
Maidensgrove RG9 . . . . . .**179** D6
Paulerspury NN12 . . . .**17** B7
Slough SL3 . . . .**206** B3
Stokenchurch HP14 . . . . .**158** E6
Parkland Ave SL3 . . . . . .**206** D2
Parklands MK14 . . . .**21** D1
Park Lane Ct HP14 . . . . . .**158** E5
Park Lawn SL2 . . . .**198** D7
Park Lodge Ave UB7 . . . .**208** F4
Park Mdw HP27 . . . .**139** A3
Parkminster MK10 . . . .**36** A1
Park Parade SL2 . . . .**198** C3
Park Parade Ctr The
HP15 . . . .**163** A5
Park Pl
Amersham HP6 . . . .**154** F1
Seer Green HP9 . . . .**176** D5
Park Rd
Amersham HP6 . . . .**154** F2
Chesham HP5 . . . .**154** B8
Farnham Royal SL2 . . . . .**198** E3
Granborough MK18 . . . . . .**75** F6
Grendon Underwood HP18 **82** F8
Hanslope MK19 . . . .**11** B1
Hartwell NN7 . . . .**10** C8
Henley-on-Thames RG9 . .**191** E1
Milton Keynes MK11 . . . . .**32** D5
Sherington MK16 . . . .**14** A2
Stanwell TW19 . . . .**213** C1
Tring HP23 . . . .**118** F2
Uxbridge UB8 . . . .**201** E6
Winslow MK18 . . . .**65** F5
Park Rise HP4 . . . .**134** E6
Park Road E UB10 . . . . . .**201** D3
Park Road S MK18 . . . . . .**65** F4
Park Sch HP20 . . . .**101** F1

Parkside
Gerrards Cross SL9 . . . . .**188** F7
Henley-on-Thames RG9 . .**191** C2
Maidenhead SL6 . . . .**195** D1
Milton Keynes MK4 . . . . . .**46** E3
Naphill HP14 . . . .**150** B1
Parkside Wlk SL1 . . . . . .**206** A3
Park Sports Ctr OX33 . . .**122** B1
Park St
Aylesbury HP20 . . . .**115** F8
Berkhamsted HP4 . . . . . .**135** B5
High Wycombe HP11 . . . .**173** D6
Maidenhead SL6 . . . .**202** F7
Poyle SL3 . . . .**212** D6
Princes Risborough
HP27 . . . .**139** B3
Slough SL1 . . . .**205** F4
Tring HP23 . . . .**119** A3
Windsor SL4 . . . .**210** D6
Woburn MK17 . . . .**60** F7
Parkstone Lodge SL3 . . .**206** A3
Park Street Ind Est
HP20 . . . .**115** F8
Parkview
Flackwell Heath HP10 . . . .**185** B7
Maidenhead SL6 . . . .**202** F7
Park View
Newport Pagnell MK16 . . . .**22** D4
West Drayton UB7 . . . . . .**208** E6
Parkview Chase SL1 . . . .**204** E7
Park View Ct
Berkhamsted HP4 . . . . . .**135** B4
High Wycombe HP12 . . . .**172** D8
4 Leighton Buzzard LU7 . .**80** E7
Park View Rd
Berkhamsted HP4 . . . . . .**135** B4
Uxbridge UB8 . . . .**208** F7
Parkway
Bow Brickhill MK17 . . . . . .**48** D2
Marlow SL7 . . . .**184** A3
Woburn Sands MK17 . . . . .**49** A6
Parkway The SL0 . . . .**200** C4
Parkwood HP14 . . . .**150** A2
Park Wood, Gouldings
Wood Nature Reserve ✱
SL6 . . . .**194** E4
Parlaunt Park Comb Sch
SL3 . . . .**207** B3
Parlaunt Rd SL3 . . . .**207** B2
Parliament Cl HP16 . . . . .**151** B7
Parliament La SL6, SL1 . .**196** F5
Parliament Rd OX9 . . . . .**125** F1
Parmiter Cl HP19 . . . .**115** B8
PARMOOR **181** F7
Parmoor La RG9 . . . .**170** E1
Parneleys MK10 . . . .**35** F2
Parrock La MK10 . . . .**36** A2
Parrot Cl HP21 . . . .**115** B6
Parrott's La HP23 . . . . . .**133** A4
Parrs Rd HP14 . . . .**158** E4
Parry Cotts SL9 . . . .**177** E6
Parry Green N SL3 . . . . . .**206** F2
Parry Green S SL3 . . . . . .**207** A2
Parsley Cl
Aston Clinton HP22 . . . . .**117** C5
Walton MK7 . . . .**48** B5
Parslow Cl HP21 . . . .**115** D3
Parslow Ct HP21 . . . .**115** D3
Parsonage Cl
High Wycombe HP13 . . . .**173** C6
Tring HP23 . . . .**119** A4
Parsonage Ct **1** HP23 . .**119** A3
Parsonage Farm HP22 . . . .**89** B3
Parsonage Gdns SL7 . . .**183** E1
Parsonage La
Farnham Common SL2 . . .**198** D5
Windsor SL4 . . . .**210** B8
Parsonage Pl HP7 . . . . . .**165** C8
Parsonage Rd HP8 . . . . . .**177** B7
Parsons Cl MK18 . . . .**65** F6
Parsons Cres MK5 . . . . . .**46** C5
Parson's Fee HP20 . . . . . .**115** D8
Parsons La HP22 . . . .**102** B3
Parsons Rd SL3 . . . .**206** F1
Parsons Wlk HP15 . . . . . .**163** A5
Parson's Wood La SL2 . .**198** D5
Parton Cl HP22 . . . .**131** A5
Parton Rd HP20 . . . .**116** B8
Partridge Cl
Buckingham MK18 . . . . . .**52** F7
Chesham HP5 . . . .**144** E3
Leighton Buzzard LU7 . . .**104** F7
Partridge Mead SL6 . . . .**195** F2
Partridge Piece MK43 . . . .**25** C3
Partridge Way
7 Aylesbury HP19 . . . . . .**101** F3
High Wycombe HP13 . . . .**161** C2
Pascal Dr MK5 . . . .**45** F5
Pascomb Rd LU6 . . . .**93** F8
Passalewe La MK7 . . . . . .**48** D7
PASSENHAM **32** C4
Passmore MK6 . . . .**47** D6
Pastern Pl MK14 . . . .**35** A5
Pastures The
Aylesbury HP20 . . . .**102** B2
Edlesborough LU6 . . . .**92** F3
High Wycombe HP13 . . . .**161** E1

Patch Cl UB10 . . . .**201** F4
Patches Field SL7 . . . . . .**183** E5
Pateman Cl MK18 . . . .**41** C1
Patemore La RG9 . . . .**168** A1
Paterson Rd HP21 . . . . . .**115** C6
Patricia Cl SL1 . . . .**204** E6
Patrick Haugh Rd OX25 . . .**94** F7
Patricks La MK19 . . . .**31** F4
Patrick Way HP21 . . . . . .**116** A4
Patrington Cl UB8 . . . . . .**201** C2
Patriot Dr MK13 . . . .**34** B2
Patrons Way E UB9 . . . . .**189** F5
Patrons Way W UB9 . . . . .**189** F5
Patterson Ct HP10 . . . . . .**185** E7
Patterson Rd HP5 . . . . . .**144** B3
Pattison La MK15 . . . .**35** C3
PAULERSPURY **17** B7
Paulerspury CE Prim Sch
NN12 . . . .**17** B8
Pauls Hill HP10 . . . .**174** F6
Paul's Row HP11 . . . .**173** B6
Pavers Ct HP21 . . . .**115** D3
Pavilions The (Sh Ctr)
UB8 . . . .**201** C5
Pavilion Way HP4 . . . . . .**166** C8
Paxton Ave SL1 . . . .**205** C3
Paxton Cl MK46 . . . .**6** F3
Paxton Cres MK5 . . . .**46** B5
Paxton Rd HP4 . . . .**135** D4
Paynes Cl MK18 . . . .**41** D1
Paynes Dr MK5 . . . .**46** A8
Paynes Field Cl HP4 . . . .**134** D7
Payton Hos SL6 . . . .**195** E6
Peace La SL6 . . . .**195** F6
Peace Rd SL0, SL3 . . . . . .**200** A3
Peachey Cl UB8 . . . .**208** D7
Peachey La UB8 . . . .**208** D8
Peach Tree Ave UB7 . . . .**208** F7
Peacock Hay MK4 . . . .**46** C2
Peacock Rd SL7 . . . .**184** A3
Peacocks Cl HP4 . . . .**134** F6
Pea La HP4 . . . .**134** D7
Pearce Cl
Aylesbury HP21 . . . .**115** E4
Maidenhead SL6 . . . .**195** F1
Pearce Dr SL6 . . . .**195** F7
Pearce Rd
Chesham HP5 . . . .**144** B2
Maidenhead SL6 . . . .**195** F1
Pearce's Orch RG9 . . . . .**191** D3
Pearl Gdns SL1 . . . .**205** B5
Pearse Gr MK7 . . . .**48** A4
Pearson Cl HP19 . . . .**115** B6
Pear Tree Ave UB7 . . . . .**208** F7
Peartree Cl SL1 . . . .**204** F5
Pear Tree Cl
Amersham HP7 . . . .**165** F8
Seer Green HP9 . . . .**176** C4
Pear Tree Ct HP15 . . . . . .**163** C6
Pear Tree Farm Ind Units
OX27 . . . .**71** A2
Peartrees UB7 . . . .**208** D6
Peascod Pl **12** SL4 . . . . . .**210** D6
Peascod St SL4 . . . .**210** D6
Peascroft HP18 . . . .**125** D6
Peatey Ct HP13 . . . .**173** D6
Pebble Brook Sch
HP21 . . . .**115** C7
Pebble La
Aylesbury HP20 . . . .**115** D8
Brackley NN13 . . . .**38** A7
Pebblemoor LU6 . . . .**92** F3
Pebody Pl **10** MK46 . . . .**6** F3
Peckover Ct **8** MK8 . . . . . .**33** F1
Pecks Farm Cl HP22 . . . .**102** C4
Peddle Ct HP11 . . . .**172** F7
Pednor Bottom HP5 . . . . .**143** B3
PEDNORMEAD END **154** A7
Pednormead End HP5 . . .**154** B7
Pednor Rd HP5 . . . .**143** E2
Peebles HP3 . . . .**146** E6
Peel Cl SL4 . . . .**210** B4
Peel Ct
Monks Risborough
HP27 . . . .**139** B4
Slough SL3 . . . .**205** B8
Peel Rd MK12 . . . .**33** C6
Peel Way UB8 . . . .**208** E8
Peerless Dr UB9 . . . .**190** C7
Peers Dr MK17 . . . .**49** E3
Peers La MK5 . . . .**46** B6
Peggs La HP22 . . . .**117** F5
Pelham Ct SL6 . . . .**202** E7
Pelham Pl MK14 . . . .**34** F5
Pelham Rd OX9 . . . .**126** B1
Pelton Ct MK5 . . . .**46** C5
Pemberley Lodge SL4 . . .**210** A4
Pemberton Cl HP21 . . . . .**115** F5
Pemberton Rd SL2 . . . . . .**197** C1
Pembridge Chase **4**
HP3 . . . .**146** A3
Pembridge Cl **3** HP3 . . . .**146** A3
Pembridge Gr MK4 . . . . . .**45** F1
Pembridge Rd HP3 . . . . . .**146** A3
Pembroke Ho
2 Milton Keynes MK3 . . . . .**46** F1
7 Olney MK46 . . . .**6** F3
Pembroke Rd HP20 . . . . .**101** F1

Pencarrow Pl MK6 . . . . 35 A1
Pendeen Ct SL1 . . . . 205 A5
Pendennis Ct MK4 . . . . . . 57 A8
Pendles Paddocks
 HP14 . . . . 158 F2
Pendrill Ho 2 HP12 . . . . . 172 E7
Penfold HP22 . . . . 116 F2
Penfold Cotts HP15 . . . . . 163 D7
Penfold La
 Holmer Green HP15 . . . . 163 E8
 Hyde Heath HP7, HP15 . . 152 F1
Pengelly Ct 2 MK6 . . . . . . 35 A1
Penhale Cl MK4 . . . . 57 B8
Penhow Rise MK4 . . . . 45 E1
Penina Cl MK3 . . . . 46 D1
Pennington Rd HP9 . . . . . 186 B8
Penlee Rise MK4 . . . . 57 B8
Penley Cl OX39 . . . . 147 B6
Penling Cl SL6 . . . . 195 E6
Penmon MK10 . . . . 35 F1
Penmoor Cl HP12 . . . . . . 172 C8
PENN 174 E7
Penn Ave HP15 . . . . 144 A1
Penn Cl
 Chorleywood WD3 . . . . . 167 D3
 Uxbridge UB8 . . . . 201 D1
Penn Ct
 14 Marlow SL7 . . . . 183 E2
 Tylers Green HP10 . . . . . 174 B8
Penn Dr UB9 . . . . 189 F5
Pennefather Ct 3
 HP21 . . . . 115 E7
Penn Gaskell La SL9 . . . . . 177 F5
Penn Gn HP9 . . . . 175 D4
Penn Haven SL9 . . . . 188 F6
Pennine Rd SL2 . . . . 205 A8
Pennings The HP22 . . . . . 131 B5
Pennington Pl OX9 . . . . . 126 B1
Pennington Rd
 Chalfont St Peter SL9 . . 177 D3
 High Wycombe HP13 . . . 173 F4
Penningtons The HP6 . . . . 154 E2
Penn Mdw SL2 . . . . 198 F4
Penn Mead HP10 . . . . . . 174 F7
Penn Rd
 Aylesbury HP21 . . . . . . 115 D7
 Beaconsfield HP9 . . . . . 175 C5
 Chalfont St Peter SL9 . . 177 D2
 Chorleywood WD3 . . . . 167 F1
 Datchet SL3 . . . . 211 D6
 Hazlemere HP15 . . . . . 163 B3
 Milton Keynes MK2 . . . . 58 E8
 Slough SL2 . . . . 198 D1
Penn Sch HP10 . . . . 174 D7
PENN STREET 164 B5
Penn Street Works Ind Est
 HP7 . . . . 164 A4
Penn Way WD3 . . . . 167 D3
Penn Wood Sch SL2 . . . . 198 D1
Penn Wood View HP7 . . . 164 A4
Pennycress Way MK16 . . . 21 F4
Pennycuik MK17 . . . . 59 C1
PENNYLAND 35 A6
Pennylets Gn SL2 . . . . . . 199 A5
Penny Pk Rd MK16 . . . . . 22 F3
Pennyroyal MK7 . . . . 48 B7
Penrith Cl UB8 . . . . 201 D5
Penrith Way HP21 . . . . . . 116 B7
Penryn Ave MK6 . . . . 35 A2
Penshurst Cl HP13 . . . . . . 177 D1
Penshurst Cres MK6 . . . . . 47 D4
Penshurst Rd SL6 . . . . . . 202 D5
Pentewan Gate MK6 . . . . 34 F2
Pentland Rd
 Aylesbury HP21 . . . . . . 115 F6
 Slough SL2 . . . . 205 A8
Pentlands MK11 . . . . 32 F4
Pentlands Cl HP13 . . . . . . 174 B4
Pentlands The HP13 . . . . . 174 B4
Penwith Sch MK6 . . . . 34 F1
Penwood Ct SL6 . . . . 202 B7
Penwood La SL7 . . . . 183 C1
Penyston Rd SL6 . . . . 202 C7
Penzance Spur SL2 . . . . . 198 B1
Peplar Way SL1 . . . . 197 B2
Peplow Cl UB7 . . . . 208 D5
Peppard Mdw HP11 . . . . . 151 D5
Pepper Hill Fst Sch
 MK13 . . . . 34 A7
PEPPERSHILL 124 D6
Peppett's Gn HP5 . . . . . . 143 D8
Peppiatts The LU6 . . . . . . 92 B5
Pepys Cl SL3 . . . . 212 B8
Pepys Dr HP16 . . . . 151 C6
Perch Cl SL7 . . . . 194 C8
Percheron Pl MK14 . . . . . 34 F1
Perch Mdws HP22 . . . . . . 131 B8
Percy Bush Rd UB7 . . . . . 208 F3
Percy Pl SL3 . . . . 211 B6
Percy Terr HP8 . . . . 177 A7
Peregrine HP19 . . . . 101 E3
Peregrine Bsns Pk
 HP13 . . . . 174 A5
Peregrine Cl MK6 . . . . 47 B8
Perivale MK10 . . . . 35 E1
Perks La HP16 . . . . 151 C3
Permayne MK13 . . . . 34 A7
Perracombe MK4 . . . . 46 E3
Perran Ave MK6 . . . . 35 A5

Perrin Springs La RG9 . . . 170 F1
Perrycroft SL4 . . . . 209 F4
Perryfields Way SL1 . . . . . 197 B1
Perry Hill HP18 . . . . 73 A3
Perry Ho SL1 . . . . 197 B2
Perry La
 Bledlow HP27 . . . . 138 C2
 Sherington MK16 . . . . . . 14 B2
Perryman Way SL2 . . . . . 197 F2
Perry Mead LU6 . . . . 92 E6
Perry St HP22 . . . . 131 A5
Perrys The HP22 . . . . 131 B5
Pershore Croft 1 MK10 . . 36 A1
Perth Ave SL1 . . . . 205 B7
Perth Cl MK3 . . . . 46 F2
Perth Rd HP13 . . . . 173 D8
Perth Trad Est SL1 . . . . . 205 B8
Peterborough Ave 2
 HP13 . . . . 173 C7
Peterborough Gate
 MK15 . . . . 35 C6
Peterhead Mews SL3 . . . 207 A1
Peterhill Cl SL9 . . . . 177 E5
Peterley Ave HP15,
 HP16 . . . . 151 E3
Peterley La HP16 . . . . . . 151 E3
Peter's Cl HP16 . . . . 151 C6
Petersfield HP22 . . . . 116 C3
Petersfield Ave SL2 . . . . . 206 A5
Petersfield Gn 5 MK9 . . . 34 E1
Petersham Cl MK16 . . . . . 22 C2
Peters La HP27 . . . . 139 E4
Peter's Pl HP4 . . . . 134 E6
Petronel Rd HP19 . . . . . . 101 D4
PETSOE END 14 A7
Pettifer Way HP12 . . . . . . 172 D6
Pettingrew Cl MK7 . . . . . . 48 B6
Petty Cross SL1 . . . . 204 E7
Petworth MK8 . . . . 33 E1
Petworth Ct SL4 . . . . 210 B6
Petworth Ho 2 MK8 . . . . 33 F1
Pevensey Cl
 Aylesbury HP21 . . . . . . 116 B5
 Milton Keynes MK3 . . . . 57 E7
Pevensey Rd SL2 . . . . . . 205 A8
Peverel Dr MK1 . . . . 47 B3
Peveril Cl HP21 . . . . 116 B5
Pevers La MK46 . . . . 6 A1
Pheasant Cl
 Berkhamsted HP4 . . . . . 135 C4
 Tring HP23 . . . . 119 B6
Pheasant Dr HP13 . . . . . . 161 C1
Pheasant Hill HP8 . . . . . . 177 C8
Pheasant Rise HP5 . . . . . 154 D6
PHEASANTS 181 E6
Pheasants Croft SL6 . . . . 202 A4
Pheasants Dr HP15 . . . . . 163 B5
Pheasants Ridge SL7 . . . . 183 C2
Pheasant Wlk SL9 . . . . . . 177 E6
Phelps Rd MK2 . . . . 58 E6
Philbey Mews SL1 . . . . . . 204 F4
Philip Cotts SL8 . . . . 185 C3
Philip Dr HP10 . . . . 185 C7
Philip Rd HP13 . . . . 173 D7
Philipshill Wood Reserve*
 WD3 . . . . 167 A2
Philips Rd HP19 . . . . 115 A8
Phillimore Cl MK15 . . . . . . 35 B7
Phillip Ct MK5 . . . . 46 B6
Philpots Cl UB7 . . . . 208 D6
Philps Cl HP11 . . . . 171 C4
Phipps Cl
 Aylesbury HP20 . . . . . . 102 A2
 Maidenhead SL6 . . . . . 202 A2
Phipps Rd SL1 . . . . 204 E8
Phoebe La MK17 . . . . 48 E6
Phoebe's Orch MK17 . . . . 69 E7
Phoenix Bsns Ctr 3
 HP5 . . . . 144 B1
Phoenix Cl SL6 . . . . 202 D4
Phoenix Dr MK6 . . . . 46 E6
Phoenix Ho 7 MK8 . . . . . 45 E1
Phoenix House Bsns Ctr
 HP12 . . . . 172 E8
Phygtle The SL9 . . . . 177 E4
Phyllis Court Dr RG9 . . . . 191 E3
Picasso Pl HP19 . . . . 100 F2
Piccadilly Mews MK18 . . . 66 A5
Pickering Dr MK4 . . . . 46 A2
Pickford Dr SL3 . . . . 207 A5
Pickfords Gdns SL3 . . . . 205 E5
Pickins Piece SL3 . . . . . . 212 A5
Pickwick Terr SL2 . . . . . . 206 B6
Picton St MK4 . . . . 45 E1
Picts La HP27 . . . . 139 A2
PIDDINGTON
 Blackthorn 95 E7
 High Wycombe 160 B1
 Northamptonshire 4 B8
Piddington La HP14 . . . . . 171 B8
Piddington Rd HP18 . . . . . 96 A8
Pield Heath House Sch
 UB8 . . . . 201 F1
Pield Heath Rd UB8 . . . . . 201 F1
Pierson Rd SL4 . . . . 209 D6
Pigeon Farm Rd HP14 . . . 158 E5
Piggotts End 6 HP7 . . . . 165 B7
Piggott's Hill HP14 . . . . . 150 E1

Piggotts Orch HP7 . . . . . 165 B7
Piggy La WD3 . . . . 167 B3
Pightle Cres MK18 . . . . . . 41 D2
Pightle The
 Buckingham MK18 . . . . . 41 D1
 Maids Moreton MK18 . . . 41 F4
 Oving HP22 . . . . 86 D7
 Pitstone LU7 . . . . 105 D3
Pigott Dr MK5 . . . . 46 A4
Pigott Orch HP22 . . . . 85 A5
Pike Cl
 Marlow SL7 . . . . 194 C8
 Uxbridge UB10 . . . . . . 201 F4
Pike Cnr HP21 . . . . 116 C5
Pilch Field Wildlife
 Reserve* MK17 . . . . 54 B5
Pilch La MK17 . . . . 54 D4
Pilgrims Cl HP27 . . . . 139 D5
Pilgrim St MK15 . . . . 35 A4
Pilot Trad Est HP12 . . . . . 172 E8
PIMLICO 26 F6
Pimlico Ct 4 MK10 . . . . . . 35 F1
Pimms Cl HP13 . . . . 174 A6
Pimms Gr HP13 . . . . 174 A5
Pimpernel Gr MK7 . . . . . . 48 B6
Pinchfield WD3 . . . . 178 D5
Pinders Croft MK12 . . . . . 33 B5
PINDON END 10 C4
Pineapple Rd HP7 . . . . . . 165 F8
Pine Chase HP12 . . . . . . 172 B3
Pine Cl
 Berkhamsted HP4 . . . . . 135 B4
 Buckingham MK18 . . . . . 41 E3
 Hazlemere HP15 . . . . . 163 B3
 Maidenhead SL6 . . . . . 202 B7
Pine Crest Mews LU7 . . . . 80 E6
Pinecroft SL7 . . . . 183 D4
Pine Ct HP5 . . . . 154 C8
Pine Gr MK17 . . . . 49 A4
PINEHAM 35 E7
Pineham Rdbt MK15 . . . . . 35 E5
Pine Hill HP15 . . . . 162 F3
Pinels Way HP11 . . . . 172 E3
Piner Cotts SL4 . . . . 209 E4
Pine Rd LU6 . . . . 106 F8
Pines Cl
 Amersham HP6 . . . . . . 154 B2
 Little Kingshill HP16 . . . 152 B4
Pine St HP19 . . . . 115 A8
Pines The
 Felden HP3 . . . . 146 F7
 Slough SL3 . . . . 206 F5
 Tylers Green HP10 . . . . 163 B7
Pinetree Cl SL9 . . . . 177 C3
Pine Trees Dr UB10 . . . . 201 E8
Pine Wlk
 Berkhamsted HP4 . . . . . 134 D7
 Hazlemere HP15 . . . . . 163 B3
Pinewood Ave UB8 . . . . . 208 F7
Pinewood Cl
 Gerrards Cross SL9 . . . . 188 C4
 Iver Heath SL0 . . . . . . 200 C5
Pinewood Dr MK2 . . . . . . 58 E7
Pinewood Film Studios
 SL0 . . . . 200 B5
Pinewood Gn SL0 . . . . . . 200 C5
Pinewood Mews TW19 . . . 213 D1
Pinewood Rd
 High Wycombe HP12 . . . 172 C7
 Iver Heath SL0 . . . . . . 200 B4
Pinfold MK7 . . . . 48 B6
PINFOLDPOND 60 E6
Pinfold Yd MK18 . . . . 51 B6
Pinglestone Cl UB7 . . . . . 213 E7
Pinions Rd HP13 . . . . 173 E5
Pinkard Ct MK6 . . . . 47 C8
Pink Hill HP27 . . . . 149 E8
Pink La SL1 . . . . 197 B3
Pinkneys Dr SL6 . . . . 195 A1
Pinkneys Rd SL6 . . . . 202 A8
Pink Rd HP27 . . . . 149 E7
Pinks Cl MK5 . . . . 46 C8
Pinkworthy MK4 . . . . 46 D4
Pinn Cl UB8 . . . . 208 D7
Pinstone Way SL9 . . . . . . 189 B2
Pintail Cl HP19 . . . . 101 E4
Pipard MK14 . . . . 34 E7
Pipers Cl SL1 . . . . 197 C2
Pipers Corner Sch
 HP15 . . . . 162 B7
Pipers Croft LU6 . . . . 93 F7
Pipers Ct SL1 . . . . 197 C2
Pipers La HP15 . . . . 162 C8
Pipers Wood Cotts
 HP7 . . . . 153 C2
Pipit Gdns 7 HP19 . . . . . 101 E4
Pipit Wlk 8 HP19 . . . . . . 101 E4
Pippin Cl UB8 . . . . 22 B3
Pippins Cl UB7 . . . . 208 D3
Pippins Sch SL3 . . . . 212 F6
Pippins The SL3 . . . . 206 F5
Pipston Gn
 Milton Keynes MK7 . . . . 48 B7
 Walton MK7 . . . . 48 B6
PISHILL 179 D8
PISHILL BANK 168 B1
Pishill Bank RG9 . . . . . . 168 B1
PISHILL BOTTOM 168 A1

Pistone Green Bsns Pk
 LU7 . . . . 105 D2
Pistone Windmill*
 LU7 . . . . 105 F4
PITCHCOTT 86 B5
Pitchcott Rd HP22 . . . . . . 86 B6
Pitcher La MK5 . . . . 46 B8
Pitchford Ave MK18 . . . . . 41 E2
Pitchford Wlk MK18 . . . . . 41 F1
PITCH GREEN 138 B3
Pitch Pond Cl HP9 . . . . . 175 C5
Pitch The HP14 . . . . 159 D3
Pitfield MK11 . . . . 33 B3
PITSTONE 105 D4
Pitstone Green Farm Mus*
 LU7 . . . . 105 D4
Pitters Piece HP18 . . . . . 125 B7
Pitt Gn MK18 . . . . 41 F1
Pitts Rd SL1 . . . . 205 C5
Place Farm Ho HP27 . . . . 139 B6
Place Farm Way HP27 . . . 139 B5
Plackett Way SL1 . . . . . . 204 D5
Plaines Cl SL1 . . . . 204 F5
Plaistow Cres MK10 . . . . . 35 F1
Plaiters Cl HP23 . . . . 119 B4
Plantain Ct MK7 . . . . 48 B6
Plantation Pl MK5 . . . . . . 46 A4
Plantation Rd
 Amersham HP6 . . . . . . 154 E2
 High Wycombe HP13 . . . 174 A7
 Leighton Buzzard LU7 . . 70 F3
Plantation Way HP6 . . . . 154 E2
Platt The HP7 . . . . 165 B8
Playing Field Rd NN13 . . . 39 A4
Pleasant Cotts SL0 . . . . . 200 B2
Pleasant Pl WD3 . . . . 178 E3
Pleasaunce The HP22 . . . 117 E5
Pleshey Cl MK5 . . . . 46 B6
Plested Ct HP22 . . . . 116 C2
Plomer Green Ave
 HP13 . . . . 161 D2
Plomer Green La HP13 . . 161 D3
Plomer Hill HP13 . . . . . . 161 D1
Plough Cl HP21 . . . . 115 E3
Plough End HP22 . . . . . . 102 B4
Plough La
 Sarratt WD4 . . . . 156 F6
 Wexham Street SL2 . . . 199 B4
Ploughlees La SL1 . . . . . 205 E6
Ploughley Rd OX25 . . . . . 94 E8
Plover Cl
 1 Berkhamsted HP4 . . . 135 C3
 Buckingham MK18 . . . . . 52 E7
 Newport Pagnell MK16 . . 22 F3
Plover The 4 HP19 . . . . . 101 E4
Plover Wlk 6 HP19 . . . . . 101 E4
Plowman Cl MK12 . . . . . . 33 B5
Plumer Rd HP11 . . . . 172 E7
Plum Park La MK12 . . . . . 17 D8
PLUMPTON END 17 C7
Plumstead Ave MK13 . . . . 34 D3
Pluto Cl SL1 . . . . 204 E4
Pluto Way HP19 . . . . 101 D4
Plym Cl HP21 . . . . 115 C5
Plymouth Gr MK4 . . . . 46 B1
Plymouth Rd SL1 . . . . . . 204 E8
Pocketts Yd SL6 . . . . 196 B7
Pocock Ave UB7 . . . . 208 F3
Pococks La SL4 . . . . 205 E1
Poets Chase HP21 . . . . . 115 F6
Points The SL6 . . . . 202 B3
Polar Pk UB7 . . . . 213 F7
Poles Hill
 Chesham HP5 . . . . 144 A2
 Sarratt WD4 . . . . 156 E6
Police Hos SL9 . . . . 188 D3
Polidoris La HP15 . . . . . . 163 C7
Polish Ave HP22 . . . . 131 E8
Pollard Ave UB9 . . . . 189 F5
Pollard Cl SL4 . . . . 211 B2
Pollards WD3 . . . . 178 D5
Pollys Yd MK14 . . . . 22 C5
Pollywick Rd HP23 . . . . . 119 D1
Polmartin Ct 1 MK6 . . . . 35 A1
Polruan Pl
 Fishermead MK6 . . . . . . 47 A8
 Milton Keynes MK6 . . . . 35 A1
Polygon Bsns Ctr SL3 . . . 212 F5
Pomander Cres MK7 . . . . 48 B7
Pomeroy Cl HP7 . . . . 165 D7
Pond App HP15 . . . . 163 C7
Pond Cl
 Newton Longville MK17 . . 57 C2
 Tring HP23 . . . . 119 A4
 Winchmore Hill HP7 . . . 164 C3
Pond Cotts HP14 . . . . . . 171 B4
Pondgate MK7 . . . . 48 B8
Pond La
 Chalfont St Peter SL9 . . 177 C2
 Little Gaddesden HP4 . . 121 E7
POND PARK 144 A2
Pond Park Rd HP5 . . . . . 144 B2
Pondwicks HP7 . . . . 165 B8
Pony Field The HP22 . . . . 116 D1
Pool La SL1 . . . . 205 E6
Poolmans Rd SL4 . . . . . . 209 D4
Pope Ct HP23 . . . . 118 F3
Popes Acre HP17 . . . . . . 126 F5

Popes Cl
 Amersham HP6 . . . . . . 154 F2
 Colnbrook SL3 . . . . . . 212 C7
Popes La SL6 . . . . 195 C7
Pope Way HP21 . . . . 115 E4
Poplar Ave UB7 . . . . 208 F6
Poplar Cl
 Aylesbury HP20 . . . . . . 102 A2
 Chesham HP5 . . . . 144 C3
 Milton Keynes MK6 . . . . 47 E5
 Poyle SL3 . . . . 212 E6
Poplar Ho SL3 . . . . 206 F1
Poplar Rd
 Aylesbury HP20 . . . . . . 102 A2
 New Denham UB9 . . . . 201 C6
 Wooburn Green HP10 . . 185 E7
Poplars Cl HP17 . . . . 114 C5
Poplars Gr SL6 . . . . 196 B2
Poplars Rd MK18 . . . . 52 D8
Poplars The HP22 . . . . . . 131 C5
Poppy Ave MK10 . . . . 36 B4
Poppy Rd HP27 . . . . 139 A2
Porlock La MK4 . . . . 46 C4
Portal Cl UB10 . . . . 201 F5
Portal Rd HP22 . . . . 131 D6
Portchester Ct 1 MK8 . . . 33 F1
Porter's Cl MK19 . . . . 31 E4
Porters Way UB7 . . . . . . 208 F4
Portfield Cl MK18 . . . . 52 E8
Port Field Farm MK16 . . . 21 F5
Portfields Comb Sch
 MK16 . . . . 22 A5
Portfields Rd MK16 . . . . . 22 B4
Portfield Way MK18 . . . . . 52 E8
Porthcawl Gn MK3 . . . . . . 57 C8
Porthleven Pl MK6 . . . . . . 35 A2
Porthmellin Cl MK4 . . . . . 57 B8
Portishead Dr MK4 . . . . . . 56 F8
Portland Bsns Ctr SL3 . . . 211 B6
Portland Cl SL2 . . . . 197 D1
Portland Dr MK15 . . . . . . 35 C7
Portland Gdns SL7 . . . . . 183 D1
Portland Ho HP13 . . . . . . 173 D8
Portland Pk SL9 . . . . 188 D5
Portlands Alley SL7 . . . . . 183 D1
Portlands Mews 1
 SL7 . . . . 183 D1
Portlock Rd SL6 . . . . 202 C7
Portman Mews HP19 . . . . 114 E4
Portmarnock Cl MK3 . . . . 57 D8
Portnall Pl MK43 . . . . 25 E2
Portobello Cl HP5 . . . . . . 144 A2
Portobello Cotts
 Lacey Green HP27 . . . . 149 E5
 Lewknor OX49 . . . . 157 C2
Portrush Cl MK3 . . . . 57 D8
Portsmouth Ct SL1 . . . . . 205 E6
Portway
 Milton Keynes, Bradwell
  Common MK5, MK9, MK13,
  MK14, MK15 . . . . 34 D2
 Milton Keynes, Shenley Church
  End MK8, MK5 . . . . . . 45 F6
 North Marston MK18 . . . 76 B1
 Stone HP17 . . . . 114 E4
Portway Dr HP19 . . . . . . 161 B1
Portway Rd
 Stone HP17 . . . . 114 E4
 Twyford MK18 . . . . 62 D1
Portway Rdbt MK5 . . . . . . 34 B1
PORTWAYS 168 B8
Posting Ho HP23 . . . . . . 120 A5
Post Mdw SL0 . . . . 200 D2
Post Office Cotts SL2 . . . 199 A5
Post Office La
 Beaconsfield HP9 . . . . . 175 D3
 Slough SL3 . . . . 206 D7
 Whitchurch HP22 . . . . . 87 A6
Potash Cl HP17 . . . . 126 F5
Potash La HP23 . . . . 104 A5
Potkiln La HP9 . . . . 176 D1
Potter Row HP16 . . . . . . 142 C1
Potters Cl HP16 . . . . 151 B7
Potters Cross SL0 . . . . . . 200 E2
Potters Cross Cres
 HP15 . . . . 162 B2
Potters Glen MK18 . . . . . . 53 B1
Potters La MK11 . . . . 33 B4
POTTERSPURY 18 D2
Potterspury Lodge Sch
 NN12 . . . . 18 B6
Pottery Cl HP19 . . . . 115 A7
Pottery Ct HP19 . . . . 115 A7
Potts Pl 8 SL7 . . . . 183 D2
Poulcott TW19 . . . . 211 E1
Pound Cl
 Steeple Claydon MK18 . . 63 D3
 Wicken MK19 . . . . 31 A4
Pound Cotts SL7 . . . . . . 183 C1
Poundfield La SL6 . . . . . . 195 F4
Poundfield Rd NN12 . . . . 18 E2
Pound Hill MK17 . . . . 59 C1
Pound La
 Heath End HP5 . . . . . . 134 A1
 Little Marlow SL7 . . . . . 184 C4
 Marlow SL7 . . . . 183 D1

Pound La continued
North Crawley MK16 . . . . 24 B7
Preston Bissett MK18 . . . . 51 C1
POUNDON 71 E7
Pounds Cl MK43 . . . . 25 B1
Pound St HP22 . . . . 131 B4
Pound The
Cookham Rise SL6 . . . . . 195 F7
Cookham SL6 . . . . 196 A7
Slough SL1 . . . . 197 D1
Syresham NN13 . . . . 27 B7
Powell Haven MK10 . . . . . 35 E3
Powis Cl SL6 . . . . 202 B4
Powis La MK4 . . . . 45 F2
Powney Rd SL6 . . . . 202 C7
POYLE 212 E2
Poyle 14 Trad Est SL3 . . 212 E4
Poyle La SL1 . . . . 197 B3
Poyle New Cotts SL3 . . 212 F5
Poyle Pk SL3 . . . . 212 E4
Poyle Rd SL3 . . . . 212 E5
Poyle Tech Ctr The
SL3 . . . . 212 E5
Poynings The SL0 . . . . . . 207 F2
Pratt Ho HP6 . . . . 154 F1
Prebendal Ave HP21 . . . . 115 D7
Prebendal Cl 11 HP20 . . 115 D8
Prebendal Cl 1 HP20 . . . 115 D8
PREBENDAL FARM 115 B7
Precedent Dr MK13 . . . . . 34 B3
Precincts The SL1 . . . . . 197 C1
Prentice Gr MK5 . . . . 46 B3
Prescott Rd SL3 . . . . 212 E5
Prescotts The UB9 . . . . . 189 F3
Presley Way MK8 . . . . . . 45 E7
Press Rd UB8 . . . . 201 D6
PRESTON BISSETT 62 B8
Preston Ct MK15 . . . . 35 B7
Preston Hill HP5 . . . . 144 D2
Preston Rd SL2 . . . . 206 C6
Prestwick Cl MK3 . . . . 57 D7
Prestwold Ho HP19 . . . . . 115 A7
Prestwold Way HP19 . . . 115 A7
PRESTWOOD 151 D6
Prestwood SL2 . . . . 206 B7
Prestwood Cl HP12 . . . . . 172 D8
Prestwood Inf Sch
HP16 . . . . 151 C7
Prestwood Jun Sch
HP16 . . . . 151 C6
Prestwood Lodge Specl Sch
HP16 . . . . 151 D5
Pretoria Rd HP13 . . . . . . 173 C8
Priest End OX9 . . . . 125 E1
Priestland Gdns HP4 . . . 135 E6
Priestley Ct HP13 . . . . . . 173 D6
Priests Paddock HP9 . . 175 B5
Primatt Cres MK5 . . . . . . 46 B6
Primrose Cotts HP14 . . . 150 E1
Primrose Ct HP21 . . . . . . 115 B6
Primrose Dr
Aylesbury HP21 . . . . 115 B5
West Drayton UB7 . . . . . 208 D2
Primrose Gdns LU7 . . . . . 80 E7
Primrose Gn HP15 . . . . . 162 F6
Primrose Hill HP15 . . . . . 162 F7
Primrose La MK10 . . . . . . 36 C3
Primrose Lea SL7 . . . . . . 183 D2
Primrose Terr HP18 . . . . 110 A8
Primrose Way MK18 . . . . 52 C7
Prince Albert's Wlk SL3,
SL4 . . . . 211 B5
Prince Andrew Cl SL6 . . 203 B8
Prince Andrew Rd SL6 . . 196 B1
Prince Consort Cotts
SL4 . . . . 210 D5
Prince Consort's Dr
SL4 . . . . 210 D5
Prince Edward St HP4 . . 135 C4
Prince Philip Ave MK43 . . 3 C8
Prince Rupert Dr HP19 . 101 C4
PRINCES
RISBOROUGH 139 D4
Princes Risborough Prim
Sch HP27 . . . . 139 B5
Princes Risborough Sch
HP27 . . . . 139 C2
Princes Risborough Sta
HP27 . . . . 138 F2
Princess Ave SL4 . . . . . . 210 B4
Princess Gr HP9 . . . . 176 D6

Princess Margaret Hospl
The (private) SL4 . . . . . . 210 D5
Princess St SL6 . . . . 202 F6
Princes St
Piddington HP14 . . . . . . 160 B1
Slough SL1 . . . . 206 B4
Princes Terr SL8 . . . . . . 185 C3
Princes Way MK2 . . . . . . 58 C8
Princes Way Rdbt MK2 . . 58 B8
Printers End HP19 . . . . . 101 B1
Prior Gr HP5 . . . . 144 C1
Priors Cl
Maidenhead SL6 . . . . . . 203 B2
5 Slough SL1 . . . . 206 A3
Priors Pk MK4 . . . . 46 D2
Priors Rd SL4 . . . . 209 C4
Priors Way SL6 . . . . 203 B2
Priors Way Ind Est SL6 . 203 B2
Priory Ave
High Wycombe HP13 . . . 173 B7
South Harefield UB9 . . . 190 C7
Priory Cl
Aylesbury HP19 . . . . 101 C2
Denham UB9 . . . . 190 A1
Horton-cum-S OX33 . . . . 108 B5
Newport Pagnell MK16 . . 22 E4
South Harefield UB9 . . . 190 C7
Priory Common Sch
MK13 . . . . 34 B4
Priory Cotts UB9 . . . . . . 190 C7
Priory Cres HP19 . . . . . . 101 C2
Priory Ct 2 HP4 . . . . 135 C4
Priory Farm Cotts OX27 . 71 E2
Priory Gdns
Berkhamsted HP4 . . . . . 135 C4
South Harefield UB9 . . . 190 C7
Priory Rd
Gerrards Cross SL9 . . . . 188 D8
High Wycombe HP13 . . . 173 B7
Slough SL1 . . . . 204 D8
Priory Rise Sch MK4 . . . . 56 E7
Priory Sch SL1 . . . . 204 D8
Priory St MK16 . . . . 22 E4
Priory Way
Datchet SL3 . . . . 211 B7
Gerrards Cross SL9 . . . . 188 D8
Harmondsworth UB7 . . . 213 E8
Pritchard Ct MK14 . . . . . . 34 E8
Proctor Rise MK8 . . . . . . 45 D6
Progress Bsns Ctr SL1 . 204 D7
Progress Rd HP12 . . . . . 172 B7
Promenade SL4 . . . . 210 C7
Prospect Cl MK17 . . . . . . 68 D6
Prospect Cotts HP11 . . . 161 D6
Prospect Ct
Lane End HP14 . . . . 171 B5
Yardley Gobion NN12 . . . 18 F6
Prospect Pl
Castlethorpe MK19 . . . . . 19 F5
Hurley SL6 . . . . 193 F3
3 Windsor SL4 . . . . 210 D4
Wing LU7 . . . . 79 E2
Prospect Rd
Marlow SL7 . . . . 183 D2
Milton Keynes MK11 . . . . 32 C5
Prothero Cl HP21 . . . . . . 115 E4
Protheroe Field MK7 . . . . 48 D4
Providence Pl
9 Maidenhead SL6 . . . . 202 F7
2 Milton Keynes MK13 . . 34 A4
Providence Rd UB7 . . . . 208 F5
Prudential Bldgs 1
SL1 . . . . 205 F4
PUDDS CROSS 145 E2
Pudseys Cl SL6 . . . . 195 B6
Puers Field HP9 . . . . 176 E4
Puers La HP9 . . . . 176 E4
Puffin Way HP19 . . . . 101 F3
Pulborough Cl MK3 . . . . . 46 D1
Pulford Rd LU7 . . . . 80 F6
Pullfields HP5 . . . . 144 A1
Pulpit Cl HP5 . . . . 144 A2
Pulpit La HP22 . . . . 76 D1
Pumpkin Hill SL1 . . . . . . 197 E6
Pump Lane N SL7 . . . . . . 183 F6
Pump Lane S SL7 . . . . . . 184 A4
Pump Mdw HP16 . . . . . . 152 A8
Pump Pl MK19 . . . . 32 B7
Pumpus Gn MK18 . . . . . . 66 A4
Punch Bowl La HP5 . . . . 154 C7
Purbeck MK13 . . . . 34 C6
Purbeck Cl HP21 . . . . . . 116 B5
Purcel Dr MK16 . . . . 22 C3
Purse La MK16 . . . . 11 F8
Pursers Ct SL2 . . . . 205 E7
Pursell Cl SL6 . . . . 202 A3
Pursell Pl HP27 . . . . 139 B5
Pursells Mdw HP14 . . . . 161 C2
Purton Cl SL2 . . . . 198 C5
Purton La SL2 . . . . 198 C5
PURY END 17 A7
Pury Rd
Alderton NN12 . . . . 9 A2
Paulerspury NN12 . . . . . . 17 D8
Pusey Way HP14 . . . . . . 171 C5
Putlowes Dr HP18 . . . . . 100 C3
Putman Ho MK5 . . . . 46 C5
Putman Pl RG9 . . . . 191 E1
Putnams Dr HP22 . . . . . 117 D5

PUTTENHAM 103 F2
Puttenham Ct HP23 . . . . 103 F2
PUXLEY 31 D7
Puxley Rd
Deanshanger MK19 . . . . . 31 D5
Milton Keynes MK19 . . . . 32 A5
Pye Bridge End MK10 . . 36 A4
Pyebush La HP9 . . . . 187 A8
Pyghtles The HP22 . . . . . 85 B5
Pyghtle The
Olney MK46 . . . . 6 F3
Turvey MK43 . . . . 8 E6
Pyke Hayes MK8 . . . . 33 D3
Pymcombe Cl HP27 . . . . 139 B5
Pym Wlk OX9 . . . . 125 F1
Pynefield Ho WD3 . . . . . 167 F2
Pyxe Ct MK7 . . . . 48 A4

Q

Quadrangle The HP13 . . 173 E7
Quadrans Cl MK15 . . . . . . 35 A7
Quadrant The
High Wycombe HP13 . . . 162 E1
Maidenhead SL6 . . . . . . 203 A6
QUAINTON 85 B5
Quainton CE Comb Sch
HP22 . . . . 85 A5
QUAINTON HILL 75 B1
Quainton Rd
North Marston MK18 . . . . 76 A2
Waddesdon HP18 . . . . . . 99 A7
Quainton Road Sta★
HP22 . . . . 84 F2
Quaker's Mead HP22 . . . 116 F3
Quakers Mede HP17 . . . 127 A6
Quantock Cl SL3 . . . . 207 A1
Quantock Cres MK4 . . . . 46 D2
QUARRENDON 101 B3
Quarrendon Ave HP19 . . 101 B3
Quarrendon Rd HP7 . . . . 165 E7
Quarry Cl HP18 . . . . 125 C7
Quarry Cl LU7 . . . . 105 B5
Quarrydale Dr SL7 . . . . . 183 F2
Quarry Green Cl MK19 . . 31 B3
Quarry Rd LU7 . . . . 105 D2
Quarry Wood Rd SL6,
SL7 . . . . 195 A8
Quaves Rd SL3 . . . . 206 C3
Quebec Rd HP13 . . . . . . 173 E6
Queen Alexandra Rd
HP11 . . . . 172 F6
Queen Anne Royal Free CE
Fst Sch The SL4 . . . . . . 210 D4
Queen Anne's Ct 10
SL4 . . . . 210 D5
Queen Anne's Rd SL4 . . 210 C3
Queen Anne St MK13 . . . . 33 F7
Queen Catherine Rd
MK18 . . . . 52 D7
Queen Charlotte St 10
SL4 . . . . 210 D6
Queen Cl RG9 . . . . 191 E1
Queen Eleanor Prim Sch
MK11 . . . . 32 F4
Queen Eleanor St MK11 . 32 E4
Queen Elizabeth's Wlk
SL4 . . . . 210 F5
Queen Mother's Dr
UB9 . . . . 189 F5
Queens Acre
High Wycombe HP13 . . . 173 D6
Windsor SL4 . . . . 210 D3
Queen's Acre SL4 . . . . . . 210 D3
Queens Acre Ho 6
SL4 . . . . 210 D4
Queen St Mews RG9 . . . 191 E1
Queens Ave MK16 . . . . . . 22 C4
Queensbury La MK10 . . . 35 E1
Queens Cl OX9 . . . . 125 F2
Queen's Cl SL4 . . . . 211 A2
Queen's Cl HP13 . . . . . . 173 C6
Queen's Ct SL1 . . . . 205 F6
Queen's Dr SL3 . . . . 199 F4
Queen's Dr The WD3 . . . 167 F2
Queensgate HP19 . . . . . 115 A8
Queen's Gate SL4 . . . . . 210 D3
Queen's La 12 SL6 . . . . . 202 F7
Queensmead SL3 . . . . . . 211 B6
Queens Mead HP21 . . . . 116 C7
Queensmead Ho HP10 . . 174 C2
Queensmead Rd HP10 . . 174 C2
Queensmere Rd SL1 . . . 205 F4
Queensmere (Sh Ctr)
SL1 . . . . 205 F4
Queens Park Arts Ctr
HP21 . . . . 115 F8
Queen's Pk HP21 . . . . . . 115 F8
Queen Sq 6 HP11 . . . . . 173 A7
Queens Rd
Berkhamsted HP4 . . . . . 135 A5
1 Chesham HP5 . . . . . . 144 C1
Eton Wick SL4 . . . . 204 F1
High Wycombe HP13 . . . 173 C6
Princes Risborough
HP27 . . . . 139 C4
Slough SL1 . . . . 205 F6
West Drayton UB7 . . . . . 208 F4

Queen's Rd
Datchet SL3 . . . . 211 B7
Marlow SL7 . . . . 183 D2
Uxbridge UB8 . . . . 201 C2
Windsor SL4 . . . . 210 C5
Queen St
Aylesbury HP20 . . . . 116 A8
Henley-on-Thames RG9 . 191 E1
High Wycombe HP13 . . . 173 C7
Leighton Buzzard LU7 . . 80 F8
Maidenhead SL6 . . . . . . 202 F7
Milton Keynes MK11 . . . . 32 E6
Piddington HP14 . . . . . . 160 B1
Pitstone LU7 . . . . 105 D4
Tring HP23 . . . . 119 A3
Waddesdon HP18 . . . . . . 98 F6
Queen's Terr 5 SL4 . . . . 210 D4
Queensway
Bletchley MK2 . . . . 58 C8
Hazelmere HP15 . . . . . . 163 A4
Maidenhead SL6 . . . . . . 195 E2
Milton Keynes MK2 . . . . . 58 D8
Queensway The SL9 . . . 188 D7
Queen Victoria Rd
HP11 . . . . 173 B6
Queen Victoria's Wlk
SL4 . . . . 210 F6
Quickberry Pl HP7 . . . . . 165 C8
Quickley La WD3 . . . . . . 167 C3
Quickley Rise WD3 . . . . 167 B3
Quickly Brow WD3 . . . . . 167 B3
Quill Hall La HP6 . . . . . . 154 F2
Quilter Mdw MK7 . . . . . . 48 D5
Quilters Way HP22 . . . . . 130 D8
Quinbrookes SL2 . . . . . . 206 C7
Quince Cl MK7 . . . . 48 B5
Quinton Dr SL3 . . . . 34 B3
Quoitings Dr SL7 . . . . . . 183 C2
Quoitings Gdns SL7 . . . 183 C2
Quoiting Sq SL7 . . . . 183 D2

R

Raans Rd HP6 . . . . 154 F1
Rabans Cl
Aylesbury HP19 . . . . 100 E1
Olney MK46 . . . . 6 E5
Rabans La HP19 . . . . 100 F1
Rabbsfarm Prim Sch
UB7 . . . . 208 E6
Rabbs Mill Ho UB8 . . . . . 201 D3
Rachels Way HP5 . . . . . . 154 D5
Rackstraw Gr MK7 . . . . . 48 D5
Radcliffe Sch The MK12 . 33 B6
Radcliffe St MK12 . . . . . . 33 B6
RADCLIVE 51 E8
Radclive Rd MK18 . . . . . . 51 F7
Radcot Ave SL3 . . . . 207 B3
Radcot Cl SL6 . . . . 195 E3
Radcote Lodge MK8 . . . . 33 E1
Radian Ct MK5 . . . . 46 C7
Radman Gr MK12 . . . . . . 33 B5
RADNAGE 159 C7
Radnage CE Inf Sch
HP14 . . . . 159 D6
Radnage Common Rd
HP14 . . . . 159 D5
Radnage La HP14 . . . . . . 148 C2
Radnor Cl RG9 . . . . 191 E2
Radnor End HP20 . . . . . . 101 E2
Radnor Way SL3 . . . . 206 E2
Radstock Cres MK10 . . . . 36 A4
RADSTONE. 26 A6
Radworthy MK4 . . . . 46 C3
Raeside Cl HP9 . . . . 176 C5
Raglan Dr MK4 . . . . 45 E1
Ragmans Cl SL7 . . . . . . 183 C8
Ragmans La HP10, SL7 . 172 D1
Ragnall's La OX33 . . . . . 108 A6
Ragstone Rd SL1 . . . . . . 205 E3
Ragstones HP10 . . . . . . 174 A1
Railway Cotts
Steeple Claydon MK18 . . 64 A1
Wigginton HP23 . . . . 119 F5
Railway St 2 HP20 . . . . . 115 E8
Railway Terr SL2 . . . . . . 205 F5
Rainborough Gdns
HP20 . . . . 101 E2
Rainbow Dr MK6 . . . . 46 F7
Rainbow Ind Est UB7 . . 208 D6
Rainsborough MK14 . . . . 35 A8
Rainsborough Chase
SL6 . . . . 202 B3
Rake Way HP21 . . . . 115 D3
Raleigh Cl SL1 . . . . 205 A5
Ralphs Retreat HP15 . . . 162 F4
Ralston Ct 20 SL4 . . . . . 210 D6
RAM ALLEY 12 B5
Ram Alley MK16 . . . . 12 B6
Rambler Cl SL6 . . . . 204 B7
Rambler La SL3 . . . . 206 C3
Ramsay Cl MK13 . . . . 34 B3
Ramsay View HP15 . . . . 163 A3
Ramscote La HP5 . . . . . . 143 F7
Ramsey Ct SL2 . . . . 197 D1
Ramsgill Ct MK13 . . . . . . 34 C5
Ramsons Ave MK14 . . . . 34 E4
Ramsthorn Gr MK7 . . . . . 48 B6

Ramworth Way HP21 . . . 116 A6
Randall Cl SL3 . . . . 206 F1
Randall Ct SL4 . . . . 211 A1
Randall Dr MK4 . . . . 45 D2
Randolph Cl MK13 . . . . . . 34 A6
Randolph Rd SL3 . . . . . . 206 E3
Ranelagh Gdns MK16 . . . 22 C2
Rangers Ct MK8 . . . . 33 F1
Rannal Dr OX39 . . . . 147 C6
Rannoch Cl MK2 . . . . 58 D5
Rannock Gdns LU7 . . . . . 80 C7
Ranston Cl UB9 . . . . 189 F5
Rashleigh Pl MK6 . . . . . . 46 E7
Ratcliffe Cl SL8 . . . . 201 D2
Rathbone Cl MK8 . . . . . . 45 E7
Ravel Cl MK7 . . . . 48 D6
Raven Cl 3 HP19 . . . . . . 101 F3
Raven Cres HP18 . . . . . . 98 C6
Raven Rd HP14 . . . . 158 F4
Ravensbourne Pl MK6 . . 35 B2
Ravensbourne Rd
HP21 . . . . 115 D4
Ravenscar Ct MK4 . . . . . 46 C2
Ravenscourt SL7 . . . . . . 184 A3
Ravenscroft Rd RG9 . . . 191 C2
Ravens Ct
Berkhamsted HP4 . . . . . 135 E6
High Wycombe HP13 . . . 161 E3
Long Marston HP23 . . . . 104 B4
Ravens Field SL3 . . . . . . 206 D4
Ravensglass Croft 6
MK10 . . . . 36 B3
Ravenshoe Cl SL8 . . . . . 185 A3
Ravens La HP4 . . . . 135 D4
Ravensmead
Chalfont St Peter SL9 . . 177 F5
Chinnor OX39 . . . . 147 C6
RAVENSTONE 5 D2
Ravenstone Mill Rd
MK46 . . . . 12 E7
Ravens Wharf HP4 . . . . . 135 D4
Ravensworth Rd SL2 . . . 198 A2
Ravigill Pl MK12 . . . . 33 D4
Rawcliffe Ho SL6 . . . . . . 203 A6
Rawlings La HP9 . . . . 176 D7
Rawlins Rd MK13 . . . . . . 34 A4
Ray Dr SL6 . . . . 203 B7
Rayfield SL6 . . . . 203 B8
Ray Ho 5 SL8 . . . . 185 A4
Raylands Mead SL9 . . . . 188 C6
Ray Lea Cl SL6 . . . . 203 B8
Ray Lea Rd SL6 . . . . 203 B8
Rayleigh Cl MK5 . . . . 46 B6
Raylens HP12 . . . . 172 B5
Ray Lodge SL6 . . . . 203 B7
Ray Lodge Mews SL6 . . 203 B7
Ray Mdw SL6 . . . . 196 A1
Ray Mead Cl SL6 . . . . . . 196 C1
Ray Mead Rd SL6 . . . . . . 203 C8
Ray Mill Road E SL6 . . . 196 B1
Ray Mill Road W SL6 . . . 203 A8
Raymond Cl SL3 . . . . 212 E6
Raymond Rd
Maidenhead SL6 . . . . . . 202 D7
Slough SL3 . . . . 207 A3
Rayners Ave HP10 . . . . . 174 B3
Rayners Cl
Colnbrook SL3 . . . . 212 C7
Loudwater HP10 . . . . . . 174 C3
Rayners La MK9 . . . . 35 E1
Ray Park Ave SL6 . . . . . . 203 B8
Ray Park Rd SL6 . . . . . . 203 B8
Rays Ave SL4 . . . . 209 F7
Rays Cl MK2 . . . . 58 E6
Ray's Hill HP5 . . . . 133 C2
Ray's La HP10 . . . . 163 C1
Ray St SL6 . . . . 203 B7
Razzaq Pl HP12 . . . . 172 E7
Read Dr HP22 . . . . 102 C4
Reade Ct SL2 . . . . 198 C6
Read Ho HP19 . . . . 115 A7
Reading Cl HP19 . . . . . . 101 A3
Reading Rd RG9 . . . . . . 191 E1
Readings The WD3 . . . . 167 F6
Reads La LU7 . . . . 78 D1
Recreation Rd SL8 . . . . . 185 B3
Rectory Ave HP13 . . . . . 173 C7
Rectory Cl
Farnham Royal SL2 . . . . 198 C2
Marsh Gibbon OX27 . . . . 71 F3
Slapton LU7 . . . . 91 D6
Windsor SL4 . . . . 210 A6
Rectory Ct
2 Amersham HP7 . . . . . 165 B7
3 High Wycombe HP13 . 173 F5
Lewknor OX49 . . . . 157 B8
West Drayton UB7 . . . . . 208 F4
Rectory Dr HP18 . . . . 99 A6
Rectory Fields MK15 . . . . 35 D3
Rectory Gdns HP8 . . . . . 177 B7
Rectory Hill HP7 . . . . . . 165 B8
Rectory La
Amersham HP7 . . . . 165 B7
Berkhamsted HP4 . . . . . 135 C4
Bix RG9 . . . . 179 D1
Yardley Hastings NN7 . . . 1 A7
Rectory Mdw OX39 . . . . 147 D6
Rectory Orch MK46 . . . . . 7 F8

Rectory Rd SL6 . . . . 196 E1
Rectory Terr SL2 . . . . 198 C3
Red Admiral St HP19 . . . . 101 C4
Redbourne Ct MK11 . . . . . 32 F5
Redbridge MK14 . . . . 34 D7
Redcliffe Wlk HP19 . . . . . 101 B2
Redcote Manor MK7 . . . . . 48 A4
Red Cottage HP23 . . . . . . 119 D1
Red Cottage Mews 6
SL3 . . . . 206 C3
Red Ct SL1 . . . . 205 E5
Redding Dr HP6 . . . . 154 A2
Redding Gr MK8 . . . . 45 E6
Reddings Cl HP22 . . . . . . 131 B6
Reddington Dr SL3 . . . . . 206 E2
Redfern Cl SL3 . . . . 201 C4
Redfield Cl LU6 . . . . 93 E8
Redford Rd SL4 . . . . 209 D6
Redford Way UB8 . . . . . . 201 D5
Red Friars Square Sh Ctr 21
HP20 . . . . 115 C8
Redgrave Dr 2 MK4 . . . . 45 E3
Redgrave Pl SL7 . . . . 183 C2
Redhill UB9 . . . . 189 D2
Redhouse Cl HP11 . . . . . . 172 E3
Red House Cl
Beaconsfield HP9 . . . . . 175 C5
Newton Longville MK17 . . 57 D4
Redhuish Cl MK4 . . . . 46 D3
Red Kite Cl HP13 . . . . . . 161 D1
Red La OX39 . . . . 147 F3
Redland Cl MK18 . . . . 63 D8
Redland Dr MK5 . . . . 46 C7
Redland Way HP21 . . . . . 116 A5
Red Leaf Cl SL3 . . . . 206 F5
Red Leys UB10 . . . . 201 E5
Red Lion Cotts SL2 . . . . . 199 B1
Red Lion Dr HP14 . . . . . . 158 D5
Red Lion St HP5 . . . . 154 B7
Red Lion Way HP10 . . . . . 185 E6
Red Lodge Gdns HP4 . . . 135 A3
Redman Rd HP12 . . . . . . 172 B3
REDMOOR 47 A4
Redpitch Pk HP10 . . . . . . 185 F6
Redriff Cl SL6 . . . . 202 D6
Red Roofs SL6 . . . . 203 C7
Redshaw Cl MK18 . . . . . . 41 E1
Redshots Cl SL7 . . . . 183 C4
Redvers Gate MK15 . . . . . 35 B7
Redway Sch The MK6 . . . . 47 C6
Red Wing HP20 . . . . 101 E3
Redwood SL1 . . . . 197 B3
Redwood Cl
Hazelmere HP15 . . . . . . 163 B3
Wing LU7 . . . . 79 E2
Redwood Dr
Aylesbury HP21 . . . . . . 115 E7
Wing LU7 . . . . 79 E2
Redwood Gate MK5 . . . . . 46 C4
Redwood Gdns SL1 . . . . . 205 D6
Redwood Glade LU7 . . . . . 70 F3
Redwood Pl HP9 . . . . 175 D1
Redwoods The SL4 . . . . . 210 D4
Reed Cl SL0 . . . . 207 E7
Reeves Croft MK12 . . . . . 33 C4
Reform Rd SL6 . . . . 203 B7
Reform Road Ind Est
SL6 . . . . 203 B7
Regal Ct
Maidenhead SL6 . . . . . . 203 B2
14 Tring HP23 . . . . 119 A3
Regency Ct HP21 . . . . . . 116 B7
Regent Ct
3 Maidenhead SL6 . . . . 202 F7
Slough SL1 . . . . 205 E7
Windsor SL4 . . . . 210 D5
Regent Ho HP27 . . . . 139 B4
Regent Rd HP21 . . . . 116 B7
Regents Hall MK11 . . . . . 32 E5
Regents Pl SL6 . . . . 202 D6
Regent St MK2 . . . . 58 C8
Regius Ct HP10 . . . . 174 D8
Reid Ave SL6 . . . . 202 E5
Reliance La MK9 . . . . 35 B3
Rembrandt End HP19 . . . . 100 F2
REMENHAM 192 A5
Remenham Church La
RG9 . . . . 192 A4
REMENHAM HILL 192 C2
Remenham La
Remenham Hill RG9 . . . . 191 F3
Remenham RG9 . . . . 192 B5
Remenham Row RG9 . . . . 191 F2
Remenham Terr RG9 . . . . 192 C2
Remus Gate NN13 . . . . . . 38 A6
Rendlesham MK15 . . . . . . 35 C3
Rendlesham Way WD3 . . . 167 C3
Renfrew Way MK3 . . . . . . 46 F3
Rennie Cl HP13 . . . . 161 F1
Repton Cl SL6 . . . . 202 C3
Repton Pl HP7 . . . . 166 A8
Retreat La HP14 . . . . 148 D2
Retreat The
Little Chalfont HP6 . . . . . 156 D8
Milton Keynes MK11 . . . . 32 D5
Princes Risborough
HP27 . . . . 139 B4
Revel Rd HP10 . . . . 185 D8

Revesby Cl SL6 . . . . 202 D3
Reyners Gn HP16 . . . . . . 152 B4
Reynold Dr HP20 . . . . . . 102 A2
Reynolds Cl
Cranfield MK43 . . . . 24 E2
High Wycombe HP13 . . . . 173 E8
Reynolds Pl MK8 . . . . 45 D6
Reynolds Rd HP9 . . . . . . 175 D3
Reynolds Wlk HP5 . . . . . 144 A4
Rhodes Pl MK6 . . . . 46 E7
Rhondda Cl MK1 . . . . 47 E1
Rhoscolyn Dr MK3 . . . . . 57 C8
Rhuddlan Cl MK5 . . . . . . 45 F7
Rhymer Cl MK19 . . . . 10 F4
Ribble Cl MK16 . . . . 22 E4
Ribble Cres MK4 . . . . 45 E1
Ribstone Rd SL6 . . . . 202 B3
Ricardo Rd SL4 . . . . 211 B1
Richard Gdns HP13 . . . . . 173 E8
Richardson Pl 2 MK6 . . . 34 E1
Richards Way SL1 . . . . . . 204 F5
Richborough MK13 . . . . . 34 A6
RICHINGS PARK 207 E3
Richings Pl SL0 . . . . 207 E3
Richings Way SL0 . . . . . . 207 F3
Richmond Cl
Amersham HP6 . . . . 154 F1
Milton Keynes MK3 . . . . 46 D1
Richmond Cres SL1 . . . . . 206 A5
Richmond Ct
Dunstable LU6 . . . . 92 E6
High Wycombe HP13 . . . . 173 C7
Richmond Rd HP20 . . . . . 116 C7
Richmond Way MK16 . . . . 22 D3
Rickard Cl
Aylesbury HP21 . . . . . . 115 D3
West Drayton UB7 . . . . . 208 D3
Rickford's Hill HP20 . . . . 115 D8
Rickley La MK3 . . . . 58 A8
Rickley Park Prim Sch
MK3 . . . . 57 F8
Rickman's La SL2 . . . . . . 198 E6
RICKMANSWORTH 167 F1
Rickmansworth La SL9 . . 177 F5
Rickmansworth Rd
Amersham HP6 . . . . 154 C2
Chorleywood WD3 . . . . . 167 F6
Rickmansworth Sta HP19 . 115 A7
Rickyard Cl
1 Milton Keynes MK13 . . 34 A4
Whitchurch HP22 . . . . . . 87 A7
Rickyard Gr HP18 . . . . . . 83 B5
Rickyard The MK46 . . . . . 7 C3
Rick Yd The MK16 . . . . . . 13 F1
Riders Way OX39 . . . . . . 147 C6
Ride The LU6 . . . . 93 B6
Ridgebank SL1 . . . . 204 F6
Ridge Cl
Aylesbury HP21 . . . . . . 115 D5
Lane End HP14 . . . . 171 C4
Ridge Ct SL4 . . . . 210 C4
Ridgemont End SL9 . . . . . 177 E5
Ridge Side HP14 . . . . . . 160 A8
Ridge View HP21 . . . . . . 119 C5
Ridgeway
Berkhamsted HP4 . . . . . 134 F4
4 High Wycombe HP11 . 173 A6
Milton Keynes, Stony Stratford
MK11 . . . . 32 F4
Milton Keynes, Wolverton Mill
MK12 . . . . 33 A5
Wing LU7 . . . . 79 E3
Ridge Way
High Wycombe HP13 . . . . 162 C1
Iver SL0 . . . . 207 F6
Long Crendon HP18 . . . . 125 F4
Ridgeway Cl
Chesham HP5 . . . . 144 B3
Marlow SL7 . . . . 183 E4
Ridgeway Cotts MK17 . . . 67 B3
Ridgeway Cl 3 HP20 . . . . 101 E1
Ridgeway Meads HP27 . . 138 B2
Ridgeway Rd HP5 . . . . . . 144 B3
Ridgeway The
Amersham HP6 . . . . 165 C4
Gerrards Cross SL9 . . . . 188 C8
Marlow SL7 . . . . 183 E4
Ridgeway Trad Est The
SL0 . . . . 207 E6
Ridgewood RG9 . . . . 181 C1
Ridgmont HP16 . . . . 31 E5
Ridgmont Cl MK19 . . . . . 31 E5
Ridgway MK17 . . . . 49 B6
Riding Court Rd SL3 . . . . 211 D7
Riding Ct SL3 . . . . 211 C8
Riding La HP9, HP10 . . . . 174 F3
Ridings Cotts HP15 . . . . . 163 D6
Ridings The
Amersham HP6 . . . . 154 D4
Iver SL0 . . . . 207 F2
Latimer HP5 . . . . 155 D3
Maidenhead SL6 . . . . . . 202 A7
Ridings Way LU7 . . . . . . 78 B1
Riding The MK19 . . . . . . 31 E5
Rigby Lodge SL1 . . . . . . 205 E7
Rigeway View LU7 . . . . . 105 D4
Rignall Rd HP16 . . . . 151 E8
Riley Cl HP20 . . . . 115 C8
Riley Rd SL7 . . . . 183 D2

Rillington Gdns MK4 . . . . 46 B3
Rimmington Way HP19 . . 101 B1
Rimsdale Ct MK2 . . . . 58 D3
Ringlet Way HP19 . . . . . . 101 C4
Ring Rd HP10 . . . . 173 F2
Ring Road E MK7 . . . . . . 47 F7
Ring Road N MK7 . . . . . . 47 F7
Ring Road W MK7 . . . . . . 47 F7
RINGSHALL 107 B1
Ringshall Dr HP4 . . . . . . 121 C8
Ringshall Rd HP4 . . . . . . 107 B3
Ringstead Way HP21 . . . . 116 A5
Ripley Cl
High Wycombe HP13 . . . . 173 A8
Milton Keynes MK4 . . . . 45 E1
Slough SL3 . . . . 206 E2
Ripon Ho HP21 . . . . 115 F6
Ripon St 7 HP20 . . . . . . 101 D1
Risborough Rd
Great Kimble HP17,
HP27 . . . . 139 D8
Maidenhead SL6 . . . . . . 202 E8
Stoke Mandeville HP17 . . 130 B7
Risborough Springs Swim &
Fitness Ctr HP27 . . . . . 139 A4
Rise Hag Hill SL4 . . . . . . 204 A7
Riseley Rd SL6 . . . . 202 D7
Rise The
Amersham HP7 . . . . 165 C8
Gawcott MK18 . . . . 51 F4
Hazelmere HP15 . . . . . . 163 A5
Loudwater HP13 . . . . . . 174 B4
Uxbridge UB10 . . . . 201 F3
Risings The HP13 . . . . . . 162 B1
Riverbank Point UB8 . . . . 201 C6
Riverbank The SL4 . . . . . 210 B7
River Cl MK16 . . . . 22 D4
Rivercrest Rd MK19 . . . . 32 B6
River Ct SL6 . . . . 203 C7
River Gdns SL3 . . . . 203 D4
Rivermead Ct SL7 . . . . . . 194 E8
Riverpark Dr SL7 . . . . . . 183 F1
River Park Ind Est HP18 . 135 A5
River Rd SL3 . . . . 203 C6
River & Rowing Mus★
RG9 . . . . 191 F1
Riversdale SL8 . . . . 185 A1
Riversdale Cotts SL8 . . . . 185 A1
Riversdale Ct SL8 . . . . . . 185 A1
Rivers Edge HP11 . . . . . . 174 A3
Riverside SL7 . . . . 183 D1
River Side MK16 . . . . 22 D4
Riverside Cotts
West Drayton UB7 . . . . . 208 C1
Wooburn Green HP10 . . . 185 E8
Riverside Cvn Pk UB7 . . . 208 C3
Riverside Gdns HP4 . . . . 135 A5
Riverside Mews MK18 . . . 52 D8
Riverside Pl SL3 . . . . 212 E5
Riverside Pl TW19 . . . . . 213 F3
Riverside Rd TW19 . . . . . 213 E1
Riverside Way UB8 . . . . . 201 B4
Riverside Wlk SL4 . . . . . 210 D7
River St SL4 . . . . 210 D7
Riverswood Gdns HP11 . . 174 B3
River View HP10 . . . . 185 B7
Riverway SL4 . . . . 210 C2
River Wlk UB9 . . . . 201 C7
Riverwood Ave SL7 . . . . . 184 A1
Riverwoods Dr SL7 . . . . . 184 A1
Rivets Cl HP21 . . . . 115 E6
Rivetts Cl MK46 . . . . 6 E4
Rixband Cl MK7 . . . . 48 B4
Rixman Cl 2 SL6 . . . . . . 202 D5
Rixon Cl SL3 . . . . 206 F4
Rixons Mdw HP19 . . . . . . 115 B7
Roade Hill NN7 . . . . 9 F8
Roald Dahl Mus & Story
Ctr★ HP16 . . . . 152 A7
Robert Rd SL2 . . . . 187 D2
Roberts Cl
Deanshanger MK19 . . . . 31 E4
Stanwell TW19 . . . . 213 C1
West Drayton UB7 . . . . . 208 E5
Robert's Dr HP19 . . . . . . 101 D1
Roberts La SL9 . . . . 178 B5
Robertson Cl MK5 . . . . . . 45 F7
Robertson Cnr LU6 . . . . . 93 F4
Robertson Rd 6 HP4 . . . 135 D4
Roberts Rd
Haddenham HP17 . . . . . 127 B6
High Wycombe HP13 . . . . 173 B8
Roberts Ride HP15 . . . . . 163 A5
Roberts Way HP21 . . . . . 115 B6
Robertswood Comb Sch
SL9 . . . . 177 F5
Roberts Wood Dr SL9 . . . 177 F5
Robeson Pl MK8 . . . . 45 E8
Robin Cl
Aylesbury HP19 . . . . . . 101 D1
Buckingham MK18 . . . . . 52 F7
Great Kingshill HP15 . . . 151 D1
Robin Hill HP6 . . . . 135 C3
Robin Hood Cl SL1 . . . . . 204 F5
Robin Par 2 SL2 . . . . . . 198 C7
Robins Cl
High Wycombe HP12 . . . . 172 B5
Uxbridge UB8 . . . . 208 C8

Robins Hill MK6 . . . . 47 A6
Robinson Cl HP19 . . . . . . 100 F3
Robinson Cl SL6 . . . . 202 E4
Robinson Rd HP13 . . . . . 174 B4
Robins Orch SL9 . . . . 177 E4
Robins Platt OX39 . . . . . . 147 B6
Robinswood Cl
Beaconsfield HP9 . . . . . 175 C5
Leighton Buzzard LU7 . . 70 F2
Robin Willis Way SL4 . . . 211 A1
Robinwood Gr UB8 . . . . . 201 F1
Roblin Cl HP21 . . . . 115 E4
Robson Cl SL9 . . . . 177 E5
Robson Ct 4 HP11 . . . . . 152 A8
Roche Gdns MK3 . . . . . . 58 A8
Rochester Ct MK5 . . . . . . 46 A5
Rochester Mews LU7 . . . . 80 E6
Rochester Pl HP19 . . . . . 115 B8
Rochfords MK6 . . . . 46 F6
Rochfords Gdns SL2 . . . . 206 C5
Rochford Way SL6 . . . . . 204 A7
Rockall Ct SL3 . . . . 207 B3
Rock Cl LU7 . . . . 80 D6
Rockingham Cl
Pitstone LU7 . . . . 105 D3
Uxbridge UB8 . . . . 201 C4
Rockingham Dr MK14 . . . 34 E6
Rockingham Par UB8 . . . 201 C4
Rockingham Pl HP9 . . . . 175 F1
Rockingham Rd UB8 . . . . 201 C4
Rockingham Wharf
UB8 . . . . 201 B4
Rock La LU7 . . . . 80 D7
Rockleigh Ct 3 LU7 . . . . 80 E7
Rockspray Gr MK7 . . . . . 48 B5
Rodney Way SL3 . . . . . . 212 E6
Rodwell Gdns MK7 . . . . . 48 D4
Rodwell Yd 3 HP23 . . . . 119 A3
Roebuck Ave SL1 . . . . . . 204 E5
Roebuck Gn SL1 . . . . 204 E5
Roeburn Cres MK4 . . . . . 46 C1
Rogers Croft MK6 . . . . . . 47 D7
Rogers La SL2 . . . . 198 F4
Roker Park Ave UB10 . . . 201 E8
Rokesby Rd SL2 . . . . 197 F2
Rolfe Cl HP9 . . . . 175 E1
Rolvenden Gr MK7 . . . . . 48 B7
Roman Lea SL6 . . . . 195 F7
Roman Pl SL6 . . . . 202 C6
Roman Rdbt MK1 . . . . . . 47 C2
Romans Field Specl Sch
MK3 . . . . 46 E1
Roman Way
Aylesbury HP19 . . . . . . 115 B8
Bourne End SL8 . . . . . . 185 B8
Brackley NN13 . . . . 38 A7
Romar Ct MK1 . . . . 47 C2
Romney Ct 11 SL7 . . . . . 183 F3
Romney Lock Rd SL4 . . . 210 D7
Romney Rd HP21 . . . . . . 115 E4
Romsey Cl SL3 . . . . 206 F3
Romsey Dr SL2 . . . . 187 D1
Romsey Way HP11 . . . . . 173 B4
Romulus Way NN13 . . . . 38 A6
Ronald Rd HP9 . . . . 175 F2
Ronaldsay Spur SL1 . . . . 205 E8
Rookery Ct SL7 . . . . 183 D2
Rookery Mdw HP15 . . . . . 163 C7
Rookery Way MK18 . . . . . 63 F3
Rook Rd HP10 . . . . 185 D4
ROOKSLEY 34 B2
Rooksley Rdbt MK13 . . . . 34 B3
Rooks Terr UB7 . . . . 208 E4
Rook Tree Farm Ind Est
MK17 . . . . 37 F3
Rook Wood Way HP16 . . . 152 B5
Ropa Ct 6 LU7 . . . . 80 F7
Ropley Way 3 MK10 . . . . 36 B3
Rosamund's Cotts HP18 . 83 B2
Rosary The HP15 . . . . . . 163 C7
Roseary Cl UB7 . . . . 208 D2
Rose Ave
Aylesbury HP19 . . . . . . 101 C4
Hazelmere HP15 . . . . . . 163 B2
Rosebank Cl SL6 . . . . 195 E7
Rosebank Cotts HP10 . . . 174 B3
Rosebarn La HP23 . . . . . 104 D1
Rosebay Cl MK7 . . . . 48 B5
Rosebery Ave
High Wycombe HP13 . . . . 173 E5
Leighton Buzzard LU7 . . 80 E7
Rosebery Cl MK18 . . . . . . 77 B7
Rosebery Cl 4 LU7 . . . . . 80 F7
Rosebery Mews LU7 . . . . 90 D4
Rosebery Rd HP22 . . . . . 117 C5
Rosebery Way HP23 . . . . 119 B5
Rose Cnr HP14 . . . . 158 E5
Rosecomb Pl MK5 . . . . . 46 A4
Rose Cotts SL6 . . . . 202 C3
Rose Ct
Amersham HP6 . . . . 154 E2
Chesham HP5 . . . . 154 D6
Eaton Bray LU6 . . . . 92 D6
3 Olney MK46 . . . . 6 F3
Rose Dr HP5 . . . . 154 D7
Rosehill HP4 . . . . 135 B4
Rose Hill SL1 . . . . 197 A5

Rosehill Cres MK18 . . . . . 62 D1
Rosehill Ct SL1 . . . . 206 A3
Rose Ind Est SL7 . . . . . . 183 D5
Rose La RG9 . . . . 193 A1
Roseleigh Cl SL6 . . . . . . 202 A7
Rosemary Cl HP12 . . . . . 161 B1
Rosemary Ct
High Wycombe HP12 . . . . 161 B1
Walton MK7 . . . . 48 A5
Rosemary La HP17 . . . . . 127 A7
Rosemead HP22 . . . . 117 E1
Rosemoor Mews HP19 . . 114 F8
Rosemullion Ave MK4 . . . 57 B8
Rosery The 5 SL8 . . . . . 185 A3
Roses Cl LU7 . . . . 78 B1
Rose Terr HP16 . . . . 151 C6
Rosetree Cl HP16 . . . . . . 151 C6
Rose Wlk SL2 . . . . 206 C8
Rosewood Gdns HP12 . . . 172 C4
Rosewood Way SL2 . . . . 198 C7
Rosken Gr SL2 . . . . 198 B3
Roslyn Ct MK15 . . . . 35 D7
Rossal Pl MK12 . . . . 33 D4
Rossendale MK14 . . . . . . 34 D7
Rossetti Pl HP15 . . . . . . 163 C7
Rossini Pl MK7 . . . . 48 D5
Rossiter Cl SL3 . . . . 206 E2
Ross Rd
Aston Abbotts HP22 . . . . 88 C5
Maidenhead SL6 . . . . . . 202 E4
Ross Way MK3 . . . . 46 F2
Rossway La HP4 . . . . . . 134 A7
Rostrevor Gdns SL0 . . . . 200 D3
Rothersthorpe MK14 . . . . 35 A8
Rothesay Cl HP20 . . . . . . 101 E1
Rothesay Ct HP14 . . . . . 135 A4
Rothschild Ave HP22 . . . . 117 E5
Rothschild Rd
Leighton Buzzard LU7 . . 80 F8
Wing LU7 . . . . 79 E2
ROTTEN ROW 181 F2
Rotten Row MK17 . . . . . . 59 C2
Roughwood La HP8 . . . . 166 E3
Roundhead Dr OX9 . . . . . 125 F1
Roundheads End HP9 . . . 175 B4
Round Hill HP17 . . . . 114 D5
Roundhill Ct HP17 . . . . . 126 E8
Roundlands HP27 . . . . . . 149 E5
Roundwood Prim Sch (Inf)
MK18 . . . . 51 B6
Roundwood Prim Sch (Jun)
MK18 . . . . 51 F4
Roundwood Rd HP12 . . . 172 C2
Round Wood Rd HP6 . . . . 154 F2
Rouse Ct SL9 . . . . 188 F6
Routs Gn HP14 . . . . 148 D2
ROUT'S GREEN 148 D2
Rowley Cl MK11 . . . . 32 F5
Rowan Ave HP13 . . . . . . 173 D8
Rowan Cl
Aylesbury HP21 . . . . . . 115 E4
Beaconsfield HP9 . . . . . 175 B1
Hazelmere HP15 . . . . . . 163 A3
Rowan Gdns SL0 . . . . . . 200 C3
Rowan Ho 1 SL8 . . . . . . 185 A4
Rowanhurst Dr SL2 . . . . 198 C7
Rowan Pl HP6 . . . . 154 F1
Rowan Rd UB7 . . . . 208 E2
Rowans The SL8 . . . . . . 188 D8
Rowan Way SL2 . . . . 205 B8
Rowan Wlk HP5 . . . . 144 B1
Rowborough Rd HP22 . . . 131 D7
Rowland Cl SL4 . . . . 209 D4
Rowland Ho HP9 . . . . . . 175 F1
Rowlands Cl MK2 . . . . . . 58 E8
Rowland Way HP19 . . . . . 115 B7
Rowle Cl MK14 . . . . 34 E7
Rowley Furrows LU7 . . . . 80 D8
Rowley La SL3 . . . . 199 D4
Rowlheys Pl UB7 . . . . . . 208 E3
Rowliff Rd HP12 . . . . 172 C6
ROWSHAM 102 D8
Rowsham Dell MK14 . . . . 21 F2
Rowsham Rd HP22 . . . . . 102 C5
Row The
Cholesbury HP5 . . . . . . 133 D2
Cold Brayfield MK46 . . . . 8 B6
Lane End HP14 . . . . 171 B4
Newton Blossomville MK43 . 8 B3
Winchmore Hill HP7 . . . . 164 C3
Rowton Heath MK5 . . . . . 45 C5
Roxburgh Way MK3 . . . . 46 F3
Roxhill Rd MK43 . . . . 25 F3
Roxwell Cl SL1 . . . . 204 E5
Roxwell Path 5 HP20 . . . 101 F2
Royal Buckinghamshire
Hospl HP19 . . . . 101 D1
Royal Cl UB7, UB8 . . . . . 208 F7
Royal Cotts SL6 . . . . 195 C7
Royal Cotts HP7 . . . . 164 C2
Royal Ct HP23 . . . . 120 A5
Royal Free Ct 13 SL4 . . . 210 D6
Royal Gram Sch The
HP13 . . . . 162 C1

Royal La UB8 . . . . **201** F1
Royal Latin Sch The
MK18 . . . . **52** D7
Royal Mansions RG9 . . **191** E1
Royal Mead HP17 . . . . **130** C5
Royal Windsor Racecourse
SL4 . . . . **209** E7
Royce Cl LU6 . . . . **93** F7
Royce Rd MK43 . . . . . . **24** D3
Royle Cl SL9 . . . . **177** F3
Royston Way SL1 . . . . **204** D8
Rubbra Cl MK7 . . . . . . **48** C5
Rubens Cl HP19 . . . . **100** F2
Ruby Cl SL1 . . . . **205** A4
Ruckles Way HP7 . . . . **165** C7
Rudchesters MK13 . . . . **33** F5
Ruddlesway SL4 . . . . **209** D6
Rudds Cl MK18 . . . . . . **65** A4
Rudesby La HP17 . . . . **127** A7
Rudsworth Cl SL3 . . **212** D7
Ruffle Cl UB7 . . . . **208** E4
Rugby Rise HP11 . . . . **174** A3
Rugwood Rd HP10 . . **173** F2
Rumptons Paddock
HP18 . . . . **82** F6
Runford Ct MK5 . . . . **46** C5
Run Furrow HP17 . . . . **127** A7
Runnymede MK14 . . . . **21** F2
Runrig Hill HP6 . . . . **154** E4
Rupert Ave HP12 . . . . **172** E4
Rupert Cl RG9 . . . . . . **191** E3
Rupert House Sch RG9 **191** E2
Rupert's La **191** E3
Rupert Way OX9 . . . . **126** A1
Ruscombe Gdns SL3 . . **211** A7
Ruscote HP4 . . . . **135** A3
Rushall Rd OX9 . . . . **126** A1
Rushbeds Wood Wildlife
Reserve★ HP18 . . . . . . **96** D4
Rushbrooke Cl HP13 . . **162** F2
Rushburn HP10 . . . . **185** F6
Rushendon Furlong
LU7 . . . . **105** E5
Rushes Mead UB8 . . **201** C4
Rushes The
Maidenhead SL6 . . **203** C6
Marlow SL7 . . . . . . **194** C8
Rushfields Cl 12 MK4 . . **45** F1
RUSH GREEN **200** E8
Rushington Ave SL6 . . **202** F5
Rushleys Cl MK5 . . . . **46** A8
RUSHMERE **70** E4
Rushmere Cl MK17 . . **48** D2
Rushmere La HP5 . . **145** B3
Rushmere Ret Pk MK1 . . **47** C2
Rushmoor Ave HP15 . . **163** B3
Rushton Ct 5 MK6 . . **45** F8
Ruskin Ct MK16 . . . . **22** C2
Rusland Cir MK4 . . . . **46** C2
Russel Ct HP14 . . . . **161** C8
Russell Ave HP21 . . **115** C6
Russell Cl
Little Chalfont HP6 . . **166** D8
Tylers Green HP10 . . **163** B1
Russell Ct
Aylesbury HP21 . . **115** E6
Chesham HP5 . . . . **144** D2
Maidenhead SL6 . . **202** F7
Wendover HP22 . . **131** B5
Russell Dr TW19 . . . . **213** D1
Russet Rd SL4 . . . . **202** C3
Russets The SL9 . . . . **177** D1
Russett Hill SL9 . . . . **188** E8
Russwell La MK17 . . **59** C6
Rustics Cl MK18 . . . . **73** B5
Rustlings Gate HP14 . . **171** C5
Rutherford Cl
Uxbridge UB8 . . . . **201** F1
Windsor SL4 . . . . **209** F6
Rutherford Gate MK5 . . **46** C5
Rutherford Rd HP21 . . **115** E4
Ruthven Cl MK2 . . . . **58** C4
Rutland Ave
High Wycombe HP12 . . **172** D6
Slough SL1 . . . . . . **205** C8
Rutland Ct 2 HP11 . . **173** A6
Rutland Gate SL6 . . **202** C6
Rutland Ho 8 MK3 . . **46** F1
Rutland Pl SL6 . . . . **202** C6
Rutland Rd SL6 . . . . **202** D6
Rutland St HP11 . . . . **173** A6
Ryans Mount SL7 . . **183** C2
Rycote La OX9 . . . . **136** D5
Rycote Lane Ind Est
OX9 . . . . **136** C4
Rycroft
Milton Keynes MK4 . . **46** E3

Rycroft *continued*
Windsor SL4 . . . . **209** F4
Rydal Way
High Wycombe HP12 . . **172** B5
Milton Keynes MK2 . . **58** D5
Ryder Cl HP3 . . . . . . **146** A4
Rydings SL4 . . . . . . **209** F4
Ryding The MK5 . . . . **46** A4
Rye Cl
Aylesbury HP21 . . **115** D4
Maidenhead SL6 . . **202** A4
Ryecote Chapel★ OX9 . **136** D6
Ryecroft Rd HP5 . . . . **154** A7
Rye Ct 9 SL1 . . . . . . **206** A4
Ryefield Terr SL3 . . **212** D7
Ryeland MK11 . . . . . . **32** E6
Ryeland Cl UB7 . . . . **208** E7
Ryemead Way HP11 . . **173** F4
Rye The LU6, LU7 . . . . **92** B8
Rye View HP13 . . . . **173** C7
Rylstone Cl
Maidenhead SL6 . . **202** C3
Milton Keynes MK13 . . **34** B3
Ryman Ct WD3 . . . . **167** C3
Rymill Cl HP3 . . . . . . **146** A3
Ryton Pl MK4 . . . . . . **46** C3
Ryvers End SL3 . . . . **206** F3
Ryvers Rd SL3 . . . . **206** F3
Ryvers Sch SL3 . . . . **206** D3

S

Sabina Cl HP12 . . . . **172** E6
Sacred Heart RC Prim Sch
RG9 . . . . **191** D1
Saddington MK6 . . . . **47** D6
Saddlers Pl MK41 . . . . **35** A5
Sadleirs Gn MK17 . . **49** B5
Sadlers Mews SL6 . . **203** B7
Saffron Cl SL3 . . . . **211** B6
Saffron Rd HP13 . . **173** C6
Saffron Rd HP13 . . **173** C6
Saffron Rise LU6 . . . . **92** E6
Saffron St MK2 . . . . **58** D7
Saham Croft Cl MK18 . **65** E4
Sailing Club Rd SL8 . . **185** A3
St Abbs Ct MK4 . . . . **56** F8
St Adrian's Cl SL6 . . **202** B4
St Agnes Gate HP22 . . **131** A5
St Aidan's Cl MK3 . . **57** E6
St Albans Cl 7 SL4 . . **210** D6
St Alban's Rd MK18 . . **65** F4
St Alban's St SL4 . . **210** D6
St Andrew's Ave SL4 . . **209** F5
St Andrew's CE Inf Sch
MK14 . . . . **34** E8
St Andrew's CE Prim Sch
Chinnor OX39 . . . . **147** C7
Uxbridge UB8 . . . . **201** D4
St Andrew's Cl
High Wycombe HP13 . . **162** F1
Old Windsor SL4 . . **211** A1
Wraysbury TW19 . . **211** E1
St Andrews Cotts 1
SL4 . . . . **210** A5
St Andrew's Cres SL4 . **209** F5
St Andrews Ct
Colnbrook SL3 . . . . **212** D7
2 Slough SL1 . . . . **205** E3
St Andrews Ho OX39 . **147** C6
St Andrew's Rd
Chinnor OX39 . . . . **147** C5
Milton Keynes MK3 . . **57** E7
Uxbridge UB10 . . . . **201** E5
St Andrews Way SL1 . . **204** D6
St Andrews Way Ind Est
HP19 . . . . **101** C1
St Anne's Cl
Henley-on-Thames
RG9 . . . . **191** D1
Wendover HP22 . . **131** B5
St Anne's Rd
Aylesbury HP19 . . **115** B8
South Harefield UB9 . . **190** C8
St Ann's HP10 . . . . . . **174** C2
St Ann's Ct HP10 . . **174** C2
St Anthony's Cl HP19 . **115** B8
St Anthony's Ct HP9 . . **186** C8
St Anthony's Pl MK4 . . **57** B8
St Anthony's RC Prim Sch
SL2 . . . . **198** B1
St Augustine's RC Prim Sch
HP11 . . . . **173** A4
St Augustus Cl MK3 . . **57** E7
St Bartholomews MK10 . **36** A1
St Bartholomew's CE Sch
HP23 . . . . **119** D1
St Bees MK10 . . . . . . **36** B1
St Bernadettes RC Prim Sch
MK10 . . . . **47** F8
St Bernards Cl HP13 . . **173** C6
St Bernard's Prep Sch
SL1 . . . . **206** B4
St Bernard's RC Gram Sch
SL3 . . . . **206** C4
St Bernard's RC Sch
HP11 . . . . **173** A4
St Bernards Rd SL3 . . **206** C3

St Birinus HP10 . . . . **174** A2
St Botolphs 2 MK10 . . **36** B1
St Brides Cl MK6 . . . . **35** C2
St Catherine RC Prim Sch
UB7 . . . . **208** D4
St Catherine's Ave MK3 **57** D6
St Catherines Ct 3
SL4 . . . . **210** A5
St Catherine's Ct HP19 **115** B8
St Chad's Rd SL6 . . **202** B4
St Christopher Rd UB8 **208** D8
St Christopher's Cl
HP16 . . . . **152** B3
St Christophers Ct
WD3 . . . . **167** D5
St Clement Cl UB8 . . **208** D7
St Clement Danes Sch
WD3 . . . . **167** D7
St Clement's Dr MK3 . . **57** D6
Saint-Cloud Way SL6 . . **203** A7
St Columba's Cl SL6 . . **202** B4
St Cuthburt La UB8 . . **208** D7
St David Cl UB8 . . . . **208** D8
St David's Cl
Iver Heath SL0 . . . . **200** D4
Maidenhead SL6 . . **202** A4
St David's St NN13 . . **38** A8
St David's Par SL6 . . **202** A4
St David's Rd MK3 . . **57** E6
St Dunstans MK6 . . . . **47** A6
St Edmund Campion RC
Prim Sch SL6 . . . . **202** B5
St Edmunds HP4 . . **135** C3
St Edmund's Ct HP19 . **115** B8
St Edwards Ct MK4 . . **34** F7
St Edward's RC Fst Sch
SL4 . . . . **210** A6
St Edward's RC Jun Sch
HP21 . . . . **116** A7
St Edward's Royal Free
Ecumenical Mid Sch
SL4 . . . . **210** A6
St Elmo Cl SL2 . . . . **198** D1
St Elmo Cres SL2 . . **198** D1
St Ethelbert's RC Prim Sch
SL2 . . . . **206** A7
St Faith's Cl MK17 . . **57** D3
St Francis Rd
Beacon's Bottom HP14 . **159** D3
Denham Green UB9 . . **189** F4
St George's CE Inf Sch 3
HP7 . . . . **165** E8
St George's Cl
High Wycombe HP13 . . **173** D7
Windsor SL4 . . . . **209** E6
St Georges Cres SL1 . . **204** D6
St Georges Ct 2 HP12 . **172** D8
St George's Dr UB10 . . **190** F1
St Georges Ind Est HP7 **165** F8
St Georges Lodge SL6 . **196** B7
St George's Rd SL6 . . **57** E6
St George's Sch SL4 . . **210** D7
St Georges Way **33** D7
St Giles Mews MK1 . . **32** D6
St Giles St MK13 . . . . **33** F7
St Govans Cl MK4 . . . . **57** B8
St Helena Ave
Milton Keynes MK3 . . **58** C3
Milton Keynes MK17 . . **58** C3
St Helen Cl UB8 . . . . **208** D8
St Helens Gr MK10 . . **47** F8
St Hilda's Ct HP19 . . **115** B8
St Hilda's Way HP10 . . **174** A2
St Huberts Cl SL9 . . **188** E2
St Huberts Cotts SL9 . . **188** E4
St Huberts La SL9 . . **188** F2
St Hugh's Ave HP13 . . **173** F6
St Hugh's Pl HP14 . . **158** F4
St Hugh's Pl HP14 . . **158** F4
St Ives Cres MK4 . . . . **57** B8
St Ives Rd SL6 . . . . **203** A7
St James Cl MK19 . . . . **11** A2
St James Ctyd 8 SL7 . . **183** E2
St James Pl SL1 . . . . **204** C7
St James & St John CE
Prim Sch
Akeley MK18 . . . . **41** F8
Chackmore MK18 . . **41** B4
St James St MK13 . . . . **33** F7
St James Way HP22 . . **102** B3
St John's Ave HP10 . . **174** B8
St John's CE Comb Sch
HP27 . . . . **149** E6
St John's Cl HP10 . . **163** B1
St John's Cl UB8 . . **201** D4
St John's Cres MK12 . . **33** D5
St Johns Dr
Stone HP17 . . . . **114** B5
Windsor SL4 . . . . **210** A5
St John's La MK19 . . **31** B4
St John's Manor Ho
HP15 . . . . **162** E2
St Johns Rd
Slough SL2 . . . . . . **206** A4
Tylers Green HP10 . . **163** B1
Windsor SL4 . . . . **210** A5

St John's Rd
4 Aylesbury HP20 . . **101** E1
Hazlemere HP15 . . **162** F2
Milton Keynes MK3 . . **57** E6
Uxbridge UB8 . . . . **201** B4
St John's St HP20 . . **101** E1
St John St MK16 . . . . **22** D4
St John's Well Ct HP4 . **135** B5
St John's Well La HP4 . **135** B5
St Josephs MK46 . . . . **6** F4
St Josephs Mews HP9 . **175** F2
St Joseph's RC Comb Sch
SL9 . . . . **188** C8
St Joseph's RC High Sch
SL2 . . . . **206** A7
St Joseph's RC Inf Sch
HP21 . . . . **116** A7
St Katherine's Way
HP4 . . . . **134** F7
St Laurence Cl UB8 . . **208** C8
St Laurence Rd MK18 . **65** F4
St Laurence Way SL1 . **206** A3
St Lawrence Cl HP3 . . **146** A4
St Lawrence View MK13 **34** A4
St Leger Cl MK14 . . . . **34** E8
St Leger Dr MK14 . . . . **34** E7
ST LEONARDS **132** E3
St Leonard's Ave 2
SL4 . . . . **210** C5
St Leonard's Hill SL4 . . **209** E4
St Leonards Rd HP6 . . **154** E4
St Leonard's Rd
Oakley Green SL4 . . **209** D1
Windsor SL4 . . . . **210** C4
St Leonards Wlk SL0 . . **200** D3
St Louis RC Comb Sch 15
HP20 . . . . **101** F2
St Luke Cl UB8 . . . . **208** D7
St Luke's CE Prim Sch 2
SL6 . . . . **202** F8
St Luke's Rd
Maidenhead SL6 . . **202** F8
Old Windsor SL4 . . **211** A1
Uxbridge UB10 . . . . **201** E5
St Margaret Ct MK2 . . **58** E8
St Margarets Cl MK16 . **22** E4
St Margaret's Cl
Berkhamsted HP4 . . **135** D3
Iver Heath SL0 . . . . **200** D3
Tylers Green HP10 . . **174** C8
St Margaret's Ct SL0 . . **200** D3
St Margaret's Gate SL0 **200** D3
St Margarets Gr HP15 . **151** E1
St Margaret's Rd SL6 . **202** A7
St Margaret Way SL1 . **204** F4
St Marks Cl HP13 . . **173** D7
St Mark's Cres SL6 . . **202** B7
St Mark's Hospl SL6 . . **202** C7
St Mark's Pl SL4 . . . . **210** C5
St Mark's Rd
Aylesbury HP21 . . **115** C7
Henley-on-Thames RG9 . **191** E1
Maidenhead SL6 . . **202** D7
Windsor SL4 . . . . **210** C5
St Martin Cl UB8 . . **208** D7
St Martin's Cl UB7 . . **208** D3
St Martin's Rd SL3 . . **206** D3
St Martin's St MK2 . . **58** C8
St Mary & All Saints CE
Prim Sch HP9 . . . . **175** E3
St Mary Magdalene RC
Prim Sch MK12 . . . . **33** A5
St Mary & St Giles CE Sch
MK11 . . . . **32** E6
St Mary's Ave
Berkhamsted HP4 . . **134** D6
Milton Keynes MK3 . . **57** E7
Milton Keynes, Stony Stratford
MK11 . . . . **32** E6
St Mary's CE Comb Sch
HP7 . . . . **165** A8
St Mary's CE Prim Sch
SL1 . . . . **206** A3
St Mary's CE Sch HP19 **115** A8
St Marys Cl
East Claydon MK18 . . **74** F8
Mursley MK17 . . . . **67** D6
St Mary's Cl
Lee Common HP16 . . **142** D5
Maidenhead SL6 . . **203** A7
South Harefield UB9 . . **190** B8
Wavendon MK17 . . **48** E7
St Mary's Farnham Royal
Prim Sch SL2 . . . . **198** C2
St Mary's Fst Sch HP4 . **134** E6
St Mary's Glebe LU6 . . **92** E4
St Mary's RC Prim Sch
Maidenhead SL6 . . **195** F2
Uxbridge UB8 . . . . **201** C4
St Marys Rd MK18 . . **74** F7
St Mary's Rd
Denham Green UB9 . . **189** F5
Slough SL3 . . . . . . **206** E4
South Harefield UB9 . . **190** B8
St Mary's Row 7 HP20 **115** D8
St Mary's Sch SL9 . . **188** E7

St Mary's Sq 3 HP20 . . **115** D8
St Mary
High Wycombe HP11 . . **173** B6
Milton Keynes MK13 . . **33** F7
St Marys Wavendon Prim
Sch MK17 . . . . . . **48** E7
St Mary's Way
Chalfont St Peter SL9 . . **177** D1
Chesham HP5 . . . . **154** B8
Leighton Buzzard LU7 . . **80** D7
St Mary's Wlk 10 SL6 . . **202** F7
St Matthew Cl UB8 . . **208** D7
St Matthew's CE Prim Sch
UB7 . . . . **208** E5
St Matthews Ct MK3 . . **57** E6
St Michael's CE Comb Sch
LU7 . . . . **68** E1
St Michaels Cl
Edgcott HP18 . . . . **72** F2
Halton HP22 . . . . **131** C8
Stewkley LU7 . . . . **68** E1
St Michael's Cl HP22 . . **117** C1
St Michael's Ct
Ashton NN7 . . . . . . **9** F8
Slough SL2 . . . . . . **197** D1
St Michaels Dr
Milton Keynes MK7 . . **47** F6
Walton MK7 . . . . . . **47** F6
St Michael's Gn HP9 . . **175** E3
St Michaels Wlk MK18 . **63** E3
St Monica's RC Comb Sch
MK14 . . . . **34** D6
St Nicholas CE Comb Sch
SL6 . . . . **196** E1
St Nicholas Cl
Cublington LU7 . . . . **78** B1
Little Chalfont HP7 . . **166** B8
Uxbridge UB8 . . . . **208** D7
St Patrick's Cl SL6 . . **202** B4
St Patrick's Way MK3 . **57** E6
St Paul Cl UB8 . . . . **208** D8
St Pauls Ave SL2 . . **206** A5
St Paul's CE Comb Sch
HP10 . . . . **185** D4
St Pauls Cl MK11 . . . . **32** D6
St Pauls Ct SL6 . . . . **202** F6
St Pauls Gdns SL6 . . **202** B8
St Pauls RC Sch MK6 . . **46** F7
St Paul's Rd MK3 . . **57** E6
St Pauls Yd MK16 . . **22** D4
St Peter's Ave HP19 . . **101** C1
St Peter's CE Comb Sch
SL1 . . . . **197** B2
St Peter's CE Mid Sch
SL4 . . . . **210** F1
St Peters Ct
Loudwater HP11 . . **174** B1
Speen HP27 . . . . **150** C4
St Peter's Cl
Burnham SL1 . . . . **197** B1
Old Windsor SL4 . . **211** A2
St Peter's Cir SL9 . . **177** E2
St Peter's Gate NN13 . . **38** A7
St Peters Hill HP23 . . **119** A4
St Peter's RC Prim Sch
SL7 . . . . **183** D3
St Peter's Rd
Brackley NN13 . . . . **38** A8
Maidenhead SL6 . . **195** D2
Uxbridge UB8 . . . . **208** D8
St Peter St SL7 . . . . **183** E1
St Peters Way
Chorleywood WD3 . . **167** B5
Milton Keynes MK13 . . **34** A8
St Pirans Sch SL6 . . **195** E1
St Rumbold's La MK18 . **52** C8
St Stephens Dr MK15 . . **35** B7
St Stephen's Rd UB7 . . **208** D5
St Teresa's Cl HP27 . . **139** B4
St Teresa's Sch HP27 . **139** B4
St Thomas Aquinas RC
Comb Sch MK4 . . . . **57** E7
St Thomas Ct MK4 . . **45** F1
St Thomas More RC Prim
Sch HP4 . . . . . . **135** A4
St Thomas Wlk SL3 . . **212** D7
St Vincents MK17 . . **49** C4
Sakura Wlk MK15 . . **35** C6
Salcey Forest Trail★
MK16 . . . . **4** C2
SALCEY GREEN **11** B7
SALDEN **67** C3
Salden Cl
Drayton Parslow MK17 . **68** C6
Milton Keynes MK5 . . **46** B6
SALFORD **37** C3
Salford Rd MK17 . . . . **49** D7
Salisbury Ave SL2 . . **205** C8
Salisbury Cl
Amersham HP7 . . . . **165** E8
Princes Risborough
HP27 . . . . **139** C3
Salisbury Ct SL6 . . . . **202** E5
Salisbury Gr MK14 . . **21** F2
Salisbury Mews SL2 . . **198** C1
Salisbury Rd
High Wycombe HP13 . . **162** E1
Uxbridge UB8 . . . . **201** B3
Sallowsprings LU6 . . **93** F2

Salmons La HP16 . . . . .151 D6
Salop Rd MK3 . . . . .46 F2
Saltash Cl HP13 . . . . .174 B4
Salters Cl
  Ludgershall HP18 . . . . .96 C8
  Maidenhead SL6 . . . . .203 A7
Salter's Cl HP4 . . . . .134 F6
Salters La HP18 . . . . .96 C8
Salters Mews MK14 . . . . .34 F6
Salters Rd SL6 . . . . .203 B7
Salters Row HP10 . . . . .186 A4
SALT HILL 205 D5
Salt Hill Ave SL1 . . . . .205 C5
Salt Hill Cl UB8 . . . . .201 E7
Salt Hill Dr SL1 . . . . .205 C5
Salt Hill Mans SL1 . . . . .205 D5
Salt Hill Way SL1 . . . . .205 D5
Salton Link MK4 . . . . .46 B2
Saltwood Ave MK4 . . . . .45 E1
Samphire Ct MK7 . . . . .48 A6
Sampsons Gn SL2 . . . . .197 F2
Sampsons Hill HP7 . . . . . . .164 E2
Samuel Cl MK16 . . . . .22 F3
Sanctuary Rd HP15 . . . . . . .163 B5
Sandage Rd HP14 . . . . .171 B5
Sandal Ct MK5 . . . . .46 A5
Sandbrier Cl MK7 . . . . .48 B6
Sandbrook La HP23 . . . . . . .104 C1
Sandels Way HP9 . . . . .175 D4
Sandelswood End HP9 . . . .175 D5
Sanders La MK12 . . . . .18 D3
Sanderson Rd UB8 . . . . . . .201 C6
Sandford Gdns HP11 . . . . . .173 B4
SANDHILL 64 C2
Sandhill Rd
  Buckingham MK18 . . . . . . .64 C4
  East Claydon MK18 . . . . . .74 F8
Sandhill Way HP19 . . . . . . .115 A8
Sandholme MK18 . . . . .63 E2
Sandhurst Dr MK18 . . . . . . .52 C7
Sandisplatt Rd SL6 . . . . . . .202 A6
Sandlers End SL2 . . . . .198 B1
Sandles The SL4 . . . . .205 B1
Sandleswood Cl HP9 . . . . . .175 D4
Sandmartin Cl MK18 . . . . . . .41 E1
Sandon Cl HP23 . . . . .118 F4
Sandown Ct
  8 High Wycombe
  HP12 . . . . .172 E7
  Milton Keynes MK3 . . . . . . .57 D6
Sandown Rd SL2 . . . . .204 F8
Sandpiper 1 HP19 . . . . . . .101 E4
Sandpipers Pl SL6 . . . . . . .195 E6
Sandpit Hill MK14 . . . . .50 F6
Sandpit Hill Cotts
  HP23 . . . . .133 B2
Sandpit La MK27 . . . . .138 B4
Sandpits La HP10 . . . . .174 C7
Sandringham Ct
  8 High Wycombe
  HP13 . . . . .173 B7
  Newport Pagnell MK16 . . . . .22 B3
  Slough SL1 . . . . .204 D7
Sandringham Pl MK2 . . . . . .58 C8
Sandringham Rd
  Maidenhead SL6 . . . . .195 E2
  Stanwell TW6 . . . . .213 E2
SANDS 172 B7
Sands Bank Nature
  Reserve* HP12 . . . . .172 A7
Sands Farm Dr SL1 . . . . . . .197 C1
Sands Ind Est HP12 . . . . . .172 B7
Sandstone Cl MK18 . . . . . . .73 B5
Sandwell Ct MK8 . . . . .33 C2
Sandy Cl
  Buckingham MK18 . . . . . . .52 F8
  Milton Keynes MK14 . . . . . .34 D8
Sandycroft Rd HP6 . . . . . . .155 C1
Sandygate Cl SL7 . . . . .183 D3
Sandygate Rd SL7 . . . . . . .183 D3
Sandy La
  Aspley Heath MK17 . . . . . . .49 B2
  Leighton Buzzard LU7 . . . . .70 F3
  Long Crendon HP18 . . . . .125 B6
Sandy Mead SL6 . . . . .203 C1
Sandy Rd MK18 . . . . .73 B5
Sandy Rise SL9 . . . . .177 E2
Sandywell Dr MK15 . . . . . . .35 A6
San Remo Rd MK17 . . . . . . .49 F4
Santen Gr MK2 . . . . .58 D4
Saracens' Wharf MK2 . . . . . .47 E1
Sargeant Cl UB8 . . . . .201 D2
SARRATT 156 F4
Sarum Complex UB8 . . . . . .201 B3
Satis Ho SL3 . . . . .211 C7
Saunders Cl MK7 . . . . .48 B6
Saunders Ct 1 MK18 . . . . .173 F6
Saunders End HP6 . . . . . . .153 C5
Saunders Pl HP19 . . . . .115 A7
Saunders Rd UB10 . . . . . . .201 F4
Saunders Wood Copse
  HP14 . . . . .158 F4
SAUNDERTON 149 C1
  Bledlow Ridge 149 C1
  Princes Risborough 138 E1
SAUNDERTON LEE 149 A4
Saunderton Vale HP14 . . . .149 C1
Savage Croft MK10 . . . . . . .35 E3

Savay Cl UB9 . . . . .190 A4
Savay La UB9 . . . . .190 A5
Savernake Rd HP19 . . . . . . .101 D3
Savill La MK4, MK5 . . . . .45 F2
Savill Way SL7 . . . . .183 F2
Savoy Cres MK9 . . . . .34 F3
Savoy Ct SL6 . . . . .195 F1
Sawley Ho 5 MK3 . . . . .46 F1
Sawmill Cotts SL3 . . . . .199 F2
Sawmill Rd HP27 . . . . .138 D7
Sawpit Hill HP15 . . . . .163 B5
Sawyers Cl MK18 . . . . .202 A2
Sawyer's Cl SL4 . . . . .209 E7
Sawyers Cres SL6 . . . . .202 A2
Saxeways Bsns Ctr
  HP5 . . . . .143 C3
Saxhorn Rd HP14 . . . . .171 C4
Saxon Cl
  Amersham HP6 . . . . .154 D1
  Dunstable LU6 . . . . .93 E8
  Milton Keynes MK19 . . . . . .11 A2
  Slough SL3 . . . . .206 F4
  Uxbridge UB8 . . . . .208 E8
Saxon Ct
  High Wycombe HP12 . . . . .172 D8
  Stanwell TW19 . . . . .213 A2
Saxon Gate MK9 . . . . .34 E2
Saxon Gdns SL6 . . . . .196 D1
Saxon Lodge SL1 . . . . .204 F5
Saxon Park Ind Est MK1 . . . .47 D2
Saxon St
  Milton Keynes, Ashland MK1,
  MK6 . . . . .47 C7
  Milton Keynes, Heelands MK6,
  MK13, MK14 . . . . .34 C5
  Milton Keynes MK2 . . . . . . .58 C8
Saxon Way
  Harmondsworth UB7 . . . . .213 C8
  Old Windsor SL4 . . . . .211 B1
Saxon Way Trad Ctr
  UB7 . . . . .213 C8
Sayers Gdns HP4 . . . . .135 A6
Saye & Sele Cl HP18 . . . . . . .82 F6
Sayward Cl HP3 . . . . .144 D2
Scafell Rd SL2 . . . . .204 F8
Scarborough Way SL1 . . . . .205 B4
Scardale MK13 . . . . .34 C5
Scarlett Ave HP22 . . . . .131 E6
Scatterdells La WD4 . . . . . .146 F1
Scatterill Cl MK13 . . . . .34 A4
Scholars Way HP6 . . . . .154 F1
Scholars Wlk
  Chalfont St Peter SL9 . . . .177 E4
  Slough SL3 . . . . .207 A4
School Cl
  Asheridge HP5 . . . . .143 E5
  Brackley NN13 . . . . .39 A4
  Cryers Hill HP15 . . . . .162 C6
  High Wycombe, Downley
  HP13 . . . . .161 D2
  High Wycombe HP11 . . . . .173 A4
  Holmer Green HP15 . . . . .163 C7
  Ickford HP18 . . . . .124 A3
School Dr MK17 . . . . .57 C3
School End
  Chetwode MK18 . . . . .61 D8
  Great Horwood MK17 . . . . .55 A3
School Hill
  Charndon OX27 . . . . .73 A6
  North Marston MK18 . . . . . .76 B2
School Ho TW19 . . . . .213 C1
School La
  Amersham HP7 . . . . .165 A8
  Buckingham MK18 . . . . . . .52 C8
  Castlethorpe MK19 . . . . . . .11 A2
  Chalfont St Giles HP8 . . . .177 B7
  Chalfont St Peter SL9 . . . .177 D1
  Chearsley HP18 . . . . .112 B2
  Cookham Dean SL6 . . . . .195 B7
  Cookham SL6 . . . . .196 B7
  Dinton HP17 . . . . .113 F2
  Eaton Bray LU6 . . . . .92 F6
  Leighton Buzzard LU7 . . . . .68 E1
  Little Marlow SL7 . . . . .184 C5
  Maidenhead SL6 . . . . .195 E1
  Medmenham SL7 . . . . .193 B6
  Milton Keynes MK5 . . . . . . .46 B8
  Oakley HP18 . . . . .109 D5
  Penn Street HP7 . . . . .164 B5
  Preston Bissett MK18 . . . . .62 B8
  Seer Green HP9 . . . . .176 D4
  Shabbington HP18 . . . . . .124 D3
  Sherington MK16 . . . . .14 A2
  Slough SL2 . . . . .205 F6
  Turville RG9 . . . . .169 F3
  Twyford MK18 . . . . .62 C4
  Upper Winchendon HP18 . . .99 A1
  Waddesdon HP18 . . . . .99 A6
  Weston Turville HP22 . . . .116 F1
  Wexham Street SL2 . . . . . .199 B5
  Yardley Gobion NN12 . . . . .18 E6
School Rd
  Harmondsworth UB7 . . . . .213 D8
  Tylers Green HP10 . . . . . .174 D8
  Wooburn Green HP10 . . . .185 E8
School St MK13 . . . . .33 F7
School The HP23 . . . . .118 C8
School Way HP10 . . . . .174 B2
Schorne La MK18 . . . . .76 B2

Schumann Cl MK7 . . . . .48 C4
Scotch Firs MK7 . . . . .48 C6
Scotlands Dr SL2 . . . . .198 B6
Scotney Gdns SL3 . . . . .57 E8
Scotsgrove Cotts OX9 . . . . .126 A4
Scotsgrove Hill OX9 . . . . . .126 A1
Scotswood Cl HP9 . . . . .175 D5
Scott Cl
  Farnham Common SL2 . . . .198 C7
  West Drayton UB7 . . . . . . .208 F2
Scott Dr MK16 . . . . .22 A5
Scott End HP19 . . . . .100 F2
Scott Evans Ct MK18 . . . . . .66 A5
Scotts Cl
  Marsh Gibbon OX27 . . . . . .72 A3
  Stoke Hammond MK17 . . . . .69 E8
Scotts Cnr NN13 . . . . .39 A4
Scotts Farm Cl MK18 . . . . . .41 E4
Scotts La
  Adstock MK18 . . . . .53 F1
  Buckingham MK18 . . . . . . .41 E3
  Marsh Gibbon OX27 . . . . . .71 E2
Scriven Ct MK15 . . . . .35 E7
Scriveners La NN12 . . . . .17 A8
Scrubb's La HP14 . . . . .160 B7
Seabrooke Ct MK8 . . . . .45 D6
Seacourt Rd SL3 . . . . .207 B2
Seaford Rd TW6 . . . . .213 D2
Seagrave Ct MK7 . . . . .48 A4
Seagrave Rd HP9 . . . . .175 C4
Sears The LU6 . . . . .92 B5
Seaton Dr HP21 . . . . .115 D4
Seaton Gr MK10 . . . . .36 A4
Secklow Gate MK9 . . . . .34 F3
Second Ave MK1 . . . . .47 C2
Second Cres SL1 . . . . .205 C8
Second St HP11 . . . . .173 C4
Sedgemere MK8 . . . . .33 D2
Sedgemoor Dr OX9 . . . . . . .126 A1
Sedgmoor Cl HP10 . . . . . . .185 A7
Sedgmoor Gdns HP10 . . . .185 A8
Sedgmoor La HP10 . . . . . . .185 B7
Sedgmoor Rd HP10 . . . . . . .185 A8
Sedley Gr UB9 . . . . .190 C7
SEDRUP 114 F3
Sedrup La HP17 . . . . .114 F4
Seebeck Cl MK5 . . . . .46 C7
Seeleys Cl HP9 . . . . .175 C4
Seeleys Ct HP9 . . . . .175 D3
Seeleys La HP9 . . . . .175 D3
Seeleys Rd HP9 . . . . .175 C4
SEER GREEN 176 D4
Seer Green CE Comb Sch
  HP9 . . . . .176 C4
Seer Green & Jordans Sta
  HP9 . . . . .176 C3
Seer Green La HP9 . . . . . . .176 E3
Seer Mead HP9 . . . . .176 D4
Sefton Cl SL2 . . . . .198 F4
Sefton Paddock SL2 . . . . . .199 A5
Sefton Park Cotts SL2 . . . . .199 A4
Sefton Park Sch SL2 . . . . . .199 B5
Sefton Way UB8 . . . . .208 C7
Selbourne Ave MK3 . . . . . . .57 F7
Selbourne Ho 10 SL8 . . . . .185 A4
Selby Gr MK5 . . . . .46 B5
Selim Ct 4 SL1 . . . . .206 B4
Selkirk Ave HP19 . . . . .101 D2
Selkirk Gr MK3 . . . . .46 F2
Selwood Cl TW19 . . . . .213 C1
Selwood Gdns TW19 . . . . . .213 C1
Selwood Way HP13 . . . . . . .161 E2
Selworthy MK4 . . . . .46 D3
Selwyn Cl SL4 . . . . .209 E5
Selwyn Ho HP21 . . . . .116 B6
Selwyn Gr MK3 . . . . .58 B8
Selwyn Pl SL1 . . . . .204 E6
September Ct UB10 . . . . . . .201 D3
Serjeants Gn MK14 . . . . .34 F6
Serles Cl MK6 . . . . .47 A6
Sermed Ct SL2 . . . . .206 C5
Serpentine Ct MK2 . . . . .58 D5
Servite Ho SL6 . . . . .203 B8
Seven Acre Ho HP10 . . . . . .174 C2
Seven Acres HP18 . . . . .125 B7
Seven Gables MK18 . . . . . . .65 D6
Sevenhills Rd SL0 . . . . .200 C6
Seven Hills Rd SL6 . . . . . . .200 C6
Severalls Ave HP5 . . . . .144 C2
Severn Cres SL3 . . . . .207 B1
Severn Dr MK16 . . . . .22 E4
Severn Ho HP13 . . . . .173 F7
Severn Way MK3 . . . . .57 D8
Sewell Cl HP19 . . . . .100 F2
Seymour Cl
  Flackwell Heath HP10 . . . .173 F2
  Maidenhead SL6 . . . . .202 B3
Seymour Court La SL7 . . . . .183 B5
Seymour Court Rd SL7 . . . .183 C4
Seymour Ct
  Berkhamsted HP4 . . . . . . .134 E6
  Tring HP23 . . . . .119 A4
Seymour Ho
  High Wycombe HP12 . . . . .172 E4
  Slough SL3 . . . . .206 E4
Seymour Park Rd SL7 . . . . .183 D3
Seymour Plain SL7 . . . . . . .183 C5
Seymour Rd
  Berkhamsted HP4 . . . . . . .134 E6
  Chalfont St Giles HP8 . . . .177 C6

Seymour Rd continued
  Slough SL1 . . . . .205 D4
SHABBINGTON 124 D3
Shackerstone Cl MK10 . . . . .36 B4
Shackleton Ct 6 TW19 . . . .213 E1
Shackleton Pl MK6 . . . . .34 E1
Shackleton Rd
  High Wycombe HP12 . . . . .172 E5
  Slough SL1 . . . . .205 F6
Shaftesbury Cres MK3 . . . . .47 A1
Shaftesbury Ct
  Maidenhead SL6 . . . . .202 E5
  6 Slough SL1 . . . . .205 E4
  Winslow MK18 . . . . .65 F3
Shaftesbury Ho HP21 . . . . .116 C7
Shaftesbury St HP11 . . . . . .172 F8
Shaggy Calf La SL2 . . . . . . .206 A6
Shakespeare Cl MK16 . . . . .22 A5
Shakespeare Lodge
  SL1 . . . . .204 F5
Shakespeare Orch HP18 . . .82 F6
Shakespeare Way
  HP20 . . . . .116 A8
Shallowford Gr MK4 . . . . . . .46 D4
SHALSTONE 39 E6
Shamaa Ho 13 SL1 . . . . . . .205 F4
Shamrock Cl MK7 . . . . .48 B6
Shannon Ct
  Chesham HP5 . . . . .144 C1
  Milton Keynes MK14 . . . . . .35 A6
Shantock Hall La HP3 . . . . .145 E1
Shantock La HP3 . . . . .145 E1
Shantung Pl HP5 . . . . .154 C6
Shardeloes HP7 . . . . .164 D8
Sharkham Ct MK4 . . . . .46 D4
Sharman Row 8 SL3 . . . . . .206 F1
Sharman Wlk MK13 . . . . .34 A3
Sharney Ave SL3 . . . . .207 B3
Sharp Cl HP21 . . . . .115 E5
Sharp's Cl HP18 . . . . .99 B6
Sharrow Vale HP22 . . . . . . .172 E7
Shaw Cl
  Aylesbury HP20 . . . . .116 A8
  Newport Pagnell MK16 . . . . .22 A5
Shaw Ct
  Aylesbury HP21 . . . . .115 E3
  Old Windsor SL4 . . . . .211 A2
Shawfield Ct UB7 . . . . .208 E3
Shaw Gdns 11 SL3 . . . . . . .206 F1
Shaws Cl HP16 . . . . .151 D5
Shaw The SL6 . . . . .195 E6
Shearmans MK11 . . . . .33 A4
Sheehy Way SL2 . . . . .206 B6
Sheelin Gr MK2 . . . . .58 D4
Sheepcoat Cl MK5 . . . . .46 A5
Sheepcote Cl HP9 . . . . .175 A1
Sheepcote Dell Rd
  HP15 . . . . .163 E7
Sheepcote Gdns UB9 . . . . .190 A5
Sheepcote La HP10,
  SL1 . . . . .186 A2
Sheepcote Rd
  Eton Wick SL4 . . . . .205 A1
  Windsor SL4 . . . . .209 E5
Sheepfold La HP7 . . . . .165 D7
Sheephouse Rd SL6 . . . . . .196 B2
SHEEPLANE 60 C2
Sheeplane MK17 . . . . .60 C2
SHEEPRIDGE 184 E7
Sheepridge La SL7, SL8 . . .184 E7
Sheep St MK18 . . . . .66 A4
Sheering Gr MK13 . . . . .34 B8
Sheerness Ct MK4 . . . . .57 A8
Sheerstock HP17 . . . . .126 E5
Sheerwater HP19 . . . . .101 E4
Sheet St SL4 . . . . .210 D6
Sheet Street Rd SL4 . . . . . .210 C2
Sheffield Dr HP21 . . . . .115 E6
Sheffield Rd SL1 . . . . .205 C7
Shelburne Ct HP12 . . . . . . .172 E4
Shelburne Rd HP12 . . . . . . .172 E4
Sheldon Ct MK8 . . . . .33 F1
Sheldon Rd HP18 . . . . .124 A3
Sheldon Way MK4 . . . . .46 E3
Shelduck Cl 3 HP20 . . . . . .101 E3
Shelley Cl
  Medmenham SL7 . . . . .193 B2
  Newport Pagnell MK16 . . . . .22 B4
  Slough SL3 . . . . .206 F1
  Wooburn Green HP10 . . . .185 E8
Shelley Dr MK3 . . . . .57 F7
Shelley Rd
  Chesham HP5 . . . . .144 B2
  High Wycombe HP11 . . . . .172 E5
  12 Marlow SL7 . . . . .183 F3
Shellfield Cl TW19 . . . . .213 A2
Shelsley Ave MK6 . . . . .47 C5
Shelsmore MK14 . . . . .35 A8
Shelton Ct
  Slough SL3 . . . . .206 C3
  Woburn Sands MK17 . . . . .49 B4
SHENLEY BROOK END 46 A3
Shenley Brook End Sch
  MK5 . . . . .46 A3
SHENLEY CHURCH END . . .45 E6
Shenley L Ctr MK5 . . . . .46 C5
SHENLEY LODGE 46 C5

Shenley Rd
  Milton Keynes, Bletchley
  MK3 . . . . .46 E1
  Milton Keynes, Loughton
  MK5 . . . . .46 A7
  Whaddon MK17 . . . . .56 C8
Shenley Rdbt MK5 . . . . .46 A5
SHENLEY WOOD 45 F4
Shenston Ct 13 SL4 . . . . . .210 C6
Shenstone Dr SL1 . . . . .197 D1
Shenstone Hill HP4 . . . . . . .135 E5
Shenton MK10 . . . . .36 C3
Shepherd Cl HP20 . . . . .102 A2
Shepherds MK11 . . . . .33 A4
Shepherds Cl
  Beaconsfield HP9 . . . . . . .175 F1
  Hurley SL6 . . . . .193 F3
  Uxbridge UB8 . . . . .201 C1
Shepherds Ct SL4 . . . . .209 E5
Shepherds Fold HP15 . . . . .163 D8
Shepherds Gate HP16 . . . .152 A2
Shepherds La
  Beaconsfield HP9 . . . . . . .175 F1
  Hazlemere HP15 . . . . .162 F5
  Hurley SL6 . . . . .193 F4
Shepherd's La WD3 . . . . . . .167 E2
Shepherds Row MK18 . . . . .66 A4
Shepherds Way HP5 . . . . . .154 D6
Shepherdswell Sch MK6 . . .35 B2
Sheppards Cl MK18 . . . . . . .22 C4
Sheppards Gn MK5 . . . . . . .45 F6
Shepperton Ct MK19 . . . . . .19 F5
Sheraton Dr HP13 . . . . .162 D1
Sheraton Ho WD3 . . . . .167 C5
Sherborne Ct SL3 . . . . .212 E6
Sherborne Ct SL2 . . . . .202 E5
Sherbourne Dr
  Bow Brickhill MK7 . . . . .48 B4
  Maidenhead SL6 . . . . .202 C3
  Windsor SL4 . . . . .209 F3
Sherbourne Wlk SL2 . . . . . .198 C8
Shereway HP19 . . . . .115 B8
Shergold Way SL6 . . . . .195 F6
Sheridan Cl HP21 . . . . .115 D3
Sheridan Ct
  High Wycombe HP12 . . . . .172 C3
  Maidenhead SL6 . . . . .203 B8
  Slough SL1 . . . . .204 E6
Sheridan Gr MK4 . . . . .45 D2
Sheriff Cl HP19 . . . . .115 B8
Sheringham Ct SL6 . . . . . . .202 E7
SHERINGTON 14 A2
Sherington CE Fst Sch
  MK16 . . . . .14 A2
Sherington Rd MK16 . . . . . . .22 C7
Sherman Rd SL1 . . . . .205 E8
Shernfold MK7 . . . . .48 B7
Sherrell Cotts HP18 . . . . . . .99 A7
Sherwood Cl SL3 . . . . .206 E3
Sherwood Ct
  Colnbrook SL3 . . . . .212 D7
  10 Slough SL3 . . . . .206 F1
Sherwood Dr
  Maidenhead SL6 . . . . .202 A6
  Milton Keynes MK1, MK2,
  MK3 . . . . .47 B1
Shields Cl HP10 . . . . .163 B1
Shifford Cres SL6 . . . . .195 E3
Shilling Cl MK15 . . . . .35 A7
Shillingridge Pk SL7 . . . . . .182 E5
Shinfield Cl MK18 . . . . .63 D2
Ship Hill SL4 . . . . .186 E4
Ship La LU7 . . . . .105 D3
Shiplake Ho SL8 . . . . .185 B4
Shipley Rd MK16 . . . . .22 B4
Shipman Ct MK15 . . . . .35 B7
Ship Rd LU7 . . . . .80 E6
Ship St HP11 . . . . .173 A7
SHIPTON 66 B3
SHIPTON 66 B3
Shipton Hill MK13 . . . . .34 B6
SHIPTON LEE 84 D7
Shipton Rd UB10 . . . . .201 E8
Shire Ct MK14 . . . . .35 A5
Shire La
  Chalfont St Peter HP8,
  SL9 . . . . .178 B6
  Cholesbury HP23 . . . . . . .133 B4
  Chorleywood WD3 . . . . . .167 C4
  North Crawley MK16 . . . . . .24 E4
Shires Bsns Pk The
  NN13 . . . . .38 A6
Shires Rd NN13 . . . . .38 A6
Shirley Ave SL4 . . . . .209 E6
Shirley Cl HP20 . . . . .101 D2
Shirley Moor MK10 . . . . .48 B8
Shirley Rd SL6 . . . . .202 C5
Shirwell Cres MK4 . . . . .46 D5
Shogmoor La RG9 . . . . .170 C1
Shootacre Cnr HP27 . . . . . .149 A8
Shootacre La HP27 . . . . . . .149 A8
SHOOTERSWAY 134 E4
Shootersway HP4 . . . . .134 E4
Shootersway La HP4 . . . . . .134 E3
Shootersway Pk HP4 . . . . . .134 F3

Shop La NN7 . . . . 1 B6
Shoppenhanger's Rd
  SL6 . . . . 202 E4
Shoredich Cl UB10 . . . . 190 F1
Shoreham Rise SL2 . . . . 197 D1
Shoreham Road (E)
  TW6 . . . . 213 E2
Shoreham Road (W)
  TW6 . . . . 213 E2
Shorham Rise MK8 . . . . . . 33 E2
Shortborough Ave
  HP27 . . . . 139 B5
Short Ditch HP17 . . . . . . 127 A7
Shortfern SL2 . . . . 206 C7
Short Hale LU7 . . . . 105 D3
Short Massey MK46 . . . . . . 6 E5
Short Rd TW6 . . . . 213 E1
Short St HP11 . . . . 172 F7
Shortway
  Amersham HP6 . . . . 154 D2
  Chesham HP5 . . . . 144 B2
Shotfield Rd HP14 . . . . . 171 C4
Shothanger Way HP3 . . 146 D6
Shouler Cl MK5 . . . . 46 A5
SHREDING GREEN 207 C7
Shrewsbury Cl MK10 . . . . 36 A2
Shrimpton Cl HP9 . . . . . 175 D6
Shrimpton Rd
  Beaconsfield HP9 . . . . . . 175 D6
  High Wycombe HP12 . . . . 172 B3
Shropshire Ct MK3 . . . . . . 46 E1
Shrubbery Cl HP13 . . . . . 173 B8
Shrubbery Rd HP13 . . . . . 173 B8
Shrublands Ave HP4 . . . 135 A4
Shrublands Rd HP4 . . . . 135 A5
Shucklow Hill MK17 . . . . . 55 E3
Shugars Gn HP23 . . . . . . 119 B5
Shupp's La HP18 . . . . 112 B1
Shutlanger Rd NN12 . . . . . 9 A8
Shuttleworth Gr MK7 . . . 48 D6
Siareys Cl OX39 . . . . 147 C6
Sibleys Rise HP16 . . . . . . 152 D8
Side Rd UB9 . . . . 189 D4
Sidings Ind Est The
  NN13 . . . . 38 A8
Sidings The
  Loudwater HP11 . . . . 174 B3
  Milton Keynes MK2 . . . . . . 47 E1
Sidlow Cl MK11 . . . . 32 F4
Sidney Cl UB8 . . . . 201 C5
Sidney Ho HP14 . . . . 171 C5
Sidney Rd SL4 . . . . 209 C4
Sidney Terr HP12 . . . . . . 131 B5
Silbury Arc MK9 . . . . 34 E3
Silbury Bvd MK9 . . . . 34 D2
Silbury Rdbt MK9 . . . . 34 C1
Silchester Ho SL6 . . . . . 203 B8
Silco Dr SL6 . . . . 202 E6
Silicon Ct MK5 . . . . 46 C5
Silk Mill Way HP23 . . . . 119 A5
Silk St HP18 . . . . 99 A6
Silkwood Ct SL1 . . . . 205 F6
Sillswood MK46 . . . . 6 E4
Silsden Cres HP8 . . . . . . 177 D7
Silverbeck Way TW19 . . 213 A2
Silver Birch Cl UB10 . . . 201 E8
Silver Birch Dr HP27 . . . 149 E5
Silverbirches La MK17 . . 49 A2
Silver Birch Way HP22 . 116 B4
Silver Cl SL6 . . . . 202 A5
Silverdale Cl
  ◢ Aylesbury HP20 . . . . . 101 D1
  Tylers Green HP10 . . . . . 163 A1
Silver End MK46 . . . . 7 A3
Silver Hill HP8 . . . . 177 B8
Silvermead HP18 . . . . . . 123 D5
Silver St
  20 Aylesbury HP20 . . . . 115 D8
  Cublington LU7 . . . . 78 B1
  Milton Keynes MK11 . . . . . 32 D5
  Newport Pagnell MK16 . . 22 D4
Silverstone Mews SL6 . . 202 C4
Silverstone Motor Racing
  Circuit★ MK18 . . . . 28 F8
Silvertrees Dr SL6 . . . . . 202 A5
Silverweed Ct MK7 . . . . . 48 B5
Simatt Ho HP10 . . . . 174 C2
Simdims MK43 . . . . 25 A1
Simmons Cl SL3 . . . . 207 A2
Simmons Ct
  Aylesbury HP21 . . . . 115 E4
  High Wycombe HP12 . . . . 172 E7
Simmons Rd RG9 . . . . . . 191 D3
Simmons Way
  Lane End HP14 . . . . 171 C4
  Thame OX9 . . . . 125 F1
Simms Croft MK10 . . . . . . 36 A2
Simnel MK6 . . . . 47 B6
Simon Dean HP3 . . . . . . 146 A4
Simonsbath MK4 . . . . 46 D2
Simons Lea MK13 . . . . 34 B4
Simon's Way MK18 . . . . . . 39 E7
Simpson Cl SL6 . . . . 203 B8
Simpson Dr MK6 . . . . 47 E5
Simpson Pl HP21 . . . . . . 115 F5

Simpson Rd MK1, MK2,
  MK6 . . . . 47 E3
Simpson Rdbt MK6 . . . . . 47 D5
Simpson Sch MK6 . . . . . . 47 D5
Simpsons Way SL1 . . . . . 205 E5
Sinatra Dr MK4 . . . . 45 E3
Sinclair Ct MK1 . . . . 47 B3
Sinclair Rd SL4 . . . . 210 C4
Singers La RG9 . . . . 191 E1
SINGLEBOROUGH 54 F5
Singleborough La MK17 . 54 F3
Singleton Dr MK8 . . . . 33 E3
Singleton Way 8 HP19 . 115 A8
Singret Pl UB8 . . . . 201 C1
Sion Terr MK18 . . . . 51 B6
Sipson Rd UB7 . . . . 208 F3
Sipthorp Cl MK7 . . . . 48 C6
Sir Henry Floyd Gram Sch
  HP21 . . . . 115 C7
Sir Henry Peakes Dr
  SL2 . . . . 199 A8
Sir Peter's Way HP4 . . . . 107 E6
Sir Robert Mews SL3 . . . 207 A1
Sir Sydney Camm Ho
  SL4 . . . . 210 B6
Sir William Borlase's Gram
  Sch SL7 . . . . 183 C1
Sir William Ramsay Sch
  HP15 . . . . 163 A3
Sissinghurst Dr MK4 . . . . . 45 E2
Sitwell Cl MK16 . . . . 21 F5
Six Cotts MK18 . . . . 29 E5
Sixth St HP11 . . . . 173 C4
Sixty Acres Rd HP16 . . . 151 C6
Skeats Wharf MK15 . . . . . . 35 A7
Skeldon Gate MK14 . . . . . 35 A4
Skeldon Rdbt MK9 . . . . . . 35 A4
Skelton Cl HP9 . . . . 186 A8
Skene Cl MK2 . . . . 58 C4
Skerries Ct SL3 . . . . 207 A2
Skimmers Cl HP15 . . . . . 163 C6
Skimmers End HP15 . . . . 163 C6
Skimmers Field HP15 . . . 163 C6
Skip La UB9 . . . . 190 E3
Skipper Cl HP19 . . . . 101 C4
Skippon Way OX9 . . . . . . 125 F2
Skipton Cl MK15 . . . . 35 C6
SKIRMETT 170 A1
Skittle Gn HP27 . . . . 138 A2
SKITTLE GREEN 138 A3
Skydmore Path SL2 . . . . 197 F1
Skye Cres
  Milton Keynes MK17 . . . . . 58 C3
  Milton Keynes MK17 . . . . . 58 C3
Skye Lodge SL1 . . . . 205 E5
Skylark Rd UB9 . . . . 189 C3
Skyline Mews HP17 . . . . 172 C4
Skyport Dr UB7 . . . . 213 D7
Skyway 14 Trad Est
  SL3 . . . . 212 C4
Slade Hill
  Aylesbury HP19 . . . . 115 A7
  Mixbury NN13 . . . . 38 D1
Slade La MK11 . . . . 33 A4
Slade Oak La UB9 . . . . . . 189 C5
Slade Rd HP14 . . . . 158 E4
Slade The MK17 . . . . 57 D3
Slad La HP27 . . . . 149 F3
Slated Row MK12 . . . . 33 B7
Slated Row Specl Sch
  MK12 . . . . 33 A7
Slatepits Croft MK46 . . . . . 6 E5
Slater St HP13 . . . . 173 C6
Slattenham Cl HP19 . . . 115 B7
Slave Hill HP17 . . . . 126 C1
Slayter Rd HP14 . . . . 171 C4
Slickett's La LU6 . . . . 92 F3
Slipe The LU7 . . . . 105 A7
SLOUGH 205 D5
Slough & Eton CE Sch
  SL1 . . . . 205 D3
Slough Gram Sch SL3 . . 206 B3
Slough Ice Arena SL1 . . 205 D4
Slough Interchange Ind Est
  SL2 . . . . 206 A5
Slough La MK14 . . . . 160 C6
Slough Mus★ SL1 . . . . . 206 A4
Slough Rd
  Datchet SL3 . . . . 211 B8
  Iver Heath SL0 . . . . 200 E3
  Slough SL4 . . . . 205 E1
Slough Sta SL1 . . . . 205 F5
Slough Trad Est SL1 . . . . 205 B7
Sly Corner HP16 . . . . 142 E4
Smabridge Wlk MK15 . . . 35 D7
SMAE Inst The SL6 . . . . . 202 B6
Small Cres MK18 . . . . 52 F8
Smalldean La HP27 . . . . 149 E2
Smarden Bell MK7 . . . . . . 48 B8
Smeaton Cl
  Aylesbury HP19 . . . . 101 A1
  Blakelands MK14 . . . . . . 22 A3
Smewin Cl HP11 . . . . 172 E7
Smith Cl HP20 . . . . 116 B7
Smith Ctr The RG9 . . . . . 191 B5
Smithergill Ct MK13 . . . . . 34 C5
Smithfield End MK17 . . . . 66 F4

Smithfield Rd SL6 . . . . . 202 A3
Smith's La
  Waterperry Common
    OX33 . . . . 122 F7
  Windsor SL4 . . . . 209 E6
Smithsons Pl MK9 . . . . . . 35 B3
Smithy The MK19 . . . . 31 E4
Snaith Cres MK5 . . . . 46 B7
Snakeley Cl HP10 . . . . . . 174 C1
Snakemoor Nature
  Reserve★ HP17 . . . . . . 126 D6
Snape Spur SL1 . . . . 205 E7
Snells La HP7 . . . . 166 C2
Snells Wood Ct HP7 . . . . 166 C2
SNELSHALL EAST 57 B7
Snelshall St MK4 . . . . 56 F8
SNELSHALL WEST 57 A7
Snowball Hill SL6 . . . . . . 202 A1
Snowberry Cl MK12 . . . . . 33 D5
Snowden Cl SL4 . . . . 209 D3
Snowdon Dr MK6 . . . . 46 D7
Snowdrop Way HP15 . . . 162 F7
Snowhill Cotts HP5 . . . . 144 F7
Snowshill Ct MK14 . . . . . . 21 F2
Soames Cl MK46 . . . . 7 F7
Soane Wlk HP13 . . . . 173 A8
Soho Cres HP13 . . . . 185 D4
Soho Mills Ind Est
  HP10 . . . . 185 D4
Sokeman Cl MK12 . . . . . . 33 A5
Solar Ct MK14 . . . . 21 E1
Solesbridge Cl WD3 . . . . 167 F6
Solesbridge La WD3 . . . 167 F6
Somerford Cl SL6 . . . . . . 203 B8
Somerford Pl HP9 . . . . . . 175 D3
Somerlea SL6 . . . . 196 C3
Somersby Cres SL6 . . . . 202 E3
Somerset Cl MK3 . . . . 46 F1
Somerset Lodge 3
  SL6 . . . . 202 F6
Somerset Way SL0 . . . . . 207 F4
Somers Lees 13 HP19 . . 115 A8
Somerville Rd SL4 . . . . . 205 C1
Somerville Way HP15 . . . 188 B5
Sophie Gdns SL3 . . . . . . 206 D4
Sorensen Ct MK5 . . . . 45 E4
Sorrell Dr MK16 . . . . 21 F4
Soskin Dr MK14 . . . . 34 D6
Sospel Ct SL2 . . . . 198 C3
SOULBURY 69 E3
Soulbury Rd
  Burcott LU7 . . . . 79 D4
  Leighton Buzzard LU7 . . . . 80 D7
  Stewkley LU7 . . . . 68 F1
Southampton Road E
  TW6 . . . . 213 F1
Southampton Road W
  TW6 . . . . 213 E1
South Bank NN13 . . . . 38 C7
South Bank Rd HP4 . . . . 134 F6
Southbourne 1 MK4 . . . . 173 C7
Southbourne Dr SL8 . . . 185 A3
Southbridge Gr MK7 . . . . 48 A7
South Cl
  Medmenham SL7 . . . . 193 D7
  Slough SL1 . . . . 204 D6
  West Drayton UB7 . . . . . 208 F3
Southcliffe Dr SL9 . . . . . 177 E5
South Common Rd
  UB8 . . . . 201 E6
Southcote Way HP10 . . . 163 B1
South Cottage Dr WD3 . 167 F4
South Cottage Gdns
  WD3 . . . . 167 F4
Southcott Lower Sch
  LU7 . . . . 80 D8
Southcott Village LU7 . . . 80 D8
Southcott Way MK6 . . . . . 47 D5
SOUTHCOURT 115 D6
Southcourt Ave LU7 . . . . . 80 D6
Southcourt Ho LU7 . . . . . . 80 D7
Southcourt Rd LU7 . . . . . . 80 D7
Southcroft SL2 . . . . 198 B1
South Dr
  Beaconsfield HP9 . . . . . . 186 B8
  High Wycombe HP13 . . . . 173 D6
South Eighth St MK9 . . . . 34 E2
South End La LU6 . . . . 92 B4
South Enmore Rdbt
  MK6 . . . . 35 B3
Southern Cotts TW3 . . . . 213 D2
Southern Perimeter Rd TW6,
  TW19 . . . . 213 D2
Southern Rd
  Aylesbury HP19 . . . . 101 C1
  Thame OX9 . . . . 125 E1
Southern Way MK12, MK13 . . 33 D5
Southfield Cl MK15 . . . . . . 35 E7
South Field Cl SL4 . . . . . 204 C3
Southfield Cotts HP17 . . 130 C3
Southfield Dr HP15 . . . . 163 A6
Southfield Gdns SL1 . . . 204 B8

Southfield Rd
  Aylesbury HP20 . . . . 116 B8
  Flackwell Heath HP10 . . 174 A1
  High Wycombe HP13 . . . 161 D1
  Princes Risborough
    HP27 . . . . 139 C3
South Fifth St MK9 . . . . . . 34 E1
South Fourth St MK9 . . . . 34 D1
Southgate Ho SL6 . . . . . 202 F8
South Gn SL1 . . . . 205 E6
South Hall MK18 . . . . 41 E3
SOUTH HAREFIELD 190 D6
SOUTH HEATH 152 E8
South Hills HP18 . . . . 96 A1
South Ho MK1 . . . . 47 D3
South La LU7 . . . . 78 E7
Southland Dr MK2 . . . . . . 58 E6
Southlands Rd UB9 . . . . 189 F1
South Lawne MK3 . . . . . . 57 F8
Southlea Rd SL3, SL4 . . . 211 B5
South Maundin HP14 . . . 162 A7
South Meadow La SL4 . . 210 C8
South Ninth St MK9 . . . . . 34 F2
South Overgate Rdbt
  MK6 . . . . 35 B3
South Park Ave WD3 . . . 167 C4
South Park Cres SL9 . . . 188 E7
South Park Dr SL1 . . . . . 188 E6
South Park Dr SL9 . . . . . 188 E7
South Park Gdns HP4 . . 135 B5
South Park View SL9 . . . 188 F7
South Path SL4 . . . . 210 C5
South Pk SL9 . . . . 188 F5
South Pl SL7 . . . . 183 C1
South Rd
  Amersham HP6 . . . . 154 C3
  Chorleywood WD3 . . . . . 167 C4
  Maidenhead SL6 . . . . . . 202 E6
  West Drayton UB7 . . . . . 208 F3
South Row
  Fulmer SL3 . . . . 199 E8
  Milton Keynes MK9 . . . . . 34 E1
  Milton Keynes MK9 . . . . . 46 D8
South Saxon Rdbt MK9 . . 34 F1
South Secklow Rdbt
  MK6 . . . . 34 F2
South Second St MK9 . . . 34 D1
South Seventh St MK9 . . 34 E1
South Side SL9 . . . . 188 D8
South Sixth St MK9 . . . . . 34 E1
South St
  Castlethorpe MK19 . . . . . 19 F5
  Wendover HP22 . . . . 131 B4
South Tenth St MK9 . . . . . 34 F2
South Terr
  Milton Keynes MK2 . . . . . . 58 C8
  Windsor SL4 . . . . 210 E6
South Vale NN7 . . . . 1 A5
South View
  Cookham Rise SL6 . . . . . 195 E7
  Eton SL4 . . . . 205 B1
  High Wycombe HP11 . . . . 161 D2
  Wooburn Green HP10 . . . 185 D8
Southview Rd SL7 . . . . . . 183 E4
South View Rd SL9 . . . . . 188 D7
South Way HP9 . . . . 186 A8
Southwick Ct MK8 . . . . . . 45 F8
Southwick St MK9 . . . . . . 34 E1
Southwold Ct HP21 . . . . . 116 A6
Southwold Spur SL3 . . . 207 C4
Southwood Gdns SL6 . . 195 E5
Southwood Rd SL6 . . . . . 195 E5
Southwood Sch MK14 . . . 34 E5
Sovereign Beeches
  SL2 . . . . 198 B6
Sovereign Cl MK18 . . . . . 75 F7
Sovereign Ct
  Aylesbury HP19 . . . . 101 D2
  High Wycombe HP13 . . . . 173 D6
Sovereign Dr MK15 . . . . . 35 A7
Sovereign Hts SL3 . . . . . 212 A8
Sovereign Lodge MK15 . 35 A7
Spackmans Way SL1 . . . 205 D3
Spa Cl HP10 . . . . 118 B8
Spade Oak Farm SL8 . . . 184 E3
Spade Oak Mdw SL8 . . . 184 E4
Spark Way MK16 . . . . 21 F5
Sparrow Cl HP21 . . . . . . 101 F3
Sparrow Hall Bsns Pk
  LU6 . . . . 92 D3
Sparrow Hall Farm LU6 . 92 D3
Sparsholt Cl 5 MK4 . . . . 46 C2
Spearing Rd HP12 . . . . . 172 C7
Spearmant Ind Est
  HP12 . . . . 172 B6
Spearmint Cl MK7 . . . . . . 48 B5
Specklands MK46 . . . . . . 46 A8
Speedbird Way UB7 . . . . 213 B7
Speedwell Pl MK14 . . . . . 34 E4
SPEEN 150 C4
Speen CE Sch HP27 . . . . 150 B4
Speen Rd HP14, HP16,
  HP27 . . . . 150 D2
Speldhurst Ct MK7 . . . . . 48 B7
Spencer MK14 . . . . 34 C8
Spencer Cl UB8 . . . . 201 C2
Spencer Gdns OX27 . . . . 72 E5
Spencer Rd SL3 . . . . 206 F3
Spencers Cl SL6 . . . . 202 D8

SPENCERSGREEN 132 C7
Spencers La SL6 . . . . 195 E6
Spencers Rd SL6 . . . . . . 202 D8
Spencer St MK3 . . . . 33 F7
Spencer Villas SL1 . . . . . 204 F5
Spenlows Rd MK3 . . . . . . 47 A3
Spens SL6 . . . . 202 F8
Spenser Ho HP21 . . . . . . 115 F6
Spenser Rd HP21 . . . . . . 115 F6
Sperling Rd SL6 . . . . 195 F1
Spickett's La HP18 . . . . . 113 A3
Spier's La OX27 . . . . 71 F2
Spiert The HP17 . . . . 114 D5
Spindle Cl HP15 . . . . 163 A3
Spindle Ct HP12 . . . . 172 E7
Spinfield La SL7 . . . . 183 B2
Spinfield Lane W SL7 . . . 183 C1
Spinfield Mount SL7 . . . . 183 B1
Spinfield Pk SL7 . . . . 183 C1
Spinfield Sch SL7 . . . . . . 183 B2
Spinners Wlk
  Marlow SL7 . . . . 183 C1
  Windsor SL4 . . . . 210 C6
Spinney SL1 . . . . 205 B5
Spinney Bglws LU7 . . . . . 91 C6
Spinney Cl
  Steeple Claydon MK18 . . . 63 C3
  West Drayton UB7 . . . . . 208 F3
Spinney Cotts OX33 . . . . 123 B1
Spinney Cres LU6 . . . . . . 93 F8
Spinney Hill Rd MK46 . . . 4 C7
Spinney La MK17 . . . . 49 F4
Spinney The
  Beaconsfield HP9 . . . . . . 175 E1
  Berkhamsted HP4 . . . . . 134 F3
  Chesham HP5 . . . . 144 D2
  Gerrards Cross SL9 . . . . 188 D3
  High Wycombe HP11 . . . . 173 A4
  Holmer Green HP15 . . . . 163 D3
  Milton Keynes MK13 . . . . . 34 A4
  Winslow MK18 . . . . 66 A6
Spire View TW19 . . . . . . 213 D1
SPITAL 210 B3
Spitfire Cl SL3 . . . . 207 A2
Spittal St SL7 . . . . 183 D2
Spoondell LU6 . . . . 93 F7
Spoonley Wood MK13 . . . 33 S5
Sportsman Cl MK18 . . . . . 63 D3
Spout La TW19 . . . . 213 A3
Spout Lane N TW19 . . . . 213 B3
SPRIG'S ALLEY 147 F1
Sprigs Holly La HP14 . . . 159 B8
Springate Field SL3 . . . . 206 E4
Springbank Ct MK16 . . . . 12 B7
Spring Cl
  High Wycombe HP13 . . . . 173 F7
  Latimer HP5 . . . . 155 D3
  Maidenhead SL6 . . . . . . 195 F2
  Milton Keynes MK17 . . . . . 55 A2
Spring Coppice HP14 . . . 171 C6
Spring Coppice La
  HP27 . . . . 150 D5
Springdale Cotts SL8 . . . 185 B2
Springett Pl HP6 . . . . 154 F2
SPRINGFIELD 35 B2
Springfield Bvd MK6 . . . . 35 B2
Springfield Cl
  Aylesbury HP21 . . . . 115 C8
  Chesham HP5 . . . . 154 C7
  Windsor SL4 . . . . 210 B5
Springfield Ct 8
  ◢ Leighton Buzzard LU7 . . 80 C7
  ◢ Milton Keynes MK6 . . . 203 B7
Springfield Gdns
  Chinnor OX39 . . . . 147 C7
  Deanshanger MK19 . . . . . 31 E4
Springfield Hollow
  HP14 . . . . 158 E5
Springfield Pk SL6 . . . . . 203 C1
Springfield Rd
  Chesham HP5 . . . . 154 C7
  Dunstable LU6 . . . . 93 D5
  Leighton Buzzard LU7 . . . 80 E7
  Olney MK46 . . . . 6 F4
  Slough SL3 . . . . 212 B7
  Stokenchurch HP14 . . . . 158 F4
  Windsor SL4 . . . . 210 B5
Spring Field Rd HP4 . . . 135 A6
Springfield Rdbt MK6 . . . 35 A2
Springfields
  Amersham HP6 . . . . 154 C2
  Padbury MK18 . . . . 53 C1
  Tylers Green HP10 . . . . . 163 C2
Springfields Cl SL3 . . . . 212 B7
Springfields Ct SL3 . . . . 212 A7
Springfield Way MK43 . . 25 C2
Spring Gardens Rd
  HP13 . . . . 173 E5
Spring Gdn La HP4 . . . . 134 D3
Spring Gdns
  Bourne End SL8 . . . . 185 A4
  Marlow SL7 . . . . 183 E3
  Newport Pagnell MK16 . . 22 C4
  Wooburn Green HP10 . . . 185 E8
Spring Gr MK17 . . . . 49 B5
Spring Hill SL6 . . . . 202 E3
Springhill Rd HP18 . . . . . 83 A8

Spring Ho SL7 . . . . . . 183 E3
Spring La
  Alderton NN12 . . . . . 9 A2
  Clifton Reynes MK46 . . . . 7 C3
  Cookham Dean SL6 . . . 195 C5
  Farnham Common SL2 . . . 198 C5
  Flackwell Heath HP10 . . . 173 F3
  Great Horwood MK17 . . . . 55 A2
  Olney MK46 . . . . 6 F3
  Slough SL1 . . . . 204 F5
Spring Mdw HP18 . . . . . 97 A1
Springs Cl HP17 . . . . . 130 B2
Springside 2 LU7 . . . . . 80 E7
Springs La HP17 . . . . . 130 B3
Spring Valley Dr HP14 . . 162 A7
Springwater Mill HP11 . . 173 E4
Springwood HP27 . . . . . 150 C4
Sprinters L Ctr HP16 . . . 151 A7
Sproggit Ind Est TW19 . . 213 F1
Spruce Ct 7 SL1 . . . . . 205 F3
Spruce Dene HP15 . . . . 162 F2
Spruce 1 HP19 . . . . . . 100 F1
SPURGROVE 170 E2
Spurgrove La RG9 . . . . . 170 E2
SPURLANDS END 163 A8
Spurlands End Rd
  HP15 . . . . 163 A8
Spur The SL1 . . . . 204 D8
Spurt St HP18 . . . . . . 112 F3
Square Close Cotts
  RG9 . . . . 169 F3
Square The
  Akeley MK18 . . . . . . 41 F8
  Aspley Guise MK17 . . . . 49 E4
  Brill HP18 . . . . 110 A8
  Great Missenden HP16 . . 152 B7
  Harmondsworth UB7 . . . 213 B6
  Long Crendon HP18 . . . 125 C6
  Milton Keynes MK12 . . . 33 D6
  Preston Bissett MK18 . . . 62 B8
  Waddesdon HP18 . . . . 99 A6
  Yardley Hastings NN7 . . . 1 A6
Squires Cl MK6 . . . . . . 47 A6
Squirrel La LU7 . . . . . . 172 C5
Squirrel Rise SL7 . . . . . 183 D6
Squirrels Way SL6 . . . . . 18 E2
Stablebridge Rd HP22 . . . 117 F3
Stable Cl MK18 . . . . . . 50 C7
Stable Cotts SL7 . . . . . 194 C5
Stable La HP9 . . . . 176 C4
Stable Rd HP22 . . . . . . 131 E7
Stables Ct SL7 . . . . . . 183 B1
Stables The MK19 . . . . . 20 F3
Stacey Ave MK12 . . . . . . 33 D6
STACEY BUSHES 33 E4
Stacey Bushes Trad Ctr
  MK12 . . . . 33 E4
Stacey's Ct HP16 . . . . . 177 C8
Staddle Stones HP27 . . . 139 B4
Stadium App HP21 . . . . 115 E7
StadiumMK (MK Dons FC)
  MK1 . . . . 47 C3
Stafferton Way SL6 . . . . 203 A6
Stafford Ave SL2 . . . . . 198 C1
Stafford Cl SL6 . . . . . . 204 B7
Stafford Gr MK5 . . . . . . 46 B6
Stafford Keep HP19 . . . . 115 A8
Stag Ct WD3 . . . . 167 C5
Stag La
  Berkhamsted HP4 . . . . 135 B5
  Chorleywood WD3 . . . . 167 C3
  Great Kingshill HP15 . . . 151 D1
STAGSDEN WEST END 16 F4
Stagshaw Gr 6 MK4 . . . . 46 B2
Stainby Cl LU7 . . . . . . 208 E3
Stainton Dr MK13 . . . . . 34 C4
Stamford Ave MK6 . . . . . 35 B2
Stamford Rd SL6 . . . . . 202 C6
Stanbridge Cl HP27 . . . . 127 A7
Stanbridge Cl MK11 . . . . 32 F5
Stanbridge Rd HP27 . . . . 127 B6
Stanbrook Pl MK10 . . . . 36 A1
Standfield Cl HP19 . . . . 115 A8
Standing Way
  Milton Keynes, Coldharbour
    Spinney MK3, MK4 . . . 46 E3
  Milton Keynes, Kingston
    MK10 . . . . 36 C1
  Milton Keynes, Peartree Bridge
    MK10, MK4, MK6 . . . . 47 C7
  Milton Keynes, Snelshall East
    MK4 . . . . 57 B7
Standring Pl HP20 . . . . . 101 F2
Stanhope Cl HP22 . . . . . 131 B7
Stanhope Heath TW19 . . 213 C1
Stanhope Rd
  Aylesbury HP20 . . . . . 116 A8
  Slough SL1 . . . . 204 D7
Stanhope Way TW19 . . . 213 C1
Stanier Rise HP4 . . . . . 134 F7
Stanier Sq 5 MK2 . . . . . 58 C8
Stanley Ave HP5 . . . . . 154 B8
Stanley Cl
  Marlow SL7 . . . . 183 F3
  Uxbridge UB8 . . . . . . 201 D3
Stanley Cotts SL2 . . . . . 205 F5
Stanley Ct MK46 . . . . . . 6 F3
Stanley Gdns HP23 . . . . 118 F3

Stanley Green E SL3 . . . . 206 F2
Stanley Green W SL3 . . . 206 F2
Stanley Hill HP7 . . . . . . 165 E7
Stanley Hill Ave HP7 . . . 165 E8
Stanley Ho SL4 . . . . . . 211 A2
Stanley Rd HP12 . . . . . . 172 C7
Stanley Spencer Gall★
  SL6 . . . . 196 B7
Stanmore Gdns MK16 . . . 22 B2
Stanstead Pl HP7 . . . . . 165 C8
Stanton Ave MK13 . . . . . 34 A6
Stanton Ct MK13 . . . . . . 34 A8
STANTONBURY 34 D7
Stantonbury Campus
  MK14 . . . . 34 C7
Stantonbury Campus L Ctr
  MK14 . . . . 34 C7
Stantonbury Cl MK13 . . . 34 A8
Stanton Gate MK14 . . . . 34 D8
Stanton Mid Sch MK13 . . 34 B7
Stanton Way SL3 . . . . . 206 E2
Stanton Wood Rdbt
  MK14 . . . . 34 D4
Stanway Cl MK15 . . . . . . 35 B6
STANWELL 213 C1
Stanwell Cl 7 SL3 . . . . . 206 F3
Stanwell Fields CE Prim
  Sch TW19 . . . . 213 E1
Stanwell Gdns TW19 . . . 213 D1
STANWELL MOOR 212 E1
Stanwell Moor Rd TW6, TW19,
  UB7 . . . . 213 B4
Stanwell Rd SL3 . . . . . 212 C4
Stanwyck La 4 MK4 . . . . 45 D2
Stapeley Ct 1 MK4 . . . . . 45 F1
Stapleford Mill★ LU7 . . . 70 B5
Staple Hall Rd MK1 . . . . 47 E1
Stapleton Cl SL7 . . . . . 183 F4
Stars La HP17 . . . . 113 E2
Startins La SL6 . . . . . . 195 C8
STARTOP'S END 104 F1
Starveall Ct UB7 . . . . . 208 F3
Starwood Ct 1 SL3 . . . . 206 A3
Staters Pound MK15 . . . . 35 A7
Statham Pl MK6 . . . . . . 46 F8
Station App
  Amersham HP6 . . . . . 154 C1
  Chorleywood WD3 . . . . 167 D5
  Denham UB9 . . . . . . 189 D4
  Gerrards Cross SL9 . . . 188 E6
  Great Missenden HP16 . . 152 A7
  Little Chalfont HP7 . . . 166 D8
  Maidenhead SL6 . . . . 202 F6
  Marlow SL7 . . . . 183 E2
  Wendover HP22 . . . . . 131 B4
  West Drayton UB7 . . . . 208 E5
Station Byd HP20 . . . . . 115 D8
Station Cotts
  Denham UB9 . . . . . . 190 A4
  Winslow MK18 . . . . . . 66 A5
Station Hill SL6 . . . . . . 195 F7
Station Par
  Beaconsfield HP9 . . . . 175 D3
  Cookham Rise SL8 . . . . 195 F6
  Denham UB9 . . . . . . 190 A4
Station Rd
  Aldbury HP23 . . . . . . 120 B5
  Amersham HP6 . . . . . 165 C8
  Beaconsfield HP9 . . . . 175 C8
  Berkhamsted HP4 . . . . 135 D4
  Blackthorn OX25 . . . . . 81 A4
  Bourne End SL8 . . . . . 185 A3
  Bow Brickhill MK17 . . . . 48 C2
  Buckingham MK18 . . . . 52 C7
  Castlethorpe MK19 . . . . 19 F5
  Cheddington LU7 . . . . 91 A1
  Chesham HP5 . . . . . . 154 C8
  Chinnor OX39 . . . . . . 147 C6
  Cookham Rise SL6 . . . . 195 F7
  Gerrards Cross SL9 . . . 188 E6
  Haddenham HP17 . . . . 127 A6
  Henley-on-Thames RG9 . . 191 E1
  High Wycombe HP13 . . . 173 C6
  Ivinghoe LU7 . . . . . . 105 C5
  Leighton Buzzard LU7 . . . 80 E7
  Little Kimble HP17 . . . . 129 C2
  Long Marston HP23 . . . 104 B4
  Marlow SL7 . . . . 183 E1
  Marsh Gibbon OX27 . . . . 71 F3
  Mursley MK17 . . . . . . 67 B7
  Newport Pagnell MK16 . . 22 C4
  Padbury MK18 . . . . . . 53 B1
  Princes Risborough
    HP27 . . . . 139 A2
  Quainton HP22 . . . . . . 85 A4
  Slough, Langley SL3 . . . 207 A4
  Slough SL1 . . . . 204 E7
  Stoke Mandeville HP22 . . 116 B2
  Swanbourne MK17 . . . . 67 A4
  Taplow SL6 . . . . 203 F7
  Tring HP23 . . . . 119 D4
  Uxbridge UB8 . . . . . . 201 D1
  West Drayton UB7 . . . . 208 E4
  Winslow MK18 . . . . . . 66 A5
  Woburn Sands MK17 . . . 49 B5
  Wraysbury TW19 . . . . 212 A1
Station Rd Ind Est MK18 . 66 A5
Station Rise SL7 . . . . . 183 E2
Station Sq MK9 . . . . . . 34 C1

Station Terr
  Buckingham MK18 . . . . 52 C7
  Milton Keynes MK14 . . . 21 E2
Station Way E HP20 . . . . 115 D7
Station Way W HP20 . . . . 115 D7
Staunton Ho MK17 . . . . . 60 F7
Staunton Rd SL2 . . . . . 205 D8
Staveley Cl HP21 . . . . . 116 C6
Staverton Gr MK10 . . . . . 36 B2
Stavordale 2 MK10 . . . . 36 A1
Stayning La MK14 . . . . . 34 F6
Steeple Cl MK4 . . . . . . 57 A8
STEEPLE CLAYDON 63 C3
Steeple Claydon Sch
  MK18 . . . . 63 E3
Steinbeck Cres MK4 . . . . 56 F7
Stephenson Cl
  Aylesbury HP19 . . . . . 115 B7
  High Wycombe HP13 . . . 161 F1
  Leighton Buzzard LU7 . . . 80 E6
Stephenson Dr MK17 . . . 210 B7
Stepnells HP23 . . . . . . 105 A1
Steppingstones LU6 . . . . 93 F8
Sterling Bus Pk MK18 . . . 52 D6
Sterling Cl MK15 . . . . . . 35 A6
Stevens Cl
  Holmer Green HP15 . . . 163 B7
  Prestwood HP16 . . . . 151 D5
Stevens Field MK7 . . . . . 48 D6
Stevens Ho 8 MK7 . . . . 165 B7
Stevenson Rd SL2 . . . . . 187 D2
Stewart Ave SL1 . . . . . 205 F8
Stewarts Dr SL2 . . . . . 198 B7
Stewarts Way SL7 . . . . 183 D7
STEWKLEY 68 E2
Stewkley La MK17 . . . . . 67 E4
STEWKLEY DEAN 68 B1
Stewkley Rd
  Cublington LU7 . . . . . 78 C1
  Hollingdon LU7 . . . . . 69 C2
  Wing LU7 . . . . 79 B3
Stilebrook Rd MK46 . . . . 6 F5
Stile Mdw HP9 . . . . . . 175 E3
Stile Rd SL3 . . . . 206 D3
Stilliters Farm Rd MK43 . 37 E8
Stilwell Dr U88 . . . . . . 201 F1
Stirling Ave HP20 . . . . . 101 E1
Stirling Cl
  Uxbridge UB8 . . . . . . 201 C2
  Windsor SL4 . . . . . . 209 D5
Stirling Ho SL2 . . . . . . 202 A8
Stirling Ho
  2 High Wycombe
    HP13 . . . . 173 F7
  Milton Keynes MK3 . . . . 57 D7
Stirling Rd
  High Wycombe HP12 . . . 172 D5
  Slough SL1 . . . . 205 A8
  Stanwell TW6 . . . . . . 213 F1
Stockaway HP21 . . . . . . 87 C1
Stockdale MK13 . . . . . . 34 C5
Stockdales Rd SL4 . . . . 204 F2
Stocken Cl MK46 . . . . . . 6 F4
Stock Field HP15 . . . . . 163 B3
Stockfields Pl HP14 . . . . 158 D5
Stockgrove Ctry Pk★
  LU7 . . . . 70 F7
Stockhall Cres LU7 . . . . 68 D2
Stocking Green Cl MK19 . 11 A3
Stocking La HP14 . . . . . 161 E7
Stock La MK17 . . . . 45 B1
Stocklake HP20 . . . . . . 101 F1
Stocklake Ind Est HP20 . 101 F1
Stocklands Way MK16 . . 151 D5
Stockley Academy UB8 . . 208 F7
Stockleys La MK18 . . . . 51 B6
Stockport Rd WD3 . . . . . 167 C2
Stocks Cl MK18 . . . . . . 65 F4
Stocks Rd HP23 . . . . . . 120 C7
Stocks The MK19 . . . . . . 19 E2
Stockwell HP17 . . . . . . 127 A6
Stockwell Furlong
  HP17 . . . . 127 A6
Stockwell La
  Longwick HP17 . . . . . 139 A8
  Wavendon MK17 . . . . . 48 D7
Stockwells SL6 . . . . . . 196 D1
STOKE BRUERNE 9 A8
Stoke Bruerne CE Prim Sch
  NN12 . . . . 9 A8
Stoke Common Rd SL2,
  SL3 . . . . 199 B8
Stoke Court Dr SL2 . . . . 198 F4
Stoke Farm La HP11 . . . 115 C3
Stoke Gdns SL1 . . . . . . 205 F5
Stoke Gn SL2 . . . . 199 A1
STOKE GOLDINGTON 9 A8
Stoke Goldington CE Fst
  Sch MK16 . . . . 12 B6
STOKE GREEN 199 B1
STOKE HAMMOND 69 E8
Stoke Ho 2 SL1 . . . . . . 205 F3
Stoke La MK11 . . . . 59 C1
Stoke Leys Cl HP21 . . . . 115 E3
STOKE MANDEVILLE 116 F4
Stoke Mandeville Comb Sch
  HP22 . . . . 116 A1

Stoke Mandeville Hospl
  HP21 . . . . 115 F4
Stoke Mandeville Sta
  HP22 . . . . 116 B2
STOKENCHURCH 158 E5
Stokenchurch Pl MK13 . . 34 C3
Stokenchurch Prim Sch
  HP14 . . . . 158 E5
Stoke Park Ave SL2 . . . . 198 C2
STOKE POGES 198 F6
Stoke Poges La SL1 . . . . 205 E7
Stoke Poges Sch SL2 . . . 198 F5
Stoke Rd
  Ashton NN7 . . . . 9 E8
  Aylesbury HP21 . . . . . 115 E6
  Leighton Buzzard LU7 . . . 70 D1
  Newton Longville MK17 . . 57 F3
  Slough SL2 . . . . 205 E7
Stokesay SL2 . . . . 205 F6
Stokesay Ct MK4 . . . . . . 45 E2
Stokes Croft HP17 . . . . . 127 A4
Stokes End HP17 . . . . . 127 A7
Stokes La HP17 . . . . . . 127 A7
Stokesley Rise HP10 . . . 185 E8
Stoke View SL1 . . . . . . 205 F5
Stoke Wood 2 SL2 . . . . 198 F8
Stolford Rise MK4 . . . . . 46 B1
Stompits Rd SL6 . . . . . 203 C1
Stomp Rd SL1 . . . . 204 B8
STONE 114 C5
STONEBRIDGE 33 F7
Stonebridge Field SL4 . . 205 B1
Stonebridge Gr HP10 . . . 35 E1
Stonebridge Rd HP19 . . . 101 B3
Stonebridge Rdbt MK13 . 33 E8
Stone CE Comb Sch
  HP17 . . . . 114 D5
Stonechat HP19 . . . . . . 101 D5
Stone Cl UB7 . . . . 208 F5
Stonecroft HP6 . . . . . . 153 C4
Stonecroft Ave SL0 . . . . 207 C2
Stonecroft Ct MK14 . . . . 34 E4
Stonecrop Pl MK14 . . . . 34 E4
Stone Ct MK46 . . . . . . 13 E8
Stonefield Pk SL6 . . . . . 202 C7
Stonefield Rd MK11 . . . . 161 C8
Stonegate MK13 . . . . . . 34 A5
Stonehaven Rd HP19 . . . 101 B2
Stone Hill MK8 . . . . . . 33 D1
Stone House La SL6 . . . . 184 C1
Stoneleigh Cl MK4 . . . . 45 E1
Stonemasons Ct 11 MK46 . 6 F3
Stone Pit Cl MK46 . . . . . 6 E3
Stonepitts Pk HP18 . . . . 111 B3
Stones Row HP11 . . . . . 173 B6
Stones Way MK17 . . . . . 68 C6
Stone View HP22 . . . . . . 86 D7
Stoney Cl HP4 . . . . 134 F6
Stoneycroft HP23 . . . . . 120 C5
Stoney Dean Specl Sch
  HP7 . . . . 165 F8
Stoneyfield SL9 . . . . . . 188 C3
Stoney Gr HP5 . . . . . . 144 D1
Stoney Grove HP5 . . . . . 144 C1
Stoney La
  Berkhamsted HP1 . . . . 146 B8
  Bovingdon HP3 . . . . . 146 C5
  Chipperfield WD4 . . . . 146 F1
  Cholesbury HP5 . . . . . 133 F1
  East Burnham SL2 . . . . 198 A4
Stoney Meade SL1 . . . . . 205 B5
Stoney Ware SL7 . . . . . 194 E8
STONOR 179 F6
Stonor Ct MK4 . . . . 45 F8
Stonor Ho & Gdns★
  RG9 . . . . 180 A7
STONY GREEN 151 A4
Stony Hill NN12 . . . . . . 17 C8
Stony La
  Little Chalfont HP6 . . . 155 F1
  Little Kingshill HP16 . . . 152 C3
Stookslade HP22 . . . . . . 89 A3
Stopps Orch HP27 . . . . . 139 C5
Stork Cl 2 HP19 . . . . . . 101 C3
Stornaway Rd SL3 . . . . . 207 C2
Stotfold Ct MK11 . . . . . 32 E4
Stour Cl
  Aylesbury HP21 . . . . . 115 C4
  Milton Keynes MK3 . . . . 57 E8
  Newport Pagnell MK16 . . 22 E4
  Slough SL1 . . . . 205 B3
Stourhead Gate MK4 . . . 45 E2
Stovell Rd SL4 . . . . . . 210 B7
Stowe Ave MK18 . . . . . . 41 B3
Stowe Cl MK18 . . . . . . 41 C1
Stowe Ct MK14 . . . . . . 34 C8
Stowe Landscape Gdns★
  MK18 . . . . 40 F7
STOWE PARK 40 E6
Stowe Rise MK18 . . . . . 41 C1
Stowe Sch MK18 . . . . . . 40 F7
Stowe View MK18 . . . . . 51 A7
Straight Bit HP10 . . . . . 185 B8
Straight Mile Rd OX33 . . 108 A5
Straight Rd SL4 . . . . . . 211 B1
Strande Pk SL6 . . . . . . 195 F5

Strande View Wlk SL6 . . 195 F5
Strand La SL6 . . . . 195 F5
Strand The HP27 . . . . . . 85 B5
Strangers La MK18 . . . . 51 A6
Strangford Dr MK2 . . . . 58 C4
Stranraer Gdns SL1 . . . . 205 E5
Stranraer Rd TW19 . . . . 213 E1
Stranraer Way 1 TW6 . . 213 E1
Stratfield Ct
  Maidenhead SL6 . . . . 203 B8
  Milton Keynes MK8 . . . . 33 F1
Stratfield Rd SL1 . . . . . 206 A4
Stratford Arc MK11 . . . . 32 D6
Stratford Ave UB10 . . . . 201 F3
Stratford Cl
  Aylesbury HP22 . . . . . 117 C5
  Slough SL2 . . . . 197 D1
Stratford Dr
  Aylesbury HP21 . . . . . 115 B6
  Wooburn HP10 . . . . . 185 D4
Stratford Gdns SL6 . . . . 202 C4
Stratford Rd
  Buckingham MK18 . . . . 41 E1
  Cosgrove MK19 . . . . . 19 D1
  Deanshanger MK19 . . . . 31 F4
  Maids Moreton MK18 . . . 42 C2
  Milton Keynes MK12 . . . 33 C7
  Nash MK17 . . . . 44 C1
  Old Stratford MK19 . . . . 32 B5
  Whaddon MK17 . . . . . 45 A2
Stratfords Way MK17 . . . 127 A6
Strathcona Cl HP10 . . . . 185 C7
Strathcona Way HP10 . . 185 C7
Strathnaver Pl MK12 . . . 33 D4
Strathspey Gate MK10 . . 36 C3
Stratton Chase Dr
  Chalfont St Giles HP8 . . 177 B8
  Chalfont St Peter HP8 . . 177 A8
Stratton Gn HP21 . . . . . 116 B6
Stratton Rd
  Beaconsfield HP9 . . . . 175 D2
  Princes Risborough
    HP27 . . . . 139 A3
Strauss Gr MK7 . . . . . . 48 C4
Strawberry Cl HP16 . . . . 151 D5
Straws Hadley Ct HP22 . . 89 B2
Streamside SL1 . . . . . . 204 F5
Streamside Wlk HP21 . . 115 C6
Streatham Pl MK13 . . . . 34 C2
Stretton Cl HP10 . . . . . 174 C8
Stretton Pl HP6 . . . . . . 154 F1
Stringers Cotts 1 SL9 . . 177 D2
Stringfellow SL4 . . . . . . 24 E2
Stroma Ct SL1 . . . . . . 204 D6
Stroud Cl SL4 . . . . 209 D4
Strudwick Dr MK6 . . . . . 46 F8
Stuart Cl
  Milton Keynes MK2 . . . . 47 D1
  Windsor SL4 . . . . . . 209 F5
Stuart Ct HP6 . . . . 154 D1
Stuart Rd HP13 . . . . . . 173 C6
Stuart Way
  Thame OX9 . . . . . . 126 A1
  Windsor SL4 . . . . . . 209 F5
Stubble Hill HP19 . . . . . 115 A8
Stubbs Cl SL6 . . . . 195 B6
Stubbs End Cl HP6 . . . . 154 E2
Stubbs Field MK5 . . . . . 46 A3
Stubbs Wood HP6 . . . . . 154 E3
Stuchbury Cl HP19 . . . . 115 A8
Studbridge Ct HP14 . . . . 158 C4
Studham La HP4 . . . . . . 107 D4
Studland Ct HP21 . . . . . 116 B5
STUDLEY GREEN 159 E3
Studley Knapp
  Milton Keynes MK7 . . . . 48 B5
  Walnut Tree MK7 . . . . . 48 B7
Studridge La HP27 . . . . 150 B4
Sturges Cl MK7 . . . . . . 48 A5
Sturman Ho HP6 . . . . . 154 C2
Stylecroft Rd HP8 . . . . . 177 D8
Styles Cl OX27 . . . . . . 71 E2
Styles Ct HP18 . . . . . . 99 A7
Sudbury Chase MK10 . . . 35 A6
Sudgrove Ho MK15 . . . . 35 A6
Suffield Rd HP11 . . . . . 172 F6
Suffolk Cl
  Milton Keynes MK3 . . . . 46 F1
  Slough SL1 . . . . 204 E7
Suffolk Ct
  Maidenhead SL6 . . . . 202 F8
  Marsh Gibbon OX27 . . . . 71 F3
Suffolk Ho HP10 . . . . . 185 E6
Suffolk Rd SL6 . . . . . . 202 D4
Sulby Cl HP21 . . . . 115 C5
Sulgrave Cres HP23 . . . 119 C5
Sulgrave Ct 3 MK8 . . . . 45 F8
Sullivan Cres MK7 . . . . . 48 C5
Sultan Croft MK5 . . . . . 46 A4
Sumburgh Way SL1 . . . . 205 E8
Summerfield Sch MK13 . . 34 C3
Summergill Ct MK12 . . . 33 A5
Summerhayes MK14 . . . . 34 F7
Summerhouse La UB7 . . 213 D6
Summerlea SL1 . . . . . . 205 B5
Summerleaze Rd SL6 . . . 196 B1

Summerleys LU6.................92 E4
Summerleys Rd HP27 ..138 F4
Summerlin Dr MK17.....49 B5
Summerson Ct MK6.....46 F5
Summerson Rd
 Bleak Hall MK6 ....47 A5
 Milton Keynes MK6 .....46 F5
Summers Rd SL1.........197 C2
SUMMERSTOWN 72 B2
Summit Ctr UB7 ....213 D7
Sumner Ct MK5..........46 A8
Sunbury Cl MK13.........34 A6
Sunbury Ct SL4 ....210 D8
Sunbury Rd SL4...........210 D8
Sun Cl SL4....................210 D8
Sun Cres HP18............109 D5
Sunderland Ct
 Milton Keynes MK4 .....45 F1
 11 Stanwell TW19 ......213 E1
Sunderland Rd SL6 .....202 B8
Sun La SL6 ....202 F7
Sunningdale Cl HP12 ..79 B5
Sunningdale Way MK3 .57 D8
Sunnybank SL7 ....183 D4
Sunny Bank
 Cheddington LU7 ....104 F7
 Hazlemere HP15 ....162 F6
Sunny Brook Cl HP22 ..117 D6
Sunny Croft HP13........161 C2
Sunnyhill Rd WD3........178 D4
SUNNYMEADS 211 E4
Sunnymeade Ave HP5 ..144 E3
Sunnymeade Cotts SL6.196 B1
Sunnyside Cotts HP5 ..145 A5
Sunnyside Rd HP5 ......144 C1
Sunny View NN7 ....1 B6
Sun Pas 15 SL4 ....210 D6
Sunray Ave UB7..........208 D4
Sunridge Cl MK16.........22 C3
Sunrise Parkway MK14 ..34 E6
Sunset Cl MK2 ....58 C7
Sunset Wlk MK9 ....34 E2
Sunters End HP12........172 A7
Sunters Wood Cl HP12 .172 B5
Surly Hall Wlk SL4 ......209 F6
Surrey Ave SL2 ....198 C1
Surrey Pl
 Milton Keynes MK3 .....46 F2
 Tring HP23..................119 A3
Surrey Rd MK3 ....46 F2
Sussex Cl
 Aylesbury HP19 ....101 A3
 Chalfont St Giles HP8 ..177 B8
 High Wycombe HP13 ...162 D1
 Slough SL1..................206 B4
Sussex Ho SL2............198 C6
Sussex Keep SL1 ....206 B4
Sussex Lodge 17 SL6 ..202 F6
Sussex Pl SL1..............206 B4
Sussex Rd MK3 ....46 F1
Sutcliffe Ave MK6........34 E1
Sutherland Gr MK3.......46 F3
Sutherland Grange
 SL4.............................209 D7
Sutherland Grange Nature
 Reserve★ SL4 ....209 D7
Sutherland Wlk HP21 ..115 F5
Sutleye Ct MK5 ....46 A5
SUTTON........................207 C1
Sutton Ave SL3 ....206 C4
Sutton Cl
 Cookham SL6..............196 B7
 Maidenhead SL6 ....202 C5
 Tring HP23..................119 B6
Sutton Ct MK4 ....46 C1
Sutton La SL3..............207 B1
Sutton Pl SL3...............212 B8
Sutton Rd SL6 ....196 B6
Swabey Rd SL3 ....207 A2
Swains Cl UB7 ....208 E4
Swains La HP10...........174 B1
Swains Mkt HP10.........174 A1
Swakeleys Dr UB10 .....201 F8
Swakeleys Rd UB10 .....201 E8
Swale Rd HP21 ....115 C5
Swallow Cl MK18 ....52 E7
Swallowdale SL0..........200 D2
Swallow Dr HP15 ....163 B5
Swallowfield MK8.........33 E1
Swallowfield Lower Sch
 MK17 ....49 B5
Swallow Fields SL0 .....200 D1
Swallow Ho SL7 ....184 A2
Swallow La
 Aylesbury HP19 ....114 F8
 Stoke Mandeville HP22.116 A1
Swallow St
 Iver Heath SL0............200 D1
 Iver SL0......................207 D8
Swallowtail Wlk HP4 ..134 F7
SWANBOURNE 67 B3
Swanbourne CE Fst Sch
 MK17 ....67 A3
Swanbourne House Sch
 MK17 ....66 F3

Swanbourne Rd MK17...67 D4
Swanbrook Ct SL6 ......203 A7
Swan Bsns Pk MK18.....52 C6
Swan Cl
 Aylesbury HP19 ....101 F3
 Blackthorn OX25 ....81 A3
 Buckingham MK18........52 E7
 Chesham HP5 ....144 B4
 Ivinghoe Aston LU7......92 A1
 Whitchurch HP22..........87 B5
Swan Cotts HP17.........129 D1
Swan Ct
 Buckingham MK18 ....65 F5
 Chorleywood WD3 ......167 C5
 Datchet SL3 ....211 B6
 Leighton Buzzard LU7 ..80 E6
 Olney MK46 ....7 A4
 West Drayton UB7.......208 D4
Swan Hill HP18 ....112 F3
Swan Hill Cotts HP18...112 F3
Swan La
 Lee Gate HP16...........142 C8
 Marsh Gibbon OX6.......72 A3
Swan Mews HP22 ....131 B5
Swann Rd HP22 ....131 B5
Swan Pool & L Ctr MK18 52 D7
Swan Rd
 Iver SL0......................207 F7
 West Drayton UB7.......208 D4
Swanson Dr MK4.........45 D3
Swansons LU6.............92 F3
Swan Terr
 Milton Keynes MK11 ....32 D5
 Windsor SL4 ....210 A7
Swan Wharf Bsns Ctr
 UB8............................201 C3
Swanwick La MK10 ......36 B3
Swayne Rise MK10.......36 A2
Sweetcroft La UB10 ....201 F6
Sweetlands Cnr MK7....48 B8
Swift Cl
 Aylesbury HP19 ....101 F3
 Newport Pagnell MK16 ..22 A5
Swift Ho SL7................184 D4
Swimbridge La MK4.....46 D4
Swinden Ct MK13.........34 B4
Swing Gate Fst Sch
 HP4............................135 D3
Swing Gate La HP4......135 D2
Swinnerton Ho RG9 ....191 E3
Switchback Cl SL6.......195 D2
Switchback Road N
 SL6.............................195 D3
Switchback Road S
 SL6.............................195 D2
Switchback The SL6.....195 D2
Sycamore Ave MK2 .....58 E8
Sycamore Cl
 Amersham HP6 ....154 D2
 3 Bourne End SL8 ......185 B3
 Buckingham MK18.......52 F7
 Chalfont St Giles HP8 ..177 A7
 Long Crendon HP18.....125 C6
 Maidenhead SL6 ....202 C3
 Stewkley LU7 ....68 D2
 West Drayton UB7.......208 F6
Sycamore Cnr HP6......154 D2
Sycamore Ct
 Aylesbury HP19 ....101 D1
 High Wycombe HP12 ...172 C4
 Windsor SL4 ....210 A7
Sycamore Dene HP5 ..144 D3
Sycamore Dr
 Marlow Bottom SL7.....183 D5
 Tring HP23..................119 B4
Sycamore Ho
 Amersham HP6 ....154 D2
 Princes Risborough
 HP27 ....139 B3
Sycamore Leys MK18...63 E3
Sycamore Pl HP6 ....154 C1
Sycamore Rd
 Amersham HP6 ....154 D2
 Chalfont St Giles HP8 ..177 A7
 High Wycombe HP12 ...172 C4
Sycamore Rise
 Berkhamsted HP4 ....135 D3
 Chalfont St Giles HP8 ..177 A7
Sycamores The HP3.....146 F8
Sycamore Way HP15 ..163 A3
Sycamore Wlk SL3 ......206 E7
Sydney Gr SL1.............205 C7
Sygnus Ct 9 SL6 ....196 F2
Syke Cluan SL0 ....207 E4
Syke Ings SL0.............207 E4
Sykes Croft MK4..........46 C1
Sykes Rd SL1...............205 B8
Sylvana Cl UB10 ....201 F4
Sylvester Rd SL6.........195 E2
Sylvia Cl HP16.............152 B4
Symington Ct MK5.......46 B5
Syon Gdns MK16.........22 C2
SYRESHAM 27 B8
Syresham St James CE
 Prim Sch NN13 ....27 C8

Tabard Gdns MK16.......22 C2
Tachbrook Rd UB8.......201 C3
Tacknell Dr MK5 ....46 A4
Tacks La HP17 ....126 F6
Tadmarton MK15.........35 A6
Tadmere MK8 ....33 D1
Tadros Ct HP13...........173 D6
Talbot Ave
 High Wycombe HP13 ...161 D2
 Slough SL3..................206 F4
Talbot Ct
 Milton Keynes MK15 ....35 C1
 Windsor SL4 ....210 B4
Talbot Pl SL3 ....211 C6
Talbot Rd HP22...........117 E5
Talbots Dr SL6.............202 B6
Talbots Hyde MK6........6 E4
Talland Ave MK6..........34 F1
Tallis La MK7 ....48 C5
Tall Oaks HP6 ....154 D2
Tall Pines LU7 ....70 F2
Tall Trees SL3.............212 E6
Tamar Cl
 Aylesbury HP21 ....115 C4
 Loudwater HP13 ....174 B4
Tamar Ho
 High Wycombe HP13 ...173 F7
 Milton Keynes MK3 .....46 E1
Tamarisk Ct MK7.........48 B5
Tamarisk Way
 Aylesbury HP22 ....116 C4
 Slough SL1..................205 B5
Tamar Way SL3...........207 B2
Tamworth Stubb MK7 ..48 D5
Tancred Rd HP19.........162 A1
Tandra MK6 ....47 B5
Tandy Rise MK8...........45 D6
Tandys Ct MK43...........8 E5
Tanfield La MK10 ....36 A3
Tangier Ct SL4 ....210 D8
Tangier La SL4.............210 D8
Tankard Cl MK16..........22 C4
Tank House Rd MK18...66 B6
Tanners Dr MK14 ....22 A2
Tannery Rd HP13 ....174 A4
Tannery Road Ind Est
 HP13...........................174 A4
Tannery The MK18.......65 F4
Tansley La MK17 ....49 B5
Tansman La MK7..........48 D5
Tanton Ho HP16 ....151 F8
Tapestries Hall SL4 ....211 A2
Tapestries The SL4......211 A2
Taplin Way HP10..........163 C1
TAPLOW.......................196 E1
Taplow Common Rd
 SL1.............................197 A3
Taplow Rd SL6.............204 A7
Taplow Sta SL6 ....203 F7
Tapping Rd HP14 ....171 C5
Taranis Cl MK7............48 C7
Tarbay La SL4 ....209 B5
Tarbert Cl SL4.............58 C5
Tarmac Way SL4 ....213 B7
Tarragon Cl
 Milton Keynes MK7......48 B6
 Walton MK7................48 A6
Tarry Ct MK13 ....34 B6
Taskers Row LU6.........92 F4
Taskers Row Cotts LU6.92 F4
Task The MK46 ....7 A4
Tatchbrook Cl SL6.......203 A8
Tate Rd SL1................177 F5
TATHALL END 11 E2
TATLING END................189 B3
Tatling Gr MK7.............48 A6
Tattam Cl MK15...........35 C2
Tattams La MK17.........67 B3
TATTENHOE 57 A8
Tattenhoe La MK3 ....57 D8
Tattenhoe Pavilion MK4.57 A8
Tattenhoe St MK5........45 E4
Tattershall Cl MK5 ......46 A6
Tattlers Hill HP22 ....89 B3
Taunton Deane MK4 ....46 D2
Taurus Cl MK18...........63 D2
Tavelhurst MK8 ....33 E1
Taverner Cl MK7..........48 D5
Tavistock Cl
 Maidenhead SL6 ....202 A8
 Woburn Sands MK17....49 B6
Tavistock Mews HP12 ..172 E7
Tavistock Rd UB7........208 D5
Tavistock St MK2 ....47 D1
Tavistock Wlk HP20.....101 E2
Taylor Rd HP21 ....115 D5
Taylors Cl SL7 ....183 F2
Taylors Cnr HP18 ....99 A7
Taylors Ct SL6.............202 B8
Taylors La
 Little Missenden HP7....153 A3
 Stewkley LU7 ....78 E7
 St Leonards HP23 ....132 C3
Taylors Mews MK14.....34 F6
Taylors Rd HP5 ....144 D2

Taylor's Ride LU7 ....70 F2
Taylors Turn HP13 ......161 D3
Taymouth Pl MK9 ....35 B3
Tay Rd MK3.................46 E1
Teale Cl OX25.............94 E7
Teal Ho HP11...............173 C6
Teasel Ave MK14.........34 E5
Tedder Cl UB10 ....201 F5
Tedder Rd HP22 ....131 D5
Teesdale Rd SL2.........204 F8
Tees Rd HP21..............115 C5
Tees Way MK3.............46 D1
Teign Cl MK16 ....22 D4
Teikyo Sch UK SL2......199 D5
Telford Cl HP11............100 F1
Telford Dr SL1..............205 A4
Telford Way
 High Wycombe HP13 ...162 A1
 Milton Keynes MK14 ....22 B2
Telston Cl SL8..............185 A5
Temperance Terr MK11..32 C6
Templars Pl 2 SL7 .....183 E1
TEMPLE........................194 C5
Temple Cl
 Buckingham MK18 ....41 E2
 Milton Keynes MK3 .....57 D7
Templecroft Terr HP17 114 A4
Temple End HP13........173 A8
Temple Gate SL7 ....173 A7
Temple Ho RG9 ....191 E3
Temple La SL7 ....194 D6
Temple Mill Cotts SL7..194 C5
Temple Mill Island SL7.194 C5
Temple Orch HP13 ......173 B7
Temple Pk SL6.............193 F3
Temple Rd SL4 ....210 D5
Templeside Gdns HP12 172 E8
Temple Sq 17 HP20 ....115 D8
Temple St
 Aylesbury HP20 ....115 D8
 Brill HP18....................96 B1
Temple Way SL2..........198 C7
Templewood HP14.......150 B1
Templewood Gate SL2 .198 C7
Templewood La SL2 ....198 E8
Tenby Gr MK4 ....45 D1
Tene Acres MK5...........45 F6
Tennant Ct MK8...........45 D6
Tennis La MK18............46 A4
Tennyson Dr MK16 ......22 A3
Tennyson Gr 1 MK3 ....57 F7
Tennyson Rd
 Aylesbury HP21 ....115 F6
 High Wycombe HP11 ...173 A5
Tenterden Cres MK7 ...48 B7
Tenzing Dr HP13..........173 F6
Terrace The
 Aspley Guise MK17......49 E5
 Bray SL6.....................203 C3
 7 Tring HP23...............119 A3
Terrent Ct SL4.............210 A5
TERRICK.......................130 C5
Terrick Row HP17........130 B5
TERRIERS.....................162 E2
Terrington Hill SL7.......183 B2
Terry Dr HP19..............101 C3
Terry Orch HP13..........173 C8
Terry Pl HP18...............208 C8
Terry Rd HP13.............173 C8
Terry's La SL6 ....195 F8
Testwood Rd SL4 ....209 D6
TETCHWICK..................82 F2
Tetherdown HP16........151 C5
Tewkesbury La 1 MK10..35 F1
TEW'S END...................17 C8
Tews End La NN12 ....17 B8
Thackeray End HP19 ...100 F2
THAME.........................125 E2
Thame Ho 6 HP13.......173 B7
Thame Rd
 Aylesbury HP17 ....127 C2
 Aylesbury HP21 ....115 D7
 Blackthorn OX25 ....81 A3
 Brill HP18....................110 B7
 Chilton HP18...............111 B3
 Chinnor OX39.............147 B8
 Haddenham HP17 ....126 D5
 Long Crendon HP18,
 OX9 ....125 D4
 Longwick HP27 ....138 E4
 Piddington OX6...........95 D6
 Thame OX9 ....136 C7
Thame Road S HP21...115 D6
Thames Ave SL4 ....210 D7
Thames Bank SL3........203 C7
Thamesbourne Mews 3
 SL8.............................185 A3
Thames Cl
 Bourne End SL8...........185 A4
 Milton Keynes MK3......58 E8
Thames Cres SL6 ....196 B2
Thames Dr MK16..........22 E3
Thamesfield Gdns SL7 .183 E1
Thames Ho
 Datchet SL3................211 B6
 Henley-on-Thames RG9.191 E3

Thames Ind Est SL7.....183 F2
Thames Mead SL4 ....209 E6
Thames Rd SL3 ....207 B3
Thames Reach SL7......193 D6
Thames Side
 Henley-on-Thames RG9..191 E2
 Windsor SL4 ....210 D7
Thames St SL4.............210 D7
Thames Valley Athletics Ctr
 SL4.............................205 E1
Thames Valley Hospl
 (private) SL3 ....199 C4
Thames Valley Univ (Slough
 Campus) SL1 ....205 E5
Thane Cl MK14 ....34 C7
Thanestead Copse
 HP10 ....174 C2
Thanet Cl HP10............174 C2
Thatcher Cl UB7..........208 E4
Thatchers Dr SL6.........202 A5
Theatre Wlk MK9 ....34 F3
thecentre:mk (Sh Ctr)
 MK9 ....34 E3
THE CITY......................159 D6
THE GREEN
 Milton Keynes 47 D8
 Newport Pagnell 22 C3
 Whipsnade..................107 F8
Thellusson Way WD3....167 F2
THE SWILLET................167 B3
Theydon Ave MK17......49 B4
Thicket The
 Tylers Green HP15......163 A1
 West Drayton UB7.......208 E7
Third Ave
 Marlow SL7 ....183 F2
 Milton Keynes MK1 .....47 B2
Third Cres SL1 ....205 C8
Third St HP11...............173 B4
Thirkleby Cl SL1...........205 C5
Thirlby La MK5 ....46 A6
Thirlmere Ave
 Milton Keynes MK2 .....58 D6
 Slough SL1..................204 C8
Thirsk Gdns MK3.........57 C6
Thistle Cl HP21............115 C5
Thomas Bourne Ho 1
 HP4............................135 D4
Thomas Coram CE Mid Sch
 HP4............................135 D2
Thomas Ct
 Berkhamsted HP4 ....134 E6
 Maidenhead SL6 ....202 A2
Thomas Dr MK16..........22 A6
Thomas Harding Jun Sch
 HP5............................154 B7
Thomas Hickman Sch
 HP19...........................101 A3
Thomas Rd HP10..........185 D8
Thomas Valentine Ho
 HP8 ....177 B7
Tompkins La SL2 ....198 A5
Thompson Cl SL3.........207 A2
Thompson Rd UB10 .....201 E5
Thompson St MK13 ......34 A7
Thomson Cl HP21.........115 B6
Thomson Wlk HP21 ......115 B6
Thornaby Pl HP10........185 E8
Thornbank Cl TW19 .....213 A2
THORNBOROUGH 54 A8
Thornborough Inf Sch
 MK18 ....54 A8
Thornborough Rd MK17..55 B8
Thornbridge Rd SL0.....200 C4
Thornbury Pl HP11.......173 A4
Thorncliffe MK8 ....33 D1
Thorndike SL2..............205 B8
Thorn Dr SL3...............206 E7
Thorne Rd HP14...........171 C4
Thorne Way
 Aston Clinton HP22......118 A3
 Aylesbury HP20 ....101 F2
THORNEY.....................208 B3
Thorneycroft La MK15...35 B5
Thorney Ctry Pk★ UB7.208 B3
Thorney Lane N SL0.....207 F6
Thorney Lane S SL0.....207 F5
Thorney Mill Rd SL0,
 UB7.............................208 B3
Thornhill MK18 ....54 B8
Thornhill Cl HP7 ....165 B7
Thornhill Rd UB10 ....201 F8
Thornlea Croft MK46....6 F3
Thornley Croft MK4......46 C2
Thorns Cl HP27...........139 D5
Thorns Rd HP27 ....139 E5
THORNTON....................43 C1
Thornton Ave UB7 ....208 F3
Thornton Chase MK14 ..34 E6
Thornton Cl UB7..........208 F3
Thornton Coll Convent of
 Jesus & Mary MK17.....43 C5
Thornton Cres HP22.....131 A5
Thornton Rd MK17........44 A1
Thorntree Dr HP23.......118 F4
Thorntree Rd HP21......116 A4
Thorpe House Sch SL9 188 E7
Thorpeness Croft MK4 ..56 F8
Thorwold Pl MK5 ....46 B6

Thrasher Rd HP21.........115 D5
Three Close La MK4.......135 C4
Three Gables HP9.........175 E2
THREE HOUSEHOLDS........176 F7
Three Households HP8....176 F6
Three Oaks CI UB10.......190 F1
Three Points La MK18....74 A6
Thresher Gr MK12.........33 A5
Thrift La SL6............202 D1
Thrift View MK43.........25 C2
Thrupp CI MK19...........20 A6
Thrush CI
  [6] Aylesbury HP19.......101 F3
  High Wycombe HP12.......172 C4
Thurlby Way SL6..........202 D3
Thurley Cotts SL2........199 B3
Thurne CI MK16...........22 E3
Thursby CI MK15..........35 D7
Thurston Rd SL1..........205 E7
Thyme CI MK16............21 F5
Tibbys La HP18...........112 F3
Ticehirst CI MK7.........48 B7
Ticehurst CI MK7.........48 B7
Tichborne WD3............178 D5
Tickford Arc MK16........22 D4
TICKFORD END.............22 F4
Tickford Park Prim Sch
  MK16...................22 D3
Tickford St MK16.........22 E4
Tidbury CI MK17..........49 A4
Tiddenfoot Waterside Pk★
  LU7....................80 E4
TIDDINGTON...............136 A7
Tierney [5] MK4..........45 D2
Tierney [3] SL7..........183 E1
Tiffany CI MK2...........58 D6
Tiggywinkles Wildlife
  Hospl★ HP17............127 A4
TILBROOK.................48 C3
Tilbrook Ind Est MK7.....48 B3
Tilbrook Rdbt MK7........48 B2
Tilbury Wlk SL3..........207 B3
Tilburywood CI HP13......161 C2
Tilebarn CI RG9..........191 C1
Tilecotes CI SL7.........183 C2
Tilehouse Comb Sch
  UB9....................189 F5
Tilehouse La UB9.........189 E6
Tilehouse Way UB9........189 F4
Tilers Rd MK11...........33 B2
Tilling Cres HP13........174 A7
Tillman CI MK12..........33 C5
Tilstone Ave SL4.........204 E2
Tilstone CI SL4..........204 E1
Tilsworth Rd HP9.........175 C1
Timber La MK17...........60 F7
Timberley La HP10........142 A8
Timberscombe MK4........46 D3
Timbers Wlk SL6..........202 B5
Timber Way OX39..........147 C6
Timberwood SL2...........187 D1
Timbold Dr MK7...........48 A7
Timor CI MK11............32 D6
Timothy's CI MK12........33 C7
Timpson CI HP15..........162 D8
Timpson La MK46..........7 C3
Timpsons Row MK46.......7 A3
Tindal Rd HP20...........101 E2
TINGEWICK................51 B7
Tingewick Rd
  Buckingham MK18........52 B8
  Radclive MK18..........51 E7
Tingewick Road Ind Est
  MK18...................52 B8
TINKERS END.............47 D6
Tinkers Dr MK18..........65 F3
TINKERS END..............65 F3
Tinkers La
  Berkhamsted HP23.......134 A6
  Windsor SL4............209 D5
Tinkers Wood Rd HP13....161 C4
Tintagel CI MK4..........47 A8
Tintagel Ho SL1..........205 C4
Tintern CI SL1...........205 C3
Tinterne CI HP21.........116 C6
Tippet CI MK7............48 D4
Tiree Ct
  Milton Keynes MK3......58 C3
  Milton Keynes MK3......58 C3
Tiree Ho SL2.............205 B8
Titchmarsh CI MK6.......46 E8
Tithe Barn Dr SL6........203 E1
Tithe CI SL6.............203 C1
Tithe CI SL3.............207 A2
Tithe La TW19............212 A1
Titmus Rd HP22..........131 E7
Tiverton Cres
  Aylesbury HP19.........101 C3
  Milton Keynes MK4......45 E1
Tobermory CI SL3........206 E2
Tockley Rd SL1...........197 B2
Todd CI
  Aylesbury HP21.........115 B6
  Holmer Green HP15......163 B6
Tolcarne Ave MK6........35 A1
Toll Bar Cnr HP27........138 D7
Tollgate SL6.............202 A6
Tollgate CI WD3..........167 F5
Tolman Ct HP21...........115 B6

Tomlin Rd SL2............197 E1
Tomo Ind Est UB8.........208 C7
Tompion Rd HP19..........100 F1
Tompkins CI
  Aston Clinton HP22.....117 E4
  Milton Keynes MK5......46 B3
Tompkins La OX27.........71 E2
Tom Scott Ho HP5.........144 B2
Toms Hill Rd HP23........120 C5
Toms Hill Rd HP23........120 D5
Toms Turn HP15...........162 F5
TONGWELL.................35 C8
Tongwell La MK15, MK16..22 C2
Tongwell Rdbt MK15......35 D8
Tongwell St
  Milton Keynes, Broughton
    MK10.................36 A3
  Milton Keynes, Northfield
    MK15.................35 F5
  Milton Keynes, Pineham
    MK15.................35 E7
  Walnut Tree MK7.......48 C6
Toot Hill CI MK5.........46 A5
Top Angel MK18...........52 D5
Topaz CI SL1.............205 B5
Top Farm CI HP9..........175 A1
Topland Rd SL9...........177 D3
Top Mdw
  Bow Brickhill MK7......48 B3
  Milton Keynes MK3......47 A3
Topping La UB8...........201 D2
Top Pk SL9...............188 C5
Top Station Rd NN13.....38 A8
Top Station Road Ind Est
  NN13...................38 A8
Torbay HP22..............85 B4
Tornay Ct LU7............91 D6
Torquay Spur SL2.........198 B2
Torre CI MK3.............47 A2
Torridge Rd
  Aylesbury HP21.........115 D5
  Slough SL3.............212 B8
Torridon CI MK2..........58 C4
Torrington Rd HP4........135 B4
Tortoiseshell Way
  Aylesbury HP19.........101 C4
  Berkhamsted HP4.......134 F6
Torwood HP4.............134 F4
TOTTERIDGE..............173 F8
Totteridge Ave HP13.....173 F8
Totteridge Common Cotts
  HP13...................173 F8
Totteridge Dr HP13......173 E8
Totteridge Ho HP13......173 E8
Totteridge La HP13......162 E1
Totteridge Par HP13.....173 E8
Totteridge Rd HP13......173 D7
TOTTERNHOE..............93 B7
Totternhoe Knolls &
  Quarry★ LU6............93 B8
Totternhoe Lower Sch
  LU6....................93 B7
Totternhoe Rd
  Dunstable LU6..........93 E2
  Eaton Bray LU6........92 D7
TOUCHBRIDGE.............95 E1
Towan Ave
  Fishermead MK6........47 A8
  Milton Keynes MK5......35 A1
Towcester Dr NN12.......18 B3
Towcester Rd
  Buckingham MK18.......41 E4
  Old Stratford MK19....32 B7
TOWERAGE................171 F8
Tower CI
  Berkhamsted HP4.......135 A3
  Emberton MK46.........13 C5
  Flackwell Heath HP10..185 C7
Tower Cres MK14.........34 F6
Tower Ct TW19...........213 A2
Tower Dr MK14...........34 F7
Towergate CI UB8........201 E7
TOWER HILL..............146 F2
Tower Hill WD4..........146 F1
Tower Hill Bsns Pk
  OX27...................71 D7
Tower Ho
  Iver SL0...............207 E7
  [4] Slough SL1........205 E4
Toweridge La
  High Wycombe HP12.....172 C8
  West Wycombe HP14.....160 F1
Tower Rd HP7............165 A4
Towersey Way HP21......115 B7
Towers Lea HP11.........173 C7
Tower St HP13...........162 D2
Town Bridge St HP5......154 B8
Town CI MK18............50 D6
TOWN END................159 C8
Town End Cres MK16.....12 B5
Town End Rd HP14........159 C8
Town Farm LU7...........105 A7
Town Farm Barns
  HP27...................139 B3
Town Farm CI OX49.......157 B8
Townfield HP5...........154 C7
Town Field La HP8.......177 C7
Townfield Rd [5] HP13...173 C7

Town La
  Stanwell TW19.........213 D1
  Wooburn HP10..........185 D4
Townlands Hospl RG9....191 D2
TOWNSEND
  Haddenham HP17........127 A7
  North Marston HP22....76 B2
TOWN'S END.............71 D2
Townsend
  Haddenham HP17........127 A7
  Marsh Gibbon OX27.....71 E2
  Quainton HP22.........85 A5
Townsend CI MK43.......37 F8
Townsend Cotts
  Great Horwood MK17....55 B3
  Middle Claydon MK18...74 C8
Townsend Gr MK43......34 B8
Townsend La OX27.......71 E2
Townsend Piece HP5....101 C1
Townsend Rd HP5.......144 C1
Townside
  Edlesborough LU6......92 F3
  Haddenham HP17.......126 F5
Town Sq [8] SL1........205 F4
Tozer Wlk SL4..........209 D4
Tracy Ave SL3..........206 F1
Tracy Way MK4..........45 E3
Trafalgar Ave MK3......46 E2
Trafford CI HP16.......152 A6
Trafford Rd HP16.......152 A7
Tram Hill HP18.........96 B2
Tranlands Brigg MK13...34 B4
Transcend [10] SL4.....202 C5
Trapp's Ct HP5.........154 C6
Trapp's La HP5.........154 C6
Travell Ct MK13........34 B3
Travic Rd SL2..........197 F2
Travis Ct SL2..........198 B2
Travis Gr MK3..........58 A8
Treacher's CI HP5......154 B8
Treadaway Bsns Ctr
  HP10...................174 C1
Treadaway Hill HP10....174 B1
Treadaway Rd HP10......174 B1
Trebah Sq HP19.........114 F8
Treborough MK4.........46 D2
Tredington Gr MK7......48 B4
Treefields MK18........52 E8
Treehanger CI HP23.....119 B4
Trees Ave HP14.........162 A6
Treeside CI UB7........208 D2
Treesmill Dr SL6.......202 C3
Trees Rd
  Bourne End SL8........185 B3
  Hughenden Valley HP14.162 A6
Trelawney Ave SL3......206 E3
Tremayne Ct MK6........47 A8
Trenchard Ave HP22.....131 D6
Trenchard St HP19......115 A8
Trenches La SL3........207 A6
Trengothal Ct NN13.....26 D4
Trent Dr MK16..........22 D4
Trentishoe Cres MK4....46 C3
Trent Rd
  Milton Keynes MK3.....46 E1
  Slough SL3............212 B8
Trent Villas Est SL3...211 B6
Tresco Rd HP4..........134 F5
Tresham Ct MK5.........46 A7
Tressell The SL6.......202 D6
Trevelyan Mid Sch SL4..210 C3
Trevelyan Way HP4......135 B6
Treves Gn HP21.........115 E5
Trevithick La MK5......46 B5
Trevone Ct MK6.........47 A8
Trevor Ct TW19.........213 A2
Trevose Ho SL2.........198 B1
Trewarden Ave SL0......90 B1
Triangle Bsns Pk HP22..130 D8
Trident Ind Est SL3....212 E4
TRING..................119 C3
Tring Bsns Ctr HP23....118 E4
TRINGFORD..............118 F8
Tring Ford Rd HP23.....119 A7
Tring Hill HP23........118 C3
Tring Park Sch for the
  Performing Arts
  HP23...................119 B3
Tring Rd
  Aylesbury HP21........116 B7
  Berkhamsted HP4.......134 D7
  Dunstable LU6.........93 E7
  Edlesborough LU6......106 E8
  Long Marston HP23.....104 C3
  Wendover HP22.........131 C5
  Wilstone HP23.........104 C1
  Wingrave HP22.........89 C1
Tring Reservoirs (Wildlife
  Trust Reserves)★
  HP23...................118 E2
Tring Sch HP23.........119 B4
Tring Sta HP23.........120 A5
Trinity Ave SL7........183 D3
Trinity CE Prim Sch
  RG9...................191 D1
Trinity CI
  Old Stratford MK19....32 B7
  Stanwell TW19........213 D1

Trinity Ct
  Aylesbury HP19........101 D1
  Chesham HP5..........154 C7
  Marlow SL7...........183 D3
Trinity Ho SL8.........195 F6
Trinity PI SL4.........210 C5
Trinity Rd
  Hazlemere HP15.......162 F3
  Marlow SL7...........183 D2
  Milton Keynes MK11...33 B7
Trinity St Stephen CE Fst
  Sch SL4..............210 B6
Tripps Hill CI HP8.....177 A7
Trispen Ct MK4.........47 A8
Trooper Rd HP23.......120 C5
Troutbeck MK6.........47 C8
Troutbeck CI SL2......206 A6
Trout CI SL7...........194 C8
Trout Hollow HP7......148 E8
Trout La UB7...........208 C5
Trout Rd UB7...........208 D6
Trubys Gdn MK6........47 A7
Trueman PI MK6........46 F8
Truesdale Dr UB9......190 C7
Trumper Way
  Slough SL1...........204 F5
  Uxbridge UB8.........201 C4
Trumpton La MK7.......48 C7
Trunk Furlong MK17....49 D6
Truro CI SL6...........202 A7
Trust Cotts HP4........107 A1
Trustees CI HP9........189 F5
Tubwell Rd SL2.........199 B4
Tucker CI HP13........173 C8
Tuckers Dr HP15.......163 C7
Tudeley Hale MK7......48 B8
Tudor CI
  Amersham HP6.........154 D1
  [5] Leighton Buzzard LU7..80 F7
  Maidenhead SL6.......196 C2
  Piddington HP14......160 C1
  [3] Stanwell TW19....213 E1
Tudor Dr HP10.........185 D7
Tudor Gdns
  Milton Keynes MK11...32 E4
  Slough SL1...........204 D8
  Steeple Claydon MK18.63 D3
Tudor Hill HP10........185 E6
Tudor Orch HP10.......134 E6
Tudor Pk HP6..........154 D2
Tudor Rd HP15.........163 C3
Tudors CI MK18........73 B4
Tudor Way SL4.........209 E6
Tuffnell CI MK15......35 E7
Tuffnell Gn MK10......35 E1
Tulip Way UB7.........208 D2
Tulkers CI HP16.......151 D5
Tulla Ct SL2..........58 C4
Tummell Way MK6......58 C6
Tunbridge Gr MK7......48 B8
Tunmers Ct SL9.......177 C2
Tunmers End SL9......177 C2
Tunmers Ho SL9.......177 C2
Tunnel Way LU7.......105 C2
Tuns La
  Henley-on-Thames RG9.191 E2
  Slough SL1...........205 C4
Turks Head Ct SL4.....210 C7
Turnberry CI MK3......57 D7
Turner CI HP20........101 F3
Turner Rd SL3.........206 C3
Turners Dr HP13.......173 E8
Turners Field HP13....161 E3
Turner's Mdw HP22....117 B6
Turners Mews MK14....34 F6
Turners PI HP15.......161 C6
Turners Wlk [4] HP5...144 C1
Turners Wood Dr HP8...177 D7
Turner Wlk [12] HP20..101 F3
Turneys Dr MK12......33 A6
Turneys Orch WD3.....167 D4
Turnfields HP18.......124 A3
Turnfurlong HP21.....115 F7
Turnfurlong Inf Sch
  HP21..................116 A6
Turnfurlong Jun Sch
  HP21..................116 A6
Turnfurlong La Cotts....116 A6
Turnfurlong Row HP21..116 A6
Turnham Way HP19.....115 B7
Turnip CI HP18........112 B2
Turnmill Ave MK6......35 B2
Turnmill St MK6.......35 B2
Turnoak Pk SL4........209 E3
Turnpike CI MK17......49 A5
Turnpike End HP21....115 F6
Turnpike La UB10......201 E3
Turnpike Rd HP12.....172 C4
Turnpike The HP10....109 D5
Turnpike Way HP12....172 D4
Turnstone Way HP19...101 E3
Turpins Gn SL6........202 A5
Turpyn Ct MK6.........47 D8
Turton Way SL1.......205 D3
TURVEY................8 F6
Turvey CI HP22........117 C5
Turvey Lower Sch MK43..8 E6
Turvey Mill MK43......8 F5

Turvey Rd
  Astwood MK16.........15 F5
  Turvey MK43..........3 E2
TURVILLE..............169 F3
TURVILLE HEATH........169 A3
Turville Rd MK45......46 B8
Turville Rd HP21......116 C6
TURWESTON............38 C8
Turweston Rd NN13....86 A1
Tuscans CI MK18......73 B5
Tweedale CI MK17.....67 C7
Tweed CI HP4..........135 B5
Tweed Dr MK3.........46 D1
Tweed Rd SL3.........212 B8
Tweenways HP5.......144 C1
Twelve Leys HP22....89 B3
Twinches La SL1......205 B5
Twinflower MK7.......48 B6
Twist The HP23.......119 D2
Twitchell La HP22...117 E5
Twitchell Rd HP16...152 A7
Twitchell's La HP9...176 F5
Twitchen La MK4.....46 D3
Twizel CI MK13.......33 E6
Two Dells La
  Ashley Green HP5.....145 A4
  Chesham HP5.........155 B8
Two Gates La HP5.....143 D7
TWO MILE ASH.........33 D2
Two Mile Ash Sch MK8.33 C1
Two Mile Dr SL1......204 E4
Two Ponds La HP4.....134 C7
TWYFORD..............62 C1
Twyford CE Fst Sch
  MK18..................62 C2
Twyford La MK7.......48 C5
Twynham Rd SL2......202 B7
Tyburn Ave MK6......35 B2
Tyhurst MK10.........36 A2
Tyle PI SL4...........211 A2
Tyler Cres HP15......163 B2
Tylers Gn MK13.......34 D3
TYLERS GREEN........163 C1
Tylers Green Fst Sch
  HP10..................174 D8
Tylers Green Mid Sch
  HP10..................174 B8
Tylers Hill Rd HP5...154 F8
Tylers Rd HP15.......163 B2
Tyler Wlk [3] SL3....206 F1
Tylsworth CI HP6.....154 D1
Tyndale Mews SL1....205 B4
Tyneham CI HP21.....116 B4
Tynemouth Rise [3]
  MK10.................36 A1
Tyne Rd HP21.........115 D4
Tyne Sq MK3.........46 D1
Tyrell CI
  Buckingham MK18.....52 C7
  Milton Keynes MK19...20 A5
Tyrell Gdns SL4......209 E4
Tyrells Gdns MK17....69 E8
Tyrells Rd MK17......69 E8
Tyrill MK14..........34 C7
TYRINGHAM...........12 F2
Tyson PI MK6........46 E8
Tythe CI LU7........78 E8
Tythe Gdns LU7......78 E8
Tythe Mews LU6......92 E3
Tyzack Rd HP13......162 F1

U

Ufton Court Yd SL8...185 B4
Ufton Ct SL8.........185 B4
Ullswater CI SL1.....204 C8
Ullswater Dr LU7.....80 C7
Ultra Ave MK3........47 A1
Ulverscroft MK10....36 B2
Ulverston Cres MK10..36 B2
Ulyett PI MK6........46 E8
Umberville Way SL2...197 F2
Underhill CI SL6.....202 E6
Underwood Cotts HP7..164 C2
Underwood PI MK6....46 C8
Underwood Rd HP13...173 D8
Union Bldgs UB8.....201 B2
Union Bsns Pk UB8...201 B5
Union Ct [11] HP4....135 D4
Union Ind Est HP12...172 A7
Union St MK9.........22 D5
University Way MK43..24 D1
Univ of Buckingham The
  MK18.................52 C7
Univ of Buckingham The
  (Verney Pk) MK18.....52 E7
Up Corner HP8.......177 C8
Up Corner CI HP8....177 B8
Upcroft SL4..........210 B4
UP END..............24 A8
Upland Ave HP5......144 B3
Uplands SL3.........183 D6
Uplands CI
  Gerrards Cross SL9...188 E3
  High Wycombe HP13...173 E8

Uplands Ct HP5 . . . . 144 C1
Uplands The SL9 . . . . . . 188 E2
Upminster CI MK10 . . . . 35 E1
Upper Abbotts Hill
  HP19 . . . . 115 A7
UPPER ARNCOTT 94 E7
Upper Ashlyns Rd HP4 . 135 B3
Upper Barn Farm HP18 . 84 B1
Upper Belmont Rd HP4 144 B3
Upper Bourne End La
  HP1 . . . . 146 B7
Upper Bray Rd SL6 . . . . 203 C3
Upper Church St HP18 . 112 F3
Upper Coombe LU7 . . . . 80 E8
Upper Dr HP9 . . . . 175 D5
UPPER DUNSLEY 119 C4
Upper Fifth St MK9 . . . . 34 D2
Upper Fourth St MK9 . . . 34 D2
Upper George St HP5 . . 144 C1
Upper Gladstone Rd 2
  HP5 . . . . 144 C1
Upper Green St HP11 . . 172 E7
Upper Hall Pk HP4 . . . . 135 E2
Upper Hartwell HP17 . . 114 E5
Upper Hollis HP16 . . . . 151 F7
Upper Hundreds Way
  HP20 . . . . 115 E8
Upper Icknield Way
  Askett HP27 . . . . 139 E7
  Halton HP22 . . . . 117 F2
  Monks Risborough HP27 139 D6
  Pitstone HP23, LU7 . . . 105 E1
  Princes Risborough
    HP27 . . . . 139 B2
  Saunderton HP27 . . . . 148 F7
Upper Lees Rd SL2 . . . . 198 B2
Upper Lodge La HP15 . 162 F6
UPPER
  MAIDENSGROVE 179 A7
Upper Mdw 2 HP5 . . . . 144 B1
UPPER NORTH DEAN . . 150 E2
UPPER POLLICOTT 111 E8
Upper Ray Mdws Wildlife
  Reserve★ OX25 . . . . . 81 C4
Upper Rd UB9 . . . . 189 D4
Upper Riding HP9 . . . . . 175 B2
Upper Second St MK9 . . 34 D1
Upper St
  Quainton HP22 . . . . . . 85 A5
  Tingewick MK18 . . . . . 51 B6
Upper Stonehayes MK14. 34 F8
Upper Thames Way
  SL8 . . . . 184 F3
Upper Third St MK9 . . . 34 D1
Upper Tring Pk HP23 . . 119 D1
Upper Ventnor Cotts
  SL6 . . . . 195 C8
Upper Way MK17 . . . . . . 59 C2
Upper Weald MK19 . . . . 45 A8
UPPER WINCHENDON . . 99 B1
Upperwood CI 1 MK5 . 46 A3
Upper Wood CI MK5 . . . 45 F3
UPTON
  Slough 206 B3
  Stone 114 A4
Upton CI
  Henley-on-Thames RG9 . 191 E1
  5 Slough SL1 . . . . . . 205 F3
Upton Court Rd SL3 . . 206 B2
Upton Gr MK5 . . . . 46 C4
Upton Hospl SL1 . . . . . 205 F4
Upton House Sch SL4 . 210 C5
UPTON LEA 206 A7
Upton Lea Par SL2 . . . . 206 B6
UPTON PARK 205 F3
Upton Pk SL1 . . . . 205 F3
Upton Rd
  Dinton HP17 . . . . 114 A3
  Slough SL1 . . . . 206 A3
Upton Terr HP17 . . . . . 114 A3
Upway SL1 . . . . 197 D7
Ushercombe View MK18 50 D6
UXBRIDGE 201 E5
Uxbridge Coll UB8 . . . . 201 E6
Uxbridge High Sch
  UB8 . . . . 201 D3
Uxbridge Ind Est UB8 . 201 B3
UXBRIDGE MOOR 201 B4
Uxbridge Rd
  Iver Heath SL0, SL3 . . . 200 B2
  Rickmansworth WD3 . . 178 F7
  Slough SL1, SL3 . . . . . 206 C7
  Uxbridge UB10 . . . . . . 201 F2
Uxbridge U Sta UB8 . . 201 D5

V

Vache La
  Chalfont St Giles HP8 . . 177 C8
  Milton Keynes MK5 . . . . 45 F6
Vale CI SL9 . . . . 177 D2
Vale Ct MK43 . . . . 25 D2
Vale Gr SL1 . . . . 205 E3
Vale House HP19 . . . . . 115 C8
Vale Ind Ctr The HP19 . 101 C1

Valens CI MK8 . . . . 45 E7
Valentine Ct MK8 . . . . . . 45 E7
Valentine Way HP8 . . . . 177 D7
Vale Park Dr HP20 . . . . 115 E8
Vale Rd
  Aylesbury HP20 . . . . . 101 E2
  Chesham HP5 . . . . 144 C4
  Windsor SL4 . . . . 209 F6
Vale Ret Pk HP20 . . . . . 115 E8
Valerian Rd MK16 . . . . . 21 F4
Vale Rise HP5 . . . . 144 C3
Vale The SL9 . . . . 177 D2
Valley CI
  Brackley NN13 . . . . 38 A8
  Whipsnade HP4 . . . . . 107 E7
Valley Cres NN13 . . . . . . 38 A8
Valley Ctr The HP13 . . . 173 C6
Valley End SL3 . . . . 199 C1
Valley Rd
  Berkhamsted HP4 . . . 134 F6
  Brackley NN13 . . . . 38 A8
  Buckingham MK18 . . . . 52 F8
  Finmere MK18 . . . . 50 D6
  Henley-on-Thames RG9 . 191 C1
  Hughenden Valley HP14 162 A5
  Uxbridge UB10 . . . . . . 201 E3
Valley Rise NN13 . . . . . . 38 A8
Valley View HP5 . . . . . . 144 B2
Valley Way SL9 . . . . 188 D5
Valpy CI HP23 . . . . 119 D1
Van Der Bilt Ct MK13 . . 33 F6
Van Diemens CI OX39 . 147 C7
Vandyke CI MK17 . . . . . . 49 B6
Vane Rd OX9 . . . . 126 B1
Vanguard CI HP12 . . . . 172 D7
Vanguard Ho 8 TW19 . 213 E1
Vansittart Rd
  Bisham SL7 . . . . 194 E7
  Windsor SL4 . . . . 210 B6
Vantage CI MK16 . . . . . 22 F3
Vantage Rd SL1 . . . . . . 205 B5
Vanwall Bsns Pk SL6 . . 202 C5
Vanwall Rd SL6 . . . . . . 202 C4
Varnell Terr MK11 . . . . 181 C2
Vaughan Copse SL4 . . . 205 D2
Vaughan Gdns SL4 . . . 204 F2
Vaughan Way SL2 . . . . 197 E1
Vauxhall MK13 . . . . 34 B6
Vellan Ave MK6 . . . . 35 B1
Venables La MK5 . . . . . . 35 B7
Venetian Ct MK7 . . . . . . 48 C7
Ventfield CI OX33 . . . . . 108 A5
Venus CI SL2 . . . . 197 F1
Venus Hill HP3 . . . . 156 B8
Verbena CI UB7 . . . . . . 208 D1
Verdi CI MK7 . . . . 48 D5
Verdon Dr MK15 . . . . . . 35 B7
Verdon Rd SL2 . . . . 198 B2
Verity PI MK4 . . . . 34 F1
Verley CI MK6 . . . . 47 C8
Vermont PI MK15 . . . . . 22 C1
Vermont Rd SL2 . . . . . . 197 F1
Verney Ave HP12 . . . . . 172 D4
Verney CI
  Berkhamsted HP4 . . . 134 F5
  6 Buckingham MK18 . . 41 D1
  Marlow SL7 . . . . 183 D2
  Tring HP23 . . . . 119 C4
Verney Farm CI MK18 . 74 F8
Verney Junc Bsns Pk
  MK18 . . . . 64 E3
VERNEY JUNCTION . . . 64 F4
Verney Rd
  Slough SL3 . . . . 207 A2
  Winslow MK18 . . . . . . 65 E4
Verney Wlk HP21 . . . . . 115 D6
Vernier Cres MK5 . . . . . 45 E5
Vernon Bldg 7 HP11 . . 172 F7
Verona CI UB8 . . . . 208 C7
Verwood Rd HP20 . . . . 101 E2
Veryan PI MK6 . . . . 35 B1
Vicarage CI
  Cookham SL6 . . . . 196 B7
  Seer Green HP9 . . . . . 176 D3
  Steeple Claydon MK18 . 63 D2
  Wendover HP22 . . . . . 131 B5
Vicarage Ct
  Hanslope MK19 . . . . . . 11 B2
  Steeple Claydon MK18 . . 63 D3
Vicarage Dr SL6 . . . . . 203 C4
Vicarage Flats SL4 . . . 210 D8
Vicarage Gdns
  Leighton Buzzard LU7 . . 80 E6
  Marsworth HP23 . . . . 105 A2
  3 Milton Keynes MK13 . . 34 A4
Vicarage La
  Bovingdon HP3 . . . . . 146 B4
  Ivinghoe LU7 . . . . 105 F5
  Piddington OX25 . . . . . 95 E6
  Steeple Claydon MK18 . 63 D2
  Wing LU7 . . . . 79 E2
Vicarage Rd
  Aylesbury HP21 . . . . . 115 D5
  Henley-on-Thames RG9 . 191 E1
  Leighton Buzzard LU7 . . 80 E6
  Maidenhead SL6 . . . . 202 F8
  Milton Keynes, Bradwell
    MK13 . . . . 34 A4

Vicarage Rd continued
  Milton Keynes, Fenny Stratford
    MK2 . . . . 58 E8
  Milton Keynes, Stony Stratford
    MK13 . . . . 32 D6
  Pitstone LU7 . . . . 105 D2
  Whaddon MK17 . . . . . . 56 B8
  Wigginton HP23 . . . . . 119 D1
  Winslow MK18 . . . . . . 65 F1
  Yardley Gobion MK12 . . 18 E6
Vicarage St MK17 . . . . . 49 C4
Vicarage Way
  Colnbrook SL3 . . . . . . 212 D7
  Gerrards Cross SL9 . . . 188 F5
Vicarage Wlk MK11 . . . . 32 D6
Vickers Ct 9 TW19 . . . 213 E1
Vickery CI HP21 . . . . . . 115 E5
Vickery Way HP21 . . . . 115 E5
Victor CI SL6 . . . . 202 B8
Victoria CE Fst Sch
  Berkhamsted HP4 . . . 135 C4
Victoria Cotts SL6 . . . . 195 C8
Victoria Cres SL0 . . . . 208 A6
Victoria Ct
  Henley-on-Thames RG9 . 191 E1
  High Wycombe HP11 . . 172 F8
  4 Marlow SL7 . . . . . . 183 E2
  Slough SL1 . . . . 205 E5
  4 Windsor SL4 . . . . . 210 D6
Victoria Dr SL1, SL2 . . 197 F6
Victoria Gdns
  High Wycombe HP11 . . 172 F4
  4 Marlow SL7 . . . . . . 183 E2
Victoria Ho SL4 . . . . . . 211 A2
Vanwrights HP18 . . . . 125 D6
Victoria Rd
  Berkhamsted HP4 . . . 135 C4
  Chesham HP5 . . . . 144 C1
  Eton Wick SL4 . . . . . . 204 F1
  Farnham Common SL2 . 198 C6
  Leighton Buzzard LU7 . . 80 E6
  Marlow SL7 . . . . 183 E2
  Milton Keynes MK2 . . . 47 E1
  Slough SL2 . . . . 206 B5
  Uxbridge UB8 . . . . . . 201 C5
Victoria Row MK18 . . . . 52 D8
Victoria St
  Aylesbury HP20 . . . . . 115 F8
  High Wycombe HP11 . . 172 F7
  Milton Keynes MK12 . . 33 D6
  10 Slough SL1 . . . . . . 205 F4
  Windsor SL4 . . . . 210 D6
Victor Rd SL4 . . . . 210 C4
Victory CI MK1 . . . . 47 B2
Victory Rd
  Berkhamsted HP4 . . . 135 A5
  Steeple Claydon MK18 . 63 D2
  Wendover HP22 . . . . . 131 B5
Vienna Gr MK13 . . . . . . 33 E6
Village CI MK16 . . . . . . 13 F2
Village Ct LU7 . . . . 80 D6
Village La SL2 . . . . 187 D4
Village Mews 2 HP3 . . 146 A4
Village Rd
  Coleshill HP7 . . . . 164 F3
  Denham UB9 . . . . 190 A2
  Dorney SL4 . . . . 204 B3
Village Way HP7 . . . . . . 166 D7
Villa Park (Mobile Home
  Pk) MK43 . . . . 37 F7
Villiers Bldgs 8 HP20 . 115 D8
Villiers CI MK18 . . . . 41 E2
Villiers CI SL4 . . . . 210 A7
Villiers Rd SL2 . . . . 205 D8
Villier St UB8 . . . . 201 D3
Vimy Ct LU7 . . . . 80 F7
Vimy Rd LU7 . . . . 80 F7
Vincent Ave MK8 . . . . . . 45 E8
Vincent Dr UB10 . . . . . . 201 F4
Vincent Rd HP19 . . . . . 101 A3
Vincents Way HP14 . . . 161 D6
Vine CI
  Hazlemere HP15 . . . . . 163 A3
  Stanwell TW19 . . . . . . 213 A2
Vine Ct SL2 . . . . 199 A6
Vine Gr UB10 . . . . 201 F5
Vine La UB10 . . . . 201 F4
Vine Rd SL2 . . . . 198 F6
Vine Row MK43 . . . . 8 E6
Vine St UB8 . . . . 201 C4
Vine The HP18 . . . . 124 D3
Vineyard Dr SL8 . . . . . 185 A5
Vineyards The HP27 . . . 138 A2
Viney La HP18 . . . . 114 F8
Vinlake Ave UB10 . . . . . 190 F1
Vintners Mews MK14 . . 34 F6
Violet Ave MK8 . . . . 208 F8
Violet CI HP27 . . . . 149 D6
Violets CI MK16 . . . . . . 24 B6
Virage HP22 . . . . 117 F4
Virginia CI MK16 . . . . . . 22 A2
Virginia Gdns HP14 . . . 159 F8
Viridian Sq HP21 . . . . . 115 E7
Viscount CI SL0 . . . . . . 201 F2
Viscount Ct 12 SL4 . . . 210 C6
Viscount Ind Est SL3 . . 212 E4
Viscount Way MK2 . . . . 47 C1

Vitalograph Bsns Pk
  MK18 . . . . 41 F4
Vivaldi Ct MK7 . . . . 48 D5
Vivien CI SL6 . . . . 195 F6
Volta Rise MK5 . . . . 46 C4
Vyne Cres MK8 . . . . 33 F1
Vyners Sch UB10 . . . . . 201 F8

W

Waborne Rd SL8 . . . . . . 185 B4
WADDESDON 99 B7
Waddesdon CE Sch
  HP18 . . . . 99 A6
Waddesdon CI 8 MK8 . 45 F8
Waddesdon Green
  HP21 . . . . 115 E4
Waddesdon Hill HP18 . . 99 C3
Waddesdon Manor★
  HP18 . . . . 98 E5
Waddesdon Manor Flats
  HP18 . . . . 98 E6
Waddesdon Village Prim
  Sch HP18 . . . . 99 A6
Wade Dr SL1 . . . . 205 A5
Wadesmill La MK7 . . . . 48 A4
Wadhurst La MK10 . . . . 36 B1
Wadworth Holme MK10 . 35 E3
Waglands Gdn MK18 . . 52 D7
Wagner CI MK7 . . . . 48 C4
Wagstaff Way 12 MK46 . . 6 F3
Waine CI MK18 . . . . 52 D7
Wainers Croft MK12 . . . 33 B4
Wainwrights HP18 . . . . 125 D6
Waivers Way HP21 . . . . 116 A5
Wakefield CI MK14 . . . . 34 F7
Wakefield Cres SL2 . . . 198 F6
Wakelins End SL6 . . . . 195 E7
Wakeman Rd SL8 . . . . . 185 A3
Walbank Gr MK5 . . . . . . 46 A3
Walbrook Ave MK6 . . . . 35 B3
Waldeck Ho SL6 . . . . . . 203 A7
Waldeck Rd SL6 . . . . . . 203 A7
Walden Croft MK6 . . . . 47 E4
Waldens CI 4 SL8 . . . . 185 A3
Walducks CI LU7 . . . . . . 78 E8
Walford Rd UB8 . . . . . . 201 D3
Walgrave Dr MK13 . . . . 34 B4
Walker Ave MK12 . . . . . 33 A6
Walker Cres SL3 . . . . . 206 F1
Walker Ct SL6 . . . . 202 D7
Walker Rd SL6 . . . . 203 A4
Walkers Rd HP27 . . . . . 138 D7
Walkham CI HP13 . . . . 174 B4
Walkhampton Ave MK13 . 34 A4
Walk House CI MK43 . . . 25 B1
Walk The
  Eton Wick SL4 . . . . . . 205 A1
  Winslow MK18 . . . . . . 65 F4
Walkwood End HP9 . . . 175 C1
Walkwood Rise HP9 . . 186 C8
Wallace CI
  Marlow SL7 . . . . 183 F4
  Uxbridge UB10 . . . . . . 201 E3
Wallace Dr LU6 . . . . 92 E6
Wallace End HP21 . . . . 116 A6
Wallace Mews LU6 . . . . 92 E6
Wallace St SL4 . . . . 33 E2
Wallace Wlk SL4 . . . . . 205 F1
Wallbridge CI HP19 . . . 115 B7
Wall Brown Way HP19 . 101 C4
Waller Rd HP19 . . . . . . 175 F2
Wallinger Dr MK5 . . . . . 46 A3
Wallingford MK13 . . . . . 34 B5
Wallingford Gdns HP11 173 B4
Wallingford Rd UB8 . . . 201 B2
Wallington Rd HP5 . . . 144 B1
Wallis Ct SL3 . . . . 206 A3
Wallmead Gdns MK5 . . 46 B7
Walney PI MK4 . . . . 45 F1
Walnut CI
  Great Missenden HP16 . 152 A7
  Long Crendon HP18 . . 125 C7
  Newport Pagnell MK16 . . 22 C3
  Stoke Mandeville HP22 . 116 C2
Walnut Cres HP27 . . . . 138 D7
Walnut Dr
  Maids Moreton MK18 . . 41 F4
  Milton Keynes MK2 . . . . 58 E8
  Wendover HP22 . . . . . 131 B6
Walnut Gr HP10 . . . . . . 185 E6
Walnut Lodge SL1 . . . . 205 D4
Walnut Sch The MK8 . . 45 D5
WALNUT TREE 48 C6
Walnut Tree CI
  Bourne End SL8 . . . . . 185 B2
  High Wycombe HP22 . . 172 C8
  Uxbridge UB10 . . . . . . 201 F8
Walnut Tree Ct HP22 . . 116 C3
Walnut Tree Ho HP11 . . 174 B2
Walnut Tree La HP22 . . 138 D6
Walnut Tree Rdbt MK7 . 48 C7
Walnut Way
  Bourne End SL8 . . . . . 185 B2
  Hyde Heath HP6 . . . . . 153 C4
Walpole Rd SL1 . . . . . . 204 D7
Walsh's Manor MK14 . . 34 D7

Walsingham Gate
  HP11 . . . . 173 A4
WALTER'S ASH 150 C1
Waltham Dr MK10 . . . . 36 A1
Waltham Ho 4 MK3 . . . 46 F1
WALTON
  Aylesbury 115 F7
  Milton Keynes 47 F5
Walton CI HP13 . . . . . . 162 E1
WALTON COURT 115 C5
Walton Court Ctr HP21 115 C5
Walton Dene HP21 . . . . 115 F7
Walton Dr
  High Wycombe HP13 . . 162 E1
  Walton MK7 . . . . 47 F6
Walton End MK7 . . . . . . 48 C6
Walton Gn HP21 . . . . . . 115 E7
Walton Gr SL4 . . . . 211 A2
Walton Heath MK3 . . . . 57 D7
Walton High Sch MK7 . 48 C6
Walton La SL2 . . . . 197 F3
WALTON MANOR 48 A6
WALTON PARK 48 A4
Walton Park Rdbt MK7 . 48 B4
Walton PI HP22 . . . . . . 116 F3
Walton Rd
  Aylesbury HP21 . . . . . 115 F7
  Caldecotte MK7 . . . . . 48 B3
  Milton Keynes MK10 . . . 36 A2
  Walton MK7 . . . . 48 B6
  Wavendon MK10, MK17 . 48 D7
Walton St HP21 . . . . . . 115 C5
Walton Terr HP21 . . . . . 115 E7
Walton Way HP21 . . . . . 116 A7
Wandlebury MK14 . . . . 35 A8
Wandsworth PI MK13 . . 34 D3
Wannions Ct HP5 . . . . . 145 A1
Wantage CI LU7 . . . . . . 79 E3
Wantage Cres LU7 . . . . 79 E3
Wappenham Rd NN13 . 27 B8
Wapping HP18 . . . . 125 D6
Wapseys La SL2 . . . . . . 187 F4
Warbler CI HP19 . . . . . . 114 F8
Warburg Nature Reserve★
  RG9 . . . . 179 B5
Ward CI SL0 . . . . 207 F7
Wardes CI HP16 . . . . . 151 C5
Ward Gdns SL1 . . . . . . 204 E5
Wardle PI MK6 . . . . 46 E8
Ward Rd HP7 . . . . 165 B7
Ward Rd
  Brackley NN13 . . . . 38 A5
  Milton Keynes MK1 . . . 47 B3
Wardrobes La HP27 . . . 149 D8
Ward Royal 6 SL4 . . . . 210 C6
Ward Royal Parade 3
  SL4 . . . . 210 C6
Wardstone End MK4 . . . 46 B2
Ware Leys CI OX27 . . . 71 E3
Wargrave Rd HP9 . . . . 191 F1
Warmington Gdns MK15. 35 B5
Warmstone CI HP18 . . . 99 B6
Warmstone La HP18 . . . 99 B6
Warneford Ave HP22 . . 131 D5
Warner CI SL1 . . . . 204 E5
Warners CI MK17 . . . . . 59 D1
Warners Hill SL6 . . . . . 195 D8
Warners Rd MK17 . . . . 57 D3
Warren Bank MK6 . . . . 47 E5
Warren CI
  Buckingham MK18 . . . 52 E7
  Slough SL3 . . . . 206 E3
  Stone HP17 . . . . 114 B5
Warren Ct
  Farnham Common SL2 . 198 C2
  Maidenhead MK17 . . . 55 E5
Warrendene Rd HP14 . 162 A8
Warrender Rd HP5 . . . . 144 E2
Warren Farm Cotts
  MK18 . . . . 50 A7
Warren Field SL0 . . . . . 200 C3
Warren Ho HP19 . . . . . 101 B1
Warren Nature Reserve★
  HP10 . . . . 185 E5
Warren Parade SL2 . . . 206 C5
Warren Rd
  Ickenham UB10 . . . . . 201 F8
  Little Horwood MK17 . . 55 F5
  Yardley Gobion NN12 . . 18 F6
Warren The
  Chalfont St Peter SL9 . . 177 F3
  Chartridge HP5 . . . . . . 143 E3
  Hazelmere HP15 . . . . . 163 A5
Warren Wood Dr HP11 . 173 C5
Warren Yd MK12 . . . . . . 33 A6
WARRINGTON 2 B1
Warrington Ave SL1 . . . 205 C7
Warrington Rd MK46 . . . 7 B7
Warwick Ave
  High Wycombe HP12 . . 172 B6
  Milton Keynes MK10 . . . 36 C3
  Slough SL2 . . . . 198 C1
Warwick CI
  Aston Clinton HP22 . . . 117 E5
  Maidenhead SL6 . . . . 202 B4
Warwick Ct
  Beaconsfield HP9 . . . . 175 D3
  Chorleywood WD3 . . . . 167 F6

Warwick Ct continued
7 Windsor SL4 . . . . .210 C5
Warwick Dr LU7 . . . . .79 E2
Warwick Ho **7** HP13 . . .173 F7
Warwick Pl
  Milton Keynes MK3 . . . . . . .57 E7
  Uxbridge UB8. . . . . .201 C5
Warwick Rd
  Beaconsfield HP9 . . . . . . .175 D3
  Hanslope MK19 . . . . .11 A3
  Milton Keynes MK3 . . . . . . .57 F7
  Pitstone LU7 . . . . .105 D2
  West Drayton UB7 . . . . . .208 E5
Warwick Row HP20 . . . . . .102 A1
Washfield MK4 . . . . .46 D3
Wash Hill HP10 . . . . .185 E3
Wash Hill Lea HP10 . . . . . .185 E4
Wash Hill Mobile Home Pk
  HP10 . . . . .185 E3
Washingleys MK43 . . . . . . .25 C2
Washington Ct SL7. . . . .184 A3
Washington Dr
  Slough SL1. . . . . .204 D6
  Windsor SL4 . . . . .209 E4
Washington Row HP7 . . . .165 C7
Wastel MK6 . . . . .47 B5
Watchcroft Dr MK18 . . . . .41 E2
Watchet CI MK4 . . . . .46 D3
Watchet La
  Holmer Green HP15. . . . . .163 B7
  Little Kingshill HP16 . . . . .152 C1
Waterbeach CI SL1. . . . . .205 D7
Waterbeach Rd SL1. . . . . .205 D7
Waterborne Wlk LU7. . . . .80 F7
Water CI MK19. . . . . .32 B7
Watercress Way MK10. . . .36 B3
WATER EATON 58 D5
Water Eaton Rd MK2,
  MK3. . . . . .58 C7
WATEREND 159 C5
Water End Rd
  Beacon's Bottom HP14 . .159 D3
  Beacon's Bottom, Waterend
    HP14 . . . . .159 C5
Waterfield MK3. . . . . .167 C2
Waterford CI MK3. . . . . . . .46 E1
Waterford Ho UB7 . . . . . .208 C3
Water Gdns The HP15. . . .162 E2
Waterglades The HP9 . . . .175 C6
WATERHALL 58 D4
Waterhouse CI MK16. . . . .22 D4
Water La
  Berkhamsted HP4 . . . . . .135 C4
  Bovingdon HP3 . . . . .146 B1
  Ford HP17 . . . . .128 B7
  Leighton Buzzard LU7 . . . .80 F7
  Sherington MK16. . . . . . . .13 E1
  Speen HP27 . . . . .150 C4
Waterlily **5** HP19 . . . . . .101 E4
Waterloo Ct MK3. . . . . . . .46 E2
Waterloo Rd
  Leighton Buzzard LU7 . . . .80 E6
  Uxbridge UB8. . . . . .201 C4
Waterlow CI MK16 . . . . . . .22 C2
Waterman Ct SL1. . . . . . .204 E5
Water Mdw HP5 . . . . .154 B7
WATERMEAD. 101 F4
Watermead HP19 . . . . . . .101 E4
Watermeadow HP19 . . . . .101 F3
Water Meadow Way
  HP22 . . . . .131 B6
Watermill Way HP22 . . . . .116 F2
WATERPERRY 123 B1
Waterperry OX33 . . . . . . .123 B1
WATERPERRY
  COMMON 122 F8
Waterperry Gdns★
  OX33. . . . . .123 B1
Waterperry Mews
  HP19 . . . . .114 F8
Waterperry Rd HP18 . . . . .123 D5
WATERSIDE. 154 D6
Waterside
  Berkhamsted HP4 . . . . . .135 D4
  Chesham HP5 . . . . .154 D6
  Edlesborough LU6. . . . . . .92 F4
  Milton Keynes MK6 . . . . . .47 C8
  Uxbridge UB8. . . . . .208 C8
  Wooburn Green HP10 . . . .185 E7
Waterside Comb Sch
  HP5. . . . . .154 D6
Waterside CI HP5. . . . . . .154 C7
Waterside Dr SL3. . . . . . .207 A4
Waterside Lodge SL6 . . . .203 C8
Waterside Pk MK12 . . . . . .33 C7
Waterslade Pens HP17 . . .126 F6
Waters Reach SL6 . . . . . .196 A1
WATER STRATFORD 40 A1
Water Stratford Rd
  MK18 . . . . .51 A7
Water Tower CI UB8 . . . . .201 E7
Watery La
  Beachampton MK19. . . . . .44 B6
  Brackley NN13. . . . . .38 A7
  Marsworth HP23 . . . . . . .104 F1
  Wooburn Green HP10 . . . .185 E8
Watling St
  Bletchley MK2 . . . . .47 D1

Watling St continued
Bow Brickhill MK17 . . . . . . .58 F8
Granby MK6. . . . . .47 A3
Milton Keynes, Kiln Farm MK8,
  MK11. . . . . .33 B2
Milton Keynes, Shenley Lodge
  MK6. . . . . .46 C6
Pottersbury NN12 . . . . .18 C3
Watling Terr MK2. . . . . .47 E1
Watlington Ct HP16 . . . . . .152 A8
Watlington Rd OX49. . . . . .157 E4
Watling Way Pool MK11. . . .32 F4
Watlow Gdns MK18 . . . . . . .41 E2
Watson CI MK8 . . . . .45 D6
Watten Ct MK2 . . . . .58 E4
Wattleton Rd HP9. . . . . . .175 E1
Watts CI MK19 . . . . .11 A3
Watts Gn HP18. . . . . .112 B2
Wavell CI MK15. . . . . .35 B7
Wavell Gdns SL2. . . . . . . .197 F2
Wavell Rd
  Beaconsfield HP9. . . . . . .176 B1
  Maidenhead SL6 . . . . . . .202 B6
WAVENDON. 48 E7
Wavendon Fields MK17. . . .48 F6
Wavendon GATE. 48 E6
Wavendon Gate Comb Sch
  MK7 . . . . .48 D6
Wavendon House Dr
  MK17. . . . . .49 B8
Wavendon Rd MK17. . . . . .37 C2
Waveney CI MK16. . . . . . . .22 B8
Waverley Croft MK10. . . . . .36 A1
Waverley Rd SL1. . . . . . . .205 C8
Waverley Wlk MK20 . . . . .101 D2
Waxwing CI HP19 . . . . . . .101 E3
Wayfarers Pk HP4 . . . . . . .134 F4
Waylands TW19. . . . . .211 E1
Wayside
  High Wycombe HP13 . . . .173 D7
  Speen HP27 . . . . .150 C4
Wayside Ct HP6. . . . . .154 C1
Wayside Gdns SL9 . . . . . .188 D4
Wayside Mews SL6 . . . . . .202 F8
Wealdstone PI MK6 . . . . . .35 A2
Weasel La MK3 . . . . .57 C6
Weatherby LU7 . . . . .80 F7
Weathercock CI MK17. . . . .49 B5
Weathercock Gdns
  HP15. . . . . .163 C7
Weathercock La MK17. . . . .49 C4
Weavers End MK19. . . . . . .11 B2
Weavers Hill MK11. . . . . . . .33 A4
Weavers Rd HP23 . . . . . . .118 E4
Webb CI
  Chesham HP5 . . . . .144 B1
  Slough SL3. . . . . .206 D2
Webber Heath MK7 . . . . . .48 D4
Webbs Home CI MK10 . . . .36 A2
Webbs Mdw HP19. . . . . . .115 A8
Webster CI
  Maidenhead SL6 . . . . . . .202 A5
  Thame OX9 . . . . .125 F1
Webster Rd HP21. . . . . . . .116 A6
Websters Mdw MK4. . . . . . .46 C1
Wedgewood St HP19 . . . . . .35 E1
Wedgwood Ave MK14 . . . . .22 A1
Wedgwood Dr HP14. . . . . .162 A6
WEEDON 87 D1
Weedon CI SL9 . . . . .177 B2
Weedon Hill HP6. . . . . . . .153 D4
Weedon La MK18. . . . . . . .154 A3
Weedon Rd HP19 . . . . . . .101 C2
Weekes Dr SL1. . . . . .205 B4
Weill Rd HP21. . . . . .116 A4
Weir La
  Blackthorn OX25 . . . . .81 A4
  East Claydon MK18 . . . . . .74 E5
  Whitchurch HP22. . . . . . . .86 F6
Weirside Gdns UB7 . . . . . .208 D5
Welbeck Ave HP21. . . . . . .116 C6
Welbeck CI MK10. . . . . .35 F1
Welbeck Rd SL6 . . . . .202 D5
Welburn Gr MK4 . . . . .46 B2
Welby CI SL6 . . . . .202 A4
Welden SL2 . . . . .206 C7
Welders La
  Chalfont St Giles SL9. . . . .177 A3
  Seer Green SL9 . . . . .177 B3
Welford Way HP18 . . . . . . .112 F3
Welland CI SL3 . . . . .212 B8
Welland Dr MK16 . . . . .22 E3
Welland Ho MK3 . . . . .57 E8
Welland Rd HP21 . . . . . . .115 C5
Wellbank SL6. . . . . .196 E1
Wellbrook Mews HP23 . . . .119 B4
Wellcroft HP6. . . . . .153 D3
Wellcroft Rd SL1. . . . . . . .205 B5
WELL END 184 F5
Well End Cotts SL8. . . . . .184 F5
Weller Ct HP6. . . . . .154 C2
Weller CI HP16. . . . . .93 C7
Weller Rd HP6. . . . . .154 E2
Wellesbourne Gdns
  HP13. . . . . .162 D2
Welles La MK4. . . . . .45 D3
Wellesley Ave SL0. . . . . . .207 F4
Wellesley Ct SL0. . . . . . . .207 F4

Wellesley Ho SL4 . . . . . .210 B6
Wellesley Path SL1 . . . . . .206 A4
Wellesley Rd SL1 . . . . . . .206 A4
Wellesley Way TW19 . . . . .173 F7
Welley Ave TW19 . . . . . . .211 E3
Welley Rd SL3, TW19. . . . .211 E3
Wellfield HP15. . . . . .163 B3
Wellfield CI MK15. . . . . .35 D8
Wellfield Rd MK14. . . . . . .171 B8
Wellhayes MK14 . . . . .34 F8
WELL HEAD 93 D5
Well Head Rd LU6. . . . . . . .93 C6
Wellhouse Rd SL6 . . . . . . .195 E2
Wellhouse Way HP14. . . . .161 E6
Wellingborough Rd MK46 . .6 F5
Wellington Ave HP27. . . . .139 B4
Wellington CI **1** SL6. . . . .202 B8
Wellington Pl
  Aylesbury HP21. . . . . .115 E4
  Milton Keynes MK3 . . . . . .58 B7
Wellington Rd
  Aylesbury HP21. . . . . .115 E4
  High Wycombe HP12 . . . .172 E4
  Maidenhead SL6 . . . . . . .202 D7
  Uxbridge UB8. . . . . .201 C4
Wellington St SL1. . . . . . .206 A4
Well La LU7 . . . . .80 A1
Well Mdw HP19 . . . . .101 D4
Wells CI SL4 . . . . .210 A7
Well St MK18. . . . . .52 D8
Welsh La MK18 . . . . .40 C5
Welsummer Gr MK5. . . . . . .46 A3
Welton Rd HP21 . . . . .116 B7
WENDOVER 131 C4
Wendover CE Jun Sch
  HP22 . . . . .131 B6
WENDOVER DEAN. 141 C5
Wendover House Specl Sch
  HP22. . . . . .131 C3
Wendover Rd
  Bourne End SL8 . . . . .185 A5
  Burnham SL1 . . . . .204 B8
  Ellesborough HP17 . . . . .130 D3
Wendover St HP11 . . . . . .172 F7
Wendover Sta HP22 . . . . .131 B4
Wendover Way
  Aylesbury HP21. . . . . .115 F6
  High Wycombe HP11 . . . .173 B6
Wendover Woods (Forest
  Wlks)★ HP23 . . . . .131 F6
Wenford MK10. . . . . .36 C3
Wenlack CI UB9 . . . . .190 A1
Wenning La MK4. . . . . .46 B2
Wentworth CI HP13 . . . . . .173 C8
Wentworth Cres SL6 . . . . .202 A5
Wentworth Ind Ctr SL2 . . .198 A1
Wentworth Way MK3. . . . . .57 C7
Wenwell CI HP22. . . . . . . .118 A3
Werner Ct HP21. . . . . .115 E4
Werner Terr MK18 . . . . .73 B6
Werth Dr MK17. . . . . .49 B2
Wescott Way UB8 . . . . . . .201 C3
Wesley CI HP20 . . . . .102 A2
Wesley Dene **4** HP13 . . .173 B7
Wesley Hill **1** HP5 . . . . .144 B1
Wessex Ct
  4 Stanwell TW19 . . . . .213 E1
  11 Windsor SL4 . . . . . .210 C6
Wessex Prim Sch SL6 . . . .202 B4
Wessex Rd SL8 . . . . .185 B2
Wessex Road Ind Est
  SL8 . . . . .185 B2
Wessex Way SL6 . . . . .202 B4
Wessons Hill SL6 . . . . . . .195 C7
West Acres HP7 . . . . .165 D7
Westanley Ave HP7 . . . . . .165 D8
West Ave HP10 . . . . .163 C1
Westborne Ct MK13 . . . . . .34 A6
Westborough Ct SL6. . . . .202 C6
Westborough Rd SL6 . . . . .202 C6
Westbourne St **6**
  HP11 . . . . .172 F7
Westbourne End MK17 . . . .57 C3
Westbrook Hay Prep Sch
  HP1. . . . . .146 D7
WESTBURY 39 B4
Westbury CI
  Bicester OX27 . . . . .71 E2
  Newport Pagnell MK16 . . . .22 B4
Westbury Court Bsns Ctr
  OX27. . . . . .71 C4
Westbury Ho **3** HP20 . .101 D1
Westbury La MK16. . . . . . . .22 A5
Westbury Mill NN13. . . . . . .38 F4
Westbury Terr OX27. . . . . . .71 F2
West CI SL7 . . . . .193 D7
Westcliffe MK8 . . . . .33 C2
West Comm SL9 . . . . .188 D6
West Common Ct SL9 . . . .188 E6
West Common Rd UB8 . . .201 D6
WESTCOTT 98 C7
Westcott CE Sch HP18 . . . .98 A7
Westcott Venture Pk
  HP18. . . . . .98 A6
West Cres SL4 . . . . .209 F6
WESTCROFT 45 E2

Westcroft
Slough SL2. . . . . .198 B1
Tring HP23. . . . . .119 A3
Westcroft Rdbt MK4 . . . . . .46 A2
Westcroft Stables★
  HP27. . . . . .150 B3
West Ct
  Bray SL6 . . . . .203 C4
  High Wycombe HP13 . . . .161 D3
West Dales MK13 . . . . .34 C5
West Dean SL6 . . . . .202 F8
Westdean La HP5 . . . . . . .143 C3
Westdown Gdns LU6 . . . . .93 F7
West Dr HP13. . . . . .173 D8
WEST DRAYTON 208 D3
West Drayton Park Ave
  UB7 . . . . .208 E3
West Drayton Prim Sch
  UB7. . . . . .208 E5
West Drayton Sta UB7. . . .208 E5
West Edge OX27 . . . . .71 E2
WEST END 63 C2
West End CI MK18. . . . . . . .46 A2
West End La SL2 . . . . .198 F4
West End La SL2 . . . . .198 E4
West End PI HP22. . . . . . . .116 E2
West End Rd
  Cheddington LU7 . . . . . . .104 F7
  High Wycombe HP11 . . . .172 F7
  West End St HP11 . . . . . .172 F7
Western Ave
  Buckingham MK18 . . . . . . .41 C1
  New Denham UB9 . . . . . .201 D8
Western Dene HP15. . . . . .163 A5
Western Dr
  Hanslope MK19 . . . . .11 A3
  Wooburn Green HP10 . . . .185 E5
Western House Prim Sch
  SL1 . . . . .204 F5
Western La MK18 . . . . .65 F3
Western Perimeter Rd
  TW6 . . . . .213 A3
Western Perimeter Road
  Rdbt TW19 . . . . .213 C2
Western Rd
  Great Horwood MK17 . . . .55 A3
  Milton Keynes, Fenny Stratford
    MK2. . . . . .47 D1
  Milton Keynes, Wolverton
    MK12. . . . . .33 C6
  Tring HP23 . . . . .118 F3
West Farm Way MK46 . . . . .13 E8
Westfield
  Aylesbury HP21. . . . . .115 E3
  Hyde Heath HP6 . . . . . . .153 C4
Westfield Ave MK19 . . . . . .31 D5
Westfield Bglws SL7 . . . . .192 F6
Westfield Cotts SL7 . . . . . .192 F6
Westfield Fst Sch HP4. . . .134 F5
Westfield Rd
  Beaconsfield HP9. . . . . . .175 C1
  Berkhamsted HP4 . . . . . .134 E6
  Dunstable LU6. . . . . .93 F8
  Maidenhead SL6 . . . . . . .202 B7
  Milton Keynes MK2 . . . . . .58 C7
  Pitstone LU7 . . . . .105 C3
  Slough SL1. . . . . .198 B1
  Wheatley OX33 . . . . .122 A1
Westfields
  Buckingham MK18 . . . . . . .52 C8
  Princes Risborough
    HP27. . . . . .139 D2
Westfield St SL6 . . . . .202 A5
Westfield Wlk HP12 . . . . . .172 D6
West Furlong MK18 . . . . . . .53 A1
Westgate Cres SL1. . . . . . .204 F6
Westgate Ct HP13. . . . . . . .174 A4
Westgate Ret Pk SL1. . . . .205 A5
Westgate Sch The SL1. . . .205 A5
Westhill MK14 . . . . .34 D8
West Hill MK17 . . . . .49 D4
Westhorpe Rd SL7. . . . . . .183 F3
WEST HYDE. 178 E3
West Hyde La SL9. . . . . . .178 A4
West La
  Bledlow HP27 . . . . .138 B1
  Emberton MK46. . . . . .13 E8
  Henley-on-Thames RG9 . .191 D2
Westland CI TW19 . . . . . . .213 E1
Westlands Ave SL1. . . . . . .204 F7
Westlands CI SL1. . . . . . . .204 C7
Westlands Rd HP27 . . . . . .149 E5
WEST LEITH. 118 F2
West Leith HP23 . . . . .118 F1
WESTLINGTON 113 E1
Westlington La HP17. . . . .113 E1
Westlington Lea HP17. . . .113 E2
Westmead
  Monks Risborough
    HP27. . . . . .139 B5
  Windsor SL4 . . . . .210 B4
West Mead SL6 . . . . .195 F2
Westminster CI
  Brackley NN13. . . . . .38 A7
  High Wycombe HP11 . . . .173 B4
Westminster Cres NN13 . . .38 A7
Westminster Dr
  Aylesbury HP21. . . . . .115 F6

Westminster Dr continued
Milton Keynes MK3 . . . . . . .47 A2
Westmorland Ave
  HP21 . . . . .116 B6
Westmorland Ho MK3. . . . .46 F7
Westmorland Rd SL6. . . . .202 D6
Westmount Ave HP7 . . . . .165 C8
Weston Ct HP22 . . . . .117 C5
Weston La OX9 . . . . .136 F8
Weston Rd
  Aston Clinton HP22 . . . . .117 C5
  Lewknor OX49 . . . . .157 A8
  Olney MK46. . . . . .6 E3
  Ravenstone MK46 . . . . .5 E2
  Slough SL1. . . . . .204 F8
WESTON TURVILLE. 116 E3
Weston Turville CE Sch
  HP22. . . . . .116 E3
Weston Turville Resr
  Wildlife Reserve★
    HP22. . . . . .130 F8
WESTON UNDERWOOD . . .6 B1
Weston Way HP22 . . . . . . .116 A2
Weston Way Ind Est
  HP22. . . . . .116 A2
Westover Ct HP13. . . . . . . .161 E4
Westover Rd HP13 . . . . . . .161 D2
West Pas **11** HP23 . . . . .119 A3
Westpits MK46. . . . . .13 E8
West Point SL1 . . . . .204 D5
West Puxley CI MK19. . . . . .31 D5
West Rd
  Berkhamsted HP4 . . . . . .135 A5
  Cranfield MK43 . . . . .24 D2
  Maidenhead SL6 . . . . . . .202 E7
  West Drayton UB7. . . . . . .208 F3
  Woburn Sands MK17 . . . . .49 A5
West Richardson St **2**
  HP11 . . . . .172 F7
Westrick Walk HP16 . . . . .151 C5
West Ridge SL6. . . . . .185 B4
Westridge CI HP5. . . . . . . .144 A1
Westron Gdns HP23 . . . . .119 B4
Westside La MK16 . . . . .12 B6
West Side Rise MK46. . . . . .6 F4
West Spur Rd UB8 . . . . . . .201 D2
West Sq SL0 . . . . .207 F7
West St
  Adstock MK18 . . . . .53 F1
  Aylesbury HP19 . . . . .101 C1
  Buckingham MK18 . . . . . . .41 C1
  Dunstable LU6. . . . . .93 F7
  Henley-on-Thames RG9 . .191 E5
  Leighton Buzzard LU7 . . . .80 F7
  Maidenhead SL6 . . . . . . .202 F7
  Marlow SL7 . . . . .183 D1
  Olney MK46. . . . . .6 F4
  Steeple Claydon MK18. . . .63 D2
West Way
  Chesham HP5 . . . . .144 D2
  Hardwick HP22 . . . . .87 B3
  High Wycombe HP13 . . . .173 B8
West Way HP9 . . . . .174 F1
West Waye HP13. . . . . .162 C1
West Well CI MK18. . . . . . . .51 A6
West Well La MK18. . . . . . . .51 A6
West Wlk MK9 . . . . .34 E2
Westwood HP12 . . . . .172 B3
Westwood CI
  Little Chalfont HP6. . . . . . .166 D8
  Milton Keynes MK8 . . . . . .45 F8
Westwood Dr HP6 . . . . . . .166 D8
Westwood Gn SL6 . . . . . . .195 F6
Westwood Rd SL7. . . . . . . .183 C1
Westwood Wlk **6**
  HP20. . . . . .101 F2
WEST WYCOMBE 160 F2
West Wycombe Comb Sch
  HP14. . . . . .161 A1
West Wycombe Park★
  HP14. . . . . .161 A1
West Wycombe Rd
  HP12. . . . . .161 C1
  HP14. . . . . .160 C8
Wetherby Gdns MK3 . . . . . .57 D6
Wethered Pk SL7 . . . . .183 D1
Wethered Rd
  Burnham SL1. . . . . .204 B8
  Marlow SL7. . . . . .183 D2
Wexford Ct **2** SL6 . . . . .203 B7
Wexham Court Prim Sch
  SL3 . . . . .206 C8
Wexham Park Hospl
  SL3. . . . . .199 C1
Wexham Park La SL3. . . . .199 C1
Wexham PI SL2 . . . . .199 D6
Wexham Rd SL2 . . . . .206 B6
Wexham Sch Sports Coll
  SL2 . . . . .206 C8
Wexham St SL3. . . . . .199 B3
WEXHAM STREET. 199 C4
Wexham Woods SL3 . . . . .199 C4
Weybourne Rd **1** MK10 . .36 A4
Wey La HP5 . . . . .154 B7
WHADDON. 45 A1

Whaddon CE Sch MK17 . . 56 B8
Whaddon Chase HP19 . . 101 D2
Whaddon Hall MK17. . . . 45 B2
Whaddon Rd
　Milton Keynes, Shenley Brook
　End MK5 . . . . 46 A3
　Mursley MK17 . . . . . 56 C3
　Nash MK17 . . . . 44 D2
　Newport Pagnell MK16 . 22 B3
　Newton Longville MK17. 57 D3
Whaddon Way MK3 . . . 46 F2
Whales La OX27. . . . . 71 E2
Whalley Dr MK3 . . . . . 47 A2
Wharf Cl
　Old Stratford MK19 . . . 32 B7
　Wendover HP22. . . . 131 B5
Wharf Ct UB8. . . . . . 201 C1
Wharfe La RG9 . . . . . 191 E2
Wharf La
　Berkhamsted HP4 . . . 134 C8
　Bourne End SL8. . . . 185 A3
　Old Stratford MK19 . . . 32 C7
Wharf Rd HP22 . . . . . 131 B5
Wharf Row HP22. . . . 118 B4
Wharfside MK2. . . . . . 47 E1
Wharfside Pl MK18. . . . 41 E1
Wharf The
　Leighton Buzzard LU7 . 80 E6
　Milton Keynes, Giffard Park
　MK14. . . . . 21 E2
　Milton Keynes MK2 . . 58 E6
Wharf View MK18 . . . . 41 E1
WHARLEY END 24 D1
Wharton Ho **2** HP20 . . 101 D1
Whatmore Cl TW19 . . . 213 A1
Wheatbutts The SL4 . . 204 F2
Wheat Cl HP21. . . . . . 115 E3
Wheatcroft Cl MK6. . . . 47 A5
Wheatfield Cl SL6. . . . 202 A4
Wheathouse Copse
　MK17. . . . . 55 A3
Wheatlands Rd SL3 . . . 206 C3
WHEATLEY. 122 A1
Wheatley Cl MK4. . . . . 46 C2
Wheatley Park Sch
　OX33. . . . . 122 B2
Wheatley Rd OX33 . . . 122 A3
Wheatley Way SL9 . . . 177 E4
Wheatsheaf Par SL4 . . 211 A2
Wheatstone Cl SL3. . . . 206 A3
Wheeler Ave HP10 . . . 174 C8
Wheeler Cl HP20. . . . . 116 B8
WHEELER END. 171 B6
Wheeler Pl HP9. . . . . 175 F2
Wheelers End OX39 . . . 147 C6
Wheelers Flats HP10 . . 174 D8
Wheelers La MK13 . . . . 34 A6
Wheelers Orch SL9 . . . 177 E4
Wheelers Pk HP13 . . . 173 D7
Wheelers Yd HP16 . . . 152 A7
Wheelwright Mews
　MK14. . . . . 34 F6
Wheelwright Rd HP27. . 138 D7
Wheelwrights HP22. . . 116 F2
Wheelwrights Pl SL3 . . 212 C7
Wheelwrights Way
　MK19. . . . . 32 C7
Wheelwrights Yd HP22. . 85 A5
WHELPLEY HILL 145 D5
Whelpley Hill Pk HP5 . . 145 D5
Whet Stone Cl MK13 . . 34 B4
Whichcote Gdns HP5. . . 154 D6
Whichert Cl HP9. . . . . 175 C6
Whichford MK14. . . . . 22 A1
Whielden Gate HP7 . . . 164 E4
Whielden Gn HP7 . . . . 165 B7
Whielden Hts HP7 . . . . 165 A7
Whielden La
　Coleshill HP7 . . . . . 164 E5
　Winchmore Hill HP7 . . 164 D3
Whielden St HP7 . . . . 165 B7
Whinchat HP19 . . . . . 101 E3
Whincup Cl HP11 . . . . 172 F4
Whinneys Rd HP10 . . . 174 C3
Whipass Hill HP9 . . . . 176 A5
WHIPSNADE 107 F8
Whipsnade Park Homes
　LU6. . . . . 93 F1
Whipsnade Rd LU6. . . . 93 F6
Whipsnade Tree
　Cathedral★ LU6 . . . 93 F1
Whitby Cl MK3. . . . . . 47 A2
Whitby Rd SL1. . . . . . 205 C6
WHITCHURCH 87 B6
Whitchurch Cl
　Maidenhead SL6 . . . 195 E3
　Westcott HP18. . . . . 98 B7
Whitchurch Comb Sch
　HP22. . . . . 86 F7
Whitchurch Ho **5** SL6. . 202 F7
Whitchurch La HP22. . . 86 D8
Whitchurch Rd LU7 . . . 78 B1
Whiteacres Dr SL6. . . . 203 B1
White Alder MK12. . . . 33 E5

Whitebaker Ct MK14 . . . 34 F6
Whitebeam Cl HP22. . . 116 C3
Whitebrook Pk SL6 . . . 196 C4
Whitechurch Cl HP17 . . 114 C5
White Cl
　High Wycombe HP13 . . 161 D1
　Slough SL1. . . . . . . 205 D5
White Cotts MK18. . . . 29 D4
White Cres HP22 . . . . 131 D7
Whitecross Green Wood
　Wildlife Reserve★
　OX5. . . . . 94 C2
Whitecross Rd HP17 . . . 126 F5
Whitefield La HP16. . . . 152 A6
Whiteford Rd SL2. . . . 205 E8
Whitegate Ct MK6 . . . . 47 B6
Whitehall SL6 . . . . . . 196 B1
Whitehall Ave MK10. . . 36 D1
Whitehall Cl UB8. . . . . 201 C4
Whitehall Inf Sch UB8. . 201 C4
Whitehall Jun Sch UB8 . 201 C4
Whitehall La TW19 . . . 212 A1
Whitehall Rd UB8. . . . 201 D3
Whitehall St **2** HP20. . . 101 D1
White Hart Cl
　Chalfont St Giles HP8 . . 177 A7
　Ludgershall HP18. . . . 96 B8
White Hart Field HP22. . 85 B4
White Hart La HP17 . . . 127 A5
White Hart Mdw HP9. . 175 E1
White Hill
　Ashley Green HP4,
　HP5. . . . . 145 C7
　Beaconsfield HP9, HP10 . 185 F8
　Chesham HP5 . . . . . 144 D1
　High Wycombe HP13 . . 162 B2
　Remenham Hill RG9. . . 192 A2
White Hill Cl
　Chesham HP5 . . . . . 144 D1
　Marlow Bottom SL7 . . . 183 C6
Whitehill Ct HP4. . . . . 135 D5
Whitehill La LU7. . . . . 105 D3
White Hill La LU7 . . . . 105 D3
White Horse Ct HP6. . . 154 C2
White Horse Dr MK4 . . . 46 C2
White Horse La HP22. . . 87 A6
White Horse Rd SL6 . . . 203 B1
Whitehorse Yd MK11. . . 32 D5
White Hos MK18 . . . . . 50 D6
Whitehouse Cl HP10 . . 174 A1
White House Cl SL9 . . . 177 E3
Whitehouse La HP22. . . 174 E2
Whitehouse Way
　Iver Heath SL0. . . . . 200 D2
　Slough SL3. . . . . . . 206 D3
Whitelands Ave WD3 . . 167 C5
Whitelands Rd HP12. . . 172 D7
Whitelands Way HP12. . 172 D2
WHITELEAF 139 D5
Whiteleaf Hill Nature
　Reserve★ HP27 . . . 139 E4
Whiteleaf Way HP27 . . 139 E5
Whiteley SL4 . . . . . . 209 E2
Whiteley Cres MK3. . . . 57 F6
White Lilies Island SL4 . 210 B7
White Lion Cl HP7 . . . . 166 A8
White Lion Rd HP7 . . . 166 B8
Whitelock Ho RG9 . . . . 191 E3
White Lodge Cl SL7 . . . 183 C6
White Paddock SL6 . . . 202 A2
Whitepit La HP10 . . . . 185 D7
White Rock SL6. . . . . . 196 B1
Whites Cl MK18. . . . . . 63 D3
Whites Croft MK6. . . . . 46 F6
Whites La SL3 . . . . . . 211 B8
White Spire Specl Sch
　MK3. . . . . 46 F1
Whitethorn Ave UB7. . . 208 F6
Whitethorn Cl HP22 . . . 130 A8
Whitethorn Pl UB7. . . . 208 F5
Whitethorns MK16. . . . 22 B3
White View **14** MK19. . . 101 F3
Whitewood Rd HP4 . . . 135 A4
WHITFIELD 26 D3
Whitfield Rd HP14 . . . . 162 A6
Whitfield Way WD3 . . . 167 F1
Whitley Cl TW19 . . . . 213 E1
Whitley Ct HP21 . . . . 115 E4
Whitmees Cl MK46. . . . 6 E2
Whitmore Rd MK4 . . . . 45 E2
Whitsun Pasture MK15. . 35 B7
Whittaker Rd SL2. . . . 197 E1
Whittenham Cl SL2 . . . 206 A5
Whittington Chase MK4 . 45 E1
Whittle Ct MK5 . . . . . . 46 C7
Whittle Parkway SL1. . . 204 D2
Whitton Way MK16. . . . 22 C3
Whitworth La MK5 . . . . 46 B7
Whurley Way SL6 . . . . 195 E2

Whybrow Gdns HP4. . . 135 E6
Whyteladyes La SL6. . . 195 E6
Whytingham Rd HP23 . . 119 C4
WICKEN 31 B3
Wicken Park Rd MK19. . 31 B2
Wicken Rd MK18. . . . . 30 E1
Wickets The SL1. . . . . 202 C7
Wicket The SL1. . . . . . 205 E3
Wick Rd HP23 . . . . . . 133 D8
Wickstead Ave MK8. . . 45 D6
Widbrook Rd SL6 . . . . 196 B3
Widdenton View HP14. . 171 C5
Widecroft Rd SL0. . . . . 207 E2
Widewater Pl UB9 . . . . 190 C6
Widgeon Ho HP11 . . . . 173 C6
Widmere Field HP16 . . 151 C5
Widmere La SL7 . . . . . 183 A6
WIDMER END. 162 E6
Widmer End Comb Sch
　HP15. . . . . 162 F6
WIDMOOR 185 E3
Widmore Cl HP5 . . . . 143 E5
Widnell La OX25. . . . . 95 C7
Wigan's La HP14. . . . . 148 C6
Wiggington Ho SL4 . . . 210 D7
WIGGINTON 119 D1
WIGGINTON BOTTOM. . 133 D8
Wigginton Bottom
　HP23. . . . . 133 E8
Wiggles La HP23. . . . . 118 F7
Wigmore Ct HP19 . . . . 101 A2
Wigmore Rd HP19 . . . . 101 A2
Wigwell Gdns MK17 . . . 55 A2
Wilberforce Mews **7**
　SL6. . . . . 202 F7
Wildacre Rd MK5 . . . . 46 A4
Wilderness The HP4 . . . 135 C4
Wildgreen N SL3. . . . . 207 A2
Wildgreen S SL3. . . . . 207 A2
Wildwood Ct WD3 . . . . 167 F5
Wilford Cl MK15. . . . . 35 C2
Wilford Rd SL3 . . . . . 206 F2
Wilfrids Wood Cl HP10 . 185 B6
Wilks Croft MK5 . . . . . 45 F7
WILLEN 35 D7
Willen La MK14 . . . . . 34 F8
Willen Prim Sch MK15 . 35 C7
Willen Rd
　Milton Keynes MK10 . . 35 F3
　Newport Pagnell MK16 . 22 D3
Willets Rise MK5 . . . . 46 A5
Willetts La UB9. . . . . . 200 F7
Willey Ct MK11 . . . . . . 32 F4
William Bandy La LU7. . 79 F3
William Burt Cl HP22 . . 116 F1
William Ellis Cl SL4 . . . 211 A1
William Fiske Ho **4**
　HP4 . . . . 135 C4
William Harding Cl
　HP21. . . . . 116 A5
William Hartley Yd SL3 . 199 B1
William Hill Dr HP22 . . 102 C4
William Ho **4** HP13 . . . 173 F5
William Moulder Ct
　HP5. . . . . 144 B3
Williams Circ MK7 . . . . 48 A4
Williams Cl
　Aylesbury HP19 . . . . 101 D1
　Hanslope MK19 . . . . 10 F3
William Shakman Ho
　HP8 . . . . 177 B8
William Smith Cl MK15 . 35 C3
William St
　Berkhamsted HP4 . . . 135 D4
　Slough SL1. . . . . . . 205 F5
　Windsor SL4 . . . . . . 210 D6
William Sutton Ho MK5 . 46 A6
Williams Way HP27 . . . 138 D6
Willis Rd HP17 . . . . . . 127 A6
Willmott Cl HP19. . . . . 101 D4
Willoners SL2 . . . . . . 205 A8
Willoughby Rd SL3. . . . 207 B3
Willoughby's Wlk HP13 . 161 D2
Willow Ave
　High Wycombe HP10 . . 172 B4
　New Denham UB9 . . . 201 C6
　West Drayton UB7. . . 208 F6
WILLOWBANK 201 C7
Willowbank Terr **6**
　HP21 . . . . 115 E8
Willowbrook
　Slough SL4. . . . . . . 205 D2
　Wendover HP22. . . . 131 B7
Willow Chase
　Chesham HP5 . . . . . 144 B1
　Tring HP23. . . . . . . 119 A4
Willow Cl
　Chalfont St Peter SL9 . . 177 E1
　Colnbrook SL3 . . . . . 212 C7
　Flackwell Heath HP10 . . 185 C6
　Maidenhead SL6 . . . 195 D1
　Moulsoe MK16. . . . . 36 B8
Willow Crescent E UB9 . 201 C7

Willow Crescent W
　UB9 . . . . 201 C7
Willow Ct
　2 Aylesbury, Quarrendon
　HP19. . . . . 101 A2
　Aylesbury, Walton Court
　HP21. . . . . 115 C6
　High Wycombe HP11 . . 173 E4
　Walter's Ash HP14. . . 161 C8
Willow Dr
　Buckingham MK18 . . . 52 F7
　Maidenhead SL6 . . . 203 B2
Willow End HP22 . . . . 116 F2
Willowford MK13 . . . . . 33 E5
Willow Gate HP18. . . . 112 B2
Willow Gn MK19. . . . . 32 B6
Willow Herb HP19 . . . 101 E4
Willow Ho LU7. . . . . . 80 E7
Willow La
　Amersham HP7 . . . . 165 F6
　Milton Keynes MK11 . . 32 C5
Willowmead HP17 . . . . 114 F5
Willowmead Cl **10** SL7. . 183 F3
Willowmead Gdns SL7 . 183 F3
Willowmead Rd **8** SL7 . 183 F3
Willowmead Sq **9** SL7 . 183 F3
Willow Parade SL3. . . . 207 A3
Willow Pk SL2. . . . . . 199 A5
Willow Pl SL4. . . . . . . 210 C8
Willow Rd
　Aylesbury HP19 . . . . 101 D1
　Brackley NN13. . . . . 38 A6
　Chinnor OX39. . . . . . 147 C6
　Great Horwood MK17 . . 55 A3
　Poyle SL3. . . . . 212 C5
　Thame OX9 . . . . 125 F1
Willow Rise HP17 . . . . 127 A7
Willows Rd SL8 . . . . . 185 B4
Willows Riverside Pk The
　SL4. . . . . 209 C2
Willows Sch The MK6 . . 35 A2
Willows The
　Amersham HP6 . . . . 154 B4
　4 Bourne End SL8 . . . 185 B3
　Edlesborough LU6 . . . 92 F3
　High Wycombe HP12 . . 172 E8
　Windsor SL4 . . . . . . 209 D7
Willow Way
　Loudwater HP11 . . . . 174 B2
　Milton Keynes MK2 . . 58 C7
　Princes Risborough
　HP27 . . . . 139 A3
　Wing LU7 . . . . 79 E3
Willow Wlk HP15 . . . . 163 A3
Willow Wood Cl SL1 . . 197 B3
Willow Wren MK14. . . . 21 F2
Wilmar Cl UB8. . . . . . 201 D5
Wilmin Gr MK5 . . . . . 46 B7
Wilmot Rd SL1. . . . . . 197 B2
Wilsley Pound MK7 . . . 48 B8
Wilson Ct MK8. . . . . . 45 E7
WILSTONE. 104 D8
WILSTONE GREEN. . . . 118 D8
Wilstone Rssr★ HP22,
　HP23. . . . . 118 C7
Wilton Ave MK3. . . . . . 58 A8
Wilton Cl UB7 . . . . . . 213 D8
Wilton Cres
　Beaconsfield HP9. . . . 175 E3
　Windsor SL4 . . . . . . 209 D4
Wilton Hollow HP9. . . . 175 F3
Wilton La HP9 . . . . . . 176 E4
WILTON PARK 175 E3
Wilton Rd HP9 . . . . . . 175 E3
Wiltshire Ave SL2 . . . . 198 C1
Wiltshire Lodge **2** SL6. 202 F6
Wiltshire Rd **2** SL7. . . 183 F3
Wiltshire Way MK3. . . . 46 E1
Wimbledon Pl MK13. . . 34 D3
Wimblington Dr MK6. . . 47 A4
Wimborne Cres MK4 . . 45 F2
Wimpole Rd UB7. . . . . 208 D5
Winbury Ct SL6 . . . . . 202 E7
Winbury Pl SL6 . . . . . 203 B3
Winbury Sch SL6 . . . . 203 B3
Wincanton Hill MK3. . . 57 C6
Winchbottom La
　High Wycombe HP10 . . 173 B1
　Little Marlow SL7, HP10 . 184 B7
Winchendon Rd HP18. . 112 B2
Winchester Circ MK10. . 36 B1
Winchester Cl
　Amersham HP7 . . . . 165 E8
　Poyle SL3. . . . . 212 E5
Winchester Ct HP11. . . 174 B3
Winchester Dr SL6 . . . 202 B3
Winchester Ho HP21 . . 115 F6
WINCHMORE HILL. . . . 164 D2
Winch Terr SL4 . . . . . 209 D5
Windermere Cl
　Aylesbury HP21 . . . . 116 B6
　Chorleywood WD3 . . . 167 D4
Windermere Dr MK2 . . 58 D5
Windermere Gdns LU7 . 80 C7
Windermere Way
　Slough SL1. . . . . . . 204 C7
　West Drayton UB7. . . 208 E5

Windmill Cl
　Aylesbury HP19 . . . . 115 B8
　Buckingham MK18. . . 41 F1
　Ivinghoe LU7 . . . . . . 105 F5
　Windsor SL4 . . . . . . 210 B5
Windmill Dr HP15. . . . 162 F6
Windmill Hill
　Chipperfield WD4. . . . 156 F7
　Coleshill HP7 . . . . . 164 F2
　Princes Risborough
　HP27 . . . . 139 A2
Windmill Hill Dr MK3. . 57 D7
Windmill Hill Rdbt MK4 . 46 C1
Windmill La HP15. . . . 162 F7
Windmill Par HP15. . . 162 F7
Windmill Rd
　Chalfont St Peter SL9 . . 177 D3
　Cookham Rise SL6. . . 195 E6
　Fulmer SL3. . . . . . . 199 D7
　Haddenham HP17 . . . 126 F6
　Slough SL1. . . . . . . 205 D5
　Thame OX9 . . . . 126 E1
　West St HP18 . . . . . 96 A1
Windmill Way
　Cranfield MK43 . . . . . 25 C3
　Tring HP23. . . . . . . 118 F4
Windmill Wood HP6 . . 154 A2
Windrush Ave SL3 . . . 207 B3
Windrush Cl
　Ickenham UB10 . . . . 201 F8
　Milton Keynes MK15 . . 35 A6
Windrush Ct
　Aylesbury HP21 . . . . 115 D4
　High Wycombe HP13 . . 173 F6
Windrush Dr HP13 . . . 173 F6
Windrush Ho SL6 . . . . 185 B4
Windrush Way SL6. . . . 203 A8
WINDSOR. 210 E6
Windsor Ave
　Leighton Buzzard LU7 . 80 F7
　Newport Pagnell MK16 . 22 C4
Windsor Boys' Sch
　Performing Arts Coll The
　SL4. . . . . 210 B6
Windsor Bsns Ctr SL4 . . 210 C7
Windsor Castle★ SL4. . 210 E7
Windsor Cl
　Bovingdon HP3 . . . . 146 A3
　Burnham SL1. . . . . . 197 C1
Windsor Cres HP10 . . . 174 C2
Windsor Ct HP6. . . . . 154 D1
Windsor Dr HP13 . . . . 162 D1
Windsor End HP9 . . . . 186 E8
Windsor & Eton Central Sta
　SL4. . . . . 210 D6
Windsor & Eton Riverside
　Sta SL4. . . . . 210 D7
Windsor Girls' Sch SL4 210 A4
Windsor Great Pk★
　SL4. . . . . 210 B2
Windsor Hall SL4 . . . . 210 D6
Windsor Hill
　Monks Risborough
　HP27 . . . . 139 C5
　Wooburn Green HP10 . . 185 F5
Windsor Ho **4** SL1. . . . 205 F3
Windsor La
　Burnham SL1. . . . . . 197 C1
　Little Kingshill HP16 . . . 152 C3
Windsor Rd
　Aylesbury HP21 . . . . 116 A7
　Chesham HP5 . . . . . 144 B3
　Datchet SL3. . . . . . . 211 A7
　Gerrards Cross SL9 . . 188 C3
　Maidenhead SL6 . . . 203 C2
　Oakley Green SL4 . . . 209 A7
　Pitstone LU7 . . . . . . 105 C3
　Slough SL1. . . . . . . 205 E4
　Wraysbury TW19 . . . 211 E3
Windsor Royal Sta **1**
　SL4. . . . . 210 D6
Windsor St
　Milton Keynes MK2 . . 58 C7
　Milton Keynes, Wolverton
　MK12. . . . . 33 C6
　Uxbridge UB8. . . . . 201 C5
Winemar Cl MK19 . . . . 11 A3
Winfold La MK4. . . . . . 46 B1
WING 79 F2
Wingate Ave HP13 . . . 173 E7
Wingate Circ MK7. . . . 48 A4
Wingate Cl HP13. . . . . 173 E7
Wingate Wlk HP20 . . . 116 A8
Wingbury Ctyd Bsns Village
　HP22. . . . . 89 D5
Wing Cl SL7 . . . . 183 C5
Wingfield Gr MK10. . . . 36 A2
WINGRAVE. 89 C3
Wingrave CE Comb Sch
　HP22. . . . . 89 A3
Wingrave Cross Rds
　HP22. . . . . 88 F2
Wingrave Rd
　Aston Abbotts HP22 . . 88 E4
　Long Marston HP23. . . 104 D1
　Tring HP23. . . . . . . 119 B5
Wing Rd
　Cublington LU7 . . . . . 78 C1
　Leighton Buzzard LU7 . 80 D5

Wing Rd continued
  Stewkley LU7 ....78 F6
Winkers Cl SL9 ......177 F2
Winkers La SL9 ......177 F3
Winkfield La SL4 ......209 A1
Winkfield Rd SL4 ......209 E2
Winnock Rd UB7 ......208 D5
Winsford Hill MK4 ....46 E3
WINSLOW 66 B4
Winslow CE Comb Sch
  MK18 ....66 A5
Winslow Field HP16 ....151 F8
Winslow Gdns HP13 ...174 A7
Winslow Rd
  Granborough MK18 ....75 F7
  Great Horwood MK17 ....54 F1
  Little Horwood MK17 ...55 D1
  Nash MK17 ....66 F3
  Swanbourne MK17 ....89 B3
  Wingrave HP22 ....89 B3
Winstanley La MK5 ....46 C4
Winstone Cl HP6 ....154 B5
Winstone Gdns HP4 ....134 F4
Winston Ho HP11 ....174 A4
Winterburn MK13 ....34 B5
Winter Cl 6 SL7 ....183 E5
WINTERHILL 46 D8
Winter Hill SL6 ....184 C1
Winter Hill Rd SL6 ....195 A4
Winters Way HP15 ....163 D7
Winterton Dr HP21 ....115 E4
Wintoun Path SL1 ....197 E1
Winvale SL1 ....205 E3
Winwood
  Slough SL2 ....206 C7
  Windsor SL4 ....209 F6
Winwood Cl MK19 ....31 E5
Winwood Dr HP22 ....85 A5
Wise La UB7 ....208 D2
Wisewood Rd MK4 ....45 C4
Wishart Gn MK7 ....48 E5
Wisley Ave MK13 ....34 D3
Wistmans MK4 ....46 D4
Witan Cl MK9 ....34 D2
Witan Gate MK9 ....34 D1
Witchell HP22 ....131 B4
Witham Cl MK3 ....46 D1
Witham Way HP21 ....115 C4
Witheridge La HP9,
  HP10 ....175 B7
Withey Cl SL4 ....209 E6
Withington MK13 ....46 E3
Withycombe MK4 ....46 E3
Withycroft SL3 ....206 E7
Witney Cl UB10 ....201 F8
Wittington Cotts SL7 ..193 D6
Wittmills Oak MK18 ....41 E1
Witton Ho WD3 ....167 D4
Wivelfield LU6 ....92 E6
Wixon Path HP19 ....115 A8
Woad La MK14 ....34 E8
WOBURN 60 F7
Woburn Ave MK12 ....33 C6
Woburn La MK17 ....49 E4
Woburn Lower Sch
  MK17 ....60 F7
Woburn Rd
  Aspley Heath MK17 ....59 C2
  Little Brickhill MK17 ....59 E6
  Sheeplane MK17, LU7 ....60 C1
WOBURN SANDS 49 A5
Woburn Sands Rd MK17 48 D3
Woburn Sands Sta
  MK17 ....49 A5
Wodehouse Wlk MK16 ..22 A5
Wolf La SL4 ....209 E4
Wolfscote La MK4 ....46 B3
Wolsey Gdns MK13 ....34 A4
Wolstan Cl UB9 ....190 A1
Wolston Mdw MK10 ....35 F3
WOLVERTON 33 C5
WOLVERTON MILL 33 A6
Wolverton Rd
  Castlethorpe MK19 ....20 B5
  Milton Keynes, Giffard Park
    MK16 ....21 E2
  Milton Keynes, Stony Stratford
    MK11 ....32 E6
  Milton Keynes, Wolverton MK18,
    MK19 ....33 D8
  Newport Pagnell MK16 ....22 B4
Wolverton Sta MK12 ....33 E7
WOOBURN 185 D4
Wooburn Common Rd HP10,
  SL1 ....186 A2
Wooburn Grange HP10 185 D3
WOOBURN GREEN 185 F7
Wooburn Green La
  HP9 ....186 A8
Wooburn Manor Pk
  HP10 ....185 E5

Wooburn Mead HP10 ..185 E6
Wooburn Mews HP10 ..185 E5
WOOBURN MOOR 174 E1
Wooburn Town HP10 ..185 D4
Woodall Cl MK10 ....35 E3
Woodbank HP27 ....149 C5
Woodbank Ave SL9 ....188 D5
Woodbank Dr HP8 ....177 D7
Woodbine Cl HP27 ....138 E5
Woodbine Cotts SL9 ..188 D8
Woodbridge Ho UB8 ..201 C5
WOODBURN
  COMMON 186 B3
Woodbury Cl SL8 ....185 C3
Woodchester Pk HP9 ..175 C6
Wood Cl SL4 ....210 C3
Woodcock Ave HP14 ..161 B8
Woodcote SL6 ....202 D6
Woodcote Gn HP13 ....161 D2
Woodcote Lawns HP5 ..144 A3
Woodcroft Rd HP5 ....144 D3
WOOD END
  Little Horwood 55 B2
  Nash 55 C8
Wood End Cl SL2 ....187 D1
Wood End Fst Sch MK14 34 D8
Wood End Rd MK16 ....23 E1
Woodfield HP27 ....149 D6
Woodfield Dr SL6 ....202 A6
Woodfield Pk HP6 ....154 B3
Woodfield Rd HP27 ....139 C4
Wodford Cl HP19 ....115 E7
Woodford Way SL2 ....198 A2
Wood Gn MK10 ....47 F8
WOOD GREEN 27 F2
Woodhall Cl UB8 ....201 D7
WOODHAM 83 E1
Woodhill Ave SL9 ....189 A5
Woodhill Ct
  Amersham HP6 ....154 D2
  Gerrards Cross SL9 ..188 E4
Woodhouse Ct MK14 ..34 D6
Woodhurst Dr UB9 ....189 F6
Woodhurst Rd SL6 ....196 B1
Woodhurst South SL6 ..196 C1
Wood La
  Aspley Guise MK17 ....49 D4
  Iver SL0 ....207 C8
  Milton Keynes MK14 ....34 E8
  Slough SL1 ....205 A4
  South Heath HP16 ....152 E8
  Tingewick MK18 ....51 B6
  Weston Underwood MK46.. 6 A2

Wood Lane Cl
  Flackwell Heath HP10 ..173 F1
  Iver Heath SL0 ....200 B2
Woodlane Gdns HP10 ..174 A1
Woodley Ct HP7 ....165 D8
Woodley Headland MK6 ..47 C7
Woodley Hill HP5 ....154 D5
Woodman Cl LU7 ....79 F3
Woodmans Cl MK19 ....31 E4
Woodmans Croft HP19 115 A8
Woodmoor End SL6 ....196 B7
Woodpiece Rd OX25 ....94 E7
Woodpits La MK46 ....6 E5
Wood Pond Cl HP10 ..176 C4
Wood Rd MK43 ....3 F7
WOODROW 164 D5
Woodruff Ave MK14 ....34 C4
Woodrush Cl MK6 ....47 B4
Woodside
  Aspley Guise MK17 ....49 D3
  Eaton Bray LU6 ....92 E6
  Flackwell Heath HP10 ..185 C6
  Milton Keynes MK11 ....32 C6
Woodside Ave
  Amersham HP6 ....154 D3
  Beaconsfield HP9 ....175 C4
  Flackwell Heath HP10 ..185 C7
Woodside Cl
  Amersham HP6 ....154 D1
  Beaconsfield HP9 ....175 C3
  Chalfont St Peter SL9 ..177 E1
  Loudwater HP11 ....174 B2
Woodside Hill SL9 ....177 E1
Woodside Jun Sch &
  Amersham Music Ctr
  HP6 ....154 D1
Woodside Rd
  Amersham HP6 ....154 D1
  Beaconsfield HP9 ....175 C3
  High Wycombe HP13 ..174 A8
Woodside Way
  Leighton Buzzard LU7 ....80 C6
  Tylers Green HP10 ....174 C8
Woods La NN11 ....18 E3
Woods Pl
  13 Tring HP23 ....119 A3
  Wendover HP22 ....131 B4
Woodspring Ct 2 MK10 ..35 F1
Wood St
  Milton Keynes MK13 ....33 F7
  Waddesdon HP18 ....99 A7
  Woburn Sands MK17 ....49 B4
Woodstock Ave SL3 ....206 D2
Woodstock Cl
  High Wycombe HP21 ..116 B6
  Maidenhead SL6 ....195 F1
Woodstock Ct MK13 ....34 B7
Woodstock Dr UB10 ..201 F8
Woodview Cl HP12 ....161 B2
Woodville SL9 ....147 C5
Woodville Cres NN12 ..18 E6
Woodward Ho 4 MK2 ..58 C8
Woodward Pl MK4 ....34 A1
Woodway MK27 ....149 D6
Wood Way HP9 ....174 F1
Woodway Farm Ind Est
  HP18 ....124 F8
Woodways HP17 ....127 A6
Woodwicks WD3 ....178 D5
Woollerton Cres HP21 ..131 D5
Woollerton Ct HP27 ....139 B4
Woolmans
  Fullers Slade MK11 ....33 A4
  Milton Keynes MK11 ....33 A4
Woolrich Gdns MK11 ....32 E5
WOOLSTONE 35 D3
Wooster Rd HP9 ....175 D4
Wooton Ct MK13 ....33 F8
WOOTTON BOURNE
  END 25 F8
Wootton Dr HP10 ....185 E8
Wootton Gn OX27 ....72 E6
Wootton La HP17 ....113 E1
Wootton Way SL6 ....202 C6

  Ickford HP18 ....123 F4
  Oakley HP18 ....109 D4
Wormsley Cres HP14 ..158 C4
WORMSLEY 99 C5
Wornal Pk HP18 ....123 C8
Worple The TW19 ....211 F1
Worrelle Ave MK10 ....36 A3
Worster Rd SL6 ....195 E6
Worth Ct MK10 ....36 B1
Worthies The HP7 ....165 B7
Worthington Rd LU6 ....93 F8
Wotton End HP18 ....96 C7
Wotton Path HP21 ....115 E3
Wotton Rd HP18 ....97 E1
WOTTON UNDERWOOD ..97 C4
Woughton L Ctr MK6 ..47 F7
WOUGHTON ON THE
  GREEN 47 D8
WOUGHTON PARK 47 E6
Wraxall Way MK10 ....47 D5
Wray Ct MK4 ....46 A2
WRAYSBURY 211 E1
Wraysbury Dr UB7 ....208 D6
Wraysbury Prim Sch
  TW19 ....211 E1
Wraysbury Sta TW19 ..212 A1
Wren Cl MK18 ....52 F7
Wren Ct SL3 ....207 A3
Wren Dr UB7 ....208 D3
Wren Path HP19 ....114 F8
Wren Rd HP16 ....151 C5
Wrensfield SL7 ....183 C2
Wrens Pk MK10 ....36 B2
Wren Vale HP13 ....173 A8
Wren Wlk LU6 ....92 E4
Wright SL4 ....209 C4
Wrights Cl HP14 ....171 B5
Wright's La HP16 ....151 C5
Wright Sq SL4 ....209 C4
Wrights Yd HP16 ....152 A7
Wright Way SL4 ....209 C4
Wroxton Ct MK4 ....45 F2
Wyatt Cl HP13 ....172 F8
Wyatt Rd SL4 ....209 D4
Wyatt's Rd WD3 ....167 F5
Wychwood HP16 ....152 B4
Wychwood Gdns HP12 ..172 C4
Wychwood Rise HP16 ..152 B4
Wyclands Ho HP12 ....161 B2
Wycombe Abbey Sch
  HP11 ....173 A6
Wycombe Air Pk SL7 ..171 F2
Wycombe Cl HP21 ....116 B6
Wycombe End HP9 ....175 E1
Wycombe High Sch
  HP11 ....172 F8
Wycombe Hospl HP11 ..173 A6
Wycombe Ind Mall
  HP11 ....172 F7
Wycombe La HP10 ....185 E2
WYCOMBE MARSH 173 B4
Wycombe Mus★ HP13 ..173 B7
Wycombe Mus & Gdn 18
  HP13 ....173 B7
Wycombe Rd
  Beacon's Bottom HP14 ..159 D3
  Holmer Green HP15....163 B6
  Lacey Green HP14 ....149 B4
  Marlow Bottom SL7 ....183 E4
  Marlow SL7 ....183 E4
  Prestwood HP15 ....151 C5
Wycombe Ret Pk HP11 ..173 F4
Wycombe Sp Ctr HP11 172 F3
Wycombe Swan Theatre
  HP11 ....173 B6
Wycombe View HP10 ..174 A2
Wye Cl
  Aylesbury HP21 ....115 C5
  Milton Keynes MK3 ....46 E1
Wye Ct 2 SL8 ....185 A3
Wye Est HP11 ....173 E5
Wye Gdns HP12 ....172 D8
Wye Rd HP10 ....185 A3
Wye River Bsns Ctr 8
  HP11 ....172 F7
Wye Valley Sch The
  SL8 ....185 B4
Wykeham Gate HP17 ..126 F5
Wykeham Rise OX39 ..147 D6
Wykeham Way HP17 ..126 F6
Wykeridge Cl HP5 ....144 B4
Wylands Rd SL3 ....207 A2
Wylie End MK13 ....34 A7
WYMBUSH 33 F2
Wymering Rd HP11 ....116 C6
Wymers Cl SL1 ....197 B3
Wymers Wood Rd SL1 ..197 A3
Wymondham MK10 ....36 B1
Wynbury Dr HP13 ....162 E1
Wyndale Cl RG9 ....191 E1
Wyndham Ave HP13 ....161 F2
Wyndham Cres SL1 ....197 B3
Wyness Ave MK17 ....59 E5

Wynford Gn HP21 ....115 F6
Wyngates LU7 ....80 E5
Wyngrave Pl HP9 ....175 C5
Wynne-Jones Ctr HP21 115 F8
Wynn Gr HP15 ....163 B3
Wynnstay Gdns SL7 ....183 E5
Wynnswick Rd HP9 ....176 C5
Wynyard Ct MK6 ....46 E7
Wyre Cl HP17 ....127 A5
Wyvern Sch MK12 ....33 C6
Wyvern Way UB8 ....201 C4

X

Xscape★ MK6 ....34 F2

Y

Yalts Brow MK4 ....46 B2
Yardley Ave LU7 ....105 D4
Yardley Gn HP20 ....101 F2
YARDLEY GOBION 18 E5
Yardley Gobion CE Prim
  Sch NN12 ....18 E6
YARDLEY HASTINGS 1 B6
Yardley Hastings Prim Sch
  NN7 ....1 A7
Yardley Rd
  Cosgrove MK19 ....19 D2
  Olney MK46 ....6 E6
  Potterspury NN12 ....18 F4
Yarmouth Rd SL4 ....205 C6
Yarrow Pl MK14 ....34 C4
Yarrowside HP7 ....166 B7
Yeates Cl
  Thame OX9 ....125 F1
  Winslow MK18 ....65 F1
Yeats Cl MK16 ....21 F5
Ye Meads Cotts SL6 ....203 E5
Ye Meads SL6 ....203 E5
Ye Meads Ho SL6 ....203 E5
Yeomans Cl NN13 ....38 A8
Yeomans Dr MK14 ....22 B1
Yeovil Ent Ctr SL1 ....204 F8
Yeovil Rd SL1 ....204 E8
Yew Ave UB7 ....208 E6
Yewtree Cl LU7 ....105 C5
Yew Tree Cl
  Beaconsfield HP9 ....175 F1
  Botley HP5 ....145 A1
  Eaton Bray LU6 ....92 F5
  Maidenhead SL6 ....202 E8
  Newton Longville MK17 ..57 C3
  Stoke Mandeville HP22 ..116 A1
Yew Tree Dr
  Bovingdon HP3 ....146 B3
  Hazlemere HP15 ....162 F6
Yew Tree Rd
  Slough SL1 ....206 A3
  Uxbridge UB10 ....201 F4
Yew Wlk HP15 ....163 A3
Yiewsley Ct UB7 ....208 E5
Yolsum Cl HP17 ....126 E6
Yonder Slade MK18 ....52 D6
York Ave
  Slough SL1 ....205 C7
  Windsor SL4 ....210 B5
York Cl HP7 ....165 F8
York Ct 5 LU7 ....80 F7
Yorke Cl HP22 ....117 C5
York Ho
  High Wycombe HP13 ..173 F8
  Milton Keynes MK3 ....57 F7
York Pl HP21 ....115 D7
York Rd
  Henley-on-Thames
    RG9 ....191 D2
  Maidenhead SL6 ....203 A7
  Marlow SL7 ....183 D2
  Milton Keynes MK11 ....32 D5
  Uxbridge UB8 ....201 D5
  Windsor SL4 ....210 B5
Yorkshire Cl MK3 ....46 F1
York Way HP12 ....172 E4
Youens Rd HP12 ....172 C5
Young Cl HP21 ....116 A6

Z

Zealand Ave UB7 ....213 E7
Zetland Ct SL6 ....203 B8
Zodiac Bsns Pk UB8 ....208 D7
ZSL Whipsnade Zoo★
  HP4 ....107 E8